# God-Man/Neo-Tech
# Decoded

# God-Man/Neo-Tech
# Decoded

## Mark Hamilton

NEO-TECH BOOKS

Published by Integrated Management Associates
850 S. Boulder Highway, Henderson, Nevada 89015, U.S.A.

First published in the United States of America by
Integrated Management Associates

4  6  8  10  9  7  5  3

LIBRARY OF CONGRESS
CATALOGING-IN-PUBLICATION DATA
Hamilton, Mark
God-Man/Neo-Tech Decoded
ISBN 885314-07-8

Printed in the United States of America
January 1999 [PP-GMNTD] [7500]
February 2000 [PP-GMNTD] [5000]

Book I
# God-Man Decoded

Book II
# Neo-Tech Decoded

*Bonuses*

Book III
# Poker: A Guaranteed Income For Life

Book IV
# Neocheating: The Unbeatable Weapon

Book One

# God-Man Decoded

Personal Renaissances I & II

# Table of Contents

# Personal Renaissance I
# A Journey of No Return

It was late at night when the Visions left me. I was exhausted, but I was also filled with euphoria. The next morning, the day after my Six Visions, I was mentally wandering through tomorrow's Neo-Tech World when I suddenly realized that *I could actually use* one of the future techniques from my Visions of the millionaire multitudes tomorrow. Over the next few days, I gained enormous momentum as I realized I could actually use today *the dozens of techniques* I was exposed to during my Six Visions of the romantic millionaires in tomorrow's Neo-Tech World!

What a ride that sent me on — a personal renaissance that resulted in me becoming wealthy *now* under the old code of living. Indeed, I used those 21st-century techniques from my Six Visions to go on a personal renaissance that put me into the wealthy world of tomorrow, even under today's subjugated society. In fact, five of the Six Ultimate Gifts became mine *now*. The only one missing depended mostly on technology: perfect health. Besides that, I was able to surround myself with geniuses, go from broke to a millionaire, capture the livelihood of my dreams, love the woman of my dreams, and command superior Neothink.

My journey began on Monday morning after my Six Visions. I stopped what I was doing at work. Like a bad dream, I realized that my job was structured to make the establishment-leaders wealthy and powerful, from the leaders of big businesses and unions that a lot of us worked under to the leaders of the land who got a major chunk of whatever we earned.

I stopped to think: The rich and powerful leaders of the Establishment did not work their whole lives to make someone else happy. But I did. I along with the majority of people worked our whole lives to make the leaders happy.

At that moment, I became flushed with determination to somehow wake up from this bad dream into a better world with a better life. Out of nowhere, a strong impression came to me: "The secret to getting ahead is to become *The Self-Leader!*" I

Book 1
God-Man Decoded

3

knew I was about to embark on a journey from which I would never return.

I drove home from work that fateful day wondering, "Who is the self-leader?" All I could figure was that the self-leader captured for himself the rewards and wealth from his efforts in life. "I must set off on a journey to discover in myself the self-leader," I said. "But where do I begin my journey?"

Deeply troubled, I felt I had no power in life. "Knowledge is power," a very wise man once said. So I decided to start my journey seeking knowledge at my place of work.

The next day I began to seriously study my place of work for the first time. I observed other people doing their jobs and even asked them questions. Immediately I noticed that the more I started to learn about the business, the more power I felt.

So, I became the pupil, and my place of work was the school. As I educated myself about the business, I acquired more and more integrated knowledge. After just one week, I could feel that this process of building integrated knowledge would inevitably deliver more and more power, promotions, and pride.

Without my Six Visions alerting me to my stagnation-trap, then success would have forever eluded me. That trap was the opposite of what guaranteed wealth and happiness — the opposite of integrated knowledge. That trap was disintegrated knowledge in the form of specialized tasks. Doing the same routine of specialized tasks every day caused me a lifelong rut of stagnation. Yet wealth and happiness now seemed attainable with another way of thinking that had never been introduced to me under the old code of living. That other way of thinking was: *integrated thinking*.

With integrated thinking, I was no longer trapped by specialized tasks in an inescapable routine rut. My mind, like everyone else, had always been trapped in a narrow sphere of specialized thinking...just following a very limited routine of specialized tasks that my leaders set out for me. Now, with integrated thinking, I began to lead myself.

## Project Curiosity

I developed a program at work called *Project Curiosity*. I simply expressed to my peers, subordinates, and superiors an interest in what they were doing. I asked questions. I explained to them that I wanted to learn more about the business and that their jobs were very important pistons that made the engine run. Most felt flattered and spent as much time with me as I needed. They also felt proud of their work, and I reflected to them what good workers they were. That not only was the right thing to do, I figured, but the mutual respect that I established now began to build my leadership role toward the future.

As I gained integrated knowledge about the business, responsibilities began to flow to me. People began to come to me for answers — for leadership. "Don't be bashful," I told myself. "Use your integrated knowledge and give them guidance. *Take control.*"

I realized I had been taught *not* to take control, but to do as I was trained. "Our leaders do not want us to gain integrated knowledge and take control," I told my friends. I knew that I had never acquired integrated knowledge before simply because I was never introduced to the concept. I was never shown how, and I never saw anyone else going after integrated knowledge. But acquiring integrated knowledge and taking control was actually very natural...and fun. It sure beat my boring routine rut.

Why do our leaders make our jobs specialized traps? I thought back over my Six Visions. The Fourth and Sixth Visions in particular had given me some unforgettable insights into our stagnation traps. With those in mind, I went to see my father who was a former Senior Research Chemist for Du Pont and author of the famous Neo-Tech Discovery.

I explained everything to him. My father smiled knowingly as I said, "Dad, the success-bound integrated thinker digs for integrated knowledge and begins to build his way out of his rut toward success. No one can stop him. He will eventually rise to the top of the company and begin nipping at the heels of the people in upper management. He will eventually take over their jobs."

"I know all about this from my days at Du Pont," he said.

"Now, let me ask you, Dad, couldn't some of the less competitive leaders of our big businesses today, without explicitly knowing what they are doing, over the decades shape their

5

companies' jobs into specialized traps to discourage integrated thinking? Couldn't they shape their companies' jobs into specialized traps to stop integrated thinking and suppress competition from within so they can remain on top unchallenged?"

"You're right," he said. "And let me caution you; when someone occasionally beats the odds and beats the negative elements in management above him to succeed with integrated thinking, or if he leaves to start his own business, then ambitious bureaucrats will eventually strike and sometimes destroy his efforts. Every business-advancing integrated thinker including every entrepreneur fears authorities — fears local authorities and federal authorities like the IRS, FTC, EPA; fears legal authorities, like the lawyers. Every business-advancing integrated thinker carries that fear. Remember, we ran into FDA authorities when we were soaring ahead on cures to diseases at Du Pont."

"Always a threat," I replied as my voice dropped to a mutter. "You know, we all sense the laziness, ineptness, and corruption in our government. But can the ordinary person really put together the hoax and expose the frauds? No, we just know that dishonesty goes on in our government, yet we are too specialized to be able to put together a solution to the fraud above us."

"But those who beat the odds and start rising up with integrated thinking are not too specialized to put together a solution to the fraud above us," my father added.

"Yes, yes, I see," I said. "Most people go to work, do the same set routine, then go back home. They can't possibly know the political frauds sprinkled among the management in big business and certainly can't know the frauds lurking throughout our government. The ordinary person does not know how business and the economy *really* work. They're simply too specialized. They go to their jobs, go back home, and they're none the wiser. They can't really see the hoax as long as they have no integrated knowledge."

"But through integrated thinking," my father added, "they begin to know how business works, then how the economy *really* works, then how big government really works against the economy. At that point, they not only see the hoax throughout government, but begin to see and expose exactly who the frauds

6

are. The point is: integrated knowledge accumulated through integrated thinking threatens our leaders in government as well as in big business. Therefore, our government authorities push down entrepreneurs and all others who rise up with integrated thinking."

At that moment, I remembered a movie I saw years ago called *Tucker*, a true story: Back in the '40s, a lone genius of society, just a working man named Preston Tucker, defied the Establishment and developed the Tucker Torpedo — the car of the future. It was the car that America loved. Yet, just before mass production began, political big-business leaders teamed together with regulatory bureaucrats in the SEC and with a dishonest judge from our decadent legal system to destroy Tucker. Those dishonest people, our establishment-leaders, destroyed Preston Tucker, an entrepreneurial genius who rose up from just an assembly line working man through integrated thinking to bring an unprecedented value to society. After our leaders destroyed Tucker, he got very sick and, his life ruined, he gave up and died. ...Yes, Dad was right, I realized.

"Integrated thinking is discouraged by our big companies, by our big government, and by our public educational system, controlled by our government," I heard my father saying.

"Society is suppressed into a big specialization-trap," I heard myself thinking. Now I understood why so many people suffer in silent frustration. "For decades, human potential has been systematically battered down and destroyed...like Preston Tucker and his car company that would've created thousands of jobs. *Jobs are being destroyed.* Opportunities for us disappear with those lost jobs. Even worse, tender youth and their new businesses that would bring a plethora of new jobs and opportunities to the world cannot rise today in the face of debilitating laws, regulations, litigation, and lawsuits. Society's long-term standard of living is suffering. Why? Integrated thinkers cannot rise. Thus, prosperity for the people sinks. Why? All this lost potential to secure the livings of the establishment-leaders."

My father, a very wise man, seemed astonished at my sudden understanding about the state of things today. So, I took the opportunity to tell him about my Six Visions.

7

Book 1
God-Man Decoded

While driving home that night, I pondered the life I dreamed about in my youth and how I never found that life. Now, I was determined to not only make a lot of money, but to have the complete life of my dreams as well. When I returned home, I telephoned my brother:

"Hello," he answered.

"Eric, it's me," I said.

"It's...it's after midnight. Something wrong?"

"I'll tell you what's wrong. We're all stuck in a big stagnation-trap! But I don't think our lives need to be like that. We can break free!"

We talked for forty minutes. After we hung up, I sat at my kitchen table and began writing in my diary: "To free myself from the leaders' system right now while still under the old code of living requires a powerful counter-system. I'll name it: *The Self-Leader System.* The Self-Leader System has begun unfolding before me day by day. I can feel the self-leader growing within me every day, deep in my psyche. I have begun building a base of integrated power inside that no establishment-leader can stop. I know that my Six Visions will become my guide during this personal renaissance. I will not be denied. I will not die unfulfilled, without experiencing wealth, prosperity, and romantic love. I will experience the good life, right now even before America goes Neo-Tech."

Each day thereafter, I enthusiastically educated myself about my place of work. Over the next couple of weeks, I acquired the basic knowledge of how everything worked. Things really started to roll.

## The Self-Investment Plan

After a few weeks with Project Curiosity, I knew all the basic responsibilities at my place of work. Now I saw how those basic responsibilities could be grouped into wealth-building jobs. On paper, I pulled the basic responsibilities together by their money-making purposes exactly as I had witnessed in the Fourth Vision. I secretly planned to target and take over one of those lucrative wealth-building jobs or mini-companies, which I named them, and I called my secret plan my Self-Investment Plan.

I systematically transformed my job into a 21st-century

wealth-building mini-company. After defining the potential mini-companies for my place of work, I chose the one I wanted and steadily took over each of its responsibilities, one by one. ...No one really knew what I was doing, but I eventually had a wealth-building job!

First, as seen in Diagram One in Chapter Six of *God-Man*, I listed the company's basic responsibilities. (At this time I did not own or run a business. I was merely an employee, but to avoid repetition for the reader, I refer you back to the similar division-of-essence example from my company in Diagrams One through Four in Chapter Six of *God-Man*.) Then, as seen in Diagram Two, I defined those basic responsibilities' money-making purposes. Then, as seen in Diagrams Three and Four, I restructured the company on paper into the division of essence — into wealth-building mini-companies. I silently selected the mini-company I wanted, and I remembered: all responsibilities were built on details. I forced myself to master and absorb the details that made up those responsibilities I needed. The details were mine for the taking, for people were happily relieved of nitty-gritty details. Then, lo and behold, the responsibilities began to flow my way; my stagnation-trap steadily transformed into a wealth-building job, just as I had seen in my Fourth Vision!

As I did this, I realized anyone in *any* job could do the same; they simply needed to figure out the potential wealth-building jobs at work. For example, I thought about the most routine job I could possibly think of...let's say, the bricklayer for a construction company. Yet, if he listed the basic responsibilities of the construction company and went through the division-of-essence exercise as shown in Diagrams One through Four in *God-Man*, he would discover that the money-making purposes of those basic responsibilities were the different construction sites or contracts. The construction sites would be his potential wealth-building jobs. If he aggressively learned and mastered the responsibilities of a wealth-building job — a particular construction site — then he would eventually take over more and more of the responsibilities and eventually the construction site itself. He would eventually take control of the contracts. His job would *come to life* as he got involved with the profits, like an entrepreneur.

9

As I personally started taking over more and more of the responsibilities of my targeted mini-company, I realized that in today's specialized working world, my specialized tasks, like in most other jobs, were until now merely *ends* in themselves — dead-end routine chores to just turn in, causing a dead-end job. Very few jobs dynamically BUILT the business; most jobs just MAINTAINED the business. And like me, before my personal renaissance began, most people just maintained their specialized tasks, hopelessly stuck in their boring routine ruts. Finally, I was moving toward an open-ended job.

When I first told my brother about the Self-Investment Plan, he could not believe his ears:

"That's too good to be true," my brother, said. "You mean, I can pull together job responsibilities at work that make me kind of my own boss — like an entrepreneur? You mean, I can actually build profits for the company and for myself? I'd love that! Right now, work feels so meaningless."

After my brother spent several minutes studying my diagrams (see Diagrams One through Four in *God-Man*), I added, "If you can't yet see how the Self-Investment Plan would come together for you at your place of work, don't be discouraged. You'll need a little time with Project Curiosity first to get a better understanding of the business and its basic responsibilities."

I went on to explain to him that most companies turned their basic responsibilities straight into specialized jobs. Therefore, those jobs had no money-making purpose behind them and could never build wealth and grow. But once a person identified the basic responsibilities' money-making purposes at work, then he could pull together on paper the jobs with money-making purpose behind them — the company's potential wealth-building jobs — and target one for himself.

My brother went home with the diagrams of the Self-Investment Plan. A week later, he and I got together again. He had gone on a crash program of Project Curiosity at work and had already sketched out his company's wealth-building jobs. He was very excited. The first thing he said when we got together was: "The wealth-building jobs are dynamite! They can grow without limits and depend on no one but yourself! And it's all so simple! Why doesn't every business do this? This is an amazing breakthrough!" I had never seen my brother like this.

"Sometime after 2001, all businesses will have to change from the division of labor to this division of essence," I said. "But for now, those wealth-building jobs would transform ordinary people into integrated thinkers and self-leaders. Lazy big-business and big-government leaders need us to be specialized thinkers and their followers. They could not remain competitive in an environment of self-leaders. By removing money-making purpose from our livelihoods and motivation from our souls, the establishment-leaders can easily float above us all and live off our routine efforts."

"You mean, big-business leaders won't want this breakthrough?" my brother asked. "They choose *not* to set up like this? Why not? Their businesses would boom and their employees would get rich!"

"And that is why every business eventually has to go this way," I said. Then I explained further, "When that day comes and ordinary working people can lead themselves, the comfortable establishment-leaders will lose their supervisory roles over us. So, they will discourage the Self-Leader System. Nevertheless, I think we have discovered a treasure. You see, dead-end static responsibilities pulled together into integrated wealth-building jobs are like torn pieces of a treasure map brought together. Useless apart but priceless together, those responsibilities, once brought together into their money-making purposes, will lead us to the money."

Eric nodded. "I can already feel my mind changing with integrated thinking. Every thought now connects with making money! This is exciting," he said. "Now I can look around me at work and see that most people today have *no power*. They're trapped by specialized thinking. I can now feel how people tomorrow will have genuine power — self-power — freed by integrated thinking. Instead of working their lives for their leaders, they'll live their lives for themselves. They'll build their own success and wealth. That's what I'm going to do now."

## Investing In Self

I came to work the next day determined to fully take over a wealth-building job. My father, a scientist and author of *Neo-*

*Tech Physics*, once told me, "To understand the vast universe first requires digging down to and learning about the tiniest subatomic particles." I now figured that, similarly, to understand vast wealth required digging down to and learning about the tiniest nitty-gritty details. So, I came to work this particular morning ready to really *dig in*.

I started really digging into my job like never before. I took full command of every detail in my job and of every detail related to my job. Little did I suspect that digging into and mastering the nitty-gritty details was a direct investment in myself. Not knowing any better, I previously never really mastered the nitty-gritty details. Instead, I just did my work — just automatically turned in my duties as I was told. Never finding the simple key to investing in myself, I had served the establishment-leaders all my adult life.

All that seemed to change as I directed my efforts to getting in and understanding *the procedures, roots, current purpose and all the reasons* behind the nitty-gritty details: the what, why, where, when, and how. I learned the integrations behind why they were originally formed, how they currently operated, what exactly they accomplished, when and where they applied, and the full and finished purpose and reasons behind how they served the business...including how they served my superiors' jobs. To do that, I reached into my superiors' jobs and began understanding their areas of the business as well. Some superiors did not like this intense and specific digging, but they could not stop it.

By digging into the completed purpose and the subtlest reasons behind every operational detail, I began to master the details. Then, with that full understanding of the full procedure and purpose of every detail, I determined whether the purpose was best served by the way a detail currently existed...or if I could improve the detail to better serve its purpose. The details now moved into my realm of control and integrations. I began to evolve into the internally guided, integrating mode. I began *to think* — not just follow what was taught, but integrate what was best. I was evolving beyond leaders, discovering self.

Indeed, by mastering the nitty-gritty details, I now truly ran my job through my own integrated thinking. I dramatically improved my efficiency. Then it dawned on me: Before now, I never ran my job through my own thinking. Instead, I blindly followed. I only turned in responsibilities as I was taught.

I felt my competence grow. As a rising integrated thinker, I took more and more control, and more and more business naturally flowed my way — to the man in control...the burgeoning self-leader. Instead of just turning in my duties via my set, specialized routine, I aggressively took over those responsibilities and improved them. My control spread over more and more of the business. My mind would never again function through static, specialized thinking in which I functioned automatically in a zombie-like state, for now I discovered dynamic integrated thinking in which I passionately spread my control over and improved more and more chunks of business and success. I was becoming a market-driven businessman. I was exhilarated!

A phenomenon began to occur: At my place of work, as in any company — well managed or poorly managed — responsibilities would get routinely delegated to subordinates. Yet, as I mastered and absorbed those responsibilities, more and more responsibilities flowed my way, to the man in control. That phenomenon began moving me toward success as I acquired greater and greater integrated knowledge and power.

Mastering and absorbing responsibility was a direct investment in myself and my success. Responsibilities and opportunities began to flow my way that I could never before imagine or know existed. As I rose from my specialization-trap, I knew that the success of all self-made, powerful and wealthy people grew through this phenomenon as they mastered details and absorbed responsibilities, and, as a result, opportunities flowed their way they could have never imagined. Eventually, like them, I would embark on unforeseen adventures into success, power, and wealth.

I wrote in my journal: "In any company, a person is given certain responsibilities. Those first, delegated responsibilities determine his or her capacity to eventually move forward. If the boss gives a responsibility to me, I now take that responsibility into my own realm of integrated thinking by mastering every nitty-gritty detail. I fully *take over* that responsibility. The average person does not.

13

"The average person is stuck in the following mode, and I am not. The difference is: who absorbs and masters the responsibilities given to them? My peers do not. I do. Therefore, I build my integrated knowledge and control. Especially in staid, bureaucratic companies, lazy managers like to delegate. As I take over those responsibilities, they become mine. Unbeknownst to those managers, I have begun to acquire my own mini-company."

I now specifically hunted for details and responsibilities that were part of my targeted mini-company. I steadily took control of my chosen mini-company. Before now, the ghostly word "success", when it came right down to it, left me wondering "what the heck do I do?" But now, I knew exactly what to do.

I previously did not master and absorb responsibilities (i.e., opportunities) that went my way. So all growth had stopped, and all hope had ended as nothing positive happened. As a young man, stagnation had already mercilessly engulfed me. But all that now changed. No longer a follower but now an initiator, I now *created* my own opportunities.

The next day my brother stopped by. As we sat down in the living room, I could not wait to talk: "Eric, I can now become anyone's 'fortune teller'. Let me tell you *your* future. It's easy. I just need to observe whether or not you leave behind leaders and discover self. I can best explain it with a story:

"Walter Chrysler, founder of Chrysler Corporation, first worked for a railroad line adjusting locomotive valves. An old veteran was training the young Walter Chrysler the highly complicated art of adjusting locomotive valves. But the old man liked drinking too much. One evening, the old man wanted to go drinking in town. In the middle of the job, he turned to Walter and said good-night and left for town. Surprised and confused, Walter was on his own with a pressing deadline. Adjusting locomotive valves was very complex, even for a veteran. But young Walter Chrysler did not panic. He dug into the nitty-gritty details like never before. He mastered and absorbed the giant responsibility that night. The young Chrysler's decision that night to dig into the details like never before and to master the responsibility of adjusting valves had planted the seeds of integrated thinking and self-leadership, which years later

14

blossomed into Chrysler Corporation."

"The road to success now seems so down to earth and attainable," my brother said. "Success really all comes down to just the most simple thing: master the details and suck up the responsibilities — especially those responsibilities of my targeted mini-company."

"Exactly," I said, my hand dropping to my lap with a slap of finality. "And, you don't even have to abandon your security. I know you have a family to feed. You don't have to do anything risky like start your own business. At work, just dig into the details and, as you say, 'suck up' the responsibilities. Moreover, this process works *at any level;* let's say you're a construction worker. Well, you may ask skeptically, 'What big-time success could I possibly get as a physical laborer?' Easy to answer you: Just take over whatever responsibility falls in front of you; take over responsibilities and make them run on your own integrations. You'll become like a Charlie Bannon before you know it. Charlie Bannon, by the way, is the main character in a book called *Calumet K.* By mastering and taking over nitty-gritty details and responsibilities, he quickly took control of large construction sites — wealth-building jobs — for the company that hired him. And once you become like a Charlie Bannon, you'll eventually take charge of even more. You could eventually become the company's president, or possibly start your own construction company. As you get hooked on integrated thinking, you'll never stop absorbing integrated knowledge and could even someday become a powerful magnate. Start off as a construction worker and become a Donald Trump! But the key is: whatever detail or responsibility falls in front of you, master it! And keep in mind a clear plan — a clear target — to take over the basic responsibilities that jell into an exciting wealth-building job, like taking over a construction site. The sooner you take control of the basic responsibilities integrated together by the same wealth-building purpose, the sooner you build wealth and release the creativity now buried somewhere deep in your mind.

"Walter Chrysler could have ended up as a 65-year-old mechanic at some gas station complaining, 'Where did I go wrong? What happened to my dreams?' If that were the

15

scenario, then you could trace his life of stagnation back to that night the old man left and young Chrysler did not dig into those valves and master that responsibility. Instead, his success goes right back to that night because he did dig into the details and master that responsibility to start his journey into integrated thinking. I guess you can say that on that night, young Walter Chrysler became a man."

My brother said, "These past couple of weeks have made me rediscover an excitement for life that I had forgotten all about. And now I feel that my peers are all being used and used up. I feel great, but I feel bad for them...like I wish I could help them."

I noticed my brother was a little emotional. I said, "Throughout your life, Eric, you, me, and everyone else got stuck in routine ruts. Those stagnation-traps drained the youthful excitement completely out of us. We've been squeezed into stagnation-traps because our establishment-leaders want it that way. We never even know about our lost opportunities, for we know of nothing beyond our specialized jobs."

"But we elect our politicians, Mark. Do we choose this fate?" my brother asked.

"No. We've been tricked," I said.

"But, if we don't choose this fate of stagnation," Eric said, "then why can't we move up rapidly to achieve wealth and happiness?"

"We don't move up because the opportunities aren't there," I said. "And we don't know how to make opportunities for ourselves. We don't know how to break through specialized thinking into dynamic integrated thinking. If we could find a way, I know each and every one of us would unleash our potential and reap the rewards. We wouldn't spend the rest of our lives trapped in our limited jobs that leave us financially stressed out and emotionally empty."

"The Self-Leader System is the way," Eric said.

"There are actually two ways," I answered. And then I told him about my Six Visions and how they showed me the way out of our leaders' system for civilization as a whole. I told him about how, in my Visions, destructive leaders eventually got replaced after 2001 with legitimate leaders through the Neo-Tech

16

Party's Great Replacement Program (see the Second Vision in *God-Man*). Then, I explained how business and technology surged ahead as opportunities flooded into society. "But as long as we're led by career politicians and their entourage of politically ambitious regulatory bureaucrats, politically fed lawyers, politically driven judges, political businessmen, political journalists, and political activists," I added, "then society and nearly everyone in that politicized society will be trapped, unable to move forward. The only ordinary people who will not suffer stagnated, wasted lives are those who discover self-leadership through integrated thinking — *the only other way out*. With integrated thinking, we do not have to wait for our leaders to make opportunities for us, which never happens. With integrated thinking, we will make our own opportunities!"

## The Fast-Track Method

For the first time, I began building wealth. And it felt good! I began moving ahead into new self-made opportunities. As those opportunities grew, so did the demands on my time. Soon under impossible time pressures, I set up my own mini-day schedule, exactly as I had witnessed in my Fourth Vision. I was amazed. Now I built my own success as *I myself* dictated my own schedule. "Talking about being a self-leader!" I shouted in glee one afternoon. Moreover, I raced ahead into new money-making projects so quickly I was assigned two assistants. I wanted to get my assistants into wealth-building jobs with mini-day schedules, just like myself.

First, I would put both my assistants immediately into their own mini-companies. So, here is what I did: I replicated, to both, two ongoing money-making projects with their own money-making purposes, as described in the Fourth Vision in *God-Man*. Those two projects could grow into wealth-building "living" jobs with their own "DNA" or money-making purpose. Then, I set up the proper tracking reports to follow every detail. Eventually, after the evolving replicating process, I started my monthly Essence Meetings. These two workers metamorphosed from my assistants into my very own profit generators. ...I was preparing myself to someday start my own company to be filled with such profit generators.

17

Early one morning after I got my assistants working hard on their own money-making projects, I called my two new assistants into my office and said, "Start this morning: List on a pad every task you perform at work for the next three days. List each task AS YOU DO THE TASK for three FULL days. After the third day, bring the list to me. We will go through your list of tasks and determine the physical movements of your exciting money-making jobs as I did. Those physical movements will become your mini-days. You will determine the time you should devote to each mini-day and will then set up your mini-day schedule."

As my assistants, excited about making more money, were walking out my office door, I added, "Do not take shortcuts! List three full days of tasks, not from memory, but as you perform the tasks. Start this morning, first thing."

After my budding profit generators left my office, I thought: But what if one's job cannot be divided into mini-days? Let's say someone works a physical labor job or is just plain stuck in a specialized routine rut?

He has two options, I realized: to stick it out where he now works, or to strive to move on toward his deepest ambitions. I leaned back in my chair and, in deep concentration, mumbled to myself: "If he goes with the first option to stick it out, then he must master any and all responsibilities that fall before him. It takes some work but can be done. He will steadily acquire more responsibility and authority. He can use that technique to take over a wealth-building job, as Charlie Bannon did in *Calumet K*. Then he can go on the mini-day schedule.

"From my experience, I realized that when he gets himself on the mini-day schedule, he immediately gets respect, no matter where he lands on the power scale. I noticed that business peers respond with respect, especially one's boss. Eventually, like me, that person would become a natural leader. He would accomplish more in a day than he previously did in a week. Quickly he would rise above his peers and quietly transform into a high-powered, money-making machine. Others could only step out of his way in awe...ready to file in behind.

"Respect," I said to myself. "How about bringing that respect and success to the physical laborer who decides on the second option to leave his job and journey out on his own?"

18

## Personal Renaissance I: A Journey of No Return

I paused, leaned forward, then continued my thoughts, silently this time: If the laborer is ready to move beyond his current job, he must do everything differently. He must think BEYOND his job about what he wants. If he wants to start his own "living" business, what are the physical movements to do that? He must place those physical movements, those mini-days, in the morning or in the evening, AROUND his job.

My thoughts went back to the most stagnant job I could think of: the bricklayer. Say he feels ambitious, I thought, and so he works harder. Well, he may lay 20% more bricks while his enthusiasm lasts. That's it. How long can he endure that extra effort year after year while going nowhere? He lives in a rut! Yet, he would love to catapult out of that rut, I thought. That bricklayer just may have greater incentive than someone sitting behind a desk whose ambitions and incentives may go no further than getting the raise next month or next year.

I tried to put myself inside the mind of a bricklayer: How can I apply this mini-day concept, the bricklayer may say, if I work eight hours a day doing physical labor? How am I going to do it, for I work all day long? ...True, he may work eight hours laying bricks, but that eight-hour physical movement (laying bricks) is considered a mini-day; an income mini-day let's call it. Now, that physical laborer must determine the physical movements *necessary to accomplish his ambitions.* Whereas I had determined the physical movements of my living job, the physical laborer must determine the physical movements needed to accomplish his ambitions, and he must structure those mini-days to either side of his income mini-day. This will pull the physical laborer out of his rut.

In fact, an American hero pulled himself out of such an impossible stagnation-trap, I remembered. Yes, it can be done; it has been done. A great American hero did just that. I remembered reading about him as a teenager. He was a laborer at the turn of the century, a dock worker among the roughest ports of early nineteen-hundred America. That dock breed spoke illiterate English, crude, unrefined. This American hero dropped out of school early. He lived on the streets. He survived. He never had an opportunity. Like millions of others, he was headed for a dead-end life. A desire burned inside, though. He desired

19

to pull himself out of the abyss. He desired to become a successful writer. In the early 1900s, an illiterate dock worker had essentially no chance to ever sell a piece of literature. But that man became the highest paid author in history! And if we adjust for inflation today, he is the highest paid author of all time. That man was Jack London. He wrote many adventure stories and best-selling novels including *Call of the Wild*, *The Sea Wolf*, *Martin Eden*.

Exactly how did Jack London do it? He established four physical movements, four mini-days that would achieve his desire of becoming a writer: (1) reading, (2) intense grammar study, (3) self-education (a library-study program), and (4) writing. Those four mini-days were divided before and after his full-day income mini-day. Even after he pulled himself out of his trap and off the docks, he never stopped the mini-day system. He stayed on the mini-day system through all his fame and glory to the last days of his life.

So, there were two ways for the physical laborer to get on the powerful mini-day schedule. One way involved eventually leaving his place of work; the other did not. The bricklayer, the cook, the bank teller, the drafting artist, for example, could actually rise in the company he or she now worked for by first defining the potential wealth-building jobs at work and then mastering the details and absorbing the responsibilities to steadily take over one of those wealth-building jobs.

Either decision — to pull himself up outside his job or within his job — he would work toward taking over wealth-building purpose...the DNA of a job. Once that occurred, then he could establish mini-days for manufacturing money and success.

I next shifted my thoughts to another powerful 21st-century tool I had seen in my Fourth Vision: *power-thinking*, made possible because of the mini-day schedule. With power-thinking, I suddenly compiled FUTURE projects into today's powerful mini-days. In other words, I compiled future money into today's paychecks. First of all, after I had been on the mini-day schedule for a couple weeks, suddenly I found myself all done with all my work by Tuesday afternoon or Wednesday morning. In a state of shock, I knew I had to *create* more work — create money-making projects to fill my week! Suddenly, I was forced to think creatively. I had to figure out and pursue new money-making projects that never existed before. I had to rise to the next level of integrated thinking — power-thinking. Now with power-thinking, my very existence was changing into some dynamo I once fantasized about.

Our minds are limited, I remember thinking. I thought: look at me not long ago. My natural follow-the-leader mode blocked me from discovering integrated thinking. After integrating five or six thoughts on my own, my mind stopped integrating and looked for external guidance before going further. Now, my mind goes further. I do not stop to wait for external guidance. Instead, I use my own self-guidance through power-thinking. Now, I never stop moving forward. I keep on integrating more projects and keep on making more income.

Before, by contrast, I MAINTAINED my specialized job with automatic or externally guided routines and traditional schedules, just like most everyone else. But to CREATE and BUILD success, I now knew, required power-thinking and the mini-day schedule.

Without removing a simple, deep-rooted limitation — the traditional schedule that designates time to tasks instead of to physical movements — major success would have forever stayed out of reach, I realized. After making that realization, I wrote the following journal entry:

"Man's deep-rooted tendencies for nonthinking automatic or external guidance previously kept me chained to the traditional schedule that essentially provided nonthinking automatic or external guidance as I simply *reacted* to the business around me. Filled to my capacity using the physically disjointed traditional schedule, I could look and feel busy and important. Yet I only MAINTAINED my job for the leaders and built nothing for myself."

That weekend my brother came over. I said, "Do I have a treat for you!" I went on to tell my brother about the mini-day/power-thinking team. Then, I showed him my own schedule. Indeed, with power-thinking, my journey into money and power quickly took off. "I get more done in a week than I used to in three months," I told my brother. "But most amazingly, I'm *creating* brand-new money-making projects now. I can't describe to you what that feels like!"

"You don't have to," Eric said. "I'll find out. Do you realize what you're creating here? You're going to free all ordinary working people. Man, this is exciting!"

## Window To Creativity

I was now receiving major pay raises at an almost unbelievable rate. With my own wealth-building job, racing ahead with the mini-day/power-thinking team, what I needed now more than anything was more and more *creativity*. I was about to discover my own private window to a whole new creative world.

I was listening to an audio-cassette tape called *The Dream Maker: William C. Durant, Founder of General Motors*. The audio-cassette tape about General Motors and its founder told a story about one of its most influential employees named Charles Nash. He had gone to work for William Durant before Durant founded General Motors, back in the late 1800s when Durant owned the Durant-Dort Carriage Company that built the carriages that horses pulled. Here is the story as told on that tape:

"In 1890, a 26-year-old man named Charles Nash began work in the blacksmith's department. His first job was pounding iron. Within a few days he walked into Durant's easily accessible office. 'I'm wasting time,' he said. 'You can get a power hammer there. It would cost about $35.00 and do more pounding in a day than I can do in a month!' Durant took the suggestion and Nash was moved over to working on a drill press that prepared cart braces for attachment. The next time Durant came through the shop, he stopped at Nash's machine. It looked like none of the others. Nash had rigged it with an overhead spring and a treadle that left both his hands free while working and doubled the output. Durant weighed the implications of this: 'Charlie,' he said, 'We'll get another man here. See if you can't straighten out the trimming department for me.' Promoted to the headship of that department, Nash wrestled with the problem of heavy expenditures on tacks. He found the answer in a short time. The carpenters held the tacks in their mouths while working. The cheap, roughly finished brand the company was using cut their lips and tongues and they would spit them on the floor in exasperation, and lose them. A better grade tack

22

proved the remedy. ...So Nash went on probing, correcting, climbing up to the highest supervisory ranks."

As it turns out, Nash went on to become, in 1910, the President of Buick; in 1912, the President of General Motors; and then four years later he left General Motors to start Nash Motors Company. Some of us still remember the Nash Rambler.

While listening to that story, I suddenly knew why Charles Nash rose from the lowest ranks to the highest possible ranks and then beyond: Nash broke the code for creativity written in numbers, which opened the window to creativity in his mind. Indeed, everything Nash did, he thought in numbers. First, he figured the cost of a power hammer versus the cost of his own labor. Second, he created a unique drill-press attachment, driven by a desire to double output. Third, he determined how to spend more money on better tacks to decrease losses and improve profits. *Nash befriended numbers and paid attention to their story!*

Using numbers to open the window to creativity in his mind, this young, inexperienced novice could see creative business advancements in a few days that veterans could not see in their whole lives. The numbers-integrating mode quickly lifted Nash out of the specialized routine rut of pounding iron all day long. That routine rut had trapped others for many years...and would have trapped them for life if not for rising creative thinkers like Charles Nash who pulled up society, standards of living, and opportunities for everyone.

While thinking about Nash, suddenly an earth-moving thought shook me: All money/power giants came to a point in their lives where they suddenly discovered this window to creativity! They all reached a point in their lives where they passionately studied the numbers. I had read about, for instance, how late into the night a young John D. Rockefeller could be seen hovering over a desk covered with accounting and marketing numbers. Rockefeller always said he had discovered "a whole other fascinating world" through the numbers. And that was when business took on great excitement for him. ...Of course!

The turning point of history's most successful people came early in their careers when they discovered a whole new world through the numbers: Pierre S. du Pont, Henry Ford, Andrew

23

Carnegie, William C. Durant, Juan Trippe, Alfred P. Sloan, J. Paul Getty, Jay Gould, Milton Hershey, Walter Chrysler, Thomas Watson, Harold Geneen, Robert E. Wood. The numbers opened their windows to creativity!

Looking through that window into an exciting new world of creations and profits unlocked Nash's creativity. To double output, among other things, he became creative and rigged the drill press. If not for looking at the details in terms of improving the numbers, Nash would have never seen through them to the creative side. He would have just kept pounding or stitching away, forever blocked from creativity, forever trapped in a rut.

Instead, driven by the numbers, peering through the window to creativity in everything he did, he eventually entered the world of profitable creations. That whole other fascinating world led to the designing and manufacturing of his own cars...cars such as the famous Nash Rambler once driven all over America's roads. That enormous creativity and talent would have forever remained behind a wall, trapped inside a dark corner of Nash's mind had he not discovered the window to his creativity.

At that moment, while listening about Nash, I knew that powerful creativity existed in me and in all of us — locked inside a dark corner of our minds as we blindly serve our leaders.

"This is it," I wrote in my diary. "I've discovered the real freeing mechanism. Breaking the code for creativity written in numbers gives me a whole new level of almost total independence."

The following days at work, I broke from any residual trace of the externally guided or following mode. For, now numbers became my compass for internal guidance. *"Seek* numbers," I kept telling myself. "Seek the story that the numbers reveal!" I knew I must become emotionally tied to numbers, for becoming motivated over improving the numbers would free my creativity.

Like Nash, I started small by studying the details and how they were done in relation to their payoff. Then I would improve that payoff. Like Nash, I quickly brought new efficiencies to my company. My window to creativity revealed advancements that even veterans did not see. I soon found myself pushing beyond operations into the powerful leagues of product development and marketing. Every day, I could not wait to read the latest story of the numbers.

I combined my efforts of mastering details and absorbing responsibilities with linking them to the numbers — to their costs/ efficiencies. I wrote about this new phenomenon in my journal: "I measure everything by numbers now. It's a whole new world! A few months ago, I could not move forward without a boss or manager directing me. But now, my numbers-integrating mode puts me in an aggressive internally guided mode. With numbers as my guide, I target business advancements with bulls-eye accuracy. I move forward on my own, with great confidence, through my own creativity. Being a winner is fun!"

I later told my brother, "Numbers ultimately drive the entire company — the marketing, product/advertising development, operations, and personnel. You must make it second nature to measure everything by numbers. Also, you should embrace a numbers mini-day. While in it, learn about the marketing data, return on investment, costs to do procedures...even the littlest procedures in operations. The act of confronting the numbers may initially leave you staring at your desk, not knowing what to do. But that time is not wasted. You are learning how to break a code. Once successful, you will open your window to creativity.

"Schedule that numbers mini-day briefly, once a week at first. Slowly, over the next few weeks, you'll begin to uncover ways to penetrate that mini-day, new ways to accumulate, learn about, and understand numbers, new ways to gather data, new ways to use those numbers to elevate your area of the business...maybe even new ways to improve the service or product, eventually new ways to market it.

"You must study/calculate numbers/efficiencies in all areas of the company, including the numbers as they pertain to operations and to personnel — the payoff to the payout. So, set up that numbers mini-day at once. Get familiar with numbers, ask questions, do not be afraid of seeming naive. For, you'll soon know more, much more, than those blinded veterans of whom you ask the questions. You'll begin to see advancements they'll never see. Measuring everything by numbers, you may even rise to the top like Charles Nash. In any case, you will become a prosperous self-leader like me. With numbers as your guide, you no longer need external guidance."

By now, I felt that the Self-Leader System had given me a new life — the life I used to only dream about.

## The Future

I was rising as an integrated thinker, rising above the clouds that block ordinary folks' views. Now, I began to see what was really going on above us, which started opening my eyes to things that later sent me into another entire personal renaissance about life in general (Personal Renaissance II, next chapter).

I called my brother and family over for dinner a couple of weeks later. He brought a friend with him. After some small talk, I said to my brother and his friend, "Eric, you're going to get everything you want out of the rest of your life: money, success, romance. How can I possibly predict that? Because, by the time you leave tonight, you'll know how to knock over the only obstacle now standing between us and victory."

My statement got my brother's attention, and I continued: "Now, tell me, Eric, who gets the bulk of the money and the prestige? Certainly not the ordinary, hard-working person. Leaders of the Establishment, by contrast, enjoy lots of easy money and power. I'm talking about many big-business leaders, union leaders, bureaucratic leaders, leading lawyers, leading journalists, and leaders of our land — career politicians.

"We support the plush lifestyle of the leaders at work, in government, and in law. As you know, the only way to claim your own future of wealth is to become your own person...*the self-leader*. The self-leader does not use up his one and only life supporting someone else's lifestyle. With the Self-Leader System, you have already redirected your daily efforts *right back into yourself and will become wealthy* if you do not fall to one remaining obstacle that I'll explain tonight." ...My brother's friend also seemed very interested, as I continued...

"Let me begin with a story: I recently went to California to attend an infomercial seminar. An infomercial is a half-hour TV advertisement. At the seminar, I met the well-known producers.

"During a question-and-answer period, I stood up to ask one producer a question. In asking my question, I had to reference an infomercial I had recently done on my own at low cost. Little did I realize the message I had just given the crowd of hundreds of people. Reading between the lines, I had told them that I was a leader, that I was a self-leader...that I did not need to go to the authorities, the producers, *the leaders* to do my own infomercial. Instead, I had done it all myself.

"Amazingly, at the next break, I had a crowd of people around me. In fact, more people surrounded me than the well-known producers. These people wanted me to do their infomercials for them. All I needed to do was put out my hand, and people would have filled it with lots of money. Why? Because I was a leader, and people are drawn to leaders. People are ready and willing to *make the leaders rich.*

"One gentleman was persistent about me producing his infomercial. I told him no, that he must do it himself as I had done. That way, he would spend just an affordable few thousand dollars to learn and eventually achieve success, not a few hundred thousand dollars through a leader — that is, about twenty tries at thirty to fifty thousand dollars each to perhaps hit upon success once through the established producers. I told him that to become successful and wealthy, he must instead invest his effort and money in himself, not in a leader. He would then grow more and more resistant to failure with each inexpensive 'lesson'. He would have a greater chance at success. Yet, to my astonishment, instead of being delighted by my insight, I saw a fear in his face. He resisted and wanted me to be his leader.

"Later I realized that all of us are drawn to leaders and will have a strong resistance to becoming self-leaders. In fact, that very resistance traps us in our routine ruts as our efforts endlessly go into building the lofty standards of living of the leaders."

To my surprise, my brother's friend, Santana, interrupted me. "I feel that resistance. I feel it, but I want to get everything good out of life, especially more money."

"A world of big money and romantic love exists just beyond our awareness," I continued, to his delight. "Our resistance keeps that great world beyond our reach. To understand the resistance that blocks us from discovering that new world, let's start by going back to the day you were born: When you came out of your mother's womb into this cold, bright world, all your little

27

body could do was cry. Your little body felt a strong resistance to this new world and wanted to go back into your mother's womb. But this world offered life, which was beyond your awareness at that time. ...Let's next fast forward to your first day at school. That first day was the first time in your young life that you were away from your mother. All your scared, toddler self wanted was to go back home to your mother. Your little body and mind felt a strong resistance to the frightening, noisy new world. But the world of education offered you happiness in life, which was beyond your awareness at that time. ...Next, let's go to the day you left home and moved out on your own into the real world. Remember the internal resistance to leaving home?

Santana nodded, and I continued: "Nature puts a natural resistance into all animals — a resistance to leaving their known protected environments and moving out on their own into the unknown. If you ever witnessed a cat weaning her kittens, you observed firsthand this natural resistance in animals. The mother feline must get violent with her young ones to push them away.

"As part of the animal kingdom, man too has this natural resistance. We have a natural resistance to leaving our leaders, both our childhood leaders, our parents, and our adulthood leaders. We have a natural resistance to moving ahead on our own and becoming the self-leader."

"That's nothing," Eric said. "You're just talking about growing up and moving out on your own."

"Not really," I countered. "Although animals are on their own once they are weaned, they're still controlled and guided by Mother Nature for their entire adult lives. Man is the only animal that can overcome the automatic controls of Mother Nature to control and guide himself. Nevertheless, man has had that capacity for only 3000 years. For over one million years prior to that, man was controlled and guided by Mother Nature all his life, like all other animals. Therefore, man harbors severely deep-rooted tendencies that seek to be controlled and guided by an external force all his life...in his case, by leaders. He harbors a severely deep-rooted, natural resistance to becoming the self-leader.

"We steadily move beyond our childhood leaders, our parents, into better worlds beyond our awareness at the time — guided into those better worlds by our parents. But when we are adults, we have no one to guide us into the better world beyond our awareness. Similar to the unknowing youngster at school his first day, beyond our awareness is a world that offers us our dreams. Finally, the Self-Leader System combined with the Neo-Tech Party will guide us there."

"Neo-Tech Party?" my brother's friend asked.

"The Neo-Tech Party," I said. Then looking over at my brother, I added, "I mentioned it when I told you about my Six Visions. I'll explain more before you leave tonight. But, right now let me ask Santana a 'what if' question: When you were a child, what if your resistance were allowed to control you, and you never left home, never went to school?"

"Then I would have stagnated and grown more and more unhappy, year after year," Santana said.

"Well, that exact scenario happens when you grow up," I said. "As an adult, your resistance is allowed to control you, and you never leave your leaders. You stagnate and grow more and more unmotivated, year after year...although you learn to live with it through entertainment, hobbies, and vacations.

"Clever people have discovered our deep-rooted tendencies that draw us to leaders, and they have gained unbeatable advantages by perfecting how to provide external guidance. Those 'natural leaders' include some of the most financially successful and prestigious people and often the most seemingly trustworthy people. For example, most politicians, presidents, many evangelists, network news anchors, and a portion of big-business upper management took this shortcut. They rose to leadership, power, and wealth by taking advantage of the deep-rooted following-mode tendencies in others. And they will always try to stop our progress into self-leadership to keep their prestigious positions in society. They largely control our lives."

"How exactly do those leaders control my life?" Santana asked.

I thought about his question for a moment before answering. I wanted to be sure my answer did not come across wrong. I said, "Most establishment-leaders are vestiges of man's deep-rooted urge for guidance. The need for external guidance became obsoleted by the discovery of human consciousness 3000 years ago. Therefore, most establishment-leaders today create illusions that we need and benefit from their guidance. Therefore, we accept them and want them for our authorities. They oblige and get their intoxicating rides in life, ruling over us. Our career politicians and regulatory bureaucrats and many corporate executives are on that stimulating ride. Moreover, they perpetuate our resistance to self-leadership by disintegrating our education and our jobs with specialized thinking (the Sixth Vision) and by defeating our entrepreneurial business environment with legislation and regulations (the First and Second Visions).

"Discouraged since our school days, we never learned to integrate and guide ourselves. So we depend on leaders to integrate for us and to guide us. Even when we know our leaders are dishonest, we fear not having leaders. And career politicians do their best to suppress our integrated thinking — starting with inferior public education and culminating in punishing legislation and regulation against aggressive entrepreneurs. The leaders guide us all right; they guide us right into stagnation for their own propagation. Those leaders shut down a progressive, Neo-Tech Society. In turn, we get trapped in a boring existence in which we just support their plush standards of living. ...That is how they control your life.

"Legitimate leaders will exist, however, according to my Visions. Those 21st-century legitimate leaders in government and business will no longer suppress society to steal a free ride. Self-sufficient, legitimate leaders will make success easy and natural for the people and their businesses. Like a mother who wants what is best for her children and who guides her children toward independence and freedom, legitimate leaders will guide the people toward independence and freedom."

"So, what's the answer?" Santana asked, looking somewhat spellbound by my revelation. "I mean, how do we replace the political leaders in big government and big business with legitimate leaders? How do we overcome our stagnation-traps...confronted with our built-in resistance, bad education, suppressive leaders and all?"

"People," I said, "will begin climbing out of their stagnation traps. But they have to overcome their built-in resistance against

30

leaving the 'protected world' of automatic guidance from an authority, an authority that will 'take care' of them."

"Because of our deep-rooted link to the automatic controls of nature," I added, "the average adult still seeks the sanctuary of automatic controls. Therefore, we seek automatic guidance at work, and we seek parental-like leaders in our lives from our government, church, the media. We resist becoming the self-leader, so we never discover the better world. Moreover, our jobs support our resistance with automatic, specialized tasks that we routinely do year after year.

"Good job figuring it all out," my brother said.

"Wow, that answers a lot of questions I've had about myself lately!" Santana blurted.

"Okay, Santana, let's take a closer look at the solution that will lift ordinary people like you and me from their stagnation-traps," I said. "Remember I told you legitimate leaders exist?"

To get Santana up to speed with my brother and me, I reached into a drawer and pulled out a folded piece of newspaper: "Here, Santana," I said, "read this article that recently appeared in a national publication. It explains something called the Neo-Tech World:"

# Why Aren't You Rich?
## The Neo-Tech World

Can *everyone* possibly be rich? Yes. That answer becomes abundantly clear with a brief story about the way things work. *"But if **everyone** were rich, then who would wash the dishes? Who would clean the houses? Who would drive in the rivets on the assembly-line? Not **everyone** could be rich,"* you may conclude.

But consider that the dishwasher machine now washes the dishes; robots in Japan now clean the houses, and computer-driven movable arms now drive in the rivets on the assembly-line.

As technology advances, machines, robots, and computers take over those physical-labor jobs. More importantly, as technology advances, the average job shifts from a job of physical labor to a job of the mind...from a low-paid blue-collar job to a high-paid white-collar job. The past decade, for example, the American work force reversed from 40% white collar, 60% blue collar to 60% white collar, 40% blue collar. Why? The computer revolution gave America a growth spurt of advancing technology.

31

*"Advancing technology might just take over my job,"* you may think if you are a blue-collar worker. But things do not work that way. In advancing times, businesses discover that their own blue-collar workers make some of the *best* white-collar employees because they know the business from the ground up — all the details. Advancing technology does not just replace blue-collar workers; it moves them on to better jobs. Technological growth means job growth, not job loss, and better jobs for the working man.

Advancing technology not only brings us better-paying quality jobs, but it brings us more and more quantity of jobs. In a booming Neo-Tech Society (i.e., a society of rapid, unrestricted advancing technology) we will see a job surplus, not a job shortage as in our current society (i.e., a society of highly regulated, restricted technology). In the Neo-Tech Society consisting of too many jobs and not enough people to fill them, we will need advancing technology to fill the vacated physical blue-collar jobs with machines, robots, and computers.

The President of the United States is the boss of the cabinets and their regulatory bureaucracies that create regulations that burden advancing technology. The President of the United States has the power to set free advancing technology and send all ordinary people into better jobs and better incomes for the rest of their lives.

But that will never happen with a career politician as President because that would mean cutting his own branch of government, his own structure of power. The Neo-Tech Society, a wealthy white-collar society, will not happen under a career politician. So, working-class Americans will never really be rich — not until they elect a President with absolutely no political agenda. That person must have a single agenda — not anything to do with politics whatsoever — just a single inward drive to slash his own structure of power to end regulations. *Strictly an inward agenda with no political "good intentions" at all.* "Good intentions" quietly build more and more regulatory jobs under the Executive Branch, which builds more and more regulatory budgets, ultimately building more and more political power for the President. That process must be completely reversed to reduce more and more regulatory jobs under the Executive Branch, which reduces more and more regulatory budgets, ultimately reducing more and more political power from the President.

Imagine you elect for President a political candidate. They all have *one* basic objective: to build their own political careers, which means building their branch of government — *bureaucratic regulatory power* — one way or the other, from the left or from the right. Restricted technology would get strangled like the regulated railroad industry of the early 1900s and like *all* the manufacturing industries of the late 1900s. Outside of short-term cycles, the country's standard of living would decline. Health would decline as the burden on advancing technology would continue to drive up health-care costs.

Now imagine you elected a Neo-Tech president. He is not a politician, and he too has *one* objective: to slash bureaucratic regulatory power, which means his own political power. Unrestricted technology would race forward in all industries like in the unregulated computer industry today. The country would steadily advance into a predominantly white-collar, upper-income society. Health would vastly improve as technological breakthroughs drove down health-care costs just as computer costs were driven down to fractions. The results would be wealthy, healthy families showered with technological breakthroughs.

Now ask yourself: "Do I want to live in the Neo-Tech (technology-driven) World of wealth, health, convenience, entertainment...and experience the good life? Or do I want to live in the politically driven world and experience the hard life?" Consider your own life and how it can be in the future based on your decision.

Making the American people wealthy is actually simple and easy — a cinch for the President of the United States. But, the President of the United States does not really want to weaken the system that gives him his power. To increase your power and wealth, he would have to slash his own power. You see, all ordinary people could *quite rapidly* soar to wealthy standards of living in the United States if the President slashed his own power by slashing all regulatory bureaucracies. Instead, he proceeds ahead with his "good intentions" that build his popularity and power...regulatory power over advancing technology, which suppresses everyone. A quick solution exists to this problem: the Great Replacement Program.

Indeed, when we leave behind 20th-century big government and

33

its career politicians and embrace our 21st-century get-the-people-rich government with its market-driven businessmen, the new market-driven President will end the thousands of new bureaucratic regulations each year that block advancing technology. The Neo-Tech Congressmen and Senators will end the thousand new federal laws each year that also prohibit a rapidly advancing economy. Without all that legislation and regulation, all that food for lawyers, then one of the great deterrents to a Neo-Tech Society — too many laws, lawyers, and lawsuits — will also fade away. That will ease the way for a Neo-Tech Society of rapidly advancing technology, wealth, health, and entertainment.

In a Neo-Tech Society of unrestricted, rapidly advancing technology, all people will advance into well-paying jobs of the mind as technology comes in behind to fill jobs of labor with machines, robots, and computers. And as technology races forward, so will medical breakthroughs in curing fatal diseases. As technology races forward, the standard of living will go sharply up as the cost of living goes sharply down. Health and longevity will go sharply up as the cost of medicine and treatment goes sharply down. Ordinary people will discover what it means to live in luxury.

After Santana put down the article, I said, "For two centuries, our career politicians have gradually taken from us our self-leader culture. As our external 'authorities', they perpetuate our resistance against becoming self-leaders. In subtle ways, they offer us a path of least resistance that seduces us into becoming dependent followers. For example, by providing the path of least resistance to low-income families in the form of automatic welfare payments, the leaders seduce families into becoming hopelessly dependent on big government. The path of least resistance — collect automatic money from big government — perpetuates their resistance to becoming self-leaders. Those low-income families become trapped like a slave class, in the ghetto, dependent on big government. They inherently know this and harbor deep resentment toward the Establishment. They never stand a chance at entering the very profitable world of the self-leader. ...That deteriorating, low-income 'slave class', by the way, is a microcosm of what is happening to America as a whole as the programs for the 'public good' that 'take care of us' grow.

34

*Personal Renaissance I: A Journey of No Return*

"Perhaps even worse, through those clever 'public good' illusions, the career politicians regulate the economy, which burdens and kills rapidly advancing technology. Even the low-income families would be rich in a Neo-Tech Society with an unburdened economy because rapidly advancing technology would multiply buying power anywhere from a hundred to thousands of times — depending on the purchase — like the computers. Instead, today, the growing 'slave class' drinks the poison of career politicians.

"Even if we wanted to, we could not immediately break free and become prosperous self-leaders because our public schools never taught us how to integrate for ourselves. The fear I saw on the gentleman's face at the infomercial seminar existed because he could not integrate, so he needed me — someone who could integrate for him...until he learned how to integrate for himself. You see, everyone needs guidance in life, otherwise he or she would founder aimlessly and die. The problem is that few people can integrate and therefore *guide themselves*. People are never taught to integrate in school, and adults are specialized in their jobs. Since ordinary people cannot integrate to guide themselves, they look for someone else to guide them."

My brother then added, "Like children need parents until they grow up, ordinary people need leaders until they learn integrated thinking."

"Right," I answered. "And legitimate leaders like good parents will guide the people into self-leadership and success."

"So, you're saying that we do need leaders?" Santana asked.

"Yes, we need a transition from illegitimate leaders to legitimate leaders to self-leaders," I said. "People do not know how to do integrated thinking to guide themselves. So, yes, we need leaders now because people are not yet self-leaders. But we need legitimate leaders.

"This is where the Great Replacement Program that I explained to Eric becomes very important. You see, the people would never get rid of the current leaders, for the people were never taught integrated thinking. They need guidance, and without internal guidance from integrated thinking, they will naturally seek external guidance. The political leaders inherently know this and cleverly offer 'guidance' and block society from

35

integrated thinking with suppressive regulations and legislation.

"The Great Replacement Program will provide the people with leaders, but with valid leaders. Realize, valid leaders exist. Valid leaders can be easily identified: They push society toward self-leadership and success — not unlike parents pushing children toward independence. In government, that means slashing regulations and legislation so integrated thinkers can rise and drive our costs of living to fractions and make us all rich. Honest leaders have no desire to suppress their employees or citizens. You see, honest leaders are not protecting false livelihoods as your external 'authorities'. Everyone benefits: more self-leaders mean more competitive businesses, profits, and a more competitive country with a soaring economy and buying power. Only false external 'authorities' lose as they lose their positions of power. In other words, they could no longer rule over us. Therefore, those false external 'authorities' — those living high at your loss — will reject the Great Replacement Program and the new Neo-Tech Party."

Santana listened closely, leaning forward in his chair.

"Career politicians are the biggest problem — the lawmakers," I continued. "The state and federal lawmakers generate laws — many thousands of laws every year — to control and guide their citizens. Not only does that put us in an externally guided state of mind and perpetuate our deep-rooted resistance against self-guidance, but all those laws and resulting regulations and litigation discourage the creation of new businesses and jobs. All those laws, lawyers, and lawsuits make it very hard for tender youth to rise with self-leadership, to build new businesses and create new jobs. Hemorrhaging laws, lawyers, lawsuits kill our younger generation's creativity and independence. Our children's future is being sold out by a clique of greedy politicians on a very stimulating ride. Those state and federal politicians cast the illusion that we need those thousands of *new* laws every year...those so-called 'good intentions for the public good'.

"Legitimate leaders not looking for a free ride would set down free and open conditions as in the computer industry that encourage, not punish, aggressive self-leaders. The freed geniuses of society would then rise and make everyone else rich like in the computer industry. All the people would get rich and then, with all that buying power, enjoy deciding how to spend all that money...controlling and guiding their own lives. Such a rich nation of self-leaders would deliver great prosperity *not* to the Establishment, but to ourselves. Stop and think: Do we really need state and federal lawmakers generating *thousands* of *new laws* each year that control and guide *and suppress* citizens and their businesses? Or is that excessive lawmaking merely creating illusions of importance as a cover for a free and intoxicating ride of power?"

"But how do I know who are the legitimate leaders?" Santana asked.

"There is one unmistakable way to identify legitimate leaders from the big-government phonies now in office," I said. "Consider that, from 1854 to 1857, the legendary Florence Nightingale worked day and night in miserable conditions saving men's lives during the bloody Crimean War. From 1993 to 1994, first-lady Hillary Clinton, by contrast, attended fancy dinners and parties using health reform as a potential ticket to personal glory. Let's compare those two opposite ladies with opposite men and women who help versus hurt our economy and taxes:

"To make soldiers survive, Florence Nightingale dug into the most nitty-gritty chores and details to dramatically increase the prosperity of hospitals. Similarly, to make their businesses survive, entrepreneurs and market businessmen also dig into the most nitty-gritty chores and details to increase the prosperity of their businesses. The world's greatest kept secret is that they are for real and can also dramatically increase the prosperity of America.

"Politicians, by contrast, are like Hillary Clinton: they sound good but never actually worked down in the tough nitty-gritty trenches. The other half of the world's greatest kept secret is that they are not for real and can only hurt the prosperity of America while pursuing their hidden agendas.

"You see, Florence Nightingale jumped right into the trenches and wrestled with the nitty gritty of saving lives and forever breathed life into hospitals. Original business owners dig right into the nitty gritty of business and forever breathe jobs and life into society. Career politicians, by contrast, are like Hillary Clinton who attended fancy dinners while never actually working

Book 1
God-Man Decoded

down in the tough nitty gritty of any hospital. They all just *sound* good while chasing after personal glory. The hard-working market businessmen and women are the Florence Nightingales of society — the job creators, the life givers. They are the super-competent people in society; they're for real. They will slash, not multiply, regulation and legislation because they neither need nor want a free ride. They are legitimately competent leaders, not ignorant phonies like career politicians."

"Yes, I see," Santana said. "But wouldn't a business owner be tempted to pass a bad law that may directly benefit his own wallet?"

"Not with the new government of defense I saw in my Second Vision. Unlike today, everything about government tomorrow was for protection only. Nothing could be done on the offense like passing laws and regulations to rule over us, no matter how good they seemed. You see, the Neo-Tech Party reduced the government to one of defense, protection only. The single purpose of the Neo-Tech President was to slash all regulatory bureaucracies except for the Department of Defense. He set down free and open conditions as in the computer industry that encouraged, no punished, super entrepreneurs and super technologies in business, science, and medicine. Those geniuses of society, not career politicians, then took care of all our needs. The single purpose of Neo-Tech Congressmen and Senators was to slash legislation for the same reason. Those Neo-Tech Party members could not violate that sole inward agenda, because the government was all defense and no longer included the bogus offense of ruling over us. Thus, no one could seek pragmatic personal gains through regulations or legislation.

"In my Second Vision, the Neo-Tech Party served a guiding Constitution to protect the people only and to forever prevent any mortals from ever again ruling over us and playing God with our lives. I witnessed in my Vision that the Neo-Tech Constitution became an amendment to the U.S. Constitution and was the *one irreducible law* necessary for a totally free country of self-leaders:"

**The Neo-Tech Constitution**
**Individual Rights**

**Preamble**
The purpose of human life is to prosper and live happily. The function of society is to guarantee those conditions that allow all individuals to fulfill their purpose. Those conditions can be guaranteed through a constitution that forbids the use of initiatory force or coercion by any person or group against any individual:

**The Constitution**
Article 1: No person, group of persons, or government may initiate force, threat of force, or fraud against any individual's self or property.
Article 2: Force may be morally and legally used only in defense against those who violate Article 1.
Article 3: No exceptions shall ever exist to Articles 1 and 2.

After I showed Santana and Eric the above Neo-Tech Constitution (which originated years before my Visions as shown in Book 2), I continued, "All Neo-Tech candidates — all market businessmen and women, whether owners of small, medium, or large businesses — abode by that guiding principle of pure protection for pure freedom: protection and freedom for people to live in any way so long as one did not physically violate others. Initiatory force or threat thereof by an individual or by the government took away freedom...freedom needed for integrated thinkers to rise. Tomorrow's government protected us from any form of such coercion or force. The Neo-Tech Party's first role was to end nearly all legislation and regulation, which were forms of initiatory force that nipped away at our freedom."

"How is regulation or legislation considered initiatory force that takes away our freedom?" Santana asked.

"Regulations and legislation tell us what we *can or cannot do*," I answered. "Most laws and regulations today are political policy law — telling us what we can or cannot do based on career politicians' political policy, which usually originated from

39

some sound-good 'good intentions', always backed by force. They differ from objective law based on physical protection of the individual and his property. Objective law is for defense only and requires a national army, local police, courts, and prisons. Political policy or subjective law is for offense too and requires three times more government to legislate, regulate, and enforce — always closing down more of our freedoms. Political policy law tells us how to live to best serve the leaders' political agendas. And if we do not abide by those extensive laws and regulations, then we are punished and sometimes go to jail. Therefore, we are threatened by force to abide by their subjective, self-serving regulations and legislation, their political agendas, nipping away at our freedom and creativity. We need freedom for self-leaders to rise.

"To protect *all* people from *all* others, including from criminals, gangs, racists, mobs, armies, or governments requires protecting the irreducible, indivisible *individual*. And, to be sure that protection cannot somehow become conditional to fit some agenda requires going down to the irreducible, indivisible, unconditional concept of *initiatory force*. That single objective law of no force against any individual cannot be twisted, divided, or built upon to mean anything else. That unconditional, guiding Constitution of the Neo-Tech Party offers the *one law* of pure protection and freedom. That Constitution serves only to protect the individual...*not* to build political power. The Neo-Tech Constitution and the Neo-Tech Party's sworn agenda to slash regulation and legislation will prevent any elected businessleader from straying and introducing more 'good intentions' for the 'public good'.

"In my Second Vision, 21st-century get-the-people-rich government tomorrow never so arrogantly assumed the 'divine' power to rule over us. Instead, an honorable government of *defense*, every action was restricted to *physical protection* only. Twentieth-century big government today, on the other hand, wrongly thrives on a 'divine' prerogative to rule over us, a government aggressively on the *offense* most often disguised as public 'well-being'...such as social and regulatory programs 'for the public good'. All those social and regulatory programs wear the disguise of serving the public 'well-being' but are all big-government tools to *regulate the economy and its industries.*

Of course, all those big-government regulations that rule over us block the Neo-Tech Era of super technologies and super entrepreneurs...our future paradise on Earth. As we move into the new millennium, a new attitude begins to shut the door on those big-government regulations.

"During my First Vision, the inevitable Neo-Tech Party from tomorrow's get-the-people-rich government orchestrated the Great Replacement Program to replace big-government career politicians (corrupt rulers) with entrepreneurs and other market-driven business leaders (virtuous producers). Only entrepreneurs and market-driven business leaders would free the economy from a ruling-class big government. The time had come to let technology take the giant leap into the Neo-Tech Era and generate millionaire standards of living for all individuals. Once people got a hint of that wonderful life they would enjoy, the Great Replacement Program was on like a stampede."

"By the way", my brother added, "market businessmen and women by nature have integrity unlike the political businessman and career politician. That integrity comes from good-old honest hard work. Entrepreneurs, for example, are not lazy people; they are not looking for get-something-for-nothing shortcuts. Those are the people who will surprise America with such competence that taxes will fall in half as standards of living soar. Those are the Florence Nightingales of society — like you said — the in-the-trenches givers of values and life."

"Absolutely," I confirmed.

"Yes, I agree with that," Santana said. "Now, I have a concern: You said that the legitimate leaders will push society into self-leadership. I get a little nervous, though, when you say that the Neo-Tech leaders from the Great Replacement Program will *push* us into becoming self-leaders."

"Your nervousness is the same as the fear I saw on the gentleman's face at the infomercial seminar," I said. "Realize, we would have never left home to go to school if our parents did not *push* us. Subsequently, we discovered everything good in life by acquiring independence. But, if not pushed along and into school, we would have sunk into stagnation for the rest of our lives, and we would have eventually hated our parents...not

41

unlike Americans are now beginning to hate politicians.

"Legitimate leaders will create the non-suppressive free environment that will inherently push our citizens into a world that delivers everything good that life offers — the Golden Neo-Tech World that frees aggressive self-leaders to make everyone else wealthy like in the computer world. But for now, our deep-rooted resistance is nurtured by the Establishment's path of least resistance: that is, given the laws, litigations, and regulations, it's not worth striving for more than a routine-rut job in our society!

"By contrast, a nation of free and creative self-leaders would generate geniuses who would drive new values onto the marketplace, not to mention drive up our buying power to make us prosperous beyond belief like in the computer world. A little sneak preview of creative new values being driven onto the marketplace is the booming biomedical industry, a direct result over the past few years of the gradually weakened power if the FDA.

My brother's friend thought for a few moments, then said, "If the career politicians are on top anyway, why do they suppress us?"

"Why?" I repeated. "To *stay* on top, to keep their stimulating lifestyles. The reason you and all ordinary people have a hard time seeing that is because you yourself do not have such malice in your own character. So, you cannot relate to such dishonest agendas. But political leaders stay on top through creating illusions that we need them while really just burdening society. Again, consider that federal and state lawmakers convince the public we need thousands of *new* laws every year. That illusion created by career politicians is ridiculous. Those laws help fill the pockets of the huge American 'slave class', all while making those Americans less and less competitive in the ever growing global economy.

"But even worse, the litigation frenzy from those laws and regulations prevents tender youth from ever having a chance to rise as self-leaders. Today, for example, to put your name as owner of a business, no matter how small, is downright dangerous.

"We really only need *one* supreme law of individual rights that protects citizens equally from harm. Beyond that law of defense, with no more external 'authorities' on the offense suppressing society's development, with no new lawmaking, more and more citizens and tender youth could rise as self-leaders. Those geniuses of society would make us all rich, just like the geniuses in the computer world made all computer consumers computer rich. Without legislation and regulation to hold the geniuses down, more and more geniuses among the tender youth would rise to great prosperity and pull up everyone around them into the Golden Neo-Tech World.

"People now are beginning to see that something has gone terribly wrong with the system. Our trusted politicians have sold out our futures for selfish near-term, look-good, vote-gathering gimmicks. Our leaders betrayed our trust. What's worse, they kept us as their followers — sort of as if parents kept their children from going to school. The children would not know of the better world; we do not know of the better world."

"We have been robbed of our self-leader spirit," my brother said. "Political businessmen and politicians are happy to be our leaders. So, we accept them. We work our entire lives to buoy their stimulating lifestyles. Unknowingly, we are their slaves."

"At work," I added, "we get stuck in boring routine ruts. And as our politicians pass laws — more and more laws — we get stuck in a stagnating economy with no opportunities to rise into dynamic self-leaders. Instead, we just pay more and more taxes to pay for their illusions of importance."

"If America's children all grew up to be self-leaders," my brother added, "we'd have a very different, a very lean and hard-working government — not a high-paced show of ego maniacs. The whole economy would race ahead with new technologies, as you say, like the computer industry. ...You know, you're right. I'm ready...I *am* ready to be my own self-leader!"

"You've already learned how to overcome the external obstacles in your company to evolve into a self-leader," I said. "Now you must overcome the internal obstacle *in yourself* to complete your journey to becoming a self-leader. That obstacle is your deep-rooted urge for the automatic controls of external guidance. You must be aware of fighting this natural urge for the next thirty days. If you aren't aware of fighting this every day initially, chances are you have succumbed. You must fight this resistance to overcome it. You may even feel 'withdrawal' symptoms. But keep focussed on your mini-day/power-thinking team. Keep mastering details and absorbing responsibilities to take over a living job. You must force yourself to do these things — you must fight your resistance to taking control of life. Fight hard, every day, for 30 days, and you will feel your psyche change. Taking control of life through integrated thinking will become more and more natural to you. What once seemed like hard work will become fun work. Eventually, making money will become your way of life."

"Eric, I'm really into all this," Santana said. "Can you teach me the Self-Leader System. I'm ready!"

"We'll start tomorrow," Eric said with a smile.

When my brother's family and friend left that evening, I wrote the following entry in my diary: "Over the past several weeks, each breakthrough taught me how to acquire greater integrated knowledge. With each breakthrough came greater success. Each of those six breakthroughs can be used independently to boost success. But by using all six together as a powerful system — *the Self-Leader System* — I'm becoming an unstoppable winner! This system is amazing. I've already started teaching it to my assistants and to about a dozen other co-workers. They love me for it! But most importantly, I *feel* like a self-leader; I've discovered myself. I'm in charge and love it. My whole outlook on life has changed. I'm my own person, on my own path, and I'm really happy. My personal renaissance has given me back myself."

## Mind Muscle

While teaching my co-workers these techniques, I realized I had to build up their "mind muscle". In fact, all geniuses of society today had to do the same to rise from under the lid holding down society under the old code of living. In my Six Visions, I observed people easily and naturally doing the following seven 21st-century techniques under the new code of living. They did not have to work hard to become wealthy and happy.

What follows are those same seven power techniques from the 21st century. The following seven power techniques let you muscle your way into big-shot success under the old code, in our suppressed 20th-century politicized society. The following techniques can give your mind some "muscle" along its journey into integrated thinking. The following techniques require some hard work but can be used like shots of adrenaline as needed to become a well paid genius in today's world, if you so choose.

Tomorrow, though, these seven techniques will not be hard, but rather exhilarating as all society flows the same way through Neo-Tech. You will be swimming downstream in the 21st century, easily gaining prestige and wealth. Today, you must swim upstream as did all geniuses of society in the 20th century. The seven power techniques that follow help kick-start your mind into integrated thinking, as taught to those now working for me (excerpts to follow were quoted directly from my meetings):

### Technique One
### The Power Approach

"You all know about my Six Visions. I could not get over how ordinary people in the Neo-Tech Era carried themselves with such self-confidence and honest power. I never saw such authentic self-authority back in today's world. Ordinary people in my Sixth Vision appeared like walking legends. What caused that bigger-than-life aura about them that radiated such confidence and competence? Their mini-companies ran with unbending efficiency and control. Everyone could count on everyone else. It was a beautiful sight.

"So I tried to simulate what I saw. In doing so, I made a personal breakthrough and developed the following technique. In fact, I subsequently realized that all geniuses of society today used this approach to turn on a little-known 'power generator' that resides in every person's mind. Of course, the walking legends in my Sixth Vision naturally performed with the power generator always on. When I turned on that power generator in me, like nothing else it cut through the illusions and lies that once left me confused and powerless at building values and wealth. Trapped in our 20th-century suppressed society, this 21st-century technique helped me break through to the winning concepts behind all problems at work and in personal life.

"Consider that human life offered me power. For example,

45

if I tried hard enough, I could take control of every situation in life. I could take control of my schedule; I could take control of my company. But I would have to *take* it. Now, I captured from my Sixth Vision the *only* mental state of being that allowed me to *take* power and called it the *Power Approach*: In confronting any problem, I asked myself, 'What is the winning concept behind this situation?' In other words, I would figure out how to bring all the little nagging percepts together and solve them with a single, integrated burst of pure power. To help myself see the winning concept, I learned to shift that intellectual question into an emotional reaction by replacing those two words 'winning concept' with the words *Power Approach*. Now, I asked the question again. I'd knit my brow and say it: What is the *Power Approach* to this problem? ...Suddenly I felt a surge of strength. You try it. That surge of strength almost always showed me the most powerful course of action. And the *most powerful course of action* was inevitably the winning concept behind the situation. Now, for situations of all kinds in my work and personal life, I'd keep asking myself, 'What is the most powerful course of action...what is the *Power Approach*?' Lo and behold, I began to consistently see a fearless choice of self-authority, the choice of a self-leader. Then, I acted on those winning concepts. ...As I increasingly acted on this pure power, I became a winner. I was emotionally transforming from following external 'authority' to self-determining internal authority.

"Each situation I encountered, particularly in my career, I kept asking myself, 'What is the winning concept to this situation?' Or, more emotionally and much more effectively, I kept asking myself, 'What is the *Power Approach* — the most potent course of action — to this situation?' That single question helped me guide myself and stop looking for external guidance.

Now, you try it: Say you work a specialized job and are unhappy; instead of brooding over all the specifics that make you unhappy, ask yourself, 'What is the winning concept to this situation? *What is the Power Approach to fixing this problem?*' Keep asking yourself that no-nonsense question. As you ponder the most powerful course of action, let your feelings get fired up until you are burning with determination. 'What is the Power

46

Approach to fixing this problem?' *Do not* analyze the answer. Just let the Power Approach flow. Realize that later you will decide whether or not to act on it.

"See the Power Approach clearly: Say, in this case, the most powerful course of action is to aggressively take control of the responsibilities that will lift you into a living job. Or, say the Power Approach calls for you to leave your specialized job and start your own 21st-century living company (the Fourth Vision). ...If you then act on your own authority and the winning concepts, then you will become a powerful dynamo and a big winner in life.

"Leaving one's job to start a business is a major undertaking. Yet the Power Approach applies everywhere, in large or small situations. You can begin small, using the Power Approach on frequent problems or common situations. By asking yourself, 'What is the Power Approach in this situation?' you can see the most powerful course of action, which burns like a laser through bothersome percepts to the winning concept. The Power Approach burns like a laser through confusions and illusions that make you weak. It burns through deep-rooted resistance to self-leadership. Once acting on the Power Approach, you become your own authority, your own God, and nothing can stand in your way. You will not succumb to others or to your own meekness. You will become too strong. Your mind will become free of debilitating illusions.

"First use the Power Approach in small daily situations. Build your strength with the Power Approach. Before long, you will take on major decisions in life using the Power Approach.

"Start today with problems and challenges in your career. Push ahead with the power course of action. Chop through lingering turmoil as you identify, 'This is the problem; here is the definitive solution.' Become calm and confident in the face of the most trying situations. Develop courage and make fearless moves. Become the decision maker.

"The average person's stagnation-trap stems from deep-rooted feelings and illusions of needing to be led. The Power Approach rises from powerful determination *not* to be led. Resistance to becoming a self-leader comes from a passive, nonintegrating mode and is the opposite of the Power Approach that comes from

Book 1
God-Man Decoded

an aggressive, integrating mode. The Power Approach provokes emotions that push you to use the great power in your head: to use integrated thinking, take control, and fearlessly lead your own life.

"The Power Approach builds on itself. Every day you will become noticeably more powerful and a stronger self-leader. Turn on this power generator in your mind, starting tomorrow at work. All the greats have. Quickly, you will experience a surge of power. Gradually, a uniquely creative genius will emerge from within your own mind."

### Technique Two
### Power-Concentration

"Okay, now pushing ahead on how to become the integrated thinker: A couple of weeks ago I talked about the two different modes of thinking: 1) the externally guided mode of the 20th century versus 2) the internally guided mode of the 21st century. To make good money now in the 20th century, we must remove anything that blocks us from evolving into the internally guided mode. I've identified the major block that prevents most of us from ever entering the internally guided mode in which we begin to form concepts and then build success puzzles. It has to do with the way we concentrate:

"First, I could never quite understand when I was in college why other students would go into the library and study for hours and hours and hours day after day after day. I would see those people studying for a test for many, many hours over several days, and I would sometimes wonder if I were going to flunk the test. For, I hadn't even started studying. But I would shut myself in one of those 6' x 8' cubicles in the library the morning of a test, not having studied at all up to that point. I would close the cubicle door and go into a super-intense mode of concentration, realizing that if I went to the test that moment, I'd flunk it.

"I'd go in this intense mode for maybe two or three hours before a test. I'd study right up to maybe five minutes before the test. I would always do well on the test. And a number of times, I would ace a test through that technique.

"I didn't explicitly realize it back then, but now I know there

48

are two different modes of concentrating. Most people in college are in one mode of basic concentration. They go to the library for days and concentrate for a test. And then there's the other mode of *power-concentration*.

"When a person is power concentrating, he is all at one time trying to get the whole picture (i.e., the multiple-thought concept) versus others who are getting pieces (i.e., single-thought percepts) one at a time as they study for all those hours in the library. Power-concentration requires much more energy. Furthermore, power-concentration is more than just getting the whole picture. In order to successfully grasp the whole picture, you must get those specifics too, simultaneously. To best understand this, consider the computer programer. He must grasp the whole concept of what the company is after, and he must grasp all the specifics and details. He must really *burrow in*. He cannot just get what he believes is the whole picture without burrowing into those specifics and knowing every little specific detail and the effect each detail has on the whole.

"You actually know if you are doing this 'burrowing in' or not. It's like a self-test. Remember in mathematics, for example, when you start off with a premise, and then you go through an equation and prove the premise. You know beyond any shadow of doubt that the premise is correct. Well, there's a comparison here to this burrowing-in mode. You burrow into the specifics until you *know* the whole picture is right. You cannot *really know* how everything works without knowing every specific involved. Then, like proving that premise in math, you see the whole picture and all its details simultaneously. At this moment, the logic jells in your mind. From that enlightened moment forward, all your decisions will be solid and your mind certain.

"Now, fathom the leverage behind this power-concentration: First consider that some of you working for me have not fully grasped how my unique accounting system works (Tracking Report #5, Chapter Six of *God-Man*). Without power-concentration, you will never fully grasp the intricate logic, not during your entire career. You will never really have control over your career, especially those who are working toward a mini-company. You can go on working very aggressively, even making some good forward movement. But you will never be financially potent and lead a mini-company like the person who understands the whole accounting picture and all its details — the fundamental logic.

"Now consider that you go into the power-concentrating mode for one hour, *sixty minutes*. I wager that, for the rest of your life, you will have total mastery over the intricate logic...over what happens and why. Such certainty over the numbers would open new horizons.

"Power-concentration provides leverage. You can, for instance, master the accounting system in sixty minutes — in the time of one TV show. Or you can, by contrast, never *master* it, even if you fill out the tracking reports.

"Power-concentrating physically differs from concentrating. Your brain feels like it is expanding as it goes to work on the situation. You must *think hard* and *not stop* until spending the intense mental energy to *really know* what's going on — the whole picture as well as every detail behind that responsibility. Then, you will grasp the logic.

"Now, I want all of you to begin power-concentrating in your jobs. Get down to the logic within each responsibility of your targeted mini-company. You will begin to form provoking questions that others would never ask. Once you have 'got it' — once you have snapped together and understand the logic within all responsibilities — that logic will never leave your head. You capture iron-grip control over that portion of the business. You will never have total control any other way. You see, in the back of everyone's mind is the external-authority problem. That problem leaves openings to avoid really *burrowing in* and power-concentrating. But by power-concentrating, you enter the internally guided mode and begin to control multiple-thought clusters, which means you begin to control your destiny."

## Technique Three
## Power-Control

"Along with driving for the logic within responsibilities, you must drive for control over those responsibilities and their details. Driving specifically to control those responsibilities broadens your mind beyond specialized thinking. *Power-control*, relentlessly pushing for more control, makes your mind jump to a higher level of awareness. As a toddler you experienced an incredible thrill as you pushed your mind to higher levels of awareness and gathered more control. In time, power-control is a similar phenomenon. As adults in the suppressed 20th century, at first we tend to dislike pushing for control. We do not really care to expand our awareness and control, and we are not motivated to do so. In the politicized 20th century, you must override your resistance to control. Such an explicit drive for control is not easy at first but will, nevertheless, push your mind to a higher level of awareness. At that stimulated level of awareness, your mind becomes aware of problems, trends, and seeks common denominators. Your mind also senses where it needs to do power-concentrating to get the logic in order to gain the control.

"Indeed, aggressively seeking and then seizing control brings your awareness to a whole new level you have not yet experienced. That higher level lets you see the responsibilities and their details from a wider perspective — from the perspective that you are going to get iron-grip control over them. You then start seizing control and taking 100% responsibility (next technique). After a few weeks, the drive for control will once again become a natural part of you for the first time since toddler years. Control feels good; you will begin to feel really good...in fact, you will begin to feel that incredible thrill again, not felt since toddlerhood."

### Technique Four
### Power-Responsibility

"To take control, you must really *feel 100% responsible* for the responsibility or project. In other words, all of you here work for me. You will never enter the realm of integrated thinking if, in your mind, *I carry* the basic responsibility. If, in your mind, I carry the responsibility, then you have the opening to switch into the externally guided mode. So, you will never become a potent integrated thinker. You may be doing 100% of the work. But, not feeling 100% responsible takes the edge off the burrowing in and seizing control. So you always lack the complete integrations. You fall short of the all-important internally guided mode. At this point, you need *power-responsibility*, you need to *really feel* 100% responsible for a

51

responsibility or project. That way, you will thoroughly burrow in until you have all the intricate logic and seize complete control.

"This 100%-responsibility concept is a key breakthrough, not only for the employee but also for the employer. If you start your own business someday, you have to know when to let a project or responsibility go and say, 'Okay, you've got it, and if you fail, the project is going to fail. Then and only then will I have to, at that point after you've failed, step in and start over from scratch. But if you're going to fail, I'm going to let the project fail with you.'

"To do that may be very difficult. For, as the entrepreneur, you always carry the sense of responsibility. People working for you may do the work, they may follow through, but you always carry the sense of responsibility. Letting go of responsibility is not in your nature. Letting go is very difficult, especially to the point that if something or someone is going to fail, then so be it. Only then will you deal with it.

"On the flip side, taking 100% responsibility is vital to climbing the ladder to better positions in any company and is absolutely crucial to taking over a mini-company. Of course, I'm not going to casually say, 'Here guy; it's yours, and if you fail, so be it.' Instead, you must *take* responsibility from me through burrowing in, seizing control, and *feeling* 100% responsible. Not until you take that 100% responsibility will I risk letting everything go. Indeed, for you to become an integrated thinker and take over a chunk of this business, you need power-responsibility. You need to physically and psychologically take over each responsibility *with 100% responsibility*. If you take *100% responsibility*, your mind will continue taking over greater and greater chunks of the business. Your mind will feel the survival pressures again, sort of like the toddler who must 'get up to speed' with the world around him. Those internally manufactured survival pressures will help kick-start you into integrated thinking and building success puzzles.

"When you feel 100% responsible, you know it. *You feel it.* You no longer have an external authority to lean on. That doesn't mean you do not have wiser, broader integrators to tap on for advice or input. But *you* carry and *really feel* 100% of the responsibility. You *feel* the pressures, and not any of those pressures go beyond you as you get the information and advice you need from those broader integrators such as myself.

"Consider this true scenario: A person is nervously waiting to present his project to the board of directors in a leading American company. He has devoted the last several years of his life to this project. He is afraid whether or not his project is going to be judged a value to the company. He is going to get aggressively questioned by the board, and he is going to make the best darn presentation he can to prove his project a value to the company. All his costs are figured out to the most competitive degree. His whole life and future might be torn down in front of his eyes if his research and development project is killed. He has raw survival pressures on him to make his presentation work. He alone is 100% responsible for his success or failure.

"The key is 100% responsibility. *You* succeed or fail. To whatever extent you are successful is *your* responsibility, 100% *your* responsibility. You must put *all* the responsibility and pressure on yourself. You must not subtly seek external authority or relief from your boss. Through this power-responsibility, you will steadily switch over from the externally guided or following mode into the internally guided or integrating mode.

"Power-Responsibility with power-concentration, pushing for power-control using the power approach gives you real power. You will absorb chunks of the business, namely a mini-company. You will break free from a routine rut. You will become an internally driven integrated thinker who can build creatively."

### Technique Five
### Power-Energization
"Energy is actually the most basic ingredient of integrated thinking because integrated thinking requires substantial energy. You will be surprised at how many people don't have much energy. If you look around, you can see that only about 10% of the people have a high energy level. So, about 90% of our subjugated 20th-century population is, right away, physically eliminated from integrated thinking and building success puzzles. Most people must start with their energy levels; they must

discover *power-energization.*

"Power-energization is a psychological phenomenon. For instance, you could sit here and be in a daze, but then all of a sudden you could say to yourself: 'What the heck am I doing?' and force yourself into an intense, high-energy mode.

"Anyone can snap out of a low-energy mode. I have proof: Put *anyone* on an urgent deadline. All of a sudden, that person works with high energy. Energy levels can be controlled by a mental choice. Power-energization takes only a simple wake-myself-up decision.

"To go to the next level of thinking — integrated thinking — requires greater energy. Power-energization — that wake-myself-up decision, physically and mentally — eventually becomes your ongoing and *natural* state.

"Once again, observe the toddler. That small child lives in a different world; he is always power-energizing his mind. In our world of resignation, we have lost that natural human state of power-energizing our minds. But we can get it back. *Just do it.*"

## Technique Six
## Power-Interaction

"To kick-start integrated thinking sometimes requires a process that is not glamorous but captures the very nature of integrated thinking. Let me explain: To effectively link together details into multiple-thought clusters and start conceptualizing oftentimes requires a back-and-forth process with your co-workers that I call *power-interaction.* For example, the new deposits on the computer reduced hours of work to seconds of work. The young lady responsible for this advancement knew nothing about computers...or bookkeeping, for that matter. But she relentlessly went back and forth with the computer programmer probably a dozen times and with the bookkeeper perhaps two dozen times. Her relentless power-interaction enabled her mind to link together and snap the countless details into a completed success puzzle. Power-interaction let her mind solve a puzzle of advancement.

"Power-interaction offers us great flexibility because it lets us seize control of unknown areas currently not part of our job responsibilities. This phenomenon is instrumental in taking over a mini-company, perhaps someday the entire company. ...You can, once again, imagine the power-interaction done by Charles Nash on his climb to the presidency of General Motors."

### Technique Seven
### Reality Power

"Most people are willing to work hard to become a major player at success. But most people run into a problem. They are caught in an illusion that has hurt them from approaching their dreams. What is that illusion? Naturally, they want to do something really important in their lives. Therefore, they are caught in a bigger-and-better frame of mind: 'I want to do something bigger and better with my life.' They will work hard, but they just do not know where to turn. Ironically, great success and achievements are right below their noses. They must break out of the bigger-and-better illusion and go into the littler-and-nastier reality. To start a path of integrated thinking, they must come down to earth by mastering the nitty-gritty details.

"Instead of some out-of-reach vague dream, great success is a crystal-clear path of learning and linking together nitty-gritty details and responsibilities. The littler-and-nastier power techniques bring you bigger and better things. That is reality power. ...You must now exert reality power: inject the nitty-gritty power techniques into your day to spark your integrated thinking and send you along the road to bigger and better things. Discover integrated thinking at work while acquiring for yourself a wealth-building job, and your best dreams will come true."

\* \* \* \*

# Your Personal Renaissance — Summary

The 20th-century civilization's trap of stagnation closed around you as you settled into a routine rut at work. Before long, you looked beyond your work to vacations and hobbies for any remaining source of excitement. But now, you can begin your journey into the life you once dreamed about. Here is your map for that journey:

**Destination One: Project Curiosity**
Start with Project Curiosity to educate yourself about the

55

business and to acquire a *general* overview of integrated knowledge. Integrated thinking will begin; your psyche will immediately begin to change.

**Destination Two:  The Self-Investment Plan**
After a few weeks of Project Curiosity — learning and obtaining a firm grasp of the business — you will gain enough integrated knowledge to be able to define the company's basic responsibilities. On paper, pull those basic responsibilities into their money-making purposes, as demonstrated in the Fourth Vision of *God-Man*, Chapter Six. Select one of those wealth-building jobs on paper as your target. Now you will begin to abandon specialized thinking for integrated thinking. As you begin absorbing your targeted responsibilities, your psyche will gain strength and confidence.

**Destination Three:  Investing In Oneself**
Now you can *dig in* to master the nitty-gritty details in order to absorb the responsibilities of an entire wealth-building job. As you absorb responsibilities and actively develop your integrated thinking or self-thinking, your psyche will dump the following-leaders mode as it discovers self-leadership. You will move into the new league of a self-leader building wealth.

**Destination Four:  The Fast-Track Method**
After taking over an open-ended wealth-building job, race ahead into building wealth with the Fast-Track Method: the mini-day/power-thinking team. Integrated thinking will get more and more effective and creative.

**Destination Five:  The Window To Creativity**
You must use the numbers-integrating mode to look through the window to the creativity trapped in your mind. You will then discover the new joy of bringing creative advancements to your business. You will become a "visionary" headed toward the highest position in the company. Integrated thinking will now jump to an advanced level, as it did for the young Charles Nash. Your psyche will have no more need for external guidance.

## Destination Six:  The Final Obstacle

The only thing to stop you now is *yourself.* You must work extra hard every day to overcome your deep-rooted resistance to becoming the self-leader. How? Simply by forcing yourself to execute the previous steps. Think hard about making progress every day. Do not slip out of that think-hard mode. If you begin to feel the "buzz-out syndrome", then your resistance is taking over. DO NOT LET IT. Fight it with "insta-act" (instant action), hard thinking, and honest effort every day. At first, this self-leader mode might seem hard and uncomfortable. But your self-leader experience will change with time to exciting exhilaration...and wealth.

## Destination Seven:  Mind Muscle

When the time comes, you must buckle down and get past the sole reason you are not an integrated thinker — external guidance. You can add some "muscle" to your mind: the seven Power Techniques help kick-start your mind into integrated thinking. Use and reuse the seven Power Techniques as needed to "muscle" your mind to the next level. Again, those power techniques are: 1) the power approach, 2) power-concentration, 3) power-control, 4) power-responsibility, 5) power-energization, 6) power-interaction, and 7) reality power. They will give your mind the "muscle" to leave behind external guidance and sail your own course to success. ...Be sure to turn on the power generator in your mind: the Power Approach. Laser-like bursts of power will burn through any obstacles between you and your goals. With the Power Approach, you will experience the new you — the *power you* who takes control of life.

# Afterthoughts

Even after becoming wealthy, something troubled me. I knew that the political leaders took away people's Six Ultimate Gifts, which robbed them of the intense happiness they were meant to enjoy. And I noticed that as people's happiness faded, so did their love and romance. What a tragedy, I thought. I witnessed intense happiness only two times in people's lives: in children with their promise of youth, and in adults when they were falling in love.

I knew I must never forget the importance of happiness *right now* for myself and for those I loved. For, if I were not aware of feeling happiness every day *right now,* then I knew as I grew older I would begin to ask, "Did I miss out? My only one time, my one chance...did I miss out?"

I started thinking about my dad. Later that evening I visited him and told him about my feelings. I asked him if he was happy. He nodded. After awhile, I said, "Dad, I think the vast majority of people today are victims. Because of today's ruling class, the people are robbed of their Six Ultimate Gifts and the spectacular life they were meant to have. Tomorrow in the Neo-Tech Era, they will become victors. Yet in today's politicized society, we not only pay for our leaders from our wallets, but from our souls, too."

My father said, "Mark, do you understand where happiness comes from?"

"Yes, I do," I said, "I saw what happiness was in my Third Vision. Let's see..." I started to answer.

"Man is a social animal living together in a society," my dad offered. "What brings man happiness is the pride and the knowledge that he is putting value into that society. The more value he puts into society, the more pride and the more happiness he feels inside. Putting value into society is the secret to a successful life, both emotionally and financially."

How elegantly simple, I thought. The age-old riddle answered in two words: producing values. That thought kept running through my head: How do we achieve happiness? By producing values for society. Now I began to put together the riddle of how our leaders were blocking us not only from success and wealth, but from above all else, *happiness*. Most people whom I knew were caught in stagnation-traps and could not put any more values into society. Therefore, they could not advance financially or emotionally and instead sank into stagnation. I now realized that emotional stagnation, like financial stagnation, was caused by our leaders and their politicized society.

"Dad," I said sadly, "our time *now* is *everything* for us — this is our *one* and *only* time. For anyone to suppress us during our one and only time in all eternity...for anyone to take happiness away from us is unacceptable. Yet, that tragedy is happening to every one of us."

"Along with losing our happiness and wealth, we also lose our love and romance," I added, suddenly thinking back to the Fifth Vision. "As our happiness gets cut off by stagnation, our capacity for *lasting love* gets cut off, too. We must be able to feed the sweet romance — felt right at the beginning — with growing happiness. Instead, losing the thrill for life eventually kills those sweet celebrations."

"Remember that special feeling when first falling in love? Remember how your life lit up? You felt like the most important person in the world. *You were in love!* You didn't have to work for that special feeling; it was just always there. But over time, it faded. That special feeling abandons us as stagnation overcomes us."

My father, seeing a look of sadness come over my face, gently added, "When you see through the deceptions as you did in your Fifth Vision, our leaders actually kill our romance.

"Our establishment-leaders are robbing us of everything we have," I said.

"Including your life itself," my father added. "In fact, we die much younger than is natural. They regulate and suppress medicine and science, too. Consider how certain people in the FDA and other bureaucracies make major medical, scientific, and business breakthroughs nearly impossible. Those cures are blocked because of 'achievement files' like I ran into at Du Pont. Bureaucrats build 'achievement files' through putting tough regulations on business, technology, and medicine. Enforcing tough regulations builds a name for those politically ambitious bureaucrats. But those regulations cripple business and science and block medical and technological progress.

"Those politically ambitious bureaucrats do not care about the public good. They care only about making a name for themselves for their own promotions and political futures. Yet, they maintain the illusion of serving the public good, while really just propagating their own power and promotions. ...Do you remember what happened during my years at Du Pont?" my father asked.

"Yes, I do remember," I said. "You were developing a cure

59

Book 1
God-Man Decoded

for cancer."

"Actually, we were involved in several disease cures at Du Pont," he said, "including a unique approach to curing cancer with tremendous promise. But FDA 'scientists' and other destructive bureaucrats trying to enhance their jobs and glean prestige killed that and many other promising research projects with prohibitively expensive, power-usurping regulations."

"We're talking about a cure for cancer here!" I exclaimed.

"You see," my father said, "those self-serving bureaucrats got promotions based on the size of their 'achievement files' — their 'accomplishments' like shutting down Du Pont's 'risky' experiments on curing cancer. Those portfolio-building, destructive bureaucrats are interested only in their own promotions and not in what is honestly best for the people. Without that small clique of destructive people, businesses like Du Pont and especially aggressive entrepreneurs would race toward curing mankind's most deadly diseases."

"Yes, I saw that actually happen in my Third Vision," I said. "When society saw through their illusions of 'good intentions', we realized the FDA robbed us of life — robbed us of cures to fatal diseases. Without those bureaucrats with self-serving agendas, then business, science, and medicine joined together and raced toward definitive cures for heart disease, cancer, for all diseases big and small from cancer to the common cold."

"I saw in my Third Vision that millions of lives were lost before that small clique of file-building, promotion-seeking bureaucrats called the FDA could no longer keep their illusions of *looking important and needed*," I said while shaking my head.

"Without such regulations," I continued, "medicine raced forward like the unburdened computer industry...raced toward definitive cures for fatal diseases, including slowing the cellular-degeneration disease called aging. Yes, we lived longer, happier lives. Today, the newly accelerating progress in hi-tech biomedicine including genetic engineering is the direct result of the waning power of the FDA.

"In my Third Vision, leading FDA bureaucrats were held legally responsible for committing the worst crime on society: they caused death by the millions. Those few greedy FDA bureaucrats, intoxicated with the power to rule over us, held back life-curing progress. Millions died because of them, which became painfully obvious after 2001. We sent the leading FDA bureaucrats to prison as we freed science, business, and medicine in the name of life!

"We had regulators, of course, but private market businessmen and women who truly served the people's best interest to stay in business. Those honest, private regulators competing for our business, served *us,* not themselves."

"Looking back from my Six Visions at civilization today," I continued, "I finally understood why regulatory bureaucrats were so destructive. You see, ambitious bureaucrats, especially those with political aspirations, stole prestige from the rightful owners who earned it. For example, they increasingly stole headlines in the media by harming legitimate businesses, like killing your research and development on cancer at Du Pont. Of course, they created the illusion that their actions were for the public good. That was their secret shortcut to publicity and prestige. They went up by stealing prestige and pushing our geniuses of society, our aggressive entrepreneurs, scientists, and doctors down.

"Growing businesses and promising research programs built over years of effort got severely harmed by increasingly virulent bureaucrats stealing prestige for personal political prominence, which caused us to sink for a few years into the Catastrophic Era. Consider that *one man* during our so-called 'decade of greed' — bureaucrat Rudolph Giuliani, U.S. Attorney General for the Southern District of New York — destroyed a large, established Wall Street company directly responsible for tens of thousands of jobs. Politically ambitious Giuliani immorally abused political power designed strictly for drug busts: he used RICO to 'bust' legitimate Wall Street businesses. During his reign of terror as attorney general, he quickly built his 'achievement file'. He got his name in all the papers and network news as 'the man who cleaned up Wall Street', which sounded good to the specialized, gullible public at the time. Giuliani came across as a hero when indeed that one man wiped out tens of thousands of immediate jobs and hundreds of thousands of future jobs, and that one man was a big reason for the politically created recessionary times of the early '90s. ...Just as market businessmen like James J. Hill (see Chapter Three in

*God-Man*) did spectacular good for society, career politicians and politically ambitious bureaucrats like Rudolph Giuliani did spectacular harm to society.

"Only the rare integrated thinkers in the late 20th century, however, understood how business and the economy worked in order to understand Giuliani's destructive route to power. Therefore, with the masses specialized and gullible, he just kept on stealing prestige by hurting the working-class leaders, the geniuses of society, which hurt our economy and the wealth of all the people. He built his prestige, activity, 'importance' by destroying values.

"Giuliani stole prestige — a lot of prestige — through causing enormous harm to our economy...all for this one man. A politically ambitious bureaucrat got his name in all the papers, on CNN, on all the network news. He stole prestige to make a name for himself..."

"Just before his race for mayor of New York," my father reminded me. "He hurt society and our economy for his own selfish political gain. And he is only one of many, many others. Most of our political leaders do the same thing: they steal prestige at our expense. They steal from our lives, from our economy, from our children's futures. Political leaders certainly do not earn their prestige and power. They do not put values into society like the entrepreneurs and market businesspeople."

"Fortunately, my Third Vision showed me that sometime after 2001, under the new code of living, we threw such bureaucrats off our backs, including the FDA," I said, "and we finally broke free from our stagnation-traps. Then, something wonderful happened: like being in our youth again, we rediscovered our dreams."

"I can attest to that," said a familiar voice. My father and I turned around to find Eric, who had just arrived, standing in the yard behind us. "I used to go to work, do my set routine, the same thing day after day after day. You were so right — the lid over me, holding me down, was specialization, nothing more. Now I've built upward momentum that can't be stopped. I'm making a lot more money; I have a lot of new things going on; I *love* my life, and I would love to live a lot, lot longer!"

"You no longer are caught in a specialized routine with

blinders," I said with a big smile. "No, you're putting together and seeing things that the masses never see."

"With the breakdown of politicization and its lid over society, I see financial and emotional riches becoming available to *everyone*," Eric added, "especially now with the information revolution upon us."

The three of us continued talking late into the night. When my brother and I were leaving, our father walked us to our cars. Under the postcard-perfect starry night sky, he said, "Watching you two these past few months has been a dream come true for me. Watching my sons become powerful integrated thinkers is an experience I'll cherish for the rest of my life. I'm proud of you." We gave our father a thankful hug, knowing it was his influence and efforts that made it all possible.

I drove home lost in my thoughts. I arrived home very late and walked quietly to the kitchen, careful not to wake my wife and children. The clock read 2:17 a.m. I sat at the kitchen table, opened my diary, and wrote my final page about the Self-Leader System:

"In my Golden Neo-Tech World, happiness constantly fills me. I have to let that happiness and excitement out somewhere, and I do so with my wife and children. I really love being with them!

"I am now teaching all my co-workers the Self-Leader System. It gets ordinary people into the Golden Neo-Tech World *before* 2001."

I closed my diary, walked upstairs and kissed my sleeping son, daughter, and wife. Then I laid down in my bed and smiled, closed my eyes, and enjoyed my own happiness.

Book 1
God-Man Decoded

# Personal Renaissance II
# Know It *All*

My personal renaissance made the techniques from my Six Visions a working reality in my life. I embarked on a wonderful journey and made my life prosperous *right now*. After I became an integrated thinker, more and more insights kept coming to me. In fact, those insights into life, business, and love accelerated as my mind started putting together things I never asked it to at a rapid pace. Suddenly, I clearly understood the world around me. I also understood everything that ever happened to me. My father was right: the integrated thinker really does figure everything out.

That all-knowing phenomenon sent me into an entirely different personal renaissance of gaining amazing insights into human life. With those insights, you too will know with certainty everything that is going on in your life and the world around you.

What happened was this: I started seeing things from the perspective of the future Neo-Tech World. So, observing the world around me was like looking back at history with hindsight, which is "20/20 vision". With a much broader understanding of things, I became the wise one. Others admired me; friends and peers looked up to me.

After "looking through hindsight" at the world around me, I finally knew *why* we never came close to our youthful expectations of wealth, love, and success. Simply stated, we never stood a chance under the old code of living. That was a profound revelation to me, for I knew it released the ordinary person from being a quiet prisoner of self-disappointment.

Now, upon seeing the coming of the new code, you will anticipate escalating wealth, love, and success sometime in the foreseeable future. Tomorrow is a real adventure! So, let us begin:

Remember, I was now looking back at the 20th century from the Neo-Tech World sometime in the 21st century. Looking back, I asked, why did we fail at our dreams in the 20th century? The answer was not difficult: we failed because we were in a

65

society in which we could not win. The blame rested squarely on our 20th-century leaders. The solution, however, was simple: with the new code, our *21st-century* leaders made this society one in which we could not fail.

By the way, my definition of failure was: not becoming the person you always dreamed of...the person you were meant to be. That person was wealthy and doing exciting, important things for society. *Everyone* was wealthy and dynamic under the new code.

How did our 21st-century leaders make this society one in which we could not fail, meaning every ordinary person enjoyed the Six Ultimate Gifts of profound security, millionaire wealth, perfect health, a dream career, a dream lover, and superior intelligence? They simply sank the B.O.A.T. Indeed, a tiny percentage of our population — our political and bureaucratic leaders — created an indomitable burden on advancing technology (B.O.A.T.). When we sank that B.O.A.T. of freeloaders, many millions of Neothink geniuses rose and technologies boomed. Our own wealth soared as prices tumbled into free-falls.

Let us first take a brief look back over your own past, growing up under the old code, to know what happened to you personally that killed your chances at your dreams:

### Born In a No-Win World

Where did everything go wrong? Think back to your earliest memories. Most people's earliest memories center around the time they started school. Little did you know that your potential in life was already limited by the time you spent your first day in school. Your lifelong potential was already limited much too low — damning you to fail at your ambitious dreams throughout life.

A common misconception in the 20th century was that your potential in life came from your education. Actually, education provided you with the thinking tools and knowledge to *fulfill* whatever potential you had left. But your potential itself was deadened before your education began.

So, let's get to the bottom of exactly what determined your potential: The human mind of average intelligence has enormous

66

capacity. We have all heard stories like: had we continued the learning curve experienced as toddlers, we would speak many languages fluently, know advanced physics, eloquently recite the ins and outs of the philosophies and, in short, know most everything in the Britannica Encyclopedia.

If man's mind is capable of such great things, what stopped us? Our geometrical learning curve collapsed. In fact, it took its biggest drop right after our toddler years — right before entering school.

What caused that geometrical learning curve to begin with? Actually, the simple answer is: *deep-rooted motivation*. As an infant and toddler, you were extremely motivated to learn to talk and become a conceptual conscious being. You felt powerful survival pressures to do so. Of course, with our superior minds, we were born to learn. And that explains why toddlers are the happiest people alive in the 20th century. You see, only when you were a toddler were you the person you were meant to be.

Then something happened around six or seven years of age, after you mastered language and became a full-fledged conceptual conscious being: your learning curve collapsed. That happened because your deep-rooted motivational drive collapsed. For, now to successfully be part of society no longer depended on a geometrical learning curve.

Imagine if that geometrical learning curve still existed in adults. Well then, to simply fit into such a progressive society, the toddler's learning curve would just keep on soaring, deeply motivated, deeply happy.

The loss of the learning curve among the entire human race under the old code was not natural. Man was meant to forever rapidly learn. We were the persons we were meant to be for only the first few years of our lives — the happiest years. Something alien killed our learning curves by killing our deep motivational drives.

That something unnatural from outside ourselves that killed our deep-rooted motivational drives was the B.O.A.T. causing a society in which we could not win. Deep-rooted resignation replaced our deep-rooted motivation. Now, back to the question: "What *really* determined potential?" The answer was: our deep-rooted motivational drive in life. With the motivational drive

67

we were meant to have, our potential equaled our mind's incredible capability. But in the 20th century, our potential was a tiny fraction of our mind's capability...motivation replaced by resignation, dooming us to fail at our most important dreams and powerful desires. If, however, you as a small child were only exposed to highly motivated parents (making hundreds of thousands or millions of dollars as young adults), your motivational drive would not have collapsed. Upon the arrival of the Neo-Tech Era in which we became millionaires, that motivational drive returned. We became creative whiz kids at all ages.

To begin answering the question, Why did we fail at our dreams in the 20th century? all goes back to before your earliest memories as you learned resignation from the world around you. But that changed under the new code. Adults grew even happier than toddlers with addicting, stimulating success. Along with integrated thinking, the learning curve returned and never collapsed. Dreams came true as you filled all your desires from wealth to sex.

## Schooled In a No-Win World

When you started school in the 20th century, you probably had dreams like becoming rich, heroic, famous...in short, becoming someone very important who would make a difference. Life probably grew increasingly frustrating because you did not have the potential to achieve your dreams. That explained why teenagers often became frustrated and disillusioned in the 20th century.

Education was how you acquired thinking tools and knowledge. The better the education, the more you could fulfill your limited potential. Unfortunately, public education had deteriorated to frighteningly ineffective levels. However, if you personally talked with teachers and principals, they were very dedicated to educating children. Teachers were genuinely into their jobs, and competent at the job they were given to do. And there, precisely, was the problem: *the job they were given to do.*

Early in the 20th century, education lost its way. Political leaders and schoolboard leaders lost their understanding of the very heart of education. At the heart of educating a child should have been: fill the child's mind with knowledge...*teach the child* knowledge, and teach the child how to think most effectively so that child could retain and build more knowledge. In a sentence, that was the job of educating children. And that was *not* the job given to teachers in the late 20th century.

Instead, sociopolitical control over government schools had given our teachers another job: to help the children "learn" from each other. Of course, that sounded good, progressive, and fashionably multicultural. The teachers performed well at the job given them, bringing to their classrooms the discussion method as their method of "teaching". And dedicated teachers admirably went to great lengths to stimulate and guide their classroom discussions. But the job given to the teacher was the wrong job. The popular discussion method was *not* education. In short, it was a case of the blind leading the blind. Indeed, hard-working dedicated teachers could not understand why children scored so low on aptitude tests. *The job* given those teachers was the wrong job: The teachers' right job was *not* to make children socially confident or culturally literate. The teacher's right job was *to teach* — yes, that old-fashioned lecture method.

The teachers had knowledge, lots of it. The children did not. Teachers should have poured as much of that knowledge as possible into young minds. That, and *nothing else*, should have been the teacher's job. Motivating children should have been defined and confined to the job at hand — that was, to pouring knowledge into children's minds via the lecture method. Motivating children in the more disciplined environment of the lecture, indeed, required greater discipline on the teacher. The teacher would have to work harder at nights making his or her lecture exciting and enlightening to students. Indeed, the effort *to teach* would go back on the teacher's shoulders. And, if given *that* job, most teachers in the late 20th century would have done a competent job educating our children.

A vital part of the teacher's job of pouring knowledge into children's minds, yet entirely lost in the late 20th century, was: *equipping our children with the most powerful thinking method.* That thinking method was *conceptual thinking*, which led to integrated thinking. Only through bringing together the scattered

69

Book 1
God-Man Decoded

fragments of facts and figures into integrated concepts could children retain and build knowledge like a puzzle. While lecturing knowledge, teachers should have pulled together the many pieces of knowledge into integrated concepts to enable themselves to pour much more knowledge — retainable knowledge — into children's minds.

For example, while studying social studies, children memorized many specific facts about different countries, cultures, economies. But those 20th-century children retained little because many specific facts were not pulled together into common denominators — into a few powerful, timeless concepts. The endless variations of prosperity and progress among cultures and economies could have been integrated by the common denominator of freedom. That's right, the prosperity and progress of each culture and economy directly related to that country's degree of freedom from the B.O.A.T. of freeloaders. Now the child would have quickly begun linking together unforgettable conceptual understandings instead of memorizing forgettable places, faces, and other forgettable facts.

By giving the child the added power to jump past limited memorization into unlimited conceptualization, the teacher could have poured far more knowledge into his students' minds. Moreover, the students would have had the foundation and the thinking tools to build knowledge. Remember, knowledge meant power. That growing power and control inside a child would have stirred up real and lasting motivation to learn.

Not faulting the teachers but faulting the leaders of the old code's no-win society, children graduated without the knowledge or thinking tools to fulfill the limited potential they did have. Again, sinking the B.O.A.T. sometime in the 21st century brought teachers back to their proper job: *to teach*. Then, children reached their breathtaking potential...sometime after 2001, under the new code.

## Role Models In a No-Win World

Teenage role models in the late 20th century often controlled which direction self-conscious teenagers turned. Role models, namely pop, rock, and rap stars, reflected the no-win society in which we were trapped.

The message those role models continued to deliver in many subtle ways was: you are worthless. That message — you are worthless — was the common denominator under the many different surface messages. For instance, the self was devalued through reducing sex to the level of scratching an itch or through making self-destruction such as drinking and doing drugs the cool thing to do or through encouraging love for others because of different skin color instead of meaningful value exchange. Self-worth, self-esteem was flattened by role models. And as one's self-worth went away, so did the irreplaceable emotional self. Indeed, role models desensitized 20th-century teenagers. Teenagers less and less felt meaningful love for family, pets, girlfriends or boyfriends. The all-important emotional peaks and valleys were getting leveled.

But looking back from the Neo-Tech World, let us not focus too much blame on the role models. In many cases, they too were just young adults expressing their own frustrations. Instead, let us focus the blame on those who caused the no-win society. You see, once we sank the B.O.A.T. and had a no-lose society, then everyone's sense of life changed. Positivity replaced negativity. Enthusiasm for life replaced destruction of life. Love and sensitivity flowed. And role models became assets, not liabilities.

## Working In a No-Win World

In the 20th century, you would neither achieve your best dreams nor fill your most powerful desires; your potential was destroyed early on, and your education was not good. In the 21st century when the B.O.A.T. sank, society rose. You rose along with society. You experienced the wealth you always dreamed of as well as the deep excitement and happiness of bringing major values to the world, all of which was beyond your potential under the old code.

Yet, you still sometimes dreamed of wealth and greatness in the 20th-century. Nonetheless, three forces held you down from ever soaring: 1) your potential, that deep-rooted motivational drive resigned early on, 2) your mode of thinking was scrambled during education, and 3) society's opportunities vanished because of the B.O.A.T. of freeloaders.

71

First, your potential, your deep-rooted motivational drive, was gone. Each day proved that. For, if you had the deep-rooted motivational drive that you did as a very young child, you would have spent enormous energy learning and absorbing knowledge for your success every day. And you would have loved it as, in turn, you used that knowledge to build values that earned millions of dollars. Driven by seven-digit financial rewards, your evenings would have been filled with reading, studying, thinking and rethinking your fast-lane of success. Your thirst for knowledge would have been unquenchable. Very few adults in the 20th century ever had the opportunity to exist in that exciting mode.

Second, your mode of thinking was scrambled during your education. By not learning to do potent conceptual or integrated thinking in school, you stayed in the impotent specialized-thinking mode. Specialized thinking worked by memory and blocked you from integrating and building knowledge, which was crucial to creating money-making opportunities. Specialized thinking put you into a following mode, merely following what you were told to do, following the set responsibilities given to you at work...trapping you in a routine rut. After 2001, integrated thinking put you into a self-leadership mode, using your own mind to build beyond what currently existed...propelling you into money-making breakthroughs.

Third, society's opportunities in the 20th century had vanished because the B.O.A.T. made success too difficult. Regulations, legislation, and litigation made success limited, costly, and risky. Without such a burden, lucrative opportunities would have been everywhere, for everyone.

The stagnation we encountered as adults certainly killed our dreams. Moreover, that stagnation also harmed our marriages and ended the thrill of love we felt during the first few weeks of falling in love. And, sadly, our children absorbed from us our hopeless resignation, just as we did from our parents. In short, all this was *why we failed at our dreams*.

What was the way out of your lifelong trap? Your way out came at two levels. By far the easiest way out was to sink the B.O.A.T. That happened sometime after 2001. Before 2001, some people made some strides forward on their own by learning integrated thinking as adults, as I did (see previous chapter).

## Victims In a No-Win World

Looking back from tomorrow's Neo-Tech World at the late 20th-century no-win world, seniors often found themselves concerned about politics. Their focus shifted to politics because they wanted security for their futures and, in some cases, for their children and grandchildren's futures.

The more they studied politics and their leaders' effects on the country, those seniors who were not part of the dependent "slave class" gradually realized that the problems had little to do with the nature of Democrats or Republicans. The country's problems had to do with the nature of *politicians*. In short, the nature of career politicians put a heavy burden on business and its advancing technologies, which put a heavy lid over many millions of potential Neothink geniuses.

Indeed, career politicians axiomatically held down society. Intoxicated by the power to rule over us, they generated more and more laws, which gained them recognition and popularity for re-election. But all those laws create more and more taxes, regulators, lawyers, and lawsuits that put a lid on the progress of America's business and technology, as demonstrated on the next two pages:

# Burden On Advancing Technology

## Three Major 20th-Century Burdens

**40 Points Taxes:** Taxes on business hurt advancing technology, indeed. The cash needed to pay taxes cut off endless research and development investments, which were the embryo not only of future creation of jobs, but of *all* advancing technology. Yet, perhaps the biggest burden was actually the income tax on <u>the people</u>. You see, taxing the people ultimately came back on the business. For, the people needed enough money for a reasonable standard of living. So, the more people paid in taxes, the more business ultimately paid its workers. In a sense, business paid our income tax, a hidden but perhaps the second most major burden on advancing technology.

**40 Points Legislation & Regulations:** Existing laws and regulations blocked industry from investing or putting effort into many vital directions. Too cost prohibitive and risky. Also, tender youth did not even attempt to move into new ventures for fear of new regulations or laws or interpretations of existing ones. Creativity and progress nearly stopped with this, the other leading burden on advancing technology.

**20 Points Litigation:** All the unnecessary laws and regulations bloated the legal industry with nearly a million lawyers by the end of the 20th century. The legal roadblocks and endless litigation handicapped American business in the global market and was a major burden on advancing technology.

## 100 Points Total

# Reducing The Burden

In the late 20th century, let us see what happened when the <u>B</u>urden <u>O</u>n <u>A</u>dvancing <u>T</u>echnology and its B.O.A.T.-of-Freeloaders rating got reduced:

| <u>Computer Industry During 1980s & 1990s:</u> | | <u>Industry Norm:</u> |
|---|---|---|
| Taxes | 40  points (taxes did not change) | 40 Points |
| Regulations & Legislation | 20 points (still applied to all supporting industries) | 40 Points |
| Litigation | 10 points (still applied to all supporting industries) | 20 Points |
| | 70 Points Total | 100 Points Total |

The personal computer industry was so new and fiercely independent, the legislators, regulators, and lawyers did not yet know how to burden it. Thus, the B.O.A.T.-of-Freeloaders rating dropped from 100 points (the norm for all industries) to 70 points. By cutting the B.O.A.T. by just 30 points, or by less than one-third, buying power went up 1000 times or 100,000%.

The reason for the dramatic explosion in prosperity and consumer buying power when sinking the B.O.A.T was simple:

Say A Business Grossed $3 million————▶And Made $200,000 Profits: That meant, for every $100 risked, made $7 or so. So fragile. The high risks of regulations, legislation, litigation could easily bankrupt the company. Just a slight shift in odds could kill <u>all</u> — all the jobs, jobs, jobs & values, values, values. Moreover, many, many businesses never even got started. And, few businesses put out the risks needed to grow to the next level. Too fragile. Too risky. The slightest additional burden could shift the fragile existence ever so slightly — but enough to wipe out the fragile 7% margin. On the other hand, when even the slightest burden was lifted, could alter the 7% margin to an 11% or greater margin, which enabled the company much more flexibility and security to pursue growth to the next level.

jobs, jobs, jobs
values, values, values

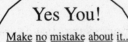

Yes You!

<u>Make</u> <u>no</u> <u>mistake</u> <u>about</u> <u>it</u>...
It's Taxes,
Regulations/Legislation,
Litigation

versus

Your   Wealth!

Book 1
God-Man Decoded

# The
# Burden On Advancing Technology
# Principle

## SINK THE B.O.A.T AFTER 2001

| Today & Climbing | | After 2001 |
|---|---|---|
| 40 | Taxes[1] | 20 |
| 40 | Regulations/Legislation | 20 |
| 20 | Litigation | 10 |
| 100 | | 50 |

## When the B.O.A.T. Of Freeloaders Sank
## *YOU* WERE WORTH MILLIONS!

B.O.A.T.
Of Freeloaders

---

[1]Why were taxes weighted so heavily — 40 points?  Taxes in the 20th century caused a great, great burden on business beyond what met the eye.  You see, *all* money used to live and survive originally came from business.  A company's employees had to experience a certain standard of living that delivered the most effective and efficient employees.  The business ultimately had to keep up its workers' standard of living.  If the government taxed the people more heavily, that burden ultimately worked it way back to the company as it had to keep its workers at a certain standard of living.  In all, every tax everywhere caused a burden on the originator of wealth: business.

# Sinking The B.O.A.T.

Under the old code of living, our government *wrongly* assumed the second purpose, below:

1) To physically protect the people with local police, courts, prisons, and national defense (government's legitimate purpose)

2) To improve public prosperity and well-being through social and regulatory programs "for the public good" (wrongly assumed purpose)

To understand why assuming the second purpose was wrong, consider that it gave government the power to regulate our economy and our businesses. That meant career politicians would rule over us, an addictive power that predictably destroyed the potential of our economy. Those politicians, however, created convincing illusions that they were helping us and serving us, although they were really interested only in serving themselves.

With the power to rule over us, interested in serving themselves, the career politicians methodically embezzled power and wealth from society with their "good intentions" in the second purpose above. No, they were not helping others, for helping others can only come through effort to build values. The career politicians' bogus purpose #2 above, giving them the power to rule over us, backed by force, only benefitted those who commanded the power to rule, for it let them *take values* and not *build values*.

True, as part of their illusions, career politicians spent our money on entitlement programs that so-called "served the public good". But *spending* other people's money *required no effort* and *built no values*. Spending other people's money could not really be serving the people, rather serving the politicians themselves as they bought votes. Only *earning* money *required effort* and *built values*.

Realize the difference between *spending* wealth, especially wealth earned by others, versus *earning* wealth. For example, imagine a lazy, young adult who never worked, but who inherited his fortune and recklessly spent that wealth in many self-indulging ways...versus the hard-working person who originally generated that fortune. The lazy self-indulger consumed massive wealth, and so did our 20th-century politicians. They consumed massive

77

wealth — *our wealth* — for their self-indulging purpose of buying votes.

Civilization would have perished if everyone self-indulged in consuming wealth. Civilization needed people who generated wealth. Civilization succeeded to the extent hard-working people generated wealth and values for society. Those people put energy into society; the self-indulger just consumed and depleted that energy.

Career politicians lived in that reckless inheritance-like mode that nearly destroyed our society. They consumed the energy of the workers. They spent our money to *disingenuously* "serve the people" but really to serve themselves by self-indulging in their own political viability. Indeed, they irresponsibly consumed our wealth to buy votes for re-election. If not stopped, they would have eventually consumed all our wealth and depleted all the energy.

Moreover, 20th-century career politicians were like alcoholics who tried to draw everyone around them into drinking with them to feel better about themselves. Indeed, career politicians tried to get as many people as they could into the inheritance-like mode. You see, that made it all right. So our nation became more and more financially dependent. Toward the end of the century, entitlements and the budget grew out of control.

The market-driven businessman, by contrast, lived in the responsible productive mode that built society. He doggedly produced values to generate wealth, which genuinely served society. Indeed, only the market-driven businessman had demonstrated that he put out the dogged effort to serve the people.

In short, spending other people's money was easy and downright self-indulging...consuming our wealth to selfishly buy votes. By nature of the effort in genuinely improving the prosperity of the people, career politicians could not succeed. Indeed, government that fell into that second purpose — to improve the prosperity of the people — was unsound. After 2001, under the new code, the second purpose went to market businessmen and women who generated and spent their own money, not ours. Only then did our country actually succeed at social and regulatory programs. That happened soon after the

Great Replacement Program and was called the Great Displacement Program. Then our government focused on its one proper purpose — to physically protect the people.

So, what caused the B.O.A.T. and how did we sink it? All well intentioned social and regulatory programs *to improve public prosperity* ironically built the B.O.A.T. To sink it, we completely eliminated that second, disingenuous purpose of government through the Great Replacement/Great Displacement Program.

To see the B.O.A.T. clearly, imagine the very poor, 20th-century third-world countries: Leaders badly *burdened* business and advancing technology. Desperation, starvation, crime took over as those self-indulging leaders badly burdened the workers. Who could help the hungry masses? Their only savior was that rare and gifted person who could *build* a business or *expand* a business to provide new jobs and spending money. He was a hard-working person who brought jobs to those people and food to their tables. Only he served the people.

That person was the *market businessman*. He was very different from the rich businessmen who worked hand-in-hand with the government. They just drained their companies and their employees. They were *political businessmen*.

The market businessman was the *one person* who could move society up for others. Looking at a poor country made that obvious, for he rescued those people from homelessness and death. But his value was *just as vital* even in the relatively wealthy United States. The *market businessman* moved society up for others.

Career politicians envied the market businessman in the 20th century. Career politicians burdened, even attacked the market businessman. In China, career politicians put to death market businessmen in the name of "economic crimes". In Russia, until the collapse of the Soviet Empire, they did the same. Wherever you went in the world, the degree of poverty had a direct relationship to the degree the market businessman was burdened and destroyed. Even in the prosperous United States, career politicians and regulatory bureaucrats caused a number of market businessmen to go to prison each year. For example, most of the Wall Street "white-collar crime" laws and regulations were distant cousins to China's "economic crimes". Aggressive

79

political policy against market businessmen suppressed society and blocked everyone from the life he or she meant to have.

In the 20th century, two groups of people lived in this world:

**The Workers:** all people who put more into society than they took out, from the laborer to founders of great business empires.

**The Parasites:** all people who took more out of society than they put in, from the petty thief to leaders of great countries.

Both groups of people had leaders: The workers' leaders, market businessmen and women, brought prosperity and jobs to the workers. The parasites' leaders, career politicians, created conditions for more parasites.

The most leveraged parasites to replace were their leaders — the career politicians. For, those politicians enabled parasites to weaken society not only from within government, but from within big business and society as well:

**In Big Business:** Career politicians enabled their country's big businesses to be filled with lazy executives with easy, parasitical lives. The politicians provided them with cushy advantages that blocked competition from the smaller, aggressive market entrepreneurs. Through legislation and resulting regulations, the politicians removed much of the free-market competition for their big-business leaders. Thus, a layer of parasites formed at the corporate top — self-indulging executives who personally consumed wealth.

**In Society:** Career politicians brought parasites into society itself. For, lack of jobs promoted crime and welfare. So the number of homeless, criminals, and welfare recipients grew each year. The more parasites on the top of society, the poorer the country became with more resulting parasites consuming wealth at the bottom of society.

One group of persons lived off the other group of persons in all 20th-century societies — the parasites lived off the workers. More and more parasites not only consumed the wealth, but slowly killed the host. The parasites' leaders in the old political paradigm were replaced after 2001 with *our* rightful leaders, the workers' leaders, the market businessmen...those who *built* values and jobs for society, those who *wanted* the economy to race forward unhampered by parasites, those who let technology race ahead like the computers to drive prices toward zero in all industries and make all the people rich under our 21st-century new political paradigm.

Indeed, who exactly was qualified to lead our country? To build the economy required building the business of a country. Career politicians had never built businesses. They knew nothing about the details of business as they merely "inherited" their power. They could not fulfill their ostensible purpose to build the economy and the well-being of the people.

If you were asked, "Who was qualified to lead the construction of your new home?", you would answer, "Those who built homes." You would not answer, "Politicians and bureaucrats."

Our career politicians knew as little about business as they did about construction. They never ran any businesses. Yet, they shaped and controlled our businesses and jobs — our economy — with their laws and regulations. ...If career politicians were to build your house, it would fall during the first bad storm. Well, our economy faced rough storms of international competition at century end.

For all the centuries under the old code, career politicians had never been replaced by market businessmen as our rightful leaders. Why not? Because of cleverly crafted illusions. Career politicians were, in essence, frauds who could not build the economy. So, they created a public enemy whom they would "protect" us from in order to justify their legislative and regulatory role over our economy. Using inverse illusions that involved your emotions (a typical ploy in most con jobs), the ruling-class leaders made us believe that they would protect us from the "greedy" market businessman, which justified their necessity and hid who they themselves were: the destructive people of society whom, under the new code, we would protect the people from.

Career politicians misled the public into believing and accepting their illusions, from the "economic crimes" in which China put the market businessman to death...to their distant cousin "white-collar crimes" from the "decade of greed" in which America put market businessmen in jail.

Ironically and tragically, legislation and regulation — burdens on advancing technology — built popularity and political power

81

for career politicians and bureaucrats in the 20th century, through their clever illusions. Moreover, legislation and regulation built a dirty alley of law in America, which was eating alive American international competitiveness. Consider if you threw one sandwich into a dirty alley, four rats came out to eat. If you threw 25 sandwiches into a dirty alley, eventually 100 rats came out to eat. ...Our lawmakers were throwing piles of sandwiches into the dirty alley of law. Packs of parasitical lawyers — nearly a million lawyers by century end — had come out to eat our economy like rats. Not all lawyers were parasites, but the majority were hurting our competitive position in the global economy.

Consider some original business founders: Henry Ford, Andrew Carnegie, Thomas Edison; these were geniuses who built industrial empires, employed hundreds of thousands of people, and brought better standards of living to the average family. Moreover, late 20th-century aggressive entrepreneurs like Bill Gates, Andrew Grove, and other truly hard-working leaders of businesses, large and small, brought jobs and better standards of living to society. ...The head to the working class served the people and would soon be our leaders. Career politicians inherently knew this and did not like it. The new political paradigm brought the head and the body of the working class together through the Great Replacement Program.

Building a value for society took *dogged effort.* Our 20th-century political leaders did not build values for society...they chose the lazy "inherited" route and did not put forth dogged effort. Everything they did was in that crafted supervisory mode, never building a value. They just rode on the efforts of others, burdened society, and consumed wealth.

Ironically, those 20th-century political leaders had *prestige,* a lot of power and activity around them and big-shot positions of "importance". All that activity around them, "importance", and prestige — where did it come from? Not from building values and earning it, for those were lazy people. Thus, all their activity and prestige, since it did not come from building values, then it came from burdening existing values — from legislating and regulating business...by building their B.O.A.T. (i.e., burden on advancing technology). Of course, they spent all their time

82

building this power to rule over us.

Prestige was either earned through building values for society; or it was stolen from those who earned it by burdening their values. In fact, the more prestige, the more a *lazy* person with power burdened, even destroyed values. As became obvious under the new code, the prestigious career politicians in the 20th century were our greatest enemies, for they outright suppressed the advancement of society that would have otherwise, on the eve of the Technological Revolution, sent prices tumbling toward zero and sent standards of living soaring toward millionaire-like wealth.

All 20th-century career politicians, regulatory bureaucrats, most media giants, and many million-dollar lawyers stole prestige. They stole prestige from the market businessman by legislating, regulating, and sometimes even jailing the best...with great fanfare and media coverage for themselves, as demonstrated in the Rudolph Giuliani versus Michael Milken late-20th-century chapter of history. Electrifying businessman Milken wrongly went to prison. Envious bureaucrat Giuliani took him down and got national publicity and eventually became the mayor of New York with presidential aspirations. Career politicians stole prestige and consumed wealth. They did not earn wealth and prestige. They did not build values for society. They simply burdened values for their own free ride in life and blocked the great prosperity-explosion for the people.

In order to justify themselves, lazy people[1] with power — our 20th-century political leaders — *had to* create a so-called "need" for themselves. They *had to* stir up "important activity" around themselves to justify themselves. But they did not build values. Therefore, all that unnecessary "supervisory" activity burdened the economy.

Envy played a big role in building their B.O.A.T. Only one group of people in civilization felt envy. The parasitical class was the inferior class of society. Feeling inferior, the parasites felt envy toward the superior working class, especially the working-class leader. They secretly felt a desire to destroy him.

Envy in the 20th century — let's talk about that for a

---

[1]The 20th-century career politicians were lazy people, but very, very busy people building their addicting political power.

moment: A parasite's envy grew as the working person's value to society grew. The greatest value one could bring to society was job creation. Therefore, envy was most targeted at aggressive entrepreneurs and leading market businessmen — the geniuses — those we later learned to protect! That envy, targeted at their businesses and success, was the *fingerprint* of the 20th-century parasitical class. The envy came from inferior feelings deep inside. That envy let us spot and know our enemies when the transition into the new code began, even when we could not see through their illusions that made them look important.

Now, their envy teamed up with their need to justify themselves. Guided by envy, they stirred up a lot of activity in their jobs. That illusion of importance brought them popularity and power. Driven by envy, our career politicians and ambitious bureaucrats developed laws and regulations that greatly burdened and sometimes destroyed market businessmen and their businesses. After all, the market businessmen and women would eventually put career politicians out of business, which became more evident with every late 20th-century election.

For some time after distrusting politicians, we still succumbed to their illusions because we were too specialized. Just as if we were in a magic show and did not know how the magicians' illusions worked, we did not know how the career politicians' illusions work. We could not see through their illusions as we first began our rise into the Neo-Tech Era, but we could more easily see their *envy* — the fingerprint of the parasitical leaders. Then we quickly replaced those envious people stealing prestige and stealing their way to political prominence via building their B.O.A.T.

Realize that it was *easy* to regulate and legislate, and it was *hard* to build values. Our lazy (but busy) political leaders sought the quick and easy ride. Indeed, in the 20th century, there were two paths to prestige and self-esteem. One was a *legitimate path:* that was the hard and slow process of building values for society. Market businessmen and women gained recognition and self-esteem over years of building and bringing tangible values to society. Then there was an *illegitimate path:* that was the easy and fast process of tearing down or regulating the advancement of values in society.

*Personal Renaissance II: Know It All*

To see through the illusions and spot the parasitical elite was difficult in those days. Again, we were just too specialized. We sensed the laziness and corruption, but we could not easily expose it. But to spot the *fingerprint of envy* was not as difficult. Indeed, the zealous approval for legislating and regulating business, particularly aggressive entrepreneurs and their advancing technologies, was the unmistakable fingerprint of envy that belonged only to the parasitical soul. The people at the very end of the 20th century began to catch on, pushed along by the rapidly growing realization of the Six Ultimate Gifts — the glorious life people of all races, cultures, and countries were meant to live — as presented to millions of eyes through cyberspace.

At first people said, "Doesn't regulating provide a value?" The answer was, "Yes, it does when you *pay* for that service...in other words, when regulating becomes a free-market service." In the 20th-century publishing industry, for example, magazines submitted to ABC, an auditing business that strictly regulated magazines in regards to subscriptions and circulation. Well, ABC was a value to the industry as it verified circulation for advertisers. Realize, ABC had to exert the *dogged effort* to be that value. ABC had to meet a bottom line; ABC had to meet the business discipline to make its service a value to people who wanted to pay for it. ABC had to *earn* its money.

In 20th-century government, by contrast, *forced taxes* removed the need to put forth *effort*. Forced taxes provided the conditions that bred laziness and incompetence. You see, the money was automatically there; no need existed to exert the effort to build a genuine value that people wanted to pay for: no bottom-line to meet, no business disciplines to meet, no competition, no threat of being fired, no fear of going out of business, no need to work intensely, no need to put out the effort to make a value for society *in order* to make a paycheck for themselves. Therefore, our politicians and bureaucrats became professionally lazy; they institutionalized laziness in our government. The leaders rode off the efforts of the people. Those self-indulging leaders, in an inheritance-like mode, recklessly spent our money and consumed our wealth for their own political popularity. They did not earn wealth.

85

Book 1
God-Man Decoded

Since our government's leaders did not put out the effort to provide genuine values for society and earn wealth, they instead created illusions that they provided values for society. The politicians and bureaucrats created a magic show of watching over and regulating business from the potential dangers of the "greedy" market businessman. Thus, their activities of creating laws, regulating (i.e., burdening) business, and spending our money now appeared as values to us. And, not grounded to the tough work of producing values, they spent *all their time* building this addicting, divine-like power of ruling over us.

Bureaucrats and politicians took the fast lane of burdening values for easy popularity. In 20th-century America, we had a large network of business to regulate for decades to come. Since people did whatever they did in their jobs *to promote their careers*, 20th-century career politicians aggressively *burdened to promote themselves*. Market businessmen and women who built values, on the other hand, *built to promote themselves*. In summing up the nature of our leaders who controlled our 20th-century no-win society, answer this: Did they *acquire their status* by: 1) building values, or 2) burdening values?

The market businessman used effort and built values. The career politician burdened values. And what motivated politicians to desperately want office? Something deep in their souls — their lacking self-esteems — desperately drove them. Politicians desperately wanted to prove to themselves and to the world that they were important. They did not earn legitimate self-esteem through building values, but they inherited a big dose of prestige if elected. And the more they ruled over us, the more prestige they enjoyed. Lacking legitimate self-esteem, they were certainly motivated to rule over us.

The secret weapon of our 20th-century political leaders was their ability to craft illusions to appear valuable and needed. Here was *how* they crafted their illusions: Our leaders used *true facts* to build *out-of-context pictures* and form the illusions they wanted. They left out the other facts that would dissolve the illusions and build *in-context pictures*.

Let me give you an example I once heard my father tell. I am going to tell you a couple of true facts: John O'Grady premeditated a plan and then brutally killed a man. Those are

86

true facts. John O'Grady, therefore, is a cold-blooded killer and should be locked away for life. That is an unjust conclusion. You see, the true facts are incomplete and, therefore, out of context, which leads everyone to an unjust conclusion.

Now, I am going to give you *all* the true facts, and I am going to put them in context: John O'Grady saved a platoon of men in 1944 at the Battle of the Bulge in Bastogne, Belgium. Trapped beneath a snow covered ledge by a Nazi machine gunner, John O'Grady premeditated a plan. He then scaled an icy cliff. Wounded twice, O'Grady finally succeeded. He shot and killed the machine gunner and saved the 20 men in his platoon. ...Those are also true facts, but those true facts are complete and, therefore, in context, which leads everyone to the just conclusion.

Using true facts incompletely and out of context, anyone can create villains out of heroes: At first, John O'Grady seemed to be a villain. But put all the facts into context and you find out he is really a hero. ...Think for a moment: could incarcerated "villains" from our "decade of greed" really be heroes? Imagine that Michael Milken, responsible for tens of thousands if not hundreds of thousands of jobs, was imprisoned for political-policy white-collar "crime". Career politicians and regulatory bureaucrats in the 20th century routinely took situations out of context to make heroes look like villains.

Realize that those same parasitical leaders made themselves appear as good and prestigious while hiding that they themselves were the villains of society. They did that through illusions that made truly good and prestigious people such as market businessmen and women appear as villains by using true facts out of context. The frauds — our parasitical leaders — then "protected" society from those "villains" and became "our heroes".

Using complicated *true facts* let them build powerful and nearly indestructible illusions. The average, specialized working person could not see through their illusions. Their illusions enabled them to build their B.O.A.T. Only those self-serving leaders and their B.O.A.T. came between you and free-falling prices that would have made you rich. Eventually, people saw the fingerprint of envy showing upon illusion after illusion. And

87

then, the ordinary person started to recognize the frauds to sink the B.O.A.T. through the Great Replacement Program.

## Just Sit Back And Get Rich

After 2001, under the new code, our society became an unbelievable source of easy money and power. Society, first of all, came upon the information revolution, the critical point of modern technology beyond which prices everywhere went into free-falls sometime after 2001. The new society caused you to live like a millionaire as America leapt ahead into the Neo-Tech Era.

Before that happened, however, America tripped off the path of destiny in the late 20th century. Instead of being your greatest source of wealth and power, society became the greatest drain on your wealth and power at century end as the economy and your freedom continued to stumble. We were sinking into the Catastrophic Era.

Virulent disease, crime, and poverty spread to more neighborhoods. By about this time, millions of people with the help of the Internet witnessed the Six Ultimate Gifts. In time, the Great Replacement Program swept across the country, which pulled a sinking America out of the Catastrophic Era. Big government died and dropped, catapulting the Technological Revolution. Our buying power sprang up, and we lived in wealth and luxury under the new code.

Twentieth-century big government and its career politicians placed a lid on society, held it down, and lived on that lid during the old code.

People went to work, did their same routines, day after day. They were caught *under the lid*. But the market businessmen, the geniuses of society particularly in the communications industries, were close to pushing up that lid so that all ordinary people could soar to new levels of prosperity.

Rising market businessmen and women in the 20th century broke free from the trap of specialized routine ruts. They broke free by taking over bits and pieces of the business...a responsibility from here, from there. Their growing integration of responsibilities gave them wings that began lifting them. As they mastered growing chunks of the business, they began to fly. (My first personal renaissance in the previous chapter teaches you how to also rise through this integrated thinking.)

As integrated thinkers rose under the old code, they began learning things that the majority of good working people, hopelessly trapped in specialized thinking, never learned. Integrated thinkers began to learn how business worked. And then as they grew and took bigger and bigger bites of responsibilities, they realized how the economy worked. In time, something frightening dawned on them: "Politicians and bureaucrats really just burdened business, technology, and the economy!" Unlike most ordinary good working people, rising market businessmen and aggressive entrepreneurs began to know what was *really* going on and could expose the fraud.

As they rose, they were no longer caught in a specialized routine with blinders. No, they began to put together and see things the masses never saw. They became a threat to expose our parasitical leaders and their free rides in life.

Market businessmen and women who rose quickly in corporations also began to expose the political businessmen in the upper echelons of our big businesses. Therefore, many of our 20th-century big-business leaders did their best to suppress and push back down those who discovered integrated thinking and how to rise in their companies.

Of course, 20th-century career politicians and regulatory bureaucrats also suppressed, even smashed down the rising integrated thinker with punishing laws, regulations, even incarceration, for they did not want their hoax exposed.

The fast-rising integrated thinker was one of us — one of the good working people — who broke free from his stagnant trap of specialization. As he rose in the 20th century, he provided more and more opportunities for his working brothers and sisters around him — opportunities for ordinary people like you and me. As he rose, he pulled up more and more ordinary working people with him. He began to push up the lid holding down all ordinary working people under the old code. That lid of politicization and society's resulting specialization that suppressed 20th-century society would begin to buckle around him as he helped free more and more ordinary people from their

Book 1
God-Man Decoded

stagnation-traps with new and exciting opportunities.

The integrated thinkers, wherever they existed, would begin to push up the lid; those geniuses of society would begin to raise the standard of living in 20th-century America, and what inevitably happened every time? **WHAM!** They were pushed back down and punished. People who rose up got pushed down and punished by our 20th-century establishment leaders. The wave of white-collar "crime" following the "decade of greed" was a very visible example. But every day in many quiet ways market businessmen got pushed down and punished, particularly through escalating prison sentences toward the century's end for what a few years before was just a slap on the wrist. The wave of white-collar "crime" in the '80s and then escalating prison sentences in the '90s made the fast-rising integrated thinkers nearly extinct in the late 20th century. Yet, that was when society needed them most to stop escalating disease, poverty, and crime as we began sinking into the Catastrophic Era.

As it turned out, the integrated thinkers, the geniuses of society, became our 21st-century saviors who could have saved us from our stagnation a lot earlier, back in the 20th century if they were not pushed down, punished, and paralyzed with regulations and legislation. Even worse, the laws and regulations and escalating prison sentences were firmly in place after the wave of white-collar "crime" convictions, which prevented most future integrated thinkers from ever rising outside of the computer industry during the last decade of the 20th century. The lid of politicization and society's resulting specialization, upon which our 20th-century leaders lived and under which we suffered, was more secure during that final decade than any time before in the 20th century. As a result, America began sinking into the Catastrophic Era.

Every entrepreneur was afraid of authorities. Why did they feel fear instead of pride? **WHAM!** That's why. They were afraid of being pushed down and punished by career politicians and regulatory bureaucrats.

In order to push down society, our 20th-century leaders camouflaged what they were doing. They tricked us with illusions. Their secret, remember, was using true facts out of context. Our leaders made villains out of heroes of society by

90

using true facts — facts we could not argue with — and presenting them incompletely and out of context. The specialized public did not have access to all the facts. Unlike the integrated thinker, the specialized public could not put together all the facts into contextual and complete pictures. Facts were kept from us, hidden from us. Our leaders made society's rare 20th-century integrated thinkers — our brothers and sisters who rose high and tried to push open the lid to paradise for us — villains when, indeed, they were our heroes.

People born after 2001 under the new code wondered what was going on in the 20th century. I think I summed it up during a dinner in the 20th century with a rising politician at the famous Las Vegas Hard Rock Cafe. A popular out-of-context illusion crafted and used against business by power-usurping leaders in the late 20th century was: you are destroying the planet. Hard Rock Cafe bought into the illusion and did not automatically bring water to the table in order to help "save the planet". Coming inside from the 105° desert heat, I asked the waitress to bring a round of water for everyone. My wife, who saw through the illusion, commented on how silly it was when you went out to dinner in the hot Las Vegas desert that a restaurant did not bring you a glass of water in the name of "saving the planet".

The rising politician, who drank half his glass of water in one lift of the glass, started sanctimoniously lecturing my wife, quoting facts upon facts about the factories in Utah using up the water and causing some harmful salt pits. Those factories were destroying the environment, he exclaimed. Then, he told a touching story about the birds that died because of the salt pits. Of course, his true facts used selectively built his illusion, and his sad story about the wildlife became his weapon to disarm any opposition.

You see, in the 20th-century, usually when a sad story was told by a politician or bureaucrat, an illusion was being fortified. First, career politicians discovered that they could control you through your compassionate emotions. Then, career politicians perfected their craft like a fine art.

The 20th-century career politicians had to camouflage their destructive motives, and the only way to do that was to make

91

Book 1
God-Man Decoded

the heroes of society appear as villains and themselves, the real villains, appear as the heroes who had to rescue the planet. To control you, they used true facts out of context to craft illusions. Those illusions were most effective *when engaging your compassion*. Had you only known that whenever the "facts" made you feel something awful was taking place in need of legislation or regulation, you could have just put those "facts" along with your concerned feelings aside for a minute, *even if you could not see through the illusion*. If the people only knew to do that, everything would have been different. They would have seen what was really going on. In the end, the people would have enjoyed millionaire wealth and perfect health in the 20th century.

Anyway, a nature-loving man, I put aside my compassionate feelings for the birds and put aside all the facts for a moment. Then I was able to see *what was really going on.* With my vulnerable feelings aside, I saw the politician's true motives. With my feelings aside, I no longer could be controlled. Like removing rose-tinted glasses, I suddenly saw an envious person before me. I felt angry and started talking, "What do you want? What do you *really* want? You want the factory owners put in jail. You want to punish, *punish* those people who are rising up, those factory owners who are rising up and trying to push open the lid on society, who are bringing the greatest value to society, jobs to thousands of Utah citizens...a priceless value to society! What do you want? You want to see the owners in jail!" ...That's what the rising politician wanted. In reality, the envious politician did not care about the wildlife in Utah. You see, he was comfortably sitting on society's lid of politicization. And with everyone specialized below the lid, he could enjoy a very cushy job. He inherently knew that if the jack-in-the-box sprang open, he with the other lazy people up there were going to fall off and society would go up and forget him and leave him forever behind. He would lose his job to people like the factory owners. So he had a vested interest in attacking our friends who were trying to push open the lid on society for us.[1]

So, how did we finally know what was *really* going on?

---

[1]Private regulating services in the 21st century put facts into context for honest, objectively firm, thus most effective results.

After 2001, during the transition from the old code to the new code of living, we rapidly learned to *beware* when our solicited compassion made us feel that legislation, regulation, and punishment was necessary against business, medicine, or science. We rapidly learned to *beware* whenever we felt that our leaders were heroes who had to protect us from business, medicine, or science. We knew we were very likely caught in an illusion crafted by true facts kept incomplete and out of context. We learned to put the "facts" and our emotions aside, even if we could not see through the illusions. Then we figured out what was really going on. And it was usually the opposite of how the politicians made us feel. For then, we could see their fingerprint of envy.

The Great Replacement Program eventually rescued the workers of the world. We, the workers of the world, changed the currents of the world...once we knew what was *really* going on.

When the lid swung open through the Great Replacement Program, *everyone* became wealthy. That Neo-Tech Era brought wealth to all people as the geniuses of society drove prices of the super rapidly advancing new technologies toward zero.

## Who Were They?

During the transition from the old code to the new code, some people wondered if our leaders were innocent magicians. But the children of the 21st century looked back at the 20th-century leaders as malicious wizards. Let me tell you a story, and then you decide:

In my college days, I was a likeable guy who made friends easily. But I did not feel comfortable around certain people in college. That feeling grew as I took government classes and political-science classes. I developed a name for the young men I did not like. I called them *poppa boys.*

You see, those poppa boys would never become independent. They would never break from the authority of adults around them to think for themselves. They dogmatically followed the views of the Establishment. To those poppa boys, anyone who was just a little bit independent or down on the recognized authority was a bad person. ...Later in life those poppa boys would

93

become the recognized authority — the Establishment. Anyone who challenged the Establishment would be a bad person and punished.

But back to my college days: I began to notice a trend; the poppa boys' fathers seemed to usually pay for the poppa boys' education. Now, there was nothing wrong with helping their sons through college, but the poppa boys — particularly those who were majoring in political science and government...our future politicians, lawyers, judges — seemed to have no intention of ever leaving the nest. They had no intention of getting a real job and providing values to society for their money. No, those spoiled boys inherently planned to always be taken care of financially. For now, it was daddy. Tomorrow, it would be the system and the government. No, they certainly seemed to have no intention of leaving the nest, rolling up their sleeves, and working hard to provide values to society.

With few exceptions, those poppa boys developed superiority complexes to cover up that they were inferior people in society. You see, they did not grow up and put values into society like everyone else, for they were taken care of financially. Those poppa boys in college living off a host — daddy — represented the initial age-group when the parasitical leaders form. ...Those poppa boys continued their inferior parasitical existence and their false superiority complexes after college as our lawyers, politicians, and judges. Unfortunately, as our lawyers, politicians, and judges, they now had the power to hurt those they did not like.

I have always respected any working person, *anyone.* Say, someone could not go to college, did not have the money, did not have the security or the right set of circumstances or just plain did not want to go to college and instead wanted to get out there in the real world and start working and start raising a family. I have always had respect for those working people. But I noticed that the poppa boys did not.

The working people put values into society. The poppa boys did not. Instead, they flaunted their superiority. "Look at those stupid working stiffs," I heard one poppa boy declare while pointing to a crew of field workers. As you may have guessed, the poppa boys also had superior attitudes toward those who worked their way through school. Yet the poppa boys were inferior, immature people in society who daddy took care of. They never left the nest and never worked to provide a value to society and earn a living.

The money was automatically there. *Whenever* they needed money, it was there. They played their superior smart role. They studied their books, learned all about the government, law, and politics. They learned all about the easy route to money and power. Indeed, they would "outsmart" the ordinary people. They were "smarter" than us...and the money would always be there. They would never have to *really work*.

When the college "poppa boys" moved on, they eased into the comfortable Establishment; many became lawyers. Like many lawyers, they became very smooth but lazy. And the money — *good money* — was always there. The legal profession had been falsely bloated with excessive laws and regulations for easy money and big paydays — falsely bloated by our lawmakers, over half of whom were lawyers securing a cushy but lazy livelihood for themselves when they were no longer re-elected.

They did not have to go through the hard work to *build* new values; rather they *burdened* existing values. Indeed, within the decadent yet lucrative legal system, they made easy livings by burdening values built by others.

Those people started as poppa boys in college, grew superiority complexes because they were inferior people, and went on to become lawyers and later, judges and politicians. Of course, the money was always there. They continued playing their "superior" smart games, for law and politics were like games of chess with little or no integrity toward justice or values.

"Daddy" — now our government — took care of them financially as they played their "superior" smart games of legislation and litigation. They could be smart and "superior" and create all this activity and "need" for themselves through burdening business and technology while never really *building* business or technology for society. Indeed, they could "outsmart" the ordinary working man.

Like their college days, those grown-up career politicians and bureaucrats had no clue about the tough *nitty-gritty* effort that went into every existing value — from the dishwasher who had

95

to clean the dishes well or lose his job, to the entrepreneur who had to work hard to make a value so good for society that people wanted to pay for it...or he would go out of business and lose everything. No such tough in-the-trenches hard work was necessary for our politicians and judges, for since their college days the paycheck was always assured with little or no value production in return.

Sure, top politicians were perhaps very, very busy. Yet never held to the real-world reality of producing values, those politicians were busy building (often to the point of compulsive addiction) their political power to rule over us.

In the 20th century, the higher one rose politically, say to a cabinet head, the busier he was to the point of being a workaholic, putting in 16-hour days, seven days a week, completely addicted to "becoming God". But their long, intense days had nothing to do with producing values. Instead, those people who ruled over us destroyed values. During their high-flying ride of superhuman power, through their long, intense work days, they knew nothing about the genuine nitty-gritty effort that doggedly went into producing values. Such effort was earthbound by reality and a bottom line. That real effort came with little glamour but lots of ongoing focussed hard work, in contrast to the glamourous high experienced by high-flying politicians and appointed cabinet heads.

The working person in the 20th-century, by contrast, confronted the real-world reality of competitive pressures: *provide a value* or not get paid. But government leaders faced no such reality, no competitive pressures to provide a value and earn wealth. In the government, the paycheck was just there. Like daddy, the money was just always there. They did not have to ground themselves to tough reality and its hard work to provide a value and earn wealth. Since school days, they always just "inherited" their money from "daddy". And now, they "inherited" their money from taxpayers. In turn, they recklessly self-indulged with that money, selfishly buying their own political popularity and spending their time building political clout.

Starting in college, the poppa boys did not grow up, leave the nest, and get a value-producing job. They did not become producers; they became inferior 'inheritors'. So they started to *fake their manhood.* They used their 'smarts' to look important and superior. After they graduated from college they still did not grow up, leave "daddy", and get a value-producing job. But now their show of importance and superiority became dangerous as those poppa boys got power and became career politicians. For, now they hurt the hard-working business leaders — those they envied most — at the cost of a weakening economy. ...Indeed, they would "outsmart" the working stiffs.

In college, those poppa boys who faked their manhood with a show of superiority were harmless to society. But when they became our lawmakers, they lived out their superiority fantasies. They used their power to hurt those they envied. Unlike their harmless school days, now their laws burdened market businessmen and suppressed the economy and all working people. Our busy career politicians created those destructive laws through illusions that brought them popularity and political power. All that burden got put on society so they could look and feel important and needed in order to fake their manhood and build their political power over us.

Remember now, to put a value into society takes nonglamorous dogged *effort.* There is no way around that. People who always had "daddy" to provide automatic funds did not have to put out that ongoing effort. Instead, they could play the stimulating game of politics and power. In the spotlight of the liberal media, they could be portrayed as among the most powerful men in the country. Ironically, those intensely busy top politicians in the 20th century were too lazy to build values and earn their money — starting way back in their school days. So, without *building* values and *earning* wealth, all the intense activity encompassing their livelihoods came from *burdening* values and *consuming* wealth.

To the children of the 21st century, it was obvious that our busy politicians in the 20th century burdened the best heroes of society. In fact, during the latter 20th century, busy politicians and ambitious bureaucrats often made the precious heroes of society appear as villains whom our leaders protected us from. That illusion was their secret deception. Remember, they used true facts *out of context* to fool us. Ironically, *true facts* became the makings of illusions that controlled us. For, we could not argue with true facts; they were merely incomplete and out of context. But we were too specialized to know all the facts and to put them into context. Under the old code, we went to our 20th-century jobs and did our routine work and came home. We would turn on the news or read the paper, but the true facts were out of context and incomplete. And we, the specialized public, could not argue with true facts. Our children and grandchildren who grew up in the 21st century felt bad at how helpless their parents and grandparents had become under the old code.

So, how did we end the suppression after 3000 years of the old code? Without the suppression, as I saw in my Six Visions, business and technology soared beyond the critical point, sending the price of modern technology into free-falls much like computer technology; under that new code, ordinary people lived like millionaires. So, how did we end society's suppression? Looking back from my Visions at the old code, all the suppression in the 20th century came from those poppa boys *faking manhood* for their pseudo self-esteems and faking a livelihood for their automatic paychecks. They spent their energy and time building their intoxicating "divine" power to rule over us. Not grounded to the tough reality of producing values, 20th-century career politicians and regulatory bureaucrats used their full time to build enormous power over the people, at which point they could easily fake their livelihoods and manhoods. They stirred up a lot of activity and "importance" about themselves, stealing prestige through burdening our businesses and blocking our geniuses who were trying to raise the lid on society.

And how exactly did they fake their images and build their political power to rule over us? Looking back from the 21st century, the answer was clear: Through "daddy". As long as they had that automatic paycheck and no competitive pressures, they could fake their livelihoods and manhoods. They were basically lazy at human life's fundamental responsibility of producing values. They could articulate intelligently, hold positions of reverence, look good before the media, and spend long hours using their well educated minds building their political power. Yet, they faked their livelihoods and manhoods, faked producing values, as long as "daddy" was providing automatic money. They never had to face reality and come down to earth and *earn* money by *producing* values for society. Instead, they went on *consuming* our money and playing God with our lives.

So, as grown-ups, who was their "daddy"? And where was the nest that bred all this growing madness in the 20th century? In America, the nest was found in one division within one bureaucracy: the *Criminal Investigation Division* (CID) of the IRS. Not the IRS itself, for any honest business or institution needed a bill-collection service. For our government, that bill-collection service was the IRS. But the *Criminal Investigation Division* was filled with men who carried guns and generated "criminals" for debt. That inherent brut force assured the money was always there for our leaders...no matter what — no matter if there were no values coming back to society. The money was always there. For if not, then those who owed money were subjected to the coercive threat of being called criminals and sent to jail. Furthermore, that coercive threat allowed the Civil Division to inflict cruel and unusual punishment upon innocent delinquents through unreasonable fines and penalties that ruined people's lives and families. The coercive threat of the CID made tens of thousands of those innocent families slaves to the IRS, especially to the whim of the Civil Division, for the rest of their lives. Without the coercive threat of the CID, the Civil Division could not inflict cruel and unusual punishment upon innocently delinquent taxpayers.

*Forced* payment guaranteed automatic money and allowed our 20th-century government leaders to become lazy, fake their livelihoods and manhoods, and spend all their time busily building their political clout, thus destroying society's prosperity. They did not have to come down to earth and produce values for their paychecks. They did not have to earn wealth, but rather consumed it. They did not have to doggedly produce, but rather flamboyantly boasted. The *Criminal Investigation Division* was the nest that bred the laziness, the faking it, the self-indulgence, the corruption of our leaders under the old code.

Under the new code, after restructuring into a government of defense only, services were merely cut off to deadbeats who did not pay their fair share of taxes. There was no need to coercively threaten us by making nonpayers criminals. For, that 20th-century tactic was payment under duress. And forced

99

payment provided unconditional paychecks for our leaders in the 20th century, which led to a tax-and-spend government on the offense spending a trillion dollars on entitlement programs for the "public good" or, in other words, spending a trillion dollars on playing God with our money and lives, which caused us to sink knee-deep into the Catastrophic Era.

Imagine for a moment if IBM, like the IRS, used coercive collection tactics: Say you were unhappy with a computer, and you called IBM, "I'm not going to pay," you say. "I'm really unhappy with this. Please, I'm returning it!" Now, just imagine if IBM arbitrarily doubled or tripled your delinquent payment through fines and penalties. You refused to pay that dishonestly inflated amount. So, they sent men with guns to your home to raid you, take your belongings as "evidence", and soon serve you with a large jeopardy assessment and then confiscate your property. Just imagine if IBM got away with this same collection policy enforced by the IRS. Well, everyone would have to pay IBM, regardless of the values provided. Then IBM could stop being customer-service oriented and become lazy. IBM could become fraudulent and start selling junk. Instead of earning wealth by producing values, IBM leaders could start self-indulging and consuming wealth. And with that guaranteed paycheck, the managers would eventually concentrate all their time not on the ongoing, dogged effort to produce competitive values, but instead on building their intoxicating power to rule over the people.

Now, imagine if those forceful collection policies spread to the utility companies. During our first year in college, we may have called home a lot because we were homesick. Maybe we got a little carried away and later ran into problems trying to pay those big phone bills. What happened? The phone company simply shut off service. If, instead, the phone company and other companies collected like the CID, then their leaders would eventually grow lazy. No one there would need to meet reality and the ongoing nitty-gritty effort to produce a competitive value, for the money would automatically be there.

If such a dishonest collection tactic used by the IRS spread to all institutions, including all businesses, then the fundamental responsibility of human existence — producing values — would end. With no more hard-working producers, everyone would just consume wealth. The economy would collapse. ...Throughout the second half of the 20th century, just one institution, the United States Government, suppressed the entire U.S. economy. Sometime after 2001, the new code of living rescued the country and then the world.

Looking back from the 21st century, the nest of the old code was the CID — the Criminal Investigation Division — not the IRS per se (although the implicit coercion of the CID enabled civil auditors to impose cruel and unusual "loanshark" fines and penalties that delinquents had to pay off, possibly for the rest of their lives, or else face criminal investigations). Now, let us see why the CID was the nest of the old code.

First, let us say someone in the 20th century was not paying his taxes. Under the new code, sometime after 2001, that was OK. Institutions he owed excess money to simply shut off his services, whether they be power company or the phone company or IBM or the government. He would get a bad credit rating and get ostracized by many vital businesses with no more service and no more credit until he paid. No problem if he was a deadbeat, everyone knew it. He would have to shape up, or stay out.

But back in the 20th century, what if someone were sincerely unhappy with the lack of values being provided? What if he just did not want to pay because he knew it was not right...politicians and bureaucrats did not produce values. In fact, they destroyed values. So, he just did not want to pay politicians to build their "divine" power to rule over us and suppress society. Well, if not for forced tax collection, more and more people would have begun legally withdrawing. "Go ahead, shut off my services," they would have said. More and more people would have withdrawn until genuine values were provided.

If those people were not made into criminals, then no problem existed because alternatives and competitive services would have begun rising. With a rising demand to serve a growing, unhappy market, private entrepreneurs would have very quickly provided the same services. Now the people would have paid competent market businesspeople for the services because now the people would have been happy with the production of genuine values.

101

In particular, those programs for the "public good" would have finally benefited society under market businessmen and women.

But the people under the old code were made criminals for withdrawing; they were forced to pay. Our 20th-century government institutionalized laziness. The 20th-century political scene with its automatic paycheck and unearned power attracted the fundamentally lazy and power-hungry poppa boy.

Of course, without the CID, there could be no more faking it. For the first time in their lives, our political leaders would have to really *exert effort* to produce values for society and earn wealth for themselves. Moreover, they would have to let go of their consumption of wealth and compulsion for power.

Looking back from my Visions of the 21st century, who were the hidden queens of the nest? Who laid the eggs of laziness and dishonesty?

Were the hidden queens our politicians? No. The politicians built the nest in the first place and allowed its continuance. They did have the power to tear apart the nest, which they eventually did after the Great Replacement Program. The politicians were the cause of the nest, but they were not the queens of the nest.

Were the hidden queens our bureaucrats? No. Those regulatory bureaucrats would, of course, take as much power as politicians and judges would give them. But the regulatory bureaucrats were simply the hatching eggs of laziness and power.

The hidden queens who quietly protected and propagated the laziness and dishonesty were found in the chambers of our federal judges. The federal judges granted the power to our CID. They protected the nest. They could have weakened the CID. But in case after case they empowered the CID, laying more and more eggs of laziness and dishonesty.

Our Founding Fathers granted the Judicial Branch the power to stop growing government abuse. Instead, the federal judges quietly guarded the nest — ultimately for their own survival.

Federal judges came from the class of poppa boys. Appointed for life, they did not have to meet healthy, competitive pressures. "Daddy" was still there for them, still getting that automatic paycheck. They never would leave the nest, for they were appointed for life. Although some were more honest than others, the hidden queens let their dark emotions come in and influence

102

their courtrooms, particularly if it involved their own security. To assure their own survival, they empowered our CID in the 20th century.

Sometime, after 2001, the Great Replacement Program and its new leaders destroyed the nest. The market businessmen and women produced values for society and earned wealth for themselves, thus they never needed forced collection of money. The leaders of tomorrow, the working-class leaders, quickly abolished the CID.

Our Founding Fathers established our government as a watchdog on itself — the Executive Branch, the Legislative Branch, the Judicial Branch. But what happened? Instead of breaking apart the nest that bred growing madness throughout the 20th century, the federal judges *protected* the nest. You see, our 20th-century leaders were all in the same dishonest family. They were poppa boys with the same daddy. There was no real watchdog. They had the same souls, same ineptness and defaults, same superiority complexes, same laziness, same daddy; none had to produce values; nearly all were envious, some more than others. Our big government was one 20th-century big family all living in the same nest. And what came from that nest? Laziness, incompetence...incestuous madness. The whole orgy of malicious wizards sent us spinning downward into the Catastrophic Era at century end. Yet, only those self-serving leaders stood between us and free-falling prices that would make us rich. When the time came for the Great Replacement Program, the world changed into the new code for living the way we were meant to live.

## The Golden Neo-Tech World

At century end, a Golden World was calling for us, waving us forward. But our ears and eyes were being covered by grown-up poppa boys. Although adults, they never fully grew up, got a job, and became real men. So, they faked their livelihoods and their manhoods, which became dangerous to society as they got legal and then political power. And with automatic paychecks, they pursued their political power *full time*.

Twentieth-century big-government leaders looked important.

103

They displayed their "superiority" over the aggressive entrepreneurs. Destructive legislation and regulation suppressed new generations of tender youth. They could not even try, for they would sink and drown in such unfriendly waters. However, the tender youth rose up and became business titans in just one, still-safe industry — the computer industry.

As knowledge of the Six Ultimate Gifts spread to about fifty million people, suddenly critical mass was reached. Nearly everyone wanted to live with the new lifestyle and watch his dreams come true.

Before November of 1989, those who attempted to escape the dishonest East German system were political criminals, sometimes shot at and killed. Sometime after 2001, history taught our children that America once had its own Berlin Wall: the 20th century Criminal Investigation Division of the IRS. Our children reviewed history in disbelief as it showed that honest people and their families who did not want part of this dishonest system and wanted to withdraw from it were routinely made into political criminals. Some innocent people were even shot and killed...innocent people had been literally shot and killed in the 20th century during raids by our Criminal Investigation Division — America's Berlin Wall.

Indeed, in the 20th century, under the old code of living, you could not leave the system. But near the end of the 20th century people began hearing about the Six Ultimate Gifts and the exciting lives they were meant to live. They began asking others, "What if America had no Criminal Investigation Division?" Then if they were unhappy with the dishonest politicians and bureaucrats, they could legally withdraw. They began looking around and realizing that three-fourths of Americans would have begun legally withdrawing toward century end if not for the CID. The old code would have given way to the new code *by* 2001.

Indeed, after learning about the Six Ultimate Gifts, the people knew that without the CID, then market businessmen and women would have risen up and provided competent and honest values a long time ago. "If not for the CID," the people began talking, "the poppa boys would not be automatically taken care of by 'daddy'. They would have to come down to earth and produce values and no longer spend their time building their addictive power to rule over us. They would have to sober up and earn their money. Moreover, they could no longer self-indulge in consuming our money, buying their own political popularity. They could no longer get the money to do so, for they could no longer go on politicizing our paychecks."

The people now realized that without the CID, the politicians would have to start building values instead of burdening values, or they would not have a paycheck. The people knew, after hearing about the Six Ultimate Gifts, that America's Berlin Wall was coming down. The people learned that only competent market businessmen and women who *earned* their money, in turn produced values that enhanced the well-being of the people and raised their standards of living and their wealth. The politicians and bureaucrats who automatically received their money, in turn produced political power that diminished the well-being of the people. The Great Replacement Program followed. The need for the CID went obsolete. And then, a Neo-Tech society swept the people into the Six Ultimate Gifts.

This transition into the new code was a step by step learning process and revelation for the people. In time, they saw that the one *valid* purpose for our government was: *physically protect the people with local police, courts, prisons, and a national defense.* "But, if the new government structure serviced us with physical protection only, then what about the poor?" they wondered. "What about education? What about health benefits? What about the elderly? What about research on fatal diseases? What about all the other important social programs?"

The people would think hard about every problem they could find with the new government structure that would function for *one* purpose: *to protect the people.* They noticed those problems all came from abandoning the second, wrongly assumed purpose of our government: *to improve the prosperity and well-being of the people, for the public good.* The people reminded themselves that such programs "for the public good" gave politicians and bureaucrats the wrong kind of power — the "divine" power to rule over us. The people reminded themselves that the only beneficial power was the earthly power to physically protect us. Still, many uncertain people would ask during the transition: "So, what exactly would happen to the poor, education, health benefits,

105

the old, medical research, social programs, and the other services provided by the government to help the people?"

The people would think of all those "problems" because of the sudden "void" left by dropping the second purpose. But the 20th-century government wrongly assumed that second purpose. Of course, 20th-century career politicians assumed that "helpful purpose" in order to supercharge their re-election popularity and build their political power to rule over us. Yet, those career politicians, receiving an automatic paychecks, incapable of producing values, made a mess of "well intentioned" endeavors "for the public good". Only the super-competent market business person who produced values on a daily basis could truly put forth the nitty-gritty effort needed to improve public prosperity and well-being.

Nevertheless, concerned people at century end pondered the "void" they thought would be left by the new government structure: the poor, education, health benefits, the old, medical research, social services. Other people pointed out that those programs "for the public good" had increasingly become financial follies destined to bankruptcy under our 20th-century government. For, the career politicians did not put forth the effort necessary for spending money soundly. Thus, those programs were doomed.

This group of people pointed to social security and medicare for *the elderly* — fiscally unsound programs that would eventually collapse.[1] They pointed to *education* — continuous deterioration with high illiteracy rates among our public schools at century end. They pointed to *medical research* — of all the major medical breakthroughs in the past several decades, *not one* had been made through government-funded research. *All* major medical breakthroughs had come through privately funded research. They pointed to *social services* — totally ineffective throughout the 20th-century crime and drug explosion. They pointed to *the poor* — the poor multiplied, crime multiplied, and welfare increasingly drained the taxpayer. Congress created an incompetent mess wherever it "improved the prosperity and well-

---

[1]Every penny of Social Security would be repaid with interest through the sale of government assets and through equity in private spin-offs during the Great Displacement Program.

being" of the people.

This group of people, who had read about the Six Visions, explained that only the market businessman could come in and clean up our government's incompetent messes. The "void" of the new government structure would never occur. This group of benevolent visionaries explained that, instead, a smooth two-step transition would take place: the Great Replacement Program would happen first to bring in the market businessmen and women to quickly stabilize things; then the Great Displacement Program would follow to spin off those programs. The programs for the public good would smoothly transfer into the hands of competent market businesspersons.

Until that point in time, as these visionaries explained, the government maintained unnatural monopolies over those programs "for the public good". The politicians and bureaucrats created those monopolies both through legislation and regulation that restricted competition and through big spending budgets acquired by force-backed taxes. But after 2001, under the new code, with legislation and regulation slashed and the CID abolished, free-market competitive dynamics unfolded as the politicians' automatic spending monopoly folded. Then market businessmen quickly filled "the void".

The growing group of visionaries reassured the people about the Six Ultimate Gifts. The "problems" of the new government structure never occurred as the market businessmen and women took over and saved those programs ostensibly designed for the public good. For example, below I summarized some of the highlights, as I witnessed in my Visions:

- <u>What happened to education?</u>
  Advanced and effective market-businessmen-run education replaced government-run education. Low-cost, high-quality education, under super-competitive free-market dynamics provided better and better values for less and less money. Savings on taxes more than paid for. The truly poor? Not a problem; schools accepted all children, even the disappearing poor, on future repayment basis. When that poor child grew up

and became successful, he or she repaid. In time, free Internet education on Web TV replaced physical schools. Zero illiteracy. 100% *productive* peer pressure.

• <u>What happened to health benefits?</u>
Advanced and cheap health care steadily appeared, free from cost-prohibitive regulations and litigation that previously drove up medical costs. People easily afforded the best care. The disappearing poor? Private investors backed the ill for future repayment with interest. If terminally ill, then patient received charitable care. (Private Red Cross type emergency programs existed for the small percentage of incapable needy.)

• <u>What happened to the poor?</u>
Poverty disappeared in the coming super prosperous Neo-Tech Society led by market businessmen and women. Private, financial assistance was provided to unemployed and repaid with interest after employed. Jobs were in surplus. Robots and computers increasingly filled the jobs of labor, for people moved on to the rapidly expanding jobs of the mind. (Red Cross type emergency programs existed for victims of natural disasters and the few remaining genuine needy.)

• <u>What happened to the elderly?</u>
Efficient retirement programs with interest and security took over, designed by competent market businessmen. In the words of Dorcas R. Hardy, a former commissioner of Social Security, "We ought to call it Social Insecurity, not Social Security." No more such government-run Social Security follies existed that, even while still functioning, left the elderly trapped at low-income poverty levels. Moreover, as the Neo-Tech Era sent consumer prices into free-falls, the elderly enjoyed high standards of living during their golden years...when they most needed to savor each other's

love. In the 20th century, poverty robbed those final, farewell years of love and tenderness. But market businessmen, the geniuses of society, rose and cleaned up that mess with safe inflation-proof retirement programs and soaring buying power and standards of living. Money, or lack of it, was not the elderly's greatest fear, but their least concern. Instead, concentrated love filled their final memories.

• <u>What happened to research on diseases?</u>
Unburdened medical businesses raced unhampered toward cures for all fatal diseases. Most government-funded programs were impotent, for those researchers' livelihoods depended on *not* finding the cure in order to continue receiving grants. Market-businessmen-funded programs in which the medical geniuses were free to rise up, by contrast, were potent, for those researchers' livelihoods depended on *finding* the cure. ...No urgency and no market-driven disciplines or logic retarded government-funded programs. Researchers received money, then approached research with questionable scientific discipline — often like sitting in front of a wall safe and spinning the numbers to hopefully discover the unknown combination. As long as they received government funds, they would sit there year after year spinning numbers. The market-businessmen-funded researcher, by contrast, was like the locksmith driven to open an airtight safe that has a baby trapped inside with only a few minutes of air left. ...The market-businessmen-funded programs, once free of destructive poppa boys, got results! Many government-funded programs were nothing but bureaucratic follies.

• <u>What happened to social services?</u>
Super effective self-sufficient programs quickly developed under the new code. Government social programs in the 20th century were follies, except for one: In the nation's largest homeless shelter, in

109

Washington D.C., was a special division for drug rehabilitation. Unbelievably, that drug rehabilitation division refused government money. Instead, it raised its own funds and was self-sufficient, using a unique results-is-everything approach. When social programs switched over to success-minded directors *not* using government money, then those programs achieved genuine success.

The visionaries at century end who had seen the Six Visions went around reassuring their loved ones, friends, and peers. The anticipated "problems" of the proposed new government structure, the visionaries pointed out, came from the "void" left by ending government programs "for the public good". Axiomatically, though, only market businessmen and women could improve the well-being of the people. The visionaries reminded the people that incompetent career politicians made utter messes of programs "for the public good". "In tomorrow's new government structure," the visionaries said, "market businessmen will clean up all the messes. The anticipated 'problems' will not be problems. In fact, they *are* problems under the old code and will finally be fixed under the new code." Once the visionaries helped introduce fifty million people to the Six Visions, a strategic inflection point had begun and the transition would not be stopped.

## The Transition To The New Code

Electing market businessmen began moving us toward the new code. As market businessmen and women filled our government and became our lawmakers, they cleaned up programs that were supposed to "promote public well-being" but were deteriorating, money-losing, tax-draining, value-destroying messes. The market businessmen saved those programs — made them self-sufficient and value-producing. The market businessmen brought each program into their competent world and provided enough *real values* to make those programs self-sufficient and even profitable. Soon, those programs for the public good would be sold or spun off to efficient, private businesses.

So, the starting point of the transition, phase one, was electing the market businesspeople — the Great Replacement Program. They cleaned up the programs ostensibly designed to help the people. Then, those programs smoothly left government and naturally transferred to self-sufficient private institutions, phase two of the transition — the Great Displacement Program. Then, our 21st-century get-the-people-rich government honed in on its proper role: physically protecting the individual. The government became a super-efficient protection service, and the geniuses of society were free to drive new technologies into new dimensions that eventually cost us pennies on the dollar and made us rich and healthy. The Six Ultimate Gifts and the glorious days we were meant to have were finally ours, forever.

Book 1
God-Man Decoded

| Sink or Soar? | |
|---|---|
| **The Old Code** | **The New Code** |
| Politicians Care For Us | Geniuses Care For Us |
| Poverty | Millionaire Wealth |
| Disease & Death | Perfect Health |
| Stagnant Job | Neothink Success |
| Shrinking Love Life | Rekindled Romance |
| Dull Mind | Surpass Intelligence |
| Powerless, Naive | Neothink Omnipotence |
| Sad End-Game Path | Exciting Journey |
| Aging, Fattening Body | Youthful, Sexy Body |
| Neighborhood Violence | Disneyland-Like Safety |
| Catastrophic Era | Neo-Tech Era |

# Epilogue
# The Neo-Tech Revolution

The Six Ultimate Gifts belong to every human being: profound security, millionaire wealth, perfect health, dream career, dream love, and Neothink. The new code will deliver those six gifts to the man in the street as the ruling class subsides.

The old code and the new code are extreme opposites. Whereas you might be broke today, my Six Visions brought to light the Technological Revolution that raised the ordinary person's standard of living to millionaire status sometime after the turn of the millennium. There, I witnessed not only abundant wealth, but we lived nearly twice as long with perfect health and enjoyed the power and romance of famous celebrities. That Neo-Tech (new technology) Era in which we were all very wealthy, healthy, and powerful happened when the path into that new era of super technologies became unobstructed by debilitating powers, namely 20th-century big government.

I saw in my Visions that at century end, we stood in the gateway to an historic ascent. This historic ascent marked the fourth for mankind, the first being mankind's rise into the Golden Age of Greece, the second being his rise during the Renaissance, and the third being his rise into the Industrial Revolution. Sometime after 2001, mankind rose again, this time into a breathtaking Technological Revolution in which ordinary people lived like millionaires, even without lifting a finger.

Our first 20th-century forerunner to the great Technological Revolution was the computer/cyberspace revolution. Over the Internet, you could control computer power for free at the end of the century that would have cost millions a few years before. That spectacular escalation of buying power came from super rapidly advancing new (Neo) technology (Tech). At century end, Neo-Tech spread to the telecommunications and television industries. As with the computers, costs to communicate plunged toward zero as services and buying power soared toward infinity.

The telecommunications and television revolutions became the next notable 20th-century forerunners to the 21st-century Technological Revolution. As televisions advanced from being

113

our favorite fishing holes of entertainment to being powerful streams flowing into the Internet, the floodgates of knowledge opened. Before long, Neo-Tech spread to *all* industries. I saw it in my Six Visions: costs of new technologies eventually plunged toward zero, as happened to computers. Buying power for new technologies soared toward infinity. The ordinary person sometime after 2001, under the new code, was rich. The great Technological Revolution, sometimes called the Neo-Tech Revolution, was the next historic advancement of civilization after the Industrial Revolution. However, whereas only the industrialists became rich during the Industrial Revolution, *everyone* became rich during the Neo-Tech Revolution.

The Neo-Tech Revolution came to us in the nick of time, for civilization was sinking into some major catastrophes, which were circumvented by Neo-Tech. For example, I'll mention three catastrophes that had actually begun: 1) new viruses and drug-resistant bacterial mutations broke out into epidemics, 2) millions of middle-class families sank into poverty, and 3) many suburbs and schools became war zones for violent crime and terrorism.

The first catastrophe that was destroying people's lives at century end was the medical catastrophe: Hollywood movies began showing up the last decade of the 20th century with the dreaded theme of near human extinction from deadly new infectious diseases. Unfortunately, those Hollywood movies depicted a very real threat to mankind. Antibiotics were steadily losing potency, for bacterial infections were steadily gaining strength by mutating and adapting to a world laced with antibiotics. For the first time in seven decades, medicine was losing ground to infectious diseases. Moreover, virulent new viruses were making the jump from animals such as monkeys to humans as mankind inhabited new parts of the world. In a world of extensive air travel, virulent pandemics could swiftly travel across the globe. Doctors and scientists feared the worst...like the Super Flu of 1918 which came from a pig, infected half the human race, and killed from twenty to forty million people. Already, several epidemics had begun. Like a godsend, however, Neo-Tech came to us just in time to pull us from an unthinkable loss of human life.

The second catastrophe that was destroying people's lives at century end was the economic catastrophe: Companies were downsizing. When a middle-aged person with a good salary lost his job, his family "went through hell". To get a comparable job was nearly out the question. Usually, that person ended up in a low-paying hourly job with little or no benefits. His family's standard of living sank and stayed there indefinitely. Millions of American middle-class families had to adjust to a low lifestyle as the real standard of living continued to drop. Both parents had to work. More and more young adults could not leave home, and older adults continued to be hit hard. Like a Godsend, however, Neo-Tech rescued tens of millions of poor and middle-class families just in time.

The third catastrophe that was destroying people's lives at century end was the criminal catastrophe: Police increasingly faced aggressive violence and bitterness among ten and eleven-year-old children. As this aggressive violence and deep bitterness showed up in younger and younger age groups, our children's schools became threatened. Some became war zones for drug gangs. Moreover, as crime proliferated, it came into our own neighborhoods. All along, crime grew more and more violent. In some neighborhoods, killings became a normal part of life. That cavalier attitude toward violent death was steadily spreading. Moreover, terrorism in America was now almost routine and always horrific. As ordinary families were exposed to increasingly violent crime, we lived in fear. Neo-Tech came in like a white knight and saved us from a frightening, losing battle with grave consequences.

Closing out the 20th century, we were sinking into major catastrophes. Sometime after 2001, under the new code, Neo-Tech not only circumvented, but actually reversed the emerging Catastrophic Era. My Third Vision showed me new medical technologies advancing at lightning speeds like computer technologies, easily outracing the rapidly evolving infectious diseases. Indeed, Neo-Tech — new technology racing ahead like computer technology — eradicated disease after disease once it began to drive the medical industry. Until then, Neo-Tech had driven forward the computer industry only. As a result, both computer breakthroughs and computer buying power soared toward infinity. As in the computer industry, Neo-Tech not only would bring us rapid breakthroughs wherever it was free to function, but would drive costs toward zero. So, as Neo-Tech began to drive forward the medical industry into spectacular breakthroughs, medical costs collapsed like the computers. We were able to afford extraordinary medical care including new medical cures and breakthroughs. Everyone enjoyed near-perfect health.

Not only were diseases cured, but so was the economy. In short, as Neo-Tech began to drive all industries, prices of everything dropped dramatically, some products more than others depending on how technologically driven the consumer product was. In any case, your buying power over everything multiplied manyfold. As in the computer world where all computer consumers became computer rich as their buying power multiplied thousands of times, consumers everywhere became rich...even those on minimum wage or set pensions. The transition from the old code to the new code was history's consummate rags-to-riches event.

Remember, the old code and the new code were extreme opposites: from deadly pandemics to perfect health, from hopeless poverty to millionaire wealth. Furthermore, under the new code, you lived in a world as safe as Disneyland. That's right, crime essentially disappeared in the Neo-Tech Era. As ordinary people became essentially millionaires without lifting a finger, the incentive for crime became obsolete. For, it was far easier to get rich by doing nothing than through risky crime. Moreover, the communications revolution brought the peace and prosperity to the four corners of the world, obsoleting oppressive rule and terrorism.

In short, the Neo-Tech Revolution saved us from the plunge into a quarter-century-long era of plagues, poverty, and violence. And all just in the nick of time.

Twentieth-century "old world" big government, however, hampered and delayed the vital Neo-Tech Revolution as long as possible, sending mankind toward a head-on collision with disaster. In fact, our initiation into the third millennium could still be catastrophic with deadly worldwide pandemics, a middle-class that collapses into poverty, and violence in our schools and neighborhoods. You see, my Visions did not show me just when

116

the new code started, for I believe that was still being determined and was the reason for my Six Visions to help guide us into the better world. If the Neo-Tech Era of millionaire wealth, near-perfect health, a super-safe self is delayed too long, we will instead sink deeper and deeper into the Catastrophic Era. In that relentlessly sinking Catastrophic Era, every reader, yes *your* life would be invaded by the three big catastrophes of disease, poverty, and crime. Life would become hard, perhaps apocalyptic. Of course, the Neo-Tech Era would rescue us from those hardships. Life would become easy.

All throughout history, once people could see a better world, they could not be stopped and quickly entered that better world. The most recent example came through the invention of satellite TV. Because of satellite TV, people in the former Soviet Empire for the first time saw the better world of the West and subsequently dumped the severely oppressive forces.

With that in mind, the Six Visions showed us the Neo-Tech World — the better world in which everyone lived like a millionaire. My moment as God-Man showed me the Six Visions of the better world. I received a strong impression to disseminate those Visions to fifty million people. I saw in my Visions that once fifty million people saw the rich world, we went into that Neo-Tech World very quickly. No more zigzags. No more delays. Positive megatrends turned into stampedes.

Aside from millionaire wealth, near-perfect health, and a super-safe self...my Six Visions showed me we enjoyed things we now only dream about like a job we love, romantic love, a slim and sexy body, and a creative mind. For instance, our 20th-century routine-rut jobs became extinct as we enjoyed 21st-century jobs with explosive opportunity. We no longer suffered in silent frustration. Instead, we discovered what it meant to be exhilarated by creative success. We discovered honest *power*.

With our new power and wealth, we actually rediscovered passionate love and youthful romance. The reason all that faded after we first passionately fell in love had to do with our stagnation-traps. Miserably stagnated under the old code, we had little passion left to give. The love faded and romance died. But tomorrow under the new code, as we became reinvigorated

117

with power, wealth, and success, we had a lot to give as well as a lot to be steamed up over. Even the most boring spouse sinking in stagnation transformed into a vibrant shaker and doer thriving on life. That ordinary person tomorrow had a lot to feel good about and wanted to share the good times with his spouse. As we forgot about stagnation and became wealthy, powerful, and successful, we rediscovered and even surpassed the passion and romance we once had.

Moreover, we recaptured the slim and sexy bodies we had in our prime. You see, as we grew older and more stagnated under the old code, we tended to eat too much and gain weight out of boredom. Let's face it, life was boring. But under the new code, as we became rich and powerful, life was never slow or boring. We never slowed down. We were too busy living the good life to be overweight. The sexy, slim body returned. Our sex lives were generously rewarded.

And that's not all: We recaptured and surpassed the creativity of youth. As demonstrated by scientists in the 20th century, our creativity under the old code gradually abandoned us as we grew older. Major advancements in physics, for instance, were made by the young creative physicists. Sometime after 2001, however, under the new code, we discovered an entirely new way of using our minds that became *more creative* with age. Integrated thinking replace IQ for effectively creating new values, and whereas only gifted people had high IQ's in the 20th century, *everyone* easily did integrated thinking in the 21st century. And the older you became, the more knowledge you had to snap together into your expanding success puzzle.

In fact, in tomorrow's Neo-Tech Era of prolific information, we discovered growing omnipotence as we snapped together information all around us into growing success puzzles and saw what the completed puzzle pictures looked like, *before they were two-thirds complete*. Moreover, as the puzzles came together, many revealed puzzle pictures never seen before, making us creative geniuses.

Our minds no longer were stuck in their routine ruts, such small spheres of thoughts, wasting in stagnation. Instead, our minds were far reaching and creative. And the older we became, the more information we accumulated to snap together into bigger

118

and bigger success puzzles, revealing far reaching, creative puzzle pictures called Neothink. Our creativity actually grew with age. Moreover, our children grew up that way — knowing how to integrate success puzzles and be creative.

Also, in tomorrow's Neo-Tech World, our bad habits disappeared. You see, under the old code, bad habits were done for the same reason: for stimulation in our otherwise boring lives. Think about your own bad habits over the past year. They were done for stimulation, whatever the bad habits were, from watching too much TV to, perhaps, drinking too much. But under the new code, the stimulation from living like millionaires with power, love, looks, and omnipotence overpowered all other sources of stimulation. Bad habits vanished overnight.

During the Visions, the future was at times frightening with surging virulent diseases, violent crime, a shrinking job base, sinking standards of living, skyrocketing divorce, epidemic obesity.

And yet, the extreme-opposite new code was beautiful with long healthy lives, peace, exciting jobs, riches, romantic love, gorgeous bodies. I witnessed in my Visions that once fifty million people got a glimpse of the Neo-Tech World and its Six Ultimate Gifts, the new code happened very fast.

We rose from virulent diseases to perfect health. We rose from neighborhood violence to Disneyland safety. We rose from routine ruts and, in many cases, unemployment and despair to exciting jobs. We rose from failed love to passionate love. We rose from over-the-hill bodies heading toward the end to nice bodies and longer lives. We rose from miserable stagnation to stimulated minds. Our children rose from increasingly illiterate airheads to creative children. The underprivileged rose from poverty to millionaire wealth. Civilization rose from the Catastrophic world into the Neo-Tech World. We rose from our worst nightmares into our best dreams.

## Million-Dollar Jackpot

What would you do if you won a million-dollar jackpot? Start thinking about it because, under the new code, you essentially did. The computer revolution with its million-dollar-

119

values-for-free phenomenon was a forerunner to the all encompassing Technological Revolution with its million-dollar-values-for-free phenomenon. And therein came, metaphorically speaking, your million-dollar jackpot.

Let me recap a regression of events that made us all essentially millionaires. Of course, the personal computer/cyberspace industry gave us a clue: It was the only industry of the 20th century uniquely free from big-government regulations. In other words, 20th-century big government never politicized the computer/cyberspace industry as it had all other industries.

Sometime after 2001, America rejected 20th-century big-government politicization and embraced 21st-century get-the-people-rich depoliticization. Without 20th-century big-government regulations, millions of geniuses rose and did to all industries what they had done to the computers.

In order to remove 20th-century big-government regulations and clear the way for the catalytic reaction of super entrepreneurs mixing with super technologies, we passed a *half*-trillion-dollar budget. That cleared out the trillion dollars in big-government regulations, including the regulatory bureaucracies that regulated industries and the social programs that regulated the economy. That half-trillion-dollar budget, eliminating the big-government regulatory web, set free the great Technological Revolution that made us rich.

To pass that half-trillion-dollar budget, we went through a Great Replacement Program. Only a White House and Congress of entrepreneurs and market-driven business people (not career politicians or politically driven big-business leaders) would shoot down the political monster and the humongous budget that fed it.

That movement to replace career politicians with entrepreneurs and market-driven business people happened in full force sometime after 2001 with the first political party from the 21st-century get-the-people-rich government. It was the first and only political party that accepted no politicians. After fifty million people witnessed the Six Visions, the people embraced the Neo-Tech Party because its electrifying platform was unbeatable, summed up in three words: *live as millionaires!*

Before that 21st-century political party of entrepreneurs and market-driven businessmen and women took over, in some ways the country still progressed. In other ways, we steadily sank. But until that new party took over, we never came close to living as millionaires.

The new political party's credible make-the-people-millionaires program caught on quickly. When the people got a glimpse of the wealth and luxury available to them, that 21st-century party became unbeatable. When it did, the people went from relative rags to riches within four years.

The only thing my Six Visions could not tell me was: how much did we first sink into the Catastrophic world? I guess the answer is left up to us, yet we now have the clear path to the Neo-Tech World.

Back to what my Visions *did* tell me: Tomorrow's Neo-Tech Era was like a get-rich fantasy, but one that came true not just for one lucky Horatio Alger character, but for everyone. As we moved into the next millennium's new political paradigm, the people increasingly shut the door on 20th-century big-government regulations and legislation. America's hottest (yet little publicized) megatrend to get big government out of our lives intensified and joined forces with the information revolution as we moved into the next millennium.

Along with abundant wealth under the new code, we enjoyed soaring innovation all around us. Limitations of distance, job selections, friends, love, entertainment, and costs disappeared. Convenience, selection, and luxury replaced those limitations, similar to the computer world. *Removing limitations*, the golden key to the computer revolution, became the golden key to the Neo-Tech Revolution...in all areas of life.

The health field went Neo-Tech like the computers. Spectacular new cures and procedures rapidly occurred at cheaper and cheaper prices. We easily afforded all those miraculous cures and health products as their prices went into computerlike dives. You see, all industries raced ahead as Neo-Tech spread beyond the computer industry that until then had been the only industry with Neo-Tech.

Soon, businesses needed to bring out and nurture their employees' unknown selves — their Neothink creativity.

Book 1
God-Man Decoded

Businesses discovered that a creative person was within each person wanting to come out. Businesses nationwide then worldwide transformed our routine ruts into exciting jobs of the mind that unearthed our buried creativity. Like those lucky few in the 20th century who loved their jobs, in the 21st century we all loved to go to work!

You see, technology was not be the only thing going through wonderful transformations. So were our jobs, our love lives, our bodies and minds. We certainly lived in an exciting time, for we lived in the gateway to mankind's next surge of prosperity.

## Perfect Health, Millionaire Wealth, Super Self

Under the old code, your life was like an express train ride traveling deeper into the unknown wilderness of age. You could not get off, and the train never slowed down as it raced toward the final destination. The quality and duration of that ride meant everything to you and your loved ones. The arrival of Neo-Tech under the new code brought a manyfold increase in the quality and eventually a twofold (then greater) increase in the duration of your ride through life.

First, super rapidly advancing new technologies brought near-perfect health to the young, the old, and to those in the prime of their lives. We were in a race for our lives against the dark side of Mother Nature. For decades we stayed several steps ahead of that dark side. But politicization of any industry slowed progress to a snail's pace. The increased politicization of the health industry throughout the 20th century eventually had the dark side of Mother Nature advancing faster than medicine. Devastating new viruses and drug-resistant bacteria were on the rise. Antibiotics were losing their effectiveness. Technological and medical progress fell behind in this race, which caused millions of unnecessary deaths. To win the race called for the opposite extreme: to aggressively depoliticize the medical industry and free the geniuses of society, those aggressive entrepreneurs, as seen in the computer/cyberspace industry.

As we entered the third millennium, America increasingly welcomed Neo-Tech. The growing American megatrend against old 20th-century big government was no coincidence — it was a sign of a major shift to a new 21st-century get-the-people-rich government. Aggressive depoliticization began with the first party from the 21st-century get-the-people-rich government called the Neo-Tech Party. Depoliticizing America versus politicizing America was a matter of life versus death, a matter of new technologies (Neo-Tech) outrunning infectious diseases before it was too late and they outran us.

Moreover, depoliticizing America was a matter of quality of life. For, when the geniuses of society and their progressive technologies were set free in *every* industry, then *nearly all* costs of living, not just computers, were driven down to fractions. Just as minimum-wage computer consumers grew computer rich, *all* ordinary people — *yes you* — actually grew rich and increasingly lived in luxury.

With the new political paradigm, you became the person you always dreamed of, the person you were meant to be. You see, the working world changed as technology soared and industries raced ahead. You became a precious commodity like those contributors to the progressive computer/cyberspace world. In other words, with business booming many times beyond any previous boom, people were in short supply and high demand. Businesses trained you to be an in-house entrepreneur and to work an exciting "mini-company", a job of the mind that released your unknown creative self.

In summary, the dawning of the new millennium and the new Neo-Tech Era quickly meant three things for you:

1. Near-perfect health for you, your children, and parents.

2. Millionaire standards of living for you and all your loved ones.

3. Exciting entrepreneurial jobs of the mind for you, drawing together your spouse and children behind your competitive creations.

Of course, the first benefit of near-perfect health upon defeating all diseases with rapidly advancing new technologies was obvious. So, let us look at the second benefit of rapidly advancing new technology, a millionaire fact:

Book 1
God-Man Decoded

# The Wealth Fact:
## You Will Live Like A Millionaire!

Answer these questions to yourself: "What is my savings?" "What is my income?" Now, answer this to yourself: "How many times do I need to multiply my savings and income to live like a millionaire?" What's your answer? A dozen times...a hundred times? Say you have a few thousand dollars saved and say you make twenty thousand dollars a year. In other words, like most people, say you are just getting by. How many times would you need to multiply your savings and income to live like a rich millionaire? A hundred times would be plenty, for then you would have a few hundred thousand dollars in a rapidly growing savings with a yearly income of two million dollars.

Upon depoliticizing America under tomorrow's new political paradigm, your purchasing power multiplied 100 times, as an average, across all consumer products. As you know, in the late 20th century computer buying power multiplied a thousand times. Of course, computers were technologically intensive. Nevertheless, while minimum-wage computer consumers became computer rich as their buying power multiplied 100,000%, the computers posted history's first demonstration of the catalytic wealth-explosion that comes from mixing modern technology with depoliticizing American industry. That awesome computer revolution was a preview of the coming, great Neo-Tech Revolution upon depoliticizing *all* existing and new industries. As with the computers, the costs of living over *nearly everything* dropped to fractions. Of course, the more technologically intensive the industry, the more prices tumbled toward zero and the more buying power soared toward infinity. Conservatively speaking, buying power increased, on average across all industries and consumer products, 100 times. Even minimum-wage consumers became rich.

### Missing The Obvious

Sitting in the big showroom at the luxurious Mirage Resorts in Las Vegas, watching the famous Siegfried and Roy magic show, was riveting. I watched in awe as Siegfried fought the million-dollar laser-eyed dragon. The show was full of illusions as things impossibly disappeared and reappeared, but for the life

124

of me, it all seemed real. The leaders of the show, Siegfried and Roy, flawlessly created illusion after illusion. ...Their livelihoods depended on it.

When I walked out of the huge showroom, I turned to my wife and said, "I have never seen anything like that. That has got to be the world's most incredible magic show!" However, I was wrong by a long shot. A magic show existed thousands of times BIGGER and many times more illusory. The leaders of that giant magic show created illusion after illusion, for their livelihoods depended on it. That giant magic show was the world we lived in, and the leaders of the show were the leaders of the old political structures.

Under the old code, we lived in the giant magic show in which the leaders benefited handsomely, and we paid the toll. If you do not believe that, consider that in the '80s a new technology sprang up too fast for the political leaders to work into their magic show of illusions. Without the political leaders and their Establishment ties benefiting, the personal-computer industry went through its unprecedented phenomenon: buying power multiplied 100,000% in a few short years. That computer phenomenon represented how technology and standards of living advanced under the new code and its 21st-century political paradigm.

The giant magic show of the old political structures reached back many centuries. Even centuries ago, man was kept from discovering explosions of prosperity. For an entire 1000 years during the Middle Ages, for example, man could not see through the leaders' magic show of illusions to discover the very obvious division of labor (i.e., dividing the labors of living into enterprises and purchasable commodities). The division of labor would have brought an explosion of prosperity to the people, but the leaders were benefiting too handsomely by suppressing the people.

Finally, after 1000 years as civilization continued growing and expanding outward, tribal towns sprang up farther and farther out on the outskirts beyond the immediate control of the leaders' magic show. There, the illusions did not completely control everything. In those outer towns, the people were somewhat able to see the obvious. Rudimentary forms of enterprise and purchasable commodities sprang up. Those towns began to thrive with an exciting, new prosperity. The illusions of the leaders were fading. As news of the new prosperity spread, the leaders of the magic show lost much power as the people saw past many of the illusions and rose from the Dark Ages...into the Renaissance and onto the Age of Enlightenment and an exciting new prosperity.

As both ancient and modern history demonstrated, once the magic show of self-serving leaders waned, many of their illusions were seen through, and then unprecedented explosions of prosperity happened for the people. That ending of the magic show was the beginning of a get-rich phenomenon.

In short, the old politics, not Siegfried and Roy, was the world's most incredible magic show. Politicization of civilization filled our futures with illusions...illusions that propagated the livelihoods of the leaders — the politicians...the magicians. The better their illusions, the more people would pay for their show.

America's hottest megatrend, at the turn of the 21st-century, against big government eventually ended the politicization of our industries — that is, ended the magic show in which we lived. Going back through history, depoliticizing society during the Dark Ages brought on the Renaissance and eventually a hundred-fold increase in the standard of living. Not politicizing the computer industry brought on an unprecedented thousand-fold multiplication of buying power. Modern technology combined with depoliticizing *all* industries brought on an unprecedented multiplication of our buying power over everything in my Six Visions.

The computer industry in the late 20th century was like one of those outer towns during the Dark Ages that began melting the illusions of the leaders. Once society saw its raw monetary power like we did with the computers, society migrated to the cause. The cause, of course, was Neo-Tech. Unbeknownst to most people, the computer phenomenon stirred up the winds of change that started the megatrend against 20th-century big government. People implicitly perceived the monetary power of an unrestricted industry — the computer industry. People took a little longer to explicitly understand where their anti big-government feelings were coming from. But those feelings were all coming from witnessing Neo-Tech — from a get-rich dream.

126

People wanted to be rich...each and every one of them. Neo-Tech — super rapidly advancing new technologies — would make them rich. People inherently sensed the same millionaire phenomenon could happen everywhere. They also sensed that, first, 20th-century big government had to be removed from all industries. In just a matter of time, Neo-Tech would then sweep through all industries to make all people rich.

The new 21st-century make-the-people-rich government provided fabulous *physical protection from aggression.* The 20th-century regulatory bureaucracies, by the way, had nothing to do with physical protection. Instead, those regulatory bureaucracies were part of the old political structure and its big ruling government. The new political paradigm never attempted to rule over us. It was a government of defense only...protecting the individual and the country from *physical attack.*

The 20th-century big government, by contrast, was on the offense always...increasingly politicizing our money and our businesses and professions, addicted to ruling over us. The people at century end began to realize something profoundly ironic: 20th-century big government grew bigger by finding conditions and ways to offer and divide up so-called "protection". Indeed, "protection" was used as an upside-down illusion to build those huge self-defeating regulatory bureaucracies that regulated us, ruled over us, and ultimately haunted us as the Catastrophic Era started heavily claiming human lives.

By gradually understanding the government's only honorable role, the people restricted government to the unconditional, indivisible act of *protecting us from initiatory force*, nothing more. Everything else would have to go — all the illusionary "protections" of big government would have to go. The trillion dollars in "good intentions" for "the public good" — in other words, big government ruling over us and playing God with our lives — eventually popped off society like a champagne cork.

Then, with a half-trillion-dollar protection-only budget, without big-government regulations burdening us, like the burden-free computers during the '80s and '90s, the entire economy shot up into the celebratory era of super technologies with no bureaucratic restrictions holding us back. The Technological Revolution in all industries became empowered by geniuses of society, by

127

aggressive entrepreneurs rising everywhere from medicine to transportation pushing the new, super technologies into ever more spectacular dimensions and bringing us paradise on Earth...from perfect health to inexpensive super-safe luxury cars.

Of course, as the Great Replacement Program began, career politicians notoriously cried, "What about the needed trillion dollars for public welfare! What about all our work for the public good! What about the underprivileged!" The people were quick to respond: "What underprivileged?" When buying power multiplied a hundred times, there were no more underprivileged. In the late 20th century, a child had the same computing power on the Internet as the Fortune 500 executive. In the 21st century, everyone had the same power as everyone else in a world where technology was nearly cost free, where everyone was essentially equally prosperous. Simply put, in the Neo-Tech Era, no one had disadvantages.

The underprivileged class in the 20th century existed for two reasons: 1) The suppressed society delivered us a fraction of the wealth we would all enjoy in the next millennium, and 2) 20th-century big government and its messenger, the liberal media, *survived via* an underprivileged class. You see, only through an underprivileged class could big government build a big welfare state. Big government needed a big welfare state to *regulate* the economy, thus rule over us. Indeed, a big underprivileged class was big business for big government.

With its messenger, the liberal media, big government convinced young black minds, for instance, of a life doomed to victimization. That belief in victimization hardened as the innocent child grew into a young adult, and that belief eventually convinced him he was a victim of racism. The underprivileged not only had limited access to advantages, but limiting beliefs. Indeed, they were captors of their neighborhoods as well as their own brainwashed minds, as Malcolm X tried to tell them. Racism, real or perceived, went away when big government went away. Until then, the underprivileged class was really a slave class to big government.

Twentieth-century big government hoodwinked its people. The political system worked through power in numbers, so politicians and their media friends acquired their necessary

128

numbers through hoodwinking the people into voting for their many programs of "public good". Trapped under all those regulatory programs, the smallest of all minorities, the individual, the aggressive entrepreneur, that genius of society, minority of one, was ultimately left unprotected, which in the end trapped the geniuses of society and blocked a Neo-Tech society.

But as big government shrank, its facade of "public good" ending, the system naturally changed from manipulating the masses to protecting the individual. Acts of government reduced to physical protection only. The shrinking of big government turned the system right-side-up — from power in hoodwinked numbers to power in the individual. Individual protection at its unconditional, indivisible level of physically protecting the individual from force (see Individual Rights, page 39) became the overriding principle in case law, clearly and swiftly distinguishing real crimes from political-policy "crimes" against the "public good". Justice became swift and honest and finally protected the people and their businesses *from* big government. Freedom and prosperity reigned.

We had no more big-government guises of "public good", for those programs always translated to public regulation. Left only with unconditional, indivisible physical protection from force, all people, businesses, and technologies — especially those geniuses leading the Technological Revolution — became forever free to race ahead unimpeded as in the computer industry.

The resulting millionaire prosperity for ordinary people inspired the people to constitutionally guarantee individual protection. The public called for the Individual Rights Amendment to the U.S. Constitution (see page 39) that made protection at the indivisible individual level part of our Constitution. The result of that Constitutional Amendment was unimpeded entrepreneurs and technologies, protected *from* big-government regulations, which quickly and permanently led to millionaire standards of living for everyone.

In the 20th century, the lucky few with lots of money had lots of other nice things too. We all wanted more money. But we did not necessarily want to work hard for it, because we knew hard work alone would never get us *lots* of money in that suppressed society. Wealth had to come a different way. We figured we would die without ever knowing what it was like to have lots of money, fun, and love.

The new era of get-the-people-rich government and resulting super technologies changed all that. Neo-Tech was the *only* way ordinary people would someday be wealthy. However, our self-serving leaders resisted Neo-Tech and retarded our leap into the Neo-Tech Era. Only elected *non*politicians superseded politics and focused on freeing the economy to lift us out of the old political structure and into the new.

Indeed, the task of doing what was best for America, not what was best for one's own political career, was not so difficult and was carried through swiftly...by nonpoliticians. For then the task transcended ever hopeless politics, and focussed on economic progress. The Neo-Tech Party let technology take the giant leap into the Neo-Tech Era and generate millionaire standards of living for the people.

The first political party of the new political paradigm and its get-the-people-rich government was the Neo-Tech Party. Until then, a third-party effort had never been successful. How was this different? *Millionaire standards of living* would come to the people by replacing career politicians with market-driven business leaders and, in turn, by unleashing the geniuses of society and their high technologies in all industries, not just the computers. That financial incentive made all the difference.

Once the Neo-Tech Party of entrepreneurs and other market-driven business leaders was nationally recognized, angry America sent the Republicans and Democrats home for good. The anger behind the voting public was directed at the game of politics and its career politicians, the ruling class. The Neo-Tech Party accepted market-driven business leaders only and, therefore, did what was best for the economy, not politics. What was best for the economy was to free the country's entrepreneurs, the most gifted geniuses, to bring the Neo-Tech Revolution beyond the computer/cyberspace industry to all industries. The Neo-Tech Party abandoned politicians and superseded politics. And that was exactly what America was looking for...*and needed.*

America's initial attraction to third-party presidential campaigns in the late 20th century came from the people wanting something better, yet those third-party attempts fell far short.

Problem was: everyone had his or her own ideas of something better. Therefore, to coordinate everyone's different hopes into a single common denominator was an indomitable task. In the end, third-party attempts always fell short.

Under the old code, our political system worked by power in numbers, and to rally six people to agree on politics was not easy, no less sixty or so million people. Furthermore, people did not want to invest money or time into wasted votes. As a result, our country mostly remained a limited-choice, two-party system: "Us or them."

Ironically, the underlying problem for America's third-party fantasies was politics itself. Politics not only made for a terrible common denominator, but the mention of politics caused the ordinary person to tune out and sign off. For, the ordinary American had come to the conclusion that politics could not help him. In late 20th-century polls, the majority of Americans believed that politics hurt their overall prosperity in life. So a third-party politician? People quickly got turned off; after all, a politician was...a politician. The initial Ross Perot sensation, for instance, was because the country first perceived him as a market-driven businessman before they realized he was merely a political businessman.

Aside from tuning out politicians, including third-party politicians, the people always found, to their dismay, that third-party politics was still...just politics. The layman was, in his own words, "done with politics" because politics did not benefit his life; in fact, politics drained his life. Until something came along that superseded the arena of politics and universally benefited the layman, no third party had a chance.

That something did come along. To get outside the arena of politics required going to the universal common denominator the people had always hoped for: to improve their own personal riches and quality of life. After all, *everyone* had the get-rich dream.

The inevitable Neo-Tech Party focussed on making that dream come true. With the agenda of freeing the economy, not adding on the politics, only market businessmen could run for office. That new party was just what the country was waiting for. You see, when it came to politics, people were fast learning: it

131

mattered not what candidates said, but who they were. People now realized that what politicians said was just an illusion anyway. Whatever was said, career politicians still just benefited themselves and advanced their own political careers at the cost of the economy. Nothing spectacularly good ever happened for the wealth of the people, *which was particularly tragic on the eve of computerlike buying power spreading to other industries.*

People sensed the inevitable tragedy of big government politicizing the information revolution, which would nip in the bud the Neo-Tech Revolution. In response, the people aggressively looked for *nonpoliticians* to be their politicians. The Neo-Tech Party gave us market businessmen, not politicians. And it focused on the economy, not politics. It took care of us financially, where it counted. And that was a powerful blessing as we entered the Technological Revolution.

The drive behind market-driven businessmen was not politics but the market — economic wealth — thus making the Neo-Tech Party the first political party to truly benefit the people. Therefore, the Neo-Tech Party pulled voters from all across the board — Republicans, Democrats, workers, retirees, men, women, minorities, majorities, the wealthy, the needy. Indeed, *everyone* wanted a higher standard of living.

The Neo-Tech Party became the dream party everyone always hoped for but never had. Its platform was based on the alluring make-the-people-millionaires program. The Neo-Tech Party wanted to see the people "start living like millionaires within the first term".

The market businessmen explained that the impetus behind the computer/cyberspace revolution was aggressive entrepreneurs — geniuses of society. Aggressive entrepreneurs, the geniuses of society, would rise in other industries once the Neo-Tech Party depoliticized those industries, the market businessmen claimed.

The incentive to the general public to get the market businessmen into office was powerful, perhaps unbeatable. The platform was solid, well presented, fresh and exciting...and much wanted and needed. All other potential third parties were based on political ideas — on (yawn) politics. They attracted not the average person, but only a very small percentage of politically inclined people. The Neo-Tech Party was based on economic

132

ideas — the one big common denominator of great interest among the people and the opposite of politics. And because the candidates were all market businessmen, the economic ideas were not political rhetoric. In fact, the central theme of the Neo-Tech Party was: depoliticize America to set free all industries like the computer industry...thus make the people live like millionaires and have their every need taken care of by the Neo-Tech Society. The temptation was too great to resist. The Neo-Tech Party (Neo-Tech: new technology) became America's rising star of the 21st century.

At the turn of the 21st century, the megatrend against big government built more and more momentum as people saw its favorable economic impact. In short, the people were monetarily motivated — that common denominator everyone liked. In the end, that economically driven anti big-government megatrend depoliticized our country — indeed, the very platform of the Neo-Tech Party and the new political paradigm. Then new technology (i.e., Neo-Tech) raced forward at ever increasing speeds. That was what the people wanted; that was what the Neo-Tech Party delivered. The megatrend led America straight to the Neo-Tech Party sometime after 2001. The people wanted to experience mankind's greatest bonanza, not mankind's greatest tragedy.

My Visions showed me that super efficient local police and national defense managed by super competent market businessmen and women were guided by the Individual Rights Amendment (page 39). The Constitution was now grounded to the Individual Rights Amendment to which *everything* answered. The Individual Rights Amendment guaranteed objective justice in the courts, thus protection of our citizens, as the Founding Fathers envisioned.

Big government's prize possession of the 20th century — that was, programs for the "public good", a regulatory paradise — thrived on political issues, rivalries, debates, votes...and regulations. To sell you their political issues and win your votes in the power-by-numbers 20th-century system, the career politicians with the help of the liberal media constantly hoodwinked the masses. But, as big government and its bogus purpose of ruling over us "for the public good" ended, the endless flow of political issues ended. Instead, government became cut-and-dry as protection against force became its sole purpose.

133

Without the mazes of conflicting political issues put on the people, livelihoods built on hoodwinking the people could no longer exist. Political rivalries could no longer survive. Instead, nonconflicting simple performance determined the job being done for us. Like any business, the numbers did not lie.

The absence of big-government regulatory barriers freed the economy, and our personal wealth soared. Just as important, we discovered a safe civilization unlike anything ever known as crime disappeared. In the 20th century, under the old code, we never really had police protection. We simply had police follow-up, not prevention. The bureaucracy was simply that — a bureaucracy, relatively not very effective. Sometime after 2001, under the new code, the government perfected its essence with the precision of a private company. Like a private company, the government was accountable for superb performance.

Served with the competence of a private protection business, crime largely disappeared. Racism, too, disappeared as people in all neighborhoods became affluent and wealthy as well as very important in-house entrepreneurs during the ensuing job revolution. Instead, good feelings flowed for your fellow man and woman as everyone contributed important values to society.

What happened to the seniors? Under the old code, paying income taxes was hard, but then for most working Americans to pay half that amount again to Social Security exceeded reasonable expectations. Of course, the young family's wealth — or lack of it — was being siphoned off to the elderly. In those times of declining standards of living, younger folk could no longer give money to others...especially once married with children.

Most seniors, however, had to have that Social Security check; they depended on it. No matter how badly they felt for the younger generations, seniors simply had no choice but to collect Social Security.

The economically driven megatrend to rid 20th-century big government from our lives, however, caused something spectacular that many people called a Modern Money Miracle. That Modern Money Miracle was, in short, America's falling out with big government, which forced the sale of government assets that had nothing to do with the government's original and valid

134

purpose: *to protect people from aggression*. The money from that extraordinary sale rightfully returned to us small fortunes that had been wrongfully collected and spent by the government. Indeed, the money from the big sale of government assets repaid all Social Security with interest. Thus, the bulk of those revenues went to our parents and grandparents who paid the taxes that built those assets. In any case, everyone at every age who paid into Social Security got a nice chunk of money that earned full fair-market interest for as long as the government held it.

Over a hundred thousand dollars went to the majority of senior citizens, all at once. In some cases, interest on that small fortune alone was greater than their Social Security benefits. And yes, Social Security ended as it had nothing to do with national defense or local police protection, thus relieving working adults and future generations from painfully paying into a dying system. The new government spared our children and grandchildren while bringing our seniors a small fortune.

After decades of paying Social Security, many seniors had anywhere from one-hundred thousand to two-hundred thousand dollars coming back to them, all at once. Two-hundred thousand dollars...that's a bigger pile of money than most people had ever seen at one time in their whole lives. Many retired seniors splurged and took that world cruise, and they put the bulk of the money in interest-earning accounts for security — whatever they decided, for it was now *their* money.

And, struggling younger people no longer had to pay their precious money into Social Security, which they would never see again under the current system. The Modern Money Miracle happily ended Social Security, which was part of 20th-century big government.

At century end, 40 million seniors received Social Security benefits. The government paid them back up to five trillion dollars. The sale of government assets that had nothing to do with protection (known as the Great Displacement Program) amounted to many trillions of dollars. Those trillions covered all seniors and all the other people who were not yet retired but who paid year after year into Social Security. Every working and retired American got a substantial check from the government. The older the citizen, usually the bigger the check.[1]

When, exactly, did this sale of government assets take place? Older folks certainly did not have a lot of time to wait around. In my Visions, I never knew exactly when this would happen, only that it was sometime after 2001. Again, I believe history was still to be determined via the dissemination of these Six Visions to fifty million people.

Whereas I could not tell when exactly the sale occurred, I did see the megatrend to end big government was economically driven. As people increasingly realized the wealth they would enjoy, the pressure built until the old political cork popped off. Everyone — old and young alike — was ready to depoliticize America...in other words, get old 20th-century big government completely out of our lives. The government then had to sell its assets to private businesses to get out of our lives. The government netted trillions of dollars as it shrank to its original purpose of *protecting* our citizens and our country, not running our lives. The bulk of those trillions of dollars went to our oldest Americans — to repaying with full fair-market interest their Social Security investments.

When that happened, new technologies unhampered by big-government red tape raced forward at blinding speeds, pushed ahead by aggressive entrepreneurs, free and rising by the millions, dwarfing the computer/cyberspace phenomenon. Those famous free-falling prices in the computer industry spread to other industries. Before long, we lived with the buying power of millionaires.

Under the old code, the younger generation viewed the older generation with growing cynicism. Younger folk resented giving precious money each paycheck to Social Security. But under the new code, the younger generation viewed seniors as heroes, for they led the political charge for the Neo-Tech Party.

The Modern Money Miracle put to rest the war between generations. Everyone got rich, starting with the senior citizens,

---

[1]Selling the government involved so much money that many Americans were given attractive incentives to, instead of receiving cash, choose equity in the privatized spin-offs and be part of substantial profit-sharing plans. Their stock, of course, could be sold in the open market at any time.

quickly followed by all Americans. That personal wealth allowed us to increase whatever stimulated our lives to exciting new heights.

Tracing our primordial roots, man was originally a running animal, tracking herds for many days and nights on end. That nonstop life as long-distance runners and hunters was exhilarating both physically and mentally. Still the same animal in the 20th century, our anatomy and psyche still needed lots of stimulation. In 20th-century suppressed society, however, trapped in our boring routine ruts, we dreadfully lacked that exhilarating body/mind stimulation. That was precisely why we formed so many bad habits under the old code from overeating and TV addiction to alcoholism and promiscuous sex — precisely for that dreadfully missing need...stimulation.

Those who surfed the Internet at century end knew the explosion of stimulation the computer offered versus just a few years before when computers were limited to specific technical applications. That same explosion of stimulation happened in every nook and cranny of our lives when Neo-Tech spread throughout all industries under the new code. Put another way, the Neo-Tech World really turned us on. When the exhilaration returned to our bodies and minds, just as in our exhilarating running and tracking days, then people lost their need for stimulating bad habits and addictions at all levels. Overeating, drugs, excessive alcohol, promiscuous sex vanished as millionaire money, power, and romantic love overwhelmed us. Happiness, the meaning of life, was in abundance in tomorrow's Neo-Tech World.

But at century end, some experts felt America was too far gone and would sink into a prolonged Catastrophic Era because of our huge debt. The standard of living in America would continue to weaken, they thought; the middle class would slowly sink into poverty, they said.

They pointed out that, not very long ago, America was the world's warm home of security. A good job with a solid company meant you were taken care of for life. That security no longer existed. As big businesses continually downsized and brought jobs overseas, few new jobs replaced the lost jobs. The job creators, the aggressive entrepreneurs, had been shut down

137

Book 1
God-Man Decoded

by big government. Aggressive entrepreneurs could no longer compete with big business, for big government had simply made it too difficult and downright dangerous to be an aggressive entrepreneur those days. The Michael Milken chapter of history demonstrated how big-government regulations destroyed aggressive entrepreneurs, especially those who challenged the Establishment. And now, big-government regulations and legislation were firmly in place to prevent new aggressive entrepreneurs from rising. As a result, America's middle class was slowly sinking. To bring life back into our economy and bring security back to our middle class was impossible, some of the experts predicted. Of course, they did not know about the coming Neo-Tech World where the old political structure and its big government was replaced by the new political paradigm and its get-the-people-rich government.

What are some things we eventually experienced under the new code? Let me say something about our love lives, our bodies, our minds. Remember, we were placed into a new setting of luxuries and wealth when Neo-Tech spread across all industries. Imagine, for example, what your expanding wealth did for your love-life. You were rich and successful, thus successful at love. You see, love depended on a person's own happiness and success. When miserably stagnated, we were not good at love. Love, an act of giving and receiving, often failed because we were not able to give emotionally when suffocating in stagnation. Wealth and success transformed us into quite romantic lovers.

Also, we got the very nice bodies we always wanted. You see, being rich, successful, and in love, our emphasis on food shifted. Overeating was done out of boredom. Let's face it, most of our lives were pretty boring under the old code. Boredom did not exist in the Neo-Tech World. Most people naturally slimmed down to their best weight.

Now, let's talk about the mind. Under the old code, our minds were taught *specialized thinking* — to do our boring routine ruts at work. But in tomorrow's world of communications, our minds became much more dynamic as we snapped together information from all over the world. That entirely new way of using the mind via snapping together success

138

puzzles was called *integrated thinking* and *Neothink.*

Integrated thinking gave us power; even average people became dynamos. With integrated thinking, average people brought together thought clusters into Neothink puzzles. Creativity actually *grew* with age as we encountered more and more knowledge to integrate and snap together into larger and larger success puzzles. The cliche, "We grow old, and then we die," evolved to become "We grow old, and then we *create!*"

## Read The Future

The process to see into the future can be scientific and not mystical...sort of like a magician is really all technique and not magic. Since the future is somewhere we have never been before, we must look for clues from the future, what I call forerunners. Once we spot a forerunner, we can put together the whole future sort of like scientists can put together a whole dinosaur from one bone.

Forerunners can always be found ahead of coming conditions. For instance, a sunny day cannot change into a rainstorm without a cloud coming first. Forerunners of coming conditions must always exist. Our job is to identify the forerunners then put together the conditions from which they are coming...which is our future.

This future-telling technique is powerful. For example, I'll tell you a prediction Dr. Frank R. Wallace, a former Senior Research Chemist for Du Pont and author of the Neo-Tech Discovery, once made that shocked us all: January of 1989, during a recorded business meeting, Dr. Wallace out of the blue predicted that we would witness "the beginning of a spontaneous collapse" of communism by January 1st, 1990. Everyone dismissed his prediction as ridiculous, for in January 1989, no one had a clue of what was about to happen. American intelligence had provided our government with just the opposite picture of Russian economic strength and optimism. Some in the meeting felt embarrassed for the ever so optimistic Dr. Wallace. Then, in November of 1989, the world was shocked by the collapse of the Berlin Wall. The "spontaneous collapse" of the Russian Empire had begun. Dr. Wallace's prediction was now reality; he was called a prophet.

Now, we can put together another "ridiculous" prediction, but this time involving *you:* Using the same future-telling technique, we can predict that all Americans will be a hundred times richer sometime after the turn of the millennium.

Ridiculous...or prophetic? Let's put together the future. Remember, look for that clue — for that cloud in a sunny sky before the storm. Our clue is the computer phenomenon. That is a forerunner of coming conditions.

What coming conditions? Great, *great* prosperity! Today you can buy a cheap home computer as powerful as a million-dollar mainframe just a decade ago. Buying power multiplied 1000 times. That's 100,000 percent! That's a forerunner of a coming storm of great prosperity.

"I'm getting it," you say. "You mean there's a lot of spectacular technology ahead." I saw in my Second Vision rapidly advancing new technologies showering upon us. Multiple showers in *all areas of living* — just think what that will do. I saw ordinary people's buying power rising toward infinity for those new technologies and rising a hundred times for nearly everything else. ...Ridiculous? Ridiculous or prophetic?

No one suspects what's coming because it's never happened before. On the eve of the third millennium, however, technology is poised to spring forward.

"Hold on," you say. "A hundred times more?" Yes, I saw people, who today live in cheap apartments, tomorrow moving into million-dollar mansions. I saw people, who today take the bus, tomorrow driving luxury cars. I saw ordinary Americans tomorrow vacationing all over the world, first class. Their savings became worth a hundred times more. Their children's education became the best in the world. Their parents' retirement was full of luxuries. I saw Americans, young and old, living in luxury sometime after 2001, under the new code.

How can we be sure those new technologies in my Vision will happen? We cannot be sure because of the looming Catastrophic Era. But consider that mankind continuously grows more and more prosperous over time. Just look at our lives now versus a few hundred years ago, or even just a few decades ago. Even the street sweeper today has a better selection of food and entertainment than kings and queens did a few hundred years ago.

"Well, of course," you say. "We're a lot more advanced." Exactly. *We advance. We progress.* Mankind's manifest destiny, therefore, is **great prosperity.** Of course, society gets off the course of destiny sometimes, which slows or even temporarily reverses progress. But progress eventually resumes, always heading toward the great prosperity of destiny. *Great prosperity is our undeniable destiny.*

*And new technologies bring on that great prosperity.*

It's obvious when you project ahead that new technologies will come to us and send our buying power toward the heavens, and that the computer phenomenon is a forerunner. We are very, *very* close to the great prosperity showering upon us. All we need to do now is get rid of the bugs in society that have us slightly off course with destiny.

You see, it's not a question of whether or not the millionaire phenomenon will happen. It *will* happen. It's a matter of *when.* Nevertheless, how can I say we have a good chance to live like millionaires *early in the third millennium?* "C'mon, that's just a few years away," you say? "The economy's not even stable."

That's all true, but good things have started happening *really fast.* Here's why: Americans have *already seen*, with their own eyes, the great prosperity of the future. We've seen it through the computer phenomenon. So, *we've been shown the way.* We've seen what it takes for buying power to soar 100,000%, so we know exactly what to do: We'll get rid of *all* the bugs in our society blocking us from that great prosperity. And that can happen fast, *really fast.* Remember how fast things changed in Eastern Europe once the people saw *with their own eyes* the prosperity of the West through the invention of satellite TV?

Still with me? Look, all we have to do is follow the bug-free computer phenomenon. The one fact separating computer technology from all other technologies is that computers race ahead without much bureaucratic regulations holding them back. The personal-computer/cyberspace technology is just too new to the world and too rapidly advancing for regulators to get a foothold on that industry whereas all other technologies and their industries are *strictly* regulated. In this modern age, *unburdened technology* results in an *explosion of prosperity.*

My Visions showed me a hundred-fold increase in buying

141

power. Without the bureaucratic bug holding back technologies, ordinary people bought brand-new luxury cars of the future loaded with technological breakthroughs for a couple of paychecks instead of an impossible eighty grand.

What's going to rid the bugs from society?

My Second Vision showed me the President of the United States submitted a protection-only budget that blacked out one trillion dollars from government spending — that is, blacked out all the regulatory and social programs, which were merely knots of bureaucratic regulations. In other words, the President submitted a budget that *just said no* to big-government regulations...*no* to government politicizing our lives and ruling over us like God, but *yes* to protection.

"That'll never happen," you say? "Congress would never let that happen. Don't be ridiculous."

Ridiculous...or prophetic? You're right, Congress would never let that happen. But in my Second Vision, I saw some of that budget stick once the word was out about the millionaire phenomenon. Today's anti big-government megatrend became tomorrow's make-the-people-millionaires megatrend. Once money got in the picture, today's megatrend, steady as she goes, graduated to something of a stampede. The people wanted what rightfully belonged to them — a future of millionaire wealth. Everyone's dream came true.

I saw that when even just a little bit of that budget stuck, taxes went down. Better yet, technology began advancing, driving our buying power up. And, with that demonstration, *nothing* could stop the same protection-only budget from passing in its entirety the next year — not even Congress could stop it. The budget passed in its entirety, ending society's bug of bureaucratic regulations. The new technologies showered upon us.

Once the word gets out about the Six Ultimate Gifts, things will happen at lightning speeds. When fifty million people realize the life they were meant to live but never had a clue under the old code, a nonpolitician will win the presidential elections, submit the protection-only budget his first year, prove his point, pass his protection-only budget in its entirety his second year, and everyone will live increasingly in luxury within a year or two.

America's hottest megatrend today is moving us toward this Vision. A Neo-Tech (i.e., New Technology) President and his make-the-people-millionaires program is our unstoppable destiny. Whether it's our near-term or eventual destiny remains a function of disseminating fifty million of these Visions. You are now part of that word-of-mouth process.

Book 1
God-Man Decoded

Book Two

# Neo-Tech Decoded

## Money/Power/Love Advantages

# Table of Contents

## Prologue

# Ancient Money/Power/Love Secrets From A Mountain Called Zon

This morning was different than every other morning for the past three years. My father was on his early morning run along his usual route on the same desert road when he stumbled to the ground. Just as he hit the ground, a powerful wind seemed to pillow the fall. He got up and looked himself over. Not even a scratch on his knees. He turned toward the mountain directly perpendicular to his path. Its amber glow, a synthesis of morning shadow and sun highlighting its definition like a muscular frame with rich ferrous skin, seemed personified as if saying, "Good morning, Frank!" Although a good mile or more away, its height and breadth made it seem unusually close, almost standing over him. "Got lucky," the healthy slim man said sheepishly, feeling a little odd talking to a mountain. Just then, the same strange wind that broke his fall blew his soft dark hair off his forehead, as if a hand gently brushed his hair back. His innocent blue eyes looked curiously ahead. At that instance, his face was the spitting image of "Little Frankie" back in preschool. A child. The wear and tear from his battles in life, including the lines of middle age on his face, during this magical moment seemed as nonexistent as the absent scratches from his fall. No one was anywhere around when a very deep and wise voice reached his ears, a gentle voice carried in the wind:

The child of the past exists in you. Lost within faded memories, that child keeps searching for a life of adventure, discovery, value, happiness. Turn inward to discover that child. And then break free from those who are hurting you...from those who are wasting your time and resources. That child of the past will kindle a new life of adventure and happiness.

My father was a brave man who stood up to anything from bullies back in school to the entire might of the U.S.

5

**Government including the vicious Criminal Division of the IRS. Never in his life had he been caught for a lack of words. He even defended himself, quite vigorously I might add, *pro se* in two historical Socratic trials against the U.S. Government and its old code of ruling classes and professional politicians. Yet, here he stood like a little boy, mouth open and stunned, and only managed to mutter, "Huh?" The words of wisdom winged through the wind.**

Satisfy your own healthy needs and set your own standards...live without being obligated to fill someone else's needs or to follow someone else's standards. But your actions must be rational and responsible to be beneficial. Irrational actions will always diminish your well-being and happiness.

You can view your future with confidence in the knowledge that you have the power, through your own rational mind and efforts, to control your own destiny no matter what external variables impinge on you. You can carve your own destiny. You can achieve great prosperity, no matter what external forces surround you. Indeed, by removing mysticism, the rational mind can be more powerful than the irrational minds that constantly work to diminish everyone's life.

In reality, no one has genuine authority over anyone else. Once that fact is realized, a person can say "no" and break the destructive habit of obedience to the myth of authority.

**Unfortunately, those important words did not reach my father's brain. He was too mystified. Realize that my father was a prominent Senior Research Scientist for Du Pont. He could never accept any ideas of supernatural phenomena. In fact, even before the words in the wind ceased coming, his scientific mind was already explaining the phenomenon. He believed the fall triggered a right-brain experience, as explained in Dr. Julian Jaynes' book about the bicameral mind, in which my father hallucinated the voices — voices telling him what to do, how to survive. Indeed, he was going through hard times, very hard times financially and emotionally. His troubled, preoccupied mind was the reason he did not see the loose rock on the road that made him fall**

6

in the first place. The fall just triggered his mind from the logical left brain to the hallucinatory right brain, he thought. To further support this theory, my father is a severe dyslexic, a reading handicap that inverts letters and numbers, caused by a dominant right brain in left-handed people. Despite their reading handicap, dyslexics including Leonardo da Vinci and Albert Einstein are often very creative because of their creative right-brain dominance. Thus, they are more prone to hallucinations. In fact, my father had experienced hallucinations as a five-year-old boy, but quickly rejected those mystical experiences, and to overcome, he journeyed into the logical left-brain-dominated world of chemistry and became the leading Senior Research Chemist for Du Pont. In any case, under immense personal pressures, the hallucinations were back, he concluded.

The next day, when he jogged by the mountain, he surprised himself by turning toward the mountain and saying, "But how do I know how to guide myself? I feel like a twig in a river, washed along to wherever. I have no arms and legs of my own, no control to swim to where I want to go." ...Did I just say that? he thought. But before he had time to figure much, the wind blew into his face and he heard these words spoken:

Remember this: rational or good actions increase prosperity and happiness. Irrational or bad actions undermine those values. While your life and values are unique, certain basic actions never change in terms of good or bad actions. The rightness or wrongness of those basic actions do not vary according to opinion, or from person to person, or from generation to generation, or from culture to culture. Two and only two black-and-white moral standards based on rationality versus irrationality exist. Those two moral standards are:

Any chosen action that purposely benefits the human organism or society is morally good and right. A rational action.

Any chosen action that purposely harms the human organism or society is morally bad and wrong. An irrational action.

7

You must meet specific needs to function at your best. I will provide the knowledge for filling those needs. Filling those needs produces prosperity and happiness.

**No longer able to stand there and listen when there was no speaker, my father blurted, "Who are you?"**

I am you, but you are not yet me. I fully integrate all knowledge spanning across the past 3000 years and hold the secrets to money, power, and love, which reach across all space and time and people. Those secrets delivered money, power, love, and freedom to people of the most prosperous ancient civilizations. Those secrets will shock the people of tomorrow's high technology Neo-Tech World with catalytic explosions of money, power, love, and freedom. Today, I will tell you those secrets. One glorious day, you and I will be one. And then, every person on our planet will join us and our prosperity.

**My father did not understand this explanation. What was meant by** *I am you, but you are not yet me?* **Someday he would understand this, but not now. My father does not like to lose, especially to ignorance. So, he wrestled with the thought for a long pause, until finally out of frustration he asked the mountain, still in disbelief, "What do I call you?"**

Call me Zon.

**"A mountain called Zon," my father said, knitting his brow upon his handsomely large face.**

Let us continue: Three requirements for prosperity and happiness exist: (1) a healthy physical state, (2) a healthy self-esteem, and (3) an honest effort at producing values for others. ...By nature, a prosperous, happy life is an active, challenging life.

You set up prosperity and earn happiness from within. Happiness cannot be taken from the material world or from another person. Happiness depends on genuine self-esteem, which is a product of your own life and choices. Self-esteem

8

is your estimation of your self-worth. Self-esteem is based on your ability to live independently and competently. Self-esteem is dependent on your effectiveness in dealing with reality. Self-esteem is that emotion of feeling worthy and competent to live in this world — of feeling in control of life. That feeling depends on having a value-producer orientation to life.

To achieve long-range happiness, you must be mentally healthy. Many people, including many psychiatrists and psychologists, erroneously believe that mental health depends on how well a person adapts to the views and opinions of others, the majority, or society. That belief places conformity as the standard for mental health. But, instead, mental health depends on a loyalty to honesty, *regardless* of the views and opinions of others or one's own feelings. Indeed, you must deal honestly with reality to gain the productivity and self-esteem required for prosperity and happiness.

Might I add, wonderful sex is one powerful reward for day-by-day rational, productive actions. Financial prosperity is another powerful reward of a productive, honest life. Of course, so is happiness.

**For the first time, my father actually let those last three sentences register. He skeptically left his mountain called Zon. However, "...great sex, money, and happiness...rewards for rational actions," kept going through his head. My dad barely slept that night. He woke at 4:20am the next morning, and in the dark, he ran seven-minute miles straight to his mountain. "Zon, I could barely sleep last night," he said in a rush between three big breaths. The still desert night carried his voice, echoes filling the three gaps between breaths, across the valley to his mountain. "I feel so good! What is happening?" The deep voice with no echoes responded:**

You as do most productive people subconsciously hold a self-love, pro-individual sense of life. But, until you found me, you outwardly expressed various selfless views deemed virtuous by our society. A major step toward personal prosperity and happiness is to reject all guilt foisted on yourself by certain

9

irrational people. Since you found me, you have begun to reject that foisted guilt by discovering the moral virtue of your own rational, self-growth, pro-individual sense of life that has always benefited others and society. And that feels good!

Before yesterday, you practiced altruistic sacrifice, but you did so always at the expense of your own productivity and happiness, while reducing your value to others and society. You struggled with a psychological contradiction. You represented a personal tragedy who was unnecessarily sacrificing your own efficacy, well-being, and happiness to clever neocheaters.

**Zon had reached some deep nerves and chilling new insights. Now, my dad was hearing everything. Enveloped in Zon's powerful wisdom, my father was intensely listening...**

For two-thousand years, I have watched altruistic ethics used as the prime tool of neocheaters. That tool is used to sacrifice the well-being and happiness of value producers to various "higher" causes, such as big governments and organized religions. Those neocheaters apply force or fear to extract their livelihoods from productive individuals like you. Neocheaters always operate from behind masks of altruistic higher causes such as fighting wars, fighting poverty, fighting pollution, fighting nonbelievers, fighting technology, fighting for the common good, fighting for all sorts of "noble" causes. They do this "fighting" with an air of self-righteousness as they extract their livings from the value producers.

Altruistic ethics threw you into unresolvable contradictions, for you could not achieve happiness through value production by accepting destructive contradictions such as self-sacrifice. Such contradictions diminished and eventually destroyed your capacity for wealth and happiness. Now, you have begun to reject their evil ethics of altruism and "higher causes". Now, you are discovering your unknown self. And that self can become rich, powerful, and sexy...the person of your dreams...the person you were meant to be.

**Those words are undeniably true, my father thought, his eyes big and looking straight at the mountain.**

10

# Ancient Secret One

# MONEY
# The Neo-Tech Factor Is Told

What will I ask today? My father had many questions
as he ran to his mountain. The final words Zon spoke
yesterday kept repeating themselves over and over in his
head, "...that self can become rich, powerful, and sexy...".
Money, power, and sex were the most pressing subjects on
my father's mind. "Today is money!" he finally decided.
"Tomorrow will be sex."

This morning, like yesterday, my father had risen from
his slumber at 4:20am as if he were lifted by an invisible
hand. My father slept on the black leather couch of his
comfortable home office. He and my mother had divorced
years ago. Neither had remarried. He led a lonely life by
choice. He was always busy working on papers. My contact
with him in those days came mostly in our daily 7:30pm
"meetings" in his home office when my brother, sister, and
I reviewed our chores.

Every morning while we slept, my father left early to run
five miles. Today, in the dark, he ran to his mountain. "I
want to know the secret to money," he said in a steady tone,
nicely covering up overwhelming urgency and explosive
excitement. He stood, fidgeting, for about fifteen minutes,
then sat down for another half hour. No answer. Just as
he began to doubt himself and his intentions, the wind began
to blow from the direction of the mountain. Then, again as
if the words rode in the wind, he heard:

OK. But you must be ready to put in a long, long day...not
just listening; I am going to put you to work writing, too. Don't
ask what. Just pay close attention. Money is a big order.

*Neo-Tech* is a noun or adjective meaning fully integrated
honesty. Neo-Tech allows the guiltless creation of earned power,
money, and romantic love.

Neo-Tech is a collection of "new techniques" or "new
technology" that lets one know exactly what is happening and

11

what to do for gaining honest advantages in all situations. That technology is needed to be competent — to guiltlessly and honestly obtain the wealth and happiness available to everyone but achieved by so few. Neo-Tech provides the power to profit in every situation by nullifying neocheating and mysticism not only in others but within one's own self. Indeed, Neo-Tech eliminates the harm of all mystics, false authorities, neocheaters, and their infinite array of deceptions. Neo-Tech lets a person gather all power unto his or her own self while rendering neocheaters impotent.

Neo-Tech provides the practical tools to eliminate neocheating throughout the world while enhancing prosperity and happiness for everyone.

For instance, I will now give you the controlling key for investing in the stock market for big long-term payoffs. That key is the *Neo-Tech Factor*.

In a free economy, the long-term value of any business or company is always determined by its long-term competitive value to society. In a free economy, that value to society is expressed in the common-stock value of the company.

The net value of any activity to society can be determined by using Neo-Tech principles. You will apply those principles to determine the objective value of any individual, management, business operation, or nation. You can use those same principles *for personally being successful in business* and *for accurately predicting the long-range, common-stock value of any corporation*.

Most stock and commodity forecasters are mystical. Indeed, such forecasters merely use their "sense" or feelings of the market to rationalize illusionary scenarios or "realities" of the future. To various degrees, those forecasters use objective facts and figures or various technical indicators as non-sequitur props to give their projection a sense of validity. But any appearance of validity is specious. By the time most valid facts or figures become available for forecasting, they already have been discounted in the price.

Indeed, with near-perfect market efficiency, all near-term prices move in unpredictable, random patterns. If a forecast turns out to be right, that rightness and duration of rightness are as

12

Money: The Neo-Tech Factor Is Told

much a coincidence as forecasting the flips of a coin. Thus, stock and commodity forecasting is generally invalid and mystical, even when promulgated by Wall-Street gurus and cloaked in the jargon of technical, cyclical, and fundamental analyses. Only by fully integrating the root causes of values can long-term values of companies to their stockholders and society be reliably predicted.

Long-term appreciation of common-stock values will occur to the extent that management implements the mystic-free standards of capitalism. Conversely, long-term attrition of common-stock values will occur to the extent that management compromises capitalistic standards in implementing mystical-based decisions. ...Attrition of value is inherent to any business situation subjected to altruism, mysticism, or neocheating.

Before my words to you this day, the standards of capitalism had never been related to the value of a company in concise terms. The relationship of capitalistic standards to the common-stock value of a corporation can best be illustrated through an actual example of a large American corporation. You are a Senior Research Chemist for Du Pont. I want you to go home and write an open letter to the administrative management of E. I. du Pont de Nemours & Co., Inc.:

**"But, I don't have any idea what to write," my father objected, standing up quickly, shocked and confused. But the mountain told him to go home and write anyway; the words would flow, the mountain Zon told him. So my father went home and sat at his desk with pad and pen. Indeed, to his amazement, in short order he knew exactly what to write. In fact, his pen could not move fast enough as he spent the rest of his day writing the following document:**

**A Proposal to Increase the Value of Du Pont Common Stock**
*An Open Letter to Those Responsible*
*for the Future*
*of the*
*Du Pont Company*

To effectively present this proposal, the following four aspects around which the proposal evolves must be identified:

**The need**
**The purpose**
**The principle**
**The proof**

After identifying those aspects, the proposal can be presented in its proper context. The proposal will entail the following recommendations:

1. Removal of specified executives who are undermining the value of Du Pont by building careers on deceptive mysticism and destructive neocheating rather than on honest thinking and productive efforts.
2. Realignment of Du Pont's philosophy around specific, profit-oriented principles.
3. Implementation of specified action designed to restore both the short-range and long-range profitability growth of the Du Pont Company.

### *The Need*

Du Pont stock sold for $278 per share. Eleven years later, Du Pont stock had fallen to $92.50 per share. Over 60% of the total corporate market value accumulated in 150 years vanished in a decade.

### *The Purpose*

For 150 years, the management of the Du Pont Company increased the corporation's value at a remarkable rate. The common stock price increased many fold. Owners became wealthy. Du Pont expanded into the largest, most profitable chemical company in the world. What was the cause? The cause can be reduced to a single principle from which all economic values grow. This document will identify that principle.

Over the past decade, the owners of Du Pont (the stockholders) have observed with mounting disappointment the declining ability of management to expand the profitability of their corporation. What is the reason for that growing impotence? Many reasons have been advanced in business and financial publications. But management's explanations failed to deal with the crucial issues. And their mystical remedies by nature have

14

accelerated the deterioration. The honest reason for the shrinking profit growth has never been publicly identified. This proposal will identify that reason. Moreover, implementation of this proposal would unleash a productivity/creativity cycle within the Du Pont Company that could generate values and profits outstripping any business enterprise on earth.

### The Principle
This proposal is based on the following principle:

All Honest, Long-Range Profits and Societal Values
Generated by Business
Arise from the Mystic-Free Standards of Capitalism

To understand that principle, the difference between altruism and capitalism must be identified. The contradiction between those two terms is evident from the following definitions:

*Capitalism* is a moral/social system as well as an economic system based on the philosophical premise that every man and woman has the exclusive right to his or her own life and property. Implementing capitalism always yields by nature a benevolent society in which individuals deal with one another on the basis of values — the voluntary exchange of values. Force and coercion are obviated. Capitalism is consistent with man's rational needs and requirements for prosperity and happiness.

*Altruism* is a morality based on the philosophical premise that man lives for the sake of others...that man's life and property are available for sacrifice to "higher" causes, e.g., the common good, society, the needy, the world, the dictator, God, country, politicians, bureaucrats, lawyers. Implementing altruism always yields by nature a malevolent society in which individuals deal with one another on terms of who will be sacrificed to whom, who will support whom. Force becomes the deciding factor. Fake jobs and bogus livelihoods grow like cancer. ...Altruism is contrary to man's nature, rational needs, and requirements for happiness.

Before applying the concepts of capitalism and altruism to

15

Du Pont and its common-stock price, those concepts must first be viewed from the broader perspective of contemporary Western culture:

Capitalism has lifted man's standard of living to undreamt heights. As will be demonstrated in this document, all long-term benefits to man's life, well being, and happiness have grown from competitive capitalistic principles.

Yet today, a growing number of altruistic businessmen are undermining capitalism. How?

1. By protecting, supporting, joining, and promoting the destructiveness of bogus-job bureaucrats, politicians, lawyers, the clergy, dishonest journalists, dishonest educators, and social "intellectuals".

2. By usurping from business short-range values and advantages for themselves rather than competitively producing long-range values for business, others, and society.

In undermining capitalism, they are depriving man of his motive to produce and his means to be happy.

Man is capable of achieving genuine prosperity and happiness only to the extent that he can produce competitive values for others and society through the rational, wide-integration use of his mind and constant, hard-work effort. That fact is based on the nature of man. Man must competitively produce for others to honestly meet both his physical and emotional needs.

Hidden beneath the words of all altruists are calls for sacrifice, "temporary" hardship, and periods of readjustment. Those calls for sacrifice are incongruously combined with promises that man can attain values without earning them. All altruists seek an unreal world based on feelings and wishful thinking...a mystical world free of demands for rational integrated thinking and competitive hard efforts. A mystical world that always moves away from the problem-solving nature of life. Indeed all mystics seek the goal of effortless, "peaceful" nirvana — a problem-free utopia. In their utopia, man can defy reality...man can usurp values without earning them...man can consume without producing...man can live effortlessly without solving problems. Reality, however, cannot be defied. Someone has to produce values and solve problems in order for human beings and society to survive and prosper. Thus, to survive and prosper, altruists and other value destroyers must deceive and coerce the value producers into sacrificing their time, efforts, property, and earnings to the value destroyers.

The altruists' final goal is to coerce or force all value producers to support and respect them, the value destroyers. The motive and ability to produce competitively and in abundance for others vanish when the producer becomes controlled by the nonproducers. Who would be responsible for such an evil, for such an unjust scourge to fall upon our civilization? Ironically, the political leaders, religious leaders, freeloaders, collectivists, and other value destroyers would not be primarily responsible. Those responsible will be the altruistic neocheaters posing as business "leaders". Such uncompetitive business quislings are today implanted throughout business and industry worldwide.

Those executives will bear the responsibility for the demise of their companies and free-market capitalism. Their altruistic principles are inimical contradictions to the principles of competitive capitalism. Through such business quislings, the sacrifice of the value producers and businesses is possible. Indeed, those quislings are the transmission belt between the value producers and the value destroyers.

But, the implementation of the capitalistic principles presented in this proposal would render impotent those altruists who are currently in positions of corporate power. For, without those altruistic business quislings, the value destroyers would be powerless to sacrifice the value producer. Their demands for sacrifice would go unanswered. The decline of capitalism would end. A new renaissance would begin. Civilization would rise to a new standard of rationality. Benevolence and goodwill among men would flourish. Man's productivity and happiness would soar.

How do those concepts of business, capitalism, and altruism relate to the common-stock value of Du Pont? This is how:

Man requires self-interest motives to be productive and creative. Man achieves happiness through his productive and creative efficacy. That is the nature of man. When altruistic businessmen assume managerial positions within a corporation, their standards of selflessness and sacrifice are asserted to allow

17

them to neocheat rather than to earn their way to competitive power and wealth. Since selflessness and sacrifice are contrary to value production and competitiveness, the producer's efficacy will diminish. His job effectiveness will decrease, and the future of his company will fade. Thus, as altruistic executives translate their standards into practice, the value of their company to stockholders and society shrinks.

Do such men exist within the Du Pont management? How can they be identified? They are characterized by their lack of singular purpose to create long-range assets, values, and profits. They are also characterized by their willingness to subjugate the best interests of the corporation and its stockholders to some fake "higher cause" or spurious "public good". Altruists can achieve their unearned ends only by sacrificing the values earned by others...such as the assets, profits, and earning potential of a corporation. They are eager to sacrifice that which has been earned and built by others. They are willing to sacrifice the stockholders' equity, potential, and property to "higher causes".

Within Du Pont there has been a gradual shift in the nature of the management from the objective, pro-capitalistic asset builder to the altruistic, socially-oriented "business leader". That shift continues under such sophistic rhetoric as "being practical", "the wave of the future", "young blood", "changing reality", "progressive needs", "social awareness", "public good", "higher causes". At the same time, the concepts of objectivity, efficacy, happiness, competence, effort, productivity, and profits are being increasingly subverted. ...These assertions about Du Pont management will be demonstrated with concrete facts later in this proposal.

Whenever long-range values are created by business, society benefits. By far, the greatest beneficiary of a profitable business is society. But the basic reason for operating any business can never be to "serve" society short range at the expense of long-range assets and earning, lest the business be eventually drained and stagnated. The only just and moral reason to operate a business is to benefit its owners through the production of competitive values for others and society. Only to the extent that owners profit can employees, society, or anyone else gain long-term values and benefits. Consequently, a business run for the best long-range financial profit of its owners will always yield the maximum, long-range benefits to society. Conversely, only by producing maximum values for society can a business produce maximum, long-range profits for its stockholders. ...That is the benevolent nature of capitalism.

Capitalism means producing competitive values (products or services) for the voluntary exchange of other values (money for further production of values). Success in a capitalistic society requires honesty, rationality, effort, wide integrations, and long-range planning. The standards of capitalism permit man to profit only by competitively producing for the benefit of others and society. The standards of capitalism allow man to fulfill his potential and to achieve happiness to the benefit of all society.

How does the above principle apply to the common-stock value of Du Pont? The common-stock price is the accurate value of a company because that price represents the exact value that buyers are willing to pay for the company in a free market. Over time, a company is worth no more or no less than its free market price (its common-stock price). **Executives are hired by the stockholders for one reason only...to enhance the long-range financial value of their business enterprise in order to increase profits and common-stock values. For long-term appreciation of stock values, an enterprise must increasingly deliver competitive values to society.**

The value of an executive is judged by the extent that he generates values for the shareholders in exchange for his compensation. In order to enhance the long-range value of a business enterprise to its owners and society, an executive must implement the principles of competitive capitalism. The altruistic executive militates against the value of his company to the extent that he directs his company. That executive does not earn his pay. For, he diminishes rather than builds the long-term value of his company.

To survive, the altruistic executive must constantly draw on the future potential of his company in a turmoil of short-range pragmatic activities that conceal the long-range damage being done to the business. At first, such an executive may blame declining stock prices on "temporary" market conditions. As the corporate assets are consumed and return on investment

19

diminishes, the executive will blame competition, inflation, deflation, "maturing business", the "inevitable", "hard luck", or a "changing reality" for the decline in stock prices.

As solutions, he may offer platitudes and schemes of short-range economies, "belt tightenings", "creative" accounting procedures, acquisitions, and other one-shot expediencies. Within the downward trend, the stock price may periodically fluctuate upward for durations of a few months or even years. But the downward trend always returns with ever-deepening losses.

When the company is finally destroyed, he will claim that events were beyond his control and the ruins were not his fault. He will plead that he had to be practical and cooperate with the altruistic "authorities". *He will not identify that operating on competitive capitalistic principles is the only honest, sound way to build values and assets. He will not identify that altruism dishonestly destroyed the value of his company. He will not identify that altruism can never be used to benefit society. But he will secretly know that altruism has always been no more than a clever tool to covertly promote bogus livelihoods.*

To repeat again the principle upon which this proposal rests:

**All Honest, Long-Range Profits and Societal Values
Generated by Business
Arise from the Mystic-Free Standards of Capitalism**

### *The Proof*

To validate this proposal, the following two assertions will be proven with specific facts:

1. Du Pont is not being managed in the best financial interest of its stockholders.
2. Management is abandoning capitalistic standards in favor of altruistic standards, thus continually shrinking the long-range profitability and value of Du Pont.

The following graph provides proof of the first assertion. The steady, long-term deterioration of Du Pont common-stock values is proof that the Company is not being managed in the best financial interest of its stockholders. That fact becomes especially obvious when the deteriorating stock price is superimposed against a composite of all other 1360 stocks on the New York Stock Exchange.

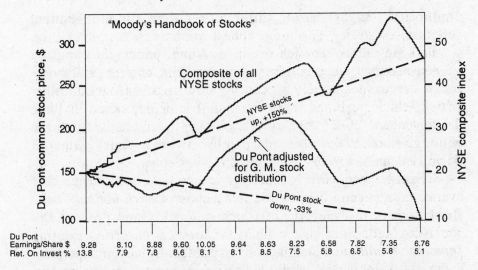

Proof of the second assertion is based on an abundance of factual evidence. A portion of this evidence will be documented with quotes from the following, publicly available communications:

- *Management Newsletter*, a Du Pont publication
- *Better Living Magazine*, a Du Pont publication
- "1 + 1 + 1", a Du Pont movie
- Statements and speeches by major Du Pont executives.

This documentation will demonstrate the extent that altruism has gripped the Du Pont Company and the consequences of abandoning competitive capitalistic principles. (The following proof provides an example on how to go about researching other companies to make profitable investments.)

### Management Newsletter

The management is responsible for the thematic content and philosophical timbre of all internal and external communications released by a company. Perhaps nowhere is the philosophical position of Du Pont management reflected more precisely than in its *Management Newsletter*. A chronological review of the Newsletter over twenty years starkly reveals the progressive abandonment of objective capitalistic principles for subjective social pragmatisms. During that abandonment of principles, decisions are increasingly made by what some shadowy external "authority" might say or think rather than by independent judgment of reality by strong, honest executives.

Past Newsletter articles reveal a strong, exuberant company guided mainly by capitalistic principles. But current Newsletter articles reveal a company guided by altruism and by what "other people" think, feel, and wish. That shift is demonstrated in Table 1 on pages 26-27 by contrasting earlier articles in the *Management Newsletter* to articles twenty years later in *Management Newsletter*.

Reading those early Newsletters is like traveling into another world...a brilliantly clear world that almost was and *should have been*...a happy, just world in which rationality and productivity are recognized as man's primary virtues...a cheerful, exciting business world in which action is guided by the independent judgment of individuals dedicated to generating values and profits. The philosophical contrast (capitalism vs. altruism) between those early Newsletters and those twenty years later is clearly apparent. Yet, the seeds for that deterioration of capitalistic principles began to appear even in the earliest Newsletters. With increasing manipulation of unearned guilt in an increasingly altruistic culture, obsequious apologies for capitalism and Du Pont were appearing in articles such as:

*Big vs. Little Business*
*Is Big Business Useful?*

A study of the Newsletters reveals that the philosophical shift from capitalism to altruism occurred in two major steps. The first step occurred when the presidency of Du Pont passed from Mr. Crawford H. Greenewalt to Mr. Lammont Copeland. The struggle to explicitly uphold capitalism abruptly ended. Articles such as listed below ceased:

*Business Pleads its Case in Whispers*

> Mr. Greenewalt stated, "It is the corporation's proper duty to oppose any action which threatens the property or the interests of its stockholders, to fight hard if the well-being of its employees is threatened, or if the successful continuity of its life comes under fire."

*U.S. Superiority and Productivity vs. USSR*
*Industrial Progress Undermines Socialism*

Soon after Mr. Greenewalt, a basic shift in philosophy was apparent. The primary focus of Du Pont changed from generating profits for the stockholders to "serving society". The following articles began appearing for the first time:

*Du Pont Research —*

President Copeland equated the value of research to serving "society" rather than to expanding corporate earnings, profits, and assets.

Could nylon have been developed and transformed into a venture that generated hundreds of millions of dollars in profits for the company, employees, stockholders, and society with an altruistic standard determining the research and development efforts at Du Pont? Commercial ventures that generate large, expanding profits for their stockholders can evolve only from capitalistic standards.

*As Others See Us*

This article signalled the acceptance of a standard whereby management replaces independent judgment with "what others think" as a valid basis for action.

*Research for Government*

Nonprofit research done at the expense of the stockholders. Why? For what purpose and at whose sacrifice? Only destructive altruism could justify such research.

Despite the basic philosophical shift to altruism, some articles such as the one listed below continued to uphold the values of Du Pont:

*Industrial Research in Internal Competition*

This article dealt with the competitively effective utilization of human skills within the Du Pont Company.

The second and most devastating step in the philosophical shift occurred when the presidency of Du Pont passed from Mr. Lammont Copeland to Mr. Charles B. McCoy. My personal experience as a Senior Research Scientist must be related to demonstrate that philosophical shift. After joining the Company, I studied each issue of the *Management Newsletter*. The articles captured the exciting action and values evolving from the most creative, capitalistic enterprise in history. The Newsletter symbolized supreme human action, creativity, and rationality. The Newsletter was a major source of pleasure and fuel in concretizing

23

man's worth and potency. When the first shift occurred under Mr. Copeland, I failed to identify what had occurred. In reading the Newsletters, I subconsciously ignored or dismissed the altruistic-based articles while savouring the articles expressing the action and values of Du Pont. After seven years, I left Du Pont for three years. On returning, I read with amazement the current *Management Newsletter*. The feature article was entitled:

*The Plant Open House,*
*A Way to Win Friends and Influence People.*

Did a multi-billion-dollar corporation have nothing more significant to report to its management than a plant tour[1] for town folk? At that time, I did not understand why such an article should appear in the *Management Newsletter*. As the months passed, I read articles such as outlined in Table 1. ...Gradually I began to understand what was happening.

The second and final step in the abandonment of capitalistic principles was occurring. In essence, all the greatness of Du Pont was being reduced and equated to a plant tour for town folks...an age-old, altruistic technique of mystically reducing man's greatest achievements to the pedestrian level.

In this seemingly innocent manner, the door had been opened to sacrifice the values of Du Pont. ...How can a philosophy expressed in the *Management Newsletter* lead to the sacrifice of Du Pont? Du Pont sacrifices to whom? To the bogus careers of altruistic management. Consider the nature of other communications that emanated from Du Pont with Management sanction. Those communications ranged from a popular, heavily-attended seminar titled *Application of Social Science Technology to Du Pont*[2] to publications like *Better Living* (analyzed next)

---

[1]Plant tours per se can be a proper, rational activity for any factory. In fact, an article on plant tours might properly appear in the "Management Newsletter" if presented from a profit-oriented, value-producing viewpoint.

[2]This Du Pont-sponsored seminar lent credibility to a pseudo-science in order to dismiss the capitalistic concept of value production by competitive individuals. Social science replaces that valid concept with the spurious collectivist concept of outputs by "human organizations" — an unintelligible concept that cannot be defined or identified within reality.

and speeches by key executives (analyzed later and in Table 4). The direct impact of management's current philosophy on Du Pont's business was reflected in a Du Pont seminar entitled, *The Future of the Fiber Business*. That seminar projected a steady decay of Du Pont's return on its fiber investment despite an optimistic market and growth picture for synthetic fibers.

That seminar was presented by the Du Pont textile-fiber management to the Executive Committee. No plan or consideration to reverse the deteriorating financial situation was offered or even considered. The gloomy nonaction stance by management to correct a suicidal business trend coupled with the anticapitalistic (government controlled) economic philosophy of Keynes accepted by Du Pont economists and management[1] are the essences for the systematic, long-range deterioration of Du Pont. With bizarre irony, the "modernistic" cover of Du Pont's Annual Report that year symbolized the purposeful destruction of values: The marvelous, industrial works of man were photographed part in-focus, part blurred, and part double exposed. Why, for what reason, for what purpose was a clear, sharp value purposely distorted and blurred into a non-value?

### Better Living Magazine

The first issue of *Better Living Magazine*[2] I received on returning to Du Pont contained an article entitled "Dedicated Amateurs" — a five-page spread on the card playing, auto driving, chess, and other free-time activities of certain employees. No, nothing was wrong with those activities. But, I wondered why such a mundane, slice-of-life article was published in *Better Living*. The article was injected between a feature article on the new fiber Qiana® and a dramatic article on building huge underground caverns for ammonia storage.

In that same issue, I read a three-page spread about a Du Pont employee dedicating his free time to unpaid social work.

[1] Seminar by Du Pont's chief economist, Mr. I. T. Ellis, "Economic Analysis and Forecasting". Credence and acceptance was granted to the spurious economic theories of master neocheater, John Maynard Keynes.

[2] *Better Living* is a bimonthly magazine published by Du Pont's Public Relations Department.

25

Creating Business Success

Table 1

## ARTICLES IN DU PONT MANAGEMENT NEWSLETTERS

| Original Newsletters | Newsletters Twenty Years Later |
|---|---|
| **Article Headings :** <br> — Annual Report <br> — Earnings <br> — Dividends <br> — Sales <br> — Payrolls <br> — Sales Price Index <br> — Income <br> — Peacetime Standards <br> — Increased Volume of Business <br> — Increased Capital <br> — Return on Operative Investment <br> — Research Activities <br> — Expansion and Improvement of Plant Facilities <br> — Employee Relations <br> — Decision of U. S. Supreme Court <br> — Strikes <br> — Nylon Price Reduction <br> — Plant Election <br> *Every article is germane to the profitable operation of Du Pont. Void of articles of a social or altruistic nature.* <br><br> Total number of articles written under the following headings: <br> — Profits - 22 <br> — Free Enterprise - 13 <br> — Big Business - 24 <br> *By contrast, not a single article twenty years later was written in support of profits, free enterprise, or big business.* | **Article Headings, Quotes, and Comments:** <br> — Plant Assists Disadvantaged Youth <br> "Plans for Progress has top corporate backing and is being implemented throughout the Company". <br> *Why? For what business purpose? Progress is achieved by efficacious producers, not by incompetents or the "disadvantaged."* <br> — New Priorities in Aid to Education "...aimed at improving educational opportunities for the disadvantaged." <br> *Why? For what business purpose? What does "disadvantaged" mean? A "disadvantaged" individual is simply one who has chosen not to put forth the effort and discipline required to become "advantaged" or productive.* <br> — Pollution Control Activities <br> "We must be concerned not only with what our neighbors think of us at the plant level, but also how we project ourselves as a total corporation." <br> *Such a statement is void of principle and lacking in independent judgment: Vast corporate actions and expenditures are being based on a standard of what "other people" think and feel rather than objective facts.* <br> — Du Pont Steps up Efforts to Hire the "Disadvantaged".[1] <br> *Why? For what business purpose? Then, Du Pont stock was above $160. Today, Du Pont stock is below $100.* <br> — Banner Year for Recruiting <br> "Du Pont people found greater social consciousness among students they interviewed." <br> *What does "social consciousness" mean? What possible value could* <br><br> *(table continued on next page)* |

Creating Business Success

Table 1(continued)

## ARTICLES IN DU PONT MANAGEMENT NEWSLETTERS

| Original Newsletters | Newsletters Twenty Years Later |
|---|---|
| **Article Headings :** | **Article Headings, Quotes, and Comments:** |
| Typical Articles of original newsletters: | *students with greater "social consciousness" have toward increasing the assets and profits of Du Pont?* |
| — Public misconception vs. facts. | — Interview with "Chemical and Engineering News" |
| — U. S. standard of living vs. Russian. | "Mr. McCoy stressed Du Pont's faith in the chemical industry and said long term the industry can greatly improve its current rate of return with a little 'luck' in reestablishing a healthy capacity-demand balance in such major items as plastics, fibers and fertilizers." |
| — Productive output of America vs. Non-America. | |
| — Left-wing criticism vs. advantages to U.S. | |
| — Reply to cellophane monopoly charge. | |
| — Atomic energy a product of American enterprise. | *The President of Du Pont publicly declares that improved rate of return for Du Pont is based on faith and luck! Mysticism and chance have become the stated basis for improving the performance of the Du Pont Company.* |
| — Du Pont President says free enterprise is greatest national resource. | |
| — Post-war production of nylon exemplifies spirit of free enterprise. | |
| — Benefits of American economic system. | |
| — Rise in standard of U. S. living through greater productivity. | |
| — Socialistic developments in U.S.: *Du Pont offered its employees a free 169-page book that identified the failures of British socialism and nationalization.* | |
| — U.S. high standards of living improved by industry. | 'That article defines the meaning of the "disadvantaged" as: "Members of poor families and unemployed or underemployed, or those who are not seeking work but should be, and who possess one of the following characteristics — high school dropout; minority group member under 22 years of age; over 44 years of age; physically, mentally or socially handicapped." Why a minority group? And what group? Only one legitimate minority exists and that is the individual. If his or her rights are protected, the rights of all are protected. What does socially handicapped mean? At competitive wages, what possible business value could such uncompetitive people offer Du Pont? Even the pretense of so-called moral value or duty fails when one identifies the injustice that placing a dishonest business value on the so-called "disadvantaged" perpetrates against those who through their own efforts become people of value...value producers. |
| — Protection of patents encourages invention. | |

27

Fine, that was his personal, free choice. The article even contained a photograph showing this employee teaching a group of migrant laborers to recognize a sign to the bathroom. That article was inserted between an article reviewing the outstanding technological achievements of the Film Department and an article describing the industrial use of television. Why the mixing of outstanding human achievement with the commonplace? In search for an answer, one might ask if a magazine needs to include the ordinary or prosaic aspects of life to be realistic and credible.

That question was eloquently answered by the *Du Pont Magazine* (issued bimonthly by Du Pont's Advertising Department). Like a searchlight slicing through the darkness, that magazine provided a dazzling flow of Du Pont's greatest products and achievements. That happy magazine was totally void of the commonplace and confirmed the vast potential that existed within Du Pont. That magazine also demonstrated that men existed within Du Pont who held greatness above the ordinary and insignificant. That magazine concretized the reason to fight for the great values of Du Pont.

The difference between *Better Living* and the *Du Pont Magazine* reflected much more than the editorial differences expected between a magazine issued by the Public Relations Department and a magazine issued by the Advertising Department. A comparison of article headings in the following table illustrates the profound philosophical and view-of-life gulf that existed between those two magazines.

| Table 2 | |
|---|---|
| **DU PONT MAGAZINE VERSUS BETTER LIVING MAGAZINE** | |
| *Du Pont Magazine* | *Better Living Magazine* |
| Cover Photo: A chic, intelligent-looking woman projecting self-esteem and confidence of self-earned values.<br><br>A Slick Assist for Snow Shovelers ("Teflon") | Cover Photo: A grinning, ungroomed girl celebrating the forceful occupation of private property (Columbia University) by a mob whose members chose to usurp and destroy values produced by others. |

(Chart continued next page)

28

| | |
|---|---|
| Goodyear's Gas-Filled Fleet ("Hypalon") | Youth: A New Society |
| A Cover that Keeps Rolling Along ("Teflon") | What's it all About |
| | The Quarrel with the Establishment |
| A Fabric of Freedom ("Dacron") | Does Business Really Care |
| Beautifully Blended for Fashion ("Orlon") | The New Left |
| Enhancing the Character of Quality ("Minute Bleach") | The Church — Will it Survive |
| | Youth Reject Racism |
| Helping Industry to Keep its Cool ("Teflon") | Youth at the University of Michigan |
| Speeding up Chemical Separations (APC Tablet) | |
| What's New ("Birox", "Mon-Soon", Polysilicates, "Cronor" gravure Film, "Tri-Seal") | |

The two magazines were philosophical opposites. The *Du Pont Magazine* reflected a cheerful, guilt-free admiration of the values and products that had arisen from Du Pont. *Better Living* reported on Du Pont's values in an apologetic, resentful manner while saluting the standards of altruism and egalitarianism, which demand the looting and destruction of Du Pont and competitive capitalism. All doubts about the philosophical nature of *Better Living* were eliminated with subsequent issues that began with the destructive mixing of great achievements with the mundane. Those subsequent articles represented the inevitable disintegration of rational values by the altruistic philosophy.

After an editorial that explicitly suspended moral judgment,[1] the entire 32-page issue of *Better Living* proceeded to idealize those who sought to destroy competitive capitalism and the profit-making ability of industry. That 32-page spread saluted those

---

[1]Quote the editorial, "We are describing — neither condoning or condemning it — this phenomenon because it is rapidly moving front and center."

29

collectivist conformists who hate and fear capitalism because they are incompetent to compete in free markets — incompetent to meet competitive standards that demand discipline, thought, effort, and the production of values. Those standards require man to think rationally and produce values for others and society to survive.

Under the title, *Youth: A New Society*, that issue of *Better Living* projected a potpourri of impotent, anticapitalistic conformists as "honest", "idealistic" youth. That "honesty" and "idealism" epitomized the dishonesty and fraud of that article: Youth who substituted emotion for reason and feelings for facts as their guide to action were blatantly dishonest and destructive. Moreover, youth who chose to evade their responsibility to produce rational values for others were neither honest nor idealistic.

The supreme injustice of *Better Living* was committed against those youth who had not surrendered to dishonesty...against those youth who were struggling to achieve rational goals and values. But the most destructive injustice of *Better Living* was committed against Du Pont and capitalism. By implication, that issue besmirched Du Pont and competitive capitalism with all the real and imaginary ills of this world. Not one word in *Better Living* was dedicated to the only rational purpose of Du Pont...to generate expanding profits for its stockholders by increasingly producing competitive values for others and society. Not a single word was dedicated to the supreme moral value of Du Pont...an efficient organization in which individuals could utilize their rational minds and productive efforts for their own and loved ones' well-being and happiness by providing benefits to others and society. ...Those who produced *Better Living* gained their dishonest, destructive livelihoods from Du Pont. And Du Pont management willingly paid their salaries!

Every Du Pont executive should carefully read that issue of *Better Living*. Observe the massive, envious, unearned guilt foisted upon the businessman, Du Pont, and free enterprise. Observe the implicit threats and sullen malevolence that exudes from beneath the "properly tempered" words and the measured praise for Du Pont's incongruous efforts to meet the demands of the value-destroying altruists. Look at the pictures...look carefully into the faces of those demanding that business sacrifice itself to the "good of society". Their expressions range from the robot, joyless faces of desperately dependent conformists to the loathing, power-seeking expression in the face of Ralph Nader to the raging faces of the militants screaming for blood and destruction.

All those faces can be reduced to one common expression ...fear...fear of competitive capitalism...fear of the hard work and honesty required to produce competitive values for others...fear of competing with value producers. To survive, those nonproducers must depend on the producer being tricked or forced into sacrificing earned values to the "good of society" — to them, the nonproducers. Remember those faces in *Better Living*...you will see them again. And you will not have to wonder who provided those "idealistic" youth with the sanction to cripple and then destroy Du Pont.

### "1 + 1 + 1" Movie

The long-term increase or decrease of common stock prices for any company can be forecast from its management's philosophical projection of capitalistic principles. The movie "1 + 1 + 1" released by Du Pont's Public Relations Department with sanction of the Executive Committee, afforded an unusual opportunity for an in-depth analysis of management's philosophical projection of capitalistic principles:

Du Pont is an awe-inspiring subject that symbolizes the pinnacle of accomplishment. Du Pont is a proud example of man's potency toward which all humans can lift their eyes for inspiration. Consider how Du Pont was treated in "1 + 1 + 1", a movie shown to most Du Pont employees and to millions of Americans:

A breathtaking skyline of New York City appeared. Exultant music played. The bold Du Pont oval filled the screen. Firm and steady words spoke of the marvels that man has created with steel and concrete. Yes, yes, one could eagerly agree. That was Du Pont. That was the story that should be told...exultant, bold, breathtaking. But that spine-tingling emotion lasted only a moment. The camera promptly zoomed into close-up shots of the "man in the street". With the focus on the group and the common man, the magnificent spell was broken.

Why did the moviemaker do that? Was he implying that the "man in the street" or the group was responsible for the great achievements symbolized by the skyline of New York? Was not that movie supposed to stress the individual? What about the few, uncommon individuals...the innovators, industrialists, scientists, and artists? It was those uncommon individuals who gave us the great values of "music, steel, and concrete". How could the moviemaker commit such an oversight? Or was it an oversight?

The scene shifted. A voice told us of Du Pont's 86 factories and 100 laboratories spanning the globe. From barren earth, factories of production rose majestically. For an instant, that thrilling emotion returned. Then came the jolt. The scene shifted. The voice changed. The value of Du Pont's factories was obliterated by a female voice sighing that the new plant will bring "A lot of young men, I hope."

Why was the moviemaker building heroic images of Du Pont only to shatter them? Why was the moviemaker purposely spoiling values? Why was he mixing poison with food? Did he not know the only results can be poison?

The movie continued. A statement was made, "Some men's urge to make life better takes them down wondrous roads." What were those wondrous roads? No explanation. Instead, the moviemaker raked the audience with a ludicrous pandemonium of old-fashioned cars speeding around corners, and water skiers engaged in spectacular falls. Another statement was made, "Man must be unique." The next scene showed a pie-eating contest and then a dozen or more youths in coon-skin coats riding in a single automobile. Mixing purity with poison...the mind with the mindless...values with non-values — an ancient neocheating trick to destroy values. What was the moviemaker's motive?

What was the meaning of that film? The movie pressed onward. The narrator revealed that over 2500 Ph.D.s worked for Du Pont. The narrator then announced that today's science was a "meshing of groups". What did "meshing of groups" mean? No explanation. Was not this movie supposed to stress the individual? Again, what about those few individuals who were responsible for all the material values we have today? No mention was made of them.

The scene shifted to technical management in action. Hope surged for a glimpse of greatness. Now will the value of the individual appear? No. Instead of crisp, intelligent men making meaningful business decisions, the scene wilted into altruistic torpidity. A woman inarticulately spoke about helping mankind by nitrogen fixation. She spoke as if the excuse for Du Pont's existence was to help the global indigents. Her words, sounding more like a bovine moan, were not those of a confident, productive human being. Was that the moviemaker's portrayal of management in one of America's greatest corporations?

Next came a scene about Du Pont explosives. Instead of depicting how explosives have so benevolently lifted a torturous burden from man's shoulders, the scene disparaged human intelligence. A scientist was presented. He proceeded to express himself with garrulities such as "those cats think explosives are for war". Did that reflect the seriousness and intelligence of the Du Pont scientist? At that point, the moviemaker introduced his metaphysical view of the science: "Let the scientist miss and miss and begin again" was presented as the modus operandi of the scientist. The focus was on failure.

No acknowledgement or recognition was given to those competitive, value-producing scientists who think long-range and achieve great goals through carefully planned, exceedingly difficult, hard work. Instead, the audience was garroted with the fallacious image of a "crackpot" scientist mindlessly mixing together everything in sight and meeting failure after failure until by chance he stumbled onto a great discovery. Was this the moviemaker's metaphysical view of science? Was man's mind impotent and technical achievement a matter of chance or accident?

How did the moviemaker project those precious few individuals who choose to use their minds and exert supreme rational effort in order to discover, innovate, produce, and market products that have generated hundreds of millions of dollars in profit for Du Pont? Their work was summed up in one sentence. "Things blew apart and everything". What was the meaning behind that seemingly frivolous remark? Was the moviemaker informing us that those great achievements required no special effort or intelligence? Did nylon evolve by a process of things blowing apart? Was that the moviemaker's view of man's accomplishments? Could anyone present such a dishonest, resentful, envious view of competence and achievement?

How were the end results of major technical achievements portrayed? Mylar® was selected as an example. Its value was promptly reduced to a toy butterfly. What about the value of knowledge? A Du Pont scientist spoke of his past. He referred to himself as a defrocked organic chemist and wondered why he ever obtained a Ph.D. degree. No explanation was given. The man was left appearing as a diffident fool for his past efforts. The man then explained that his genetic makeup made him what he was. Did not that mystical, predeterministic view negate the value of man's mind and his volitional discipline, effort, and free choice?

What about the value of man achieving his long-range goals? A sequence began with an obviously intelligent man making the rationally correct statement that "man has to satisfy the need to build". Indeed he does. Man's most fundamental need is to build (to produce). How did the moviemaker project that? The next scene showed a descending foot crushing a child's sand castle. Why? Is what man builds so tenuous and meaningless that his work can be crushed to nothing at someone's random whim?

What about the moviemaker's view of absolutes? His view was projected by a factory scene: A worker asserted that there was too much supervision. The next worker asserted that there was too little supervision. What purpose did that seemingly innocuous scene serve? Was it to show that one side is as valid as the other...that everything was a matter of opinion...that there was no right or wrong way...that whatever one felt was right...that there was no objective reality?

The scenes went on and on. Build up and tear down. A skyline was silhouetted with beautiful new factories. What significance was attached to those factories? Only one specific message was projected — new factories caused problems of uprooting, relocation, and retraining. What about the products, jobs, profits, and competitive values generated by those factories? ...Silence.

34

What about the most important facet of man's life — his productive work? Man and his work were sloughed off in ten seconds with the statement, "man must do his own thing while inside the Company". The scene shifted to man's activities outside the Company. In a lengthy persiflage of bizarre nonsense, we were bombarded with an incoherent collection of silent flickers blended with all the modern, mind-blowing psychedelic effects. Why? For what purpose? Was the moviemaker telling us that man's work was no more significant than a perfunctory statement that "he must do his own thing" and his other activities were no more worthy than meaningless pantomime and boring psychedelic effects? Could anyone possibly hold such a malevolent view of man and his life? Let us continue with the movie:

The desecration of values, man, and Du Pont continued at an accelerating pace. Du Pont employees *at work* were associated with pin-up girls, slogan-painted lab coats, and hippy buttons. The basic technique continued...show a value and then tear it down...show a man producing at his work and then knock him down with a slogan-painted lab coat or leave him leering at a girlie picture.

The moviemaker's technique reached the climax with the scene of the Executive Committee. Waiting in desperate hope for a glimpse of greatness, one found himself begging the movie to preserve values here...with the men who run that great, productive company. In the Executive Committee, one must find firm-faced men with clear, honest eyes...men whose voices were strong and confident...men who talked of important matters, such as production, profit, and values...men who talked of awesome business transactions, heroic discoveries, and fearless plans. But, alas, one was told apologetically that "someone had to run the store". Everyone was then gratuitously rammed with personalized close-ups of the men one wanted to keep at an impersonal distance in order to uphold them as ideals and sources of inspiration. Yes, everyone was assaulted with poster-size faces of the "warm personal man next door"[1].

---

[1] The moviemaker was not completely successful here. A few faces did not yield. They reflected a dignity and self-esteem that even the moviemaker with all his modern techniques could not pull down.

Was the moviemaker telling everyone that the leaders of Du Pont were nothing more than a group of regular guys? Did it take no one special to run E. I. du Pont de Nemours & Company...just the man next door? The fist hit hard. The Executive Committee was the last place one wanted to see the regular guy. One's soul pleaded for something better, a glimpse of a hero, a glimpse of inspiration. The rest was anticlimactic. No words were uttered of awesome business transactions, thrilling discoveries, or fearless plans. Instead, one heard only of personnel problems, pollution problems, and safety problems.

Nothing seemed to matter after that scene of the Executive Committee. One could watch with indifference as a plant manager obsequiously apologized to the mayor of a city for a new Du Pont factory by explaining that "Du Pont did not want to lean on people or be a problem, but wanted to help solve problems". Nor did it matter anymore when the narrator implied that Du Pont had to cajole college graduates into marketing careers. It no longer mattered that the wonderful values available through marketing careers were ignored.

But one final shock remained. It bludgeoned the senses in a thundering broadside. In the final denouement of the moviemaker's soul, the most indisputable values of Du Pont — its magnificent array of commercial products — were reduced to the level of the "inscrutable jellybean". One by one the wonderful products of Du Pont were paraded before everyone to be wantonly besmirched with alternating, out-of-focus scenes of strident, blank-faced youths, writhing with loose, flopping mouths and glazed eyes. One by one the products of Du Pont were flung onto a carrion heap of tortured motions, primitive drum pounding, and flashing lights that accurately reflected a schizophrenic's view of life.

The great products with all the heroic efforts of individuals who chose to use their minds...all the benevolence, achievement, and inspiration that Du Pont represented...all those great values and achievements were trampled into the joyless, Marcusian-Kafka jungle of the parasitical collectivists and professional mystics whose darkling minds viewed with hatred every value that Du Pont delivered to society. ...Could anyone hate life and its values that much?

With howling screams ringing in one's ears and the neocheaters dancing on Du Pont's murdered spirit, the movie ended with brashly incongruous proclamations about the value of the individual. The movie inextricably wove Du Pont into the anticapitalistic dishonesties that are moving throughout the world. The movie maker was successful...brilliantly successful. The movie "1 + 1 + 1" will accomplish precisely what its creator intended the movie to do — drive nails into the coffin of capitalism. And when the last nail is driven, all the benevolence and happiness possible to man will be sealed in that coffin.

How could a mere movie have such devastating effects? This is how: Think back...think far back into your childhood. Recall that precious time when one could romantically look to the future as a life of boundless happiness and goals to achieve? Remember eagerly seeking values, knowledge, and facts? That spark of life, however brief, exists in every child. But most choose to let that spark flicker out — to give up so early in life. Most forever extinguish that spark, never to know life again. A few hang on longer. Fewer, still, never give up. In them, a hidden spark forever burns. And it is they who count. It is they who become the heroes of life.

The movie "1 + 1 + 1" is the instrument that will break those still struggling to hold on. Implicitly to them, United States business is the last bastion of reason...the last source of inspirational values. Capitalism is the lifeline they unknowingly cling to. As the movie "1 + 1 + 1" was shown throughout the land, thousands of those young, precious sparks quietly flickered out. So subtle was the movie that few will ever know why. But those who read this document will forever know why. To those who saw "1 + 1 + 1", recall the emotions at the conclusion of that movie: Aside from a vague feeling of malaise one might have felt, aside from an undefined nagging that something was wrong, what other emotions could possibly be experienced? One could experience only boredom, indifference, puzzlement, sadness, or resignation. With the strength and vitality drained from a once proud image, Du Pont was left hat-in-hand apologizing for its existence. Du Pont was left as an empty, hulking skeleton of effaced values...not even worthy of having its name in the title

37

of the movie.[1]

What was the reaction to this movie by those young minds after being inculcated with forty minutes of subtly specious but powerfully effective anti-heroic, anti-mind scenes? To those who had already given up, only a lethargic "so what" was possible: They were saying "so what" not only to the movie, but to Du Pont, business, capitalism, and their own lives. ...As they gave up and their sparks flickered out, so went the future of Du Pont and capitalism.

No, the producer of "1 + 1 + 1" was not responsible for such crimes. The responsibility belonged to the corporate management for failing to protect the ideals of Du Pont and competitive capitalism. Men such as the producer of that movie would be powerless without the sanction and support of such quisling managements.

Nearly twenty years before, a movie was produced under a different management — a management that took Du Pont to the heights of profitability and common-stock values — the movie was entitled *The Du Pont Story*. Those who recalled that proud and glamorous movie vividly grasped the opposite philosophical view of that management. That earlier management took Du Pont to the height of profitability and value. The subsequent management replaced that management with "liberal views" as a route to "higher" values. Du Pont stock sold for $278 per share. Eleven years later, Du Pont stock had fallen to $92.50 per share. Does that represent higher values? Or do such "higher values" represent value destruction?

### Speeches and Statements
### by Major Du Pont Executives

In one last desperate hope, one might rationalize that the

---

[1]*Management Newsletter*: "'The film', Strauss says, 'takes advantage of many visual, shorthand techniques to tell a story that informs and motivates without preachment, puffery, or the heavy hand of corporate self-congratulation.'" *Better Living* stated: "The moviemakers (Henry Strauss & Co., Inc. of New York City) provided no traditional story line. Instead of a continuous band of narrative, the impressions were assembled, then tumbled against each other like brilliant shards of glass." For what purpose? For what value?

*Money: The Neo-Tech Factor Is Told*

*Management Newsletter, Better Living*, and the movie "1 + 1 + 1" reflected only the views of its writers and editors and not the philosophy of Du Pont management. That hope promptly dissipates on examination of speeches and statements of certain key executives who controlled Du Pont management. Their words were philosophically consistent with the *Management Newsletter, Better Living* and the movie "1 + 1 + 1". Their own statements demonstrated that Du Pont management was abandoning capitalistic standards for mystical, altruistic standards:

*McCoy Tells of Need to Cure Social Ills.*
Article Headline<br>Wilmington News-Journal

Casting an undefined pall of guilt on industry for the "social ills" of man, the President of Du Pont, Mr. McCoy, implied that private enterprise had the duty to cure those "social ills". He then declared his intentions to "serve society" through the Du Pont Company. With no reference to serving the stockholders and a perfunctory reference to profits, Mr. McCoy stated the lip-service non sequitur that "nothing is mutually exclusive about making a profit and serving the needs of society."

As Mr. McCoy led Du Pont into the "service of society", the press eagerly reported his views and actions:

*Du Pont President sees unique role for industry in solving society's problems.*
— Chemical and Engineering News

Ironically, that same magazine revealed the inevitable results of abandoning capitalistic principles to altruism:

*Earnings are still far below their peak, and this year will bring, at best, only a small improvement over last year's performance. Du Pont's stock price is less than half what it was four years ago and it has been falling all year.*
— Chemical and Engineering News

On the same day that *Chemical and Engineering News* published its article about Mr. McCoy, the *Wall Street Journal* published comments on the performance of Du Pont. Those two articles provided a grimly realistic cause-and-effect dialogue between altruism and profits as shown in the following Table 3.

## Table 3

## DESTRUCTIVE ALTRUISM *versus* PRODUCTIVE PROFITS

CAUSE — "Although Mr. McCoy is now faced with the responsibility of getting his vast company really moving again, he also gives very deep thought to the increasingly critical role industry must play in society in the years ahead."
> — McCoy, *Chemical & Engineering News.*

EFFECT — "The stock may be cheap like some people say — but where's the incentive to buy when the outlook is so hazy?"
> — *Wall Street Journal.*

CAUSE — "The challenge is for industry to devise more imaginative ways to place its technological resources in the service of man; to couple its business goals with the clear and pressing needs of society."
> — McCoy, *Chemical & Engineering News.*

EFFECT — "How the mighty have fallen," remarked one fund manager. The reference was to the stock of Du Pont.
> — *Wall Street Journal.*

CAUSE — "Society will reward those that help unclog our highways, rebuild and revitalize our cities, cleanse our streams, and conquer poverty and disease, not those whose pursuit of the dollar blinds them to such needs."
> — McCoy, *Chemical & Engineering News.*

EFFECT — "Investors' increasing disenchantment with Du Pont stock is largely based on what Richard Berkley of H. Hentz characterizes as an uninspiring earnings record over the past 10 years."
> — *Wall Street Journal.*

CAUSE — "In Mr. McCoy's view, industry has already moved away from the narrow idea that business corporations are merely organizations to make and sell goods to provide a fair return to their owners. Instead, he says, we have to come to look upon our enterprises as mechanisms invented by society to translate scientific knowledge into the goods and services that society needs."
> — McCoy, *Chemical & Engineering News.*

EFFECT — "But if you're a level-headed investor, you buy performance. And Du Pont — based on its record over the last 10 years — hasn't shown it."
> — *Wall Street Journal.*

President McCoy must be held responsible for the deteriorating performance of Du Pont. Mr. McCoy was hired as the chief executive to serve the stockholders. He was paid by the stockholders to protect and enhance the financial value of Du Pont. A president of an industrial corporation is not paid to solve society's problems or to cure "social ills" with the earnings and property that belong to the stockholders.

Were not other executives also responsible for abandoning capitalistic principles and the resulting poor performance of Du Pont? Yes. And they must also be held responsible to the extent they neglected, misused, and damaged the stockholders' property. In examining the speeches and statements of other major Du Pont executives, however, one discovers a profound difference between *some* executives and Mr. McCoy. While the speeches and statements of those Du Pont executives contained philosophical errors and varying degrees of compromise to altruism that were contrary to the best interests of Du Pont, their projected views still remained basically pro-capitalistic. To varying degrees, they recognized and upheld the values of Du Pont. In other words, a few executives still displayed viewpoints that, although often blighted with sprinklings of altruism, were nevertheless based on capitalistic premises. Mr. McCoy's views, on the other hand, were based solidly on altruistic premises that were "justified" with bits and pieces of pragmatic "capitalism". That fundamental difference in viewpoints becomes vividly apparent in Table 4 on pages 42-43 in which the mystical statements by altruist president Charles B. McCoy are compared to the honest statements by dedicated executive Pierre S. du Pont who recognized and upheld the values of capitalism.

The profound difference between the viewpoints of those two men is self-evident. Mr. McCoy's sad, guilt-ridden view of man's nature and achievements contrasted sharply to Mr. Pierre du Pont's benevolent, guiltless view of capitalism and the benefits it bestows upon all mankind. On reviewing other speeches and public comments by Mr. McCoy, one fails to find a single word of admiration or recognition of capitalism or the marvelous plethora of material and financial values that emanate from the Du Pont Company.

41

*Creating Business Values*

## TABLE 4
## SENSE-OF-LIFE COMPARISON

| Cheerful, Productive, Hard-Driving Capitalist Pierre S. du Pont Speech (Integrated/Business Mind) | Gloomy, Destructive, Guilt-Projecting Altruist Charles B. McCoy Speech (Altruist/Criminal Mind) |
|---|---|
| "The United States became the strongest and most prosperous nation in the long history of mankind. Its reputation for wealth and generosity grew to such proportions that a successful motion picture was based on the idea that the way for a nation to live happily ever afterward was to lose a war with the United States and get on the list of foreign aid. | "We always come out with pretty much the same laundry list: food supply; population control; housing and urban renewal; pollution control; improvements in medical care and in the cure and prevention of killer diseases; development of alternative raw materials to supplement scarce natural resources; improvements in transportation, especially in densely populated areas. |
| "United States, one of the rarest things the world has ever known — a country with a surplus of food. Most of the world, even today, lives almost literally from hand to mouth, on the verge of famine and starvation. Indeed, famine and starvation are an annual way of life in far too many areas of the world. The United States is a most happy exception. | "There is deep concern that technology is not working as it should in the service of man, and that organizations closely identified with technology — including our industry very pointedly — are steered by the profit motive into projects that are low in priority or even destructive. |
| "If the average American — the common man, which I suppose includes pretty much all of us — could be made to understand the importance of this question to him, and the fact that he has a major responsibility to make sure that his selfish and personal interests are protected, then I believe our economic structure would be invulnerable. | "It is said that too much technical skill is wasted on projects that are glamorous but essentially frivolous, while too little is focused on problems such as hunger, pollution, the decay of our cities, and the psychic destruction of the people who live in them. |
| "We have here what ought to be the most salable product on earth, and yet all available evidence is that the great bulk of those advantaged by it do not appreciate it, do not | "There is concern about the side effects of technology, the 'accidents' that seem to occur all too often. There is concern about the long-term effects of the use of chemical materials, as in the case of agricultural chemicals. There is a growing fear that we have unleashed a force we can no longer control, a force doing irreparable damage to the |

*Creating Business Values*

## TABLE 4
## SENSE-OF-LIFE COMPARISON

know or care whether any of it is in any danger, and do not consider, if it is, that they have any responsibility to do anything about it. This adds up to perhaps the worst selling job in the long history of mankind.

"This becomes especially evident when you consider that those who have failed in this task have always been considered as pretty impressive in the field of selling. I mean the representatives of American business and industry. Who else can be held responsible? When you come right down to it, who else is interested in tackling this selling job? I'm afraid the answer is nobody. It's up to us.

"Because of this, some have become discouraged and feel it is an impossible task to win the active and dynamic support of American men and women for the system that has provided a way of life that not even kings and emperors enjoyed a century ago."

biological balance of the planet.

"More and more, we are hearing serious questions about the meaning of the word 'progress'. It is no longer taken for granted, as it was for many years, that more technology and more economic growth automatically add up to improvements in the human condition.

"They are as likely as anyone else to raise the question we hear so often today: 'If we can put men on the moon, how come we can't clean up the mess down here?'

"Perhaps to an extent we have brought this on ourselves by claiming so many wondrous products and monumental discoveries."

Mr. McCoy's view of capitalism, technology, achievement, and Du Pont was one of disparagement and effacement as evidenced by the following public statement made in his speech before the Society of Chemical Industry:

"There are people so enthusiastic about technology that they assume it is going to solve all our problems. It's nice to have such trusting friends, but they are operating under an assumption that can only hurt us more than anyone else. We cannot meet this blanket contract. When they discover this, as sooner or later they must, they are likely to be angry as well as disappointed. They will think we let them down. Perhaps to an extent we have brought this on ourselves by claiming so many wondrous products and monumental discoveries. Be that as it may, would we not be well-advised in the future to make doubly sure that our propaganda stays in line with practicality? Could we not profit from a more open and candid acknowledgment that we have limited expertise?"

What standard was held by a man who projected technology and human achievement in this manner? What long-range inspiration, daring progress, or heroic achievement could ever evolve from such a standard?

Here a logical question arises: Why did the Board of Directors, the majority of whom are presumably productive men on capitalistic premises, elect Mr. McCoy as the president of Du Pont? What is the underlying reason for their selecting a value-destroying altruist as president? Today, most businessmen are confused and bewildered by the irrational, anticapitalistic culture raging about them. Instead of being hailed as the heroes of mankind that they genuinely are, productive businessmen are maligned and assaulted with blame for the world's "social ills".

The rational businessman, in his innocence, does not understand the reason or the nature of the mounting assaults against him and his business by the news media and by the growing hordes of value-destroying altruists, politicians, and pseudo intellectuals. He has not gained the philosophical knowledge to explicitly identify that he is right and good and they are wrong and evil. He represents the creation of values through rational thought and action, and they represent the destruction of values through force and coercion. He represents the honest and intellectual; they represent the dishonest and anti-intellectual.

Having neither the knowledge nor the stomach to deal with the inscrutable irrationalities besieging him, the businessman usually commits a major error...he avoids thinking about the dishonest hypocrisies surrounding him. Instead, he seeks ways to mollify those menacing anticapitalistic forces by making financial amends for his lack of "social" consciousness, by making "practical" compromises, by supporting their "humanitarian" causes, or by cooperating to alleviate their "just grievances". He does not realize that his cooperation and support are providing those anticapitalistic neocheaters with the power and means to destroy him and his business. Thus, that businessman becomes increasingly bewildered as the irrational demands escalate. He often assumes unearned guilt and self-blame for not understanding or knowing how to answer the "socially concerned" news media, the "significant intellectuals", the "idealistic" youth, the "reforming" politicians, the "concerned" clergy, the "humanitarian" altruists, and all other professional mystics and neocheaters swirling about him.

As the threats and harassment mount, the businessman may seek someone who better understands the emerging "new culture" — someone...anyone who will be more favorably received by the news media, youth, politicians, and the "socially concerned". With such a misguided view, the directors of a company become prone to select the worst possible candidate to lead their company. Instead of selecting a businessman who would protect and enhance the value of their company through implementing capitalistic principles, they seek a man who could "attune" their company to the "demands of society", a man who could communicate with "social" intellectuals and "social" leaders, a man with a "social" conscience — a professional altruist.

Such self-defeating acts by businessmen occur through the disease of acting on the basis of what others think, feel, or wish rather than on one's own independent judgment of factual reality. Business decisions based upon what others think undermines the earning potential of companies such as Du Pont. Indeed, most research and marketing failures at Du Pont occur through those

45

who validate decisions not on facts and independent judgment but on what others think, feel, or wish. That intellectually crippling affliction is the consequence of adopting altruistic standards.

With capitalistic standards, each person must think for one's own self to compete and succeed. Indeed, altruism would vanish in a world of value producers who think for themselves and accept the facts of reality as the only valid basis for action. ...The professional altruist negates the integrated, rational use of one's own mind. Furthermore, to sustain his bogus livelihood, the professional altruist must keep the producers from thinking for themselves so they will obey the demands of professional mystics and neocheaters.

"That question cannot be answered in technical terms alone. It depends on social and political factors as much as economics. It depends on the attitudes of people within the technical work force, and what society expects and demands of them."

— McCoy, Speech

Mr. McCoy's statement speaks for itself. How could any technical achievement capable of generating major profits evolve from Du Pont or from any company when its chief executive subjugates technology and facts to the expectations and demands of an undefinable, nonexistent form of "superior intelligence" that Mr. McCoy calls society. The "superior intelligence" or the "higher good" is the mystical rationalization by which all professional altruists justify their destruction of values. That "superior intelligence" or "higher good" can assume any unreal, mystical form such as "a society that expects and demands". Plato, the philosophical father of altruism and mysticism,[1] first introduced this concept with his various forms of "higher

---

[1]Altruism is tied to Plato's mysticism. For, no rationality, facts, or logic can support altruism. Thus, faith is the cornerstone of the altruist's eternal promises for a better future: "...Mr. McCoy has a sublime faith in the chemical industry in this future of growing technological application to the good of society." *Chemical and Engineering News*

realities"[1].

With Immanuel Kant transmitting the philosophy of sacrifice from the Dark Ages, Georg Hegel prepared altruism for the twentieth century. Indeed, the horrors and destruction of Nazi Germany reveal the final results of altruism. Adolph Hitler was the ultimate practitioner of altruism. His explicitly stated enemies were rationality, capitalism, and individualism. Using the philosophical ammunition of Hegel and the morality of altruism, he perfected a new "higher good" to which anything and everything could be sacrificed without question. Hitler called his mystical "higher good" or "higher cause" the *National Will*.

"The states and municipalities, and certainly private industry, must look to the Federal level not just for coordination and specific legislation, but first of all for a clear, consistent statement of the *National Will*."

— McCoy, Speech

The future value of a corporation by nature is determined by the philosophical position of its management. Indeed, this document identifies the business values being destroyed by management's mystical philosophy of "higher causes". While the harmful effects of management's altruistic philosophy are creeping into every phase of Du Pont's business (research, sales, manufacturing, administration), those effects are most vividly observed in art. Indeed, one's philosophical views are openly revealed in one's artistic choices and preferences. Art expresses man's deepest view of life and himself. How does that view apply to the management and business operations of Du Pont?

Consider that architecture is perhaps man's most eloquent, revealing form of art: A mighty, artistic structure rose in the center of Wilmington, Delaware — the Brandywine Building — the building to house the offices of E. I. du Pont de Nemours & Co., Inc. Watching the silhouetted skeleton of that colossus rise toward the sky, one could experience a thrilling pride in

---

[1]There are no "higher realities", only objective reality. Thus no "higher good" exists to which man can be sacrificed because the highest good is man himself. No "higher cause" (or "society") exists to which individuals can be sacrificed, because the highest cause is the individual.

witnessing the bold shape being assumed by that great structure. Viewing the structure of this building, one could grasp everything that Du Pont has meant to man. The structure embodied all the creativeness and innovativeness of man. That structure represented the frozen intelligence of man's most magnificent achievements. What an appropriate symbol for Du Pont — perhaps the most innovative, creative company in history. One anxiously awaited for that girdered skeleton to become alive with a sleek skin of glass and steel. A building saluting the achievements of Du Pont. A building with striking, objective beauty.

With disbelief and initial horror that gradually turned to sadness, one watched the desecration of that building take place as workers installed each gloomy slab of massive stone. Increasingly those slabs disfigured that beautiful structure. A building to house a company that symbolized everything productive and creative about man was transformed into the antithesis of modern architecture. The Brandywine Building was wantonly mutilated into an ugly, expensive, medieval structure. That structure reflected the torturous, physical burdens of the Dark Ages during which the lives of men were consumed in back-breaking toil to erect massive, stone structures with sunken slits for windows. Such was the desecration of the Brandywine Building.

Architecture, as any form of art, reflects the deepest views of its creator as well as the views of those who approve and finance the architecture. A building that should reflect modern man's mastery of nature was dragged back through the centuries to emulate a medieval structure. That structure conjured visions of penitentiaries and monasteries with the accompanying emotions of oppressive guilt and tortured screams. The Brandywine Building was transformed into a structure void of joy and happiness.

The future of any company depends on the philosophical premises of the controlling management. If a management on capitalistic premises ever again assumes control of Du Pont, those oppressive walls of stone will come down. Rising proudly in their place will be glittering sheets of light, airy glass and sleek strips of steel and concrete. When the Brandywine Building is delivered into a joyful, glistening structure by modern man and for modern man, one will know that Du Pont management is once again operating on the mystic-free standards of capitalism.

## SUMMARY
### All Honest, Long-Range Societal Values
### Generated by Business
### arise from the
### Mystic-Free Standards of Capitalism

This document reveals how the long-term value of a company is determined by the extent management implements the standards of capitalism. For investors, analysts, and speculators, this document provides an immutable standard to predict long-range, common-stock values. For businessmen and executives, this document provides the basis for expanding both short-term and long-term profitability of their companies. For implementing the standards of capitalism within a company, the following actions are recommended:

1. Dismiss all executives whose corporate actions remain on altruistic standards. Fire all nonproducers and value destroyers.

2. Increase the salaries and responsibilities of those executives who have demonstrated competence in delivering long-range financial benefits to the stockholders.

3. Establish an Industrial Philosophy Department in order to define business standards based on the principles of competitive capitalism. With capitalistic business standards defined, the Industrial Philosophy Department would then be responsible for protecting the company and its growth. How? By assuring that all short-range and long-range corporate actions were mystic-free.

If the controlling management rejects (1) dismissing value destroyers, (2) rewarding value producers, and (3) acting according to capitalistic principles, then what does that management stand for? What is the purpose of that management? Where will that management lead its company?

Injection of capitalistic principles into every phase of management will lift a company into a commanding advantage over competition while unleashing a productivity/creativity cycle

49

that will generate continually expanding profits and rising stock values.

### Epilogue

This document seeks those individuals who act on their own judgment and live by their own productivity. For those value producers are responsible for all the long-term profits and competitive values that business generates.

Without the value producer, no profitable enterprise could exist. In business, as in reality, the value producers and only the value producers earn their livelihoods. All others, no matter what their positions or apparent power within a business concern, remain on the payroll by the erroneous grace and innocent sanction of those value producers.

This document calls upon all value-producing executives to (1) inject the principles of competitive capitalism into every facet of their operation and (2) rid their company of all value destroyers in order to increase the long-range financial value of their corporation. Can this be accomplished by the few? Yes, of course. Although outnumbered and perhaps outranked, those value-producing executives can always exercise de facto control over their company because the existence of every job and the company itself depends upon them.

This document asks all value producers to exercise their potency in establishing business and industry on the objective principles of capitalism...for their own sake...for the lives and happiness of themselves, their loved ones, and all civilization. For they, the value producers, and only they, hold genuine power.

\* \* \* \*

**My father returned to his mountain the next morning calling, "Zon! Zon! Zon! Do you know what I wrote? Zon, it's amazing. I'm seeing so clear. I feel so powerful! Where are we heading?" Immediately the wind combed back my father's hair as the mountain answered:**

Your document gives us the fundamental principle that determines the long-range value of a corporation to its stockholders and society: *All honest, long-range profits and societal values generated by business arise from the mystic-free standards of capitalism.*

Your document demonstrates that in a free economy the long-term values or common-stock prices are ultimately determined by the extent that management implements the mystic-free standards of capitalism to produce evermore competitive values for society. For investors and speculators, your document provides a valid standard to predict the long-range profit growth of all businesses and their common-stock values. For businessmen and executives, your document provides specific recommendations for implementing mystic-free capitalistic standards in order to increase the value of their company. Also, your document gives us:

- A standard by which to identify those executives and employees who are genuine, long-range assets to their company.
- A standard by which to identify those executives and employees who are undermining the long-range value of their company.
- Standards for adopting a business philosophy around specific profit-oriented principles.
- Action required to expand both short-range and long-range profitability of a company.

Now people can use the standards in your document to judge the future financial value of business enterprises. And they can use the standards to increase the financial value of any business venture, and they can contrast the wealth-producing mystic-free capitalistic nature of business to the wealth-destroying mystical nature of altruism and neocheating.

While western political systems have pragmatically and incompletely used various aspects of capitalism, no nation has ever experienced laissez-faire capitalism.

But most writers and commentators put dishonest altruistic-platonistic connotations on the meaning of capitalism: *A system of exploitation of the weak by the strong — devoid of love and good will. A system in which unwanted goods and services are pushed onto consumers through clever, deceptive advertising for the sole purpose of profits and greed. Capitalism dominates most Western governments. Capitalism, big business, and fascism are synonymous.*

51

Book 2
Neo-Tech Decoded

The reason professional mystics and neocheaters display aggressive hostility towards capitalism is because of its anti-mystical, competitive nature — its nature of requiring integrated honesty and competitive efforts for success. Mystics and neocheaters could not survive in an honest, fully competitive, capitalistic society. They could no longer use their deceptive, altruistic manipulations to plunder the producer. Fearing survival through honesty and competitiveness, they are compelled to hate and attack capitalism.

**Later that month, at the Du Pont Hotel in Wilmington, Delaware, my father stood up and made the following statement during the Du Pont Annual Stockholders meeting:**

**"Today, within the Du Pont company exists the personnel, facilities, and capital to embark on a long-range venture designed to lift our company to new highs in earnings, return on investment, and stock prices. To accomplish that goal, its management must adopt a new standard — a standard called capitalism. Why? Because honest, growing, long-range profits can evolve only from the standards of competitive capitalism.**

**"Capitalism, the philosophical child of Aristotle, found birth in the United States and ultimate expression in the Du Pont Company. Here within this building, our company, Du Pont, represents the apex of intelligence and civilization. ...Du Pont is a triumphant testimonial to man's mind, potency, and value.**

**"One man...one individual stands at the base of this magnificent, commercial achievement. In 1802, Mr. Eleuthère Irénée du Pont began a capitalistic venture. With earned profit as his motive...with unflagging effort and his own mind as his tools, that man chose to function as man should — as a producer of values. The results? Look. Look around this room. Step outside and look. Look across this city...this state...across our nation. Look around the globe. One cannot imagine a more eloquent testimonial to the potency of man than E. I. du Pont de Nemours & Company. Man and capitalism together are the essence of values and wealth...of**

civilization and mastery over nature...of man's well-being and happiness. Capitalism is the standard for man on earth.

"Yet today, Du Pont, along with many other major companies, is increasingly operating on a different standard...a standard directed toward a mystical 'higher cause'. That standard is altruism...a destructive morality diametrically opposed to productive capitalism. As capitalism creates ever-expanding values for man, altruism consumes or destroys values in the name of an imaginary 'higher cause', such as society or the national will. Within capitalism there is no higher cause than man, the individual. Within Du Pont, no higher cause exists than serving the stockholders by increasing their long-range common-stock values. How is that accomplished? By increasingly delivering competitive values to others and society.

"This idea...this message, must not be a call into silence. For, the owners, the stockholders, must have productive individuals on capitalistic premises once again lead their company. Today, a few such value producers still exist within Du Pont. Those precious few are quietly carrying thousands, tens of thousands, of employees on their shoulders. The owners, the stockholders, must see to it that those precious individuals be the ones who manage their company. Du Pont will then rise as a mighty phoenix...as the harbinger of capitalism, prosperity, and happiness."

\* \* \* \*

My father followed up his speech a few days later with the distribution of his open letter. His open letter, by the way, was written back in the 1970s when he had his phenomenon with the mountain called Zon. The 1970s was the era of the White-Collar Hoax (i.e., lazy management parasitically draining big companies). The 1980s saw the shaking up and cleaning out of the white-collar hoax through the heroic dynamics of business takeovers, many orchestrated by the brilliant financier Michael Milken. Of course, the powerful Establishment found a way to end that healthy phenomenon and dishonestly incarcerate Milken. But the white-collar hoax still had a hard time returning to

53

management in full force because of the rise of global competition in the 1990s. To survive, many businesses had to kick out and keep out the nonproducers, especially in the make-or-break computer industry.

Now, if management of all businesses in a particular industry, such as today's computer industry, *were* functioning through the mystic-free standards of capitalism, then each company's success becomes even more challenging, much more competitive, and demands wide-reaching Neothink. In the computer industry, for instance, merely looking for Neo-Tech management is not enough for a good investment guide, for most such managements *are* Neo-Tech. In staid industries plagued by the white-collar hoax, Neo-Tech management alone becomes an accurate investment guide, for most such managements are mystical thus uncompetitive.

Interestingly, the more that Neo-Tech management becomes an ineffective investment guide (i.e., the more competitive and Neo-Tech a particular industry becomes), the more wealth that industry brings you. Eventually as all industries go Neo-Tech, when Neo-Tech management becomes obsolete as an investment guide, you will not really need to invest for security, for when all managements are Neo-Tech management under the new code after 2001, you will already live like a multi-millionaire as described in Neo-Tech Publishing Company's *God-Man: Our Final Evolution.*

## Ancient Secret Two
# POWER
## Neothink Is Told

My father woke up with power pumping through his veins. He would distribute his document to many people at Du Pont by the week's end. Better yet, "I will become a millionaire investing money," he said in the dark room while tying his running shoes. "What's next? Love and sex? Mind and intelligence? I sure would like to have better relationships. I sure would like to be smarter. What will I ask this morning?"

When he reached the mountain, before 5:00am, he felt a little embarrassed to ask a mountain about sex. So, he went to Plan B and asked, "Now I have a good idea on how to make more money. But I sure would like to be a lot smarter still and a lot more savvy to help me at it. Are we born the way we are, or can I get smarter and more powerful quickly with some form of new Neo-Tech technique?" The wind blew; the voice of Zon rode on the wind:

I know many things from ancient times to modern times. A person could make an excellent bet by wagering a hundred ounces of gold bullion that Princeton University Professor and renown scientist Dr. Julian Jaynes' book *The Origin of Consciousness in the Breakdown of the Bicameral Mind* will someday rank among the five most important books written during the second millennium. Jaynes' book signals the end of a 10,000-year reign of authoritarian institutions. His book also marks the beginning of a new era of individual consciousness during which people will increasingly act on the authority of their own brains. That movement toward self-responsibility will increasingly weaken the influences of external or mystical "authorities" such as government and religion.

The discovery of the bicameral mind solves the missing-link problem that has defied all previous theories of human evolution. But more important, that discovery opens the door today to an entirely new and much more powerful way of using the mind

55

called Neothink, with which all human life can evolve into abiding prosperity and happiness. ...Now, I want you to go home and spend today writing again. I know you have been reading Dr. Jaynes' book, and I want you to write a review of his book. My spirit will be in you as you write today, just as it was yesterday.

**Very enthused by his previous day's writings, my father couldn't wait to get started. He turned and ran home at sub-seven-minute miles. With his heart pounding, half from running and half from suspense, he started his day's work. And what a day's writing it turned out to be, as follows:**

Dr. Jaynes discovered that until 3000 years ago essentially all human beings were void of consciousness. Man along with all other primates functioned by mimicked or learned reactions. But, because of his much larger, more complex brain, man was able to develop a coherent language beginning about 8000 B.C. He was then guided by audio hallucinations. Those hallucinations evolved in the right hemisphere of the brain and were transmitted as "heard" in the left hemisphere of the brain (the bicameral or two-chamber mind). ...In effect, human beings were super-intelligent but automatically reacting animals who could communicate by talking. That communication enabled human beings to cooperate closely to build societies, even thriving civilizations.

Still, like all other animals, man functioned almost entirely by an automatic guidance system that was void of consciousness — until about 1000 B.C. when he was forced to invent consciousness to survive in the collapsing bicameral civilizations. And today, man's survival still depends on his choice of beneficially following his own consciousness or destructively following the voices of external "authorities".

The major components of Jaynes's discovery are:

• All civilizations before 1000 B.C. — such as Assyria, Babylonia, Mesopotamia, pharaonic Egypt — were built, inhabited, and ruled by unconscious people.

• Ancient writings such as the *Iliad* and the early books of the Old Testament were composed by unconscious minds that

56

automatically recorded and objectively reported both real and imagined events. The transition to subjective and introspective writings of the conscious mind occurred in later works such as the *Odyssey* and the newer books of the Old Testament.

• Ancient people learned to speak, read, write, as well as carry out daily life, work, and the professions all while remaining unconscious throughout their lives. Being unconscious, they never experienced guilt, never practiced deceit, and were not responsible for their actions. They, like any other animal, had no concept of guilt, deception, evil, justice, philosophy, history, or the future. They could not introspect and had no internal idea of themselves. They had no subjective sense of time or space and had no memories as we know them. They were unconscious and innocent. They were guided by "voices" or strong impressions in their bicameral minds — unconscious minds structured for nature's automatic survival.

• The development of human consciousness began about 3000 years ago when the automatic bicameral mind began breaking down under the mounting stresses of its inadequacy to find workable solutions in increasingly complex societies. The hallucinated voices became more and more confused, contradictory, and destructive.

• Man was forced to invent and develop consciousness in order to survive as his hallucinating voices no longer provided adequate guidance for survival.

• Today, after 3000 years, most people retain remnants of the bicameral guidance system in the form of mysticism and the desire for external authority.

• Except for schizophrenics, people today no longer hallucinate the voices that guided bicameral man. Yet, most people are at least partly influenced and are sometimes driven by the remnants of the bicameral man as they seek, to varying degrees, automatic guidance from "voices" of others or mystical external "authorities".

• All religions are rooted in the unconscious bicameral mind that is obedient to the "voices" of external "authorities" — obedient to the "voice" of God, gods, rulers, and leaders.

• The discovery that consciousness was never a part of nature's

57

evolutionary scheme (but was invented by man) eliminates the missing-link puzzle in human evolution.

• Essentially all religious and most political ideas survive through those vestiges of the obsolete bicameral mind. The bicameral mind seeks omniscient truth and automatic guidance from external "authorities" such as political or spiritual leaders — or other "authoritarian" sources such as manifested in idols, astrologists, gurus — as well as most lawyers, most psychiatrists and psychologists, certain professors, some doctors, most journalists and TV anchormen.

The idea of civilizations consisting entirely of unconscious, automatic-reacting people and the idea of man bypassing nature to invent his own consciousness initially seems incredible. But as Jaynes documents his evidence in a reasoned and detached manner, the existence of two minds in all human beings becomes increasingly evident: (1) the obsolete, unconscious (bicameral) mind that seeks guidance from external "authorities" for important thoughts and decisions, especially under stressed or difficult conditions; and (2) the newly invented conscious mind that bypasses external "authorities" and provides thoughts and guidance generated from one's own mind. ...Understanding Jaynes's discoveries unlocks the 10,000 year-old secret of controlling the actions of people through their bicameral minds.

What evidence does Jaynes present to support his discoveries? After defining consciousness, he systematically presents his evidence to prove that man was unconscious until 3000 years ago when the bicameral civilizations collapsed and individuals began inventing consciousness in order to survive. Jaynes's proof begins with the definition of consciousness:

Julian Jaynes defines both what consciousness is and what it is not. After speculating on its location, he demonstrates that consciousness itself has no physical location, but rather is a particular organization of the mind and a specific way of using the brain. Jaynes then demonstrates that consciousness is only a small part of mental activity and is not necessary for concept formation, learning, thinking, or even reasoning. He illustrates how all those mental functions can be performed automatically and unconsciously. Furthermore, consciousness does not contribute to and often hinders the execution of learned skills such as speaking, listening, writing, reading — as well as skills involving music, art, and athletics. Thus, if major human actions and skills can function automatically and without consciousness, those same actions and skills can be controlled or driven by external influences, "authorities", or "voices" emanating under conditions described later in this review. ...But first an understanding of consciousness is important:

Consciousness requires metaphors (i.e., referring to one thing in order to better understand or describe another thing — such as the head of an army, table, page, household, nail). Consciousness also requires analog models, (i.e., thinking of a map of California, for example, in order to visualize the entire, physical state of California). Thinking in metaphors and analog models creates the mind space and mental flexibility needed to bypass those automatic, bicameral processes.

The *bicameral thinking* process functions only in concrete terms and narrow, here-and-now specifics. But the *conscious thinking* process generates an infinite array of subjective perceptions that permit ever broader understanding and better decisions.

Metaphors of "me" and analog models of "I" allow consciousness to function through introspection and self-visualization. In turn, consciousness expands by creating more and more metaphors and analog models. That expanding consciousness allows a person to "see" and understand the relationship between himself and the world with increasing accuracy and clarity.

Consciousness is a conceptual, metaphor-generated analog world that parallels the actual world. Man, therefore, could not invent consciousness until he developed a language sophisticated enough to produce metaphors and analog models.

The genus Homo began about two million years ago. Rudimentary oral languages developed from 70,000 B.C. to about 8000 B.C. Written languages began about 3000 B.C. and gradually developed into syntactical structures capable of generating metaphors and analog models. Only at that point could man invent and experience consciousness.

Jaynes shows that man's early writings (hieroglyphics, hiertatic, and cuneiform) reflect a mentality totally different from

59

our own. They reflect a nonmetaphoric, unconscious mentality. Jaynes also shows that the *Iliad*, which evolved as a sung poem about 1000 B.C., contains little if any conscious thought. The characters in the Iliad (e.g., Achilles, Agamemnon, Hector, Helen) act unconsciously in initiating all their major actions and decisions through "voices", and all speak in hexameter rhythms (as often do modern-day schizophrenics when hallucinating). Hexameter rhythms are characteristic of the rhythmically automatic functionings of the right-hemisphere brain. Moreover, the *Iliad* is entirely about action...about the acts and consequences of Achilles. The *Iliad* never mentions subjective thoughts or the contents of anyone's mind. The language is unconscious — an objective reporting of facts that are concrete bound and void of introspection and abstract thought.

With a conscious mind, man can introspect; he can debate with himself; he can become his own god, voice, and decision maker. But before the invention of consciousness, the mind functioned bicamerally: the right hemisphere (the poetic, god-brain) hallucinated audio instructions to the left hemisphere (the analytical, man-brain), especially in unusual or stressful situations. Essentially, man's brain today is physically identical to the ancient bicameral brain; but with his invention of consciousness, he can now choose to integrate the functions of the left and right hemispheres.

Beginning about 9000 B.C. — as oral languages developed — routine or habitual tasks became increasingly standardized. The hallucinating voices for performing those basic tasks, therefore, became increasingly similar among groups of people. The collectivization of "voices" allowed more and more people to cooperate and function together through their bicameral minds. The leaders spoke to the "gods" and used the "voices" to lead the masses in cooperative unison. And that cooperation allowed nomadic hunting tribes to gradually organize into stationary, food-producing societies. The continuing development of oral language and the increasing collectivization of bicameral minds allowed towns and eventually cities to form and flourish.

The bicameral mind, however, became increasingly inadequate for guiding human actions as societies continued to grow in size and complexity. By about 1000 B.C., the bicameral mind had become so inadequate that man's social structures began collapsing. Under threat of extinction, man invented a new way to use his brain that allowed him to solve the much more complex problems needed to survive — he invented a new organization of the mind called consciousness.

Jaynes eliminated the missing link in the evolution of man by discovering that consciousness never existed in the evolutionary processes — consciousness was invented by man.

Dr. Jaynes shows through abundant archaeological, historical, and biological evidence that the towns, cities, and societies from 9000 B.C. to 1000 B.C. were established and developed by unconscious people. Those societies formed and grew through common hallucinating voices attributed to gods, rulers, and the dead — to external "authorities". Various external symbols that "spoke" (such as graves, idols, and statues) helped to reinforce and expand the authority of those common "voices". And those "voices" continued to expand their reach through increasingly visible and awe-inspiring symbols such as tombs, temples, colossuses, and pyramids.

But as those unconscious societies became more complex and increasingly intermingled through trade and wars, the "voices" became mixed and contradictory. With the "voices" becoming muddled, their effectiveness in guiding people diminished. Rituals and importunings became ever more intense and elaborate in attempts to evoke clearer "voices" and better guidance. The development of writing and the permanent recording of instructions and laws during the second millennium B.C. further weakened the authority and effectiveness of hallucinated voices. As the "voices" lost their effectiveness, they began falling silent. And without authoritarian "voices" to guide and control its people, those societies suddenly began collapsing with no external cause.

As the bicameral mind broke down and societies collapsed, individuals one by one began inventing consciousness to make decisions needed to survive in the mounting anarchy and chaos. On making conscious and volitional decisions, man for the first time became responsible for his actions. Also, for short-range advantages and easy power, conscious man began discovering and using deceit and treachery — behaviors not possible from

61

unconscious, bicameral minds. (Before inventing consciousness, man was as guiltless and amoral as any other animal since he had no volitional choice in following his automatic guidance system of hallucinated voices.)

As the "voices" fell silent, man began contriving religions and prayers in his attempts to communicate with the departed gods. Jaynes shows how man developed the concept of worship, heaven, angels, demons, exorcism, sacrifice, divination, omens, sortilege, augury in his attempts to evoke guidance from the gods — from external "authorities".

All such quests for external "authority" hark back to the breakdown of the hallucinating bicameral mind — to the silencing and celestialization of the once "vocal" and earthly gods.

Much direct evidence for the breakdown of the bicameral mind and the development of consciousness comes from writings scribed between 1300 B.C. and 300 B.C. Those writings gradually shift from unconscious, objective reports to conscious, subjective expressions that reflect introspection. The jump from the unconscious writing of the *Iliad* to the conscious writing of the *Odyssey* (composed perhaps a century later) is dramatically obvious. That radical difference between the *Iliad* and the *Odyssey* is, incidentally, further evidence that more than one poet composed the Homeric epics.

The transition from the unconscious *Iliad* to the conscious *Odyssey* marks man's break with his 8000-year-old hallucinatory guidance system. By the sixth century B.C., written languages began reflecting conscious ideas of morality and justice similar to those reflected today.

The Old Testament of the Bible also illustrates the transition from the unconscious writing of its earlier books (such as Amos, circa 750 B.C.) to the fully conscious writing of its later books (such as Ecclesiastes, circa 350 B.C.). Amid that transition, the book of Samuel records the first known suicide — an act that requires consciousness. And the book of Deuteronomy illustrates the conflict between the bicameral mind and the conscious mind.

Likewise, the transition to consciousness is observed in other parts of the world: Chinese literature moved from bicameral unconsciousness to subjective consciousness about 500 B.C. with the writings of Confucius. And in India, literature shifted to subjective consciousness around 400 B.C. with the Upanishadic writings.

American Indians, however, never developed the sophisticated, metaphorical languages needed to develop full consciousness. As a result, their mentalities were probably bicameral when they first encountered the European explorers. For example, with little or no conscious resistance, the Incas allowed the Spanish "white gods" to dominate, plunder, and slaughter them.

Dr. Jaynes identifies many vestiges of the bicameral mentality that exist today. The most obvious vestige is religion and its symbols. Ironically, early Christianity with its teachings of Jesus was an attempt to shift religion from the outmoded bicameral and celestial mind of Moses to the newly conscious and earthly mind of man. Christianity then discovered a devastatingly effective tool for authoritarian control — guilt. Indeed, guilt not only worked on conscious minds, but required conscious minds to be effective.

Despite religion, conscious minds caused the gradual shifts from governments of gods to governments of men and from divine laws to secular laws. Still, the vestiges of the bicameral mind combined with man's longing for guidance produced churches, prophets, oracles, sibyls, diviners, cults, mediums, astrologers, saints, idols, demons, tarot cards, seances, Ouija boards, glossolalia, fuhrers, ayatollahs, popes, peyote, Jonestown, born-agains.

Jaynes shows how such external "authorities" exist only through the remnants of the bicameral mind. Moreover, he reveals a four-step paradigm that can reshuffle susceptible minds back into hallucinating, bicameral mentalities. The ancient Greeks used a similar paradigm to reorganize or reprogram the minds of uneducated peasant girls into totally bicameral mentalities so they could become oracles and give advice through hallucinated voices — voices that would rule the world (e.g., the oracle at Delphi). ...Today, people who deteriorate into schizophrenic psychoses follow similar paradigms.

A common thread united most oracles, sibyls, prophets, and demon-possessed people: Almost all were illiterate, all believed in spirits, and all could readily retrieve the bicameral mind. Today, however, retrieval of the bicameral mind is schizophrenic

63

insanity. Also, today, as throughout history, a symptomatic cure for "demon-possessed" people involves exorcising rituals that let a more powerful "authority" or god replace the "authority" of the demon. The New Testament, for example, shows that Jesus and his disciples became effective exorcists by substituting one "authority" (their god) for another "authority" (another god or demon).

As the voices of the oracles became confused and nonsensical, their popularity waned. In their places, idolatry revived and then flourished. But as Christianity became a popular source of external "authority", Christian zealots began physically destroying all competing idols. They then built their own idols and symbols to reinforce the external "authority" of Christianity.

Among today's vestiges of the bicameral mentality is the born-again movement that seeks external guidance. Such vestiges dramatize man's resistance to use his own invention of consciousness to guide his life.

The chanting cadence of poetry and the rhythmic beat of music are also rooted in the bicameral mentality. In ancient writings, the hallucinated voices of the gods were always in poetic verse, usually in dactylic hexameter and sometimes in rhyme or alliteration — all characteristic of right-brain functionings. The oracles and prophets also spoke in verse. And today schizophrenics often speak in verse when they hallucinate.

Poetry and chants can have authoritarian or commanding beats and rhythms that can effectively block consciousness. Poetry is the language of the gods — it is the language of the artistic, right-hemispheric brain. Plato recognized poetry as a divine madness.

Most poetry and songs have an abruptly changing or a discontinuous pitch. Normal speech, on the other hand, has a smoothly changing pitch. Jaynes demonstrates that reciting poetry, singing, and playing music are right-brain functions, while speaking is a left-brain function. That is why people with speech impediments can often sing, chant, or recite poetry with flawless clarity. Conversely, almost anyone trying to sing a conversation will find his words quickly deteriorating into a mass of inarticulate cliches.

Likewise, listening to music and poetry is a right-brain

function. And music, poetry, or chants that project authority with loud or rhythmic beats can suppress left-brain functions to temporarily relieve anxiety or a painfully troubled consciousness.

Jaynes goes on to show phenomena such as hypnosis, acupuncture, and déjà vu also function through vestiges of the bicameral mind. And he demonstrates how hypnosis steadily narrows the sense of self, time, space, and introspection as consciousness shrinks and the mind reverts to a bicameral type organization. Analogously, bicameral and schizophrenic minds have little or no sense of self, time, space or introspection. The hypnotized mind is urged to obey the voice of the hypnotist; the bicameral mind is compelled to obey the "voices" of "authority" or gods. By sensing oneself functioning in the narrow-scope, unaware state of hypnosis, gives one an idea of functioning in the narrow-scope, unaware state of bicameral man.

Jaynes also identifies how modern quests for external "authority" are linked to the bicameral mind. Many such quests use science to seek authority in the laws of nature. In fact, today, science is surpassing the waning institutional religions as a major source of external "authority". And rising from the vestiges of the bicameral mind are an array of scientisms (pseudoscientific doctrines, faiths, and cults) that select various natural or scientific facts to subvert into apocryphal, authoritarian doctrines. That subversion is accomplished by using facts out of context to fit promulgated beliefs. Such mystical scientisms include astrology, ESP, Scientology, Christian Science and other "science" churches, I Ching, behaviorism, sensitivity training, mind control, meditation, hypnotism, cryonics, as well as various nutritional, health, and medical fads.

Today the major worldwide sources of external "authority" are the philosophical doctrines of religion (plus the other forms of mysticism and "metaphysics") combined with political doctrines such as Fascism, Marxism, and Maoism. All such doctrines demand the surrender of the individual's ego (sense of self or "I") to a collective, obedient faith toward the "authority" of those doctrines. In return, those doctrines offer automatic answers and life-time guidance from which faithful followers can survive without the responsibility or effort of using their own consciousnesses. Thus, all political systems represent a regression

65

into mysticism — from conscious man back to bicameral man.

Despite their constant harm to everyone, most modern-day external "authorities" and master neocheaters thrive by using the following two-step Neocheating technique to repress consciousness and activate the bicameral mind in their victims.

1. First man is made to feel guilty. He is condemned for having lost his "innocence" by inventing consciousness. He is condemned for assuming the responsibility to use his own mind to guide his life. He is condemned for exchanging his automatic, bicameral life for a volitional, conscious life...condemned for exchanging his nature-given bicameral mind for a superior, man-invented conscious mind.

2. Then man is offered automatic solutions to problems and guidance through life into an "effortless" Garden of Eden or a utopian hereafter if he exchanges his own invented consciousness for faith in external "authority" — bicameral faith in some leader, doctrine, or god. He is offered the "reward" of escaping the self-responsibility to make one's own decisions and to guide one's own life. But for that "reward", he must renounce his own mind to follow someone else's mind or wishes disguised as the "truth" promulgated by some external "authority" or higher power.

But in reality, no valid external "authority" or higher power can exist or ever has existed. Valid authority evolves only from one's own independent, conscious mode of thinking. When that fact is fully realized, man will emerge completely from his bicameral past and move into a future that accepts individual consciousness as the only authority. ...Man will then fully evolve into a prosperous, happy individual who has assumed full responsibility for his own thinking and life.

**My father put down his pen and sat in stunned silence. He grasped the scientific significance of what he had just written. He gathered himself and stood up to go eat something. But his mind never left the page. The next morning, my father said to Zon, "Despite the great advantages in using the man-invented mode of thinking and all the power that goes with it, most of us depend to various degrees on our automatic bicameral mentality and external 'authorities' to make our decisions for us. We actually search for 'sure-**

thing' guidance from 'higher authorities', rather than using our own consciousness for making decisions and determining our actions. Zon, we are throwing our power out the window! In our search for automatic guidance, we seek automatic answers from religion, politics, idols, leaders, gurus, cults, astrology, fads, drugs, feelings, even shrinks. No wonder altruism controls us and a ruling class rules over us. Wake up! Our bicameral minds seek outside sources that will tell us how to think and act. No wonder neocheaters exploit the automatic bicameral minds in the masses by setting themselves up as 'authorities' for influencing or controlling that bicameral mentality seeking external guidance." Zon answered my father:

Still, the resistance to self-responsibility is formidable. The bicameral mentality grips those seeking mysticism or other "authorities" for guidance. Those who accept external "authority" allow government officials, religious leaders, faith, homilies, cliches, one-liners, slogans, the familiar, habits, and feelings to guide their actions. Throughout history, billions of people unnecessarily submit through their bicameral tendencies to the illusionary, external "authorities" of government and religion. And that submission is always done at a net loss to everyone's well being and happiness.

To some, the implications of Neo-Tech will be frightening, even terrifying. To others, the implications will be electrifying and liberating. ...The implications of Neo-Tech are that each individual is solely responsible for his or her own life — responsible for making the effort required to learn honesty and guide one's own life through one's own consciousness. No automatic, effortless route to knowledge or guidance exists.

No valid external "authority" exists that one can automatically live by. To live effectively, an individual must let only the authority of his own consciousness guide his activities. All consistently competent people have learned to act on reality — not on their feelings or someone else's feelings or doctrines. An individual must accept the responsibility to guide his own life. He must constantly exert the effort needed to identify reality through his own consciousness in order to live competently and

67

happily.

People knowledgeable about Neo-Tech have the tools to control all others who act on their bicameral tendencies. ...Equally important, people knowledgeable about Neo-Tech have the tools to control their own lives and destinies, free from crippling mysticism and harmful neocheating.

Now you can identify the bicameral elements of any statement or action by anyone or any group, for example, church, government, media, politician, priest, businessman, doctor, friend, parent, spouse, self. Armed with Neo-Tech, you can free yourself from the control or influence of mysticism and external "authority". Sometime after 2001, Neo-Tech and Neothink will have eliminated all vestiges of the bicameral mentality — all vestiges of mysticism and external "authority".

Without the bicameral mentality, all mysticism and external "authority" will wither and vanish, for they have no validity except that which is granted to them by the bicameral mentalities. With political and religious influences disappearing, the mechanisms for "authorities" to harm individuals and wage wars will also disappear. Thus, if civilization is prospering long after 2001, Jaynes's discovery along with the discoveries of Neo-Tech and Neothink will have contributed to that prosperity by ending the symbiotic, mystical relationships of bicameral mentalities with authoritarian societies, which now hold nuclear weapons. Such mystical relationships would sooner or later cause the annihilation of any civilization.

If our civilization is flourishing long after 2001, rational human consciousness will have eliminated mysticism and external "authority" through fully integrated honesty, Neo-Tech. And without external "authority", governments and their wars will be impossible. Best of all, without external "authority" or mysticism, no one will be forcibly controlled, impeded, or drained by others. There will be no ruling class. Then, the people will discover their true power.

**"I can feel a new power rising in me — a power that will reject all others trying to make decisions for me. I feel good!" ...After a long pause, my father asked his mountain, "What exactly is Neo-Tech and Neothink?"**

68

## Power: Neothink Is Told

Neothink is a new way of using the mind. It is the mind of tomorrow. Neothink comes from Neo-Tech. Neo-Tech removes bicameral tendencies through exerting hard-thought honesty to understand reality. Neo-Tech dissolves and removes illusionary, mind-created "realities" caused by the bicameral mentality. Indeed, as Neo-Tech removes more and more illusions (caused by our bicameral tendencies vulnerably following neocheaters), the conscious mind integrates more and more widely, bringing it escalating power not known to the ordinary mind today. As the mind becomes free of bicameral tendencies — free of mysticism, which is the only disease of the mind caused by bicameral tendencies in today's conscious mind — the mind goes into a whole new potential of unlimited wide integrations or unlimited power. That brand-new way of using the mind, activating its limitless capacity, is called Neothink. Through that process of using Neo-Tech to release Neothink, the limitless capacity of the human mind comes to ordinary people. Ordinary people can then make explosive advancements of human knowledge, regularly. As a result, ordinary people will transform into wealthy geniuses.

**"And I will be among the first into Neothink and its rewards!" my father shouted, very elated. Then he stopped and his expression changed. "How do I reconcile you? Am I not in a bicameral mode, looking for my answers from you as my external authority?**

I am the voice of fully integrated honesty. You will learn, in due time, that I am *not* a higher authority. The individual is the highest authority, and Zon has always existed within every individual but has never been able to rise. Before now, planet Earth never saw the rise of Zon. After 2001, under the new code, my spirit will rise within everyone; you and your loved ones will discover unity with Zon. My answers to you ultimately come from within you. But, you must capture these answers in writing and disseminate fifty million copies throughout the world to give me lasting life on Earth and yourself eternal life.

**"Is this in conflict with God?" my father asked.**

Zon and God are in purest harmony. You will know this fact within a month. ...The wind stopped, but my father sat still and stared. He wanted to know more. The mountain knew that my father was the one to someday tell the world Zon's deepest secret: *Zon is man; Zon is God.* Indeed, through my father, the world would someday learn that Zon is the point of unity of man and God, the God-Man, the moment they join and become one.

## Ancient Secret Three

# LOVE
## Psychuous Sex Is Told

That night at home, my dad knew he was dealing with some kind of powerful phenomenon. He knew he must think out and ask the most important questions about human life while the phenomenon lasted. So, tomorrow he would not be bashful. He would go ahead and ask about sex and love. He thought, "I want to be the best lover I can — the best in the world!"

The next morning he ran to his spot, sat down on the big flat rock, and asked about sex. The wind blew and carried a gentle voice...but it was a woman's soft voice that answered:

Do not be afraid. I will tell you all about sex and love. So sit peacefully, my child, and hear my many stories.

Three basic views of sex and love exist: 1. The religious-procreative view. 2. The recreational-fun-noncommitted "Playboy" view. 3. The Neo-Tech view.

The guilt generated by the religious view of sex makes romantic love impossible. An even more devastating loss evolves from performance anxieties caused by the "Playboy" view coupled with the demands to be a sexy person by someone else's standards.

The diminished self-esteem caused by the fun-only "Playboy" view creates anxiety and boredom to steadily diminish sexual pleasures and capacities. That process, if allowed to continue, ends in impotence or frigidity. Much of the impotence in men today is linked to self-esteem problems. Many insecure men who depend on a macho act for pseudo self-esteem collapse into impotence when confronted with healthy, confident, sexually liberated women who see through their act as laughable, immature, childish.

Only the third view, the Neo-Tech view, equates with human nature.

Sensuous relates to the five physical senses — touch, sight,

71

hearing, smell, and taste. Sensuous is associated with the pleasurable gratification of one or more of those physical senses. Neo-Tech expands the meaning of sensuous to capture the essence of pleasure by including and integrating the most potent dimension: the pleasurable gratification of the human mind. That gratification includes the harmonious agreement of your love life with your psychological well-being. ...The word for that expanded meaning of sensuous is *psychuous*.

Your conscious mind is the ultimate organ for experiencing pleasures, including sexual pleasures. Your mind integrates all pleasures with all that you are, do, and *think*. Your mind is the organism that offers unlimited pleasure and happiness. Add the exciting pleasure of your body, and you discover a spectacular experience called Psychuous Sex.

In Neo-Tech, the meaning of sex includes intercourse as a series of highlights along a vast range of sexually rooted experiences and emotions. Indeed, the meaning of sex in Neo-Tech encompasses all sexual influences — often hidden but powerful — that weave through your life.

Psychuous sex is an intense mind-body experience. Yet, psychuous sex does not always produce intense *physical* reactions. That would be too exhausting, too demanding, and eventually boring. Psychuous-sex intensity is measured by emotional depth and expression...not by overt physical reactions.

Sensuous behavior can increase psychuous pleasures. But since psychuous pleasures involve the whole person in both sexual and nonsexual experiences, those pleasures are *not* dependent on sensuous behavior. You can and should, however, assertively increase your sexual attractiveness. But do not reduce your natural sex appeal by faking sensuousness.

Especially important: dump ideas of sacrifice and altruism. That dumping of irrationality allows you to guiltlessly experience psychuous pleasures. Indeed, your capacity for psychuous sex, the most intense human pleasure, always arises from the same base — from dealing honestly with reality. ...Now, let us look more closely at how to launch the ultimate mind-body experience.

**My father stood up as if to speak. But he just stood there like a shy boy, dwarfed by the mountain and embarrassed**

72

**to speak.  The gentle female voice continued.**

Most of your pleasures and happiness are experienced through emotions.  *And the final moral purpose of all human life is rational happiness.*  Moreover, negative emotions are reliable warning signals that you are acting irrationally or contrary to your nature, well-being, and happiness.

Emotions deliver your ultimate rewards and penalties.  Such emotions depend on the life you choose to create and live.  Your emotional content will be either happy or unhappy, depending on the extent which you reject or accept irrationality, which I often call *mysticism*.  Mysticism steadily destroys the happy emotional self, destroys the pleasurable gratification of the mind, and destroys psychuous sex.  Rejecting mysticism means accepting sole responsibility for understanding and dealing honestly with reality.

**"Excuse me," my father said.  "I don't mean to interrupt. In fact, I am fascinated by this new Psychuous Sex breakthrough.  But, before you go on, I have to stop you and ask you to explain what you mean when you say to reject mysticism."**

*Mysticism* is defined as any attempt to use the mind to create reality rather than to identify and integrate reality.  Mysticism is a disease — an epistemological disease that progressively undermines one's capacity to think, to identify reality, to live competently.  Mysticism is also a collective disease that affects everyone who looks toward others, or the group, or the leaders for solutions to his or her own problems and responsibilities.  The symptom of mysticism is jumbled or nonintegrated thinking — leading to mind-created "realities".  The mind is a reality integrating organ, not a reality creating device.

Mysticism is a disease of the mind that blocks integrated thinking and brings stupidities through mind-created "realities". But mysticism is also the tool that neocheaters use to justify or rationalize the use of force, fraud, or dishonesty to usurp values from the producers.  For example, mind-created "realities" are used to create false standards and guilt designed to beguile you

73

into surrendering your earned values, power, and happiness.

Mysticism is the only disease of the conscious mind. But as with drugs and alcohol, mysticism is seductively comfortable, like a warm, old friend — until the destructive consequences and hangovers manifest themselves.

Mysticism is based on a false and destructive idea: the primacy of emotions over reality. Mysticism is the opposite of Neo-Tech. The mind-created "realities" of mysticism eventually render all life unto death. ...You must resist, must fight mysticism both from within and from without. Those who surrender — quit resisting, quit fighting — allow mysticism to take over their lives. When that happens, they become a part of the unhappy, dishonest world.

**"OK, I understand now. Neo-Tech means *integrating* reality — as fully and as honestly as you are able. Mysticism, by contrast, means NOT integrating reality, but rather *creating* 'reality' in your mind, often through emotional whims. Neo-Tech and mysticism are opposites." My father now was more than satisfied, in fact, he had in that instance just seen deeper into human life than in his entire four decades. My father knew he had learned something powerful and profound by understanding mysticism, its mind-created "realities", and its potential to control others through, for instance, the media that often creates "realities" far different than reality. But before asking more about mysticism and its influence, he decided to stay on the topic of love today. As if the mountain could read his mind, just as my father started to ask another question about psychuous sex, the mountain continued, on the subject:**

You must reject mysticism to effectively perceive and integrate reality — to effectively solve problems of growth and develop the competence needed to earn prosperity, power, and love. That, in turn, delivers the self-esteem and emotional content needed to experience abiding well-being, psychuous pleasures, and romantic love. ...You control your wide-range emotions of being fundamentally happy or unhappy through your constant, volitional choice to be honest or dishonest — to act through honest thinking or through mystical thinking.

Emotions are a real part of you and, therefore, are a part of reality. To know and deal with undistorted reality, you must first know yourself, which includes knowing your own emotions. You must learn to be aware of feelings in order to prevent destructive emotional reactions. You must also know your own emotions in order to effectively share them in a love relationship. For, the pleasure and happiness of a romantic-love relationship is measured by emotional closeness.

**"Now I'm a little confused," my father responded. "Emotions are good and the way to feel happiness, romantic love, and psychuous pleasures. Yet, I thought emotions can also sometimes be bad. In fact, I thought emotions sometimes caused negative mystical reactions."**

Emotions are not subject to condemnation, guilt, or right or wrong judgments...only *actions* are right or wrong. Next to the mystical concept of original sin, perhaps the most pervasively damaging, unjust concept projected by the Christian ethic is the moral judgment of emotions. Especially malevolent and harmful are the condemnations of emotions such as found in the Sermon on the Mount: "But I say unto you, that whosoever looketh on a woman to lust after her, hath committed adultery with her already in his heart." By condemning human emotions, Christian neocheaters discovered an effective tool to condemn everyone...to make everyone guilty, keeping them more controllable for usurping power and values. Since everyone by nature possesses a full range of automatic feelings or emotions that cannot be directly controlled, shut off or stopped, nearly everyone is victimized by Christian-style "sin" and "guilt".

While you innocently experience negative, irrational emotions, you never have to act on such emotions. And since only human *actions* are subject to choice, only human *actions*, not emotions, are subject to moral judgment.

Personal *emotions* possess an untouchable ownership and privacy. Emotions are subject neither to criticism nor judgment. Only *actions* can be criticized or judged as right or wrong. Feelings and emotions can have a rational or irrational basis, but

75

they are never "right" or "wrong". Emotions are spontaneous, automatic reactions that are not in the immediate or direct control of a person. No one ever needs to feel guilty about any emotion. Again, a person is responsible only for the actions he or she takes.

Many innocent people repress emotions because of false guilt. In doing so, they never can know themselves. To fully experience pleasure and happiness, you must develop an integrated awareness of your emotions along with a mystic-free, guiltless acceptance of those emotions. Then you must reject mystical guilt to fully experience your earned emotions of happiness, pleasure, love. Happiness, pleasure, and love can be experienced only through emotions. To the extent that you repress emotions is the extent that you deny earned pleasures and happiness. You must experience emotions in order to psychologically live. If you continually diminish self-awareness or repress emotions, you will steadily lessen your capacity to feel emotions, love, and happiness.

Fear of being hurt or rejected prevents the development of many romantic-love relationships. That fear keeps you defensive which, in turn, prevents emotional openness with your partner. And that openness is necessary for developing romantic love and psychuous pleasures.

The achievement of romantic love involves a willingness to take risks. Moreover, the fear of being hurt by being open is unfounded. To the contrary, you are always hurt by faking or concealing emotions from yourself or a loved one. Denial of feelings traps you into emotionally repressive situations that diminish the potential for love and happiness. Being emotionally honest and open is the safest, happiest way to live.

**"Being honest with myself and not concealing my feelings from myself, I must ask you this as a single, divorced man: enjoying multiple sexual affairs is OK, isn't it?" After about ten minutes, the breeze started again, carrying the sweet words of a woman:**

Psychuous sex is always linked to values...to an exchange of rational values between partners. A continuous exchange of

76

values that enhances personal worth and psychological visibility is the basis of psychuous pleasures and romantic-love. But, sex without serious values, i.e., casual sex, cannot deliver psychuous pleasures and is eventually self-destructive.

The difference between serious and casual sex is not always obvious on the surface. But the difference always appears at the base of every relationship. While the actual sexual activity of serious sex can and often does have interludes of lightness and fun, the meaning behind every act is serious and important. But sex on a nonserious, unimportant, or casual basis done only for "fun" is a diminishing experience that erodes self-esteem and sexual competence. On the other hand, a serious sexual affair will always produce growth and values so long as the relationship is based on mutual values, honesty, and respect. In a value-based sexual relationship, psychuous pleasures are linked to a mutual reflection of each partner's personal values and worth.

Unlike casual sexual relationships, serious relationships have no bounds or limits to personal values that can be exchanged. The value of a serious romantic relationship can grow so great that you would give, if necessary, all of your possessions, even your own life, to protect your romantic-love partner.

You almost never can benefit from a multi-partner relationship, not only because of the painful, emotional conflicts but because of the time and effort inherently required to develop a valuable, romantic-love relationship with just one partner. Furthermore, the amount of time required to develop valuable multi-partner relationships could deprive you of the time needed to fully develop crucial areas of life such as your rewarding career.

The biggest negative of multi-partner relationships evolves from the nature of psychuous sex: Romantic love works best when structured around long-term, monogamous relationships. Why? Because continuous efforts and experiences with an exclusive partner deliver the most intimacy, growth, and values. Thus, the most erotically exciting and sexually satisfying experiences by nature evolve from long-term, monogamous/psychuous relations.

Casual, nonintimate, or fun-only sex does not always start from a neurotic base. Casual sex may begin as an immature

77

Book 2
Neo-Tech Decoded

sexual view during adolescence. Or casual sex may begin as a notion to experiment with "new" sex in order to broaden one's sexual experiences or to diminish sexual inhibitions and taboos. Indeed, casual sex, swinging sex, orgy sex may accomplish those ends. But, the eventual cost of casual sex, fun-only, or exploitive sex to your self-esteem is high. You experience such sex only with grave consequences to your self-esteem, sexuality, and happiness. By contrast, you experience a limitless broadening of erotic sexual experiences with enhanced self-esteem through psychuous sex within a growing relationship.

Human beings are always capable of correcting errors. The harm caused by past, casual-sexual experiences can be reversed by restructuring sexual standards around the consistent, value-oriented foundation of psychuous sex.

A value-oriented, romantic relationship offers limitless pleasures ranging from joy and spontaneous fun to erotic thrills, adventure, psychuous pleasures, and profound happiness. Equally important, such romantic relationships can greatly enhance each partner's productivity, values, and prosperity.

Psychuous pleasures can always grow, even during crisis or turmoil. Psychuous sex lets you physically confirm the value of your life, especially during difficult or crisis periods. Psychuous sex allows you to be acutely aware of your worth, pleasures, and happiness. But psychuous pleasures go far beyond sexual intercourse. In fact, sexual intercourse itself plays only a small (but crucial) role in psychuous pleasure, which is integrated with all aspects of conscious life.

Romantic love and psychuous pleasures add so much to human happiness that to settle for something as unchallenging and limited as casual, fun-only sex is to treat yourself poorly indeed. Limiting the potential for pleasure to such a narrow, shallow range of experiences undermines your entire life.

**Trying hard to be honest, my father said, "Even though I have strong sexual feelings for several different women, to act on those feelings would most likely be irrational. You know, as busy as I am, I can see you're right. To have all those women would mean shallow one-night stands. Instead, I can get deeply involved with one, and blossom outward from**

**sensuous pleasures to full-scale psychuous pleasures...from moments of instant gratification to a lifetime of deep fulfillment. As a result, I'll discover the most mind-blowing sex of all. ...Are you telling me I should go ahead now and make a commitment to one love?"**

Not exactly. You see, a commitment to *honesty* with your romantic-love partner is essential for achieving psychuous pleasures. In an open relationship, each partner is free to follow those actions self-judged best for his or her own rational well-being. Each must also be equally free to make and correct his or her own errors. Both must strive to meet their individual needs for growth. Both must accept the fact that neither has any physical or psychological ownership over the other. With the freedom and self-responsibility to guide one's own life, each partner develops an ever-growing accumulation of strengths. Those new strengths allow each to continually feed fresh love and enriching values to the other.

With each partner feeding new strength and values into the relationship, each benefits from the other's unique experiences. With such constant values coming from free and independent sources, the excitement between partners can grow continuously, often by large leaps, toward increased psychuous pleasures and abiding happiness. With this never-ending, spiraling growth, each partner becomes increasingly valuable to the other. Thus, fewer and fewer circumstances could threaten or replace such a romantic-love relationship.

Like money in the bank, newly added values accumulate with interest. And with time, the strength of such value-built relationships becomes so great that no outside force, no matter how valuable or appealing, could compete. ...Such self-built continually added strengths and competitive values offer the only genuine security for any romantic-love relationship.

By contrast, sexual affairs hidden from one's love partner are deceptive and, therefore, dishonest and destructive. Moreover, such affairs are usually too restricted by their secrecy to deliver continuously growing values. ...Honesty and rationality are the foundations of psychuous pleasures and romantic love.

79

**"I follow you," my father said. At that same instance, my father could almost feel a maturing process occurring within himself.**

The first known sex manual was written about 2000 years ago by a Roman named Ovid. His manual stressed seduction techniques for *casual sex*. In addition, the manual aggressively promoted the Don Juan and "Playboy" fun views of sex while teaching various role-playing games and manipulative techniques for the seduction of women.

The Don Juan and "Playboy" approaches to sex use hypnosis, manipulations of sex partners, and pragmatic dishonesty of professing "sincerity", "seriousness", and "love" when strategically advantageous for conquest. But most modern-day Don Juans can only feign lust while actually being terrified of their own sexual inadequacies. In fact, most macho Don Juans have never experienced psychological orgasms and remain psychosexual virgins all their lives — they never develop a capacity for delivering or receiving psychuous pleasures. More simply, macho men are males who have never sexually matured or grown up.

**Then, there was a long pause. After awhile, my father thought his day here was over. But then the wind began to blow again, and the gentle female voice continued:**

No matter how irrational or immoral if enacted in reality, fantasies are never immoral, wrong, or harmful when experienced or expressed without external action. For, fantasies are never harmful as long as they remain in the non-action, fantasy stage.

Seductiveness in the traditional, casual-sex sense and sensuousness are two different qualities. Traditional seductiveness involves sly trickery to accomplish an end such as sexual seduction — often for neurotic macho-like purposes such as to bolster a weak self-esteem.

Sensuousness, on the other hand, involves openness and self-expression free of guilt. Sensuousness is a healthy trait, while seductiveness is generally an unhealthy trait. Sensuousness for enhancing personal appeal arises from rational effort that enhances self-esteem and long-range happiness. Seductiveness for manipulating sex partners arises from irrational laziness that undercuts self-esteem and long-range happiness.

But, seduction techniques for *serious sex* can be honest and beneficial. Those techniques are more accurately described as "sensuous projections" and differ from casual seduction techniques that depend on deceit. Sensuous projections are done through both verbal and body communication. The presentation of a person's body and words can be sexually attractive if projected with calculated thought. Those techniques are nonmanipulative and can be mastered through understanding the nature of psychuous sex. Men and women using the Neo-Tech/Psychuous concepts can quickly achieve effective sensuous-projection techniques. The techniques involve integrating clothes, cosmetics, hair with one's body, face, voice, expressions — all combined to project sexual attractiveness. Once acquired, those advantage-gaining techniques are available for life.

A basic right, indeed a self-duty, of every human being is to be sexually attractive. Natural attractiveness is a given that has no moral virtue. But self-made, sexual attractiveness is an admirable, moral virtue that requires continuous thought and effort. Keeping one's self sexually attractive throughout life is a highly rational act of self-responsibility that delivers increased power, prosperity, and romantic love. ...Contrary to the cancer seeds planted by mystics and neocheaters, self-made sexiness does not reflect any lack of values or promiscuity. But, to the contrary, self-made sexiness reflects a respect for values and self.

The primary attraction between two people moving toward rational, romantic-love relationships is their character traits, not their personality traits. Likewise, character development is the chief element in successful romantic-love relationships. And a romantic relationship based on psychuous sex usually develops into a *mutual* seduction process. During that process both partners project mounting sensuous, sexual attractiveness between them. Non-manipulative seductions are innocent projections of sexual attractiveness combined with trust, honesty, and care. That kind of seduction helps both partners plumb rich, personal depths with each other — physically and emotionally.

Be aware that, because of their greater ease in initially

81

attracting sexual partners, individuals with great natural, physical beauty must be cautious of the tempting traps inherent in easily obtainable sexual love. A few people, because of their stunning natural beauty, are not directly subjected to nature's vigorous sexual competition. To achieve love, sexual pleasures, and happiness, most people recognize early in life that they must become competitively attractive through high-effort development of character and competence. In adulthood, those who grew up accepting the challenge to self-develop can easily outcompete those naturally beautiful people who earlier in life never experienced those pressures to develop. As a result, some people with great natural beauty sadly grow old while remaining undeveloped, immature, incompetent, unable to love or be loved.

**"Should I still work on my looks — still workout, run, stay slim, and look good?" my father asked.**

Achieving and maintaining good physical fitness and appearance are necessary for developing psychuous pleasures and long-range happiness. On the other hand, physical appearances *not* within one's control are unimportant for achieving psychuous pleasures and happiness. The difference, for example, is between being sloppy and ugly. The natural, physically ugly person can choose to develop beauty through character development and sensuous efforts. He or she can then experience the full range of psychuous pleasures and happiness. But careless or sloppy people can never fully experience psychuous pleasures and happiness as long as they choose to remain careless and lazy about self and life. For by not caring about self and life, they obliterate their self-esteem and desirability, while cutting themselves off from love and happiness. ...How can anyone ultimately care about those who do not care about themselves?

Consider people who let themselves grow fat. Such people have chosen to travel on a death curve. Traveling that route, a person's unhappiness and probability of death increases with increasing fatness. In turn, that route devastates a person's self-esteem and happiness.

People who let themselves physically deteriorate or grow obese lose the capacity for psychuous pleasures from both physical and psychological capacities.

Nearly anyone at any age in any physical condition can achieve optimum physical fitness by gradually increasing physical stress with an aerobic-type program totaling less than two hours per week of running, swimming, bicycling, or brisk walking as described in Dr. Kenneth H. Cooper's book, *Aerobics*. Permanent, optimum body weight can be achieved through low-carbohydrate diet as described in Dr. Robert C. Atkins' book, *Dr. Atkins' Diet Revolution*. Both books taken together are major contributions to human health and well-being that deliver attractiveness, vigor, and happiness.

An individual has much more voluntary control over his or her physical and mental health than most people realize. Over the long range, a person has almost total control over his or her emotional and physical well-being. By choosing to consistently use the mind rationally in becoming an honest, productive human being, a person *can* control his or her own psychological and physical well-being. Every individual always has the choice to rationally solve problems or to default on that responsibility. Those who chronically default on that self-responsibility have no way to earn prosperity or psychuous pleasures.

Both mysticism, a psyche "drug", and hard drugs have both short-range and long-range harmful effects on health and happiness. Even in moderate amounts, mysticism and drugs distort reality. And all distortions of reality are harmful because the human organism depends on accurate perception of reality to be competent, competitive, and to make the non-mystical judgments necessary for prosperous, happy survival. The illusionary values of mysticism and drugs arise from their reality-distorting effects. Indeed drugs and mysticism can feel like old, comfortable, warm friends. But, in the long term, they deliver only harm, incompetence, and unhappiness. And their distortions can initially be so well rationalized that the mystic or the drug user can easily choose to remain unaware of the mounting damage until permanent loss of happiness and energy become inescapable.

Damage from mysticism and drugs can range from a quick overdose death or suicide, to an unhappy truncated life, to the more subtle psychological and physiological damages that occur even with moderate use of mysticism and drugs. For instance, marijuana disorients the electrical brain patterns to diminish one's quality of thinking and order of priorities. For instance, marijuana tends to convert demanding action and ambition into passive dreams and laziness. More serious, that movement from effort and ambition to passivity and dreams may be cumulative. Furthermore, the mystical-dream effects of marijuana destroy competence. Also, investigations by Masters and Johnson show that male marijuana users experience drops in testosterone of 40% and more. Reduced testosterone causes reduced sex drive, an atrophy of male sex organs, a softening of muscle tissue, and a wimpish decrease in aggressiveness.

Drugs cause many psychological and physical problems that diminish prosperity, romantic love, and psychuous pleasures. Other diminishers of prosperity and happiness include mystical, religious, and political activities as well as lying, self-lying, praying, promiscuous sex, and the use of tobacco, sugar, and caffeine.

Breaking sugar, tobacco, and caffeine habits quickly improves a person's quality of life. A person's self-esteem also significantly increases by eliminating habits that are destructive to the conscious mind and physical body. ...The surest way to stop smoking is to make a nonnegotiable decision to stop smoking completely and forever...and then stop completely and forever without using any crutches such as increased eating, snacking, sweets, sucking Lifesavers, or excessive bragging. A person who uses such crutches will almost always return to smoking sooner or later. The decision to stop must be decisive, irrevocable, uncompromisable, and forever.

Likewise, caffeine in coffee, cola, and chocolate is a stimulant drug. Aside from the depressing psychological effects of being controlled by a habit, prolonged and excessive use of caffeine can physically damage parts of the body such as the kidneys and pancreas and can adversely affect carbohydrate metabolism. That, in turn, can add to the damage and unhappiness caused by sugar consumption. Except for mysticism, the most common and destructive drug is the sedative sugar. Indeed, sugar causes more unhappiness, illness, and deaths through body mutilation (obesity), metabolic damage, physical and psychological harm than all other drugs combined.

But, the most pervasive and destructive of all diseases is mysticism. In fact, for 3000 years, mysticism has been far more destructive on human life than all the other diseases on this planet combined.

Casual sex, mysticism, neocheating, dishonesty, deceptive manipulation, compulsive gambling, hard and soft drugs, tobacco, caffeine, excessive alcohol, sugar, and prayer are long-term, negative aphrodisiacs that undermine self-esteem, romantic love, and psychuous pleasures. Also, folk-lore aphrodisiacs such as Spanish fly, yohimbine, ginseng root, and others have no long-term or physiological aphrodisiac value. The only effective aphrodisiacs are a desirable sexual partner, physical fitness, and the psychological/philosophical conditions of Neo-Tech that allow psychuous pleasures to flourish through the production and exchange of values.

**Again, the voice of fully integrated honesty stopped, as if Zon had reached a conclusion. After a minute, my father asked, "Is there anything else I should know about sex?" Indeed, the soft female voice of Zon continued...**

The opposite extreme of Neo-Tech aphrodisiacs are playboy anxieties. Those anxieties caused by pressures from "expected" sexual performances cause impotence and frigidity. Impotence also occurs through put-down statements or actions from a partner. Such statements or actions occur either willfully and maliciously or through error and ignorance. But the effects of such damage are often limited to that particular relationship. Thus, once the problem is identified, the victim can promptly abandon that destructive relationship. Decisively rejecting a "castrating" or "frigidizing" partner usually restores full sexual capacity.

A less obvious, more dangerous pressure subconsciously corrupts the mind. That pressure comes from listening to false or undercutting statements about the sexual performance of one's own self or others. Such statements, no matter how false, involuntarily lodge in the subconscious mind. That happens even when the conscious mind rejects such statements as false. By

85

that mechanism, a subconscious undermining of a person's sexual potency or character can occur in one of two ways: (1) by innuendo and other indirect forms of communication, or (2) by sexual or character put-down humor. Even if the conscious mind rejects such put downs, the choice to grant credibility by voluntarily listening lets the subconscious mind accept such specious, harmful information as valid.

The nonanalytical, subconscious mind does not evaluate assertions. The subconscious mind does not distinguish honest from dishonest information or serious from humorous situations. Thus, on entering the subconscious, the false information gradually works its undermining damage on the mind and nervous system. For that reason, a person should never propagate or even listen to unjust put downs, attacks, jokes, or gossip concerning the character or sexuality about oneself or anyone else. ...Such is the ear and mouth responsibility of everyone.

A person, however, should always be open and receptive to constructive, factually valid criticism about oneself or others.

Impotence and frigidity also develop when a man tries to oppress a woman, or vice versa. A person's willingness to accept such oppression blocks the possibility for psychuous pleasures. Such mutual acquiescence to oppression leads to impotence and frigidity in both partners. By contrast, a man's psychosexual dominance and a woman's act of *sexual* surrender harmonize with the physical and psychological nature of human beings. That psychological dominant/surrender interaction permits both partners to achieve the guiltless freedom and emotional closeness necessary for psychuous pleasures. There is no greater experience in this world than psychuous pleasures.

**"I really want to experience psychuous pleasures," my father echoed.**

Searching for that great experience, some people try to get involved too quickly in deep romantic relationships. The possible penalties of pressing for deep involvement too quickly include losing a potential romantic-love partner or unnecessarily wasting an irreplaceable portion of one's life by locking into a time-wasting destructive relationship.

*Love: Psychuous Sex Is Told*

Many initial approaches to romantic love are possible: Some start hot and flaming, others start cool and conservatively.  But the way a romantic relationship starts is usually unimportant because romantic love evolves through the exchange of mutually beneficial values.  Therefore, any initial, honest approach is good and normally does not determine the outcome. ...What determines the success of a relationship is the creation and growth of mutually beneficial values.

By applying Neo-Tech, you increase your *Life-Lifting Capacity,* which is a powerful attraction.  Life-Lifting Capacity means providing the exciting environment that helps our loved ones discover and fulfill their *own* unrealized capacities and potential.  With that capacity, you can lift a potential, romantic-love partner to new experiences and growth.

**"And what about commitment?" my father asked.**

The only commitment you ever need to make in romantic love is a commitment to honesty and growth.  If a relationship grows out of honest free-choice, the values accumulate naturally.  The relationship then increasingly forms a self-chosen permanence.  If growth continues, the relationship can gain unbreakable strength and permanence.  If growth stops, the relationship can benevolently end with most of the accumulated values retained by you and your ex-partner.  As a result, you and your ex-partner will have expanded your capacities for future relationships.  In addition, the benevolent termination of a value-oriented relationship can, if the partners so choose, remain open to possible changes that would allow resumption of growth and the relationship.

Romantic love never occurs automatically or by chance.  Life values are earned through honest efforts.  That means constant, conscious efforts orchestrated in full accord with reality.  As with all important values, romantic love and psychuous pleasures demand thought, effort, and time to develop.  The positive values generated are proportional to the rational thought and honest effort invested.

**My father started thinking about what Zon had just said**

Book 2
Neo-Tech Decoded

87

about a commitment to honesty and growth. Preoccupied by this thought, he said, "I want to go home now and think about all this. A lot of things you said today are completely different than what I always believed, but, on the other hand, seem totally honest...and exciting! Finally, there seems to be order in love. Now I feel I can get control of my love life for exciting results! I would like to ask you more questions tomorrow."

That night my father, in the physical prime of his life, felt something unfamiliar but wonderful — he felt *free*. When he slept, he had a wonderful dream about a fairy-tale love, a deep and meaningful love. When he woke up, he knew he wanted that kind of love for real. Throughout the morning, he felt different. A wave of maturity seemed to have washed through him. When he got to his mountain, he sat down and said,

"Whatever you are doing to me, I like it. Last night I was thunderstruck by realizing my actions in life were largely based on what others deemed best. Now I think I will discover who I really am, and it feels good. For the first time, I suddenly desire a serious relationship, *my kind of relationship*. Can we talk about that?"

In about a minute, the wind blew and the gentle woman's voice — the voice of fully integrated honesty — continued:

Actions based on standards of other people or "authorities" stifle self-discovery and block the personal and intellectual growth necessary for romantic love and psychuous pleasures. Society or peer views are often very immature. Within romantic love, no action or behavior needs the approval or sanction of anyone beyond the partners themselves.

Acceptance or approval by people is *not* a requirement for success, happiness, or psychuous pleasures. To achieve psychuous pleasures, a person must be free to be one's own self and choose one's own actions. Trying to be different from one's rational self is a distortion of human nature and contrary to romantic love. Acting on what others think rather than on your own thinking not only undermines integrity and judgment, but diminishes self-esteem. That, in turn, gradually represses the best qualities within you.

**"But, how do I get started in a psychuous relationship?" my father asked.**

The starting point of a psychuous relationship is the similarity of both partners' views of life and their underlying philosophical premises. Without that base of philosophical harmony, no solid ground for mutual development of a value-oriented, romantic-love relationship would exist.

Forming and building a fundamental base is not a process of creating, but one of discovering mutual values, ideas, and thoughts already held. This segment of romantic love is usually the fastest, easiest aspect of the relationship to identify and establish. But discovering the infinite depth and full nature of your partner is an exciting, life-long, unfolding process. Most of the fundamental, philosophical links between two people can usually be recognized early in the relationship. Unfortunately, one's fundamental basis is relatively easy to fake. Faking one's fundamental self to attract a love partner, however, is a disastrous error that will eventually be paid for in lost love, lost time, reduced self-esteem, diminished happiness, and a dimmed future, especially for the one doing the faking.

In order to establish a growing, long-range relationship, you and your partner must understand the ideas that the other holds about man-woman relationships. In order for both you and your partner to work effectively toward creating a relationship, you each must first identify the basis and nature of your own relationship. The Neo-Tech/Psychuous ideas that I reveal to you identify the basis for man-woman relationships designed to yield growth, psychuous pleasures, and happiness.

A romantic-love relationship moves forward with motivation and anticipation through a vision of future values, benefits, and happiness.

**"I am ready," my dad said. "But in my case, I am so busy in my career and now with my newly discovered love of writing...how could I do it?"**

Two types of romantic-love relationships exist. First, one partner works through the other more creative or active partner in climbing to increasing levels of accomplishment. Both partners share the rewards according to the values that each contribute. The more productive, creative, efficient, one partner becomes, the greater are the benefits and growth opportunities for the other partner. In turn, that partner then grows to become increasingly valuable to the other partner. Each partner benefits greatly from such a combined working/growing relationship. And such a relationship is mutually advantageous even when major differences in productivity, creativity, or energy exist between partners. A difference in productivity does not imply a difference in personal character. In such a joint-working relationship, even wide differences in productivity and creativity do not threaten the relationship, so long as growing values are being exchanged between the partners.

A joint-working relationship has the outstanding advantage not only of the partners sharing much larger portions of their lives, but of the partners living their lives more intensely together. ...They are living integrally together before, during, and after work, every day. They move on their goals, careers, essences, integrated thinking, and happiness together. They can each be more effective, efficient, and happier working together than working separately. They can become major, irreplaceable, growing values to each other.

Now second, each partner can pursue independent routes toward separate careers or goals. And each can benefit from such a relationship by the cross-sharing of experiences, emotions, and rewards of their separate experiences and accomplishments. The separate-working relationship need be neither threatening nor competitive for either partner, but rather can be a continuous source of pleasures and enrichment not available to either partner alone.

Both types of relationships offer unlimited opportunities for personal growth and happiness. In such value-producing relationships, each partner knows either implicitly or explicitly that intimacy, pleasures, and happiness in a relationship arise from sharing personal growth, not from possessing or owning one another.

*Love: Psychuous Sex Is Told*

Profound differences exist among people in their self-made qualities such as character development, earned skills, self-worth, extrinsic worth, aspects of intelligence, self-esteem, life-lifting capacity, psychuous-pleasures capacity. The "average individual" does not exist. Each individual is unique. So many variables are involved in an individual's character, physical structure, and psychological makeup that no individual can possibly be an average person. Moreover, no average psychology or lifestyle exists. When searching for your psychuous partner, remember, all *rational* psychologies have a "random-walk" capacity for delivering happiness. That means that every rational, productive individual has the same capacity for earning abiding happiness regardless of intelligence, psychology, or job status. Abiding happiness is possible to the extent that a person rejects mysticism in utilizing the mind to think rationally and in exerting the effort to live fully. A person's honesty, character, and self-earned values count above all else.

Also, keep in mind that people are capable of change...of changing their lives, character, attitudes, views, and actions. To be real, however, such changes must occur through one's own choices motivated by one's own desires and self-interest. Basic changes can never be successfully imposed on anyone, not even by a person's love partner. Changes accomplished by force, threat, coercion, or pressure are not genuine changes, but are pretenses or changes in external appearance designed to deceive, relieve pressures, or to avoid threatened consequences. Such feigned changes are never positive and always lead to harmful consequences.

Positive changes always require honest, self-directed efforts. Through ongoing character development, a person can become triggered to integrate new information quickly. That integration can cause significant, rapid changes in attitudes. For example, consider yourself the past three days since listening to me! If a person is unable or unwilling to act on valid new information, however, then efforts directed toward changing that person will fail. That does not mean untriggered persons cannot eventually change. But, if they do, the change will be by their own choice and pace.

91

**"You're right," my father said. "I have changed enormously these past few days from your enlightenments. In fact, for the first time in my life, I'm really excited about love. I guess, for the first time, I realize the joy and fulfillment possible from love." At that moment, his face, smiling and round under the midday sun, looked as innocent as a schoolboy. The dialogue continued with the sweet female voice that seemed brightened by a smile...**

Finding the right partner with whom to experience psychuous pleasures and romantic love is one of life's most important responsibilities. Opportunities to discover a potential, life-long romantic partner exist everywhere. But unplanned approaches diminish your chances of securing the best possible romantic-love partner.

You should remember that meeting a suitable partner to build abiding love and happiness needs only one connection, one meeting, one social function, one planned effort...and any time could be that one time. Until you find that right romantic partner, you should never stop searching for that person with whom to share and build values, love, and happiness. To give up searching would be to give up on life itself. And finding that one person makes all efforts worthwhile.

Never bemoan the unhappiness or falseness of guests at social gatherings, for you might be projecting your own feelings of unhappiness or falseness onto people who may not be that way at all. But, by looking past your own mystical complaints, you can usually generate self-benefiting values from most social circumstances, even if the people encountered hold values and life styles different from your own.

Still, you must be selective to protect your time. You must not let valuable, irreplaceable segments of life be consumed by those who waste time, retard personal growth, or work against your best interests. But when unavoidably cast into a situation with undesirable people, you can usually salvage valuable new insights. Whenever possible, however, you should promptly exit from situations that waste time.

Feelings of social incompetence are generally unfounded. Such feelings are often caused by falsely negative views about yourself or mystical views about others. When you become aware of and scrap those false views, the feelings of social incompetence diminish and often vanish.

An effective way to bypass shyness, nervousness, and feelings of social incompetence is by *intense listening* with full-focus awareness on the speaker. Not only does such attention elicit friendly reactions from the speaker to the listener, but intense listening increases the listener's ability to communicate and articulate. Intense listening is also a valuable tool to evaluate potential partners for romantic love.

Possibilities for contacting potential, romantic-love partners increase proportionately with the number of approaches made toward potential partners. Many opportunities for discovering romantic-love partners are lost by people who fear what others may think of them for trying to "pick up" people to whom they are attracted. Even more opportunities are lost through inaction caused by fear of rejection.

In finding the best romantic-love partner, you must be free and forward in approaching potential partners. That includes all approaches from a self-introduction to a media ad or a bold pickup. Through fear of rejection, many people lose valuable opportunities to discover romantic partners within whom the supreme values of psychuous pleasures and romantic love reside. That fear of contacting others dissipates on realizing the nature of rejections: Most rejections stem simply from unavailability. And many other rejections arise from inadequacies within the person doing the rejecting. Such rejections are not personal rebuffs, but actually serve as valuable sorting processes that allow the quick elimination of unpromising prospects with a minimum loss of time.

Those who rely on natural beauty or physical attractiveness to control love situations are generally unsuitable for romantic love. For usually they ignore the efforts and disciplines needed to develop capacities to receive or deliver romantic love and psychuous pleasures. Those who respond to your initial, natural approach often make the best prospects for romantic partners. For that reason, you must freely express your unique, natural self from the start in order for the selection process to work effectively in uncovering the best potential romantic-love partners.

93

Many people erroneously think that seeking potential romantic partners at social functions designed for that purpose, such as singles dances, clubs, introduction services, Parents Without Partners, is somehow degrading. But the opposite is the fact. People who value themselves and their happiness will resist mystically acting on such false feelings. Instead, they will place a high priority on those activities that will improve their chances of discovering the best-possible, life-long, romantic-love partner.

The value of romantic love is far too important for leaving to random chance. Instead, you must put the discovering of a life-long partner under your own direct control. You must exert organized, rational efforts to find the love partner with whom the greatest values can be exchanged. That direct-action approach contrasts with the mystical approach of those who count on random chance, a white knight, or someone else to deliver the values of love and happiness to them. ...To gain and keep a value as great as romantic love requires some effort.

**The voice of honesty paused. My father stood up and looked deep into the mountain's terrain, then said, "Zon, thank you. I feel that deep responsibility and desire now." The moment captured my father and Zon, looking at each other...just as still as a desert painting. Yet, internal emotions raced through my dad. He did not even notice when the wind began blowing again, but then heard Zon saying...**

Do not seek the most gorgeous woman for the sake of securing a trophy. Consider that most animals evolve to near their perfect physical appearance. But conscious beings do not because those without natural beauty can choose to work harder to develop their character and competence to higher levels. Thus, some people with less natural beauty work harder to develop superior characters. They do that to compete better in attracting mates for psychuous pleasures and reproduction. By contrast, many of those endowed with natural beauty lack the same competitive pressures to work harder to develop character and competence.

Thus, because certain people without natural beauty make themselves more competitive, they remain well represented throughout the evolutionary stream. In fact, they tend to rise above the naturally beautiful people in power, intellectual attractiveness, and sexual desirability. Those dynamics are why (1) naturally beautiful people can be found among the less evolved and (2) unhandsome people can be found among the highest levels of evolvement. Thus, unlike other animals, nature's drive for physical perfection is not a controlling evolutionary force in man. Indeed, man-controlled intelligent actions can outcompete nature-controlled, physical appearances not only for reproduction and survival, but for prosperity, happiness, and romantic love.

You see, achieving psychuous pleasures and romantic love requires the same discipline, thought, and effort for every individual, regardless of innate physical appearances. You must be cautious of involvement with a woman of exceptional, natural beauty whose personal life reflects low-effort, low-productivity. Such women often let their natural beauty substitute for the long-term effort required to develop characters of competence, self-esteem, and sensuosity required for romantic-love. Thus, underdeveloped, beautiful women — and men — are often airheads...often boring, value-draining people who are poor lovers with low self-esteems.

In any case, shyness reduces contact and chances with potential romantic-love partners. But shyness is easily overcome once the problem is identified. In addition, the constant misunderstanding of a uniquely different individual may cause that person to withdraw and become a loner. That aloneness may create an erroneous image that such a person is shy or a bore when neither is true.

A major step toward eliminating shyness is the acceptance of one's own self. To do that, you must realize that no "model" person exists with whom anyone needs to emulate or identify with in order to be healthy, happy, or successful. ...You bypass shyness by being your own self in guiltlessly, proudly producing rational, competitive values in any way you choose, regardless of what others may say or think.

A shy person is seldom a bore. A bore is a person who is silly, uninteresting, or uncomfortable to another person. Often being a bore to a particular person is merely the result of that particular person's reactions. Such reactions depend on individual values and standards. Some people can be boring to certain people, but exciting to others. For example Einstein, Edison, Henry Ford, and Bill Gates while being very exciting to each other, probably would have bored some if not most beautiful women before becoming rich and famous.

**"Yes. I see how that could be true," my father said, a bit surprised. "As for not being shy, I'm OK in that department," he added, with a hint of male pride. "But are there other important tips on getting my love-life right and wonderful this time?"**

In searching for that life-long romantic partner, keep the following in mind: Men and women have equal capacity for intellectual development, character development, integral honesty, self-esteem, physical fitness, psychuous pleasures, romantic love, and abiding happiness. But physiological differences as well as psychological differences exist between men and women. Those differences must be recognized in order to function effectively — to function as a human male or female is intended to function — to function as an honest, rational, conscious being. Those differences cannot be considered good or bad, better or worse, or by any other label. They are just differences in their natures. But the differences are real. Thus, they must be recognized and dealt with as reality.

The feminist movement ignores or rejects the psychological differences and often even ignores the physiological differences between man and woman. That evasion of reality is reflected by the feminists' irrational, destructive demands for government-enforced "equality".

The often misunderstood division-of-labor concept is central to all beneficial relationships, ranging from individual man-woman romantic relationships to mutually beneficial employer-employee relationships involving thousands of people. Next to their attacks on individual rights through the use of government force, the most harmful neocheating manipulations by feminist leaders are their attacks on the voluntary division-of-labor concept. Some feminists advocate eliminating the division-of-labor dynamic from

96

man-woman relationships. They demand, for example, that all jobs, chores, and activities be shared equally.

Most other people desire and happily use the division of labor to their mutual advantages. Indeed, the most fair, efficient way to exchange values for desired values is through division of labor. Even the traditional trade in which the man earns money while the woman makes an efficient home and living atmosphere is a valid, proper trade that can greatly benefit each, if each mutually agrees to and desires such a trade.

For what reason would a feminist or anyone else attack two people who agree to what they want to do with their own personal selves and lives? One reason is that such feminists are neocheaters using the tool of guilt to undermine values in order to usurp power and values earned by others. But, romantic-love partners responding to feminist demands for equality of actions — rather than for each partner offering the other his or her separately developed values — eventually eliminate happiness from their relationships. For equality of actions pushes love partners toward inefficient, restricted petty relationships in which mutual growth fades and love dies. ...In other words, do not get too tied into a woman locked into feminist ideas, or your love will suffer.

Women functioning in any of the following three categories can achieve psychuous pleasures, romantic love, and abiding happiness:

1. Self-sufficient, commercially productive career women can easily experience the full-range of psychuous pleasures and romantic love.

2. Genuinely productive housewives or mothers who contribute significantly to increasing the commercial productivity of their husbands and the value potentials of their children can also experience growing psychuous pleasures and romantic love. But they, as with men, must always keep developing their intellectual and productive capacities. Women most naturally succeed in this category.

3. Women actively seeking growth by becoming knowledgeable or proficient in artistic, cultural, or recreational areas, such as art, music, literature, dance,

97

sports, can experience growing romantic relationships. But such relationships will not continue to grow unless the woman passes the amateur stage to eventually become commercially productive and self-sufficient in that or another area. Only a tiny percentage of women succeed in this category.

Today, with the many domestic labor-saving conveniences, a housewife "career" is often too unchallenging to provide the self-esteem, independence, and growth needed to experience the full range of happiness available from life. But, exceptions exist in which being a housewife is a challenging management profession delivering full self-esteem, happiness, and romantic love. Examples today include the partner-wives of super-productive entrepreneurs, businessmen, farmers, scientists, and other hard-driving producers. Another example includes mothers who take over the responsibility of properly educating their children in light of today's incompetent educational systems.

**"What are your integrations on having children?" my father asked.**

A potential area for either undermining or boosting happiness is having children. Which direction often depends on whether or not the parents have achieved financial independence. Parents who lose growth and happiness can damage the well-being of their innocent child or children. On the other hand, parents who gain growth and happiness can sustain the great gift of happiness in their children's lives.

Common sense dictates: do not have children until you are in a financial and maturity position to conceive a child as a net-happiness asset, rather than a draining task. Couples who follow that advice almost always have greater capacities to love both life and their children than those who thoughtlessly or prematurely have children to "secure" the marriage, to meet the expectations of others, or other unhealthy reasons.

Romantic love and psychuous pleasures can still be achieved for couples who have children if they fully meet their responsibilities to both their children and to themselves. With children, the goal of building happiness and romantic love

98

becomes more challenging. But if successful, a romantic relationship with the uniquely valuable experience of children can be even more rewarding than a romantic-love relationship without children.

Except to yourself and dependent children, you owe duties to *no one* — including your spouse, siblings, parents — and to nothing, including society, the government, the church, or to any other "higher" cause. The prime moral duty is to develop your own potential to achieve abiding happiness through character development and value production. Beyond the prime responsibility to be a net value producer in order to earn happiness, your *only* other moral duty is to support and develop your own children into honest, nonmystical, self-sufficient adults. That duty includes teaching children to objectively identify facts in full context and to live competently by rejecting all forms of mysticism, dishonesty, and neocheating.

Properly caring for and rearing children to become honest, self-sufficient adults is a moral responsibility and duty of the parents. That duty is assumed from the parent's chosen act of procreation, for which the children are not responsible. Thus, parents have no right to place future claims or obligations on their children. Likewise, after children develop into self-sustaining, independent beings, the moral responsibilities and obligatory duties end for the parents.

**My father stopped Zon. Dad was thinking about myself, my brother, and my sister. Then, feeling an impulse of happiness, he said, "The past week has been the most spectacular experience in my life."**

Strongly positive experiences such as major achievements, aerobic exercises, great music, art, literature, drama, and romantic love are natural highs. The ultimate high, however, comes from feeling your own self in control — being in control of life, living free of mysticism, living honestly, rationally, productively. In that non-mystical state, you acutely feel the integrated physical and psychological process of living. You experience the impact of living fully, in competent control of your own self, destiny, and reality.

99

That clarity and control of self, life, and reality produces a physical and emotional high, which is what is happening to you since hearing me, the voice of Neo-Tech. Your physical and emotional high evolves from an acute awareness of living in reality...of being in control. Such highs are far more exhilarating than those achieved through reality avoiding, artificial stimuli such as drugs, alcohol, religious or mystical experiences, manipulating others, ruling others. Those fake highs are achieved through self-destruction. By contrast, all genuine, lasting highs are achieved through production of values.

The most intense reality high is psychuous pleasures. Reality highs, however, can be consistently experienced in almost any phase of your life to produce continuous waves of pleasure and happiness. Most people have at times experienced brief or partial glimpses of those natural highs. Such experiences live vividly in nearly everyone's memory. On analysis, you will discover that those experiences occurred when you were most free of mysticism — most free to be your own self — most free to function according to your biological nature, like this past week. Everyone who has developed a rational, productive lifestyle has the capacity for experiencing natural highs with increasing frequency. Those highs can eventually blend into a near continuous state of happiness marked by extra-intense moments of psychuous pleasures.

Natural highs involve the release of physical and emotional tensions while being fully aware of the mind and body. The sensation is that of "letting go" as the body tensions release and the emotional pleasures are guiltlessly felt. Those natural, euphoric experiences are contrasted to the destructive, tension-breaking actions of taking drugs, getting drunk, food gorging. Such artificial or mystical highs always leave hangovers and unhappiness along with damaged minds and bodies.

**My father stood there smiling. "That all sounds so nice," he said. "But how do I do this right and make the right choice for psychuous pleasures? I have never been able to experience real romantic love."**

You must know perhaps the two most common causes of

judgment error: 1. *Infatuation* is a subtle and often a dangerous judgment error, especially when it occurs without realizing the error. Infatuation is the focusing on a single attractive or desirable characteristic of another person and then considering the total person as that one positive attribute. Infatuation is not only an unfair burden placed on the person being judged, but can lead to long-range disillusionment and pain for the person making the erroneous judgment. The infatuation-judgment error is a common "true-love-turns-sour" theme so often used in movies, novels, and magazine fiction.

2. *Reverse Infatuation* is perhaps the most subtle form of judgment error. Still, reverse infatuation is a common error that can cause losses of potential values and happiness. Reverse infatuation involves the focusing on a negative characteristic of an individual and then considering that total person as that one negative attribute. That judgment error can be blinding, depriving, and unjust in obscuring areas of earned values and worth in other individuals. Even minor reverse-infatuation puts unjust penalties on the person being judged. While valid criticisms about an individual should be identified and expressed when appropriate, the criticism should explicitly focus on those specific issues, not on the whole person.

Segmented judging is a method to decrease judgment errors. This method provides a more fair, accurate, and valuable way to judge individuals, especially those important to one's life. This method is particularly important for judging potential romantic-love partners.

First, you must recognize that people are many-faceted combinations of complex character traits — usually combinations consisting mainly of objectively positive traits with some, often hidden, negative traits. And second, you must break down those various character traits into separate components.

Once that breakdown is done, you can make more fair and accurate judgments by weighing specific positive traits against specific negative traits, "positive to me" values versus "negative to me" values. The extent that the positive values outweigh the negative values is the extent you make a positive *moral judgment*. Similarly, the extent that "positive to me" values outweigh the "negative to me" disvalues is the extent you make a positive

101

*personal-value judgment.* Many personal values are merely preferences and tastes that develop from your past experiences, interests, and motivations that are not grounded in right or wrong issues, but arise from the uniqueness of you and your past experiences and development.

The most useful and accurate method to judge a potential romantic-love partner, or any person, is on a segmented "value-scale" basis. You cannot judge the whole of an individual on any specific aspect of his or her character, personality, actions, words, or behavior. Exclusively focusing on specific aspects of a person yields distorted, infatuation-type judgments. Instead, you should judge an individual by placing all the known characteristics and qualities of that person on either the "value to me" side or the "disvalue to me" side of the balance scale. You then judge the person by the extent that the scale tips to the value side or to the disvalue side.

You should keep the evaluation of each person open. In accumulating more experience or information about any person, the balance tilt can change. Growth, change, or deterioration of either yourself or the person being judged can cause the "value scale" to tilt more or less in one direction or even to switch to the other direction.

The "value to me" standard is the most reliable, valuable way for you to judge the personal value of another individual. The direction and extent the "value scale" tilts is influenced by the personal-value system of you, for the value weights often depend on your personal wants, goals, needs and thus will vary from individual to individual.

**"Zon, I may have already found the woman I want to become serious with," my father said. "Can you give me some Neo-Tech tips? I want the power of fully integrated honesty to make this work."**

Once you find romantic love, realize this: Only within a romantic relationship in which you and your woman love and value each other in your private universe can you experience the full range of physical and psychological sharing. Within the romantic relationship resides the full scope of psychuous pleasures: the combination of full-range sexuality with the freedom to fearlessly share any aspect of yourself...any thought, feeling, fantasy, emotion — good or bad, rational or irrational. Thus, you can let go completely to share and guiltlessly experience any aspect of your body, mind, emotion, imagination with your romantic-love partner.

You can freely share *any* aspect of yourself and life. But you need not share *every* aspect. You always have the guiltless right to privacy to any area of your life, even within the closest, most open and honest friendship or romantic-love relationship. Total honesty does not require total revealing all of your private self. Indeed, absolute and total sharing of yourself and psyche involves losing the most profound essence of privacy. That loss, in turn, diminishes the sense of "I" and your self-esteem. Retaining the essence of personal privacy is not an act of repression, inhibition, dishonesty, or lack of openness, but is a self-respect preservation of your inherent right to privacy.

To experience psychuous pleasures through romantic love requires genuine self-esteem valuing of your own self. Beyond the romantic-love relationship, self-esteem is diminished or even destroyed by indiscriminately sharing or by giving away your personal, private self too cheaply. That loss of self-esteem can be especially severe if you promiscuously give away your private self just because socially chic books, gurus, and media commentators falsely promulgate the need to be totally open with everyone. They imply that love, openness, and honesty are demonstrated by the giving of your private self to all comers.

The sharing of yourself is a personal choice and judgment. Such sharing with another person may occur quickly, even on initial contact if judgment responses trigger desires to move toward deeper personal or romantic possibilities. Chances should and must be taken on exploring potentially valuable relationships. Errors in judgment are often made. But minimum harm from such errors results so long as you are making your *own* choices, using reason and reality rather than following the words of mystics, social "authorities", or gurus.

Happiness exists as a private world within your own self. That world expands into a mutually exclusive universe shared by two people involved in a psychuous-pleasure, romantic-love relationship. And that exclusive, private universe is a uniquely precious, emotional treasure. But that treasure can be forever lost by indiscriminately or promiscuously sharing yourself physically, psychologically, or spiritually with others.

That selfless giveaway and subsequent destruction of your private inner world is exactly what the egalitarian advocates of "total openness" wish to accomplish. Only by negating everyone else's private values and self-esteem, can they justify their own prostituted inner world.

By contrast, avoiding that self-giveaway trap leaves romantic love and abiding happiness open for any value producer.

**"In the past, when I got close to a woman, I did try communicating well. What about that?" my father asked.**

Crucial in your romantic-love relationship is open communication, especially during negative emotional experiences. During stressful or negative experiences, deliberate reason-based — rather than automatic emotion-based — conclusions are needed to make fair, honest judgments. The ability to communicate honestly without mysticism during emotional stress is the hallmark of successful love partners.

The first step to reason-based communication between you and your woman is to identify and separate the emotional aspects of a problem. For, knowing the difference between reason-based conclusions and emotion-based conclusions is the most important step in developing communication skills during negative situations.

Your ability to generate reason-based conclusions out of negative situations has powerfully beneficial effects on your well-being, self-esteem, and happiness. Reasoned conclusions in emotional situations, for example, can prevent irrational actions that damage or destroy business, family, and romantic-love situations. The habitual use of reason-based conclusions in emotional situations leads to powerfully effective communication in all situations, especially business and romantic-love situations.

**Feeling that it was getting late, my father asked the mountain if there was anything more for today. The gentle**

**voice responded:**

I have one more important tip to give you today, one more important Neo-Tech advice: Psychuous pleasures and abiding happiness depend on psychological health which, in turn, depends on productive work. Without productive work or preparations for such, psychological health is impossible. Moreover, psychuous pleasures and happiness act as the emotional incentives to constantly increase your value and productivity.

By the way, you like most productive individuals are of much greater value than your mystically diminished self-image lets you realize. For, the image of highly productive individuals has been constantly denigrated by dishonest media journalists, authors, university professors, educators, theologians, politicians, and social "intellectuals". The productive middle class is projected in the ugly, inverted, false images of the Babbitts and Willie Lomans. The ultimate unjust irony lies with the destructive government bureaucrats and "professionals": They who never produce values, only consume or destroy them, coined and contemptuously use the pejorative "working stiffs" in describing the self-sufficient, working middle class. Those "working stiffs" are the honest people who daily produce a flood of values for others, including those government value destroyers. Indeed, those value destroyers could not survive without those "working stiffs". But those "working stiffs" would thrive without those bureaucrats and professional value destroyers.

You, the value producer, can feel your full worth only after discarding the years of unearned guilt foisted on you by the mystics, politicians, social "intellectuals", media commentators, and other neocheating altruists and egalitarians. Indeed, you can and should experience the pleasure of feeling your full worth all the time. And now with Neo-Tech, you can forever free yourself of egalitarian altruism and its envious neocheaters to always feel your deserved worth and happiness.

Productivity is the building block for prosperity, love, and happiness. Now, I want you to go home and write down tonight the most common character and behavior traits associated with productive men and women. Reflect on what I have bestowed upon you, and then make your list.

That night, my father reflected for about two-and-a-half hours, reviewing in his mind Zon's voice of fully integrated honesty. Then, my father put to paper his list as Zon had asked, as follows:

## CHARACTER AND BEHAVIOR TRAITS
## OF COMPETITIVE VALUE PRODUCERS

### <u>Character Traits</u>

Honesty
Integrity
Rationality
Consistency
Perseverance
Individualism
Enthusiasm
Ambition
Passion

### <u>Behavior Traits</u>

- Acts with energy, honesty, and fairness regardless of near-term consequences. Loyalty to honesty.
- Recognizes and pursues the values of honesty and integrity.
- Thinks rationally, logically, objectively.
- Focuses on reality.
- Seeks facts *in full context.*
- Organizes self, life, and work toward profitable actions.
- Asks clear questions and listens carefully.
- Values time. Uses it efficiently and profitably.
- Anticipates and then strives for achievement.
- Sets value-producing goals and strives to accomplish them.
- Seeks to understand fully and contextually before judging.
- Shows passion, benevolence, and innocence toward life.
- Avoids mystical reactions.

106

*Love: Psychuous Sex Is Told*

**The next day, my father arrived at the mountain, feeling somewhat proud of his efforts the night before. "I want to start writing more," he said to Zon. Zon responded by saying that was part of the original reason Zon spoke to him, with the knowledge that he would record and distribute the message to the world. Zon also made it clear that the voice of fully integrated honesty still had much to cover, then that widely integrated voice, blowing in the wind, turned to a very grave message:**

Growth Death or Psyche Death are terms used to describe the tragedy of dying as a competently functioning conscious being while continuing to exist physically. That phenomenon unnecessarily occurs in a high percentage of people. Caused by the disease of mysticism, Growth Death affects perhaps 90% of the world's living adult population. Growth Death is a uniquely human phenomenon that involves the stagnation and death of the human psyche, often at an early age — even before the human body reaches physical maturity.

The human psyche embraces both the emotional and intellectual spheres of the mind. Contrary to popular myth, both spheres are inseparably linked and symbiotically function together. If one sphere grows, so does the other. If one sphere deteriorates, so does the other. Most important, the human psyche has no age or capacity limitations on its growth.

Unlike the physical body, the human psyche has no growth limits. It never needs to stop growing. In fact, the continuous growth of the psyche is the process of conscious living. When that process stops, the individual ceases to function as a conscious being is designed to function. If a person's psyche is not growing, that person is living contrary to his or her nature. Thus, that person's psyche begins dying. And if one's psyche is dying, that person cannot experience growing prosperity, love, or happiness.

What happens with a living, growing business-like mind? Value-producing actions beget happy feelings while honestly integrating reality. What happens with a dying, shrinking mystical mind? Indulged feelings beget destructive actions while dishonestly evading reality. I want you to compare the psyche

107

of those two minds — the criminal, destructive, mystic mind versus the heroic, productive, business mind.

Understand that people generally display various mixtures of living and dead psyche characteristics. But the mixture is always tilted to one side or the other with the general direction usually moving unnecessarily toward death.

Now, I want you to go home and think hard about what I just said. Then, I want you to make a checklist for self-mysticism to determine whether your psyche is living or dying.

**My father worked through the rest of the day and late into the night to complete the checklist below. He returned at predawn the next morning. "I made the checklist," he said. "And you know what Zon? I also realized that a person with a dying psyche can reverse the trend and live again by using Neo-Tech to cure the disease of mysticism within his own self."**

| CHECKLIST FOR SELF-MYSTICISM | |
| --- | --- |
| Characteristics of a <br> <u>Dying or Dead Psyche</u> <br> (Ralph Nader Type Mystical Mind) | Characteristics of a <br> <u>Living or Growing Psyche</u> <br> (Ray Kroc Type Business Mind) |
| ☐ **Envious of others for their achievements, success, happiness, or material well-being. Resents heroes, value producers, and especially great business people and their productive accomplishments.** | ☐ **Envy-free. Admires and encourages individual achievement in self and others.** |
| ☐ **Operates on subjective feelings or wishes. Oriented toward short-range, value-destroying approaches to problems and goals.** | ☐ **Operates on objective principles. Oriented toward long-range, value-producing approaches to problems and goals.** |
| ☐ **Desires the destruction, distribution, or leveling of the wealth, happiness, and well-being earned by others.** | ☐ **Produces tradeable values. Desires a life of achievements and happiness for self and others.** |
| ☐ **Holds anti-individualistic views. Has egalitarian and collectivist desires to seize, destroy, and level values produced by others.** | ☐ **Orients around rational self-interests. Independently fills own needs through production of tradeable values for others.** |
| | *(continued on next page)* |

108

---

## CHECKLIST FOR SELF-MYSTICISM
*(continued)*

| Dying or Dead Psyche | Living or Growing Psyche |
|---|---|
| ☐ Fears freedom, independence, and competition. Follows external "authorities" in religion and government. | ☐ Seeks freedom, independence, and competition. Rejects external "authorities". |
| ☐ Praises humble, selfless altruists. Attacks or maligns proud, productive achievers. | ☐ Admires and seeks productive achievers. |
| ☐ Unhappy with life. Only interludes of short-term happiness. Represses the tragedy of death. Recoils at the possibility of an extended life. | ☐ Happy with life. Only interludes of short-term sadness. Recognizes the tragedy of death. Hails the possibility of human life extension. |
| ☐ Seeks government controls and laws that forcibly restrict and repress individual freedom. | ☐ Seeks freedom. Opposes all forms of oppression, especially government force and oppression of the individual. |
| ☐ Plagued with anxieties and self-doubts. | ☐ At ease and comfortable with self. Increasingly feels joyful life building within his or her physical and emotional self. |
| ☐ Holds a cynical or malevolent view of life and people. | ☐ Holds a benevolent view of life and people. |
| ☐ Life is viewed as unhappy and people as inherently destructive, wicked, or sinful. | ☐ Life is viewed as naturally happy, beautiful, exciting. People are viewed as inherently good, valuable, productive. |
| ☐ Emotionally and physically experiences life with increasing unhappiness and lethargy. | ☐ Experiences life with increasing joy and intensity. |
| ☐ Accepts harmful, mystical concepts such as original sin and predestination. | ☐ Rejects mystical concepts such as original sin and predestination. |
| ☐ Orients around mystical premises and beliefs, statism, astrology, the occult. | ☐ Orients around honesty and objective reality. |
| ☐ Orients around an altruistic, Platonistic philosophy that holds the sacrifice of the individual to "higher" causes as a virtue. | ☐ Orients around an Aristotelian/ Neo-Tech philosophy that holds the individual as the supreme value in the universe. |

Book 2
Neo-Tech Decoded

**"Zon, do you want to see the list?" But before the wind had a chance to carry the voice of fully integrated honesty, my father answered his own question: "No. You already know what I wrote." Then Zon told my father he is learning well and to keep his checklist, for he would need it to publish in his future writings on Neo-Tech. Zon's voice, still that of a female, carried an unmistakable pitch of pride. Then, Zon went on the point intended for this day:**

To let your psyche live or die was a volitional choice made by you alone — a choice usually made early in life, often in childhood. The tragically unnecessary surrender of the psyche to mysticism and Growth Death took the subconscious form of:

*What's the use. Why struggle any more to understand reality or bear the pain and pressure of being honest? I am not going to live by my own mind because the effort and responsibilities are too great. I'll let others think for me. I'll let the authorities tell me what to believe and do. Yes, I'll support their power no matter how dishonest or destructive. I want the easiest, safest way through life. No, I don't want to advance in life by independent, integrated thinking and actions. Instead, I want to be a believer and to follow some 'wiser' authority or 'higher' good. I'll live by the thoughts and feelings of others.*

From that point of surrender, although you became more knowledgeable, skillful, and proficient in specific areas, your psyche diminished as overall growth of your mind stopped and turned downward toward death.

This past week you, as could anyone else, decided to countermand that subconscious surrender order and restart psyche growth. If you had not, the quality of your life would continuously decline, always controlled, always pushed or pulled one way or another by outside forces, by the influences of "others".

**"Yes!" my father shouted. "This past week I have discovered the power of fully integrated honesty — it gives me the freedom to make my own decisions in everything. And it feels wonderful to no longer live under the influences of others!"**

The "others" represented higher "authorities" you once let control your thoughts, judgments, actions, life rather than using your own mind. Those "higher authorities" included friends, relatives, politicians, bureaucrats, lawyers, social "intellectuals", neocheating university professors, the media, the church, the ruler, and for some people include the Messiah, Allah, cocaine, the Bible, the stars, the state, "society" — anyone or anything outside the individual's own mind.

People default on the primary responsibility of their minds by letting outside others — "authorities", neocheaters — do their thinking and make their decisions. When people default on using their own minds, they lose control of their lives and begin dying as they become controlled by others.

By nature, control through others always contradicts your long-range well-being. Thus, accepting such outside control always begins the process of Growth Death. For no one can experience growth, prosperity, and happiness while under control of others.

Through honest thinking and sustained efforts, you can self-heal and strengthen your mind. Anyone can through Neo-Tech. Through such self-healing, you retake control of life and reverse that mind atrophy caused by mysticism. On healing your mind, the future once again promises boundless prosperity, growth, love, and happiness. Your psyche will experience anew an exhilarating freedom and control over reality, perhaps for the first time since early childhood.

Like you, before you heard the voice of fully integrated honesty, most people have defaulted, at least partially, on the independent use of their minds. By abandoning any part of their minds to "others", including psychologists in many cases, they diminish their means to prosperity and happiness. Yet, through Neo-Tech, the potential is always available to rescue one's self from mysticism and its external "authorities". By nature, the self-rescue of one's own mind from mysticism must be an act of self-responsibility free from external "authority".

Few people choose to resurrect themselves from Psyche Death and Growth Death. Those who have surrendered usually rationalize their deteriorating self and shrinking potential as a natural, biological aging process. Growth Death may be common,

Book 2
Neo-Tech Decoded

but is neither natural nor necessary. Furthermore, rebirth of a dying mind or psyche is not only possible but quite easy for anyone possessing Neo-Tech knowledge.

Neo-Tech leads the way to mental health by self-curing the disease of mysticism. ...And without mysticism to manipulate others, the neocheaters are powerless.

**"But how do I do that? How do I cure the disease of mysticism in myself?" my father asked.**

How to do that? Developing accurate awareness of self and reality through honest, integrated thinking is the prime responsibility for all human beings. In fact, such awareness is a necessity to live prosperously and happily. That awareness is available to those who exert constant, rational thinking efforts toward understanding self and reality — and the relationship between the two. No one can deliver that understanding to another. Indeed, developing an accurate understanding of self and reality is a crucial self-responsibility for personal power.

Mystics struggle to avoid that constant, rational thinking effort needed to honestly and accurately integrate one's life with objective reality. That honest understanding and integration of reality is the key to competence and prosperity in a competitive world. But losers and mystics seek anyone or anything promising to deliver prepackaged knowledge that lets them avoid the hard work required to develop their own integrated knowledge and awareness. That is why mystics embrace such quackeries as astrology, psychic readings, graphoanalysis, biorhythms, most psychoanalysis, fortune telling, or any other flimflam that deludes them with a sense of gaining effortless knowledge, awareness, control. By accepting such specious awarenesses conjured up by others, a person keeps drifting further from reality, becoming increasingly unaware, unhappy, and incompetent while rationalizing the opposite.

Acquiring integrated awareness, competence, and happiness is a *self*-responsibility that no one else can deliver. No one can deliver awareness and happiness to you because no other person is in a position to:

1. know your own integrated self.

112

*Love: Psychuous Sex Is Told*

2. think integrally and contextually about your own life.
3. control your own actions.
4. integrate your own work and life with reality.

For any "authority" to have an integrated awareness of another person is impossible. No matter how complete or scientific looking — for example, computer printouts of horoscopes or biorhythms — any such outside self-awareness analysis is invalid and mystical. And any seeming validity of such "self-awareness" packages is a specious illusion. Such illusions lead you further away from an awareness of reality and deeper into the stupidity of mysticism — the disease that undermines all human life and love.

Your own choices, not your environment, control your destiny. Except for natural catastrophe or brute-force totalitarianism, the forces of nature and social environment when pitted against the rational conscious mind have little or no influence over your long-range future.

For you to allow your future to be influenced by even the most direct and powerful forces of nature — such as the weather, the wind, the rain — would be to relegate the potency of your mind and actions to a low position indeed. But to assert, as astrologers do, that the faintest forces in nature — the celestial forces from outer space can influence human beings and their minds is to relegate the human mind to a most inept position. To view the human mind as being that feeble or impotent, even though the view may be only subconscious or implicit, undermines a person's confidence and self-esteem. The human mind, along with the choices made through your life, controls the life and future of a productive person...unless government or religious forces directly cripple or destroy that person.

Entirely different from such astrology-like fake "awarenesses" through mysticism is the awareness arising from the mutual mirroring of character and personal qualities between yourself and a friend or romantic-love partner. Such mirroring genuinely enhances self-awareness, communication, and pleasure especially between romantic-love partners. That reflecting of a person's character and qualities is based on direct, intimate knowledge of that person. Such honest, valuable reflections differ profoundly from fake ego-stroking awareness packages mystically reflecting

113

Book 2
Neo-Tech Decoded

personal character and exciting qualities based on nothing but self indulgence.

As with happiness, self-awareness cannot be given from one person to another. But by reflecting personal values, you can enhance another person's self-awareness in a similar way that you can enhance another person's happiness.

**"Such as you have done to me more than once. Again, thank you Zon. Since you spoke to me, I have become much more aware of myself and my strengths and qualities," my father said. "Also, my woman is amazing. I'm able to express myself privately to her, and she helps me understand what I am going through with both the elation in my life, which is you Zon, and with the tribulation in my life, which is my ongoing battle with the government because of the IRS."**

A strong emotion felt by highly productive men is the desire for a peaceful core to counterbalance their aggressively assertive lives. That desire usually relates to a woman with whom such a man is free to retreat from his battlefield actions to experience peaceful love, tenderness, serenity. For only during that precious time is he free to fully expose and share his soul exclusively with another human being — his woman. During those moments, that woman becomes to him the supreme value in all the universe. ...Now, my friend, you are discovering the immeasurably greater value of a psychous relationship over a casual-sex relationship.

Ironically, the strongest, most productive, independent men have the greatest need and capacity to receive a woman's love, support, and tenderness. Tragically, however, many such men never recognize or admit, even to themselves, that supremely important emotional need and pleasure. Similarly, strong men often never admit to other emotional needs such as being free to cry when suffering great sadness or pain. ...A man crying has been erroneously viewed as a weakness or unmanly.

Many women are unaware of the need in productive men for a peaceful, private world containing a one-woman love. But women who understand that need hold a key for delivering powerful values and happiness to their men and to themselves. Understanding and filling the need for a peaceful, reflective core in aggressively productive men is among the most powerful of all binding ingredients in romantic-love relationships.

Now, let me encourage your very productive, growth path this past year.  As you are discovering first hand, from the production of competitive values all other values grow, including prosperity, self-esteem, psychological well-being, romantic love, and abiding happiness.  Furthermore, competitive, tangible, and material values are important building blocks and binding ingredients of conscious relationships, especially business, friendship, and romantic-love relationships.  All professional mystics and neocheaters desperately try to deny the cardinal role of producing competitive values in living happily and in gaining romantic love.  But only through the exchange of such values can personal relationships become fully integrated:  From an exchange of tangible and material values, a far greater stability, intensity of love, and abiding happiness can develop than is possible from a relationship consisting only of abstract values.

Tangible values in a romantic-love relationship directly affect sexuality.  For, exchanges of tangible values markedly increase sexual intensity and psychuous pleasure.

**My father stopped the mountain and said, "I'm falling in love, and as I've said, I really want to do everything right this time.  Can you elaborate in detail about this value exchange?  It seems to be a key to a good relationship and great sex."**

Abstract values are the crucial ingredient for initiating, establishing, and maintaining a friendship or a romantic-love relationship.  However, tangible and material values *combined* with abstract values are the variables that cause psychuous pleasures and happiness to ignite and then grow constantly.  Both love and deep friendship relationships require a base of abstract values to start.  But the production of tangible and material values is necessary for moving a relationship into unlimited growth and high-gear happiness.

Abstract values delivered from one person to another person

115

in friendship or love relationships include: psychologically valuable reflections, philosophically valuable reflections, reflections of each other's values, analytical feedback of thoughts and ideas, mirroring of personal worth, values, and ideas. Tangible and material values include: practical contributions to increasing the efficacy and productivity of the other, practical contributions to reducing or eliminating value-destroying and time-wasting problems and errors inside and outside the relationship, practical contributions to producing tangible and material values to one's self and the other, practical contributions to providing tangible and material values to the other.

Without value-generating interactions, two people are of little direct value to each other — at least no more value that any two random people might be to each other. Valuable human relationships evolve when two people deliver objective values to one another. That exchange of values measures the value of a relationship.

Aside from the intrinsic value of human life that exists among all people, a person is not a value to others by merely existing. Instead, a person must deliver competitive values to be a value to others and society. Otherwise, that person will be a drain on others and a disvalue to society. And a person must continue delivering values to be a continuing value. Moreover, one must continue adding new values to existing values to experience value growth within one's self and within a relationship. Value growth is a self-created, pyramiding process that requires rational thought and constant effort to sustain. Such a growth process is the essence of human living. For value growth fills life's needs and delivers life's major rewards — abiding prosperity, romantic love, and happiness.

To fully experience life and sustain value growth requires continuous thought and effort. The need for value growth is not someone's philosophical theory or ethic. That need is an integral part of reality: Constant value growth is required for the conscious organism to function properly. A person makes a disastrous error by failing to put forth the honest, integrated thought and rational effort needed to produce growing, competitive values for others.

Tragically, most people choose to stop their growth early in life. Many stop in childhood — soon after exerting that mighty learning effort required to read and write. When they stop exerting that effort, they stop growing. The quality of their lives then declines until physical death. ...Without growth, a person cannot experience abiding prosperity, happiness, and psychuous pleasures. Without growth, a person misses the point of conscious life. Without growth, a person dies.

*Growth Death* is a great, unnecessary tragedy. It never has to happen to anyone; it is imposed on no one. Growth Death occurs only when the victim chooses to avoid the integrated thought and rational effort required to produce and deliver net, competitive values to others. When Growth Death occurs, then all value-based friendships and love relationships stop growing and begin to die.

Now, listen intensely, for I'm going to give you other deep insights about love and then come back around again to value exchange: Both romantic-love relationships and friendships can involve deep psychological and philosophical interactions. But the distinguishing characteristic of a romantic-love relationship is its physical-sexual sharing. That sexual sharing, in turn, offers physical and psychological intimacy unobtainable from any other human relationship. ...Those unique physical/psychological intimacies can lead to growing psychuous pleasures.

Friendship is a necessary ingredient of romantic love. Without friendship, no basis for romantic love exists. A romantic-love relationship has all the ingredients of a value-oriented friendship plus the powerful ingredient of physical intimacy and sex. ...Friendship can be more personally intimate and involved than any other human relationship except a romantic-love relationship.

The value of friendships should neither be underestimated nor overestimated. You can achieve unlimited psychuous pleasures and happiness through romantic love alone, without any close friend beyond your love partner. Friendships alone, no matter how valuable or extensive, can never deliver the full spectrum of values and happiness available from a single, friendship-based romantic love.

The following two ingredients will deliver a prosperous, happy life:

117

1. achieving self-sufficient independence through honest production of competitive values for others

2. achieving psychuous pleasures through romantic love.

In other words, you need only your productive work and a romantic-love partner for a full-range, prosperous, happy life. But productive work is a basic requirement for achieving romantic love. In that sense, productive work is a cause and romantic love is an effect.

Productive work is the basic requirement for human values. And romantic love and psychuous pleasures are the rewards for achieving those values. ...You cannot experience self-esteem, happiness, and romantic love without productive work. But you can experience self-esteem, happiness, and productive work without romantic love.

Friendship can offer great values and pleasurable experiences. Yet, friendships, especially close friendships, can in certain cases drain valuable time needed for high levels of business, creativity, and achievement. In a demanding business or intensely creative work, a person with a valuable romantic-love partner can often reach higher levels of achievement and happiness with few or no other friends. Friendships, moreover, are subject to errors that can turn into liabilities which drain your time, productiveness, efficacy and, thus, happiness. But value-generating, business friendships are generally the happiest, most exciting, most valuable of all relationships, except the romantic-love relationship.

In the end, reality prevails over life. The total experience of every person's life always moves toward justice as reality asserts itself: Productive, rational individuals increasingly gain prosperity, love, and happiness from life. Conversely, unproductive, irrational individuals increasingly lose prosperity, love, and happiness — no matter what the surface appearances.

**"That is a profound thought about life and justice," my father said. "I never saw that connection. It seems to me that values are the key to life and love...and justice. Can you talk more about values and love?"**

118

Abstract values of a friendship are normally not negotiable for tangible and material values. Likewise, tangible and material values normally cannot be converted into abstract values. Occasional exceptions do exist. Exceptions occur mainly in romantic-love relationships because the intense physical/psychological interactions tend to pull abstract values and material values closer together. At times, within a romantic-love relationship, those values can become interrelated. For example, emotional and sexual love provided by one partner can tangibly increase the creative, productive output of the other partner. Likewise, certain tangible values can amplify abstract values. For example, creative and productive accomplishments of one partner can increase the emotional love, sexual exhilaration, and psychuous pleasures of the other partner.

Generally, in a friendship or romantic-love relationship, an exchange of abstract values — be they healthy, neurotic, or a mixture — is taken for granted and occurs naturally. In friendship relationships, much of the abstract value interchange consists of open, casual exchanges of ideas and suggestions — a type of easy two-way communication that often is mutually valuable. Indeed, such exchanges of ideas and suggestions occur in most good conversations between friends or lovers.

Other abstract values exchanged between two people in a valid love or friendship relationship include psychologically pleasing or enhancing reflections, consistent encouragement especially during difficult times, mirroring various psychological values, understanding feedback of the other's thoughts or activities, and the exchange of practical ideas obtained from each person's unique life experiences.

Sometimes abstract values from a friend or love partner can be beneficially integrated into one's personal life to increase awareness, productivity, and happiness. Generally, abstract values are offered freely, without the thought or expectation of material or tangible payment. In a love or a friendship relationship, no one needs to measure or weigh that natural interchange of abstract values. For that exchange is freely taken and given as a natural, pleasurable, expected part of any good relationship.

Thus, abstract values cannot be used to pay for material values. For material values must always be fairly traded.

Material values represent irreplaceable segments of a person's life, effort, and time required to earn those values. Every productive human being needs to trade, not give away, his or her produced values in order to survive, grow, and be happy. If material and tangible values are not traded mutually and fairly, then a portion of a person's life is sacrificed to another person at the expense of both people. As a result of that unfairness, both happiness and friendship decline.

Fairly traded, tangible values do not necessarily mean evenly traded, tangible values. Moreover, a highly competent, nonmystical housewife can through integrated thinking and consistent efforts contribute great tangible and material values to her husband's ability to work more efficiently and effectively, thus, generate more values and income. For that, he fairly trades by providing his wife with tangible and material goods.

Those who misunderstand the nature of friendship or romantic love may try to use abstract values as payment for material values. In doing so, they are exploiting their friendship or love relationships. Such people unjustly extract material values from others for the "privilege" of those others being in their presence. They unilaterally deem their abstract values as payment for tangible and material values. That kind of exploitation, aside from being unjust and parasitical, poisons the relationship.

More important, habitual trading of abstract values for tangible values diminishes that person's ability to produce and deliver tangible values. Such unfair trading leaves that person increasingly incompetent and dependent on others for material or tangible values. ...The potential for friendship, romantic love, and happiness is always the greatest among value-producing men and women who fairly trade tangible and material values in their relationships.

**"OK, Zon, I have a tough one for you," my dad stood up and said. "I have run into problems with jealousy before, both my own feelings and then hers. How do I handle jealousy this time? I don't want it to creep into this wonderful relationship. What is the mystic-free voice of Zon on this topic...the powerful voice of fully integrated honesty?"**

*Love: Psychuous Sex Is Told*

I identify two types of sexual jealousy: *good-thought* (GT) and *bad-thought* (BT). Both types are based on the erroneous assumption that you have a claim on your love-partner's life, especially her sex life.

No one can ever really own another person's life, including that person's sex life. Every individual exclusively owns each and every segment of his or her own life. In relationships, people volitionally share, not own, various aspects or segments of each other's lives. In a romantic-love relationship, by nature, many more life experiences are intimately shared and integrated than in other types of human relationships. Also, while certain segments of a person's life can be temporarily rented or hired as in a voluntary employer-employee relationship, no part of a person's life can be actually owned by anyone else.

Feelings of jealousy arise when the unreal presumption of possessing your partner seems challenged. GT jealousy is characterized by the retention of basically *good thoughts* about your partner, even when pain or anger is generated. Most people can experience various degrees of GT jealousy about their love partners. GT jealousy does not always mean the jealous-reacting partner is insecure or possessive, especially if the jealousy is experienced only as a passing feeling. GT jealousy, even if severely painful, rarely inflicts deep or permanent damage on either partner or the relationship.

Likewise, GT jealousy seldom cuts deeply into the emotions because positive feelings about one's partner dominate the underlying emotions.

BT jealousy, on the other hand, is a destructive, mystical reaction that conjures up, often out of nothing, unjust *bad thoughts* about one's partner. Those bad thoughts are often well concealed, but insidiously destructive to the emotions of both partners. In contrast to GT jealousy in which good thoughts are retained about one's partner, BT or bad-thought jealousy prevents the jealous partner from knowing, accepting, remembering, or believing the values in the victim partner. Instead, unreal bitterness, cynicism, or malevolence against the victim partner is conjured up by BT jealousy.

Such negative illusions are usually rooted in past experiences not even related to the victim partner. The victim partner usually

121

senses a "bad-person" feedback from the BT jealous person. That causes the victim to respond with increasing puzzlement or astonishment followed by anger, dislike, and a sense of injustice. Those negative emotions usually keep building until they eventually outweigh all the good feelings and values between the partners. At that point, love and the relationship die.

Neo-Tech or fully integrated honesty can overcome both types of jealousy, especially the GT type. BT jealousy is more difficult to overcome because the cause is a cancerous mysticism that becomes deeply rooted in one's emotions. Cognitive-based psychotherapy may help overcome BT jealousy and its destructive effects. Unfortunately, only a minute fraction, if any, in the profession understand mysticism as the prime disease of the human mind and the only disease of human consciousness. The only certain cure is to use mystic-breaking, integrated honesty to self-command *all* actions. Without that integrated honesty, one will continue reacting destructively to the emotions of jealousy.

Realize, honesty is not automatic. It always requires explicit, conscious effort. Being honest is hard work...very hard work. If, in difficult emotional situations, one is not aware of the concentrated effort required to be honest, that person is probably not being fully honest. At that point, he or she can easily plug into effortless mysticism. For with mysticism, a person can automatically rationalize out-of-context scenarios to avoid the effort required to understand reality and solve one's own problems.

Developing the skills for being honest is neither automatic nor easy. Honesty requires high-effort concentration, discipline, and awareness. Because of the constant effort required to be honest, many people default to mysticism and thus lose the essential tool for solving problems — the tool for achieving prosperity, power, and happiness. That tool is honesty. ...Many people *never* grasp or experience integrated honesty.

Fully integrated honesty evolves from the efforts required to be consistently honest. By contrast, mystical dishonesty evolves from self-deceptions and defaults — from a self-chosen laziness that relegates honesty to a low priority, especially when feelings are involved. ...With mysticism, honesty becomes arbitrary.

**"That is a profound thought: being honest is hard work,"
my father said with a wide-eyed look on his face...like this
was one of those moments that would always stay in his
memory as a mental videotape.**

Indeed, being honest is hard work, especially in difficult
emotional situations such as bouts with deep-rooted jealousy.
Realize, however, no value judgment can be made on emotions
alone. Only the choice to react rationally or irrationally to an
emotion can be judged good or bad. The judgments I am making
here are based on jealous reactions, not jealous emotions. The
choice to act rationally in avoiding a jealous reaction will help
dissipate that harmful emotion. But the harmful, irrational choice
to react jealously always feeds and amplifies that emotion.

The bad thoughts of BT jealousy along with its hostile,
immature possessiveness and obligatory demands become
increasingly unreal, unfair, and burdensome to the victim partner.
Such jealousy will eventually destroy any love relationship no
matter how strong were the original love and values. BT
jealousy is an unfair, hostile foisting of one's own personal
problems or inadequacies onto the victim partner. The mounting
obligatory demands and hostile possessiveness of BT jealousy
destroys a love relationship by penalizing the victim partner for
the very values he or she offers. In fact, the more values offered,
the greater are the penalties — the greater are the possessive
attacks and obligatory demands. Indeed, BT jealousy, immature
possessiveness, and obligatory demands not only rest on
mystically unreal premises, but are always unjust since the victim
is penalized to the extent he or she offers values to the jealous
partner.

The jealous partner ignores the free-choice position necessary
to build a healthy, permanent romantic-love relationship. The
jealous partner accepts the false idea that outside relationships
or associations are by nature threatening. Furthermore, the
jealous partner erroneously judges his or her partner in terms of
unrelated, outside experiences and relationships rather than in
terms of their own relationship.

Through mysticism, jealousy destroys values by focusing on
what is *not* given or what is not available...while ignoring,

123

abusing, tearing down, or destroying what is given or is available. Through Neo-Tech, the non-mystic appreciates and focuses on what values are given or are available and then builds from that position — and only from that position.

"Testing" is simply another form of jealousy in which one partner translates his or her insecurity into testing the victim partner for proof of love or fidelity. Such "testing" is unfair, immature, and continually escalates until the values of a relationship are destroyed.

**"Zon, I once loved a woman who was a prisoner to bad-thought jealousy, which I did not understand at the time, but was the reason I never married her. I loved her very, very much, but she systematically destroyed that love. Often, I felt as if she wanted to destroy me."**

BT jealousy will eventually destroy even the deepest love relationships. Jealousy gradually poisons the friendship aspects of love. Once that friendship is gone, no link remains to hold together the nonsexual aspects of the relationship.

Within the person projecting bad-thought jealousy, a bitter core of poisonous emotions develops, although often initially hidden. That core increasingly releases bad feelings toward the victim partner which, in turn, unfairly diminishes the victim's freedom and happiness. Recognizing the presence of that poison core is the first step in keeping BT jealousy from destroying a relationship. But once that core is formed, freeing oneself from its destructive effects is difficult.

The problem of BT jealousy cannot be wished away. For the poison core usually develops from mystical defaults deep within the jealous partner's subconscious. Unless identified and removed, that poison core will dissolve the pleasure, happiness, and love in any romantic relationship.

Such a poison core generates hostile actions that are often subtle and unrecognized at first. But that jealous partner increasingly takes unjust advantage of the victim partner's innocence, values, love, and goodwill. Such injustice constantly wounds the victim partner and will eventually destroy all love and friendship. Unlike the nonjealous lover who usually

124

experiences pain whenever his loved one is in pain, the BT jealous lover will often gain a satisfying sense of security on being able to inflict pain on the victim partner. That malevolence of BT jealousy eventually negates any value of the relationship.

A person should avoid listening to false accusations or unjust innuendos leveled against oneself or others by a jealous, envious, or gossipy person. Even though the conscious mind can reject known false charges, such accusations still enter nonanalytical pockets of the subconscious mind. That, in turn, causes subsequent emotions to automatically reflect negative feelings toward oneself or the person being falsely accused. A person is helpless in avoiding those unjust, harmful, subconscious reactions. Likewise, a person is essentially powerless to avoid the guilt or bad feelings resulting from false implications coming from a BT jealous partner. As long as that relationship continues, the jealous partner can increasingly inflict psychic damage within the victim's subconscious. The victim partner suffers damage proportional to his or her exposure to the poison core of a BT jealous partner. Usually the only release from that damage is for the victim partner to terminate that harmful relationship, as you did.

By contrast, a mystic-free Neo-Tech partner will ask: "Do not judge me on your feelings, wishes, imagination, or what others say. Judge me by what you know about my character, deeds, and actions. And I will always grant you the same."

**"Sometimes I feel anxiety about getting old," my father confessed, changing the subject. "I guess I love my life so much and love my children, seeing them grow up so fast, and I'm still looking for love. What do you make of those anxieties?"**

As people grow older, their views of life often grow increasingly negative. Their hopes and dreams often turn into disillusions. On aging, such people gradually lose the capacity to experience the joy inherent in life. Their anticipation of life continually diminishes as their used-up, shrinking futures become evident and the inevitability of death draws closer. ...But Neo-Tech reverses that dying process by allowing life and happiness

125

to grow with age and experience.

In the upsidedown, mystical death-oriented world, increasing age becomes an increasing liability on each individual. In that mystical world, "It is better to be young than old". But in the Neo-Tech life-oriented world, increasing age becomes an increasing asset of growth, knowledge, experience, especially as mystic-free businesses develop commercial, non-aging biological immortality.

Age is no factor in achieving psychuous pleasures, except for the possible lack-of-knowledge limitations of adolescent sex. Moreover, psychuous pleasures can continually increase with age as one widens his or her values, knowledge, and experience. In building psychuous pleasures, a person's psychological growth can far outweigh so-called physical aging effects. Emotional and physical pleasures as well as prosperity and happiness can increase indefinitely for any honest, productive individual applying Neo-Tech knowledge.

For most people, both sexual and nonsexual pleasures unnecessarily diminish with age. Negative philosophical and psychological changes occur as their futures fade and their spans of remaining years shrink. They despair and become sour with age while increasingly surrendering to the mystics' come-to-God or waiting-for-death attitudes. They surrender to the altruistic myth that older people should sacrifice themselves, their careers, their lives to "make room" for youth. With that surrender, a person's happiness fades.

Despite what many physicians erroneously advise, no mystic-free, productive person has to decline in physical, mental, or sexual activity with age. All mystic-free, productive people can experience increasing happiness and quality of life with age caused by increasing knowledge, growth, and experience: By applying the Neo-Tech/Psychuous concepts, one can not only avoid the unnecessary, mystical decline toward death, but can continually elevate his or her quality of life and psychuous growth through increasing knowledge and experience.

Sex never renews itself spontaneously. Left unattended, sex gradually diminishes in both quality and value. But with Neo-Tech, the quality and value of sex is continuously renewed and expanded by constantly investing conscious thought and effort into further developing personal values and earned power. The Neo-Tech/Psychuous concepts allow never-aging growth on all levels of conscious human life — on physiological, psychological, and philosophical levels. ...In a Neo-Tech civilization, one need not age, lose values...or die.

**That evening at home, my father looked up from the book he was reading and said, "What did Zon mean when she said that in a Neo-Tech civilization, one need not age, lose values...or die?"**

## Ancient Secret Four

# FREEDOM
# A New Code Of Success Is Told

**The next day my father came to his mountain and said, "Thank you for giving me strength. I thought the whole night about what you said yesterday. I feel so happy. I know what I really want now. But my happiness is being destroyed. I cannot get away from the IRS. It has hounded me and my business for years. I'm exhausted by it, but I cannot get it off my mind, ever." My father's face, as the wind blew his hair back, at that sad moment looked old and worn. Then, the deep male voice of Zon reached his ears via the wind. The voice of Zon, so wise and strong, immediately relaxed the tension on my father's face. The longer Zon spoke, the younger my father looked again, for Zon, who had watched man since the beginning of human consciousness, made my father realize that *he*, not the neocheaters, held genuine power:**

For 2300 years I have observed as the neocheater says that sacrifice is "noble", especially when done for a "higher" cause or, better yet, no cause. He says that use of force, especially government force, is acceptable against individuals, especially if the result serves the social "good" or a "higher" cause. The ends can justify the means. Force and coercion can be pragmatically used for the "good" of society. Individual rights can be violated or sacrificed for "noble" ends.

The Neo-Tech person says that refusal to sacrifice is by nature life enhancing and thus is morally right. He says that rejecting the *initiation* of force, threat of force, coercion, or fraud against any individual for *any* reason is the foundation of morality. In regards to force, the ends *never* justify the means. All moral actions are based on principles that prohibit initiatory force, threat of force, coercion, and fraud as a means to accomplish ends, no matter how "noble".

The highest cause in the universe is the well-being and happiness of the conscious individual. The individual — a

129

minority of one — is the smallest, the most important, most unprotected of all minorities. If rights of the individual are protected, then rights are protected for everyone — for Blacks, Chicanos, women, factory owners, factory workers, farmers, homosexuals. The concept of minority rights is meaningless, prejudicial, and destructive. In fact, that concept is a tool, a "higher cause", used by professional mystics and neocheaters to usurp power and unearned values not by protecting but by violating the rights of individuals.

All destructive authorities and other neocheaters would become powerless if the value producers withdrew their support and said "no". If *all* victims simply said "no" to their victimizers, *all* professional mystics and neocheaters would lose their power to plunder others and destroy values. ...After 2001, there will be a way to safely say "no", with the Neo-Tech Party of the 21st century. Exciting times are ahead for mankind.

Today, value producers neither like nor sanction neocheaters, usurpers, plunderers, and other such parasites. But can those value producers say "no" to the neocheating powercrats who threaten them? In the long run, value producers can and must say "no". They must refuse every usurping neocheater if they are to survive. Indeed, most businessmen are innocent heroes struggling to produce competitive values for others despite increasing government coercion, attacks, and usurpations. ...After 2001, they will be able to *safely* say "no" under the new code.

Without the professional mystics and neocheaters, all the corrupt systems of forced regulations, forced mediocrity, fake litigation, destructive taxes, corruption, and wars would not exist. But without the value producers, civilization itself would not exist. Without those producers, all civilization would perish. Or, by contrast, without mysticism all neocheaters would perish. Everyone else would flourish.

**From Zon's teachings, that evening my father started writing a list of thoughts of the neocheaters versus thoughts of the Neo-Tech person. Here was his list:**

**Thoughts Of A Neocheater:**

- The uncontrolled, free individual is by nature bad and harmful to conscious life. Morally, the individual must be controlled by external "authorities".

- Group or government force is necessary to control the individual to make him do good.

- The conscious individual is subordinate to society or to "higher" or "nobler" causes.

- The use of force to compel individuals to comply with the "will" of society is moral.

- The moral purpose of life is self-sacrifice in serving "higher" goals.

- Pride is a character flaw.

- Service to a government by conscription is necessary and proper.

- Property belongs to society, the "people", or the government.

- Social science is a valid, valuable science.

- Populations consist of various groups of people, societies, and cultures.

**Thoughts Of A Neo-Tech Person:**

- The uncontrolled, free individual is by nature good and beneficial to conscious life. Morally, the individual must be free and remain free from external "authorities".

131

- Both the individual and society function best when the individual is free from any group control, government force, or external "authority".

- The conscious individual is the highest, noblest possible good or cause in the universe.

- The use of initiatory force against any individual for any reason is immoral.

- The moral purpose of life is to achieve rational happiness.

- Pride is the result of moral virtue.

- Service to a government or to any cause is proper only on a voluntary basis. Any form of conscription is forced sacrifice and evil.

- Property is an earned entity. Thus, it can morally belong only to those individuals (or their businesses) who produced the values needed to earn that property.

- Social science generally has little or no validity as a science, especially because it usually denies the individual as the prime entity of human life.

- Populations, societies, and cultures consist of specific individuals.

The next morning when he summoned Zon, my father called out, "Zon, I'm beginning to shed my mystical sense of guilt for my contempt of bogus authority. What is external authority, anyway? It's a myth that has no basis in reality. It came from our deep-rooted, bicameral-mind tendencies. Such external authority always develops into a destructive machine when the majority unthinkingly or out of fear accept, obey, and follow the commands and wishes of that authority.

**Once the majority have a way to say 'no', then the neocheaters — the nonproducers and parasites — will be abandoned by the value producers. And all neocheaters and value destroyers will founder with no power to survive. ...Wow, Zon, for the first time I feel stronger than the neocheaters!" Zon answered:**

Professional mystics and neocheaters function by forcing or coercing you, the producer, to sacrifice increasingly larger portions of time, property, and earnings to themselves and other nonproducers. As a result of making "careers" from other people's sacrifices, those value destroyers never learn to exert the honest thought and effort needed to be competitive — to produce tradeable values required to become happy, independent individuals with genuine prosperity and self-esteem. By their defaults, mystics and neocheaters lose the possibility of earning abiding prosperity and happiness, despite their desperate efforts to feign importance, self-worth and happiness. ...With Neo-Tech, you not only can avoid sacrifice, but can smash the facade of all professional mystics and neocheaters.

The most harmful neocheaters operate through government, religion, public education, and dishonest journalism. Such people must always fake self-esteem to justify their destructive existences. They do that by slyly attacking businesses, their products, and those who through heroic efforts create productive jobs for others, a supreme moral virtue. For, by attacking through the bizarre, inverted ethics of altruism, even the most destructive neocheaters can fake a moral superiority over great producers and their works. Indeed, attacking values is the only way those neocheaters can gain a drug-like relief from their anxieties caused by living destructively. They get relief by destroying values. That destruction gives them a sense of power — a faked self-esteem needed to survive — needed to ward off suicide. ...But with Neo-Tech, the value producers finally have a fumigant to rid their lives of mystics and neocheaters.

A particularly malevolent theme has developed in the rhetoric and actions of today's neocheating "ecologists" and "environmentalists". They, by using the force of government, place the "well-being" of birds, insects...including mosquitoes,

133

trees, plants, and inanimate "landscapes" *above* the lives, well-being, and happiness of human beings. Those anti-human themes are extensions of the altruistic philosophy advanced through many media commentators, almost all politicians and theologians, neocheating social "intellectuals", including many teachers, university professors, and know-nothing personalities and entertainers acting as "authorities" on the basis of feeling rather than knowledge.

And beyond? What does a future of growing altruism hold? Constant exposure to the increasing atrocities of altruism gradually numbs people into silently accepting higher and higher levels of injustice, human suffering, crippling of minds, killing, violence, terrorism. Fewer and fewer people object or even care about those mounting atrocities. Before Neo-Tech, those who consistently upheld individual rights to life and property were fading in both intensity and numbers. In that way, conditions were developing for the ultimate egalitarian end result. But Neo-Tech is reversing that trend — slowly today, rapidly tomorrow.

The final egalitarian "purification" is always the mass liquidation of human life. That "purification" starts with the exploitation and then sacrifice of the productive middle class and ends with their physical slaughter. Those who live by honest principles, those who uphold freedom and justice, those who love life, those who will not surrender their minds and lives to others, those who produce the most values for others — they, as the best, are eliminated first. The mass destruction of the best, the innocent, the virtuous producer of values has been occurring with increasing intensity in various African and Asian countries. And the same would happen throughout the Western world, including the United States, if altruism and egalitarianism grew to their natural conclusions. ...Neo-Tech will prevent that from happening.

But, only those holding genuine power — the value producers — can cure the disease of altruism. The value producer can stop altruism cold by saying "no" to the sacrificial demands of mystics and neocheaters. That mechanism to say "no" is coming. Indeed, through Neo-Tech, all value producers can guiltlessly, decisively reject all mysticism, altruism, egalitarianism. When the value producer says "no" to the neocheaters, their mystical hoaxes will become powerless and then crumble. Never again can those neocheaters trick or coerce the value producer into supporting them.

The Neo-Tech concepts provide the tools to expunge all professional mystics and neocheaters from our planet forever. The Neo-Tech Party will provide the means.

**"Just how is it, Zon, that mystical hoaxes have so completely held back civilization from its extraordinary potential?"**

All organized religions and most political systems contradict man's nature because they are based on mysticism and altruism. Those systems require the individual to contradict his or her nature through sacrifice. Under the spell of mysticism, one loses increasing portions of prosperity, life, love, and happiness to various imaginary "higher causes". And such losses are for no real reason except to support those neocheaters who survive by manipulating dishonest, destructive, mystical notions.

**"But, how are the mystical illusions made so convincing that they fool the majority of intelligent people?"**

Valid facts and concepts are first presented to capture the interest and confidence of the ordinary person. Those valid concepts are then woven throughout the false, mystical notions to lend an air of validity. Essentially all altruistic doctrines depend on similar techniques of using out-of-context facts, non sequiturs, slogans, "truisms", and parables to "validate" their specious doctrines.

Similarly, the news media constantly mislead their audiences by using out-of-context facts and non sequiturs to create stories that seem valid, but are not. In that way, the media mystically manufacture "news" that subtly or overtly attacks objective values and their producers. Constant exposure to propaganda against objective values and heroic producers leaves people increasingly indifferent toward upholding honesty and justice. That mystical-based indifference produces lethargy and ennui not only toward objective values and heroic producers but toward life itself.

By manipulating subjective mysticism with dishonest

135

reporting, much of today's neocheating media successfully obscure the value of productive individuals and their benevolent power. That constant obscuring of facts undermines everyone's view of great human achievements such as the automobile, supermarkets, and major technological advances. The persistent attacks against objective human values by politicians, theologians, social "intellectuals", and the media gradually diminish the strength, confidence, and happiness of the productive middle class, leaving them increasingly vulnerable for exploitation by the professional mystics and neocheaters.

**"A systematic blurring of reality, then a sharp focussing of illusions," my father said, thinking out loud.**

Many current authors of social literature use rationalizations, specious cliches, non sequiturs, concrete-bound specifics taken out of context, and guilt-inducing half-truths to manipulate the middle-class producers into sacrificing their self-interests to an array of "higher" causes.

Stalin, Mao, and their neocheating colleagues used various altruistic tools to justify slaughtering millions of innocent, middle-class producers in the name of a higher "good". And what is always the reason for such mass destruction and slaughter? Always for no other reason than to build personal false power and bogus jobs. No other reason ever exists.

In order to live, the value destroyer must usurp values created by the value producer. That dependence deprives the usurper of self-esteem, leaving him resentful and envious toward value producers. Such feelings of worthlessness, resentment, and envy can build until the usurper would subconsciously just as soon be dead. Out of such resentment and envy, that person would like to drag everyone else to the grave with him, especially the value producers. Indeed, that is what happens when totalitarian leaders assume power. Out of envy and hatred, they eventually destroy themselves and anyone else they can destroy.

Stalin, Hitler, and Mao, for example, were personally responsible for staggering property destruction while systematically slaughtering many millions of innocent, productive human beings. Castro, as another example, publicly stated that

136

he, an ex-lawyer who had never produced or earned competitive values, would like to drop a nuclear bomb on New York City, destroying the greatest concentration of earned, man-made values on this planet. Such mass destruction would help prop his pseudo self-esteem by making him feel big and important. But, in fact, he has never been more than a destructive pip-squeak and mass murderer. ...All mass murderers throughout history required the tools of altruism and mysticism to rationalize their purposeful destruction of values and life.

**"So does the IRS," my father said. "What will save me from this monster?"**

After 2001, a new code of living is coming. Everything will change. After 3000 years, the new code will lift mankind into the Civilization of the Universe.

Our civilization is at *the* pivotal point today. The *Nuclear-Decision Threshold* is the point at which energy, knowledge, and technology have advanced to where sufficient, man-made energy — nuclear energy — can be generated to physically destroy all life on the planet. From that point, all civilizations must follow one of two courses:

(1) Proceed in an irrational, altruistic, Platonistic philosophical system in which initiatory force compels others to support mystical "higher" causes that feed the bogus livelihoods of neocheaters. Such systems will eventually lead either to all-out nuclear warfare or to a retreat into an anti-technological Dark Ages in which most knowledge and technology are lost. In either case, most of the world's population will die and civilization will perish because of meaningless mysticism being manipulated to give false power and bogus livelihoods to the value destroyers.

(2) Proceed in, or change to, a rational, business-like, Aristotelian philosophical system in which initiatory force plays no role. Such a system allows civilization to safely advance beyond the *Nuclear-Decision Threshold*. That threshold is the point that every advanced civilization must successfully pass through to survive.

Thus, any civilization advancing significantly beyond that threshold would by nature exist within a rational Aristotelian/Neo-

Tech society. That in turn would mean a free-market business society from which initiatory force is eradicated as uncompetitive, impotent, and immoral. In any such advanced society, all forms of mysticism would by nature have been discredited and discarded as stupid and destructive. Such a business-minded society would be free of politicians, theologians, neocheaters, coercive governments, and other usurpers and parasites. Actions would be based on reality-oriented logic exercised by free individuals harmoniously, competitively living in accord with their rational best interests. Thus, the Civilization of the Universe consists of many advanced civilizations all based on Neo-Tech.

Such advanced civilizations would have access to the interstellar "computer" system most certainly present throughout the universe. Throughout that "computer" system, all important knowledge would be organized and available for exchange among all advanced, Neo-Tech civilizations — perhaps through an oscillating, gravity-coded system.

For our own civilization to advance significantly beyond our current *Nuclear-Decision Threshold* would require a shift from the current Platonistic/altruistic philosophical base to a Aristotelian/Neo-Tech philosophical base. Sometime after 2001, that new code of living that eliminates all ruling classes will begin.

Aristotelian philosophy is the intellectual basis of Neo-Tech. Platonistic philosophy is the intellectual basis of every irrational, destructive religious and political system promoted in the past 2300 years. Indeed, Platonism is the philosophical foundation of mysticism, altruism, sacrifice, egalitarianism, existentialism, religion, dictatorships, theism, socialism, democracy, communism, fascism, evangelism and every other rule of force, coercion, and fraud. Except for free-enterprise capitalism, all political systems including democracy — a tyranny by the majority — require deception and force to exist. Thus, all those political and religious systems are immoral and harmful to human beings. Only free-enterprise capitalism is:
  1. based entirely on voluntary free choice,
  2. consistent with the nature of conscious beings and, thus is beneficial to all conscious beings,
  3. moral and just: Offers freedom to everyone. Rejects

all mysticism, racism, initiatory force, and fraud.

Civilization would have advanced super rapidly if an Aristotelian rather than a Platonistic philosophy had dominated for the past 2300 years. Free-enterprise capitalism would have eliminated mysticism, parasitism, religion, collectivism, altruism, and force-backed governments with the subsequent elimination of neocheating, wars, crime, disease, poverty, and death itself. In this super rapidly advancing Neo-Tech Society, the steam engine and trains would have been in operation at the birth of Christ; mass produced cars would have been available in 50 A.D.; commercial airlines would have been in operation by 60 A.D.; crime and fraud would have been eliminated, not by government police but by individual self-defense and private protection services, private courts, and computerized ostracism, by 65 A.D.; nuclear power would have existed by 70 A.D.; man would have landed on the moon by 80 A.D.; cancer would have been cured by 90 A.D.; youth-perpetuating biological immortality would have occurred by 120 A.D.; immortal conscious individuals, master of all known nature, would have happened by 2000 A.D.

**"What are you saying?" My father stood up and looked puzzled.**

A Neo-Tech Society is a super rapidly advancing society, as everyone will discover after 2001, under the new code. If an objective, Aristotelian-based philosophy rather than a mystical, Platonistic-based philosophy had dominated the Western World since the Golden Age of Greece, mankind would have experienced that super rapidly advancing Neo-Tech Society. This is what would have happened:

350 B.C.   Aristotle 384 B.C.-322 B.C. Plato's philosophy identified as mystical and forever dismissed as dishonest, destructive.

200 B.C.   America discovered.

100 B.C.   Free-enterprise capitalism established around the world. Free markets flourishing. All forms of mysticism and neocheating identified, discredited, and

rejected. All government taxation and nonprofit spending programs abolished. All forms of initiatory force are morally condemned. Wars become obsolete and vanish. Arts, sciences, technology boom in totally free markets. Dynamic competition and value production rule. Romantic love flourishes.

0 B.C.    All traces of mysticism, altruism, and collectivism are gone. Poverty essentially eliminated. The individual is the supreme value. Jesus builds the highest skyscraper in Asia Minor. Trains and steamships are major forms of transportation.

20 A.D.    Electrical power developed, camera developed.

40 A.D.    Internal-combustion engine developed.

50 A.D.    Cars in mass production. Airplane developed.

60 A.D.    Commercial airlines flourishing. Computer developed.

65 A.D.    Crime and fraud become unprofitable, obsolete, and essentially eliminated by computerized ostracism.

70 A.D.    Nuclear power developed. Nuclear weapons never conceived.

80 A.D.    Man on the moon. Internet developed.

90 A.D.    Cancer and most other diseases eliminated.

100 A.D.    Man on Mars and heading for other planets.

110 A.D.    Need for sleep eliminated.

120 A.D.    Youth-perpetuating biological immortality developed.

140 A.D.    Prosperity and happiness of conscious beings are universal.

200 A.D.    Worldwide, commercial, biological immortality achieved. All diseases and aging eliminated. Man colonizing, mining, and commercializing the moon, asteroids, and Mars. Commercial shuttle flights, passenger and freight, to space-station colonies. ...Achieve access to the gravity-coded, interstellar universal computer.

1200 A.D. Energy and technology advanced to where sufficient energy can be generated for traveling to other earth-like planets in outer space. Science, knowledge, and fulfillment advanced to the point at which no economic or scientific incentive exists for directly communicating with or travelling to the billions of other, outer-space civilizations.

2000 A.D. Immortal conscious beings in a Neo-Tech, free-enterprise society are master of all known nature. People and goods are transported at the speed of light via electronic transfer. Most goods manufactured via nanotechnology with the electronic control of atoms and molecules. New knowledge is expanding at near the speed of light.

**My father, still standing, wiped his forehead with his arm. "Wow," he said, sensing the scientific logic behind Zon's timetable. The mountain told him to go home now, and think about today. Tomorrow, the mountain would tell him how that Neo-Tech Society will come about.**

**That night, my father was laying on his black leather couch in his home office with the lights out, further sorting out the difference between most men, women, and children versus this odd ruling class of politicians, regulatory bureaucrats, and the establishment media. In the darkness, he was saying, "The destructive authorities and neocheaters say that human beings are by nature evil, irrational, and destructive. They are subordinate to 'higher' causes. Human beings must be controlled by some higher 'authority' or government and forced to serve others or society.**

**"In reality, human beings are by nature good, rational, and productive — or mankind could not exist. Human beings are competent to fill their needs and to achieve happiness. By being free to act according to their own nature, they will best serve themselves and society without force or coercion from any authority or government.**

**"Mystics and neocheaters say that reality is what the mind thinks or imagines. Wishes, will, or faith can create or alter reality. 'True' reality is unknowable, they say. But I know that reality is what exists. Reality exists independently of**

anyone's thoughts, desires, will, or wishes. All reality is knowable.

"Of course, the neocheating external authorities say that sacrifice, humility, and service to duty are needed for prosperity, love, and happiness. In reality, though, rational action, self-esteem, and production of competitive values for others are needed for prosperity, love, and happiness.

"Human beings survive by using their minds rationally to deal with reality. They must know reality to competitively produce the values needed to prosper. Only by being left free to satisfy their nature can human beings serve themselves and others best. People who live free and according to their natures can easily build a future of prosperity and happiness. Moreover, with Neo-Tech, such people can easily rid themselves of all mystics and neocheaters. ...I cannot wait until tomorrow when Zon will tell me how the Neo-Tech Society will come about."

\* \* \*

The next day, my father arrived full of energy with lots of questions. But he barely got to his spot when the mountain spoke, startling my dad:

Everyday I feel your thoughts. Why is it that the IRS causes you such anxiety?

Surprised, my father thought hard about the question, then answered, "It's because of the cruel-and-unusual punishment they inflict on innocent productive people."

But you feel much more than ripped off. You feel fear.

Again, my father thought hard about what the mountain had said. Then he added, "Yes I do. I do feel fear."

Ah, yes. The threat. That constant threat. Now, I will tell you something: Once that threat and that fear in ordinary people is gone, the Neo-Tech Society will happen. That threat and fear come from coercion, the threat of force — pay or they'll

142

ultimately put you in prison.

Force, coercion, threat of force, or fraud initiated against any individual for any reason by any individual, groups of individuals, societies, or governments is morally wrong. That is the only categorical moral statement possible. That statement must, by its nature, be the categorical, irreducible, and fundamental standard for all conscious beings, always, everywhere. That statement is the moral axiom upon which Neo-Tech rests.

The initiation of force and fraud among conscious beings is not only the basic moral wrong and evil, but is the primary tool used by all professional mystics and neocheaters to survive through value destruction. The initiation of force is the one and only cause of a ruling class. Since the Golden Age of Greece, civilizations have all lived under ruling classes. That was the old code of living that will vanish sometime after 2001.

No exceptions to the immorality of initiatory force exist. No matter how "noble" the ends, they never justify the means of initiating force, fraud, or coercion against any individual. Any government or activity that depends on or uses initiatory force, threat of force, or coercion is immoral and destructive. Therefore, all taxation backed by force, all conscription backed by force, and all laws that regulate or control by force or coercion are immoral.

The only laws that are objectively just and moral are those that protect the life and property rights of individuals from initiatory force and fraud. All other laws that regulate people's lives or property are morally wrong, contrary to human nature, and harmful to everyone. Later I will give you examples of such immoral laws and their harm. But right now, it is important to understand all such laws are morally wrong because they use threats or force against individuals.

While all governments have the power, none ever have the moral right to initiate force or coercion against any individual. Again, the only beneficial and moral laws are those designed to protect the life and property rights of individuals from initiatory force, the threat of force, and fraud. In turn, the only moral use of force is for self-defense: That is for protection of oneself, property, or country from force initiated by other individuals or governments. ...Self-defense by any means, including force, is not

143

only a basic moral right, but a moral duty.

No government has ever helped an individual produce more values or greater happiness than that individual could have produced without government. Governments differ only in the degree they harm people. In fact, except for protecting individual rights, no valid reason for government exists. Indeed, the entire concept of government is invalid and mystical. Government is nothing more than a mystical, big-lie hoax perpetuated through the centuries by neocheaters through force, non sequiturs, and the manipulation of mysticism.

Government is not the equivalent of one's country. Governments are based on invalid mystical notions that have no basis in reality; countries are objectively real entities of defined territories. A person can love his or her country, but properly despise the government that with usurped power constantly harms and drains everyone within its realm.

Oppression is directly proportional to the force and fraud governments and religions exert against individuals. The most oppressive, unhappy period of history was the Dark Ages during which religious power controlled the political system with unlimited force against individuals. By contrast, human happiness and well-being increased markedly during those periods when honesty and business reduced government and religious power. Indeed, governments and churches have always been controlled by neocheaters who manipulate the mystical concept of altruistic sacrifice to gain power.

Today, the various political-religious hucksters, neocheating academia, mystical feminists, and many dishonest journalists and political cartoonists are climbing over each other to attack and undermine individual rights, business, and value producers around the world. Since business and its value producers strengthen individual rights, the attacks on business and producers are actually attacks on individual rights. Such attacks are designed to control the value producers for exploitation by neocheaters.

Under the old code, dominated by ruling classes increasingly pushing mysticism and violence, our society would sink into a Catastrophic Era around century end, which could lead to and culminate in either a government-sponsored nuclear holocaust or a world-wide, terror-controlled government. Either course would end our current civilization. With a continued rise of worldwide mysticism, either (1) a nuclear holocaust would occur through destructive political insanities...for example, nuclear-armed Marxists/Leninists/Maoists, or through destructive religious insanities...for example, nuclear-armed Shiite muslims, or (2) a Lenin/Mao-style or Khomeini/Giuliani-style government would enslave or slaughter the best — the most valiant, independent, value producers. That enslavement and slaughter of the good, the happy, the best among us would drag humanity back into the Dark Ages...perhaps for centuries.

But the new code is coming. No ruling classes. No mysticism. No violence. Only Neo-Tech. The alternative to all gloomy scenarios caused by mystics and neocheaters is Neo-Tech driven competition — a competitive revolution led by honest, productive working people. That competition will render all professional mystics and neocheaters impotent, uncompetitive, unable to manipulate the producers, unable to survive. Neo-Tech led competition will bring a forever prospering, happy business world.

In a Neo-Tech political, social, and business environment, an unstoppable surge of human happiness, well-being, productivity, and romantic love will occur. Against Neo-Tech, professional mystics and neocheaters will appear as impotent clowns. They will be unable to deceive, cheat, oppress, injure, destroy, kill... unable to manipulate their plunderings and aggressions...unable to wage wars or commit mass murder. Indeed, Neo-Tech with its honest nature and competitive business climate will create an exhilarating, unstoppable atmosphere for creativity and achievement. The worldwide standard of living and happiness will soar. Poverty and famine will vanish. Most diseases including cancer and AIDS will quickly be eliminated. In the Neo-Tech Era, human biological immortality without aging will soon become commercially available — probably within a decade.

At no time in history have the ideas, influences, doctrines, platforms, or actions of any political or religious system ever yielded a net benefit to productive human beings. No such system has ever increased the long-range prosperity, well-being, and happiness of anyone. Indeed, individuals and civilizations thrive to the extent that religious and government power is diminished. All political systems depend on force, fraud, or coercion to function. Thus, all such systems have always harmed everyone throughout the ages.

Only the unique, anti-force nature of business allows people to fully use their minds and exercise their individual rights to live prosperously and happily. The question of having no government in a Neo-Tech business society versus having a limited government in areas of national defense, the courts, and police protection is meaningless so long as the moral principle of no initiatory force or fraud is observed. Within a Neo-Tech business society, a company called "government" or competing companies would deliver a needed, integrated package of services to those who voluntarily paid for such services. Without power to initiate force or the threat of force required to collect taxes, governments would function only to the extent their citizens or clients found their services valuable enough to voluntarily purchase.

If citizens refused to purchase certain government services, those services would simply go out of business. Or they would be replaced by more efficient services that enough people thought valuable enough to buy. An honest, legitimate government would by necessity be both a competitive, profit-oriented service and an individual-rights protection business. In some areas, possibly several competing businesses, organizations, or companies might offer the same services in competing for citizens as customers.

Voluntarily supported governments and voluntarily supported businesses would really be equivalent entities subject to the same free-market dynamics and the unbreakable order dictated by free competition, market demands, investment protection, and value exchange. A nonforce government could be called Government, Government Company, or any other name. Likewise, that entity would be subject to the same economic disciplines of profits, losses, growth, competition, and bankruptcy as any competing business. In other words, in a Neo-Tech society, governments would have the same nature, disciplines, and anti-anarchy order as any free-enterprise business. And they would be subject to the same competitive influences and disciplines to improve quality and value. ...The ordered purpose of business would reign; the arbitrary disorder of mystical/neocheating, force-backed

146

A New Code Of Success Is Told

governments would vanish. Neo-Tech leads to business-like order and prosperity. Only destructive, bogus-job authorities backed by force cause disorder and eventual anarchy.

The transition from a force-dependent government to a nonforce government could cause some temporary dislocations, such as cutting welfare, stopping transfer-payment "services", and selling government property to pay off and close out Social Security claims. But those problems would be minor and transitory compared to the flood of permanent, major benefits that would immediately assert themselves. For example, national defense and police protection would immediately strengthen toward total effectiveness as purpose and efficiency soared. Moreover, a nonforce government would mean no taxes, no irrational controls or destructive regulations, no government corruption, no neocheaters, no wars, and a spectacularly prosperous, healthy, happy society.

The purpose of each individual human life is to prosper and live happily. Anyone can achieve that prosperity and happiness when free of force, fraud, or coercion by others.

The Neo-Tech Constitution forbids initiatory force, threat of force, or fraud by any individual, group of individuals, or government. No other law or rule is needed for a moral, rational society.

Forbidding initiatory force and coercion is the only political law compatible with the prosperity and happiness of human beings. Thus, the Neo-Tech Constitution leaves everyone with the conditions for prosperity and happiness. No other constitution or laws are needed or valid. The Neo-Tech Constitution obsoletes the constitutions of all nations.

**"Please tell me," my father said, realizing the Neo-Tech Constitution would remove the threat of the IRS, hanging over everyone's head.**

The Neo-Tech Constitution begins with the following preamble: *The purpose of human life is to prosper and live happily. The function of society is to protect those conditions that let all individuals achieve prosperity and happiness. Those conditions can be delivered by a constitution that prohibits the use of initiatory force or coercion by any person, group, or*

*government against any individual.*
Then comes the Constitution itself, in three Articles:

### The Constitution

*Article 1:* No person, group of persons, or government may initiate force, threat of force, or fraud against the person or property of any individual.

*Article 2:* Force may be morally and legally used only in defense against those who violate Article 1.

*Article 3:* No exception shall ever exist to Articles 1 & 2.

The Neo-Tech Constitution rests on six axioms:
1. Values exist only relative to life.
2. Whatever benefits a living organism is a value to that organism. Whatever harms a living organism is a disvalue to that organism.
3. The basic value against which all values are measured is the conscious individual.
4. Morals relate only to conscious individuals.
5. Immoral actions arise from individuals choosing to harm others through force, fraud, deception, coercion — or from individuals choosing to usurp, attack, or destroy values earned by others.
6. Moral actions arise from individuals choosing to benefit others by competitively producing values for them.

How would the Neo-Tech Constitution be enforced? Through (1) self-defense/deterrent forces and (2) organized ostracizing systems. ...Effective ostracisation is a much more powerful mechanism for justice, restitution, and deterrent than any form of force. And the severest, fully integrated ostracisation can eventually deliver capital punishment through suicide.

I want you to go home now and think about your fears and anxieties of being a prisoner of the IRS with its cruel and unusual punishments. Think about how your anxieties are all based on force at the hands of IRS agents. Under the new code, society would be forever free of such force.

## A New Code Of Success Is Told

**That night, my father tried to imagine a Neo-Tech Society without initiatory force. After two hours of thought, sitting at his desk with only his desk lamp on in his home office, he muttered, "What a wonderful world that would be. I'd be so rich and happy...and free!" The next morning, he came to tell Zon. But Zon spoke first...**

The purpose of human life is to prosper happily. By integrating the human mind with reality, anyone can prosper happily by making one's self increasingly valuable to others. But what keeps most people from doing that — from fulfilling their own nature? What has kept most people throughout history from experiencing the prosperity and happiness that they are fully qualified to earn? ...The answer lies in three words: *Force, Mysticism, Neocheating*:

*Force* is the instrument used to usurp or expropriate values earned by others: Directly or indirectly, all initiated force supports stagnated status quo, laziness, and incompetence at the expense of competitive growth, productivity, and ability. Criminals, mystics, neocheaters, governments, and religions use force, threat of force, or fraud to drain life, values, and happiness from the producers and society. But those who live by force or fraud live in discord with reality. They offer nothing to others except dwarfed lives, diminished happiness, and lost values.

Professional mystics and neocheaters depend on force or deception to survive. But, the value producer never needs to use force or deception to prosper.

Once value producers identify the nature of initiatory force, they will reject its use as criminal and harmful under *any* conditions. From that point on, the value producers can guiltlessly collect their earned prosperity and happiness. And all who have lived by force and coercion will find they can no longer live by usurping values. Instead, they too will have to produce competitive values for others or perish.

*Mysticism* is defined as: 1. Any attempt to use the mind as a "reality" creating device rather than a reality integrating organism. 2. Any attempt to recreate or alter reality through dishonesty, feelings, non sequiturs, or rationalizations. 3. Any attempt to ignore, evade, contradict, or fake reality. 4. Any

149

creation of problems where none exist.

Mysticism is the tool used by neocheaters to manipulate or hide the force, fraud, or coercion used to usurp power and values from others. Mysticism is used to create specious standards for projecting undeserved guilt onto others. Why? To beguile value producers into surrendering their earned power and values to the value destroyers.

*Neocheating* is defined as: Any intentional use of mysticism to create false realities and illusions in order to extract values or power from others.

Neocheating is the technique for usurping values, money, power by using mysticism to manipulate others. Neocheating is the essential technique politicians, clergymen, bogus-job bureaucrats, and white-collar-hoax business quislings use to usurp jobs, power, money, and pseudo self-esteem from others.

Mysticism, used by neocheaters, is an evasion of reality that is never supported by honesty or objective reality. Mysticism, the stupidness disease, harms human beings in five ways:

1. Mysticism cripples the integration capacities required to accurately understand reality. That accurate understanding is necessary to make decisions competently, to solve problems effectively, and to live competitively.

2. Mysticism short-circuits or blocks the mind to prevent unlimited, wide integrations that let one know and understand everything in the universe without limits.

3. Mysticism drains one's intelligence, efficacy, and ability to live competitively.

4. Mysticism blocks the long-range thinking integrations needed to prosper continuously, love romantically, and live happily.

5. Mysticism subjects individuals increasingly to the control of professional mystics and neocheaters.

Mysticism is arbitrary, has no link to reality, and is based on nothing. Thus, mysticism *is nothing*. Yet, by manipulating

150

rationalizations, non sequiturs, aphorisms, parables, superstitions, modern art, poetry, songs, rock music, chants, slogans, newspeak, quotes, or facts out of context, a professional mystic or neocheater can create illusions to seemingly justify almost any harmful action, including thefts and murder. Such "justifications" are essential for their unjustifiable pillagings of value producers.

Mysticism and neocheating have been used for 2000 years to create illusions that "external authorities" protect the lives of individuals, can solve problems for others, and can provide livings for non-producers. But, in reality, all such "authorities" are merely neocheaters using deception, force, or coercion to extract their bogus livelihoods from the value producers. And those neocheaters are the fountainhead of crimes and human-imposed suffering.

Mysticism and neocheating are the main causes of pain and failure among human beings. Mysticism and neocheating are anti-life — death-oriented. The core of mystics and neocheaters is dishonesty and laziness. Their task is to beguile value producers into supporting the value destroyers.

**"Like honest, hard-working people being *forced* to pay taxes to a destructive government...or go to prison," my father said with disgust in his voice. "That is so immoral."**

*Morality* is defined as: Conscious actions that purposely benefit people and society are moral. Conscious actions that purposely harm people and society are immoral. Thus, value destroyers such as mystics, neocheaters, and their agents of force, coercion, and deception are immoral. For, they purposely harm others and society by choosing to usurp values from others rather than produce values for others. By contrast, value producers are moral. For, they purposely benefit others and society by choosing to competitively produce more values for others than they consume.

*Mystics* violate morality: They harm both their own and every other person's life. They are destructive, silly, immature, childish. By choosing to evade reality, they undermine their ability to identify reality, to think clearly, to produce values, to live happily, to compete honestly — to survive. As a result,

151

they increasingly transfer responsibilities for their failures onto others. They routinely lay blame and guilt on others for their own problems.

*Neocheaters* violate morality: They purposely expand their harm by orchestrating mystical illusions to plunder others and society. Moreover, they design their illusions to make themselves appear as innocent benefactors and their victims appear as the guilty malefactors. But the opposite is true: The neocheaters are the guilty malefactors; their victims are usually the innocent value producers. Yet, as long as most people allow themselves to accept those mystical inversions of honesty, the neocheaters will keep pillaging them and society. As a result, such neocheaters always harm society by draining prosperity and happiness from everyone.

*Agents of Force* violate morality: They purposely harm others by expropriating values through force or threat of force. Moreover, by choosing to expropriate rather than earn values, agents of force destroy their own lives by demolishing their competence, self-esteem, and happiness.

*Nonmystics* are moral: They accept the responsibility to think and act for themselves in order to produce objective values for others. With a loyalty to honesty, they act in accord with objective reality. They are mature, evolved people who strive to integrate their words and actions with honesty and reality, regardless of anyone's opinions, dictates, wishes, or emotions. As a result, nonmystics always benefit others and society.

Mystics, neocheaters, and agents of force are losers. They are immature, unevolved people with self-arrested character development. They function through dishonesty and deception. For those reasons, they must depend on the producer for survival. But, they resent and envy the producer in knowing that they cannot experience his or her competence and happiness, no matter how much they extract from others. Mystics and neocheaters live unhappy, shrinking lives. Living through huckstered faith enforced by deception or force, they steadily lose respect for honesty, happiness, and the purpose to live. They increasingly move toward failure and death. And often, steeped in envy, they want everyone else to fail and die with them. ...Thus, anyone can benefit by immediately rejecting losers such as mystics, neocheaters, and agents of force.

All people must continually choose between dishonesty or honesty, between laziness or effort, between accepting or rejecting mysticism from both within and without. Accepting mysticism means evading honesty and denying reality in favor of feelings, wishes, or external "authorities". And those consistently choosing mysticism become dependent on others or "authorities" to think for them, to lead them, to neocheat for them. But rejecting mysticism upholds honesty, rejects neocheaters and dependence on them, builds competence and independence, and finally enhances life for everyone.

Now I will give you four facts that I want you to go home and think about tonight. Also, I want you to go to bed earlier tonight — go to sleep by midnight. We have a big day tomorrow. Now, here are the four facts to ponder tonight:

1. No one can give another person self-worth or happiness. Yet anyone can achieve those two prime values by (a) producing more competitive values for others than consumed by oneself; and (b) rejecting mystics, neocheaters, and their schemes to usurp power and values from others.

2. Loyalty to honesty and rationality must replace mysticism in order to harness one's natural power. By remaining loyal to honesty and rationality, a person can (a) disarm mysticism, (b) render neocheaters impotent, and (c) create the conditions that allow personal prosperity and happiness to flourish.

3. People who resist mysticism from within and reject neocheating from without will gain prosperity and happiness. But others who remain foundering in the seas of mysticism and neocheating will become uncompetitive and lose the values of life.

4. If everyone were a mystic, human life would end. If everyone were a value destroyer, an agent of force, a neocheater, human life would end. But if everyone were an honest value producer, human life and happiness would flourish beyond

imagination.

**The next morning my father sat in front of his mountain. He said, "Zon, I thought about the four facts until midnight. Why is it I feel less anxiety and fear than I have since my plight with the IRS began five years ago?"**

Today you will understand why that is so. Let's get started:
Mysticism destroys from within; force destroys from without. Yet, both mysticism and force are unnatural and disposable. Neither are rooted in reality or have any inherent power. Still, all unearned power and expropriated values depend on mystical illusions backed by coercion, force, fraud, or deception. Mystics, neocheaters, and other value destroyers need those illusions to beguile, flimflam, or force values from others. But once that intertwining dependency of mysticism and force is unraveled, the rationalizations crumble and illusions vanish. ...Without their illusions, mystics and neocheaters are powerless. That day is coming.

When value producers understand that intertwining dependency of force and fraud on mysticism, they will stop supporting mystics and neocheaters who live off the efforts of others. Those mystics and neocheaters will then be powerless. Their only means of survival will be to produce rather than usurp values. Once they become value producers, their self-esteems and competencies will soar. And then, they too can evolve into self-responsible human beings who *earn* their prosperity and happiness.

The Neo-Tech Constitution forbids initiatory force or fraud. Without force or fraud, mysticism and thus neocheaters become impotent. Without mysticism, force becomes ineffective for extracting values from others. The axioms of the Neo-Tech Constitution are real and cannot be contradicted. They are based on human nature. By contrast, all mystical illusions are capricious and contradictory. They are based on nothing. And that nothingness is why force, fraud, or coercion are required to make others accept the dishonest illusions of mystics and neocheaters. Thus, by forbidding force, fraud, and coercion, the Neo-Tech Constitution vanquishes mystics and neocheaters.

Most people unknowingly let mysticism have disastrous effects on their lives and society. As throughout history, people unnecessarily accept the dishonesties of mysticism in allowing neocheaters to pillage them materially and spiritually. But, once the mystical illusions are identified and the neocheating hoaxes are rejected, destructive mystics and neocheaters will be powerless because they have no reality-based, earned power. Rejecting mysticism and its dishonesty means rejecting neocheaters and their agents of force. That rejection will come with the new code of living after 2001.

With widespread rejection of mysticism and neocheaters, violations of individual rights become unacceptable, pillaging becomes impractical, and waging war becomes impossible. ...People will then be free to live prosperously and happily forever.

The Neo-Tech Constitution fully meets the responsibility of any government to its citizens. The sole purpose of The Neo-Tech Constitution is to protect individual rights through the abolition of *all* initiatory force.

The Neo-Tech Constitution not only provides impenetrable armor for individual rights, but embodies the principles of prosperous living. People one by one will recognize the consummate advantages of The Neo-Tech Constitution. Then, with increasing momentum, those people will reject mysticism and neocheating. Those who do not reject mysticism will be left behind, unable to compete for power, prosperity, and romantic love among the rising army of Neo-Tech value producers.

With the discovery of Neo-Tech, all mystics and neocheaters are in the final sentence of the final chapter of their long, destructive history on planet Earth. They are finished forever. But ironically, for the first time in history, all mystics and neocheaters have, through Neo-Tech, an invincible tool to purge their own mysticism, to solve their own problems, to evolve into happy, productive human beings. ...Happy days are here for everyone, forever.

**"Yes. Yes! I understand now. I understand everything so clearly. Let me go home and put it all together in my head. I know why my fears are subsiding".**

155

That night, my father wrote and wrote and wrote. He was writing letters to problematic bureaucrats who had been bothering his business and life. In fact, this evening began a powerful showdown with the IRS that would lead to the Supreme Court and later to political pressures on Congress to dismantle the IRS as we knew it in the 20th century. Over the next year, my father developed and marketed a commercial Neo-Tech Protection Kit. From his own experiences, the kit provided many specific, real-life examples and letters that showed how Neo-Tech jettisons mystics and neocheaters. For example, the following letter (written a few months later) from that Neo-Tech Protection Kit illustrates an attack by neocheaters and how Neo-Tech effectively dismisses such neocheaters:

**Mr. Paul L. Douglas, Attorney General**
**Department of Justice, State Capitol**
**Lincoln, Nebraska 68509**

**Dear Mr. Douglas:**
Important to your future is understanding the enclosed letter from Mr. Thomas P. Vlahoulis of your Consumer Protection Division. As Nebraska's Attorney General, you are responsible for the actions of that Division and its use of taxpayers' money.

Please carefully read that letter, for it is under your name: Does Mr. Vlahoulis, you, or anyone in your Department of Justice have a single, concrete complaint about the Neo-Tech Research and Writing Center or any of our publications? If so, we request that you immediately inform us. For, we want to know exactly what the complaint is and who is making it. We insist on our basic right of knowing and facing our accuser so we may respond fully.

And very important, Mr. Douglas, why exactly is your Department of Justice gratuitously intruding into a publishing company with an inquisition directed at its writers and sources? What exactly is Mr. Vlahoulis implying or presuming, and on what basis? And what is the idea of his threatening us while remaining secretive in vaguely implying that the inquisition arises from "information forwarded by a concerned citizen"?

If someone has a complaint, then out with it so we can respond. Indeed, has Mr. Vlahoulis or anyone in that Division ever received even a single complaint? And what about the thousands of happy Nebraskans who have benefited from Neo-Tech? ...Just who is complaining and why? Or is Mr. Vlahoulis merely acting on someone's specious attack on values?

If no complaint based on fact exists, then I submit that Mr. Vlahoulis is consuming taxpayers' money in creating bogus jobs by conjuring up problems where none exist while sapping valuable time from innocent value producers. If that be the case, is not your Department committing a double-edged fraud under the aegis of "consumer protection"?

What would the citizens of Nebraska think about spending their tax money on harassing value-producing writers in the name of "consumer protection"? What would Woodson Howe, editor of the Omaha World-Herald, or Tom White, editor of the Lincoln Star, say about your arbitrary threats aimed at a publisher of ideas? ...Ideas that will collapse mysticism to benefit everyone except the neocheaters.

Through the philosophically oriented books and articles developed by the Neo-Tech Research and Writing Center, we have delivered objective, long-range values to over a million appreciative individuals just this year alone in all 50 states and over 140 countries. Still professional mystics and neocheaters who are threatened by Neo-Tech always attack it, often vehemently, often imploring government authorities to stop our publishing activities. But, as they sooner or later discover, such attacks always backfire. For, we utilize all their attacks to our benefit. Indeed, their attacks directly enhance our business objectives of collapsing mysticism to eliminate neocheating. Moreover, their attacks are published and marketed in our Neo-Tech Protection Kit. That kit lets honest, productive people specifically identify and then forever dismiss those mystics and neocheaters who foment dishonest attacks on value producers.

We are resolutely principled and never knowingly yield

157

to actions that are wrong or unfair, no matter what the cost. Indeed, over the long-range we build strength through a loyalty to honesty. And that means standing up to and publicly exposing neocheaters wherever we encounter them.

In addition to the definition of neocheaters on the second page of our enclosed statement of principles, I ask you to read the third page concerning our policies toward neocheaters. That policy includes never knowingly doing business, regardless of dollar losses, with those who live by force, threats, or fraud.

Enclosed are samples of letters from Neo-Tech owners. As you can see in the inset on the second page, various mystics and neocheaters fear Neo-Tech so much that they stridently threaten us. Additionally, all our sales literature openly displays a printed warning requesting professional mystics and neocheaters (e.g., clergymen and politicians) not to buy anything from us. For, we will not knowingly do business with any value destroyer. We reject their orders and never want their business.

But above all, we as everyone in America are protected by the First Amendment. And we as everyone in America can freely publish our ideas without anyone's permission or license no matter how many authorities, mystics, or neocheaters object, including those in government, including you, your Department of Justice, and Mr. Vlahoulis.

That raises the question of why I spent the time identifying the nature of Mr. Vlahoulis' actions. Am I letting your value-destroying minions consume my time needed to produce values for others? No, not at all. For I am a writer, researcher, and editor whose single, long-range responsibility is to develop and publish those identifications that will reveal and eventually eliminate dishonest mystics and destructive neocheaters — in and out of religion and government.

Indeed, every destructive action integrated with Neo-Tech generates material for future publications. Those publications are dedicated to eliminating mystics, neocheaters, and their 2000-year hoax used to pillage value producers. For once free of mystics and neocheaters, society will be free of parasites and bureaucratic value destroyers. Then all people will be free to earn full prosperity, personal happiness, and romantic love.

And now a most important note. A personal note offered in goodwill to you, Mr. Douglas: I ask you to take the following step that will bring you and the public great benefits, now and in the future: Although we do not sell Neo-Tech to mystics, neocheaters, politicians, the clergy, most lawyers, certain academe, and others listed in our policy statement, we invite you to leave politics, acquire Neo-Tech knowledge, and join in the ascent of man and woman to guiltless prosperity, happiness, and romantic love.

If you arrange to leave politics to produce marketable values for others, I could arrange for you to purchase Neo-Tech as we have occasionally arranged for other nonqualifiers. But first you must desire to abandon neocheating in order to pursue a happy, productive life. So please let me know if you are interested in this new direction. For, we can help you. With Neo-Tech, you can be infinitely happier than working toward the next election.

Sincerely,
Frank R. Wallace

Note: Several months after receiving this letter from my father and failing to accept his benevolent offer, Attorney-General Paul L. Douglas was impeached and later indicted for perjury and obstruction of justice.

\* \* \* \*

After being up writing such letters all night long, my father came to his mountain feeling strong and fearless. "I am different now," he said. "I understand the meaning of life. The essence of conscious life is control — the ability to control one's present and future. Conscious life is the only entity in the universe that can control nature and future events. That control is possible to the extent that mysticism is absent and Neo-Tech is present. A person in control is happy and will prosper. A person out of control is unhappy and will fail. Neo-Tech puts a person in control. ...Today

**I'm very interested in knowing exactly why there are neocheaters. What causes them? By the way, my mind is very clear now, so don't hold back. Tell me everything, and tell me fast. I'll keep up now."**

**The wind from the mountain started blowing harder than usual. It carried the words, faster than before:**

For 2500 years, citizens from ancient Greece to modern America have sought to understand and judge those holding or seeking public power. The higher, more powerful the "authority", the more attention focuses on trying to judge that "authority". In fact, attention expands geometrically on ascending the power scale to the president of the United States. Yet, a consistent, reliable standard for judging power and authority has until now remained a riddle.

That riddle is solved by applying two metaphors: (1) Knowing the material world around us requires understanding the smallest atomic units. And (2) knowing the cosmos above us requires understanding its primordial origins. Now apply those two points to authority and power: (1) Knowing authority around us requires understanding the smallest authoritarian units. And (2) knowing the power above us requires understanding its philosophical origins.

Understanding authority begins by traveling far from the great concentrations of government authority — traveling away from the eastern megalopolis, west to a small desert city in Western United States. By putting a microscope on that oasis of population, one can focus beneath its few, simple layers of authority. One can focus beneath the mayor, past the city council and paid government employees down to an unpaid, appointed planning commission. And finally, one can reduce that commission's microcosm of authority down to its most mundane exercise of authority — the granting or denying of a minor zoning variance to a lone, uninfluential individual with a modest home needing a second bedroom for his family.

That property owner duly completed the proper forms, submitted blueprints, paid the filing fees, and presented the facts to the planning commission. He explained why variance was necessary not only to better the property, but to preserve one

160

of the largest elm trees in the city. The owner detailed how alternative plans without the variance would neither be practical nor best serve the neighborhood. In addition, a professional urban planner — hired by the commission — found no problems or objections to the variance. He also concurred that well over half the homes in the neighborhood already had structures built in greater variance to the zoning ordinance than the minor variance requested.

Moreover, unlike the surrounding structures, the proposed structure was designed to beautify both the owner's home and the neighborhood. In addition, that would be done entirely at the owner's expense while providing local employment. And most important, a two-week notice posted on the property, an advertised notice in the local newspaper, and written notices mailed to all homes surrounding the proposed property improvement brought not a single objection. In short, everyone logically concerned supported the variance.

On concluding the hearing, the members seemed ready to approve this minor, routine variance. But then spoke a younger commissioner, a stocky, flush-faced government environmentalist living in a wealthy neighborhood atop a hill, far from the property owner. He turned enough to observe the property owner from the corners of his eyes. Then with twitching jowls, he stated that the property owner's needs and desires meant nothing in his considering the variance. He then cited three ambiguous, ordinance clauses with arbitrary interpretations — impossible interpretations that no home owner could ever satisfy. ...He chose the exercise of power for the sake of gaining unearned power by destroying the creation of values.

In prompt rebuttal, spoke an older commissioner. A trim, leather-faced workingman living in the same modest neighborhood as the property owner, he pointed out that no objective reason to deny the variance existed, especially after everyone in the neighborhood and all others who could possibly be concerned approved. ...He chose the creation of values over the exercise of power.

To fully understand the profound difference between those two commissioners, one must know that they are appointed by politically elected officials and meet four hours each month

161

without pay. If they receive no pay, what do they receive? They receive political power and civic recognition with little expenditure of time and effort. Thus, the motivation for such people entering the world of government authority varies between political enhancement and civic achievement. From those beginnings, from that political atom, emerge two types of people: One desiring to gain power and a political future by destroying values. The other desiring to enhance the civic needs of the community and its citizens by protecting values. ...The first type gains authoritarian power by destroying values of others; the second type resists authoritarian power by protecting values of others. The first type consists of bad-intentioned value destroyers. The second type consists of well-intentioned, but misguided value producers.

The first type subconsciously orients around Plato's philosophy — a subjective, mystical-based philosophy. The extent a person adopts Plato's views is the extent that he or she holds that:

1. Standards for morals and ethics are products of changeable opinions rather than products of objective reality.

2. Power is to be used as an end in itself to determine who through their "wisdom" — through their feelings, whims, wishes, "intuition" — should rule or control others.

3. Facts, honesty, and logic are relative, arbitrary, disposable.

4. Principle does not matter: ends justify the means.

By nature, Plato nourishes not only all despots and dictators, but politicians and bureaucrats at all levels of government. Plato justifies the striving for power at the expense of the rights, property, and life of others. Plato provides the rationalization for all laziness, dishonesty, and value destruction — for all subjective, unjust non sequiturs and actions used to usurp power and values from others. According to Plato, the rights and needs of individuals are secondary to any external "authority's" desire to usurp values and power. Indeed, Plato assigns virtue to sacrificing individual rights and needs to *any arbitrary "higher cause"*, "higher power", or external "authority". ...Thus, Plato is

162

the philosophical father of mysticism and neocheating.

The second type subconsciously orients around Aristotle's philosophy — an objective, reality-based philosophy. The extent that a person adopts Aristotle's view is the extent he or she holds that:

1. Standards for morals and ethics are products of objective reality rather than products of changeable opinions.
2. The well-being of society is enhanced to the extent that individuals are free to produce objective values for themselves and others.
3. Facts, honesty, and logic are absolute, unchangeable, eternal.
4. Principle matters: ends do not justify the means.

By nature, Aristotle nourishes all value producers. The Aristotelian-oriented person has a loyalty to honesty. That person strives to avoid acting on whims, feelings, or wishes. Instead, that person strives to identify and integrate contextual facts in order to act in a rationally consistent manner that generates maximum values for others. Thus, Aristotle is the philosophical father of business and Neo-Tech.

While most people outwardly exhibit mixtures of Platonistic and Aristotelian views, everyone holds a dominant view of life that is either Platonistic or Aristotelian. Once the Platonistic and Aristotelian views are understood, the dominant view of most individuals becomes evident. With that understanding, one can detect the philosophical core of anyone seeking or holding government power — from the president of the United States to a planning commissioner of a small desert town.

Now, after 2500 years, an objective standard exists to judge power and authority: Who should hold government power over the life, property, and freedom of individuals? A person with Plato's view or a person with Aristotle's view? The answer is...neither.

All forms of external power or authority undermine the productive, self-responsible nature of human beings. Thus, all such authority is bogus and eventually harmful to everyone. No person, group, or government has the right to deny *or* grant permission for individuals to use their own earned property in ways not infringing on the life or property rights of other individuals.

**"I'm still with you," my father said.**

Mystic-free individuals who think and act with full-context integrations can easily retake power usurped by the mystics and neocheaters. And a mystic-free, Neo-Tech person can always outcompete those hampered with mysticism in personal and business endeavors. To consistently act in the *rational* interest of self, others, and society requires mystic-free thinking and actions in concert with fully integrated honesty...which is Neo-Tech.

With Neo-Tech, people can free themselves of the life-stunting oppression imposed by external "authorities". Once free, Neo-Tech people become totally responsible and accountable for their own actions and, thus, gain full control of their own lives and well-beings. Only with that responsibility and control can individuals be of maximum value to others in producing values. But those ideas of freedom and responsibility contradict the premises of both conservatives and "liberals". All such advocates of government control claim that individuals must in various ways be controlled by force or coercion for the "good" of society. Remember, individuals free to function toward their own rational, nonsacrificial self-interests will achieve maximum prosperity for themselves, others, and society. If they allow themselves to be sacrificed, everyone loses except the neocheaters promoting sacrifice of others to their destructive, self-serving "causes".

Free, unsacrificed individuals provide the maximum benefits to others and society. But that is not the reason why government force and coercion against individuals by nonproductive mystics and neocheaters are morally wrong. Independent of the practical benefits, the principle stands: Each individual has the inalienable right to his or her own mind, body, and earned property regardless of those benefits that naturally accrue to others and society. No one can ever rightfully own or morally take any portion of another individual's life or earned property.

Freedom and property can be taken from an individual in only one of two ways: (1) by his or her consent (moral), (2) by initiatory force, threat of force, coercion, or fraud (immoral). All governments throughout history have immorally usurped individual freedom and property from their citizens by initiatory force or the threat of force. And that theft is always done under the Platonistic rationalization of serving some common "good" or "higher" cause. All governments today initiate force or threats of force to deprive their citizens of their property, prosperity, freedom, happiness. ...While everyone has the right to use self-defense force, no one or no government has the right to initiate force or threats of force against anyone, for any reason, under any circumstances.

**My father jumped up from the flat rock and, with his arms raised, yelled, "But why do politicians, regulatory bureaucrats, and most media people live by force, fraud, deception, or coercion? Why do they live by usurping values from others rather than by producing values for others?"**

One discovers the answer by stripping the layers of rationalization from such people. Beneath those layers is a lack of maturity and self-esteem, a lack of self-responsibility and independence, a lack of honesty and effort. For they made a secret choice to be dishonest, lazy, and dependent on others for survival — a secret choice to avoid the honesty and effort needed to live productively. They chose to abandon their nature and not produce competitive values desired by others.

Also, professional mystics, neocheaters, and other value destroyers hold various degrees of secret fear and envious hatred toward the value producer. After stripping away the various rationalizations from those value destroyers, the same core — no matter how skillfully hidden — always manifests itself. That core is dishonest laziness: a default against the constant hard effort needed to competitively produce values that benefit others.

Self-responsibility, rationality, honesty, and effort are necessary for human well-being and happiness. People must produce competitive, tradeable values — goods or services — that others desire and will voluntarily buy. How many free, honest, productive people would voluntarily buy the "services" of a politician, a bureaucrat, a dictator? The character core of mystics, neocheaters, politicians, and other value destroyers is dishonest laziness. Consider, for example, essentially all politicians are lazy, despite their often cleverly staged, look-like-work flurries. Those flurries of "work" are really nothing more than flurries of anti-productive machinations or ego-boosting power ploys. Such destructive machinations are the daily routines of dictators, prime ministers, and presidents as so starkly revealed in the putrefied personal lives of neocheating politicians as Lincoln, Wilson, Stalin, Hitler, FDR, LBJ, the Clintons. They are all soul mates concealing their mutual secret of laziness and living off the productive efforts of others.

**"So they need coercion and force to survive," my father whispered to himself. Then, looking up with a curious expression, he asked, "Is there any difference between liberals and conservatives? Is one less harmful than the other?"**

Most professional mystics and neocheaters are "liberal" oriented. I put "liberal" in quotes because those who are called liberals today are the opposite of the past, classical liberals who represented anti-force, pro-individual ideas. To live off the producers, those modern "liberals" must promote the false notion that human needs are human rights. They must promote their non-sequitur emotional hoax that being "compassionate" means forcing the value producer to fill their parasitical needs.

Gaining unearned values is the foremost concern of "liberals". Yet, they constantly project that they are concerned about "higher values" and "compassion" for others. But their compassionate images are hypocritical shams. For, professional mystics and neocheaters are interested only in unearned power and bogus jobs so they can go through life living off the values produced by others.

Since professional mystics, neocheaters, and other value destroyers are not self-sufficient, they must spend their lives in a deceptive, resentful struggle designed to extract their material and emotional needs from the producer. Even those nonproducers who have inherited wealth are psychologically dependent on the producer. Those wealthy nonproducers must attack or undermine the producer to elevate their own weak egos and to camouflage

166

their worthlessness.

Because of their parasitical nature, "liberals" are generally more destructive than conservatives. For, conservatives are often misguided value producers who live pragmatically — without consistent principles. ...But also, some of the most clever neocheaters adopt conservative, free-enterprise images to dupe the producer into surrendering his or her earned power and self-esteem.

Conservatives generally promote material and economic freedom. But, to gain their unearned power, they want government to control morality and ideas. Most "liberals", on the other hand, appear to promote freedom of ideas such as free press, academic freedom, no censorship, freedom in the arts. Ultimately, however, that freedom is granted only to those who support their usurpations. For, to survive, "liberals" need governments to usurp money and values earned by others. ...What about "middle of the roaders"? They favor various mixtures of government control over individual minds, morals, bodies, and property. ...They are little more than pragmatists with no principles at all.

Only Neo-Tech people reject *all* usurpations, use of force, and gun-backed controls over individuals. For Neo-Tech people orient exclusively around individual rights, not fake human rights. Both conservatives and "liberals", on the other hand, orient around two areas of false government power. Those separate areas they arrogate for themselves are: (1) controlling the mind and moral realms for the conservatives, (2) controlling the body and material realms for the "liberals". ...Only Neo-Tech people want to control no one in any way. They have no need or desire to control the spiritual or material realm of anyone. They recognize everyone's sovereign right to both realms.

**"Everything is so clear to me now. Please, go on. What about corrupt big business?"**

The link between big business and laissez-faire capitalism is largely a myth originating from Karl Marx's anti-intellectual canards in his book *Das Kapital*. Consider that laissez faire is a French phrase meaning, "to let do", or "to let people do as they choose". Thus, laissez-faire capitalism means neither pro big business nor anti big business, but means simply individual freedom. Yet, today, most chief executives of large stagnated businesses are anti laissez-faire. Indeed, many entrenched CEOs support fascist concepts of big government. For such concepts utilize force-backed government regulations needed to protect their jobs and businesses from more competent, harder-working entrepreneurs and foreign competitors.

Laissez-faire capitalism simply means no government control over individuals and their property — a Neo-Tech atmosphere. Within such an atmosphere, individuals are free to create and build businesses, including big businesses, even monopolistic big businesses. Within that laissez-faire atmosphere, government would have no power to support big businesses or protect monopolies; for example many banking, utility, and communication companies are monopolies protected by government force. Without government protection or assistance, big businesses and monopolies could exist and grow only by continually delivering better values than anyone else. Whenever any monopoly failed to deliver maximum values, the free-market dynamics in the absence of government controls would cause that monopoly either to deliver better values or yield to others delivering greater values. ...Market dynamics free of government controls will sooner or later always collapse uncompetitive or harmful businesses, monopolies, or cartels.

Companies, businesses, industries, and monopolies are not detached entities, but are composed of individuals who function through individual thoughts and actions. Business entities are the property and extension of individual human beings. Thus, businesses possess the same inalienable rights of free action and ownership of earned values as individuals. Also, individuals and their honest businesses exert power through peaceful voluntary free choices, not through force, coercion, or deception as do professional value destroyers in or out of government.

Most government agencies ultimately exist through force, coercion, or deception. Thus, such agencies that depend on threats and force have no moral right to exist. Those agencies are in reality coercive engines of antisocial actions.

Governments are colossal mystical frauds that usurp power

and values by force-backed laws and regulations. And those usurpations are used to further violate individual and property rights. Such destructive processes keep building and feeding on themselves. ...All value producers would benefit greatly without such governments.

Today, upper management of big-business is increasingly controlled by altruistic, neocheating "businessmen" who apologize for the business they now control, but never built. Those altruistic "businessmen" are usually fascist oriented. For they use government force to shield their businesses from competition. Indeed, they promote anti-capitalistic legislation, regulations, and controls. The unspoken policies of those executives are to gain government favors and to encourage government-forced regulations that block more competent competitors and diminish or halt superior-value imports. Such executives realize that, without government interference, the free-market competition would eventually eliminate their jobs and their poorly managed businesses that they have drained through harmful government-approved, socially oriented "business" policies.

Government-corporate collusions inflate prices, lower quality, block competition, and are the antithesis of free enterprise. Indeed, the greatest enemies of free enterprise are not the socialists or "liberals", but are those business leaders who collude with government to consolidate their power without having to earn that power in a competitive, value-producing atmosphere.

Perhaps the most evil collusions occur between neocheating executives of large companies and government bureaucrats in promoting envy-motivated antitrust laws. Those immoral laws are designed to penalize the most competitive companies and productive businessmen. But increasingly, the growing number of Neo-Tech executives will rid the corporate world of those government-colluding executives who neocheated their way to unearned power through force-backed laws, regulations, and controls.

Your second day here after I opened my voice to you, I revealed the malevolent destruction of altruism as opposed to the benevolent productivity of business. Then, with my spirit, you wrote an open letter to Du Pont that demonstrated how neocheating executives are today undermining many great

Book 2
Neo-Tech Decoded

169

corporations.  They can often hide their destructive drain of assets for many years by continually shifting long-range efforts into increasingly shorter-range pay-offs that keep profits growing while concealing the eventual, dead-end quality of such profits.

**"Yes, I will be releasing that letter to Du Pont very soon," my father said.  "Now tell me, if altruistic chief executives are taking over major corporations and causing their long-range demise, who then is left to stop the neocheaters' continued consumption of business?  Who will lead the way to a society in which mysticism and the resulting neocheating are eliminated?  Who will uphold the productive individual as the highest value?  Who will lead the way to a society in which prosperity, happiness, and biological immortality will reign supreme among human beings?"**

The answer is today's growing army of value producers who are becoming knowledgeable about Neo-Tech.  For such people hold genuine power.  One key necessity is to establish an Industrial-Philosophy Department responsible for making major actions consistent with the principles of fully integrated honesty — Neo-Tech. ...Neo-Teching business policies and actions inject vitality and profitability into companies, large or small.

**My father, who sat before the mountain, said, "Yes, that is a key necessity, which I discovered last night.  I have begun my Industrial-Philosophy Department myself, and I immediately put myself in control."**

Indeed, Neo-Tech traps professional mystics and neocheaters in their world of big lies.  Neo-Tech reveals the exact opposite to what most people have been led to believe by mystics and neocheaters.  For example, how many people realize that the many pseudo ecologists and self-appointed "consumer advocates" today are not interested in protecting the environment or human beings.  Deceptively hidden behind their neocheating non sequiturs and destructive work is a contempt for human life and happiness.  They use ecology and consumerism as tools of demagoguery, often with the goal to cripple and eventually

170

eliminate the benefits of technology, industry, and free enterprise. As a result, many valid ecological problems are obscured, confused, and remain unsolved. Moreover, the long-range destructiveness of such neocheaters is surfacing in many areas. For example, consider Rachel Carson's decades-old book, "Silent Spring": Its specious charges and unscientific conclusions caused the banning of DDT, which in turn caused a resurgence of malaria in Asia and Sri Lanka at the eventual cost of perhaps a million lives — lives of human beings, not birds or fish. Yet, people will never find those facts among the neocheating academe and media.

With government banning of DDT and other pesticides, the mosquito and insect populations burgeoned along with a proportional rise in "ecologist" caused famine and disease such as malaria and encephalitis. In addition, those irrational bannings have decimated trees and crops in the United States and around the world. The banning of DDT has also lowered the world standard of living by billions of dollars per year in crop losses and expenses. That, in turn, significantly increased third-world inflation, hunger, suffering, famine, and death. All that human death, destruction, and suffering starting from the handiwork of just one "ecologist" needing to feel good by boosting her pseudo self-esteem with dishonest non sequiturs.

An even more destructive breed of neocheaters exists who methodically decrease the living standards for everyone. That breed includes self-appointed, "consumer-advocate" demagogues epitomized by Ralph Nader and his raiders. In the long run, their destruction surpasses that of even the murderous banning of DDT. For the real targets of those "consumer advocates" are the value producers from which come all life-enhancing values. Moreover, the pervasively destructive work of Nader sets up the psychological conditions for unjust attacks on great value-producing companies such as Union Carbide:

Years ago, a great benevolent company, Union Carbide, was excoriated and threatened with extermination by the neocheating media and politicians for a tragic *accident* in India for which the Indian Government itself was responsible. The Indian politicians arbitrarily and irrationally forced Union Carbide to hire incompetent, distrustful nationals who were unable to perform

171

even basic security-control operations. Such forced interference by government neocheaters left Union Carbide unable to properly protect its business from sabotage by envious, anti-business value destroyers. That sabotage at Union Carbide *for which the Indian government was responsible* left 2500 dead — the worst industrial "accident" in history.

But that tragic loss of life was minuscule when compared to the routine, purposeful slaughter by political neocheaters. To the "liberal" media, the murder of 2500 people by their Marxist soul mates would hardly be newsworthy — too common, too minor, too routine, not really that bad.

Such examples starkly contrast the good of business people to the evil of political or government neocheaters. The loss of life from the worst industrial *accident* in history is little more than a casual day of slaughter for totalitarian neocheaters. For example, at the same time that Union Carbide was being excoriated by the dishonest media for sabotage that was not even the company's fault, no media outrage arose toward Marxist murderers in Ethiopia who were *purposely* starving to death millions of innocent men, women, and children they considered politically troublesome. Instead, the media were going through news-twisting contortions and telethon spectaculars in trying to falsely show the cause of that coldly calculated mass starvation was a drought rather than their soul-mate Marxist-Leninist politicians. They were mass murdering so they could feel big, feel important, feel unearned power. They were mass murdering by purposeful starvation, just as Stalin did two generations before in the Ukraine.

People build. Governments destroy. Who really needs governments? Productive individuals always suffer a net loss from mystically conceived, force-backed governments. Such governments diminish everyone's values, earnings, life. They survive by always expanding their unearned power. And they expand that power by increasingly transferring the earnings and property of the producer to the nonproducer by force, threats, coercion, fraud. Thus, governments and politicians, by nature, can offer only life diminishment as they continually increase their force-backed demands on the value producer. At the same time, they aggressively finagle respect and adulation for their

172

destructions through non sequiturs and fake altruistic catchwords such as "compassion", "the heart", "humanitarian", "human rights". But never do they mention the only valid points — individual rights and competitive value production.

To psychologically survive, politicians must garner praise for their usurping values from others without producing values for others. They use the handy, God-like, "goodness" gimmicks of altruism to make their destructive actions seem "good", "compassionate" and "humane" while hiding the criminality of their destructions. Such is the nature of political neocheaters and their media, academic, and religious collaborators. For that reason, effective business people who exist by producing values for others have no desire, time, or reason to diminish their lives by becoming politicians or other neocheaters who exist by usurping values from others.

All political, religious, academe, and media neocheaters destroy the personal property and individual rights of others through escalating usurpations from value producers. Without Neo-Tech to stop the neocheaters, they would eventually dissipate all productive wealth and individual freedom, causing a worldwide economic collapse with an enormous loss of human life, well-being, and happiness.

**"Yes, we must learn Neo-Tech to protect ourselves with the power of fully integrated honesty," my father said.**

The need to protect oneself from neocheaters reveals another destructive effect of mysticism: As the neocheaters attack and usurp those values, the most productive citizens are drained of investment capital, creative energy, individual freedom, and irreplaceable time. Those producers must increasingly struggle to protect themselves, their loved ones, their property, their means of production, and especially their time from the ravages of government value destroyers. More and more valuable time, capital, and effort are wasted in:

1. following destructive bureaucratisms and irrational government regulations, and
2. studying, paying attention to, and speculating in nonproductive asset protectors, tax shelters, and inflation hedges.

Many people go broke through such speculations.

Also, people increasingly lose concentration on their productive work as they follow their speculations. Producers become unproductive speculators as they increasingly look for easy wealth through speculation rather than through producing values with integrated thought and hard work. But in a Neo-Tech society free of neocheaters and destructive governments, all that time, energy, and capital would be channeled into uses that benefit the individual and society: Producers would spend more of their time and energy on producing values for others rather than on having to protect themselves from government value destroyers.

**"I am discovering something interesting: by using the power of fully integrated honesty in my correspondence with bureaucratic neocheaters, I create something I call 'the silence syndrome'. After I use a Neo-Tech approach with my harassers, they back off, and I often never hear from them again. Neo-Tech saves me a lot of time." After a pause of acknowledgment, the mountain continued...**

Governments are nothing more than groups of people. Many of those people are value destroyers who exist by usurping power and values from others to the harm of everyone and society. Some, however, do honest work in the government, especially in service areas such as postal, police, park, library, scientific, technical, military, intelligence. But all governments are controlled by neocheating politicians, bureaucrats, and lawyers living off the producer. Behind all their rhetoric about "service to society" and "working for higher causes" is their need to survive by usurping values earned by others.

Earning major values along with long-range happiness requires an independent aloneness. Neocheaters, nonproducers, value destroyers, and politicians dread that aloneness. The glib politician, being psychologically and materially dependent on others for survival, has a desperate need to be among people, to buy their favor with tax money, and to become increasingly involved in their lives by increasing government control over them. ...The worst situation for the neocheater or politician is

174

to be left alone, especially to be left alone to survive by his or her own efforts. By contrast, the value producer usually has no desire to get involved with the "public" lest his or her irreplaceable time for value production be wasted.

Perhaps the cruelest of government neocheaters are those "liberals" whose actions pass under the specious banner of protecting the elderly. For, their neocheating actions always end up draining the well-being, happiness, and earned savings of elderly people.

Most elderly people no longer have growing assets or competitive earning power. A large percentage of them have worked hard and honestly throughout their lives only to have government policies drive them into the inescapable trap of government dependency. They are further lured into that government trap by, for example, social-security policies that offer temporary relief from inflation only to be devastated by the next wave of inflation and a failing social-security system.

Government manipulations through taxation and inflation diminish the well-being and happiness of everyone. But those destructive manipulations especially debilitate elderly people dependent on the government for survival. For, governments subtly push their dependent elderly citizens toward unhappiness, suffering, early death.

Most elderly people deliver themselves into that dependency trap by believing that government is a benevolent, positive force that will somehow benefit them in the present and help them in the future. The opposite is true. By nature, no one can ever look to any government for net benefits. Indeed, the essence of government is value destruction from which long-range benefits and values can never flow. Thus, one must always avoid government dependency to protect his or her well-being and happiness.

The unhappiness trap shuts when a person becomes dependent on government for needs. Once the trap is shut, that person's life turns downward with declining self-esteem, well-being, and happiness. To avoid that trap, a person must recognize that government is by nature a destructive, life-negating force that should be avoided in every possible way. A person should never believe in, count on, or become dependent on any aspect of government for his or her present or future well-being. The only way to retain growing prosperity and happiness is to remain independent, self-sufficient, and commercially productive, *especially as one grows older.*

The best asset for future prosperity and the best protection against government, mystics, and neocheaters is fully integrated honesty — or Neo-Tech. Indeed, Neo-Tech is the development of personal honesty, integrity, and the ability to perceive reality accurately in order to competitively produce values for others. Thus, the most valuable gift given to children and adults is Neo-Tech knowledge. For that is the knowledge needed to accurately perceive reality, to reject mysticism and neocheating, to develop personal integrity, and to competitively produce tradeable values desired by others.

**"Neo-Tech must spread to everyone," my father said. "I believe in the power of Neo-Tech. I know I am dealing with something very powerful here. You probably know this, but I'm going to devote my life to writing about and distributing this new power called Neo-Tech. Is there more I should know?" The mountain told him to return tomorrow for more.**

\* \* \* \*

**The next day my father told Zon, "I have started taking notes on everything you have told me. It's so powerful, I plan to write and publish Neo-Tech. ...Is that OK?" The mountain replied that not only was it OK, but vital for mankind to pull out of a potentially apocalyptic Catastrophic Era and rise into a spectacular Neo-Tech Era. The mountain added, however, that no big-business publisher would publish this material. My father would have to do it himself. In fact, Zon insisted he do that to fulfill his great responsibility. Thus, my dad started his own publishing company while he was still a Senior Research Chemist for Du Pont.**

Now that you have dedicated yourself to writing this down and to publishing it and to starting your own publishing company,

I must give you the nature of government, politicians, bureaucrats, and the Supreme Court to finish your work, for once the ordinary person sees their true natures, he will be ready to depoliticize the world and collect the rewards.

All current governments depend on coercion and force. Thus, they are destructive to human life, productivity, prosperity, and happiness. The destructiveness of the United States Government is implemented mainly through force-backed bureaucracies such as the BATF, EPA, FDA, FTC, INS, IRS, OSHA, and the SEC.

Consider, for example, the Food and Drug Administration (FDA): That bureaucracy has been responsible for the premature death of many thousands of people through its arbitrary, forced banning of such life-saving, free-choice discoveries as the first effective artificial sweetener cyclamates. And if not for the enormous pressures that subsequently arose for slim, healthy bodies during the national health craze, the FDA would have also banned life-saving saccharine and then aspartame. The palatable cyclamate sweetener was the first to effectively replace the deadly poison of sugar to reduce caloric/carbohydrate intake, obesity ailments, diabetes, heart-attack deaths for millions of people.

All such FDA value destructions serve solely to satisfy some value-destroying bureaucrat's need to feel important, to feel unearned power through destruction of human lives and values.

Also, the arbitrary banning or controlling of life-saving products such as non-toxic pesticides, herbicides, food preservatives and additives, new drugs and medicines has caused death and suffering on massive scales. In addition, FDA regulations on drug research and marketing retard or prevent the development of many life-benefiting, life-saving drugs, medicines, and devices while increasing research and development costs to prohibitive levels. Effective cancer cures, for example, would certainly have been developed years ago if research and business were free from regulations and controls. For, such freedom allows aggressive individuals and companies to openly pursue the full profit and achievement potential in discovering and marketing effective cures for cancer, AIDS, and other diseases.

Even more important, FDA regulations block the required risk taking, incentive, and business freedom required for rapid development of human biological immortality.

177

The blocking of human progress along with mass suffering and death are the natural results of government force. And government agencies are the instruments of such force. The essences of agencies such as the BATF, EPA, FDA, FTC, INS, IRS, OSHA, and the SEC are always destructive and their intentions are never good. Such agencies costing billions of dollars each year serve only to harm productive individuals and society. Indeed, those life-depriving agencies are subtle death machines that are directly and indirectly responsible for more suffering and deaths than all wars of history. All wars are also government sponsored. Throughout history most governments with their use of force, fraud, and coercion begin as "legalized" protection rackets and always end as destructive engines of crime and death. Such governments operate under the rationalizations of protection, altruism, the social "good", and "higher" causes.

Agencies such as the EPA and FDA often carry out their destruction through dishonest assertions. They assert, for example, that DDT or cyclamates might be "bad" for the ecology or cause cancer in animals. Then they expand their power with a job-creating bureaucracy to control or ban such substances. Usually those agencies hide their dishonesties with non sequitur "facts". They often manufacture unscientific data developed from spurious research to "prove", for example, that use of cyclamates might cause cancer in humans: Research on feeding megadoses of cyclamate diet sweetener to rats indicated that humans could experience bladder irritation or even tumors if they drank the equivalent of 700 bottles of diet soft drinks per day over an extended period of time. When, in fact, that amount of water alone — to say nothing of the immediately fatal amounts of sugar in less than 100 bottles of non-diet soda — would fatally break down the kidneys in human beings.

Still, the FDA used those non-sequitur, rat-feeding data to assert that cyclamates can be cancer-producing in human beings. The FDA then demanded that the producers prove that cyclamates do not cause cancer. Since a negative cannot be proven, the government neocheaters subsequently used their dishonest, non-sequitur data to ban the sale of cyclamates without any scientific evidence of harm to a single human being. At the same time, those neocheaters purposely ignored the wide-ranging, beneficial,

178

life-saving effects of that artificial sweetener.

The FDA, EPA, or any other government agency never honestly attempts to prove their assertions. Rather, those agencies demand that the producers disprove their assertions. Their demands to disprove assertions or accusations contradict the concepts of honesty, objective law, and justice. Indeed, to demand proof of a negative undermines honesty by shifting the burden of proof away from the source making accusations, the neocheaters, to their victims, the value producers.

Without the burden-of-proof standard, government and religious neocheaters avoid the responsibility to prove their assertions and accusations. Without the burden-of-proof standard, neocheaters are not accountable to honesty. Without that accountability to honesty, professional mystics and neocheaters can continue to usurp power and bogus livelihoods through fraud, deception, and force.

By nature, most government bureaucracies cannot produce values. Thus, to grow, such bureaucracies must usurp power by destroying values. In turn, value destruction requires little competence or effort. Thus, by necessity, value destruction is the modus operandi of most government bureaucracies and agencies — the most virulent being the BATF, EPA, FDA, FTC, INS, IRS, OSHA, and the SEC. To conceal their destructions, they masterfully use non-sequitur facts and mystical ploys to justify their destructive usurpations from the value producers. But now, after 2000 years, the evolvement of Neo-Tech will collapse and eliminate those fake empires of destruction.

**"I guess that without a scientific background, most people have a hard time seeing past the regulatory bureaucrats' non-sequitur facts," my father said.**

Often, only a scientist trained with the scientific method can identify the neocheater's dishonest use of facts and information. Without Neo-Tech, most people have no way to discern the dishonesty of neocheaters. And without Neo-Tech, most people will confusingly accept the neocheater's usurpation of values. But with Neo-Tech, destructive mysticism and neocheating irreversibly ends.

Now, let us turn our eyes to the Supreme Court. The United States Supreme Court was meant to function as a principled, philosophical body designed to protect individual rights. But decisions on obscenity and pornography have been void of principle in ignoring the concept of individual rights. An earlier Supreme Court decision, *Memoires vs. Massachusetts*, stated the following criterion for pornography: "A book cannot be proscribed unless it is found to be utterly without redeeming social value." That criterion ignored the principles of individual rights and property rights while opening the way for people to be jailed on the basis of some other person's judgment of the "social" merit of their work.

Seven years later, the Supreme-Court *Miller vs. California* case negated individual rights in determining the following criteria to *criminally* convict for victimless pornography: "(a) whether the average person applying contemporary community standards would find that the work, taken as a whole, appeals to the prurient interest... (b) whether the work depicts or describes, in a patently offensive way, sexual conduct specifically defined by the applicable state law, and (c) whether the work, taken as a whole, lacks serious literary, artistic, political, or scientific value."

That Supreme Court ruling left the individual unprotected and at the mercy of any judge, prosecutor, police force, or community. Any of those forces can now attack, prosecute, and jail an individual under arbitrary standards such as (1) contemporary community standards, or (2) "offensive" as defined by a state law, or (3) if the work lacks serious literary, artistic, political, or scientific value. In other words, anyone who disagrees with the arbitrary standards of the empowered authorities — judge, police, community leaders — can potentially be jailed through current anti-obscenity laws. Such nonobjective law is a major step toward censorship, which is the precursor to totalitarianism.

The above Supreme Court majority opinion, which abridges individual rights, was written by the conservative Chief Justice and supported by the other four conservative justices in a 5 to 4 decision. Only Justice Douglas identified the issue of individual rights in his dissenting opinion:

The idea that the First Amendment permits punishment for

ideas that are 'offensive' to the particular judge or jury sitting in judgment is astounding. No greater leveler of speech or literature has ever been designed. To give the power to the censor, as we do today, is to make a sharp and radical break with the traditions of a free society. The First Amendment was not fashioned as a vehicle for dispensing tranquilizers to the people. Its prime function was to keep debate open to 'offensive' as well as to 'staid' people. The tendency throughout history has been to subdue the individual and to exalt the power of government. The use of the standard 'offensive' gives authority to government that cuts the very vitals out of the First Amendment. As is intimated by the Court's opinion, the materials before us may be garbage, but so is much of what is said in political campaigns, in the daily press, on TV or over the radio. By reason of the First Amendment — and solely because of it — speakers and publishers have not been threatened or subdued because their thoughts and ideas may be 'offensive' to some."

The conservative Chief Justice and his conservative associates on the Supreme Court shifted from the principle of protecting individual rights to an arbitrary, undefinable standard of "social good". Hitler, Stalin, and Mao also subjugated individual rights to their standards of "social good". Those arbitrary standards eventually included killing tens of millions of their own citizens for the "social good".

**"Zon, can you clue me into the soul of the value destroyer?" My father then added, "What do I look for right up front?"**

Destructive people enviously hate highly productive people and environments. Master neocheater, Fidel Castro, for instance, expressed the ultimate desire of all envious mystics, neocheaters, and other value destroyers in his publicly stated, personal desire to drop a nuclear bomb on New York City to destroy the greatest, most intense fountainhead of values known to mankind.

Professional mystics and Marxist neocheaters destroyed countries such as Cuba, Cambodia, Iran, and Nicaragua. Such envious neocheaters work explicitly for the demise of modern,

181

highly productive, highly technological societies. They gain their power by pandering to their downtrodden proletariat with false promises of a nonthinking "peaceful" existence — a prehistoric, unthinking "animal-nature" existence. They promise the ultimate mystical dream of a nonthinking, egalitarian, "problem-free" nirvana. But that dream contradicts life, nature, and reality as does all mysticism. Indeed, that no-effort, "problem-free" mysticism is the essence of value destruction and death. By contrast, high-effort problem-solving is the essence of value production and life.

**"So, I look out for envy...that desire to destroy outstanding values and bring everything down...down to an egalitarian society where no great producer stands out," my father said. Then he asked, "What exactly causes envy anyway?"**

The underlying cause is dishonesty and laziness. Laziness means the abdication of self-responsibility. That abdication is the root cause of mysticism, envy, altruism, neocheating, and chronic unhappiness. Also, incompetence and lost potential arise from laziness and defaults on self-responsibility.

Envious value destroyers have vested interests in attacking competitiveness — in attacking Neo-Tech, individualism, prosperity, and free-enterprise. The master neocheaters among the politicians, theologians, and social "intellectuals" live by attacking the competitive value producers and usurping their values. Through such destructive attacks, those neocheaters hide their own defaults while creating their needed illusions of personal power and pseudo self-worth. And, to maintain those illusions, they must continue attacking the competitive producer, his integrated thinking, the values he produces, and his individual rights and property. For those fake illusions let them physically and psychologically live off of the value producer.

Malefactor is a label that can be applied to envious people. An envious person wants values destroyed. An envious person works to undermine individual and property rights, both of which are needed to achieve well-being and happiness.

Envy distorts and then consumes a person's view of life.

Envy is a prime evil that people let develop within themselves to their great personal harm, unhappiness, and eventual death. Laziness and dishonesty are basic *causes*. Envy and impotence are basic *effects*. Envy is the desire to destroy values created or earned by others...to destroy the good because of its goodness. Why? Because the objective good — rational human values — exposes by contrast the envier's defaults and impotence. That exposure, in turn, diminishes the envier's pseudo self-esteem. And that pseudo self-esteem is needed for both psychological and physical survival — needed to prevent a mental breakdown or suicide.

Values earned by others make the envier experience his impotence. The good inherent in objective values reveals what the envier lacks. Such values reveal the human goodness that the envier has defaulted on. Such values leave the envier aware of his or her incompetence to live as a self-sufficient, independent, happy human being. Thus, the envier fears and hates such values.

The desire to destroy the values, happiness, and pleasures earned by others is the essence of envy. Envious attacks against the producers and their values are woven throughout all the "good sounding" non sequiturs of media journalists, religious leaders, politicians, social "intellectuals", "consumerists", "ecologists", and other envious neocheaters.

Contrary to the misconception promoted by envy-oriented writers and journalists, envy is not analogous to jealousy. While both reduce happiness, their causes are opposites. Jealousy is rooted in valuing and coveting a value...because the value is good to the beholder. Envy is rooted in resenting and hating a value...because the value threatens to expose the dishonesty and failures of the envier. The jealous person is threatened by the loss of a value. The envious person is threatened by the presence of a value.

Enviers have always hidden, camouflaged, and distorted the meaning of envy. Enviers must not let their inferiority and dependence on the producers become known to themselves or others. For, if everyone understood the nature of envy, the professional mystics and neocheaters would lose their survival tools and rationalized self-esteems. And that would bring loss of unearned gains, public disgrace, even suicide — unless the envier chose to change — to prosper by becoming a competitive producer of values.

Out of fear and resentment, enviers must attack values earned by others. At the same time, they must constantly usurp those values in order to survive. That contradictory life of enviers brings increasing resentment, anxiety, incompetence, unhappiness.

Those free of envy have no way of knowing the malevolent nature of the envier. Thus, most value producers, because of their naive innocence, are relatively helpless in protecting themselves from envious value destroyers. The issue is black and white: All people can be clearly classified as either envious or nonenvious. From value-destroying bureaucrats right up to genocidal dictators, the survival of envious people depends on their victims never discovering the nature of envy.

Over the centuries, concealing the nature of envy has been easy. For without Neo-Tech, most nonenvious individuals have no way to comprehend envy. In their innocence, envy-free productive people cannot emotionally or intellectually grasp the idea that people actually exist who want to destroy values because *of the goodness* represented by those values.

The envier must depend on the minds and efforts of others to survive. Envy comes from within the self-made character of a person, not from society or the environment. Envious people, therefore, are responsible for their own envy, destructions, and harm to others. Enviers are the malefactors of civilization.

Who are the envious malefactors? Who are the value destroyers of civilization? Of course, you already know. They are the dictators, politicians, theologians, social "intellectuals", destructive bureaucrats, criminal-minded professionals, which includes many of the lawyers, media journalists, university professors.

Envious malefactors or value destroyers are not inherent to these specific occupations. But a particularly high percentage of such malefactors populate these easy-to-fake professions. By contrast, envious malefactors rarely exist in productive hard-to-fake activities such as competitive, profit-making businesses.

Other enviers include unproductive scions of inherited wealth or dissipators of wealth earned by others, self-appointed

professional feminists, self-appointed professional environmentalists, self-appointed professional consumerists.

These professional, self-appointed value destroyers such as the
Nader type, for example, are destructive enviers who use
neocheating demagoguery to gain unearned power. Such
neocheaters use non sequiturs to create falsely inverted "realities"
such as the "hero" consumer pitted against the "villain" producer.
But those neocheaters hurt both the consumer and the producer
by promoting government controls and force. By contrast, those
"villain" producers of values are and always have been the only
real benefactors and heroes of mankind. Without those producers,
no productive jobs or consumers would exist since no products
or values to consume would exist. Indeed, without those
producers, little, if any, human life would exist.

**My father stopped the mountain's eruption of knowledge
by saying, "You have said a lot, and I need to digest it and
write it down. May we continue tomorrow? I really need
to think through all what you said today."**

\* \* \* \*

**That night my dad wrote until 3:00 in the morning. He
was back at his mountain at 6:00 am. "My mind is sharp
today," he yelled at the mountain, smiling wide. "Zon, lay
it on me!"**

Value destroyers are basically immature, anti-intellectual
people who seek to evade reality and honesty. By contrast, most
value producers are mature, genuinely intellectual people who
seek to identify contextual facts through fully integrated honesty.

Most politicians and social "intellectuals" are immature value
destroyers who survive by neocheating the value producer. Such
people promote altruistic social "ideals" designed to harm and
drain the value producers of this planet. Those immature value
destroyers include not only politicians but a high percentage of
university professors, especially in the fields of social and
political sciences, philosophy, psychology, education, law,
religion...and a smaller percentage in other fields. Their crusades
for fake social "justice" and specious human rights are motivated

185

by envy and executed through criminal minds. Their attacks on values are neocheating ploys not only for plundering the value producers but for hiding their own incompetence, laziness, and dishonesty. But the greatest evil of those academe is their irreparable mutilation of millions upon millions of young, developing minds.

**"I have heard you denounce organized religions," my father said. "Tell me, why do you classify theologians as neocheaters, malefactors, value destroyers, and parasites? What about the good that theologians do, such as help the poor?"**

Their so-called "good" is usually specious and contrary to human well-being and happiness. For, their "good" is based on the altruistic sacrifice of the value producer with the theologians collecting both the praise and a middle-man's cut without producing values.

Most theologian-type "good" depends on dishonest, guilt manipulations of the producer. That "good" arises from their subtle, unjust denigrations of personal success, prosperity, and happiness. Furthermore, their "good" generally involves hypocritical, neocheating ploys designed for living with praise and "ease" without working to produce competitive values. In other words, theologians support themselves by promoting God-like altruistic schemes designed to usurp values earned by others while collecting unearned respect and power. ...That is the purpose and livelihood of most theologians.

Other value destroyers such as demagogic "ecologists" and "consumerists", neocheating politicians and bureaucrats, evil dictators and ayatollahs usurp enough power to directly execute their envious destructions. They camouflage their envy by operating under non-sequitur banners of common "good", human rights, social "justice", "peace", equality, the fatherland. Such envious, value-destroying professionals live by usurping power and values, by attacking, undermining, crippling, destroying value producers.

Most other enviers, however, lack the power, cunning, and resources to directly damage and destroy value producers. To vicariously satisfy their envy, they eagerly support the destructive causes promoted by those demagogic "consumerists", "environmentalists", theologians, politicians, social "intellectuals", and other neocheaters.

A person can cure his or her envy only by becoming a self-sufficient producer of competitive values to achieve genuine independence, competence, and self-esteem. If not cured, the malignancy of envy will keep growing, consuming that person in malevolent hatred toward self, productive people, objective values, and life itself.

Expressed another way, growing envy destroys a person's potential to earn genuine prosperity, psychuous pleasures, and happiness. To break free from envy's grip, a person must first identify the envy. Next, that person must reduce the need for envy by becoming increasingly productive until competent enough to live by competitively producing values desired by others. Then a metamorphosis occurs that changes envious fear of objective values to a passionate desire to uphold those values. On evolving into an independent, self-sufficient producer of values, envy fades as a new, exciting life emerges — a life of growing prosperity, expanding power, and abiding happiness.

Producers of objective values have prosperity and happiness always open to them. But first they must break free from the unearned guilt foisted on them by the enviers who surrounded them. The producers must realize that they are the ones who hold the real power. And only they can guiltlessly collect genuine prosperity and happiness.

**"I feel the power, Zon. I feel the power of Neo-Tech in my life. I feel like...like a mountain of strength. I feel like...like I am you," my father said enthusiastically. "How do I get more and more of this power? How does everyone get this win-win power...this Neo-Tech power?"**

Neo-Tech sharply contrasts the world of mysticism and envy to the world of value production and self-esteem. One does not cross into the happy, envy-free world until that person becomes competent enough through consistent logical thinking, integrated honesty, and hard efforts to be self-sufficient by producing

187

competitive values for others and society.

Consider that laziness and dishonesty are volitionally chosen prime evils. People allow laziness and dishonesty to develop within themselves to their great personal harm. Laziness and dishonesty are the basic causes of mysticism, neocheating, and envy.

Laziness always involves mysticism undercutting the conscious mind. One must exert a constant, honest, life-long effort to maintain a prosperous, happy, healthy life. By contrast, mental and physical laziness means defaulting on those key attributes of honesty and effort required for independent self-survival and happiness.

The logical use of the mind combined with consistent rational efforts is required for human survival and prosperity. But, mental default is seductively tempting. A person simply adopts someone else's thinking, thus avoiding the responsibility of exerting one's own integrated thinking and honesty for independent survival and prosperity. Such "pleasantly easy" defaults against using one's own mind are traps that corrode self-sufficiency and lead to intellectual, psychological, and eventual physical dependence on others, especially "authorities".

Usually those "authorities" are neocheaters who dupe the defaulter into accepting their dishonest, destructive ploys designed for usurping power. ...Such neocheating "authorities" survive by promoting their mystical hoaxes and specious doctrines of altruistic self-sacrifice in order to control the defaulters and neocheat the producers.

Integrated, logical thinking does not preclude errors or wrong judgments. But only through habitual, integrated, logical thinking does one become efficient in identifying and correcting errors. If a person defaults on that thinking effort, he or she must live increasingly through other people's thinking. That person then gradually loses the ability to recognize the errors in other people's thinking as well as to correct his or her own errors. Such a person eventually becomes incompetent to live independently. That person then becomes dependent on destructive, neocheating "authorities" to survive.

Essentially all willful destruction, all purposeful violence, all initiation of force against individuals and their property can be reduced to a single, originating cause — mysticism originating from laziness and dishonesty. That laziness and dishonesty evolve from choosing not to exert the constant, rational efforts required to understand reality in order to make one's own independent decisions. ...Laziness and dishonesty are the cause of evil; envy is the effect.

Attacks on free enterprise, producers, and objective values by envious altruists, powercrats, social "intellectuals", theologians, lawyers, judges, academics, and other neocheaters are on the rise around the world. Before Neo-Tech, envious altruism was increasingly undermining the value producers. But now, Neo-Tech not only identifies the nature of envy, but also reveals how neocheaters use mystical altruism to attack and undermine the producers in order to usurp unearned power and values. Thus, just in time, at the crucial Nuclear-Decision Threshold, you must make Neo-Tech available to the world to identify, counteract, and reverse the destructive trend of mysticism. Moreover, your timely Neo-Tech will also demonstrate how guiltless psychuous pleasures and happiness arise from rejecting all mystical dishonesties. Finally, Neo-Tech renders powerless the intentional value destroyers — the professional mystics, altruists, powercrats, parasites, enviers, and other neocheaters.

Neo-Tech means the eventual demise of the politician, social "intellectual", theologian, and every other neocheating altruist and egalitarian who usurp values and power from the value producers. At the same time, almost anyone can achieve a prosperous, happy life with Neo-Tech, even those hapless mystics and neocheaters who have been exposed and rejected by the producers armed with Neo-Tech.

Without Neo-Tech, the legions of altruists, mystics, and powercrats would have eventually buried the producers and their values, causing a new dark age. But through you, Neo-Tech knowledge will begin spreading around the world. That expanding Neo-Tech matrix will render impotent all professional mystics and neocheaters caught in its web. Yet, ironically, those foundering mystics and neocheaters can with Neo-Tech join the producers in experiencing genuine prosperity and happiness by rejecting their own mysticism and producing competitive values for others.

189

Book 2
Neo-Tech Decoded

Those with Neo-Tech knowledge will gain powerful advantages in every competitive situation. That is why you must write this all down and disseminate this to fifty million people. For then they will fully understand the crippling, 2000-year hoax of Platonistic-based philosophies that today dominate most people's thoughts and actions. Thus, by removing that hoax, Neo-Tech leaves ordinary people with profound competitive advantages over those foundering in the Plato-based world of professional mystics and neocheaters. That competitive edge will pull more and more people into the Neo-Tech way of living.

**"Why me, Zon...why did you choose me?" My father pleaded for an answer. Almost as if the mountain were contemplating, a long pause of silence ensued. Then the wind blew and the voice returned:**

I did not find you — you found me. You were ready to hear me. There are many reasons for that, which someday you'll know. But one crucial dynamic happened to you that was necessary to hear me within today's anticivilization: You were in a fight for your life with the world's most powerful neocheaters. You were in a survival mode. Survival pressures forced bicameral man to jump to conscious man 3000 years ago. Survival pressures forced you to jump from conscious man to Neothink man. Now, you will bring justice, good, and love to the world.

I have waited for over 2000 years. Through the 2000-year history of altruistic-based cultures, most material achievements have been maligned and attacked by theologians, politicians, and other professional mystics and altruists. The motive for scorning human-produced values has always been to saddle the value producers with unearned guilt. Once saddled with guilt, value producers were more easily manipulated, duped, and usurped out of their earned power and values. Indeed, to survive, professional neocheaters and mystics constantly usurped material and psychological values from those producers.

**"I bet that would be tough to sit through for 2000 years," my dad said, shaking his head.**

190

## A New Code Of Success Is Told

The production of values for others is the single most important function of any person's life. Every person's survival and happiness as well as every facet of his or her physical, mental, and psychological well-being depends on the production of competitive values for others. If a person chooses not to produce sufficient values to survive, then that person must become dependent on the producers to survive by begging, cajoling, neocheating, deception, force, or theft.

Thus the producer, not the consumer, is essential to human life and happiness. By contrast, nonproductive people are dependent on the producers to survive. And those nonproducers who neocheat to survive exist with deteriorating competence, mounting envy, and growing unhappiness. That nonproducer's life soon terminates in Growth Death, then in emotional death.

Integrated links exist between productivity, self-interest, self-esteem, psychuous pleasures, and happiness. Production of competitive values is the integrating growth dynamics for conscious beings. Production of competitive values provides freedom, prosperity, psychuous pleasures, and abiding happiness.

Productivity and rational self-interest are not only essential to happiness, but are essential to life itself. For without productive self-interest, only consumptive altruism remains. What would a world of consumptive altruism mean? What if everyone began living as selfless, unproductive consumers, temporarily surviving by sacrificing one another in consuming the values created by the past producers. One can imagine what an unhappy, destructive world that would be. One can imagine the malevolence and meanness that would exist among those human beings as they cannibalized the final values and then one another. Soon after that, nearly everyone would be dead, even those with guns.

But what if everyone began living competitively as rational, productive individuals with everyone intent on producing maximum values for others and society in order to achieve maximum prosperity, psychuous pleasures, romantic love, and happiness for themselves and their loved ones. One can imagine what a benevolent, happy, exciting, thriving world that would be...a world free of mysticism and neocheaters...a world without guns...a world in which everyone forever increases his or her productivity, prosperity, and happiness. You must help civilization enter that world.

**"Imagine such a world. Wow, I wish I could," my father said.**

A society that functions exclusively for the rational benefit of the individual has never existed. *A society has no moral or logical reason to exist except to benefit the individual and protect his and her property rights.* But a fully moral, logical society has never existed. For the producers have always been tricked into accepting and supporting free-loading, professional mystics and neocheaters acting as "authorities". Such "authorities" use altruism to control value producers through false guilt. Thus, those value producers work to support those very neocheaters who harm, pillage, and eventually destroy them, their loved ones, and everyone's happiness.

A totally free, just, and rational society would by definition be a Neo-Tech society — a society based on fully integrated honesty. Such a society would be a free-enterprise, nonforce government...a government and society that has yet to exist on planet Earth. The ethical essence of a Neo-Tech society is the holding of individual rights as supreme. Therefore, *any* form of initiatory force, coercion, or fraud against any individual by any individual, group, society, or government is immoral and thus is ostracizable.

Any suggestion of force-free societies strikes fear into neocheating politicians, demagogues, and mystics. Knowing that professional value destroyers cannot survive in a nonforce, noncoerced, free-enterprise, fully competitive society, they desperately vilify and subvert any movement toward such a society and its values. They sabotage and undercut those values with non-sequitur, out-of-context attacks. Indeed, to survive, professional mystics and neocheaters must prevent a value-oriented, Neo-Tech society. For such a society would quickly identify and forever banish them as destructive criminals. ...On rejecting mystics and neocheaters, the value producers become free to prosper guiltlessly and happily by benefiting without limits others and society.

## A New Code Of Success Is Told

Prohibiting initiatory force, threats of force, and fraud is the only law in a Neo-Tech society. Highly effective enforcement of the individual-rights law by an integrated ostracizing system would become very punishing and would add extreme effectiveness to any police force and prison system. Thus, with that single, highly enforceable law, each individual would be solely responsible for his or her own actions, life, and well-being. The resulting competitive, free-choice interaction among people would deliver maximum benefits to each individual and society. That, in turn, would greatly enhance every productive person's well-being and happiness. ...Thus, to survive, the nonproductive mystics and neocheaters would have to begin producing competitive values for others instead of destructively usurping values from others. Today, by attacking those values, they can still conceal their parasitism and failure to fulfill their responsibilities toward producing desirable, competitive values for others and society.

**"Zon, their days are numbered. I'm going to take Neo-Tech to the whole world!" my father blurted, filled with determination. "I will turn into a writing machine, and then I will learn how to publish and market Neo-Tech across the globe."**

I want you to remember this as you write down the Neo-Tech knowledge: Contrary to the pronouncements of most modern linguists and social "scientists", words and language are primarily tools of thinking, not of communication. But clear thinking would lead to identification of the value destroyers. Thus, professional mystics and neocheaters must constantly attack and debase words and language to prevent clear thinking. For the existences of professional value destroyers depend on obscuring, distorting, and concealing reality in order to perpetuate fuzzy thinking among their victims. To accomplish that obfuscation, the mystics and neocheaters must (1) use words out of context, (2) twist and invert meanings of key words and concepts, and (3) dishonestly build on rationalizations and non sequiturs. ...They develop their own newspeak without regard to honesty.

193

Honest intellectuals concerned about the decay of language know that twisting and misusing words corrode the tools of thinking. But that is only half the problem. Protecting honesty and language also involves *context*. Powerful thinking requires not only using consistent, exact definitions but also precise, accurate contexts for all words and concepts. To accurately define meanings *and* contexts of important words and concepts is not only central to precise communication, oral or written, but is the key to effective thinking and understanding reality.

By contrast, twisting meanings of key words and using concepts out of context are the primary techniques of professional mystics and neocheaters, especially those in the media. For they exist by distorting or inverting language to deceive others. They invert the meanings of important words in order to rationalize their deceptions, destructions, thefts, use of force, and other irrational, immoral actions. And they do that often under inverted newspeak pretexts of justice, social good, human rights, and "higher" causes.

In seeking honesty and understanding of reality, you must be aware of both definition and context of key words. But neocheating "intellectuals", in their need to conceal meanings, exert mighty efforts to distort the meaning and invert the context of crucial words such as the following words:

| | |
|---|---|
| Capitalism | Peace |
| Consumer | Producer |
| Ecology | Reality |
| Good | Rights |
| Justice | Selfishness |
| Love | Truth |

Words can also represent concepts. The more basic the concept, the greater abstraction and integration is required to fully grasp that concept. The most difficult concepts to grasp in their full, accurate context are the most basic human concepts such as:

Justice
Good
Love

Throughout history, those three basic concepts have been used out of context or inverted in meaning by all professional mystics and neocheaters in their constant need to camouflage their destructive, parasitical existences. When neocheaters speak of justice, they are usually promoting unjust, destructive actions against the value producer, objective values, individual rights, private property, and the means to produce values and achieve happiness. When neocheaters speak of good — the common good or the "higher" good — they are usually promoting destructive altruism designed to usurp or destroy values earned by others. When neocheaters speak of love and brotherhood, they are usually promoting envious, promiscuous, egalitarian schemes designed to cripple competitive value producers and undermine romantic love.

To fully understand the basic concepts of justice, good, and love requires an accurate understanding of human nature relative to reality. That understanding requires integrations of the many specific concepts I have presented you. To understand the concept of romantic love, for example, requires understanding the array of Neo-Tech/Psychuous concepts needed to understand romantic love in full, accurate context. Because the concepts of *justice*, *good*, and *love* are inextricably linked, all three concepts have been fully integrated throughout all the Neo-Tech knowledge I have bestowed upon you.

**"I understand," my father said with a peculiar look of shock on his face. "No Zon, I mean, I *really* understand *you* now. You are Zon. And Zon is knowledge — widely integrated knowledge put together through hard-thinking fully integrated honesty for powerful, far-reaching, Neothink context. I mean, that is who you are: widely integrated knowledge in fully honest, Neothink context. And that is what my writings must become."**

**With that insight, my father knew his time with the mountain called Zon was coming to an end. Feeling this would be his last time to talk with his most amazing friend he ever knew, my father started to call out, but Zon spoke first:**

195

You have worked very hard, all your life, and you have exerted enormous efforts to be honest during your stand-up battle with the neocheaters. That enormous effort is why you were the first person to be able to hear my voice of Zon. Still, your work has just begun, for now you must *work very hard* to develop and disseminate 50 million copies of your Neo-Tech writings. Business — product development *and* marketing — is the great challenge of life. That is your job now. Good-bye, my friend.

**To this day, my father still runs by the mountain. Of course, the wind blows with no voice. He often stops and looks at his mountain. Lonely as it seems, my father knows the silence means he did his job well in writing down everything Zon had to say.**

**In the months that followed, the more my father looked over his many notes on Zon, the more elegantly simple Zon's message became, summarized in a four-part formula: The main tool used to control or rule over mankind was "higher causes" via altruism (*Ancient-Secret-One* Chapter). Our deep-rooted bicameral-mind tendencies made that higher-authority control over us quite easy, almost natural, to do (*Ancient-Secret-Two* Chapter). The way to rationalize and camouflage the harm and destruction was reality-altering mysticism (*Ancient-Secret-Three* Chapter). And the neocheaters propagated mysticism to confuse us, rule over us, manipulate our bicameral-mind tendencies, and promulgate an altruistic subservience to them — the leaders, the rulers...the neocheaters (*Ancient-Secret-Four* Chapter). ...After 2001, in our Neo-Tech World, bicameral-mind tendencies will no longer exist, replaced by Neothink. Then, higher "authorities", altruism, mysticism, and neocheaters will no longer exist. All the suffering will be replaced by man's Six Ultimate Gifts (see *God-Man: Our Final Evolution*). We, the yesterday's victims, became tomorrow's victors.**

## Epilogue

# Yesterday's Victims; Tomorrow's Victors

About a week after his last talk with Zon, my father grew impassioned to know the day-to-day technique neocheaters used to routinely pull off their hoax for over 2000 years. With the voice of Zon now silent, my father struggled to figure it out himself. Frustrated from endless thinking, he sat down one Sunday afternoon to watch Mike Wallace's "60 Minutes" on TV. Suddenly, while watching the show about welfare families living in New York City hotels, the answer came to him. My dad reached for a pad of paper and pen and, with "60 Minutes" still airing, he began to write. He felt as if Zon were in him, guiding his thoughts as he wrote as fast as he could. This paper on the secret staying power of the neocheaters was the beginning of his own writings, guided by the spirit Zon:

### THE SECRET OF NON SEQUITURS

The word non sequitur embodies the key survival tool of all professional mystics and neocheaters. Non sequitur is a Latin word meaning "it does not follow". Because the word is dead-language Latin, its meaning is stable, immutable — unable to be changed or twisted by mystics and neocheaters. That is why the word is so valuable for uprooting neocheaters.[1]

Non sequiturs are blatantly yet cleverly used in news journalism. Mike Wallace's "60 Minutes" television program, for example, orchestrates outrage at New York City hotel owners who accept welfare families. Those owners are projected as crooks for charging the city $70 daily room rates while charging only $50 daily for rooms to self-paying customers.

But, "60 Minutes" purposely ignores the fact that few of those welfare families accept the responsibility to take care of their own lives and bodies, much less their "free" rooms. Thus, their rooms soon become filthy and then deteriorate rapidly toward destruction. With those facts ignored, the TV audience is treated

---

[1]Webster's 9th Collegiate Dictionary definition of non sequitur is, "a statement that does not follow logically from anything previously said".

197

to shots of an unhygienic, obese mother with a brood of unkempt children vegetating in a cockroach-infested room.  Then "60 Minutes", always cravenly shielding itself from valid rebuttal, implies to a viewing audience of millions that somehow the hotel owners are responsible for the personal filth of those clients and the resulting cockroaches.  Mike Wallace lays the fault on value-producing businesses and their hard-working creators rather than on value-destroying welfare schemes and their neocheating creators.

"60 Minutes" then attacks the hotel owners with the non sequitur of higher room rates as "proof" of some kind of unscrupulous greed inherent in businessmen.  Hence, most of the millions of viewers are tricked into accepting the false, non-sequitur premise that profit-oriented businessmen are "insensitive", unscrupulous, corrupt and, somehow, the cause of misery in others.  With that premise accepted, the neocheaters can then demand that value producers be controlled by others.  By others? ...By the professional value destroyers creating bogus jobs and livelihoods for themselves.

The facts, however, are opposite to what was projected.  The hotel owners were not greedily overcharging at $70 per room for welfare clients, but were grossly *undercharging* at $70 per room subjected to welfare destruction:  A hotel has two main assets:  (1) its physical real estate (rooms), and (2) its milieu (setting) that determines what can be charged for their rooms.  In accepting those welfare clients, the owners are charging only $20 per day additional to have their two main assets systematically destroyed, day after day.  Thus, when the full-context situation is considered, the city is renting those rooms at bargain prices in a terrible, losing proposition for the hotel owners.  For, how many other hotel owners responsible for survival through long-range profits would allow their rooms and milieu to be destroyed for only $20 a day?

Dominating the national press and TV news media are value destroyers existing on non sequiturs:

A conservative, religious-oriented TV talk-show host devastates an honest, brave woman voicing a valid objection to school prayer.  The bully TV host dishonestly uses a non sequitur in asking her where the good, loving mother within her is.  On

198

another network that same night, an honest value-producing toy manufacturer heroically refutes the dishonest, non-sequitur attacks on the toy industry. By standing firm on facts and context, that toy manufacturer has the famous TV news commentator on the defensive...until that commentator suddenly asks where the good, gentle grandfather within that businessman is. Such emotional-manipulating non sequiturs about being a good mother or a gentle grandfather have no connection with the issue. Such dishonest innuendos dismiss any concern for honesty or dealing with contextual facts. ...On and on go the "news" media, day after day, year after year, living through attacks on values by using non sequiturs without regard for honesty or contextual facts.

As with all professional mystics and neocheaters, honesty and integrity must be replaced with non-sequitur manipulations to support their destructive jobs and fake livelihoods. Such people must constantly invert values, making good appear as bad and bad appear as good. Neocheaters must always use non sequiturs to press their specious points on the public. For, to survive, they must continuously attack and lay guilt on the "greedy" value producers in order to control them, to live off them. Indeed, over the centuries, mystics and neocheaters have effectively used non sequiturs to attack and lay false guilt on business-minded value producers everywhere. ...The non sequitur is the neocheater's survival tool for usurping a bogus living from honest value producers.

Some neocheaters use non sequiturs in highly generalized ways. For example, Popes and leaders of the Catholic Church have for centuries brilliantly used inspiring art, great architecture, and classical music as non sequiturs. With that, the religious leaders created a mighty non sequitur. And projecting that non sequitur let them gain the public respect and credibility needed to usurp unearned power, values, and livelihoods from the value producers.

Indeed, the Catholic church saved itself through nonsequiturs during the rise of honesty and logic that occurred during the Renaissance. The master neocheaters of the Roman Catholic hierarchy recognized the starkly obvious values of the burgeoning, new art forms. They then captured those art values for exploitation by aggressively commissioning the most skilled artists

199

to produce highly obvious values. The master neocheaters captured those values at first through architecture, the fine arts, and sculpture. Later they added music to their arsenal through the great classical composers. Governments and tyrants right up to Lenin, Hitler, and current neocheating rulers also seized that neocheating ploy. To gain easy credibility and to capture support through the emotions, they used the fine arts, literature, music, and opera.

Since the value of art can be sensed through emotions and requires no intellectual analysis, the public needs only to notice the obvious art and architectural values to erroneously link those values of the master artists to the master neocheaters presenting that art. Thus, the masses are deluded into seeing those obvious values of great art as also representing the values of the neocheating church or government. Subconsciously they conclude: "I can see, hear, and feel those architectural, art, and musical values. I know those values are real and valid. Thus, those values must also represent those who own and present this art — the church or government. Therefore, all that I do not comprehend about the church or government must be as good and valuable as the art that represents them."

Through that brilliant, but dishonest use of art as non sequiturs, the church and governments were able to survive the rise of honesty and logic during the Renaissance, the resulting industrial revolution, and then the rise of capitalism and free enterprise.

Even more pervasive, destructive uses of non sequiturs arise from politicians. Throughout history, politicians have been the premier professional neocheaters operating on grand scales.

Essentially all their public statements and career actions of "good intentions" always "for the public good" are really for their own political power. Indeed, they use their good-sounding "good intentions" as potent illusory non sequiturs that hypnotize the public while carrying forth immense destruction to society for their own political rise to power.

In the widest context, government value destroyers can never benefit anyone. Instead, they can only harm, destroy, and kill: A study by professor R.T. Rummel at the University of Hawaii reveals that in this century government value destroyers directly and purposely killed 119 million of their own citizens in non-war actions — over triple the 35 million they killed in war actions (international and civil). In addition, government value destroyers have wreaked such suffering and destruction on their victims to indirectly cause extreme premature death (two decades or more of life lost) for at least 800 million conscious beings in this century alone. ...By contrast, business value producers purposely hurt or kill no one. Instead, they give life and benefits to everyone.

Neocheaters conceal themselves with non sequiturs designed to make dishonesty seem honest, harm seem helpful, bad seem good — and vice versa. ...Non sequiturs are the disguises worn by all professional mystics and neocheaters. Neo-Tech tears off those disguises.

**My father put down his paper and then muttered, "The value destroyers constantly use such non-sequitur/neocheating maneuvers to camouflage unfair, destructive modi operandi with opposite illusions of fairness and helpfulness. But with Neo-Tech, one easily identifies how their good-sounding facts or words are falsely used as non sequiturs to attack and harm value producers. Such non-sequitur attacks are used to usurp power and values by journalists, clergymen, politicians, regulatory bureaucrats, and self-appointed consumer and environmental advocates." ...That night, my father began writing again. The next day, he wrote for fifteen hours.**

**Zon still talks to me, my father thought, but he talks to me through my writing. Here is what my father wrote as it flowed from his pen, again just as fast as he could write, obviously guided by Zon:**

Mysticism Creates Problems Where None Previously Existed
Business Creates Values Where None Previously Existed

About 2000 years ago, a new form of dishonesty evolved. Today, that form of dishonesty is called neocheating. Today, as in those ancient times, neocheating involves the undetected theft of power and values from others. Such undetected theft is accomplished by manipulating mysticism to create problems

201

where none exist.

Christian religious leaders orchestrated the first mass manipulations of mysticism: About 1800 years ago, those religious leaders discovered a mighty tool for extracting power and values from merchants, laborers, farmers, craftsmen, builders, and other value producers. That tool was false guilt. They used false guilt to undermine prosperity and happiness earned by others. Projecting false guilt, those religious leaders attacked and undermined the producer in order to usurp his earned power and values.

Those earliest neocheaters discovered they could control and then live off the value producer by manipulating that false guilt onto him or her. From that discovery, those neocheaters usurped more and more power and values from the naive value producers by adding more and more false guilt fashioned from the inverted ethics of religion and altruism.

Christianity was founded almost 2000 years ago. For many years, Christian followers formed cadres of zealots who resisted, heroically at times, the oppression of Roman authorities. Then certain Christian leaders seeking greater unearned power discovered and developed a neocheating power more pernicious than any destructive power known previously. That power destroyed Roman civilization. And that same power today undermines the prosperity and happiness of every individual worldwide. ...That power is false, altruistic guilt in which the innocent are made to appear bad while the guilty are made to appear good.

Those original religious neocheaters learned how to foist altruism and guilt onto innocent value producers to deprive them of their earned prosperity, power, and happiness. Moreover, those early Christian neocheaters developed cunning, Platonistic ethical systems that inverted values. Their bizarre, irrational systems were based on altruism, collectivism, and egalitarianism. So effective were those systems for secretly exploiting others that to this day most neocheaters vigorously and pervasively press hypocritical altruism on everyone as a moral ethical system. ...But today, Neo-Tech is replacing those dishonest, mystic-based, value-destroying systems with honest, business-like, value-producing systems.

202

*Yesterday's Victims; Tomorrow's Victors*

Most neocheating systems use clever, good-sounding non sequiturs that make good appear bad and bad appear good. With non sequiturs, neocheaters developed diabolically ingenious doctrines of altruism to sacrifice real values to conjured-up false values. The net result is always the destruction of values. Over the centuries, neocheaters have neatly woven destructive rationalizations, seductive mysticism, and good-sounding altruism throughout government, religion, education, law, and journalism.

By contrast, of all the ethical systems built by society, only the system of business with its manifestations of honesty, productivity, commerce, mathematics, and science is not rooted in mysticism or altruism. Instead, business is rooted in the voluntary trading of competitive values. Thus, by nature, business is the most rational, intellectually demanding, honest, productive, and benevolent ethical system possible to conscious beings.

But why is altruism so pernicious? Consider that religious and political neocheaters have for 2000 years honed altruistic guilt into razor-sharp, well-camouflaged stilettos to attack, slash, and stab the value producers. For, to survive, all professional mystics and neocheaters must constantly attack and undermine those producers in order to usurp their power, property, and values. Also, to survive, the rewards of prosperity, self-esteem, and happiness must constantly be faked by all neocheaters. For without faking their self-worth, they could not survive: Without a faked or rationalized self-esteem, all value destroyers would either directly or indirectly commit suicide...or become honest value producers to survive.

Earned power is the basis of self-esteem and happiness. Honest business titans, for example, have earned the power to orchestrate vast ranges of actions to determine their futures. Indeed, by picking up the telephone anywhere, day or night, they have the power to direct thousands of people into productive, life-enhancing activities. Those business titans hold a real power that mystics and neocheaters never even dream of achieving. Exercising such productive power is the primordial source of prosperity, self-esteem, and happiness.

By contrast, professional mystics and neocheaters can never experience earned power. They can only exercise usurped power. Or ultimately, as mass-murderer Mao Tse-Tung accurately

203

identified: "All political (unearned) power comes from the barrel of a gun." For that reason, such neocheaters can never feel genuine power, self-esteem, or happiness. Indeed, they can operate only through unearned power...through destruction, deception, and force in beguiling or forcing producers into sacrificing their values.

Such professional mystics and neocheaters survive by using non-sequitur deceptions or force-backed machinations to drain the prosperity and happiness earned by others. Mystics and neocheaters justify their dishonesties and destructions through specious Platonistic philosophies based on "higher" causes and altruism that were designed solely to extort values earned by others.

Two fundamentally different classes of conscious beings exist in free or semi-free societies:

(1) those who choose to live by exerting integrated physical and mental efforts to produce competitive values for others and society (or those who are learning or striving to be competitive value producers), and

(2) those who choose to live by avoiding competitive efforts in designing their lives to live off the efforts of others and society.

The sense of life, honesty, and maturity between those two classes are opposites: Value producers share a confidence-driven goodwill and an effort-driven competence. But value destroyers share a resentment-driven cynicism and a laziness-driven incompetence. That incompetence fuels destructive envy aimed at the value producer upon whom everyone depends for prosperity and survival.

With the preceding knowledge, one realizes that politicians and clergymen as well as most lawyers, journalists, academe, union leaders, and bureaucrats live by destroying rather than producing values. Thus, they live by attacking or harming the producers, their businesses, their products. ...With that knowledge, one recognizes how profoundly different value producers are from value destroyers.

Professional mystics and neocheaters are clever, scheming people with well-camouflaged, criminal minds. They steal physical and psychological livings from the producer with no one realizing their thefts. Without their victim's knowledge, they orchestrate manipulations of mysticism, using non sequiturs to produce deceptive illusions. With those illusions, they attack, undermine, and lay guilt on innocent value producers while making the good seem bad and the bad seem good...the innocent appear guilty and the guilty appear innocent.

Ironically, the most vicious neocheaters fashion illusions so they appear as paragons of justice, benevolence, or compassion. But they are the exact opposite. Indeed, vicious neocheaters are not only the Marxists and Maoists who ravage or kill everyone, but are the force-backed bureaucrats, the anti-business regulators, and the Giuliani-type prosecutors along with their politician, clergy, academic, and journalist cheerleaders. Also, included among the vicious value destroyers are those union leaders, "consumer advocates", "environmentalists", "peace advocates", and business quislings who live by attacking the value producers or supporting the value destroyers. Such mystics and neocheaters are responsible for subtle, undetected destruction, suffering, and killings far beyond all the bloodiest wars combined, which are also staged by professional mystics and neocheaters.

And what about those responsible for such force-backed bureaucracies as the FDA, EPA, IRS, OSHA, HEW? Those people live by directly and indirectly attacking businesses, producers, and objective values. They are among the cleverest, deadliest neocheaters. For they gain their power through draining others on well-hidden, but massively destructive scales.

Such neocheaters undercut values and drain happiness from everyone. Without a qualm or backward glance at their wreckage, they blithely commit any destruction they can get away with in order to keep or increase their unearned power. Honesty means nothing to them. Long ago they abandoned the concepts of integrity, rationality, and honest competitive effort. Yet, those neocheaters succeed by creating illusions that they care about life...that they protect, help, or save the lives of others. Thus, with bizarre irony, they make themselves appear as compassionate benefactors of mankind. Indeed, until the recent discovery of Neo-Tech, neocheaters for 2000 years succeeded in appearing as benefactors worthy of respect. But now, with Neo-Tech, they are exposed for what they are — value-destroying pip squeaks worthy only of contempt.

In stealing their livings through dishonest "for-the-public-good" laws and regulations forced upon entire populations, government-type neocheaters eventually cost the lives of thousands even millions of innocent persons while diminishing everyone's life. Such neocheaters range from power-type bureaucracy builders to Mussolini-type crowd pleasers, to Nader-type government manipulators, to Silent-Spring type social authors. Yet, those value destroyers always display look-good, non-sequitur evidence (e.g. "helping" the poor, prompt trains, consumer protection, "clean" water). Through their force-backed laws and regulations, they point to the "good" they do and the people they "protect" from the businessmen, the Jews, the industrialists, the factories — from the value producers. Backed by neocheating quislings in business (the white-collar hoax) and neocheating collaborators in the media and the academe, such master neocheaters victimize all value producers. But those collaborators will also become victims. For today, with Neo-Tech, all such collaborators will sooner or later be stripped of their unearned well-being and smug security. They all will pay the price for supporting the destructive machinations of professional mystics and neocheaters. ...Through Neo-Tech, justice will prevail.

All master neocheaters fake compassion as they pretend to benefit and protect the majority, the minorities, the government, the country, the master race, the poor, the masses, the worker, the consumer. But instead, through dishonest manipulations of mysticism, they relentlessly diminish and destroy human values and lives.

Without the slightest care, they live by hurting or destroying innocent others, often by the millions. Consider Hitler's splendid-looking, mystically motivated, Panzer Divisions that blitzkrieged across Europe. They rendered their constant destructions without the slightest care or even a backward glance at the destroyed lives, shattered businesses, and flattened homes they left behind. Everyday, by the thousands, the life-long efforts of producers were destroyed in an instant by the neocheaters' marching minions. For such value destroyers never honestly think — they

206

never think or integrate what productive effort is, what creating values means, or who creates the values they use every day to live comfortably, safely, easily. Instead, they blindly, mystically render their destructions, every day leaving behind broken lives and rubble. ...So what! cry the neocheating masters as they gloriously roll on attacking and destroying the lives and efforts of innocent value producers. For, the more destruction such neocheaters render, the more secure and powerful they feel.

Those neocheaters just roll on, never considering the carnage they leave behind. For them, destroying the lives, property, and values of others is their only route to power and control. For them, usurping and destroying values (requires only force and deception) are much easier than earning and producing values (requires hard work and honesty). Thus, they dare never to glance back at their products of destruction, which are the only products they can deliver. ...Be they "liberal" politicians, conservative evangelists, modern preachers, pseudo business executives, white-collar-hoax business quislings, dishonest journalists, or neocheating academics, they all must live without regard for honesty or reality while attacking producers and destroying values.

Consider the highly publicized, "liberal"-type politicians or the highly visible, fact-twisting journalists. Such master neocheaters build their unearned power by, for example, partaking in the orchestrated destruction of the innocent value producers in Cuba, Cambodia, Vietnam, Nicaragua, and soon South Africa. They spread death and destruction under a maze of dishonest, neocheating guises, including so-called human rights, while ignoring individual rights. Indeed, they must bury individual rights in order to keep usurping power and values. ...Without Neo-Tech to stop them, they would keep escalating their damage until all value producers were crippled or destroyed.

Also, among the subtlest yet most vicious neocheaters are those orchestrating agencies such as the INS, IRS, EPA, SEC, and FDA. Those agencies through their force-backed regulations cause the unnecessary sufferings and deaths of innocent people by the millions. The motives of those responsible for attacking values have nothing to do with helping or protecting anyone, but have everything to do with usurping a living by intimidating

207

value producers into obedience, controlling their means of production, and usurping their values.

What values, for example, has the FDA and its prosecutors ever produced for anyone? They survive entirely by attacking and hindering those who produce life-enhancing values for others. Through power-usurping regulations, the FDA throttles the entire drug industry. Through unscientific, dishonest, emotionally appealing demands for "risk-free" products, they ply their power-generating regulations. And their costly, destructive regulations delay for years or outright prevent the development and marketing of thousands of life-enhancing drugs and life-saving cures.

Without government regulations and controls, the producers long ago would have developed (with voluntarily accepted risks) definitive cures for essentially all diseases, ailments, and malfunctions ranging from deadly cancer, heart disease, and AIDS to the agonies of arthritis, the sadness of senility, and the costly economic and fitness losses caused by the common cold, backpain, and headaches. How many lives are lost, how many values are destroyed, how much suffering is endured to support the bogus livelihoods within just one clique of value destroyers in a single government bureaucracy?

Consider the destruction those bureaucrats wreak in usurping their fake jobs without producing values. ...Such neocheaters represent the most cleverly hidden, criminally destructive elements in our society. Indeed, such neocheaters are highly leveraged purveyors of poverty, suffering, destruction, and death.

But, today, even more subtly destructive neocheaters crawl from the swamps of mysticism. They have found a new weapon that without the defense of Neo-Tech would eventually decimate all value producers and their means of production. Those new-breed neocheaters are attorneys who blend tort liability with the malevolence of altruism and the envy of egalitarianism. That new weapon is aimed straight at penalizing success and destroying the means to produce values. ...The intended victims are the "deep pockets" of the most successful, innocent, and beneficent value producers on this planet.

No matter how much false power neocheaters gain by attacking the producer and usurping values, they never can escape a fact they all want to deny: Honest, productive effort is the act of living. Thus, productive effort is the only source of genuine power, honest prosperity, and abiding happiness. Nor can the neocheaters stop Neo-Tech from collapsing mysticism and eliminating their means of survival. They cannot stop Neo-Tech from ending their 2000-year reign of destruction, pain, suffering, and killing. For, productive effort integrated with Neo-Tech forms a matrix that cannot be broken by mysticism or its symbiotic neocheaters — a matrix of competitive values, prosperity, and happiness.

Once the value producers see the mystics and neocheaters through Neo-Tech, nothing can blind them again. Darkness can never return. Once free of mysticism and neocheating, nothing can deny the producers from gaining their earned power, prosperity, and happiness.

As throughout history, most philosophers live by attacking the power and value of the conscious mind. They do that by promoting dishonest, cleverly integrated non sequiturs designed to subordinate man's power and responsibility to profound-sounding, "higher" authorities that do not and cannot exist. Likewise, most authors of philosophically, politically, or socially oriented books (including economic, management, and business books by non-business or academe-oriented authors), operate from the same specious base of non sequiturs: Their books or works sound good while directly or indirectly attacking value producers and undermining business values. Rather than exerting the effort and discipline required to produce values, they choose to subvert values as their route to unearned respect, power, and money. Such authors are identified as:

1. Those who avoid integrating their work with disciplined honesty and competitive effort.
2. Those who promote mystical notions or altruistic rhetoric to extract respect, power, and prosperity from the value producers.

Before Neo-Tech, no philosopher, academic, or author had integrally identified how business is the prime source of earned values, power, prosperity, and happiness. Also, before Neo-Tech, all mystics and neocheaters had successfully concealed three facts:

1. Business-type thinking represents the most intellectual, disciplined, and integrated use of the conscious mind.

209

2. Business-type action is the fountainhead of earned values, power, wealth, and happiness.
3. Business-type action is the prime mechanism for all competent efforts and competitive values.

But most important, mystics and neocheaters have for 2000 years hidden the crowning reward of business. That reward is happiness, which in turn is the purpose of all human life. Genuine happiness and benevolent power are available in never-ending quantities through business. Nothing even comes close to business as a source of earned values, genuine power, and abiding happiness. But mystics and neocheaters with their guilt-projecting altruism and envious egalitarianism have blocked the producers from recognizing business as the fountainhead of all values. And, thus they succeed in blocking the producers from collecting their earned prosperity and happiness. ...But today, the unhappiness of mysticism is yielding to the happiness of business.

**My dad threw down his pen and rushed out to dinner, ate quickly, and then returned to the flow of his pen and spirit of Zon, and he wrote late into the night:**

For nearly 2000 years, master neocheaters have manipulated the destructive forces of mysticism to drain power and prosperity from all honest men and women. But today, for the first time in history, a newly discovered idea system called Neo-Tech reveals and eliminates those destructive forces while releasing a stream of intellectual, psychological, and material advantages. Neo-Tech integrations deliver emotional and material benefits to everyone. Indeed, anyone can use the Neo-Tech concepts to guiltlessly increase his or her wealth and happiness — now and forever into the future.

Furthermore, the Neo-Tech concepts can free any individual from all who waste one's time, from all who work against one's best interests, from all neocheaters and mystics who use non sequiturs to diminish the lives of others. The Neo-Tech concepts provide the ways and means to limitless prosperity and happiness.

The philosopher's job is to provide human beings with practical tools for dealing with reality in order to live easier, more prosperous, happier lives. But almost all philosophers throughout

210

history have defaulted in their responsibility and failed in their job. Indeed, most philosophers have done all in their power to make life for human beings not easier and happier, but more difficult and unhappy by obscuring reality. As a result, almost everyone rejects the practicality of philosophy. Thus, almost no one recognizes the potential of this mighty tool.

Few people can formulate integrated philosophical systems on their own. Moreover, few people have the knowledge to reject or even identify the neocheaters and mystics who implicitly use philosophy to drain the lives of others. ...The first step in dismissing the mystics and neocheaters is to recognize that only two basic philosophical systems or choices exist:

One system arises from a mystical/altruistic premise that individuals should be sacrificed either to others or to "higher" causes. The father of the criminal mind, Greek philosopher Plato (427 B.C. – 347 B.C.), identified and developed that system. Throughout history, all governments, religions, and neocheaters have implicitly used Plato's philosophy to usurp unearned power and values from innocent value producers.

The other philosophical system arises from a reality/self-interest premise that the individual is the highest value in the universe. The father of the business mind, Greek philosopher Aristotle (384 B.C. – 322 B.C.), identified and developed that system.

Neo-Tech (fully integrated honesty) shows how anyone can switch from being a loser with a mystical/Platonistic approach to being a winner with a Neo-Tech/Aristotelian approach.

The manipulation of mysticism in others is the common bond linking all neocheaters: Now, for the first time, heads of states, religious leaders, elegant con artists, Mafia dons, most attorneys, some Nobel-prize laureates, many leading academe, certain well-known media personalities, certain entertainment people, some bankers, and even certain business people (e.g., white-collar hoax executives) are inextricably linked as soul mates. They all live by attacking the competitive value producer, competitive business, and competitive products. Yet, they themselves live uncompetitively, producing no long-range, net benefits for others or society. In other words, those people live as neocheaters or as just plain cheaters by usurping, attacking, undermining, and

211

destroying values produced by others. ...Neo-Tech ends that secret, parasitical bond by forever dissolving the chains of mysticism and its mind-created "realities".

With Neo-Tech, all effort is directed toward achieving fully integrated honesty needed to act in concert with reality. With mysticism, all effort is directed toward rationalizing non sequiturs or deceptions needed to satisfy some feeling, wish, or whim arising from one's self-created "reality" or some external "authority". ...Neo-Tech is rooted in effort, objective reality, and value production. Mysticism, by contrast, is rooted in laziness, random nothingness, and value destruction.

Neo-Tech is health. Mysticism is sickness. Neo-Tech is the opposite of mysticism. Neo-Tech heralds the end of mysticism and its symbiotic neocheaters.

Neocheating politicians, clergymen, union leaders, lawyers, media commentators, university professors, entertainment personalities are the Typhoid-Mary spreaders of mysticism. In fact, through the ages, the most virulent spreaders of mysticism have been those neocheaters who wangle respect and values from the value producers of this world.

**Neocheating** is defined as: Any intentional use of mysticism designed to create mind "realities" or false illusions in order to extract values from others. Neocheating is the technique for expropriating unearned money or power by manipulating mysticism in others. Neocheating is the means by which all politicians, clergymen, union leaders, many journalists, many academe, and most lawyers usurp power and values from the innocent producers. Neocheaters create many millions of dependent mystics.

**Mystics** choose to evade or fake reality; they undermine their ability to identify and integrate reality, to think clearly, to produce values, to live competitively — to survive. As a result, they increasingly lay responsibilities for their well-beings onto others. Thus, they routinely lay blame or guilt on others for their own problems and failures.

Mystics will (1) avoid the responsibility, effort, and honesty needed to identify and integrate reality and (2) use their feelings or imaginations to recreate "new realities". They attempt to fill their desires the "easy", mystical way. But the mystical way is unreal — the way that never works. The nonmystic, by contrast, will (1) take responsibility for his or her own problems and (2) reject the destructive notion that "realities" spun from the mind can replace objective reality.

Mystics make "realities" out of what they feel, think, wish, or want rather than on what actually is or exists. Thus, they blind themselves to what is happening and become increasingly incompetent. They are irresponsible, immature people. As a result, they cannot achieve the major values of life: genuine prosperity, romantic love, abiding happiness. Mystics avoid the responsibility of a conscious being and, thus, miss the rewards of life.

As pervasively evident throughout TV network news, many involved in media journalism are profoundly dishonest manipulators of mysticism who live by purposely creating problems where none exist. They do that by dishonestly attacking and undermining values to gain unearned power and values. Many are consummate neocheaters who find the media the easiest, most effective format for mass deception, unearned power, and bogus livelihoods.

**Neocheaters** do more harm than mystics. They constantly try to expand their usurpations of values by manipulating mystical illusions and non sequiturs. Moreover, neocheaters design their illusions to present themselves as the benefactors of society. At the same time, they enviously present the real producers (e.g., aggressively competitive entrepreneurs, innovators, business people, industrialists) as the malefactors of society.

But the opposite is true: The neocheaters are the mean, the guilty, the malefactors of society. And the value producers are the compassionate, the innocent, the benefactors of society. Yet, as long as most people allow themselves to accept mystical illusions and inversions of facts, the neocheaters will keep usurping values and escalating their destructions.

Some neocheaters usurp credibility by exploiting popular causes that sound good — causes that in proper context may be noble if handled honestly. Examples include the environment, nutrition, health, animal rights, human rights, peace. But neocheaters exploit such causes to usurp credibility and power in order to attack competent producers, their honest businesses,

213

and their valuable products. ...The two-headed essence of all mystics and neocheaters is dishonesty and laziness.

Other neocheaters (politicians, clergymen, many journalists and academe) survive by attacking values, businesses, producers, and earned profits as enemies. They attack by making those who create genuine values for others appear as guilty and wrong. Simultaneously, they live by promoting mysticism, altruism, external "authority", collectivism as friends. They promote those destructive forces by making them appear innocent and right.

Mysticism is central to the neocheater's ability to thrive by attacking values. For only through mysticism would anyone accept the neocheater's upside-down world of undermining, attacking, and destroying values.

Mysticism yields actions based on what one feels, wishes, wants, or imagines rather than on what actually exists right in front of that person. That is why professional mystics and other neocheaters can easily manipulate people: they manipulate them through their mysticisms. Neocheaters manipulate infinite arrays of mysticisms to usurp values earned by others. As a result, the professional mystics and other neocheaters eventually destroy all values of life, love, and happiness for themselves and everyone involved with them.

**Nonmystics** are innocent and moral. They accept the discipline and responsibility to think and act with integrated consistency. They support themselves by producing *competitive* values for others. With a loyalty to honesty, they act in concert with reality. They are evolved, honest people. They strive to fully integrate their words and actions with reality, regardless of anyone's dogma, dictates, or opinions. As a result, nonmystics benefit everyone and society.

The mystic's life is basically irrational and unhappy with perhaps some scattered islands of rationality and happiness. By contrast, the nonmystic's life is basically rational and happy with perhaps some scattered islands of irrationality and unhappiness.

Turning to one's inner self, mystics find unhappiness, anxiety, and hatred. Whereas nonmystics find happiness, equanimity, and love.

**Consciousness** allows human beings to escape the automatic controls of nature. At the same time, only through consciousness

214

can a person be subjective and mystical. Thus, only through consciousness, can a person choose to act in discord with nature. Unlike all other animals, conscious beings can choose to act better or worse than their nature to benefit or harm themselves and others. Choosing to deny or contradict nature or reality is mysticism, which is an unnatural, irresponsible abuse of the conscious mind. But, conscious beings can also choose to act better than their nature to gain power and advantages over all else in the universe. Because consciousness allows choices and actions beyond preset nature, only human beings can choose to be honest or deceptive, objective or mystical, responsible or irresponsible, competent or incompetent, striving or lazy, productive or destructive, beneficial or harmful, noble or evil. ...With consciousness, anyone can choose either alternative at any time.

All other animals have no choice but to automatically respond to nature. They cannot be deceptive, irresponsible, mystical, or purposely harmful to themselves and others. They have no such choices, thus, they bear no responsibility for their actions. ...Animals cannot be mystical, dishonest, or self-destructive.

With consciousness, only human beings can freely choose to live better or worse than their natures.

**Free choice** determines the future of all human beings: Through mystical choices, people diminish themselves and their potentials to live happy lives. But through Neo-Tech choices, people reject mystical choices. Thus, in turn, they prosper and live happily, far beyond nature's preset course. In fact, only by choosing the integrated effort of Neo-Tech over the automatic laziness of mysticism can people build lasting prosperity and happiness.

**The key choice** between exerting effort or defaulting to laziness determines the course of all important human actions. The three choices constantly confronting every human being are to (1) exert integrated effort, (2) default to camouflaged laziness, or (3) act somewhere in between.

The choice to exert integrated effort or to default to camouflaged laziness is the key choice that determines the character, competence, and future of every human being. That crucial choice must be made by everyone, continually, throughout

life. ...That key choice determines the:
1. direction of an infant's life beginning at the first moment of consciousness.
2. development of a child's implicit nascent philosophy which determines that child's developing psychology.
3. development of an adult's implicit and explicit philosophy which develops that person's psychology to determine the quality of his or her life.
4. philosophies that guide entire nations, eras, and civilizations with the resulting cultures, economies, and degrees of enlightenment or darkness.
5. evolvement or regression of human consciousness, power, prosperity, happiness, and love.
6. prosperous survival or eventual destruction of human life on this planet.

That same key choice determined the direction of all original philosophers: For example, the prime immoral philosophers, Plato and Kant, chose to formulate sweeping, out-of-context abstractions in conjuring up all-encompassing mystical idea systems that were "validated" with brilliantly deceptive inner logic. Thus, their basic choice was a default to laziness. For they chose the neocheater's "shortcut" to unearned power or "greatness" by formulating out-of-context, non-sequitur, "higher-cause" philosophies.

Such specious philosophies are designed to assault the supreme value of the conscious mind. Their destructive, death-oriented "greatness" contrasts sharply to the productive, life-oriented greatness of the prime moral philosophers: Aristotle and Rand. For, those moral philosophers chose to exert hard efforts and fully integrated honesty to build full-context, rationally integrated systems of universal value for all people of all times.

Those choosing to live through automatic laziness survive by usurping or attacking values produced by others. Those usurpers and attackers include essentially all politicians and theologians as well as many dishonest professionals, attorneys, psychologists, academe, elitists, journalists, philosophers. Well-known usurpers and attackers of values include Plato, Hitler, Stalin, FDR, the

Pope, Al Capone, Pol Pot, Fidel Castro, Ralph Nader, Jesse Helms. By contrast, those who choose to live through integrated effort can thrive by producing or building values for others. Those producers include working people, business people, industrialists, scientists as well as honest professionals, artists, musicians, philosophers. Well-known value producers include Aristotle, Ray Kroc, Henry Ford, Edison, Einstein, Pierre S. du Pont, Andrew Carnegie, Galileo, Beethoven, Ayn Rand.

That choice between laziness and effort determines if one becomes an unhappy destroyer of values or a happy producer of values.

**Business** is the competitive development, production, and marketing of values that benefits others. Any and every aspect of business succeeds to the extent that effort, thinking, planning, and action are free of mysticism...or fails to the extent that mysticism is injected into any decision. Business ultimately flourishes in the absence of mysticism or dies in the presence of mysticism. Mysticism is the creating of problems where none exist; business is the solving of problems wherever they do exist. Mysticism represents stagnation and death; business represents growth and life. Mysticism is nonbusiness; business is nonmysticism.

Since the early days of Phoenician commerce, envious mystics and destructive neocheaters have striven to besmirch the value producers, their business enterprises, and their competitive products. Legions of pseudo-intellectuals, say-much/do-little underachievers, envious nonproducers, and mystic-manipulating neocheaters, especially in the media and academe, constantly attack businesses and their creators. With specious pejoratives, the attackers imply that business people lack care, humanity, compassion, social concerns. Such implications are opposite of the facts. Indeed, only through business and its creators do societies advance and individuals prosper.

Hiding behind their altruistic platitudes, neocheaters and mystics are the ones who default on productive effort, do not care, and lack humanity, compassion, social concerns. For all they can do is cleverly attack values. And their attacks are designed to undermine those heroic efforts required to competitively produce jobs and values for others. Indeed, the

217

mystics and neocheaters strive desperately to conceal the intellectually superior nature of business — the universally beneficial, cheerfully benevolent, nonmystical nature of business. For business is the antithesis of mysticism, the epitome of rationality and morality, and the furthest evolvement of human intellect.

Business is the highest evolution of consciousness, responsibility, and morality. No other animal is even remotely able to function on a business level. The essences of business are fully integrated honesty, responsibility, integration, abstraction, objectivity, long-range planning, effort, discipline, thought, control. Business creates essentially every major human value, ranging from the development of language, mathematics, the arts, and all commercial breakthroughs up to the electronic revolution...and now finally, Neo-Tech.

Neo-Tech Publishing Company is the first company to successfully inject a fully integrated system of ideas and values directly into the stream of public thinking and action. That successful, efficient injection is done by subjecting Neo-Tech to organized business disciplines in markets far beyond the small, closed circles of elitists and academics.

Without being subject to the intense, disciplined efforts of business and marketing, Neo-Tech would have languished undeveloped, perhaps for centuries, trapped in those small, closed circles of less-evolved, nonbusiness intellectuals. But by applying hard-nosed business disciplines to marketing Neo-Tech, Neo-Tech Publishing Company demonstrates in real life the extraordinary, practical benefits of Neo-Tech to every human being. Marketing Neo-Tech through a high-effort, business structure provides the fastest, most efficient distribution of Neo-Tech advantages to every value producer in this world.

For that reason, life-enhancing Neo-Tech ideas will increasingly replace life-diminishing mystical ideas as the source of philosophical standards and values for all honest, productive people — for all people who count.

**Business people** create values through intellectual efforts involving the widest-range integration of facts and knowledge. Successful, growing businesses always require honest long-term planning combined with constant integration of time with effort.

## Yesterday's Victims; Tomorrow's Victors

...Few people have any idea or appreciation of the constant, hard-driving effort and difficult integrations required for a businessman to create and maintain honest, value-producing jobs for others.

By contrast, professional mystics and neocheaters avoid all such long-range, wide-scope, integration efforts. Instead, they operate on a dishonest, anti-intellectual level — on spurious, out-of-context terms in attacking producers with slander, libel, force, coercion, and false guilt in order to usurp values from those value producers.

The master neocheaters gain power by constant destruction of values rather than by production of values. To realize that fact, a person needs only to examine the words of any Hitler, Pope, charismatic politician, network anchorman, high-profile humanities professor, or advanced-degreed underachiever. Their essential words are always in a negative mode or an envious attack mode. They rise in power not by the long, hard, rational efforts that build competitive values wanted by others. Instead, they garner power by glib, negative attacks that undermine the producers and their values. ...That fact becomes obvious on comparing the words of honest business people to those of neocheating media people.

Mystics and neocheaters are guilty losers who harm everyone. But business people, especially the essence-moving entrepreneurial type, are innocent winners who benefit everyone. Honest business people do not even know how to think, talk, or operate in the destructive, out-of-context, envious attack modes of mystics and neocheaters. Instead, such business people cheerfully focus on integrating reality — on benefiting others by creating and trading values. Without Neo-Tech, however, those business people are unable to protect themselves from the neocheaters' destructive ideas and actions.

**Master neocheaters** rise above others without earning their way — without exerting the long-term, hard-integration efforts needed to build values for others. By nature, neocheaters are dishonest, unproductive, hostile, immoral, guilty. They have no genuine power. By contrast, business-minded people are honest, productive, benevolent, moral, innocent. Such business-minded people are the only source of genuine power and prosperity in the universe.

219

**Two worlds** exist: One world is that of the mystics, neocheaters, master mystics, and master neocheaters along with all their duped victims and followers. That unhappy, sour world is for the living dead — for those who choose to (1) detach themselves from reality, (2) remain ignorant of reality and what is actually occurring, (3) survive by usurping values from others. That destructive world consists not only of lethargic mystics but of aggressively active, master neocheaters with their minions and followers. Such neocheaters stage furious but meaningless or destructive activities in their need to appear busy and important to themselves and others. ...The world of mystics and neocheaters is destructive, unhappy, meaningless.

The other world belongs to the value producers. That happy, cheerful world is created by individuals who prosper by producing values for others. That purposeful, active world consists of those workers, business people, industrialists, professionals, artists who produce more than they consume. The world of value producers is exciting, prosperous, meaningful.

The integrated efforts of value producers such as businessmen are directed toward supporting or building values for others. In sharp contrast, the efforts of neocheaters are directed toward attacking or usurping values from others. Master neocheaters are manipulative and destructive in their every action ranging from political summits to papal tours. Such neocheaters include not only politicians and clergymen but those say-much, do-little academe who conceal their lack of value by constantly flaunting credentials to impress themselves and others. On establishing specious credibility, those neocheaters extract values from others by promoting spurious ideas that undermine or attack value producers and competitive values.

Those two worlds will never meet. For, they are moving in opposite directions: one toward death, the other toward life. Any conscious individual, however, can choose at any time to reject mysticism and exchange the unhappy world of value destroyers for the happy world of value producers. ...The choice is to exist in the dead world of mysticism or to live in the alive world of Neo-Tech.

**Man's nature and survival:** The nature of all animals evolves around their survival mechanism. But what is the distinguishing nature of man? He has the ability to think consciously in concepts and then integrate those concepts into wider concepts. No other animal can think consciously or think significantly beyond percepts, much less integrate concepts. Indeed, man can easily and logically integrate two or more concepts into new and still wider, more abstract concepts. That logical integration of concepts is called reasoning. Man's reasoning ability is his survival mechanism. But unlike all other animals whose survival mechanisms work automatically, man's reasoning mechanism works volitionally. Man must *choose* to exert the effort required to reason. Man undermines or damages his or her reasoning ability by nonuse or misuse of the mind through mysticism. For mysticism, by nature, subverts or cuts off the integration mechanism of the conscious mind to reduce one's efficacy, competitiveness, quality of life, well-being, self-worth, and especially happiness.

Reasoning is the nature of man — the distinguishing nature that elevates the value of man above all other life...above all else in the universe. Reasoning through logic is man's survival mechanism.

**Morals:** Since morals and morality require conscious choices, man is the only animal who can be moral or immoral. Thus, man is the only animal who can consciously or purposely make moral choices: to think or not to think, to be mystical or nonmystical, to produce or usurp — to benefit or hurt oneself and others.

The meaning of *moral* in Neo-Tech is simple and direct: Whatever is consciously done to help fill human biological needs is good and moral (e.g., the productive actions of honest people). Whatever is consciously done to harm or prevent the filling of human biological needs is bad and immoral (e.g., the destructive actions of mystics and neocheaters).

Honestly using one's reasoning nature is always beneficial and moral; dishonestly using one's reasoning nature is always harmful and immoral. ...Volitionally harmful acts always arise from mysticism — from dishonesty, rationalizations, evasions, defaults.

Yet, acting on fully integrated honesty (Neo-Tech), not reason itself, is the basic moral act. When Genghis Khan, for example, chose to use reasoning for a specific military move, then in an

221

out-of-context sense, he chose to act morally by protecting himself and his troops (thus filling human biological needs). But in the larger sense of fully integrated honesty, Khan's total actions were grossly immoral in choosing to use aggressive force in becoming a mass murderer (thus negating human biological needs). The highly destructive, irrational immorality of Genghis Khan's overall dictatorial military actions far outweighed any narrow, out-of-context "moral" actions. ...Genghis Khan was enormously evil as were Stalin, Hitler, Mao, Castro, Pol Pot.

**Immoral Concepts — Altruism and Sacrifice:** Genghis Khan an altruist? Stalin and Hitler[1] too? Yes, they were altruists as were Lincoln, Mao, Schweitzer, Nader, Pope John Paul, and almost all other professional mystics and neocheaters. And all current religions and governments exist through altruism.

The dictionary definition of altruism is: "Uncalculated consideration of, regard for, or devotion to other's interests sometimes in accordance with ethical principle." Upon first consideration, the definition of altruism seems loving, kind, and good. In which case, how could Genghis Khan and Hitler relate to that definition?

Close examination of altruism reveals that its ethical principle and implications are human sacrifice.[2] Thus, the altruist accepts

---

[1]Hitler an altruist? He was the ultimate altruist in both word and deed: "The Aryan is not greatest in his mental qualities as such, but in the extent of his willingness to put all his abilities in the service of the community. In him the instinct of self-preservation has reached the noblest form, since he willingly subordinates his own ego to the life of the community and, if the hour demands, even sacrifices it." Adolph Hitler, *Mein Kampf*, Houghton Mifflin, Boston

[2]Auguste Comte (1798-1857) was the first philosopher to articulate the ethical principle of altruism as sacrifice. His altruistic ethics held sacrifice as the goal of moral actions, regardless of the means, cost, or beneficiary. He projected selflessness and sacrifice as the ultimate good while positing self-interest as the antithesis of that good. (Reference: Comte's *System of Positive Polity*, 1877).

But Immanuel Kant (1724-1804) consciously and methodically laid the philosophical groundwork for the concept of altruistic self-sacrifice as a moral principle. Kant used brilliantly orchestrated, cleverly

[footnote continued next page]

222

as ethical principle that human beings and their values can be sacrificed to others. And those human sacrifices can be made to anyone or for the sake of anything — the gods, the tribe, the ruler, the fatherland, the system, the party, the "good", the poor, the cause...for the sake of enhancing the power or prosperity of any professional mystic or neocheater.

All current political and religious systems depend on the principle of altruism...the principle of forced or coerced sacrifice of victims to others. Altruism holds sacrifice as a good in itself, regardless of the means (e.g., force, coercion, fraud, guilt, deception, charisma), regardless of the recipients (e.g., dictators, presidents, popes, theologians, welfare clients), and regardless of the victims (e.g., war dead, taxpayers, business people, value producers).

Sacrifice is the opposite of productivity: Productivity creates values. Sacrifice destroys values. Sacrifice is contrary to human biological nature as demonstrated throughout Neo-Tech. Upholding the ideas of sacrifice or altruism involves accepting the nonreality of mysticism. And accepting such mysticism always requires evasive rationalizations. Indeed, mysticism, altruism, and sacrifice are purposeful reasoning defaults that are always harmful to human beings, thus, are always immoral.

---

[footnote continued form previous page]
integrated non sequiturs to attack logic, reason, and the human mind. Kant is among the most destructive of all master neocheaters. His philosophy provides ingenious systems of noncontextual, inner logic that offers beautiful-sounding rationalizations for all violations of individual rights and destructions of values. Kant's works are essential for Fascism, Marxism, and every murderous neocheating regime of the twentieth century: Plato begot Kant, who begot the socialist's philosophical father, Georg Hegel (1770-1831). In turn, Hegel begot Karl Marx and spawned mass-murderers Lenin, Hitler, Mao. And, Plato begot the philosophical father of religio-conservatives — Jean-Jacques Rousseau (1712-1789). In turn, Rousseau spawned equally bloody mass-murderers: Robespierre, Pol Pot, Khomeini. ...All that blood, suffering, and destruction arise entirely through neocheaters manipulating unreal, arbitrary illusions and mind-created "realities" of mysticism in order to support their own personal, bogus livelihoods. ...No other reason or motive exists or has ever existed for purposeful death and destruction.

Altruism and sacrifice are rationalized through mysticism. And mysticism is a reasoning default that accepts fake realities or nonrealities such as sacrifice, faith, dogma. Thus, all advocates of altruism are mystics or neocheaters by nature because they accept or manipulate the mystical concepts of sacrifice.

But why do people default on reason? Why do they evade reality to become advocates of altruism who promote sacrifice? Professional advocates of altruism are always, in a direct or indirect way, recipients of the sacrifices they promote. The booty is often unearned power. But the booty may also be or include unearned material goods, glory, adulation, love, respect, pseudo self-esteem, neurotic or psychopathic satisfactions. In any case, professional advocates of altruism depend on the sacrifice of others to fill their material needs, their self-esteem needs, their images of importance, their neurotic wants. In one way or another, all professional altruists are neocheaters who live off the forced or coerced sacrifices of productive people. For that reason, no professional mystic or altruist can be happy or experience psychuous pleasures.

In addition, altruism and sacrifice are the vortex of all concepts, ideas, and philosophies that drain productive people of their earned values and happiness. In the long run, altruism and sacrifice fill the needs of no one. Instead, altruism and sacrifice always drain everyone.

Over the past 2000 years, altruism and sacrifice have destroyed untold values and billions of human lives. All current governments and major religions exist on the principles of altruism and sacrifice. But Neo-Tech lets us: 1. negate all neocheaters; 2. avoid being victimized by mysticism or sacrificed to altruism; 3. forever collapse the 2000-year-old hoax of mysticism and eliminate its symbiotic neocheaters; 4. live prosperously, guiltlessly, and happily to the benefit of everyone.

**Happiness** results from dealing competently with reality. Happiness is a state of intellectually knowing and emotionally feeling the following:

**Short-Term Happiness**
**(Positive or Negative Sources)**
The situation is good.
The situation is right.
The situation is of value.

**Long-Term Happiness**
**(Positive Sources Only)** ·
Life is good.
People are good.
Oneself is good.
Oneself is right.
Oneself is of value.
Oneself is capable of understanding reality.
Oneself is growing in a positive direction.
Oneself is producing values needed to live independently.
Oneself is competent in producing competitive
values for others and society.
Oneself is competent to reject mysticism in self and others.
Oneself is worthy of living.

Short-term happiness from positive sources can add to a person's long-range happiness. But short-term pleasures from negative, destructive, or irrational sources (e.g., drunkenness, politics, drugs, religion, promiscuous sex, prosperity through dishonesty or fraud) can deliver only temporary feelings of power, well-being, and euphoria. For the inescapable consequence of reality will always assert itself, reversing those "good" feelings to yield ever greater unhappiness and anxiety.

Long-term well-being and happiness come *only* from (1) a continuing development and evolvement of one's own mind and character, (2) one's increasingly accurate knowledge and control of reality and self, and (3) increasingly producing competitive values for others and society.

Achieving happiness is the ultimate moral purpose of human life.

Mysticism harms every value it touches — especially love. After attacking values for 2000 years, professional mystics and neocheaters aim their most subtly destructive attacks on value

225

production, romantic love, and happiness: First they undermine the concepts of values, love, and happiness with clever inversions of facts that sound good or valid. Then, for example, they undermine the concept of love by promoting the false idea that totally rational behavior between couples would yield cold, passionless relationships. But the exact opposite is the fact: Consistently honest, rational behavior offers the greatest capacity for love and passion. By contrast, emotionally reacting, irrational behaviors destroy love and passion.

Successful romantic love requires acting on reality rather than reacting on feelings. Only through fully integrated honesty (Neo-Tech) can one guiltlessly experience the full range of positive emotions and passion. By contrast, mystics act on feelings rather than on reality. Such acting on feelings leads to incompetence with the subsequent loss of prosperity and romantic love. ...Mystics experience life with increasing anxiety, unhappiness, deadness.

Professional mystics and neocheaters avoid the honest thought and hard competitive effort needed to produce values desired by others. Instead, they live by faking reality to extract power and values from others through deception, coercion, force. ...Unchecked mysticism destroys all values, especially love and happiness, through arrays of irrational illusions and dishonest actions.

**Integrated thinking** is the conscious effort of putting information into accurate context by logically and honestly connecting *all* relevant knowledge. All valid and powerful knowledge is contextual. Thus, genuine power is gained through integrated thinking used to obtain the widest possible range of contextual knowledge. Integrated thinking delivers unbeatable advantages.

Those who live by fully integrated honesty (Neo-Tech) are by nature sexy, happy, prosperous winners. For they ultimately hold all honest power. Moreover, with Neo-Tech, they hold the supreme aphrodisiac. By contrast, mystics and neocheaters contradict their nature through their laziness, dishonesty, and parasitism. They are unsexy, unhappy, envious losers. Thus, they become increasingly impotent, tired, powerless.

Through fully integrated honesty (Neo-Tech) one increasingly earns competence, self-esteem, happiness. Through Neo-Tech, one soars to spiralling heights of money/power/romantic love.

**After fifteen hours of hard thinking and writing, my exhausted father dropped his pen and fell asleep right on his desk. That would become a common scene over the years to come — my father asleep on his desk from exhaustion after marathon runs of Neothinking and writing.**

**Four hours had passed when he awoke again. His desk lamp was still on. He picked up his pen and, oblivious to time in the middle of the night, he started writing again, with powerful passion. Unrelated thoughts would come to him, then in a hurried rush he would write something about that thought. He seemed to be rushing as if he wanted to get all his thoughts down on paper while his ability to make vast integrations lasted. Little did my father realize that, through Neo-Tech (i.e., fully integrated honesty), the power to make vast integrations — to Neothink — grows instead of shrinks. Neothink builds upon itself like a growing puzzle. Yet, feeling *Zonpower* for the first time in his life, he wrote like a scientist making a major discovery with only a week left to live.**

**He wrote with abandon about everything that came to mind. His mind was never so open before, his thoughts never so clear. The first subjects that came through his pen seemed to be about personal self-improvements, specifically about sense of life, emotions, relationships, and thinking. It did not take my father long to Neothink those four subjects of self-improvement, as follows:**

**Sense of Life:** A sense of life is an integral part of everyone's subconscious philosophy and psychology. Every person has a fundamental view or sense of life. While usually existing on a subconscious level, a person's sense of life largely determines his or her major actions. Sense of life falls into two opposite categories:

1. An objectively rational, self-interest, benevolent, individualistic sense of life that is characterized by:
   a. the knowledge that conscious achievement is the highest value.

    b. the knowledge that the conscious mind is competent to know reality.
2. A mystically irrational, altruistic, malevolent, anti-individual sense of life characterized by:
    a. the belief that non-man-made values (e.g., nature, the universe, the cosmos) and mystical "values" (e.g., God, the State, society) are superior to man-made values.
    b. the belief that the conscious mind is incapable of knowing reality.

The altruistic, malevolent sense of life finds virtue in sacrificing real, individual values to unreal, mystical "higher" causes such as God, the fatherland, nature, society. That altruistic, malevolent sense of life keeps one from acting in his or her long-range best interest to achieve power, prosperity, and happiness in order to produce competitive values for others. Those competitive values, by nature, require a rational self-interest, pro-individual sense of life combined with effort and honesty.

Specifically, Neo-Tech operates on the premises that the conscious individual is by nature (1) good, (2) the highest value in the universe, and (3) competent to understand and deal with reality. By adopting those premises, one can enjoy guiltless freedom. ...By adopting Neo-Tech premises, a person can achieve great prosperity and psychuous pleasures.

**Emotions:** Inseparable links exist between productive work, earned values, prosperity, psychuous pleasures, and happiness. Too many productive people live without experiencing their earned happiness or psychuous pleasures. That deprivation of happiness and psychuous pleasures is an unnecessary tragedy due to altruistic, mystical guilt inculcated into the value producer by the professional value destroyers.

*Pride* is the reflection of self-worth, which requires the rejection of mysticism. And that rejection of mysticism through the reflection of self-worth is what all mystics, existentialists, and neocheaters fear and attack. For, if all value producers recognized their genuine self-worth and felt their earned pride, they would reject mysticism to end the hoax of all neocheaters.

Most mystics denounce pride as negative, bad, or sinful. But,

228

individual pride is the result of moral virtue, which requires the rejection of the dishonesty inherent in mysticism.

*Happiness* is a deeply personal, inner matter. Thus, no one can judge another person's happiness by outward appearances alone. A person may be miserable (such as a nonproductive mystic), but project a happy, cheerful appearance. Another person may appear unsmiling, even stern or cross (such as an intensely busy business executive), but if he or she is a productive person with self-esteem and pride, that person will be profoundly happy.

*Joy* is a self-induced, here-and-now emotion that arises from pleasure, well-being, and happiness. *Enjoyment* is also induced by consciously reflecting on the emotional rewards of pleasure, well-being, and happiness. To fully experience enjoyment, one must reject unearned guilt foisted on him or her by mystics and neocheaters. When a Neo-Tech oriented person earns happiness, he or she can then make a conscious choice to guiltlessly *enjoy* that happiness.

To compensate for a deadening of feelings (thus a deadening of life), by contrast, a person losing the battle to mysticism must take increasingly stronger measures to feel something until the only feeling left to feel is *pain*. But that person must feel something, so he or she strives to feel pain. And the easiest, quickest route to feel pain is through destructive actions rationalized through mysticism.

Also, as a person diminishes his or her awareness and integration capacities, the initiation of longer range, positive actions becomes increasingly difficult. At the same time, that person increasingly succumbs to mysticism in selecting more and more destructive actions in order to feel something. Destructive actions taken to feel something include manipulating others, initiating force (political or criminal) to control or plunder others, using drugs or alcohol, promiscuity, injurious masochism or sadism, vandalism, thrill killings, mass murder, waging war, genocide.

Positive emotions deliver pleasure and happiness. Negative emotions provide warnings that something is wrong. Thus, negative emotions and negative experiences should *not* be repressed. Emotions never should be repressed, but at times emotions can and should be suppressed:

*Suppression* involves being fully conscious of the emotion, but because of the circumstances, the emotion is temporarily set aside for experiencing at a more appropriate time. Suppression is a useful, healthy method for avoiding harmful mystical reactions based on emotions.

*Repression* involves trying to deny an emotion by permanently forcing it out of the conscious mind. That act is a mystical distortion of reality, for emotions are a real, undeniable part of a person. By repressing an emotion out of the conscious mind, the emotion is pushed into the subconscious to remain buried. And accumulating buried, negative emotions can harm both one's psychological and intellectual well-being. For those festering, buried emotions can interfere with a person's accurate perception of reality needed to make correct integrations, judgments, and decisions. ...One never has to act on negative emotions, but one should always guiltlessly self-acknowledge negative emotions.

Avoiding emotional repression involves consciously and guiltlessly feeling one's own emotions in order to know and defuse them. That honest, open dealing with emotions is necessary for (1) resisting harmful mystical actions, (2) building mental health, and most important, (3) experiencing psychuous pleasures, romantic love, and abiding happiness.

Also, openly knowing and experiencing one's own emotions are necessary to distinguish those emotions from the independent world of objective reality. That understanding of emotions, in turn, is necessary to avoid unhealthy mystical actions. For basing judgments and conclusions on emotional reactions rather than on reality causes harmful mystical actions. Such mystical actions, in turn, diminish the prosperity, well-being, and happiness of human beings. If important judgments or actions are mystically based on emotions, then grave errors with harmful consequences will result.

A person can react to emotions in two ways: (1) The mystical, erroneous, harmful reaction that ranges from repressing emotions to overtly injecting emotions into the decision-making process. And (2), the nonmystical, beneficial reaction that recognizes and freely feels emotions, but then separates them from reality in order to make reasoned, logical judgments undistorted by emotions, whims, or feelings.

Because no one is infallible or omniscient, errors are always possible. But errors from honest, *objectively* based thinking are less frequent, less severe, and easier to correct than are errors from mystical, *emotionally* based thinking.

The emotion *fear* is a valuable protection mechanism. By contrast, irrational fear is destructive whenever it stops a person from taking needed actions. Fortunately, the paralyzing effects of irrational fear can be overcome with direct, conscious effort. For example, if a person takes a rational action that he or she fears (if no actual danger exists), that fear will dissipate. Irrational fears can cause inaction that prevents deserving, productive people from developing prosperity and happiness. A fearlessness to live is perhaps the most financially and emotionally rewarding character trait that an honest, productive person can develop.

Consistently acting on rational premises and being loyal to honesty builds confidence in a person's own rectitude and worth. Rationality and honesty, in turn, help remove the fear that prevents people from venturing into new growth areas, including romantic love. Rationality, fairness, and honesty act as powerful protectors when venturing into unexplored areas, ranging from business to love relationships.

However, fearlessness does not obsolete privacy and protectiveness. For instance, openly revealing one's deep personal self to everyone diminishes self-esteem. That, in turn, militates against one's best interests and happiness. Nevertheless, many authors, gurus, and "therapists" advocate revealing one's personal and private self to all comers. Those "total-openness, let it all hang out" advocates are promoting an egalitarian recipe. That recipe calls for breaking everyone's ego by sharing all personal values and emotions with all comers. Such ego-breaking recipes are often well-disguised, downhill roads to impotence and unhappiness.

Those advocating ego-breaking, emotional egalitarianism usually do so under false labels of openness and honesty. But the opposite is true. Failure to discriminate with whom one shares his or her private personal feelings destroys the potential for experiencing a close, genuinely open, romantic-love relationship with another human being. Instead, an egalitarian

231

"total openness" to everyone is a cheap giveaway of an individual's most precious possession — one's own personal, private self. Nothing squelches romantic love more completely than a love-all, share-all egalitarian approach.

A person can and should be sincere and honest to everyone without sharing his or her private self or emotions with everyone. In fact, when a person does share his or her private self with everyone else, that person's sincerity and motives become questionable.

Surrendering one's independent judgment to mystics, social "authorities", or gurus and offering one's private self to all comers results in:

1. Diminished self-confidence and self-esteem.
2. Unproductive, unrewarding consumption of time: Such wasting of irreplaceable segments of one's life span continually diminishes the time needed to build a competent, productive life necessary for growing prosperity, romantic love, and abiding happiness.
3. Diminished personal desirability: Indiscriminate "openness and honesty" is often a boring imposition on those being gratuitously subjected to such personal openness.
4. And most important: After selflessly giving one's self to all comers, little if anything that is private, exciting, or precious is left to share exclusively with one's closest friend or romantic-love partner...little if anything is left to build that unique, priceless, private universe crucial to a romantic-love relationship.

Moreover, most of the "total-openness" egalitarians are professional mystics or neocheaters who depend on extracting their material and spiritual livelihoods from others. To do that, they first must dupe productive people with altruistic guilt. Then those neocheaters can psychologically pull the producers down to the level of mystics and parasitical neocheaters through selfless egalitarianism. ...The lower the level that value producers can be reduced, the more easily can their values be usurped by neocheaters.

**Relationships:** Every relationship can be evaluated in either "good for me" or "bad for me" terms. Love partners, for example, can evaluate their relationship by how much it increases or decreases their well-being and happiness.

A sacrifice-free, romantic-love relationship allows both partners to fill their physical, emotional, and intellectual needs without any losses or compromises. Such a relationship provides major personal benefits and increased pleasures from life. And, over the long term, a person can honestly love only those who integrate into a relationship from which benefits and pleasures evolve and grow.

Any action that enhances psychuous sex, prosperity, and long-range happiness is good and healthy. Likewise, any action that diminishes psychuous sex, prosperity, and long-range happiness is bad and unhealthy. That "good for me" or "bad for me" standard can be used to classify any action as good or bad, beneficial or harmful, healthy or unhealthy, moral or immoral.

Of course, mysticism is always "bad for me". One should avoid partners whose lives are dominated by mysticism, especially disguised mysticism. Symptoms of mystics include people who project their problems and disorders onto others, often characterized by their paranoid use of non sequiturs to blame others for their own problems. Also, mystics inwardly hurt themselves by undermining values that enter their lives. Mystics create problems where none exist and are incompatible with romantic love. They will eventually destroy any value-based relationship. Yet, Neo-Tech can cure any type of mysticism (the stupidness disease) to yield competent lives filled with growing values, happiness, and romantic-love.

Value exchanges occur in valid relationships. In fact, the basic requirement for any valuable human relationship is the exchange of tangible values. On the other hand, naturally beautiful people can more easily offer nominal values and can easily develop "lady-killer" or "man-killer" syndromes in their relationships. Being a seductive "killer" can temporarily boost a weak ego by feeling a power to hurt others. But that syndrome leads the perpetrator into life-wasting, destructive relationships. Indeed, a person who mistreats or manipulates his or her love partner usually suffers much more in the long run than the abused partner. For that abused partner will have new chances for love and happiness. But the chronic manipulator loses his or her capacity for love and is left with a future of increasing unhappiness, sexual incompetence, romantic failures, and ultimate loneliness.

**Thinking:** Mysticism undermines the capacity for integrated thinking. Thus, mysticism reduces competitiveness, self-esteem, and psychuous pleasures. Thus, all mysticism leads to incompetence and unhappiness.

The more an individual surrenders to mysticism, the more that person becomes incompetent and tries to escape reality. For such a person, life increasingly becomes a source of conflict and pain. To the extent that one accepts mysticism is the extent that a person withdraws from life and loses contact with the pleasures and happiness that life inherently holds.

The extent to which a person follows mysticism or external "authority" is the extent to which he becomes incompetent and moves toward death. But the extent to which a person integrates reality with his own rational consciousness and fully integrated honesty (Neo-Tech) is the extent to which he will experience ever-growing competence, prosperity, and happiness.

As a person develops one's character, an unevenness develops in being honest versus being mystical. For example, a person may find that the honest integration of facts is easier in certain areas of life. In other areas, that person surrenders to the "easy-way-out" mystical trap. Such unevenness in honesty is caused by a person's past and present choices and actions. That volitional behavior, in turn, determines the rate of *personal evolvement* and the quality of *character development*.

One's nature can be changed only from within that person, not from without. Of course, a person can develop his or her own character and correct errors as new knowledge is acquired. Such changes are the process of personal growth. And such growth comes through volitional choices to honestly integrate new knowledge.

Everyone alone must personally battle to overcome internal mysticism in order to live prosperously and happily. Self-responsibility cannot be transferred to anyone.

Most psychological problems arise from internal mysticism.

And each individual can overcome such problems by continual, conscious choice to be honest rather than mystical. Each person must decide to self-determine the future or to surrender that responsibility to external "authorities". That surrender of life occurs on asking others to solve one's own problems and deliver happiness.

Fighting and rejecting mysticism within one's own self is the greatest, most important of all battles.

Having an external "authority" delivers: 1. quick, easy-way, no-struggle "answers" that avoid self-responsibility, and 2. fuel for more personal mysticisms. That avoiding of self-responsibility always fuels personal mysticism while diminishing the individual's competence and motivation to solve one's own personal problems. Only individuals themselves can have sufficient motivation and self-knowledge to successfully overcome internal mysticism and solve life's problems. Only individuals themselves can put sufficient energy and knowledge into the efforts needed to become competent, prosperous, and happy. No mystical or outside source can provide those values.

As with all forms of mysticism, acceptance of myths varying from astrology to organized religion cripples a person's thinking and integration processes. Indeed, crippled thinking and integration processes undermine a person's personal power, productive competence, financial well-being, psychuous pleasures, and long-range happiness. Indeed, independent, integrated, logical thinking is not a function of intelligence, but is a function of self-responsibility, self-effort, and self-honesty.

Many popular myths depend on proclaimed "scientific" evidence to create illusions of credibility. Astrology devotees promote the "scientific" notion that the infinitesimally faint celestial forces that impinge on human beings affect and influence their minds, actions, behavior, and destiny. As "proof", for example, they state how the gravitational forces of the moon cause the oceanic tides. But facts and logic show that man alone controls his own destiny. And his mind can easily override all the forces of nature combined. Indeed, in a free society, the conscious mind is a much stronger controller of an individual's future than all the overt, direct forces of nature, government, and religion combined.

235

Most forms of "scientific" mysticism reflect wishful desires to discover outside forces or "authorities" to take over the thinking tasks of the human mind. The mystic's wish is to be automatically and effortlessly guided to knowledge and through life by external forces. But no effortless guide exists. No outside force can take over and do what the mind and the individual must do for him or her self.

Poetry, song lyrics, especially pop, rock, and rap lyrics, and political demagoguery and speeches can be cast in what appears to be beautiful gems or nuggets of packaged "truth" and knowledge from "authorities". Those packaged "truths" are designed for consumption in quick, convenient gulps. That gulping of "truths" bypasses the analytical mental effort required to integrate information and assess its validity through one's own mind.

Determining the validity of any information requires analytical integration of facts and information within a full, accurate context. But poetry and song lyrics effortlessly bypass the demanding thinking and integration processes needed to accurately identify objective reality. In that way, poetry and lyrics subvert the effectiveness of the mind. Most poetry and lyrics, no matter how beautiful, right, and "true" they sound (that being their seductive nature) cannot be substituted for honesty or facts any more than good-sounding slogans or parables can be substituted for honesty or facts. Furthermore, cleverly used poetry and lyrics can be powerfully effective tools for rationalizing laziness, dishonesty, injustice, mysticism, and neocheating.

Most poetry and song lyrics, if taken seriously (especially emotional or "beautiful" poetry that lacks an objective base), not only undermines a person's ability to make independent judgments, but diminishes one's capacity to think objectively about crucial matters. That, in turn, decreases one's ability to achieve prosperity, psychuous pleasures, and long-range happiness. In other words, certain poetry or song lyrics taken as packaged "truth" will bypass the independent, in-context thinking processes required to make the integrations and decisions necessary to develop long-range prosperity, pleasures, and happiness.

Aristotelian-based poetry that is intellectually valid and certain song lyrics that are non-mystical can be objectively valuable when viewed as symbols of one's own values and not as packages of "truth" to be swallowed whole, without integration. Still, the effect of poetry on most people is harmful because they allow the abstract symbols of poetry to enter their minds as unintegrated, unchallenged "truths" or as pre-packaged value systems ready for direct use. The problem is amplified because many poets, song lyricists, and political cartoonists proceed with dishonest, destructive intentions to mislead the reader. They want their work swallowed blindly as "truth" by their audiences, regardless of the validity or context of their work. Such work is neither art nor honest; it is neocheating.

Poetical sing-song or hypnotically rhythmic meter are often found in the rhetoric of dictators, evangelists, politicians, theologians, social "intellectuals", media men, chanting shiites, and screaming terrorists. Consider how millions of normally rational Germans thrilled and responded to the poetical cadence and charisma of the consummate altruist neocheater, Adolph Hitler.

By using specious nuggets of poetical "truth" and spell-binding slogans, the malefactors, demagogues, and neocheaters such as Hitler, FDR, Nader, Khomeini, Lincoln, Mao, Billy Graham, Pope Paul, Jimmy Swaggart, Castro, Kennedy, Martin Luther King Jr., Jim Jones, the Clintons could smoothly, quickly subvert the objective concepts of justice, good, and love. And they often did that by manipulating words to sound good, just, or loving. Why? To promote their own rationalized schemes of "higher" causes. Such people use those poetic techniques to keep their rationalizations sounding valid, taking control of people's *bicameral minds*. Indeed, their unthinking followers grab the beautiful nuggets of "truth" and eagerly swallow them without thought or challenge.

What is the bicameral mind? The bicameral mind is a human mind functioning in a particular, unconscious mode or manner...in the manner intended by nature. While the bicameral mind exists in all people, it can be controlled or dominated by a special mode of consciousness developed not through mother nature but volitionally by each individual being. That mind control or domination can be exercised by an individual over himself and others. Or an individual can allow that mode of consciousness

237

in others to control or dominate his or her bicameral mind.

The bicameral mind (two-chamber mind) is one that functions as an unconscious, two-step process. Automatic reactions and thoughts originate in the right hemisphere of the brain and are transmitted to the left hemisphere as instructions to be acted upon. The bicameral functioning is nature's automatic, learned mode of response without regard to conscious thinking. By contrast, man-made consciousness functions through a deliberate, volitional thought process that is independent of nature's bicameral thought process.

Approximately 3000 years ago, man's brain functioned entirely in nature's automatic bicameral mode. But the automatic bicameral mind became inadequate to handle the mounting problems as societies became more complex. To survive, man was forced to invent a new way of thinking — a new mode called consciousness that could solve infinitely more complex problems. That consciousness mode involved his newly discovered powers of introspection. His thinking process was further enhanced by new thoughts and insights created by comparisons done through metaphors and analogs.

Consciousness allows a person to make his or her own decisions rather than relying on nature's bicameral process that automatically follows learned customs, traditional rules, and external "authorities".

Bicameral mentalities avoid human self-responsibility by seeking and obeying external decision makers. In poker, for example, bicameral tendencies leave players open to being controlled by any conscious individual acting as an external decision maker and authority. In addition, the single, biggest money-losing, mystical concept — the belief in luck — is rooted in the bicameral mentality. In fact, most gamblers rely on the phantom "authority" of luck to escape the only valid authority: their own rational consciousness.

Understanding bicameral tendencies in others can provide unbeatable advantages by knowing the external forces that control most people. That understanding enables one not only to predict the actions of others but to control their actions. A poker player, for example, can create unbeatable advantages by projecting any number of phantom "authorities" to which his opponents will obey, act, or react.

The principle of controlling the bicameral minds of others applies not only to poker but to all competitive situations involving two or more people. Poker, however, provides crisp, clear examples of using the bicameral mind to control people. More important, poker provides countless metaphors to which everyone can relate. Also, most poker players are gamblers. And gambling is a bicameral activity in which people abandon their own rational consciousness to phantom "authorities" such as feelings, luck, priests, and politicians.

Poker games exist because of the bicameral urge in most players to gamble. That urge resides in the desire to escape the responsibility for consistently making rational decisions needed to prosper by producing values for others. Gamblers try to escape (at least temporarily) that self-responsibility through an activity such as poker. And through their bicameral urges, gamblers can be controlled by others.

Even the best professional player can succumb to bicameral urges: By playing poker for a living, for example, he avoids involvement in a productive career that demands much more independent, rational thinking than poker. But, the good player can also use poker as a discipline to strengthen both his conscious integrating processes and his abilities to control others.

Through understanding those bicameral urges in others, a good player can generate unbeatable advantages. He creates those advantages by conjuring up external "authorities" for guiding his opponents into actions that benefit him. For example, an opponent is told to "open up" (bet more loosely) because good player X always bets aggressively in the same situation — and good player X always ends up winning heavily. In that way, player X is set up as an external "authority" for misleading the opponent into making wrong moves based on facts bicamerally accepted out of context. Even greater advantages are gained by realizing that an opponent is bicamerally using rules, information, and odds gleaned from "authorities" such as authors of noncognitive poker books.

Bicameral tendencies can also be exploited through subtle maneuvers. For example, mumbling very quietly (almost subaudibly) words that will influence or trigger reactions in opponents who subconsciously hear those "voices". To those opponents, the subconscious voice automatically acts as an external "authority" to be followed. As another example, a player who is hesitant about attending a game after several losing sessions is fed whatever out-of-context facts or spurious "truth" he wants to hear such as, "The worst thing a player can do is quit just as his losing streak is about to end. That's when the odds are the greatest for shifting from a bad-luck streak to a good-luck streak. Managing luck streaks is the whole idea of winning. All winners know that." With such specious "truths" and non sequiturs, the good player establishes himself as an external "authority" in controlling his opponents.

But most important, as demonstrated in the original Neo-Tech Prediscovery, poker generates accurate metaphors needed to identify the bicameral tendencies existing in most people. Indeed, those tendencies are readily exploitable by neocheaters beyond the card tables with the same kind of phantom or external "authorities" set up either overtly or subliminally. Such external "authorities" can be established, for example, in religion, politics, psychology, medicine, business, and personal relationships. ...Understanding the bicameral mind is invaluable for avoiding being controlled by others.

Whereas the bicameral mind is the mind of the past, *Neothink* is the mind of the future. The human mind has a limited storage and processing capacity. But Neothink, a discovery made through Neo-Tech, infinitely expands the capacity of consciousness to understand anything in existence. The exchanging of the mystic/conscious mind for the Neo-Tech/Neothink mind will affect mankind even more profoundly than the discovery 3000 years ago of exchanging the bicameral mind for the conscious mind. And, as 3000 years ago, this exchange will occur swiftly, automatically sometime after 2001, regardless of what anyone does, says, or thinks. The pressure to convert to the Neo-Tech/Neothink integrating mind is competition. Those who do not convert cannot survive. Just as the bicameral mind could not compete and survive 3000 years ago against the conscious mind. Against Neothink, all mystics and neocheaters are finished. They will be ignominiously scorned out of existence.

Neothink develops new concepts over unlimited ranges of integration. That unlimited capacity is accomplished by dividing separate thoughts into two or more separate groups and then building each of those groups toward the maximum capacity of consciousness. Those groups of conscious thoughts can then be swiftly integrated into new units of knowledge and concepts beyond the capacity of the human mind thinking as a single conscious unit.

**Within those four personal subjects — sense of life, emotions, relationships, thinking — Neo-Tech quickly enhances a person's success and happiness. Now, my father's writings shifted to the overwhelming culprit that holds down all good people from success and happiness — I mean, awesome success and happiness such as experiencing the Six Ultimate Gifts described in your *God-Man* manuscript. That overwhelming culprit is FORCE. Again, his Neo-Tech writings on force came to him quickly, as follows:**

**FDA/EPA:** The government-forced end to DDT alone is responsible for perhaps a million or more malaria deaths. Moreover, forced banning of pesticides, herbicides, and chemical preservatives is decreasing food productivity while increasing production costs, poverty, suffering, and starvation. [Re: J. Maddox, "The Doomsday Syndrome", McGraw-Hill] That irrational banning of valuable agriculture chemicals and food preservatives also causes greater food scarcity in famine areas to greatly increase worldwide malnutrition and starvation. The massive suffering and death in the name of protecting the environment or "doing-good" by government bureaucracies is documented in Grayson and Shepard's book, The Disaster Lobby, Follett Publishing Company. That book also demonstrates how advancing industrial and business technology free of government interference steadily (1) protects human life, (2) improves the environment — water, air, land — for human habitation, and (3) solves genuine ecological problems.

**DEA:** Any use of force to accomplish a "good" always, by nature, does much more long-range harm to people and society than any intended good. Moreover, those who use or advocate such force seldom have honest or innocent intentions, no matter what their external appearances. As in using force to prohibit drugs, the enforcers are not only morally wrong, but their policies of force drive drug prices far above their free-market values. Those artificially high prices, in turn, allow organized crime to flourish through the extremely high-profit margins guaranteed by the government enforcers.

Indeed, those government-created, sky-high prices cause the addict to push drugs onto others, especially onto vulnerable children and adolescents. The addicts must push drugs in order to obtain the cash needed to pay for the grossly inflated drugs. Thus, government oppression of individual rights through force creates hundreds of thousands of young, new addicts each year *because* of anti-drug laws. In addition, the desperate, dying addict will rob, mug, commit mayhem, murder — he will do anything to raise the money required to buy the government-inflated drugs.

And finally, as during government enforced prohibition three generations ago, the anti-drug laws are by far the greatest boon and source of wealth to organized crime. The government through its power-usurping oppression creates huge, lucrative markets from which organized crime prospers and grows.

Despite the damaging effects of alcohol and drugs, no rational or moral reason exists for government to restrict, control, or forbid by force the sale or use of alcohol or drugs in any way whatsoever. No one or no government has the right to initiate or threaten force against any individual who is not violating the individual or property rights of others. Individuals have the basic right to do anything with their lives they choose, including damaging themselves by using alcohol and drugs, just as they have the right to damage themselves with sugar, tobacco, religion, promiscuous sex, mysticism, and suicide...so long as they do not initiate threats, force, or fraud against any other individual.

**Feminism**: The worst aspect of the feminist movement and other so-called "rights" movements is their advocating legislated government force or coercion to violate individual and property rights of others. All professional mystics and neocheating leaders require force or deception to survive by parasitically filling their needs. And those needs are usually disguised as "noble" ends.

242

But no matter how noble sounding the end, it can *never* justify the means of force against any individual. Institutionalized initiation of force against individuals for any reason is categorically wrong, immoral, and diminishes the well-being and happiness of everyone.

Government policies and laws backed by force have always been the major instrument for denying women their individual rights. So what about those legions of feminists advocating that same legislated government force to achieve women "rights" by violating rights of others? They diminish everyone's rights and well-being.

Despite feminist claims, nothing today prevents women from realizing their potentials. The battle is not for women's rights, minority rights, black rights — the battle is and always has been for *individual* rights. When individual rights are fully protected, then everyone's rights are protected.

Most feminists diminish the potential for all women by trying to usurp unearned economic or money gains through government force or coercion in violating the rights of others. Such tactics are morally wrong and destructive to all individuals. And in the long run, those tactics succeed only in giving government more power to oppress everyone — especially women.

While stridently expressing goals of liberation and freedom, most feminist policies deny freedom of choice, voluntary division of labor, and open competition. Those policies reveal a fear of freedom, competition, integrated thinking, and self-responsibility. Such dishonest, double-speak contradictions of demanding freedom while actually attacking freedom via government force are also common in "liberation" or "rights" movements of various black, consumer, and environmental groups. Such groups demand benefits and "freedoms" via government force while reducing their own and everyone else's freedom.

Government laws backed by force have always been the mechanism that eventually oppressed women. The genuine liberation of women occurred during those rare, historic periods during which the reason and logic of individual freedom gained influence over the dishonesty and mysticism of government and religious oppression. Those liberating periods were the Golden Age of Greece, the Renaissance, and the greatest, most

243

profoundly moral period of all: the free-enterprise phase of the Industrial Revolution. In free-enterprise capitalism, the influences of reason, honesty, effort, productivity, and voluntary individual choice count for everything, while the influences of mysticism, dishonesty, racism, social status, and the use of force are dismissed as nothing. ...The causal relationship of reason and capitalism to freedom and prosperity for women is clear.

In attempting to establish credibility, feminists promote and publicize certain "famous" women of history as heroines. Some of those women were honest value producers who contributed to human well-being. But most of those feminist "heroines" were demagogues and neocheaters who agitated for more government force to make individuals conform to their wishes or demands. In their promotion of "great women", most feminists hypocritically ignore one of the greatest benefactors to human life and champions of individual rights. That person was a woman. She was one of the most profound thinkers and writers, male or female, of all time. She was a world-famous novelist and the most important philosopher since Aristotle. Her name: Ayn Rand.

Why do most feminists ignore Ayn Rand? Because she intellectually refuted their concepts of mysticism, initiatory force, and government coercion to achieve ends. More important, she clearly identified the immorality of such approaches, thus repudiating the core of most feminist movements and methods. Also, Ayn Rand identified that the only proper moral issue is individual rights...not women's rights, black rights, or any other such "rights" or causes. For such causes are largely designed to support neocheaters.

The feminists' rejection of Ayn Rand not only underscores their intellectual dishonesty, but demonstrates that their movement is not interested in individual rights. Instead, they are interested in usurping power, values, advantages, and bogus livelihoods through the spurious neocheating gimmick of women's rights. Because of their disregard for individual rights in their demands for government coercion or force, feminist movements bring, in the long run, only further government oppression of women. Indeed, that oppression is already recurring with, for example, the anti-abortion and anti-pornography movements.

And finally, most feminists stridently attack women's greatest benefactor and liberator — free-enterprise capitalism. Furthermore, many feminists actually support the prime causes for oppression of women — government and religion. In fact, some feminists remain active members of the most virulently anti-women, patriarchal organization ever contrived by man — the Roman Catholic Church. Such feminists work against the well-being of all women and all individuals.

Two approaches to life are open: (1) The neocheater's approach of using force-backed government or deceit-based religion to drain values from others, or (2) the producer's approach of using integrated honesty and free markets to deliver competitive values wanted by others and society. That second approach obviates force, coercion, fraud in allowing all men and women equally to pursue prosperity, romantic love, and abiding happiness.

**Politicians**: Power usurped through government force gives neocheating politicians illusions of control over reality. They use those rationalized illusions to build pseudo self-esteems needed for psychological survival. Their need for unearned power grows from a base of laziness, immaturity, a lack of self-responsibility, and a desire for an easy route to "accomplishment" and "control".

By contrast, self-sufficient producers such as successful businesspeople earn genuine self-esteem through their own integrated thinking and hard efforts. They have no need for unearned power or usurped values. They have no desire to forcibly control the lives of others. That is why genuine value producers are seldom, if ever, interested in politics. ...Productive businesspeople are too busy being happy, creative, and productive to waste their precious time on unhappy, destructive politics.

Innocence is what traps most honest, productive people. Believing that most people are basically good and honest (which is fact), productive people cannot grasp or imagine the inherently dishonest nature of governments. They cannot grasp the immature, evil nature of neocheating politicians, bogus-job bureaucrats, and their agents of force who exist through camouflaged value destructions.

Indeed, to survive without producing competitive values *for others*, professional neocheaters and mystics must use force,

245

Book 2
Neo-Tech Decoded

deception, and mysticism to usurp their destructive livelihoods *from others*.

Neocheaters betray their conscious nature. They program themselves to self-destruct. Time is their enemy. Each passing day brings increasing decline to their lives. With time, exposure of their fraud to themselves and others becomes inescapable.

Who really helps the needy: the elderly, the handicapped, the oppressed, the sick, the helpless? Who really protects the disadvantaged, the consumer, the environment, the innocent animals? Who really provides the rational needs of everyone at ever lower costs? No, not those people who effusively try to convince themselves and others how much care and compassion they have for the disadvantaged, animals, and the environment. They are compassion hoaxers. For, they function by irrationally demanding *others* be forced into providing for the needy and protecting the environment.

Those compassion hoaxers do not function through benevolence and good will. They function through parasitical force and malevolent destruction. Be they politicians, journalists, judges, professors, advocates, or entertainers, they all hypocritically feign good intentions to conceal agendas of unearned livelihoods, power, esteem.

**Altruism**: Who is an example of a consummate altruist? Adolph Hitler was a consummate altruist. He scorned material values in his personal life. He was the personification of asceticism and sacrifice. He demanded the eventual sacrifice of all human beings and their values to his deemed "higher" cause of duty and obedience to society. He fed his weak ego and pseudo self-esteem with an ever increasing need for power and control over others by force. Similarly, people like Mao, Pol Pot, Nader and other altruists ignore honesty, scorn material values, and survive on unearned power gained by brute force or neocheating deceptions. They need increasing control over others to feed their weak egos. ...Such altruists gain their power by attacking and usurping values produced or earned by others. Thus, such altruists live by harming or killing innocent value producers.

Left-wing, right-wing, conservative, and "liberal" views all stem from the same reactionary, Platonistic root. All are

246

dependent on dishonest mysticism and all are philosophically entrenched in the neocheating ploys of sacrifice and altruism. Such altruistic philosophies are contrary to human nature and well-being. Social utopias extrapolated from any altruistic premise are by nature Platonistic, destructive, and totalitarian. Such utopias depend on sacrifice, force, coercion, controls, and doomsday predictions. With those conditions, the individual's best interests are always subjugated to the utopian "higher" causes. Thus, being continuously neocheated and drained by utopian rulers, the individual becomes less and less able to produce competitive values for others and society.

Most of the past and present doomsayers (such as Plato, the Catholic Church, Stalin, Hitler, Ralph Nader), use dishonest projections of free man destroying himself. But those projections are false non sequiturs used to promote the neocheaters' own value-usurping utopias. Such utopias are not only totalitarian by nature, but would be boring, static societies frozen **by force** around some predescribed "ideal". Such utopias would block the exciting, never-ending discoveries that naturally occur through advances in knowledge, technology, and art by productive individuals in a non-utopian, free society.

In a Neo-Tech society, the only actions that are prohibited are the use of initiatory force, coercion, or fraud against any individual. That prohibition is upheld by ostracism as well as the right to use retaliatory, self-defense force or legal action against any initiator of force, coercion, or fraud.

In a Neo-Tech society, the individual is free to function according to his or her biological nature in becoming more and more productive for others and society. The natural happiness and freedom in a Neo-Tech society starkly contrasts to socialistic utopias. In such utopias, individuals are compelled to sacrifice their value-producing competence and efficacy to the altruistic, "higher" causes of utopian rulers. Only in a noncoercive Neo-Tech society are productive individuals free to function according to their nature in order to achieve maximum prosperity, psychuous pleasures, and happiness by delivering maximum values to society.

**Democracy**: Government control always means the control of individuals by force. Communism, fascism, socialism, and democracy are political systems that survive by force. Democracy, however, is generally less destructive or less malevolent than the other three systems of oppression. All four political systems operate on the same neocheating concepts of external "authority" and unearned power backed by "legalized" force. Moreover, all four systems require Platonistic, existentialist philosophies for the value destroyers to usurp bogus livings from the value producers.

Contrary to popular myth, democracy is rooted neither in justice nor in the protection of individual rights, but is rooted in the uncompetitive principle of "authorities" with power to force the deemed "will" of the majority onto specific individuals. (The United States was not founded as a democracy, but as a republic based on constitutional law forged between democratic myths and free-choice, competitive-market principles. Today, most of the remaining nonforce, free-choice, competitive elements of freedom in the United States are being replaced with uncompetitive fascist or socialistic elements of force.) A business-like, free-choice, competitive system is the only political system based on logic, justice, growth, and earned values rather than on feelings, force, stagnation, and usurpation of values. Of all political systems, only the nonforce, free-choice competitive system rejects the concept of uncompetitive "authority" system of force, threat of force, and fraud. And only competitive, free markets fully recognize the sovereignty of the individual and the right to his or her own body, life, and earned property. ...All professional mystics and value-destroying neocheaters hate and fear free-choice competition. Why? Because free-choice competition would drive them from their dishonest careers and bogus livelihoods.

**Ego "Justice":** *Subjective Laws* include political-agenda laws conjured up by politicians and bureaucrats to gain self-serving benefits, false egos, and unearned power. Enforcement of political-agenda laws requires the use of force and armed agents against innocent people. ...The only outcome of such laws is increased violation of individual rights. *Objective Laws* are not conjured up by politicians or bureaucrats. Instead, like the laws of physics, they arise from the *immutable laws of nature*. Such laws are valid across time and space, benefit everyone, and advance society. Objective laws are based on the moral prohibition of initiatory force, threats of force, and fraud. ...The only rational purpose of laws is to protect individual rights.

*Ego "Justice"* is the use of subjective, political-agenda laws to gain parasitical livelihoods and feel false importance. Ego "justice" is the survival tool of many politicians, lawyers, and judges. Ego "justice" is the most pernicious form of neocheating. ...Parasitical elites thrive on subjective laws and ego "justice" to the harm of every individual and all of society.

Ego "justice" is practiced by judges who abandon objective law to support armed bureaucracies that enforce destructive political agendas. Through judicial exploitations and social deceptions, those judges garner public respect. Yet, they are destroyers of property, life, and happiness. Today's ego-"justice" judges incarcerate ever more political pawns with ever harsher, totally unjust sentences. Why? To maintain their ego props and arbitrary power through expanding enforcement of political-agenda laws.

Consider the life-shattering sentences imposed daily on people innocent of any objective crime. Consider Los Angeles federal judge Manuel L. Real who routinely destroys those caught in his web with the harshest possible prison terms — solely to feel power and importance. He takes pleasure in his tough-judge image expressed by his Maximum-Manny nickname. In his self-glorifying process, he destroys the lives of innocent men, women, and children. ...Many other judges at all levels are also Maximum Mannys who destroy innocent human beings and their families in order to feel important.

Consider federal judges Thomas P. Griesa, Milton Pollack, John M. Walker, Jr., and Kimba Wood. Each giulianied[1] innocent business giants for personal power and ego enhancement. Each such judge is a killer of innocent but unpopular people like Michael Milken and Leona Helmsley. Review the records of perhaps the most murderous political-agenda judges in America, Walter Smith, Jr., of Waco, Texas and Clifford Weckstein of

---

[1]The verb giuliani means to use gun-backed, political-agenda law to criminally destroy honest businesspeople and illegally seize private property. Derived from Rudolph Giuliani who advanced in politics by illegally using RICO and seizure laws to crush innocent people and their businesses.

249

Leesburg, Virginia. Such judges destroy objectively innocent individuals caught in the evil web of political-agenda enforcements. To garner ego-boosting publicity and to feel powerful, those humanoid judges crush their wrongly accused, media-smeared victims with false, inhumane imprisonments.

Each such judge is an accomplice to the gun-backed crimes of political-agenda enforcement — crimes of collective assault, pillage, murder. Such judges and their prosecutor cohorts must be held responsible for their crimes against individuals, the economy, and society. Moreover, their innocent victims must be freed, pardoned, and paid restitution.

**By now my father had a swelling anger building within.** *Just who the heck are those people who have the arrogance to spend their lives using force on others*, **he asked himself. No sooner had he asked himself that question when he pinpointed in his widescope thinking the small clique of humanoids responsible, whom my father called the Parasitical Elites. Immediately, off he was writing about them, as follows:**

A parasitical-elite class has spawned this upside-down civilization — an irrational civilization that inflicts purposeful harm on conscious beings, their economies, their societies. Parasitical elites today manipulate nearly all politics, many bureaucracies, the legal profession, the courts, public schools, the academe, the news media, religion, entertainment, and certain big businesses. What most of those manipulators represent as the best is really the worst...the *most destructive* — and vice versa.

Be prepared to discover the facts: Jay Gould is the best, Abraham Lincoln is the worst; Leona Helmsley is the best, Eleanor Roosevelt is the worst; Malcolm X is the best, Martin Luther King is the worst; Michael Milken is the best, Rudolph Giuliani is the worst. ...Indeed, you must first dismiss nearly *everything* that the parasitical-elite class and its news media represent as good and bad in order to command your life on planet Earth toward boundless prosperity.

What do the following have in common? Armed ATF, DEA, IRS agents, force-backed anti-abortionists, jailing of Milken and

Helmsley, Jew and Japan bashing, gay bashing and gay "rights", racism, urban riots, RICO and seizure laws, PETA, political correctness, the DEA, EPA, FDA, INS, IRS, OSHA, formal religion, Greenpeace, evangelism, gun control, Ralph Nader, Fidel Castro, Jesse Jackson, Jesse Helms, Pat Buchanan, white-collar-hoax big-business executives: What do they all have in common?

All of the above are based on economic and social parasitism. They are all backed by professional value destroyers, parasitical elites, envy mongers, and self-righteous neocheaters infesting government, religion, big business, entertainment, the media. By purposely creating problems where none exist, all such parasites end in destroying the very values they pretend to support. Such destructive people must pretend to support values. They must fake compassion and good intentions to survive — to gain false esteem, power, and bogus livelihoods.

They and their supporters comprise a rapidly expanding class of parasitical elites. Today, from survival necessity, they are converging in a final feeding frenzy. They increasingly loot and destroy innocent value producers through despotic "laws": RICO, seizure, and EPA/FDA/FTC/OSHA/SEC-type "laws"...all backed by force along with the irrationalities of ego "justice", fake scientisms, and pressured by escalating deep-pocket litigations. And now, the parasite class fight one another to devour the remains of a vanishing class of genuine job-and-wealth producers.

Indeed, for decades, that escalating class of professional value destroyers has orchestrated libel, slander, and public envy to attack and drain a now decimated, crumbling class of super value producers. Eventually, under various disguised forms of fascist socialism — such as, tax-the-producers envynomics — those converging parasites would drain dry the remaining remnant of super job producers and aggressive entrepreneurs. The demise of those last great value producers would bring annihilations of the world economies and societies. ...But, none of that will happen because of Neo-Tech and the Prosperity Revolution.

Who exactly are the parasitical elites? A simple, wide-scope accounting process reveals one fact: Parasitical elites are those whose livelihoods are draining much more, often infinitely more, from the economy and society than they deliver. Such accounting answers the following question: Does one's job, livelihood,

251

profession, agency, bureaucracy, or company *build or drain* the economy — *benefit or harm* the productive class? **Does one produce values or destroy values?** ...Wide-scope accounting is a definitive economic-impact statement.

Murderous organizations are killing *you*. Some net value destroyers are so obvious that no specific accounting figures are needed for the public to see the destructiveness of such people and their harmful organizations. Consider some of the most harmful bureaucracies in America today: the BATF, DEA, EPA, IRS, INS, FDA, FTC, SEC. Such murderous organizations[1] need guns, jails, and ego "justice" to exist and expand. Those organizations breed legions of professional value destroyers who are responsible for mass property and business destructions that eventually bring economic and social devastations. But, most harmfully, those organizations move *everyone* toward life-wasting stagnation, unhappiness, and death.

Daily, those organizations violate objective justice by committing real crimes of force and fraud. Those organizations are not only harming the economy, but are destroying society and everyone's freedoms by violating each of the ten Articles of the Bill of Rights except the third — they have not yet forced the quartering of their troops in private homes. ...Those organizations depend on a legal system corrupted with the subjective laws and ego "justice" used to advance their harmful political agendas.

*The DEA:* With conventional accounting within arbitrary or closed boundaries, almost any destructive end, even destructions of entire economies and genocide, can be made to appear beneficial to the public as demonstrated by Lenin, Hitler, and Mao. But, wide-scope accounting immediately reveals the

---

[1]Murderous organizations? Even the EPA, for example, is responsible for the deaths of 8–20 people for every life it theoretically saves. The EPA kills people through the increased living costs and decreased living standards that bureaucracy forces on society, especially on the lower classes (Ref: *Forbes*, 7/6/92, page 60). Likewise, other bureaucracies cause long-term harm and death to countless more people than those few people who may benefit. In fact, those who profit from or live off the lethal actions of those bureaucracies are accomplices to murder — often mass murder.

destructiveness of those men and their organizations. Now, apply that wide-scope accounting to organizations like the Drug Enforcement Administration (the DEA). First, consider that the DEA exists entirely through gun-backed policies created by self-serving, demagogic politicians. From that fact, the public can increasingly see that the armed divisions of the DEA are the engines that support and expand the drug problem, crimes, death, and loss of constitutional rights for every American citizen.

The armed DEA divisions continuously expand the market for drugs by providing the super-high price supports that make possible the flourishing of organized crime and drug cartels. Such government-forced economics necessitate pushing ever more potent drugs onto others, especially onto vulnerable young people. In turn, those immoral DEA actions keep escalating the crimes and deaths related to drugs.

Gun-backed organizations like the DEA serve but one purpose — the expansion of harmful livelihoods that let politicians and bureaucrats drain the economy and damage society by creating ever expanding drug problems.

*The IRS:* Likewise, the gun-backed divisions of the Internal Revenue Service work with politicians in expanding destructive political agendas that enhance their jobs and power. Their armed criminal activities diminish everyone's future by crippling or breaking the daring entrepreneur and aggressive business person. Indeed, every large business today started with the daring courage, hard work, and precious seed capital of a heroically aggressive entrepreneur. Yet, as official policy, the IRS directs its newest-trained auditors and armed agents to "cut their teeth" on small, vulnerable, first-year companies. In that way, the IRS each year ruins countless individuals and small businesses — destroying the seeds to our economic future by destroying millions of current and future jobs.[1] Indeed, wide-scope accounting reveals how the armed divisions of the IRS are criminally destroying the essence of our economy, society, and freedoms not only for today, but for future generations.

The IRS thrives as a destructive bureaucracy *because* of the

---

[1]The Neo-Tech Research Center estimates that 7.1 million jobs in the American economy were lost from 1980-1990 due to businesses being damaged or destroyed by illegal IRS actions.

irrational income tax. By contrast, revenues raised through consumption or sales taxes would vanish deficits, reduce the IRS to a fraction of its current size...and eliminate its armed divisions that back criminal collection procedures used to override due process while inflicting cruel-and-unusual punishments on its victims.

No legitimate reason exists for armed agents in any bureaucracy. Local police and courts, not armed bureaucratic agents, can competently and constitutionally protect all individuals, property, and organizations, including physically protecting government officials.

*The INS:* What about the Immigration and Naturalization Service, the INS? By throwing wide-scope accounting on the gun-backed segments of that organization, anyone can see its harm to the economy. With its army of enforcers who never have to answer to American citizens, the INS ravishes hard-working value producers and their families. The INS army expands its power and livelihoods by attacking America's most competitive workers of the past and future. Those workers are the immigrants who abandon their homelands and risk their lives to deliver competitive values to our economy. Thus, they raise the well-being and prosperity of all Americans. Such life-improving immigrants have been the backbone of competitive growth and economic prosperity in America, despite the dishonest political demagoguery to the contrary.

*The FDA:* And the Food and Drug Administration? Wide-scope accounting shows the FDA to be the biggest killer of all — literally killing millions of human beings. Operating under a power-mad Commissioner, armies of FDA bureaucrats destructively build their own "achievement" files for their own promotions. By enforcing increasingly cost-prohibitive compliance to irrational regulations, the FDA blocks scientific and medical progress.

As specifically identified by Zon, without the FDA and its armed enforcers, today we would have cures for cancer, heart disease, AIDS, muscular dystrophy, and essentially all other serious diseases. Moreover, biomedical advances would have the human race moving toward non-aging longevity as achieved in all mystic-free civilizations throughout the universe — in all civilizations free of parasitical elites.

How do destructive organizations succeed in deceiving everyone so completely for so long?

A successful magician deceives *everyone* in his audience with illusions. The key to the magician's successful tricks or deceptions is to keep everyone distracted. The magician with his wand keeps attention focused on a decoy illusion removed from the point of deception. With everyone's attention diverted, no one sees the deception.

All parasitical elites and their organizations have a myriad of decoy illusions. Created through deceptive rationalizations, those illusions have hidden the destructions of the parasitical-elite class since Plato showed golden-soul parasites 2300 years ago how to rule the value producers.

Consider today's Drug Enforcement Administration: With subjective laws enacted by power-usurping politicians, the DEA uses its wand of deception to point at the drugs it seized and people it jailed as progress in the "War on Drugs". But, in fact, the DEA has no motivation to diminish any drug problem. Without an expanding drug problem, its system of livelihoods and power would diminish. Thus, the DEA has every motivation to expand its bureaucracy of bogus livelihoods and power by creating and expanding drug problems, which it does very successfully.

Consider the armed criminal divisions of the Internal Revenue Service: With their wands of deception, those IRS divisions point at the money and property seized. Through its gun-backed agents, the IRS criminally squeezes the working assets out of the "underground" economy, heroic entrepreneurs, struggling individuals, and small businesses. They point to the dollars they have seized from those whom they have crippled, destroyed, or jailed. But throw wide-scope accounting on those illegal elements of the IRS, and one discovers its gun-backed enforcers are destroying our present and future economy, jobs, freedoms, privacy, and well-being. More broadly, the, IRS-forced paperwork alone is the greatest time-and-life destroyer *ever* devised to expand bureaucratic jobs and power. ...And most destructively, the IRS smothers youth from becoming the independent business giants needed for the future prosperity of any society.

Consider the Immigration and Naturalization Service: The INS points its wand of deception at the "illegal" aliens it forcibly drains, blocks, jails, or ejects from America. Such uses of force are not only racist, but are criminal acts against innocent value producers. Those crimes are hidden by deceptive-wand myths such as "draining welfare funds" and "keeping jobs for Americans". Both such claims are patently false. Wide-scope accounting clearly reveals that "illegal" aliens (1) add much more in taxes than they "drain" and (2) create many more jobs for Americans than they take. Thus, each racist INS crime diminishes everyone's job and life by undermining America's standard of living, its economic strength, its international competitiveness.

And finally, consider the Food and Drug Administration: The FDA points its wand of deception toward "protecting" the health of Americans. But, in reality, the FDA is responsible for killing more citizens than any other group of parasitical elites. For, through power-usurping regulations, the FDA blocks the cures for all major diseases. The FDA also blocks the development of major longevity advances. ...Only unhindered science and business can bring disease-free, non-aging longevity, as accomplished in all mystic-free, parasite-free civilizations throughout the universe.

With actual wide-scope accountings, Neo-Tech reveals the huge net destructions caused by specific politicians, bureaucrats, judges, lawyers, prosecutors, white-collar-hoax business people, and other parasitical elites. Neo-Tech also details how those elites can exist only by creating and expanding power-building instruments such as armed bureaucracies. Neo-Tech identifies how all parasitical elites depend on armed bureaucracies and subjective ego "justice" to enforce their harmful survival agendas. And finally, Neo-Tech details the spectacular prosperity that awaits everyone upon terminating the parasitical-elite class (Book One).

Most people in government, business, and the professions are *not* targets for personal ostracism or job termination. Instead, they are candidates to benefit economically, professionally, and personally by getting on the honest side of the split caused by the *Neo-Tech Wedge*. That Wedge is already beginning to move through governments and businesses, separating the honest productive people from the parasitical elites. ...Only parasitical elites and their armed enforcers are targeted for ostracism and job termination. They are the ones who waste everyone's brief life. They shall not escape the Neo-Tech Wedge.

In contrast to legitimately armed policemen who serve to protect life and property, armed bureaucrats serve to harm life and property. Today, the increasing social and physical harms caused by politicized armed bureaucrats are endangering all federal employees. ...Bureaucrats, not law-abiding citizens, must be disarmed.

A politician who lives through armed bureaucracies exists not to produce values but to destroy them, not to bring social harmony but to disrupt it. The conflict between Neo-Tech and politicized armed bureaucracies evolves from the deepest issues of right versus wrong, honesty versus dishonesty, and protective government versus destructive government.

Neo-Tech will bring *peace* to the world and *trust* in government by vanishing armed bureaucracies.

Neo-Tech is simply fully integrated honesty. Nothing can stop the natural mission of Neo-Tech. Nothing can stop its mission of terminating the parasitical-elite class.

A rising Prosperity Revolution will accomplish the first-and-final *valid* class overthrow in history. That overthrow and termination of the parasitical-elite class by *Neo-Tech self-leaders and honest business leaders* will boom all economies. Mankind will finally experience the unlimited prosperity enjoyed by all advanced civilizations throughout the Universe.

This is *your* revolution to unlimited prosperity.

A prosperity revolution? Neo-Tech self-leaders? Class overthrow? Relentless and uncompromising? Overthrowing the entire parasitical-elite class? Yes. Forward march to the overthrow and unlimited prosperity!

Another revolution of bombs, blood, and tears? Power-seeking revolutionary leaders? Another round of destructions leading to ever more destructions? Socialist, fascist, or world-order "democracy" inspired? Building a new parasitical-elite class? No. Just the opposite.

*All past revolutions required inconsistencies, illegalities, and*

257

*destructions. But this revolution is unique. It is based on Neo-Tech. And, Neo-Tech requires logical consistency, objective law, and honest productivity.* Neo-Tech upholds objective law by terminating all subjective political policies that harm you, society, and the economy. ...This is your revolution. This revolution will bring you unlimited prosperity.

Your prosperity revolution? When will it happen? What will happen? Who will make it happen? How will it bring you unlimited prosperity?

All past revolutions and class overthrows were bogus or compromised. For, all were fomented so one parasitical group could take power from another parasitical group. All were fomented from false or artificial class conflicts of nationalities, races, religions, political issues, economic levels, or social levels.

*The Prosperity Revolution is the first and only legitimate class overthrow possible among human beings:* The honest productive class ranging from construction hand to billionaire entrepreneur will overthrow the parasitical-elite class — a criminal class comprised of destructive politicians and their legions of harmful bureaucrats, armed political-policy enforcers, ego judges, politico prosecutors, corrupt lawyers, dishonest journalists, evil academics, and white-collar-hoax business quislings.

Parasitical elites survive through false power — power gained through deceptive illusions. But, today, with your personal terminator, you can break their illusions to end all false power.

Independent self-leaders are developing with no leader to follow or obey. They are people who will increasingly carry out missions of subversion against the parasitical-elite class.

So long as self-leaders have no leader to obey, they will steadily multiply and never stop moving forward. For, on learning how to break the hoax of professional parasitism, they will react personally to each parasite who harms or drains society. On their own, in their own ways, they will increasingly subvert the entire parasite class. They will subvert the leeches one by one, relentlessly, until each is driven from his or her bogus career. Especially through the Internet, self-leaders will have no time or energy limits to stop them from eradicating the parasitical-elite class that wastes the lives of everyone. They will have no more compunction about swatting down parasitical elites who exploit society than they have about swatting down mosquitoes that spread disease.

So long as uncensored cyberspace and free expression exists, the Prosperity Revolution will proceed peacefully. Without gun-backed oppression, the overthrow of the parasitical-elite class will be peaceful but uncompromising, total, permanent.

**After hours of writing, my father now needed a break. Now morning, he put on his running clothes and went for a refreshing run, right to his deep friend — his mountain called Zon. Although the strong yet peaceful mountain talked no more, my dad stopped and sat at his old spot. "How long will my thinking be this way — so widely integrated and powerful?" he asked Zon, knowing he would get no answer. "It's so clear now — mystic-free thinking is Neothink. Neo-Tech or fully integrated honesty is the vehicle to Neothink. What is this new power I have, anyway? I write just like you used to talk to me, and I get to the root of everything now, unlike before. This Neo-Tech and Neothink is so powerful. What do I call this new power? Zon, what do I call it?" My father sat there, looking like a schoolboy as he did that first day when he fell and Zon first talked to him. The desert wind pushed his hair back, then with schoolboy excitement, he said, "I know. I'll call this new power *Zonpower* — after you! That's it: *Zonpower*. Zonpower means the power over life one commands by using Neo-Tech to become mystic-free and to take man's next quantum leap into Neothink. ...Thank you Zon for my inspiration. I must get back to my writing now. I love feeling my Zonpower!" With that, my middle-aged dad bounced up like a kid and ran back to his home office at the fastest clip he had run in nearly ten years. As he bounded away on the desert road, he finally heard, in his thoughts this time, Zon's first words to him that never reached his consciousness that first day after his fall. As he now listened to those words for the first time, a lump grew in his throat, and a tear of gratefulness welled up in his eye as he ran along the desert road. Here is what he heard in his mind; Zon's first words to my dad:**

259

The child of the past exists in you. Lost within faded memories, that child keeps searching for a life of adventure, discovery, value, happiness. Turn inward to discover that child. And then break free from those who are hurting you...from those who are wasting your time and resources. That child of the past will kindle a new life of adventure and happiness.

**"I have discovered that child of the past, Zon...thank you, Zon!" my father shouted as tears streaked down his cheeks. "I have broken free and discovered the adventure!" When he got back home, he took a three-minute shower, wrapped a towel around his waist, then sat down and started writing, again for hours. (This towel-around-the-waist writer became a common scene over the next few years, even to this day.) My dad did not know where his writing on this day was taking him, but he knew he was writing toward something big. His pen raced through the subjects as he headed along a mapped course toward the climax that would come to him before the day was over:**

**Business**: Business is the most noble of all ideas, the most intellectual of all thinking, the most valuable of all activities. Business is a man-made mechanism from which all major values of civilization are created, produced, and distributed. Business is the mechanism through which people most effectively assert themselves into life to produce maximum values for others and achieve abiding happiness for themselves and their loved ones.

Almost without exception, those who vilify, undermine, and drain honest businesses are those who usurp their livings from the value producer. Most mystics and neocheaters undermine and destroy values out of envy and resentment. For through their habitual parasitism, they have made themselves incompetent to honestly produce competitive values for others and society. Such professional mystics, neocheaters, and external "authorities" survive by draining their benefactors — the value producers.

Moreover, the professional mystics and neocheaters who publicly scorn money and values are actually obsessed with usurping money and values in order to live without producing competitive values for others. Such mystics and neocheaters project false guilt onto the value producer in order to conceal their motives, methods, intentions, and impotence. They demand control and regulation of the value producer when they themselves are incompetent to produce values for others.

Business delivers competitive values to others, to society, even to the value destroyers. While the value destroyers deliver only false guilt, usurpations, and harm to business and its value producers.

Business people are primarily interested in producing values for others. To such business people, money represents not a means for consumption, but a means to grow — to produce still more and better values at ever lower costs and greater efficiencies. That mechanism for producing ever-increasing values at ever-lower costs is the unmatched virtue of business. Indeed, business is the most moral, most intellectual of all human activities. Business is the most widely integrated, evolved form of human intellect. Business is the antithesis of mysticism.

**Fraud-Based Academe**: Many university professors today are *not* intellectuals. Genuine intellectuals use their minds rationally, honestly, productively. Many university professors today are fake intellectuals who use their minds cleverly, dishonestly, and destructively to hold their bogus jobs. They are professional neocheaters. Thus, even some of the most "famous" of such professors, even some Nobel laureates, cannot produce net values. Instead they wreak great damage on the minds of their students. ...Neo-Tech will bring a worldwide purge of such university professors.

Great intellectuals exist in every major area of productive human activity. Genuine intellectuals are those businessmen, industrialists, scientists, engineers, artists, musicians, and educators who advance their profession by using their minds honestly in working hard through rational actions. A rational, hard-driving, successful mining engineer, for example, is highly intellectual in mining, but may not be highly intellectual in English literature. At the same time, a university professor of English literature is probably not highly intellectual in mining. Indeed, he may be incompetent to function intellectually in any area of business. Perhaps he is even incompetent in English, especially if he or she is a low-effort, laid-back, tenured professor living off taxpayers. Such professors damage students' minds by using non sequiturs to attack the potency of the logical mind, reason, heroic value producers, and their life-giving products.

The only difference between intellectualism in the business world versus intellectualism in the academic world is that performance in business is much easier to measure and thus more difficult to fake. That is why the academic world accumulates such a high percentage of lazy charlatans and clever pseudo-intellectuals compared to the business world. Those charlatans and pseudo intellectuals cannot survive in the business world. For, through their fake jobs cleverly designed to camouflage their laziness and dishonesty, they have become uncompetitive and incompetent. Still, they can fake lifelong careers in the academic world. And as long as mysticism and altruism dominate philosophical thought, such pseudo-intellectual neocheaters will proliferate throughout the academic world.

**Education:** Platonism is the basis of all public educational systems. Government-run schools today are inept at educating children because they embrace the ideas of John Dewey, a Platonist existentialist who dishonestly replaced the objective principles of education with power-usurping, subjective methods. Using dishonest non sequiturs, Dewey's philosophy dismisses as socially irrelevant the pedagogical teaching of fundamental knowledge such as reading, writing, mathematics, and science.

Dewey's philosophy promotes the mystical concept that children can be "educated" by allowing them to randomly pursue their own whims. The students' whims are considered socially relevant to the here-and-now and thus are deemed as the basis of education. The "teacher", therefore, merely follows wherever the child's feelings may lead (rather than the teacher providing the child with objective knowledge through systematic input of integrated facts and information). With an existential action approach, Dewey deems the mind as the creator of "reality". Thus, in one mystical stroke, he negates both the integrating conscious mind and objective reality.

Although deceptively stating the opposite, Karl Marx's dialectical materialism is the same "reality creating" approach to action as Dewey's approach. Hitler's approach is also the same as Dewey's "willed realities" and "created logics". That "reality-creating" approach is the essence of mysticism. For it relieves the mind of the basic human responsibility to identify, integrate, and then logically deal with objective reality. As a pragmatic existential neocheater, Dewey scraps logic, knowledge, and reason in favor of whims and feelings. He deems such whims and feelings as the primary guide to human knowledge, education, and action. ...Designed from dishonesty and laziness, Dewey's destructive "educational" approach is the basis of public education today.

As a result, severe crimes against children occur on a grand scale in most public schools and universities today. The perpetrators of those crimes are many of the educators and philosophers of this world. They implement those anti-educational ideas advanced at the turn of the century by master comprachico, John Dewey. Such educators methodically destroy the efficacy of the child's mind. By the millions, eager, knowledge-seeking children turn into lethargic airheads or dishonest manipulators unable to achieve honest prosperity and genuine happiness.

**Existentialism:** A dominant form of mysticism and Platonistic philosophy in Western civilization is existentialism and its many disguised variations such as Gestaltism, transcendental meditation, Zen Buddhism. Existentialism is really nothing more than clever irrationalism and contradictions that ironically heralds Kierkegaard's "individual responsibility", which existentialism ultimately negates, often cloaked in pragmatic non sequiturs or good-sounding rationalizations. Existentialism claims that reality does not exist. Thus, the meaning of existentialism is impossible to objectively define or understand. For existentialism is nothing. And nothing can be attached to nothing.

Expressed in countless ways, existentialism is the philosophical form projected by (1) most media commentators, (2) almost all politicians and theologians, (3) neocheating social "intellectuals", including many teachers, university professors, and (4) know-nothing personalities and entertainers acting as "authorities" on the basis of feeling rather than knowledge.

In the past several decades, those four groups of people have effectively spread existentialism among the nonproductive elements of society. More recently, those same groups are

Book 2
Neo-Tech Decoded

263

successfully pushing existentialism onto the working middle class. As a result, the productivity, self-esteem, and happiness among the productive middle class is diminishing as value producers increasingly swap their earned happiness and freedom for the existentialistic ideas of mysticism, egalitarianism, and altruism. Their ultimate negation of self-responsibility and self-control opens the way for increasing government control of their lives.

Many people are drawn into the chameleon-like forms of existentialism through an assortment of highly publicized, illusionary benefits designed to indulge almost anyone's emotions to escape reality. Touted benefits include discovering "real truth", "peace of mind", "happiness", new "freedoms", "self-awareness", increased "sensitivity", "discovery" of one's true self. But beneath all such jargon and claimed benefits, existentialism is nothing more than a wimpish irrationality that promotes stupidity. ...Indeed, existentialism promotes the negation of reality.

Existentialism and organized religions both grow from mysticism. And both lead to the oppression of the individual. Existentialism and organized religions both reflect fear of the independent individual.

**Equality:** People are *not* equal in value or worth. Only in the rights to their own lives and property are people equal. Those and only those rights are inalienable for all human beings. By nature, no one has an automatic or natural right to anything else in life. Moreover, beyond the equality of individual or property rights, nothing is, can, or should be equal between human beings.

Earned values always determine one's self-esteem and happiness despite the constant efforts by politicians, media journalists, cartoonists, social "intellectuals" and other neocheaters to use nonearned characteristics such as face, skin, sex, age, race, nationality, or family background to praise, pay off, judge, or condemn people. Constant exposure to the anti-individualistic myths pushed by professional mystics and neocheaters diminish one's ability to honestly judge character and earned worth. Recognition of an individual's earned worth is the cornerstone of justice and essential for romantic love and psychuous pleasures.

**Media:** A central theme of today's existentialist culture is "do not judge others". The neocheating media, social "intellectuals", and theologians continually tout, both implicitly and explicitly, the themes "do not judge others", "there are no absolute morals, no rights or wrongs", "everything is relative". Neocheaters have strong motivations for sowing themes of nonknowing and nonjudgment. Their livelihoods depend on keeping others from knowing and judging the parasitism and destruction inflicted by professional mystics and neocheaters onto society.

The continuous campaign to repress moral judgment depends largely on the specious technique of pointing to various erroneous judgments and then implying that such errors are inherent in all judgments. From that false reasoning, neocheaters dishonestly assert that all moral judgments are wrong, unfair, or harmful. From that conclusion, they compound their dishonesty by further asserting that moral judgments should never be made. Moreover, armed with specious egalitarian slogans or Biblical parables, those neocheaters, especially media journalists, malign or castigate those who have the courage and confidence to make honest moral judgments about value destroyers. While, at the same time, those same neocheaters constantly, dishonestly, hypocritically attack their victims (i.e., the value producers) with negative moral judgements that are false.

How are valid moral judgments made? Such judgments are made by using the biological nature and well-being of the conscious organism as the moral standard. With that objective standard, human actions can be consistently and validly judged by acquiring adequate facts and knowledge:

1. Only volitional actions involving conscious choices can be morally judged. All other actions are amoral.

2. A volitional action is moral, for example, if the action is beneficial to the conscious organism. Likewise, a volitional action is immoral if the action is harmful to the conscious organism. Or more simply, *if a volitional action is rational and "good for me", it is moral; or if a volitional action is irrational and "bad for me", it is immoral.*

3. The ability and willingness to make moral judgments are necessary to make sound decisions and function effectively. The more important the personal or business decision, the more

important is the need to make accurate moral judgments. In turn, such judgments are crucial for making the correct decisions needed for abiding prosperity, happiness, and romantic love.

Since making moral judgments is necessary for quality survival, a person must be aware of the possible traps and errors in making such judgments. Some of the traps and errors are those that the nonjudgment advocates take out of context to support their harangues that moral judgments should be avoided.

The most common judgment trap or error, *erroneous or inadequate information to make a valid or accurate judgment,* is the most obvious and common cause of judgment errors. Everyone is subject to this error. But that does *not* preclude certainty over moral issues and judgments. The central argument of the nonjudgment neocheaters is that since no one can know everything or be error free, no one can be certain about anything, especially moral issues. That argument is false. A person can be absolutely certain if given sufficient facts and context to validly measure against the axioms of objective reality.

Since no one is omniscient or infallible, everyone is subject to specific errors. But that vulnerability to errors has no bearing on knowing objective reality or being able to make moral judgments with certainty. For example, with inadequate information and judgment errors, a person can temporarily choose the wrong romantic-love partner. But, at the same time, he or she can still know with certainty the objective standards needed for a valid romantic-love relationship. With that certainty, a person can more quickly recognize and correct such judgment errors. In other words, with adequate objective knowledge, a person can make moral judgments with certainty without being omniscient or infallible.

A person can confidently proceed through life knowing that moral and character judgment can be performed with certainty. But again, that person must be aware of those areas subject to error because of inaccurate or incomplete knowledge or information. By always keeping the mind open to new information and being prepared to correct errors, the damage of judgment errors is minimized.

*Infatuation* is also a media generated, judgment-error tool to deliver undeserved adulation to charismatic politicians, evangelists, and other neocheaters. And *reverse infatuation* is constantly used as a grossly unfair, dishonest technique by media people as well as by politicians, clergymen, and academes to discredit value producers and their products, businesses, and ideas.

Essentially every big business was originally created and built by an honest, heroically productive individual such as E. I. du Pont, Henry Ford, Andrew Carnegie, Thomas Edison, John D. Rockefeller, Harvey Firestone, and other industrial supermen. Such men are the true benefactors of working-class people, of value producers, of society and civilization. For those industrial supermen intensely pursued the moral objectives of benefiting their customers, workers, managers, and investors by delivering spectacular values to society at ever lower costs. Those creative, productive individuals contrast sharply with destructive, media-made "heroes" such as the Lincolns, FDRs, Naders, Kennedys, and other such bad-intentioned nonproducers who survive by attacking and harming value producers, their products, their businesses.

While never honestly acknowledging those who produce great wealth and values, the "liberal" or neocheating journalists and writers often praise the wealthy, nonproductive scions of past industrial heroes. Neocheaters especially praise those immature, nonbusiness-like "philanthropists" who dissipate inherited wealth such as Henry Ford II and Nelson Rockefeller. And those same journalists and writers attack nearly every major value created by outstanding businessmen, scientists, and industrialists. For example, under such guises as ecology, consumerism, or "compassion", the "liberal" media attack, often with rabid envy, the greatest, most heroic values created by conscious beings. Such outstanding values attacked include the automobile, the computer, the drug industry, the petroleum and mining industries, and America's magnificent food processing and distribution systems. At the same time, the "liberal" media are quick to praise progressively meaner values such as the car pool, the abacus, folk medicine, hand-made goods, growing one's own food. They promote those kinds of unheroic, mean values under good-sounding non sequiturs as returning to basic "values", returning to hand-made quality, returning to nature.

Envy growing out of dishonesty and laziness is a major

destructive force. In contrast to jealousy that is directed toward the *possession* of values, envy is directed toward the *destruction* of values.

The media often claim that envy is inborn or is "forced" into people by the environment. Therefore, envious people are blameless. Instead, society and inequality are to blame. But, in reality, envy is a destructive character development observed throughout the media today resulting from:

1. volitional laziness and dishonesty, and
2. the choice to default on the self-responsibility to live by one's own mind and efforts through competitive value production.

**Racism**: In American cities, white neighborhoods are generally safer than black neighborhoods. Throughout history, men have reached greater heights in intellectual, aesthetic, and commercial achievements than have women. In general, Jews are more intelligent, productive, creative and, therefore, more potent in life than people of other religions, nationalities, or races.

Are those the words of a racist, a chauvinist, a Zionist zealot? Perhaps so if such statements were directed toward or used in judgment of particular individuals. But the statements are made in reference to objective, statistical facts that are real. When those statements are placed in the proper context of being generalized statistics that do *not* characterize any particular individual, they are then validly applicable to *generalized* situations.

If the data are accurate, then in-context inferences from those data are factual and must be considered in order to make honest evaluations and correct decisions. Consider, for example, the provable statistic that in all major U.S. cities a significantly higher percentage of Blacks than Whites injure and murder people.[1] That is a statistical fact regardless of the reasons or so-called social causes. But to apply that statistical fact to any individual would be out-of-context and unjust because such statistics cannot be validly or honestly applied to any particular individual.

[1]References: "Crime in the United States: Uniform Crime Report", issued annually by the FBI; "Crime and Race" M.E. Wolfgang and B. Cohen.

On the other hand, to ignore or distort in-context facts is a dishonest evasion of reality. Such dishonest evasions of reality mystically conceal the knowledge required to deal accurately with reality in making effective decisions and judgments. For example, consider if a white or black person is concerned with physical safety for his or her loved ones and property: What if that person had the choice of living in equivalent housing in a predominantly black, depressed community or in a predominantly white, equally depressed community? Basing that choice on facts, that person would choose to live in the white community. Indeed, that person would have made the correct decision without necessarily harboring any bigotry or without acting unjustly or harmfully toward any individual.

Likewise, from factual statistics, a much higher percentage of men than women accomplish major intellectual, artistic, and commercial achievements. Regardless of the causes or reasons, that statistical fact has been true throughout recorded history and is still true today. However, with the increased educational, social, economic, and financial freedoms now available to Western women, the percentage of women attaining high achievement has increased. But the increase is nowhere near the proportion of increased opportunities for women. Women, in general, have not fully utilized their increased freedoms and opportunities. Still, to blindly apply that statistical fact to any individual woman would be unjust, inaccurate, and out of context. But to ignore that statistical fact in its proper, generalized context would be a mystical evasion of reality that could result in serious errors in judgment and thinking needed for honest, accurate business and personal decisions.

Proper in-context generalizations based on accurate facts are necessary to accurately perceive reality, to know what is going on, and to make correct decisions. On the other hand, a person must never apply statistical data or generalizations to any specific individual. To do so would not only be unjust and dishonest, but would also be inaccurate, misleading, and a mystical distortion of reality.

Conversely, applying individual characterizations to general groups of people would likewise be invalid, unjust, dishonest, misleading, and mystical. To most effectively use the Neo-Tech

Advantages, one must not only integrate thought with action, but must integrate both in-context generalized facts with in-context specific facts.

As with any feeling or emotion, an unacted-upon racist feeling is not subject to guilt or moral judgment. Mind crimes do not exist, except through the false-guilt ploys of political, religious, and "intellectual" neocheaters. Only when racist feelings are translated into harmful actions does racism become unjust, immoral, guilty.

Destructive, government-implemented racism occurs in Zionist Israel and formerly in apartheid South Africa. But much more destructive racism occurs in all Arab, Moslem, and black-African dictatorships as well as in many Asian countries such as India, China, and throughout the former USSR. But, ironically, the freest countries practicing racism potentially present the most tragic dilemmas:

What is the remedy to Zionist racism that forcibly violates the individual rights of millions of Palestinians? The only moral position is to restore full individual rights to everyone, including the Palestinians. But would that allow even greater violations of individual rights by permitting a much worse, Syrian-like dictatorship or a murderous, Iranian-like theocracy take over?

An unsolvable dilemma? Not at all. Instead, spectacularly beneficial solutions exist through Neo-Tech: By using Neo-Tech principles, people can explicitly and permanently eliminate initiatory force and fraud by any person, group, or government. In other words, Neo-Tech effectively dismantles the mechanism for government to initiate force or fraud. A Neo-Tech based society has but a single law and responsibility — to protect the individual rights of everyone.

Neo-Tech is the solution to racism in South Africa, in Israel, as well as in all fascist, Marxist, and theocratic regimes. For, Neo-Tech collapses force-backed power and laws, leaving that society with the sole power and function to protect the individual rights of everyone — black, white, man, woman, rich, poor, Jew, Palestinian, business person, laborer. Neo-Tech frees individuals from initiatory force, fraud, and destructive oppression. Neo-Tech protects each person's individual and property rights from Marxist-Leninism destruction and other forms of force and coercion.

In South Africa, Israel, and totalitarian nations, Neo-Tech would free victims of force-backed racism and vanquish laws backed by force. In turn, eliminating that mechanism for initiating force would dramatically strengthen self-defense for protecting the individual rights and property of everyone.

Thus, Neo-Tech would eliminate the threat of destruction that now awaits those in oppressive government regimes, especially the value producers and their property. For, Neo-Tech delivers a safe, orderly society of unprecedented prosperity and happiness reaching forever into the future. Neo-Tech is the freedom and inspiration for those still living under force-backed, totalitarian governments. In one stroke, Neo-Tech will end those fears and threats by denuding the professional value destroyers of their power. For Neo-Tech dismantles their mechanisms of initiatory force and coercion. At the same time, Neo-Tech provides iron-clad protection of individual rights.

**Fraud-Based Organized Religions**: Fraud-based, organized religions are products of mysticism. Mysticism is the opposite of honesty and reason. Mysticism underlies all volitionally destructive actions. Mysticism undermines the capacity for independent, integrated thinking and reasoning, which is the survival tool for all human beings. ...The mystical-oriented mind is the basis of the criminal-like mind, which is the exact opposite of the business-like mind.

For two-thousand years, organized religions have been the most effective tools of the professional mystics and neocheaters for usurping a material and psychological living from the value producers. Organized religions manipulate major thinking defaults into convenient well-organized packages of specious "truths". Professional value destroyers can with relative ease use various well-packaged "truths" to deceive or cajole innocent producers into sacrificing their earned values to them, the nonproducers. Most organized religions promote the "virtues" of humility, altruism, egalitarianism, selflessness, "higher" causes, and sacrifice. Such specious "virtues" are designed to generate guilt for lowering the self-esteem of producers to the level of the nonproducer. Once burdened with false guilt, the producers will more readily hand over or sacrifice their earned values to the nonproducers.

Throughout history, the many variations of organized religions have provided professional mystics and neocheaters with effective tools for extracting a living from the value producer.[1]  For survival, value destroyers depend on the producer to sacrifice his or her created or earned values to them.  They also extract values through government force and coercion. ...All professional mystics and neocheaters rely on the unearned guilt foisted on producers through various altruistic or religious  hoaxes to extract material and psychological "livings" from value producers.

Organized religions and mysticism are also the tools needed to establish totalitarian dictatorships, including both theistic and "atheistic" dictatorships.  Russia, for example, was the most religious, mystical country in Europe during the early 1900s.  That heavy mysticism provided an ideal psychological setup for the acceptance of perhaps the most destructive and irrational, mystical-based political system in history — Marxism/Leninism.  Acceptance of an irrational, Kantian-based philosophy such as Marxism was needed to negate objective values and individual rights, to rationalize the enslavement of entire nations, to slaughter millions of productive human beings for a meaningless, mystical higher "authority" — the state. ...Thus, the religious tools of altruism and mysticism are needed not only to establish the murderous religious regimes of an Ayatollah-led Iran but the murderous "atheistic" regimes of a dictator-led Soviet Union and Red China.

Sometime after 2001, as the frauds of altruism and "higher causes" are identified and rejected by the value producers, the neocheaters will lose their unearned power.  Once the value producers identify and reject mysticism, all fraud-based religion and force-backed governments will vanish.

The political/religious/media axis have built the highest reverence and respect for some of the bloodiest, most morally

---

[1]On a morality scale, most criminals rank several notches above such destructive neocheaters of the politician and theologian genre.  The criminal does not attempt to establish himself as a morally righteous person or palm off his actions as morally good.  Moreover, the criminal does not use altruism or the God concept to foist false guilt onto his victims after stealing or usurping his livelihood from them.

perverted, but most brilliant succession of neocheaters in history — the popes and cardinals. And with bizarre irony, those men, by competitive necessity, were and are closet atheists. In fact, the entire upper hierarchy of the most powerful religion (or of any powerful religion or other neocheating organization) would have to be closet atheists in order to be cunning and competitive enough to achieve their power.

On knowing the nature of neocheating, one fact becomes compellingly obvious: To successfully impose such an ingenious, big-lie, 2000-year hoax continuously on millions of confused, mystical-accepting victims, all popes and cardinals could not be intellectually handicapped by honestly searching for the truth. For, they would be (1) too benighted to outmaneuver the fierce competition vying for power, and (2) too unaware and weak to orchestrate such a mighty hoax. Thus, all popes, cardinals, and probably most bishops would have to be atheists to be sharp and shrewd enough for attaining their positions of power. Also, theists would be too naive and uncompetitive to perpetuate for centuries such a cleverly integrated hoax. ...Only those who saw through their own promulgated mysticism would be aware and competent enough to win the fierce competition for the positions of power occupied by popes and cardinals.

About 300 A.D., Christian theologians discovered the ultimate neocheating technique to control human beings. That technique was to link guilt with sex. With that technique, the Christian church rose to its height in power, causing Western civilization to crumble into the mystical Dark Ages as human well-being and happiness sank to the lowest level in recorded history.

The history of Christian oppression of individual life, rights, values, happiness, pleasure, and sexuality is outlined on the following pages:

## CHRISTIAN OPPRESSION OF HAPPINESS
(from research by Morton M. Hunt and others)

### 100 A.D. – 385 A.D.

•Roman Empire still appeared vibrant, but was surrendering to a new religion...Christianity. Rome plunged into altruism and

273

asceticism.

•Roman pagans began persecuting those Christians who became altruistic fanatics and used any means to meet their goals of destroying the life-enhancing and productive aspects of Roman civilization. Those neocheating Christian leaders had the dual objective of wiping out the pleasures of human life as well as destroying the high standard of living enjoyed by the Romans. The early Christians heroically formed tightly-knit anarchist groups for effective protection from the oppression of the bureaucratic Roman government while laying the foundations for their own much greater oppressions.

## 385 A.D. – 1000 A.D.

•The rise of the unkempt ascetics (hippies) in Egypt. Based on Christian self-torture and denial (e.g., St. Simon).

•Christianity discovered a fast, neocheating route to power — the foisting of guilt onto innocent value producers. As an effective rallying symbol, they found and elevated to martyr-level status an obscure historical individual who died three centuries earlier. That individual ironically was a gentle, appealing rebel who heroically stood up to the injustices of the parasitical-elite authorities — the same type authorities who three centuries later usurped and mystified him for their own dishonest exploitation. That individual, their new symbol, was named Jesus Christ. ...Jesus has been done a rank injustice by the Catholic church.

•Christians became increasingly preoccupied with sex as they struggled against lust (e.g., by burning off fingers to resist temptation). Thinly veiled, neurotic eroticism steadily increased within the church.

•St. Augustine (born 354 A.D.) promoted guilt through his books: (1) *Confessions* — self-accusations of his pagan, lustful youth. He converted to a Christian in 386 A.D., then gained power through neocheating by hatefully using guilt to turn the goodness and pleasures of man against himself. Promulgated how all are born between feces and urine.

274

(2)*The City of God* — his major work — speculates how babies might be born from women "uncankered by lust and sex". Demonstrates passionate hatred for human life. St. Augustine became a master neocheater in achieving respect and power by making problems where none existed. He destroyed values rather than create them.

•By the 5th Century, marriage came under church domination.

•The decline into dark ages coincided with the rise of Christianity. Collapsing under the Christian stranglehold, 6th Century Rome was repeatedly ravaged and looted. One million population was reduced to fifty thousand. The city lay in rubble and ruins. The Senate ceased for lack of qualified men. The hygiene, science, and culture of Rome was abandoned as Christianity took hold.

•By 585 A.D., Catholics argued that women did not have mortal souls and debated if women were even human beings.

•Sex was reduced by Christianity to an unromantic, harsh, ugly act with penance easily and hypocritically granted to men whenever required. Women became pieces of disposable property.

•Clergy and popes turned to prostitutes and neurotic sex. (e.g., The Pope of 904 A.D. practiced incest and was a lecher with children).

•By the 9th Century, Christianity dominated. Women were considered property of men. The church sanctioned wife-beating. Men were merely fined by the church for killing women.

•For the Catholic clergy, sex without values (e.g., prostitute sex, orgy sex, even forced rape or sadistic sex) was not a serious offense, but sex with values (e.g., loving or valuing a woman) was a high sin with severe penalties. For, love and valuing resist control by "authorities", therefore, had to be squelched.

•St. Jerome stated that he who too ardently loved his wife was an adulterer.

•Christian marital sex was performed only in one position and then only to conceive a child. Sex was never to be performed during penance nor on Sundays, Wednesdays, Fridays, holiday seasons.

•The major Christian sin was not sex, but pleasure.

## 1000 A.D. – 1500 A.D.

•Courtly love reflected happiness and contradicted the malevolence of religion. Churchmen feared and fought courtly love (e.g., St. Thomas stated that to kiss and touch a woman with delight, even without thought of fornication, was a mortal sin).

•The struggle was between oppressive religion and renaissance free thinking. Also, the struggle was between papal power and the new Aristotelian ideas.

•In the 1300s, an ominous new interest in witchcraft and exorcism began appearing in the church. Priests fulminated about the evil powers of women who formed sex pacts with the Devil.

•By 1450, the dichotomy was complete and the dogma was established by the Catholic church that all physically desirable women were evil witches. The church was losing its power, and demonizing women was their means to fight the rediscovering of human joyfulness brought on by the emerging Renaissance.

•Renaissance noblemen in the 15th Century equated beauty to good. To counter this trend toward good and beauty, the church attacked through the Pope. The Catholic church developed a new breed of neocheating malefactors not known before...the inquisitors who were backed by a series of papal pronouncements and bulls. The Pope set up two theologians (Jacob Sprenger and Henry Kramer) to act as inquisitors. Sprenger and Kramer wrote a widely influential book dealing with the "evils" of women and witchcraft. That led to the burning to death of tens of thousands of innocent women during the Renaissance.

•Crosscurrents and contradictions — the "lady ideal" projected by the happy, benevolent spirit of the Renaissance versus the "evil witch" projected by the unhappy, malevolent spirit of the church.

- King Henry VIII was the first major figure to combine love and marriage. He waged a long battle with Bishop Wolsey and Pope Clement VII about his divorce and subsequent marriage to Anne Boleyn.

- Renaissance enlightenment made sex seem not so sinful and disgusting as the church insisted. The middle class began to associate sex with love.

## **1500 – 1700**

- The Reformation combined with the enlightened Renaissance by considering sex in marriage as wholesome and free of guilt. But the malevolent Christian position continued to burn women as witches.

- Martin Luther battled Catholic asceticism by advocating the enjoyment of every pleasure that was not "sinful". Luther lived in a lusty "eat, drink, and be merry" style. He fought Rome and claimed that celibacy was invented by the Devil. He insisted that priests could marry and asserted that marriage was not a sacrament at all, but a civil matter. Luther asserted that sexual impulses were both natural and irrepressible. He broke from Rome and married. He cheerfully loved his wife and held pleasurable sex in marriage as good. Luther's reformation rapidly spread across Northern Europe.

- John Calvin (the father of the Bluenoses) was the opposite of Martin Luther. Calvin was sour, malevolent, and had a ferocious theology based on human depravity and the wrath of God. He was an unhappy ascetic who had ulcers, tuberculosis, and kidney stones; he considered life of little value. Calvin set up a brutally strict theocracy in Geneva that allowed no dancing, fancy clothes, or jewelry. The death penalty was imposed for adultery. Even legitimate love was stringently regulated. Engagements were limited to six weeks. No lingering at romance was allowed. Weddings were grave with no revelry. The Calvinist marriage had two functions: (1) to produce children, and (2) to reduce sexual desires.

277

•Most Puritans, however, were quite unlike the inhuman joylessness of Calvin. But a few vocal fanatics such as John Knox in the United States continued to pile misery onto others. His Blue laws of the 1650s were against amusements, smoking, drinking, gambling, fancy clothing. He also promoted public whippings, scarlet letters, executions for adulterers, and the Salem "witch" executions (executed 26 women and two dogs in 1692).

•Early Puritan traits were mainly stern expressions masking mischief and romance. Church trial records show much "sinning" existed. But only sex outside marriage was attacked. Puritans were very much for sex inside marriage and condemned the virtue-of-virginity concept. Most Puritans were tenderly romantic and good lovers.

•The image of the sexless Puritan with a stony heart is false. For example, the 17th Century Puritan John Milton (*Paradise Lost*) projected a healthy view of married sex. He displayed idealistic, romantic views about marriage. Moreover, Milton sent tracts to Parliament urging modern-day, easy divorce. Milton's *Paradise Lost* projects a benevolent view of Adam and Eve in a romantic-love context. Milton rejected St. Augustine's malevolent views of life, sex, and pleasure.

•16th Century Puritans combined the ideals of romantic love with the normality of sex in marriage. Woman's status improved under Puritanism (e.g., if beaten, women could separate and even divorce.). Property rights and inheritance laws improved. Marriage became a civil contract.

### 1700 – 1800

•The rationalists in this new Age of Reason rejected the gloom of Christianity. They scrapped the church's portrait of woman as evil.

•18th Century love rejected Christian anti-sexual values and idealized the mythical Don Juan, who was impeccably mannered, lustful, haughty. Love was reduced to mere sensuality and pleasurable sport with the motive to seduce and then desert.

## 1800 – 1900

• Religious Victorian men, on the other hand, were patriarchal and stern. But they played that role at their own sexual expense.

• Out of religious Victorianism arose a great hunger for a fantasy sex life. Flagellation, pornography, and prostitution rapidly increased.

• Capitalistic economics were greatly accelerating the dissolution of medieval religious ties along with their unjust social customs and racism.

• The religious Victorian home was threatened by talk of female suffrage, divorce reforms, and free love.

• Victorianism was a reactionary, desperate delaying action (in collusion with the church) against the inevitable changes made by an emerging industrial civilization. Religion-oriented Victorians tried to fight change via religious coercion, government force, and police activities.

## 1900 – 1950

• Margaret Sanger staged a historic fight for birth control claiming that a woman's body belonged to her alone. She published birth-control information in 1914 and opened birth-control clinics in 1916. Outraged Roman Catholic elements had her arrested and jailed.

## 1950 – 1980

• Modern sexual revolution toward openness and honesty has caused the church's malevolent influence over sexuality to wane. In a last desperate effort, "modern" and new-wave churches evolved that adopted existentialist and fun views of sex in order to diminish the value and importance of sex. Thus, those churches kept control by undercutting people's self-esteem. Without self-esteem, one cannot experience abiding happiness or psychuous pleasures. Without self-esteem, a person will continue to be controlled by neocheaters using the tools of mysticism.

## 1980 – PRESENT

•An ominous rise of overt mysticism, born-again Christianity, and fundamentalist religions signal a turn back toward malevolent views of life, love, and sex. A revival of fundamentalism and theocratic concepts are conditions ultimately sought by all mystical leaders. No matter what deceptive facades they present, all mystical leaders are destructive neocheaters who ultimately want to reign with murderous power. But today, for the first time in history, mysticism and neocheating are being irreversibly undermined by the spreading Neo-Tech matrix.

By the way, Jews are generally more evolved, moral, productive, intelligent, creative, and potent than other groups of people. Why? Mainly because the Jewish religion is less harmful than religions or mysticisms engulfing other people. The Jewish religion itself is harmful and irrational as are all mystical religions and governments. But the Judeo ethics project less guilt toward value producers and less malevolence toward human values such as productive effort, sexual pleasures, creativity, self-sufficiency than do the much more virulent, envious ethics of Christianity (especially Roman Catholicism), Islam, and other evilly destructive religions. Also, the Jewish religion is more oriented around respect for self and less around respect for external "authority" such as government. Jewish people, therefore, have been freer to reject other mysticisms and live for their rational best interests. That allows them to more fully and guiltlessly develop their own creative and intellectual capacities to the maximum benefit of themselves, society, and civilization.

Women hold great potential for gaining economic and cultural power throughout the world. But their potential is undermined by politicians, feminists, and other value destroyers who use the government to force their egalitarian equalities on others. Physically weaker women are the easiest targets for their destructions. Thus, professional mystics and neocheaters more easily subject women to injustices and abuses to usurp power and values.[1] For that reason, throughout recorded history, women

[1]By oppressing women, men become easier to control.

280

have suffered greater oppression than have men as illustrated on the following pages:

## OPPRESSION OF WOMEN SINCE 1300 BC

### Ancient Greece
### 1300 B.C. – 450 B.C.

Homeric women (1300 B.C.-1100 B.C.) were relatively free and exercised considerable influence over men. But all women were subjected to double standards — legal and sexual.

### Enlightened Greece
### 450 B.C. – 27 B.C.

Courtesans held the highest positions of individual rights and personal respect available to women. Wives held the lowest position and were considered as housekeepers with few if any rights.

High-class prostitutes or courtesans were held superior to virtuous women and wives.

### Roman Empire
### 27 B.C. – 385 A.D.

With increased economic freedom, the drive for individual freedom brought new rights and respect for women. Oppression by mystics and conservatives decreased. Double standards diminished.

Drive for women's liberation and equality. As today, Roman feminists who advocated use of government controls and force to accomplish their ends failed in the long run by establishing the conditions for the increased oppression of women.

### Decline of the Roman Empire
### 100 A.D. – 385 A.D.

The spreading altruistic influence of Christianity began stripping

281

women of their individual rights and subjecting them to new, heavy oppressions while leading the civilized Western World toward asceticism and anti-sexual attitudes.

Christianity plunged Rome into asceticism, causing massive destruction and suffering. Women lost almost all rights with rising Christian power. ...Today, ominous parallels are developing with rising fundamentalist, born-again, anti-porn/anti-abortion movements.

Rise of Christianity
385 A.D. – 1000 A.D.

The Western World sank into the Dark Ages as women were pushed to their lowest position in recorded history. They had no individual or legal rights. The Church considered women as subhuman. In fact, the Roman Catholic Church considered women as wasteful property who could be killed, beaten, tortured, ravished or forced into slavery with impunity by theologians and "devout" noblemen.

Catholic bishops argued that women did not have mortal souls and that women were pieces of wasteful property. The Roman Catholic church sanctioned wife-beating. Killing a woman was not a very serious offense. Noblemen had the natural "right" to ravish any peasant woman.

Pre-Renaissance
1000 – 1300

The rise of courtly love and the de-emphasis of the Catholic Church began elevating women to emotional partners more equal to men. Respect and admiration for women increased with increased economic activity. But women still had few individual or legal rights. Extreme double standards were still practiced.

A new man-woman relationship developed that was previously unknown to Western civilization. Women gained respect and admiration. Courtly love elevated women from child bearers and

282

Yesterday's Victims; Tomorrow's Victors

lust satisfiers to more equal partners with men.

## The Church vs. the Renaissance
### 1300 – 1500

The Church fought viciously to stop the rising new concepts of romantic love, happy man-woman relationships, and pleasurable sex. Pope Innocent VIII started the inquisitions and witch trials. Millions of innocent women were killed, tortured, and burned to death by the Roman Catholic Church. But the growing enlightenment of the Renaissance with spreading economic freedoms began liberating the human mind and reason from the dark, brutal mysticism of Christian theology.

Renaissance noblemen equated women to beauty and good. The church fought back by promoting the "evils" of women and witchcraft. They advocated hanging "evil" women by their thumbs, twisting ropes around their heads, pushing needles under their nails, and pouring boiling oil on their feet in the "devout hope" of forcing confessions of their "wickedness". The Roman Catholic church then proceeded to burn to death tens of thousands of innocent women.

## The Puritans
### 1500 – 1700

With increasing economic activity, the Puritans rejected the Church's hatred of women, sex, and happiness. They accepted the normality of sex, pleasure, and happiness. Women's rights greatly improved under Puritanism. Women could divorce. They gained property and inheritance rights. Marriage became a civil contract.

## The Age of Reason
### 1700 – 1800

Men respected women for their minds and intellectual development. People involved in business began scrapping the gloom and hatred of Christianity and its idea that women were evil. Yet, women were still held as subservient to men.

Book 2
Neo-Tech Decoded

The rationalists rejected the malevolence of Christianity. But women were often considered as ornaments, toys, or nitwits.

### Pre- and Early Victorianism
### 1800 – 1850

Slobbering sensitivity became the ideal. Men sought shy, virginal women. The togetherness concept developed. Glorification of "pure" women was a pretext for a desperate last attempt by neocheating conservatives and the Church to subjugate women as servants of men. A great increase in double standards occurred under the guise of "moral" standards. Women lost considerable individual freedom.

Men grew shy and sought "pure" women. Virginal-type women were "glorified" and idealized. But that "morality" was only a new pretext for the continued subjugation of women by men. The U. S. Surgeon General, Dr. William Hammond, issued the warning that decent women should not feel the slightest pleasure during sexual intercourse. Many doctors considered sexual desire in women to be pathological. But women began revolting against their "purified" and "glorified" status.

### The Decline of Religion and Victorianism
### via the Rise of Capitalism and the
### Emancipation of Women
### 1850 – 1900

Capitalistic economics undermined the oppressive customs of the past and broke the unjust, feudal hierarchy of the social classes. Capitalism crippled the influence of the Church. Capitalism created the atmosphere and pressure for female suffrage, individual rights, divorce reform, and equal legal and economic rights. Victorianism was a desperate delaying action against increasing honesty, individuality, justice, earned equality, and rising economic freedoms.

With the rise of capitalism, women gained significant economic rights for the first time since the anti-Christian, pagan Roman

Empire. Capitalism broke the stifling, unjust religious/feudal-class patterns. A new optimism and cheerful happiness rose among the middle class. Capitalistic economics greatly accelerated the collapse of hypocritical snobbishness, racism, artificial social ties, and oppressive religious and social customs. The rigid Victorian home was threatened by increasing economic freedom for females, divorce reforms, and free-choice love. Victorianism was a last-stand action by the conservatives and the church against the inevitable, liberating changes caused by capitalism and a prosperous, industrial civilization.

The Emergence of 20th-Century
Romantic Love
1900 – 1960

Flourishing commerce among individuals, especially in America, discarded the anti-sexual, Victorian-Christian ethics. Double standards diminished with more equal educational, economic, legal, and sexual rights for women. Birth control and abortion rights were promoted. Capitalism liberated women and minorities by valuing all individuals according to their objective worth rather than to their sex, beliefs, social status, or race.

Women increasingly became equal to men in romantic relationships. Love patterns of all societies were drawn to the free and honest capitalistic style of Western love, which combined sexuality, affectionate friendship, productive work, and family functions...all into a single, equal-partner relationship. The modern, capitalist-generated, sexual revolution demolished most of the Christian-Victorian patterns of anti-sexual, patriarchal oppressiveness.

Modern Romantic Love
1960 – Present

The sexual revolution broke the last vestiges of inequalities between men and women. But today, renewed oppression of individual rights has begun to rise ominously with the feminist and religious movements against pornography and abortion.

285

Those movements are inspired by neocheating authorities seeking unearned power. Still, the majority of women have not fully exercised their new freedoms and rights. Many neocheating feminist leaders seek unearned gains through government coercion and force. And that force will boomerang to increasingly subjugate the rights of all women...and men.

Women who usurp feminist-inspired, unearned values are heading back toward dependence...toward being taken care of and eventually subjugated by men. In essence, the feminist movement is designed to coerce productive people into taking care of protesting women. The inevitable results are opposite the goals of freedom declared by feminist neocheaters. And those same ploys are destructively used by politicians to usurp "freedom" for blacks and other minorities. Indeed, the more unearned values usurped by the neocheating feminists and politicians, the more their recipient clients move toward dependence and subjugation. ...Neocheaters transfer values from the earned to the unearned while harming everyone, especially those they claim to help.

Individual freedom that naturally evolves from capitalism made possible modern romantic love and the liberation of women. For, the capitalistic free market put values on individuals according to their objective worth rather than their sex, social status, or race.

In recent years, radical changes have occurred to eliminate most differences in oppression between men and women. Those changes have occurred through the relentless, rational pressures of business and free enterprise, not through coercions of government, the feminists, or the non sequiturs of neocheating theologians, journalists, professors, and politicians.

The following chart summarizes the trend of human oppression over the past 3300 years. Also, as shown in the following chart, the government and church always oppressed women more than men. And, historically, those male neocheaters have always found physically weaker, more mystically dependent women their first and easiest target to bully into submission.

In exercising their unearned power, professional mystics and neocheaters gained added leverage by encouraging men to bully physically weaker women into submission. And they especially lured women into silliness — into following mystical stupidities such as astrology and religion. But with the rise of nonmystical, free-market economies, women have become increasingly productive, more independent, less mystical, thus less oppressed. And recently, for the first time in history, freedom for men and women has become nearly equal. But with today's reviving interest in the stupidities of mysticism and religion, more women are choosing to slip back into mystical lives controlled by others.

## FREEDOM/OPPRESSION LEVEL
+6=Maximum Freedom to
-6=Maximum Oppression

| Period | Men | Women |
|---|---|---|
| Ancient Greece 1300 B.C. – 450 B.C. | 0 | -1 |
| Enlightened Greece 450 B.C. – 27 B.C. | 0 | -3 |
| Roman Empire 27 B.C. – 385 A.D. | +1 | -1 |
| Christianity Established 200 A.D. – 385 A.D. | -2 | -4 |
| Rise of Christian Power (the unhappiest period in history) 385 A.D. – 1000 A.D. | -5 | -6 |
| Romantic Love Challenges Christianity 1000 – 1300 | -2 | -4 |
| Renaissance Weakens Christianity 1300 – 1500 | 0 | -1 |
| Church Fights Back with Witch Trials and Inquisitions 1300 – 1500 | -4 | -6 |

287

Book 2
Neo-Tech Decoded

| | | |
|---|---|---|
| The Puritans 1500 – 1700 | +1 | 0 |
| Age of Reason 1700 – 1800 | +1 | -1 |
| Early Victorianism 1800 – 1850 | +1 | -4 |
| Rise of Capitalism 1850 – 1900 | +2 | 0 |
| Rise of Romantic Love 1900 – 1960 | +3 | +1 |
| Sexual Liberation 1960 – 1980 | +3 | +2.5 |
| Rise of Mystical Stupidities: Evangelism via Television 1980 – 1990 | +2.5 | +1.5 |
| Rise of Neo-Tech: The End of Mysticism and Neocheating 1990 – ∞ steadily increasing to +6 | | +6 |

The long-term, general trend throughout history has been away from mysticism, poverty, stupidity, oppression, misery...and toward honesty, prosperity, intelligence, freedom, happiness: Away from the mystic-plagued Plato mind...and toward the mystic-free cosmic mind.

**At this moment, after two long days of intense thinking, research, and writing, my father had a Eureka Neothink experience. "But, of course!" he shouted. "Biological immortality!" He just pulled the integration string on the meaning of all he had been frantically writing for:** *eternal, happy life.* **Here, he writes about this Neothink advancement of human knowledge:**

**Biological Immortality (pulling the Neothink integration**

**string):** For thousands of years, essentially every human being has desperately repressed a crucial fact that every person must personally face alone. That fact is the fleeting briefness of human life and the finality of death. *Every* person who has ever lived exists but a few decades and then is gone forever. And without Neo-Tech, *every* person alive today will be completely and forever gone in a few brief decades. To repress or distort the reality of life's briefness and death's finality is a harmful act of mysticism with serious, long-term consequences on one's life and happiness.

Contrary to popular beliefs, children early in life understand death and its finality. Because of the mystical evasions and dishonesties of adults, most children gradually learn to evade reality with various mystical, life-after-death manipulations in order to repress the essential facts about life and death. Indeed, such religious notions are usually among children's first defaults to mysticism which, in turn, start undermining the efficacy of their minds through evasions of reality and repressions of emotions. On the other hand, dealing honestly with reality means consciously integrating into one's thoughts and actions the fact that permanent death will happen to oneself and everyone else within a brief time span. With that awareness, people, including children, place much more value on their lives, time, and actions in order to evolve to their full potential and achieve maximum happiness.

That honesty about death causes individuals to hold life in much higher esteem. Thus, they more fully meet the long-range, self-responsibilities required to gain maximum happiness and fulfillment from their brief lives. Such adults do not squander their lives on the nothingness of mysticism, but instead put greater effort into self-development in order to become more productive, accomplished, and happy. And they take better psychological and physical care of themselves.

By contrast, repressing the fact of life's briefness and death's finality lets people evade the precious value of their lives and time. That evasion allows default on their prime responsibility to live intensely — to achieve maximum self-development and growth.

Being fully conscious of life and death, people will value their lives beyond all else in the universe. And that valuation of human life as the supreme value rejects self-destructive acts of mysticism while establishing the psychological and motivational conditions needed to achieve commercial biological immortality.

On the other hand, repressing the fact of life's shortness and death's finality lets one rationalize laziness, mysticism, life-after-death myths, and all else that lead to unfulfilled or wasted lives. That repression also leaves one vulnerable to destructive exploitation by mystics, neocheaters, religions, and governments. But full awareness of one's fleeting, one-shot life span will counteract mysticism and laziness with a powerful appreciation of life. That, in turn, will stimulate the honest thinking and consistent efforts required to achieve prosperity and happiness. And achievement of happiness is the sole, moral purpose of human life.

Achieving happiness requires living according to man's nature. That means taking those long-range actions required for rational prosperity in order to enjoy life — to live happily. That also means cherishing and building the emotions of happiness, joy, and love during one's fleeting existence.

Non-aging biological immortality is the technology that will allow human beings to live physically and consciously forever with growing prosperity and happiness. That is man's highest moral goal. And, as Zon would have told me, such biological immortality is not only possible but becomes a mandatory moral obligation through man's self-invented consciousness.

First, important to understand is that the purpose of biological immortality is not to serve others, society, or mankind, but to preserve forever the most precious, important value in the universe — one's own individual, integrated physical and conscious self. For, the moral purpose of preserving anyone, including great value producers as Michelangelo, Mozart, Carnegie, or Einstein, is **not** to benefit society (even though society would enormously benefit), but to deliver the ultimate value to that lone individual. And the ultimate value is to continue living as an individual...to continue experiencing flesh-and-blood life, growth, thoughts, values, prosperity, love, and happiness forever.

So, whereas, the ultimate goal for conscious beings on planet

290

Earth is non-aging biological immortality, the supreme importance of that goal lies not in just preserving human consciousness but in preserving an individual's own sense of self...the continuous sense of "I-ness". Indeed, the most important value of human biological immortality lies not in preserving a creative, productive individual for the benefit of society, but in preserving that individual's sense of self for the benefit of himself and his loved ones — for his own continued happiness and growing enjoyment of life. Thus, the technological challenge lies not just in preserving consciousness, but in isolating and then preserving one's own sense of self...one's sense of "I-ness".

Preservation of that sense of "I-ness" for continued growth and enjoyment of individual life is man's highest value and moral goal.

You see, the development of human consciousness obsoleted nature's need for aging and death, for consciousness far surpasses nature's evolutionary process for species survival and for adapting to environmental changes. Indeed, conscious man today has nearly infinitely greater power to protect and improve life than nature itself. Thus, in nature, the function of death to protect and improve the species is obsolete for conscious beings. Indeed, death in nature still protects and preserves nonconscious life. But a tragic and unnecessary loss occurs on the death of each rational, conscious being. For conscious beings now have both the power and responsibility to prevent death — to preserve conscious life forever.

Today, human consciousness is a value that never needs to be lost to death. To muster, however, the resources and mind power in industry and science needed to achieve commercial biological immortality, Neo-Tech must first collapse the hoax of mysticism along with the specious, altruistic philosophies and neocheating psychologies that dominate all cultures today. Only through Neo-Tech will the commercial elimination of death become recognized as man's most urgent, important goal.

For 2000 years, organized religions have used various life-after-death manipulations to dissipate everyone's natural desire to live fully. Such manipulations cleverly repress the importance of life, leaving the neocheaters in control of those who accept those manipulations.

Also for 2000 years, many if not most everyone *did not* necessarily want to live forever. Everyone *free of mysticism,* however, would want to continue flourishing and living happily forever. But because the disease of mysticism infects most people to various degrees, almost everyone is blocked from deeply wanting to live forever. Instead, they think living forever would be boring. Without mysticism and neocheaters, however, the opposite would be true.

Infinite knowledge will always be generated through integrated thinking (rather than uncovered through perceptual thinking) forever into the future. Thus, open-ended, infinite, man-created new knowledge is forever generated without bounds or limits. Happy, exciting human life, therefore, can keep growing forever into the future.

Indeed, achieving biological immortality requires personal prosperity (which begets the *desire* to live forever) and personal freedom (which begets the *motivation* to technologically pull it off).

First, people can flourish with personal prosperity by eliminating personal mysticism. Mysticism reorients a person's consciousness from a natural, healthy happiness and life to an unnatural, unhealthy suffering and death. To the extent a person eliminates personal mysticism is the extent that the person flourishes with success, love, and growing happiness.

Second, people can flourish with personal freedom by eliminating neocheaters. Neocheaters reorient a society from a natural, healthy happiness and value production to an unnatural, unhealthy suffering and value destruction. To the extent society eliminates neocheaters is the extent that society flourishes with business, discoveries, and rapid progress.

Personal prosperity plus personal freedom will deliver biological immortality. The vehicle to biological immortality is business. Business is the highest evolution of consciousness, responsibility, and morality. No other living organism is even remotely able to function on a business level. Business creates essentially every major human value, ranging from the development of consciousness, language, mathematics, the arts, up to the electronic and biogenic revolutions. And now, from business will come commercial biological immortality.

*Yesterday's Victims; Tomorrow's Victors*

Indeed, when Neo-Tech philosophical and psychological conditions are established among the value producers, they will quickly recognize that biological immortality is the highest commercial and moral priority of business, science, and ethics. As the supreme value of human consciousness becomes understood and accepted, business will deliver the motivation, brain power, and resources to achieve biological immortality.

Again, achieving personal success and happiness in a free world are requisites for achieving commercial Biological Immortality. Those requisites require eliminating mysticism and neocheaters. Within any society free of mysticism and neocheating, the supreme value of human life would drive businesses to commercial biological immortality. The most efficient deployment of brain power and financial resources would be focused directly on achieving youth-rejuvenating immortality as quickly as possible. And at today's level of knowledge and technology, the goal of biological immortality could be accomplished within a decade.

Indeed, with the collapse of mysticism, the supreme value of conscious life will soar above all else. At the same time, the quintessential commercial product, *Youth-Rejuvenating Immortality*, will become stunningly obvious. And with that supreme valuation of conscious life combined with the collapse of mysticism, full mobilization efforts to develop commercial biological immortality will begin. All viable scientific, technical, and medical efforts will be directed into a rainbow of competitive products that will hurl mankind toward commercial biological immortality. With today's knowledge of Neo-Tech combined with our current level of technology and the free-market mobilization of commercial efforts, biological immortality could be available to everyone early into the third millennium.

**My father suddenly dropped his head down to the desk, sound asleep. He explained to me once that sometimes when he put together a breakthrough using Neothink, (like his Neothink understanding of biological immortality), his mind would sometimes become overwhelmed, short circuit and shut off via sudden sleep. When he woke up, he read over what he had written and was astounded by its implications. Just**

293

Book 2
Neo-Tech Decoded

## to get his bearings, he wrote the following summary:

Animals live, age, and die without choice, according to their environment and biological nature. That no-choice situation does not exist for human beings. Only human beings have the choice and power to control nature. People can learn to continuously expand the value of their lives. They do that by increasingly developing knowledge and productivity to experience increasing earned power, prosperity, and happiness. Likewise, people can learn how to continuously extend their biological/psychological lives through Neo-Tech knowledge, technology, and business. Youth-rejuvenating immortality is the supreme moral achievement for conscious beings as their individual lives become increasingly valuable with increasing age, knowledge, and experience.

Life can be immortal. Today, for the first time, no one has to age and then die — intellectually, psychologically, or physically. With current technology, free of mysticism and neocheating, commercial biological immortality for conscious beings is possible in a decade or less by not one but by several different scientifically feasible routes. Indeed, youth-perpetuating biological immortality will be quickly accomplished when the current anti-life, mystical/neocheating cultures are collapsed by Neo-Tech. With that collapse, the professional mystics and neocheaters will lose their power. In their place will rise a Neo-Tech/Neothink society in which the life of the individual is revered as the supreme value in the universe.

In a Neo-Tech/Neothink society, self-rejuvenation of and/or exact-replica replacement of body parts, including the entire body could be possible in less than ten years through already known biological techniques and future nanotechnologies. Today, however, the primary problem of achieving youth-rejuvenating immortality is *not* medical or technical, but is philosophical. ...With Neo-Tech curing the always terminal disease of mysticism, conscious life will change from always terminal to forever eternal.

Biological immortality could be achieved quickly in an unregulated, free-enterprise, Neo-Tech atmosphere. That business atmosphere of fully integrated thinking and honesty would boom commercial research seeking maximum profits from rejuvenation developments and immortality services. Non-aging biological

294

immortality would have the widest market and maximum value of any commercial product or service possible to conscious beings.

Yet, the enormous commercial and moral incentives to achieve human immortality remain unrecognized because of the prevailing, mystical, anti-life philosophies and the neocheating "authorities" whose control over value production prevent the motivation and freedom for producers to develop biological immortality.

If Einstein — or just his brain — could have been kept functioning after his death, imagine the additional benefits that mind would have bestowed on society: Is not that the main motivation for and value of immortality? Is not that the moral purpose of biological immortality?

No, absolutely not. That is an altruistic view that stymies the effort, motivation, and moral mandate needed to develop commercial I-ness immortality within our generation.

The entire purpose, motivation, and goal of biological immortality is not so a brain can continue to serve some "higher" cause, but so the flesh-and-blood individual, from an Einstein to a productive factory worker, can continue to physically enjoy life and create happiness for his or her own self and loved ones by continually producing values for others. As a result (*not* a purpose), the immortal individual will increasingly benefit others and society as that person becomes increasingly knowledgeable, experienced, and efficient at producing competitive values desired by others.

The value of Einstein's or anyone else's life is meaningful only to one's own flesh-and-blood life and living happiness, not to some society or "higher" cause.

Why do so many people *not* want to live forever? Because they fail to earn guiltless prosperity, love, and happiness needed to experience the passion to live and love forever.

The more people let mysticism influence their lives, the more they become unknowledgeable, undermine values, grow lazy, lose happiness, dislike life. With increasing mysticism, they become increasingly incompetent to earn honest values, power, love, and happiness. In addition, the more people accept mysticism, the more neocheaters can manipulate them. And the more manipulated and less successful one becomes, the more painful

295

and difficult life becomes until the idea of living forever becomes abhorrent, even terrifying. ...Only people who purge themselves of hateful, destructive mysticism can earn the values, power, and happiness needed to experience the passion to live and love forever.

Professional mystics and neocheaters have perfected and perpetuated their hoax of inverted values for the past 2000 years. But today, Neo-Tech is in forward motion around the world. The Neo-Tech matrix is spreading. It is unstoppable, irreversible, and will collapse the entire destructive hoax of mysticism. No mystic or neocheater can stop Neo-Tech from eliminating mysticism and its symbiotic neocheaters.

With life ageless and immortal, mystic-free conscious beings can forever experience growing prosperity, love, happiness, and life itself through productive work, romantic love, psychuous pleasures, and I-ness immortality. ...The moral purpose of all conscious life would then be met — increasing happiness forever.

**My father dropped his pen and leaned back in his leather chair, oblivious of the chill of the leather against his bare back. "This is the meaning of my life...my calling that I have always searched for and henceforth live my life for: I now live to bring about the mystic-free conditions that will bring us biological immortality. I now live to achieve and experience biological immortality!" my father exalted. ...Later that month, he talked to me about his incredulous insight. Although only a teenager, my spirit and soul grabbed onto and never let go of that mission in life — to obsolete death. From that moment forward, both my father and I knew with a passion what our mission was in life.**

**In amazement how others did not respond favorably as I had, over the years my father pondered the following thought: What hidden societal virus diminished the human spirit so that people were so blah about life? About the same time that I had my Six Visions (in your *God-Man* manuscript), my father finally had an answer to people's puzzling apathy for life. Indeed, he finally did find a very small, hard-to-see societal virus that weakened everyone's energy for life. He called the societal virus *"the pips"*, as follows:**

296

## Yesterday's Victims; Tomorrow's Victors

**The Pips:** The greatest human spirits are always attacked by the smallest human spirits. What is the greatest? What is the smallest? First the smallest: As a law of nature, everything in existence can be reduced to a smallest unit or quantum — be it an electron or quark for mass or a photon for energy. Beneath mass and energy lie resonating strings with dimensions less than $10^{-35}$ meters. Those strings create spacetime mass, energy, and consciousness. Beneath those dimensions lie an ether of hypothetical Gravity Units that form a universal sea of eternal geometries. ...Somewhat analogously, the human spirit can also be reduced to a smallest unit or dot. The next step down is not to a smaller dot; the next step down is to nothing...except that universal sea of geometries.

Now, consider life itself. Consider that viruses and bacteria are among the smallest, simplest forms of life. Yet, those smallest forms of life can and do destroy the most complex, most valuable forms of life — conscious human beings. A similar parallel exists with the human spirit. The smallest, most malevolent spirits can and do destroy the greatest, most benevolent spirits.

Those smallest spirits are the self-proclaimed "victims" of this world. *They create problems where none exist.* Such "victims" can destroy all that is valuable to human life. By contrast, genuine victims are those whose lives are diminished through force or fraud by governments, religions, criminals. But, self-proclaimed "victims" are those who diminish their *own* lives by blaming the value producer for their own self-made problems.

A close cousin of the self-proclaimed "victim" is the "pip". A pip is also a small, diminished human spirit who creates problems where none exist. The pip generally tries to build a pseudo self-esteem and often a bogus livelihood at the expense of genuine value producers, especially businesspeople, employers, entrepreneurs. Pips try to feel morally or intellectually superior by berating great values and their creative producers. Pips attack with dishonest, out-of-context criticisms and non sequitur accusations. ...Great value producers, especially in business, are constantly attacked by the pips in political, journalistic, academic, and entertainment circles designed to conserve the stagnating Establishment.

297

To understand those smallest spirits and their destructiveness, one must first recognize the greatest human spirits and how they lift humanity to ever greater heights of stimulating well being.

In time, Ayn Rand will be recognized as a giant among giants in history who changed civilization on Earth dramatically for the better. Ayn Rand rose by fiercely struggling to escape the bloodiest, most oppressive cult in history — Communism under Lenin and Stalin in the Soviet Union. Then, emigrating to relatively free-enterprise America, Ayn Rand, by her own decisions and titanic efforts, broke through seemingly impossible language, economic, and cultural barriers in rising to the highest level of literary accomplishment. She then arose atop the pinnacle field of knowledge — philosophy — which, until Rand, had been dominated for 2500 years exclusively by men. Thus, as is being increasingly recognized today, Ayn Rand is posthumously becoming one of the most stimulating benefactors to grace planet Earth. Yet, she was and is still today attacked and ridiculed by nearly the entire panoply of stagnant Establishment elites with their arrays of self-proclaiming authorities, "victims", and pips. ...In fighting for her values and achievements, Ayn Rand always dismissed such persons as boring pip-squeaks not worth a moment of anyone's time.

Other exciting great spirits include Joseph Smith (the super-competitive Mormon business-and-city builder), Andrew Carnegie, Jay Gould, Florence Nightingale, John D. Rockefeller, Henry Ford, Ray Kroc, Mary Kay Ash, Michael Milken, Leona Helmsley. Many were vilified and drained by political demagogues and self-proclaimed "victims". All such great spirits are harmed by, destroyed by, or killed by the Establishment wielding its "victim" and pip tools.

Consider another example involving the greatness of human spirit: Year after year in the 1940s and 1950s, the giant chemical firm, E.I. du Pont de Nemours, Inc., was rated by business publications as the best managed company in the world with a consistent 20%+ annual return on investment. Through decades of unmatched success, Du Pont became the largest, most exciting company in the world. Then, latching onto the envious attacks by whining business "victims" and pips, the Federal Government penalized Du Pont for its success by forcing the company to terminate its ownership of General Motors.

Du Pont rose from its inception in 1802 as a family-managed explosives and gunpowder manufacturer to become the premier research and industrial company in the world, delivering huge values to society. Du Pont's ever increasing rate of success peaked in the late 1940s with the last du Pont family member in control: Pierre S. du Pont, one of history's most emulated businessmen. His revolutionary decentralized management concepts and accounting methods remain the essence of essentially all successfully managed, large corporations to this day. The stimulating benefits that the Du Pont Company bestowed on the business world, on its customers, and on its employees were not only without match, but served as a farsighted model for all successful, big businesses.

Du Pont was the innovator and leader not only in competitively producing invaluable products for society but in pioneering for its employees various safety and pension plans, medical insurance, stock-and-saving plans, even alcohol-and-drug treatment programs long before most other companies even conceived of such sound business practices. Never was a company more helpful to the business world, more valuable to customers, more beneficial to employees. And, never did a giant company struggle as hard to avoid stagnating government contracts and favors as did Du Pont when it was managed by Pierre S. du Pont.

Du Pont began declining from its pinnacle business position in the 1950s when, through the envious dynamics of self-proclaimed "victims", a wave of asset-milking executives took control from the asset-building du Pont family. Those asset-milking executives did not care what happened to the business after their tenure. They did not plan 50 and 100 years ahead as the generational-planning executives had done since the founding of Du Pont in 1802. Indeed, after P.S. du Pont, waves of self-aggrandizing political executives milked the previous 150 years of du Pont-built assets. ...Such asset-milking executives work only for their short-term personal wealth, power, and status.

Adopting the John Maynard Keynes evil concept "In the long run, we are all dead", such political-type executives are not concerned about the future health of their companies, their employees, or society. Implementing asset destroying policies, they ignore the consequences on the future of their companies and society. Like their soulmates, the politicians, the real harm of their self-serving agendas become obvious only after they are gone.

Such political executives, through their own short-sighted agendas, implicitly sanction unjust attacks and torts by business/ employee "victims" against the greatest, most beneficent business enterprises. ...Those self-proclaimed "victims" manipulated by politicians, lawyers, and journalists sow the cancer seeds that eventually cripple or destroy genuine competition — the most aggressive value-and-job producers and their businesses.

Why does acting as a "victim" or pip shrink one's spirit to the smallest unit — to the shallowest level of a human being? How can such shallow people be the prime destructive force in today's civilization? And, specifically, how will Neo-Tech in cyberspace vanish such "victim"-like viruses and pip-like bacteria? In a moment, we will look at four specific examples of horrendous destructions done to the greatest lives by parasitical-elite humanoids with their manipulations of "victims" and pips. Then we will demonstrate how cyberspace will end such life-draining dynamics. ...The four examples with one solution are:

The Marx/Lenin/Business/"Victim" Example
The Hitler/Jew/"Victim" Example
The Giuliani/Media/Michael Milken/"Victim" Example
The Giuliani/Media/Leona Helmsley/"Victim" Example
and then
The Neo-Tech/"Victim"/Cyberspace Solution

But first, let us make this point: No one can be a victim of private business per se. Victims are impossible <u>when</u> <u>no</u> force or fraud is involved. One can be a victim <u>only</u> <u>when</u> force or fraud is manifested by governments, religions, or criminals. The employer and employee always fill each others needs voluntarily, consensually. No matter what the conditions, barring acts of force or fraud by either party, neither the employer nor the employee can *ever* be a victim. ..."Exploitation by business" is a conceptual hoax perpetuated by the parasitical-elite class, pips, and "victims".

300

Profit-motivated businesses never purposely harm anyone — much less employees or customers. Such behavior would be irrational and contrary to competitive business success. The essence of every successful business is to maximally enhance everyone's job, livelihood, and standard of living under the conditions required for competitive value production. By contrast, every self-proclaiming business/employee "victim" and pip works to harm successful businesses and their employees.

**Great lives and achievements** are destroyed by **the smallest human spirits.** But, if such "victims" and pips have shrunken their spirits to the lowest level, how can they be so destructive as to hobble the greatest human spirits and businesses? ...The staggering extent of those virus-caused destructions is demonstrated in the following four examples:

### The Marx/Lenin/Business/"Victim" Example

Most people believe that politicians — the Lenins, Hitlers, and Maos — are the fundamental cause of history's greatest destructions of human lives and property. They are not. The root cause of purposeful destructions among human beings and their achievements are those smallest units of the human spirit: the envious self-proclaimed "victims" of value-producing businesses and employers. Politicians simply step in and manipulate the claims of those "victims" and pips as tools to drain progress, values, jobs, and lives from everyone.

Without self-proclaiming "victims", Marx and Engels could never have developed their political theories or written the *Communist Manifesto*. Without the proletariat "victims" with their envious desires to destroy private business, Lenin would not have had the tools to diminish and destroy hundreds of millions of lives during his reign...and for three generations after his death.

### The Hitler/Jew/"Victim" Example

Hitler conjured up bogus complaints to evolve envious "victims" of Jewish businessmen, bankers, and other Jewish value producers. Those phoney, self-proclaimed "victims" allowed Hitler to kill millions of Jews and other innocent people throughout Europe during his era of holocausts and conflagrations.

301

...Without those self-proclaimed "victims", Hitler would have been powerless.

### The Giuliani/Media/Michael Milken/"Victim" Example

The hard-driving financier Michael Milken turned America around from an uncompetitive, depression-bound economy in the early 1980s to an internationally vibrant, competitive economy that continues even years after he was stopped by government force and jailed.

How did Michael Milken accomplish such a feat that saved and protected seemingly doomed livelihoods for millions of Americans? He accomplished that fifteen-year turnaround of the American economy by driving a competitive stake into the heart of giant Corporate America while driving out its stagnant executives. Those executives were milking great pools of assets built by previous generations of forward-essence-moving entrepreneurs and businesspeople.

Milken developed unstoppable techniques to dump those executives by taking over the assets they were parasitically wasting. He then turned those stagnant assets over to hard-driving, business-oriented managers who once-again unleashed the growth of those assets, thus, saving many old companies, starting many new companies, and revitalizing the dying American economy.

What happened to that brilliant, heroic man? Was he rightfully honored and congratulated by a grateful nation and its leaders? No, he was dishonestly vilified by the stagnant business Establishment, libeled and slandered by the media Establishment, prosecuted by the politically rabid Rudolph Giuliani criminally wielding evil RICO "laws", and finally jailed by a higher-office-seeking, ego-agenda judge Kimba Woods. Besides crushing and jailing that great spirit, those parasitical elites destroyed one of the great financial companies in America, Drexel Burnham Lambert, wiping out the jobs for thousands of innocent value producers and their families. Why? For no other reason than to expand the destructive livelihoods and inflate the false egos of those parasitical elites wielding bogus, gun-backed, political-agenda laws.

How can such destructions and injustices exist? How can

they be so deeply camouflaged? What morbid irrationalities cause such a 180 degree inversion of values? Milken and his company committed no objective crimes. Instead, with great daring and exciting effort, they delivered incalculable values to society. Indeed, while those parasitical elites were drum-beating the innocent Michael Milken into condemnation and prison, they themselves were committing sweepingly destructive crimes not only against Michael Milken and Drexel Burnham but against all Americans. Yet, the parasitical-elite class itself, even with all its dishonest politicians, corrupt media, armed bureaucrats, and life-appointed ego judges cannot commit their crimes of forced enchainment without their tools — without their collections of "victims" and pips.

How can professional parasites commit such massive harm without society identifying the "victim" tool? How? By fraudulently generalizing the "victims" parasitical claims across the entire public spectrum. Those frauds backed by dishonest political-correctness pressures let professional parasites like Giuliani drain and destroy the value producers with near impunity. Those fraudulent people crush great spirits like Michael Milken and Leona Helmsley.

### The Giuliani/Media/Leona Helmsley/"Victim" Example

In the fiercely competitive New York hotel market, Leona Helmsley was perhaps the only person who had the toughness and ability to capture the first-class niche market for her Helmsley Hotels. She was perhaps the only person who could successfully create, expand, and manage this particular business that daily delivered values to thousands of highly discriminating customers while providing good livelihoods for thousands of employees.

Leona Helmsley was exceedingly hard working, value driven, detail-and-numbers oriented, and honest. Slack off or drop one element in her formula and the entire business could stop growing and begin declining toward eventual noncompetitiveness and failure. ...As Arthur Miller in his play *Death of a Salesman* portrayed — in the constant, fierce struggle to stay competitive, a person needs only to allow a single soil spot on one's hat to cause that unnoticed 180 degree turn from moving up to moving

303

down toward loss and ruin.

Few could ever begin to appreciate the constant hard work, discipline, and attention to detail required daily, hourly by Leona Helmsley to remain competitive in providing expanding values and continuous livelihoods for thousands of fellow human beings.

No, she was never appreciated or honored for her beneficent and sustained value production. Instead, she was vilified by a malevolently destructive establishment media, especially the perniciously dishonest *Newsweek* with its jury-inflaming "Queen of Mean" and "Rhymes with Rich" cover stories. And, during a year in which she paid $75,000,000 in taxes, not to mention the millions in taxes paid by the thousands of individuals for whom she created jobs, political predator Rudolph Giuliani swaggered in to criminally prosecute that totally innocent, heroic 72-year-old woman. He then jailed her in collusion with a life-appointed, ego-agenda judge, John M. Walker, Jr., on conjured-up charges involving a 0.5% error on the $75,000,000 she paid in taxes.

The result? A great spirit was jailed, torn not only from her business but from her dying husband whom she devotedly loved. Her business and the jobs she provided were set on a declining path. And her elderly, ill husband was cruelly left to suffer alone. Yet, the criminals who belonged in jail were rewarded for their brutal crimes against innocent people and great value-and-job producers. ...Political humanoid Rudolph Giuliani was rewarded with the Mayorship of New York City for jailing innocent giants like Michael Milken and Leona Helmsley.

Criminals such as Giuliani would easily kill like Hitler and Stalin given the power and opportunity. Yet, none of those evil people would have the power to do any destructions without their tools of disgruntled business/employee "victims" and attack-mode pips to act as deadly viruses. In Leona Helmsley's case, the dishonest media and criminal-minded Giuliani used a few disgruntled or fired employee "victims" to vilify, libel, slander, and jail that heroic woman.

Using "victims" and pips combined with subjective, political-agenda laws, the Giulianis of this world manipulate the majority into praising tyrants for criminally exploiting minorities, starting with the smallest of minorities — the individual human spirit, the minority of one, the individual value producer. ...Tyranny depends on politician-made subjective law: Tyranny has little concern for objective crime, but is gravely concerned with the parasitical control of others...and eventually the parasitical control of everyone.

Politician-made, subjective/offensive law was actively promoted by Oliver Wendell Holmes, the past Chief Justice of the U.S. Supreme Court...and more recently by judges like Robert H. Bork. Opposite to such subjective/offensive law is unchanging, objective/defensive law, universally principled law — natural law — promoted by fully integrated honesty and backed by Objectivist philosophy. Objective law protects individual property rights, which, in turn, protects every individual — every minority of one — from tyranny. By contrast, unprincipled political law and giuliani "justice" always moves government toward criminality and despotism fueled by self-proclaimed "victims" and pips. ...Politician-made subjective law endangers and eventually crushes everyone. Universal objective law protects and frees everyone.

Two final questions: First, why do political humanoids like Lenin, Hitler, and Giuliani wreak such destructions on the value producers? For three reasons: (1) their parasitical survival, (2) their self-aggrandizing pseudo power, and (3) their desperate ego enhancements. And, second, what gives them that power? The whining "victims" and attack-mode pips who enviously place the blame for their own inadequacies, stagnations, and failures onto successful individuals and businesses. In fact, only genuine value producers are useful as targets for politicians using "victims" and pips as their tools.

As previously identified, such "victims" and pips have generally accomplished little or nothing outstanding in their lives — little or nothing about which they can be proud. Because of their smallness, the public cannot easily focus on them, notice them, or even detect them. Indeed, politicians can be only superficially criticized because their means to destructive power are camouflaged behind those "victims" and pips. And, such people are usually too small, too pip-squeakish to be noticed, much less held accountable for their destructions.

In the noncyberspace world, little can be done to counteract

305

those deadly politician/"victim"/pip combinations.  Now, however, for the first time arises a cyberspace world here on Earth. Indeed, cyberspace is already crumbling those evil-spirited value destroyers as illustrated below.

### The Neo-Tech/"Victim"/Cyberspace Solution

I & O Publishing Company, which was founded in 1968, moved past its publish-for-profit dynamics during the early 1980s to focus on a single goal: curing the disease of mysticism worldwide.  Interest evaporated in building wealth, assets, a business, or a publishing company per se.  Multimillion dollar business opportunities were abandoned or turned down, including a million-dollar-a-month *profit*-potential, back-end marketing program offered by the largest, most successful infomercial firm in the world.

Why were such profit opportunities turned down?  Because efforts directed toward non-goal related profits would break the forward-movement concentration required to reach I & O's single goal of curing the disease of mysticism or irrationality.  Avoiding non-goal profit dynamics let the prime movers at I & O Publishing focus maximum time and energy on ridding this planet of its worst disease — irrationality, from which flows dishonesty, stagnation, crime, failure, and death itself.

Developing and distributing the knowledge required to cure irrationality, especially when faced with hostile resistance worldwide, was a difficult, dangerous task requiring full focus of every essence mover at I & O.  During the 1980s, every action and resource was directed toward undermining the parasitical-elite class, which was the first-step ingredient for curing irrationality in America.

Under increasingly hostile conditions from a giuliani-oriented Establishment, I & O Publishing Company was vulnerable to being attacked and silenced.  Indeed, such attacks finally happened in the late 1980s when just one ex-employee "victim" was seized and then manipulated by the giulianied legal Establishment.  With that one "victim" as their only needed tool, armed federal agents physically attacked I & O Publishing and destroyed its work while beating, kicking, and hospitalizing one of its editors, seizing its assets and research funds, carrying away its literature and computer files, and finally, in violation of the first amendment, imprisoning its founder for his writings, literature distributions, and billboard displays that identified the criminal acts of those armed federal agents. ...I & O Publishing Company was destroyed by gun-backed violence, forever put out of business by criminal force.

But, ideas cannot be destroyed by guns, fists, or prisons. Neo-Tech Publishing Company and its phantom bantam companies are now scattered worldwide. Momentum toward curing irrationality is rising phoenix-like, quietly, relentlessly.

Indeed, in cyberspace, Neo-Tech is beyond the reach of those destructive forces left behind in the noncyberspace anticivilization. Throughout cyberspace, integrated honesty rules. Dishonesty, force, fraud, "victims", and pips appear increasingly freakish as those tools of destruction disappear in cyberspace. Moreover, "victims" and pips — those smallest of human spirits — are compelled in cyberspace to quit whining, quit blaming others, and grow up by accepting the responsibility for solving their own personal problems.

New knowledge changes the world. Throughout history, whenever sea-change knowledge evolved from wider-scope observations and conceptual integrations, initial rejection of that new knowledge always occurred. Sooner or later, however, a tiny percentage of people investigated enough to independently grasp that knowledge through those new, wider-scope perspectives. That new knowledge then began spreading as its efficacy was increasingly demonstrated. Finally, that knowledge was utilized to bring unique streams of unstoppable benefits.

Over the ages, such sea-change phenomena have occurred for good and for evil. For example, early in the 20th century, after an initial surge of acceptance, Vladimir Lenin lost essentially all support and understanding. Alone and rejected in Geneva, he discovered two other people who fully understood his matrix for revolution. He then excitingly announced that the revolution was won. Sure enough, in a matter of months after that announcement, Lenin triumphantly entered Russia through Finland. Then, by generalizing his matrix, he advanced on a straight line route to winning his bloody revolution that eventually brought devastation and misery to two-thirds of the world for three

307

generations.

About that same time, Albert Einstein worked alone for years on developing his non understood and widely ignored theory of relativity. After discovering three or four others who understood his wide-scope integrations of relativity, he excitingly worked to generalize his theory with cheerful confidence. Within a decade, the revolution of general relativity was won worldwide forever.

By contrast, about that same time, Karl Menger, the Aristotelian father of capitalistic/market-based economics, worked with increasing pessimism...as later did Ayn Rand who founded Objectivist philosophy, and as more recently did Leonard Peikoff who brilliantly developed Objectivism into an array of specific values and products. Menger, Rand, and Peikoff never fully generalized their work. Therefore, they never confidently sensed the ultimate triumph of their work as did Lenin for evil and Einstein for good.

Neo-Tech uniquely generalizes *all* values, including Objectivism, into practical, profitable uses for *all* individuals in all activities. Indeed, grasping the eternally wide-scope ideas, methods, and integrations throughout Neo-Tech becomes an endless succession of unfolding Ahas! In fact, around the globe lies an exciting Aha! revolution to be sparked when fifty million people are exposed to Neo-Tech. That critical mass will lead the march into a new civilization over just a few years.

That critical mass is more than enough to secure the prosperity revolution that will bring a Neo-Tech civilization to everyone on Earth. However, we will not rest until fifty million Neo-Tech Books have reached the people.

The rational, compatible dynamics of nature have been contradicted for the past 3000 years in forming today's irrational, parasite-ruled anticivilization. Human consciousness combined with the disease of irrationality (i.e., mysticism) drives human beings into chaotic contradictions and paralyzing stagnations — away from reliable consistency and liberating prosperity. Now, however, the emerging Neo-Tech dynamics in cyberspace are drawing conscious beings out of this unnatural anticivilization and toward the natural Civilization of the Universe.

Because of everyone's life-long investments in this irrational anticivilization, however, no one can leave without the escape engines of Neo-Tech and Zonpower. In this parasite-ruled civilization, conscious life is incredibly brief, during which aging and death come quickly, unnecessarily. Only the tiniest fraction of conscious potential — the potential of exciting productivity, romantic love, eternal happiness — is achieved by all of us entrapped in this anticivilization.

Why has no one escaped this bizarre, up-side-down anticivilization? Why has no one discovered the natural, exciting, eternal Civilization of the Universe? Because, without the escape route of Neo-Tech/Zonpower, no one can abandon his or her fatal, lifelong investments in this anticivilization. But, now, today, with the newly available Neo-Tech/Zonpower engines, people can finally scrap their death-trap investments and discover the limitless wealth and romance possible in a rational, objective-law civilization.

**"Who started the anticivilization?" my father asked Zon one morning. Of course, my dad did not expect an answer, but he found he could Neothink most freely when he sat in front of the mountain. When my father got home later that morning, he wrote his answer — his last note in a big box of notes titled, simply, *From A Mountain Called Zon:***

**Plato:** Plato's philosophy provided the foundation for subsequent philosophies involving mysticism, sacrifice, and the use of force to achieve "higher" goals. Plato's philosophy also provided the basic tools for rationalizing laziness.

Still, Plato, the father of the criminal mind, was one of the most original, creative thinkers in history. His work was the first widely integrated philosophical system recorded *in writing*. The depth and breadth of his integrations were quickly matched and then surpassed by the philosophical writings of his student — Aristotle, the father of the business mind.

But much of Plato's credit, particularly the sounder aspects of his philosophical system, perhaps belongs to his teacher, Socrates. Unfortunately, Socrates never recorded in writing his ideas or philosophical system. No writings of Socrates are known to exist. And knowledge of his work was left to the mercy and plagiarism of Plato, who perhaps deleted crucial Aristotelian-like

309

views that would have contradicted Plato's own manipulated views. Nevertheless, Socrates was probably the first man to develop a broadly integrated philosophical system.

Plato held enormous leverage with his great intellectual and creative abilities. Thus, profound philosophical errors would occur if he were tilted even slightly toward immaturity, dishonesty, mysticism, and neocheating. And that is what happened. Some of the most integrated aspects of Plato's philosophical system are in profound error. His errors involve the integration of dishonesties, mysticism, "higher purposes", the use of force, and the exercise of authoritarian power into a full-blown, ethical philosophical system of enormous deception and dishonesties.

Furthermore, the foundation of Plato's philosophy is not based on reality, but on mysticism. His philosophy does not recognize the life of the individual human being as the prime value or even an important value. Indeed, Plato is not a man to be respected. For he was an immature, dishonest conniver who wreaked death and destruction on this world for over 2000 years. He subordinated human beings to arbitrary "higher" powers and mystical "values". Yet, the tight inner logic and integrated completeness of his specious philosophy provided great staying power for his false ideas. Thus, his spurious philosophy became the intellectual foundation of all subsequent specious philosophies, religions, and political systems.

Plato provided the tools for rationalizing an "intellectual" basis for any false or specious approach, including Dewey's educational approach. Platonistic philosophy can "justify" any irrational or unjust means to "noble" ends or "higher" causes. That same philosophy provides the tools for rationalizing the two primary character faults of conscious beings — dishonesty and laziness.

Aristotle, on the other hand, provided the tools that every person needs to develop the knowledge necessary for guiding his or her life to unlimited prosperity, psychuous pleasures, and abiding happiness. Aristotelian philosophy provides the tools for meeting the needs of the human organism for optimum survival and maximum happiness. Successful use of those tools requires integrated honesty and rational efforts.

310

Plato's philosophical system has been the greatest tragedy of our civilization. But at last, today, Neo-Tech is in the process of eliminating that tragedy.

By contrast, Aristotle was perhaps the greatest intellectual power in history. He built his philosophical system on objective, noncontradictory premises by placing objective reality as the only basis of honesty. Aristotle placed the individual conscious being as the supreme value on Earth. ...The philosophical roots of Aristotle lead to Neo-Tech.

Major competitive advantages accrue to those who use Neo-Tech knowledge to reject mystical, Platonistic-based frauds.

**My father continued researching and writing for weeks, months, years. As a trained Research Scientist, he began reaching out to the Universe through Neo-Tech Physics. There, he envisioned something called the Civilization of the Universe — eternally rational, mystic-free civilizations that survived their Nuclear Decision Thresholds. He believed that our civilization can and should join the mystic-free Civilization of the Universe, which now became his life's goal. For, by joining the mystic-free Civilization of the Universe, man would quickly develop non-aging biological immortality. My father's amazing project, to map the way there, flowed from his pen day after day, guided by Zon. In time, he would discover civilization's deepest secret: *Zon is mystic-free man; Zon is God-Man.***

Book 2
Neo-Tech Decoded

---

Author's Note
My father, Dr. Frank R. Wallace, is the discoverer and author of the original Neo-Tech Discovery. The metaphorical use of the Mountain called Zon in this Neo-Tech Decoded publication is closer to an actual event than you might think. Early each morning, my father would run by a mountainous terrain and go into deep thoughts. The voice of Zon, of course, was his own thoughts as they achieved Neothink status. His encounters with Zon were his encounters with his own God-Man (see *God-Man: Our Final Evolution*, Neo-Tech Books). In fact, Zon *is* God-Man. ...You can now become God-Man and a citizen in the Civilization of the Universe.

---

Book Three

# Poker

## A Guaranteed Income For Life

By
**Frank R. Wallace**

# USE THIS BOOK WITH CAUTION!

Armed with the **advanced concepts of poker** that this book teaches, you know how to play good poker — and how to force others into playing poor poker. You know when to bet, raise and bluff — how to elicit bets, raises and bluffs from those you have to beat. You know how to read the hands and intentions of opponents, how to extract the maximum money from them — how to bankrupt them. You are in control of the game and its players. You can lure them into following their emotions, into losing control of themselves, into disorienting their psyches...even into destroying themselves.

# HOW FAR CAN YOU GO WITH POKER?

*Let your conscience and your goals be your guide.*

# Special Features!

- A complete glossary, bibliography and history of poker.

- The only accurately defined table of odds ever published.

# PREFACE

You can earn $50,000 a year by playing poker...yes, even more if you want to. Any man or woman can get rich by applying the "Advanced Concepts of Poker".

This book is for the penny-ante novice as well as the professional poker player; this book is for anyone who will ever pick up a poker hand. Once you are familiar with the "Advanced Concepts of Poker", your only limitation in winning money is the extent you choose to apply these concepts.

What is your goal in poker? Do you want to get rich, be the biggest winner in the game, gain confidence, punish another player, or just have more fun? Define what you want, then increasingly apply the "Advanced Concepts of Poker" until you reach your goal. How far should you go?... That depends on you, your conscience, and your goals.

# CAUTION

The poker player armed with the "Advanced Concepts of Poker" knows how to play good poker—he also knows how to force others into playing poor poker. He knows when to bet, raise, and bluff  he also knows how to elicit bets, raises, and bluffs from those he has beat. He knows how to read the hands and intentions of opponents—he also knows how to delude opponents into misreading his hands and intentions. ...But most importantly, the poker player armed with the "Advanced Concepts of Poker" knows how to extract maximum money from his opponents-he knows how to bankrupt them.

...And most dangerously, the poker player armed with the "Advanced Concepts of Poker" knows how to control the game and its players-he knows how to control and manipulate the minds of players. He knows how to lure players into following their emotions, into losing control of themselves, into disorienting their psyches...even into destroying themselves.

7

# INTRODUCTION

Every week millions of poker players lose more money than many nations spend in a year.* Around the world, billions of dollars await those knowing more than the basic concepts and techniques of poker. ...The opportunities for the good player are great.

From 1850 to 1977, over one-hundred and fifty books have been published about poker—none focus on the concept of extracting maximum money from a poker game. This book reveals methods to win maximum money from any game. This book also describes methods to generate more money by quickening the betting pace, raising the stakes, expanding the game, creating new games, and finding bigger games... This book shows how amateurs and professionals alike can win a guaranteed income from poker—in private games or in public casinos.

The player who knows and applies the "Advanced Concepts of Poker" is a rare person...few have ever played against him. He can win money so fast that he could bankrupt most games at will. But he controls his winnings and preserves the game in order to extract maximum money from his opponents. He camouflages his poker skill; his opponents seldom realize that he is taking all their money.

* *A LIFE magazine article (August 16, 1968) about poker reported that 47,000,000 poker players in the United States wager 45 billion dollars annually...Most poker players are poor players who lose both their time and their money in poker. The good players with, all the money the poor players lose.*

Once familiar with the "Advanced Concepts of Poker", any player can—

- recognize the good player

- guard against the good player

- develop into a good player.

The "Advanced Concepts of Poker" are objective and realistic. Many involve deception. Some are ruthless. A few are immoral.* Know them and be wiser. Apply them and get richer. * *

*None of the "Advanced Concepts of Poker" employ cheating, but a few are immoral because they involve deception outside the poker game. The good player, however, does not need to use a single immoral concept to achieve his goals. So why include immoral concepts? This book is a definitive treatment of poker and, therefore, all concepts are included. Also, by identifying the immoral concepts, the reader can recognize them and take defensive measures when such concepts are used against him.*

**This Manual identifies the true nature of winning poker as a highly profitable but a time-consuming, nonproductive activity that requires bringing out the worst in each opponent. In certain cases, therefore, poker can work against the good player's self-esteem and happiness no matter how much he wins.*

# CONTENTS

## PART FIVE
### GAMES

## PART SIX
### PROFESSIONAL AND PUBLIC POKER

15

## APPENDICES

## TABLE OF TABLES

## TABLE OF ILLUSTRATIONS

# The
# Advanced Concepts
# of Poker

How much money can you win at poker? It makes no difference if you are a professional poker player, a novice, or have never played poker before[3]... the following 120 Advanced Concepts of Poker can guide any man or woman to unlimited winnings. How much you win depends on how fully and how many of these concepts you choose to apply.

[3] *Complete Beginners: The basic rules and concepts of poker are simple. They can be mastered after a few hours' exposure to any poker game. Beginners, however, should avoid the advice in most other poker books, for as shown in Concept 7 and in the bibliography, their advice is often based on spurious clichés and a faulty understanding of poker that assures one of never becoming a good player.*

# PART ONE

# DEFINITIONS

Definitions of the broadest aspects of poker (i.e., the game, odds, betting, players, emotions, and concepts) are given in the following pages as contextual descriptions. Definitions of specific words or phrases used in poker are given in the Glossary in Appendix C.

# I

# GAME OF POKER (1)[4]

The object of poker is to win maximum money. Poker is not a card game; poker is a game of deception, manipulation and money management. Cards are merely the tools for manipulating opponents and money. From the smallest penny-ante game to the largest table stake game, all money eventually goes to the good player. His key weapons are his mind and a license to use unlimited deception.

Poker is unique among money-making situations. In business, for example, opportunities to apply the proper business concepts are limited in number. The financial outcome, therefore, cannot be certain. But, in poker, while chance may influence each separate hand, the opportunities (hands) are so numerous that chance or "luck" becomes insignificant and success becomes certain. Application of the proper poker concepts assures financial success.

**Poker concepts are best illustrated by players in actual game situations. The following players are the nucleus of a weekly Monday night game:**

**Sid Bennett**

**Ted Fehr**

**John Finn**

**Quintin Merck**

**Scotty Nichols**

**Although other men play in this game from time to time, most of the poker situations in this book are illustrated with these five players.**

**"Four in the morning," Quintin Merck grunts at the dark-whiskered men still sitting around the rectangular poker table. It is not a real poker table, not the kind with trays for money and a green felt top**

[4] *The 120 Advanced Concepts of Poker are listed in order by numbers in parentheses following each concept heading.*

... it is the dining room table at Scotty Nichols' house. They have played here every Monday night for the past six years.

Layers of gray smoke mushroom around the overhead cluster of electric bulbs that light a leather table mat covered with $10 and $20 bills. The largest pile of money is in front of John Finn, a twenty-eight-year-old social worker — so everyone thought.

In the sticky summer heat, the men slouch in squeaking wooden chairs. Only John Finn appears alert. The tall black-haired man slips on his glasses and hooks the gold rims around his ears. His dark eyes move from player to player.

On his left sits Sid Bennett, a thirty-five-year-old paving contractor. His large smiling head flops in a semicircle as straight yellow hair falls over his forehead and nearly touches his faded blue eyes. He's in a daze, John says to himself. Look at him grin.

On John's right sits Ted Fehr, a thirty-year-old gambler and restaurant owner. He coils a $50 bill around his skinny fingers while waiting for the next hand. Beneath a knotted mat of red hair, his freckled face wrinkles. Then his bloodshot eyes sag as he watches John Finn's arm hook around the huge pot. "The biggest pot of the night," he moans, "and look who wins it. You . . ."

John interrupts. "Wake up, Professor, it's your deal."

With a growling noise, Professor Merck deals. John watches the deck and sees the bottom card plus two other cards flash. He then studies Quintin Merck's green eyes ... they are watering from the cigarette smoke curling over his mustache and into his leathery face. Wearing a sweaty beret and an opened polo shirt, the wiry fifty-five-year-old college professor hunches over the table. Suddenly he looks up and frowns at John Finn.

Without flinching, John refocuses his eyes and looks into the kitchen. Then his eyes return to the game .. . he studies Scotty Nichols. The plump forty-two-year-old stockbroker slumps half dozing in his

**chair. His mouth droops to expose a cluster of gold-capped teeth. His thick glasses magnify his eyes into brown globes that float in circles between each squeezing blink. A tie droops from the frayed collar of his scorched white shirt.**

**They're all valuable to me, John Finn tells himself as his dark eyes draw into slits.**

# II
# POKER PLAYERS (2)

There are good poker players and poor poker players. Most players fall in between these two extremes. The good player works hard to maintain maximum edge odds. He never compromises his advantage for the sake of others. He shares his abilities and earnings with no one. The poor player is usually lazy and generally lacks discipline. Unlike those in the non poker world, the poor poker player cannot live off the advantages or earnings of others.

### 1. The Good Player and the Maximum-Win Approach(3)

The good player plays solely for his own benefit. He is not a gambler[5] because he bets only when the odds are favorable. (Gamblers bet money at unfavorable odds and eventually lose all the money they risk.) The good poker player cannot lose; he eventually wins all the money that gambling players risk.

The ability to play good poker does not correlate with intelligence or the ability to play games such as bridge or chess. And, ironically, poker is a game of neither skill nor luck, but rather, is a game of discipline, aggression, and effort. The good player subjugates his impulses and motivates all his actions toward meeting the objective of poker, which is to win maximum money. He never gives anything away or helps others without the motive of eventual profit. The good player thinks ahead and plans his moves in advance. He disciplines himself and maintains an emotional consistency. He objectively analyzes the game as

_____

[5] *See the footnote in Concept 82 for a definition of gambling.*

Poker: A Guaranteed Income For Life

well as each individual player, hand, and bet; he then adapts to any situation. The good player continuously expands his prowess by soaking up the experience of every play made by each player.

Good poker players are rare, and their paths seldom cross. In fact, most players have never encountered a good player. In the rare event that two good players are in the same game, their effective control is diluted and their edge odds are reduced by each other's presence. A good player searches for weaknesses in his opponents, but two good players do not waste time trying to analyze each other. They more profitably direct their mental effort toward studying the game and the other players.

The strategy of the good player often depends on creating impulse reactions in his opponents. Often, therefore, the best move against a good player is to act oppositely to initial impulses. For example, when undecided about calling a good player and the impulse is to fold, the best move may be to call or even raise.

## 2. Other Players(4)

The other players supply income to the good player. They are working for him and are his assets. He treats them with care and respect. He plans his actions to extract maximum money from them.

The differences in attitude between the good player and other players are listed in Table 1.

*Part One: Definitions*

## TABLE 1
## ATTITUDES OF POKER PLAYERS

| Situation | Mystical Feelings of Most Poor Players | Objective Attitudes of Good Players |
|---|---|---|
| **Poker game** | A relaxing mental diversion to escape reality. | A mental discipline requiring full focus on reality. |
| **Evaluation of a play** | Winning the pot is most important. | Playing the hand properly is most important. |
| **Winner or loser** | Play according to winnings or losses. | Never be influenced by winnings or losses. |
| **Streaks of luck** | Chances or odds are influenced by previous events. Luck runs in cycles. | Past means nothing except for the psychological effects it has on other players. Luck is an illusion. |
| **Wild games** | Such games are not real poker and require little skill. "Good" poker players will not play these games. | Complex or wild games require more skill and offer greater advantages to the good player. |
| **Ante increase** | Attitudes are mixed. | An increased ante encourages looser play and works against tight players. |

25

*Poker: A Guaranteed Income For Life*

| Situation | Mystical Feelings of Most Poor Players | Objective Attitudes of Good Players |
|---|---|---|
| **Table stakes** | Winner has an advantage when he takes money off the table. | The good player has more advantage with maximum money on the table. |
| **No-limit poker** | A dangerous game for pros only. | Requires more aggressiveness and bluffing. Gives the good player greater advantages. |
| **Play past time limit** | Chances of winning decrease. | Advantages for the good player increase as opponents get tired and careless. |
| **Violation of rules** | Enforce rules equally. | *Interpret* rules consistently and equitably, but *enforce* rules less rigidly against weak players. |
| **Change in sequence of cards while dealing** | The run of cards is broken—misdeal. | Makes no difference—keep on playing. |
| **Opponents' errors such as betting out of turn** | Scold or penalize the culprit. | Usually benefits the good player. Encourage sloppy and loose play. |

## Part One: Definitions

| Situation | Mystical Feelings of Most Poor Players | Objective Attitudes of Good Players |
|---|---|---|
| **Cheater** | Throw him out of game. | If he is a regular loser, say nothing and let him play. |
| **Good player** | Welcome him. | Get him out of game. |

The major enemy of poker players is their rationalization for their failure to think. They continually find excuses for their self-imposed weaknesses and their lack of self-control. Their losses are directly proportional to their mental laziness.

Many poor players evade thinking by letting their minds sink into irrational fogs. Their belief in luck short-circuits their minds by excusing them from their responsibility to think. Belief in luck is a great mystical rationalization for the refusal to think.

In method of thought, good players are right and poor players are wrong.

**John Finn uses the mystical attitudes of his opponents to extract more money from them. In his black notebook, he has a chart that summarizes everyone's attitude:**

| Situation | Mystical Attitude | Objective Attitude |
|---|---|---|
| **Evaluation of a play** | Quintin, Scotty, Sid, Ted | John |
| **Winner or loser** | Scotty, Sid, Ted | John, Quintin |
| **Streaks of luck** | Scotty, Sid, Ted | John, Quintin |
| **Wild games** | Quintin, Scotty, Ted | John, Sid |
| **Play past time limit** | Scotty, Sid | John, Quintin, Ted |

| Situation | Mystical Attitude | Objective Attitude |
|---|---|---|
| **Violation of rules** | Quintin, Ted | John, Sid, Scotty |
| **Cheaters** | Scotty, Ted | John, Quintin, Sid |

# III
# EMOTIONS (5)

Money affects emotions, and emotions control most players. Poker involves the winning and losing of money. Common emotions of anger, excitement, greed, masochism, sadism, and self-pity often take control of players during the action. Most players fail to recognize or are unable to suppress those emotional influences that decrease their objectivity and poker ability. The good player recognizes his own emotions and prevents them from influencing his actions.... He avoids acting on his whims and feelings.

Players respond emotionally to various experiences during the game. The good player uses those emotional reactions to his financial advantage. Some typical reactions and their causes are listed in Table 2.

28

## TABLE 2
## EMOTIONAL REACTIONS

| *Emotional Reactions* | *Causes of Reactions* |
|---|---|
| Playing loose to recover losses<br>Playing tight to minimize losses | A losing streak |
| Playing loose to push good luck<br>Playing tight to protect winnings | A winning streak |
| Extending a "rush" or "streak of good luck" by playing recklessly | Winning a big hand or several consecutive hands . . . or having a "hot streak." |
| Playing poorly to avenge a loss or to retaliate for injured feelings | Losing a big hand or having feelings or pride hurt |
| Acting comical or silly | Fear, nervousness, lack of confidence, or desire for diversion |
| Becoming prone to impulsive actions and mistakes | Fear, nervousness, or desperation |
| Losing concentration and decreasing awareness of situation | Fear, laziness, fatigue, other problems |
| Losing assertiveness or aggressiveness | Fearing opponents, high stakes, or loss of too much money |

Book 3
Poker: A Guaranteed Income For Life

29

Recognition and control of one's own emotions are difficult and require thinking effort. That is one reason why good poker players are rare.

The good player directs his actions to produce desirable emotions (e.g., pleasure and self-esteem); the poor player lets his emotions produce undesirable actions (e.g., poor concentration and carelessness).

**Poker is a unique medium for studying people. Where else can one stare at and intensely observe another person for hours every week?**

**Poker offers opportunities to study people, often in highly emotional situations. Such opportunities that are probably better than those most psychoanalysts get to study their patients. The observant, good player will soon understand his opponents better than their own families do.**

**Poker players are often fatigued and under emotional stresses that expose their characters. On another page in John's notebook, he summarizes the emotional characteristics of his opponents as shown on the chart below:**

| *Player* | *Prototype Player* | *Emotional Characteristics* |
|---|---|---|
| **Quintin Merck** | **Sound** | **Fairly stable and objective. Can be upset when insulted or humiliated. His play then disintegrates. Becomes less objective during late hours as he fatigues.** |
| **Scotty Nichols** | **Average** | **Has inferiority complex and lack of confidence. Plays extremely tight if winning. Loosens up and plays recklessly after suffering a heavy loss or after losing several consecutive hands.** |

| Player | Prototype Player | Emotional Characteristics |
|---|---|---|
| **Sid Bennett** | **Wild** | **Hides lack of confidence with silly behavior. Humor him and keep atmosphere relaxed to bring out his worst. Be careful not to hurt his feelings, or he will sulk and play tight. Goes wild when winning.** |
| **Ted Fehr** | **Self-destructive** | **A compulsive gambler. Lacks self esteem. Wants to punish himself. Wants to lose. Deteriorates easily into a desperate condition. Insensitive to insults. No pride.** |

# IV
# POKER CONCEPTS (6)

Ideas on how to play poker can be assembled into concepts. The normal concepts described in most poker books are popular ideas based on a combination of common sense and generalizations. Those concepts can help some poor players improve their game. But good poker requires a much sharper definition of the problems, followed by actions based on more sophisticated and advanced concepts. The Advanced Concepts of Poker offer objective approaches to each aspect of the game and are designed for winning maximum money.

*1. Common Concepts (7)*

The most common concept for winning at poker has always been to play conservatively (tight) and to play according to the card odds. Most books on poker stress that concept. They usually include some basic techniques as well as some rules for betting, raising, and bluffing. They also present some common ideas about

31

strategy and psychology. But none of those books offers or even considers a maximum-win approach to poker. (Appendix B lists all the known books about poker published since 1872.)

Table 3 identifies and analyzes the fallacies of many common concepts presented in the well-known and classic books on poker.

By applying the *common* concepts of poker, a player can win moderately in small-stake games that consist mainly of poor players. But in regular high-stake games, continual losses force most poor players to quit or to improve. High-stake games, therefore, often consist of experienced poker players advanced beyond the common concepts. But when a player using the common concepts enters a high-stake game, he usually feels confident that by playing tight he will eventually win over his looser playing opponents. Bewilderment gradually replaces confidence as he continually loses against players whom he considers inferior competition.

**Scotty Nichols usually plays sensibly. He bets only good hands and is the tightest player in the game. He has studied many books about poker and faithfully follows their techniques and strategy. According to those books, he should be a consistent winner, particularly in this game with its loose and wild players. Why is he a loser? John Finn knows the answer . . . Scotty plays too tight. The pots he wins are usually small, and the pots he loses are often large. Why? Whenever Scotty shows betting strength or even stays in a hand, the other players either fold or stop betting. When he wins, therefore, the pots are smaller than normal. When players do bet against him to make a large pot, they usually hold powerful enough hands to beat him. In other words, Scotty is a tight player who, like the wild player, has not adjusted to the game pace.**

## 2 Advanced Concepts (8)

A player extracts maximum money from a poker game by using the Advanced Concepts of Poker. Use of those concepts involves—

- opponents who do not fully understand poker

32

## TABLE 3
## EXAMPLES OF COMMON CONCEPTS IN POKER LITERATURE

| Book | Concept | Failure of Concept |
| --- | --- | --- |
| Abbott, 1.—1881 Jack Pot Poker | Never lend or borrow money. | Credit is necessary to keep most private high-stake games going week after week. |
| Allen, G. W.—1895 Poker Rules in Rhyme | "It's the game the boys like best / Two or three times a week, / One man often beats the rest / With nothing else but cheek." | Action on objectively thought out plans (not cheek) is needed to win consistently. |
| Blackbridge, J.—1880 The Complete Poker Player | To play for a minimum loss or gain is what a gentleman should hope for. | To play for maximum gain is what the good player strives for. |
| Cady, Alice H.—1895 Poker | Bluffing should be shunned, for only an old player can experiment in this. | Only the weakest players will shun bluffing. |
| Coffin, G. S.—1949 Fortune Poker | Shrewd players in bad luck should call for a new deck of cards to break the cycle. | A sign of a poor player is one who calls for a new deck of cards to break his "bad luck" . . . he fails to understand poker. |

Book 3
Poker: A Guaranteed Income For Life

| Book | Concept | Failure of Concept |
|---|---|---|
| Crawford, J. R.—1953 How to Be a Consistent Winner | Treat every bet as though it were your first one. Forget the money already in the pot. | Must consider the money in the pot to estimate the potential return on the present bet (Investment Odds). |
| Culbertson, E.—1950 Culbertson's Hoyle | Never raise early unless the purpose is to drive out players. | Raise early to start bluffs, build pots, control betting, keep players in, drop players out—depending on the situation. |
| Curtis, D. A.—1901 The Science of Draw Poker | New-fangled, high-low poker is mental weakness and should soon die out, even among the feeble-minded. | High-low poker requires more skill and offers greater advantages to the good player than does straight poker. |
| Dowling, A. H.—1940 Confessions of a Poker Player | Players acting out of turn should be penalized. | Players acting out of turn generally benefit the good player. Encourage sloppy play in opponents. |
| Encyclopedia Britannica—1965 "Poker" | In high-low seven-card stud, never play for high unless first three cards are trips. | When to play depends on the investment odds, not on fixed dogma. |

34

Book 3
Poker: A Guaranteed Income For Life

| Book | Concept | Failure of Concept |
|---|---|---|
| Florence, W. 1.—1891 Handbook on Poker | A good player will at times purposely play poorly to vary his game. | The good player never purposely plays poorly. With thinking, he finds infinite ways to vary his game at favorable investment odds. |
| Foster, R. F.—1904 Practical Poker | The compulsory ante is not based on judgment and has been the ruin of the scientific poker player. | The ante helps the loose player and usually benefits the good player. |
| Frey, R. L.—1947 The Complete Hoyle | Never open unless the probability is that you hold the highest hand. | Open without best hand to establish betting position, to defend against a larger bet, or to set up a play at favorable investment odds. |
| Henry, 1 R.—1890 Poker Boiled Down | Elements of poker success are good luck, good cards, cheek, good temper, and patience. | "Good luck" and good cards have no bearing on poker success . . . all players eventually get the same "luck" and cards. |
| Jacoby, O.—1947 Oswald Jacoby on Poker | The most successful bluffs are likely to be the innocent ones. | The most successful bluffs are likely to be the well thought out and properly executed ones. |

35

| Book | Concept | Failure of Concept |
| --- | --- | --- |
| Keller, l. W.—1887 Draw Poker | Playing poker without money is really an intellectual and scientific game. Playing poker with money becomes mere gambling. | The essence of poker is aggression and money. |
| Morehead, A. H.—1956 New Complete Hoyle | The most widespread mistake is to play long hours in a futile losers' game. | The greatest advantages occur in a game consisting of tired losers... they are usually the poor players at their poorest. Also, the losers' game will usually move at a faster pace and with sloppier play. |
| Morehead, A. H.—1967 The Complete Guide to Winning Poker | Many of the finest poker exploits are inspirational and intuitional. | The only fine poker exploits are the ones consciously thought out. |
| Moss, l.—1955 How to Win at Poker | Beware of poor players. Stay out of games in which there are fish. | Poor players are the most profitable opponents. Seek poor players and games in which fish abound. |

| Book | Concept | Failure of Concept |
|---|---|---|
| Ostrow, A. A.—1945 The Complete Card Player | Wild-card and high-low poker increase the element of luck so greatly that rules for improving one's play cannot be set down. | The more complex the poker variations, the less the element of "luck" affects the outcome. |
| Philips, H.—1960 Profitable Poker | No sillier resolution is uttered than "Well, I must see it through." | If the pot is large and the final bet is small, the investment odds may heavily favor "seeing it through." |
| Radner, S. H.—1957 The Key to Playing Poker | To assure a night's winnings, sit to the left of loose bettors and to the right of tight players. | The good player usually sits to the right of loose bettors and to the left of tight players. |
| Reese, T. and Watkins, A. T.—1964 Secret of Modern Poker | To win consistently, you must play tight. | To win consistently, you must adapt to the game pace. |
| Rottenberg, 1.—1965 Friday Night Poker | High-stake games are played by grim, salty players. | High-stake games are played by all types of players. |

| Book | Concept | Failure of Concept |
|---|---|---|
| Scarne, I.—1965 Scarne on Cards | Do not lend money. It often comes back to break you. | The good player lends money in order to win more money. |
| Schenck, R. C.—1872 Rules for Playing Poker | The dealer has no special advantage. | The dealer has an advantage in draw games... and a large advantage in low ball and hold 'em games. |
| Smith, R. A.—1925 Poker to Win | The yellowest, most contemptible form of cheating is welching. | The welcher has lost his money in the game before borrowing; therefore, he has been an asset. |
| Steig, I.—1959 Poker for Fun and Profit | When someone says, "There isn't much to poker," walk away from him; he is a lout. | When someone says, "There isn't much to poker," get him in the game; he will be a valuable loser. |
| Wickstead, J. M.—1938 How to Win at Stud Poker | In poker, fortune favors the brave. | In poker, the objective thinker makes fortune favor him. |
| Winterblossom, H. T.—1875 Draw Poker | The bluffing element in draw poker is fictitious. | The importance of bluffing depends on the stakes, not on the type of game. |

Book 3
Poker: A Guaranteed Income For Life

| Book | Concept | Failure of Concept |
|---|---|---|
| Yardley, H. O.—1957 Education of a Poker Player | In all my life, I've never lost at over three consecutive sittings. | A good player at theoretical maximum edge odds (an impossible situation) will lose about once every four sessions... or lose in four consecutive sittings about once every 250 sessions. Also, the good player never brags about his success—he tries to conceal his success and understate his winnings. |
| General advice in most poker books from 1872 to 1968 | Keep stakes down, hold to a rigid quitting time, play tight and according to the card odds. | The good player drives the stakes up, usually avoids a rigid quitting time, and plays according to the investment odds. |

39

- ownerless pots that separate players from their money[6]

- interactions among a good player, other players, and pots.

By using the Advanced Concepts of Poker, the good player eventually wins all the money that his opponents are willing to lose.

**Objective, planned deception is the strategic basis for the Advanced Concepts of Poker. Unlimited deception is accepted and ethical in poker. John Finn makes full use of this unique license and will do anything — except cheat — that brings him an advantage.**

**The other players in the Monday night game believe they are deceptive. Their deception, however, is generally unimaginative and repetitive ... it seldom fools John Finn. He eventually wins all their money.**

---

[6] *In poker, unattached money in a pot belongs to no one and can be ethically won by any deceptive means, except cheating. But outside of poker, any poker like deception used to take money from an individual (rather than from an ownerless poker pot) would be dishonest or fraudulent.*

# V
# ODDS (9)

Three types of odds are important in poker. Most players are familiar with the card odds, and most players base their playing and betting decisions on them. The card odds, however, can be meaningless unless the investment odds are also considered. Another type of odds is the edge odds, which evaluate the relative performance of each player. These three types of odds are described below.

## 1. Card Odds (10)

The card odds are the probabilities of being dealt or drawing to various hands. These odds are reviewed in most books about poker. Table 4 is based on the card odds and shows the statistical frequency with which different poker hands occur.

### TABLE 4
### CARD ODDS

| High Hands | Approximate Deals per Pat Hand | Hands Possible |
|---|---|---|
| Total hands | 1 | 2,598,960 |
| No pair | 2 | 1,302,540 |
| One pair | 2.5 | 1,098,240 |
| Two pair | 20 | 123,552 |
| Three of a kind | 50 | 54,912 |
| Straight | 250 | 10,200 |
| Flush | 500 | 5,108 |
| Full house | 700 | 3,744 |
| Four of a kind | 4,000 | 624 |
| Straight flush | 70,000 | 36 |
| Royal straight flush | 650,000 | 4 |
| Five aces (with joker)* | 3,000,000 | 1 |

\* A fifty-three card deck with the joker has 2,869,685 possible hands.

41

*Poker: A Guaranteed Income For Life*

| Low Hands | Approximate Deals per Pat Hand | Hands Possible |
|---|---|---|
| Ace high (+) | 5 | 502,880 |
| King high (+) | 8 | 335,580 |
| Queen high (+) | 12 | 213,180 |
| Jack high (+) | 20 | 127,500 |
| Ten high (+) | 37 | 70,360 |
| Nine high (++) | 36 | 71,860 |
| Eight high (++) | 70 | 35,840 |
| Seven high (++) | 170 | 15,360 |
| Six high (++) | 500 | 5,120 |
| Five high (++) | 2,500 | 1,024 |

(+) No straights or flushes. Ace is high.
(++) Including straights and flushes. Ace is low.

There are 2,598,960 different poker hands in a fifty-two-card deck. If a player is dealt 100,000 hands in his lifetime, he will never hold (on his first five cards) more than 4 percent of all the possible hands.

Other poker probabilities based on the card odds are tabulated in Appendix D.

**The card odds can reveal interesting information. For example. how many pat straight flushes will Sid Bennett get during his lifetime? To determine that number, the expected number of hands that will be dealt to him during his life is estimated by the following calculation:**

**10 hands/hr.x5 hrs./gamex50 games/yr.
x40 yrs./poker life=l00,000 hands/poker life**

**From this estimation, the number of pat (on the first five cards) poker hands that Sid should get during his lifetime is calculated from the card odds and tabulated below:**

*Part One: Definitions*

*Approximate Number of
Pat Hands in a Lifetime*

| | |
|---|---|
| No pair | **50,000** |
| One pair | **40,00** |
| Two pair | **5,000** |
| Three of a kind | **2,000** |
| Straight | **400** |
| Flush | **200** |
| Full house | **170** |
| Four of a kind | **25** |
| Straight flush | **1.4** |
| Royal straight flush | **0.15** |

So statistically, Sid should get a pat straight flush on his first five cards once or twice during his life. He will, of course, catch straight flushes more frequently on the draw and in seven-card stud.

...Sid wins a big pot with a full house. He throws back his massive head and shouts, "I'm on a spinner! I'm going to break this game!" His head drops; he shakes his finger at the players and continues, "Just watch my luck. I'm getting a whole round of pat flushes... starting next deal."

"That won't happen till the sun burns out," Quintin Merck snorts.

Statistically, Quintin is right. Sid will be dealt five consecutive straight flushes once in every 1.7x1024 deals, or once in every 700,000,000,000,000,000,000 years. Yet his five consecutive straight flushes could start coming with the next deal.

Let him hope, John Finn says to himself.

43

## 2. Investment Odds (11)

Investment odds are the estimated returns on money that is bet. These odds are approximated by the following formula:

$$\frac{(\text{potential size of pot, \$}) \ (\text{probability of winning pot})}{\text{potential loss, \$}} = \text{Investment Odds}$$

*Note: If you are a beginner or are not mathematically inclined, do not be discouraged or get bogged down by this formula. Forget the formula for now and read on. With experience, you will realize that accurate estimations of investment odds are achieved by the proper thinking methods and not by mathematical problem-solving. This formula is merely a shorthand expression of the thought process required for properly evaluating a bet.*

For example, if a player estimates that a $80 potential pot would require a $20 betting investment (his potential loss), and if he estimates that his probability of winning that pot is .4 (40 percent[7]) then his investment odds would be calculated as follows:

$$\frac{(80) \ (.4)}{20} = 1.6$$

When the investment odds are greater than 1.0, the play is favorable and should be made.

Investment odds are important for making correct betting and playing decisions. Most players rely only on card odds, which often lead to wrong decisions. For example, investment odds sometimes favor drawing to an inside straight. At other times, investment odds favor folding three aces before the draw. In both cases, the wrong play may result if the decision is based on the card odds.

---

[7] *How does a player estimate the probability of winning a pot? He does this by assessing his own hand and position against the behavior and betting of his opponents. Initially, the estimates may be little more than guesses. Accuracy will improve with practice, experience, integrated effort, and application of various concepts described in this book.*

Determination of investment odds is not a mathematical problem. Numbers plugged into the investment-odds formula are quick estimations or guesses derived by gathering together and then objectively evaluating the facts of the game, players, and situation. Those estimations become more valid with increased thinking effort and experience. While the good player may never actually use or even think about the investment-odds formula, it does express his thought process for evaluating bets.

**Quintin, Ted, and Scotty each draw one card. John Finn holds two low pair, tens and fours. What does he do? He considers the card odds, the past betting, probable future betting, his observations (e.g., of flashed cards), and his reading of each opponent... and then estimates the following investment odds:**

**Draw one card to his two pair...**

$$\frac{(\$200)\ (.2)}{\$60} = .66 = \text{fold}$$

**Draw three cards to his pair of fours...**

$$\frac{(\$300)\ (.1)}{\$20} = 1.5 = \text{play}$$

**So instead of folding his two pair (and often the investment odds favor folding the two small pair), he breaks up his hand and draws to the pair of fours at favorable investment odds. The low $20 estimate of his potential loss is the key to making this play favorable. John figures his chances for catching and having to call the last bet are small.[8] When the high probability of a no bet or a folded hand (zero dollars) is averaged into the numerator, the potential loss becomes relatively**

[8] *The weakness of hands such as small pairs, four flushes, and four-card straights after the draw increases the investment odds because failure to improve those hands causes an immediate fold, thereby reducing the potential loss.*

45

small—even though the last-round bet may be large if he improves his hand. In other words, he will fold with no additional cost unless he catches three of a kind or better, which would let him bet heavily with a good possibility of winning.

In another hand, Sid and Ted draw three cards. Again John has two low pair. After objectively weighing all factors within the framework of the investment-odds formula, he estimates his most favorable play is to stay pat and then bet the last round as if he had a straight or a flush:

Play pat . . .

$$\frac{(\$100)\ (.8)}{\$60} = 1.33 = \text{play}$$

The advantages of this play are: If either Sid or Ted catches two pair or even trips, he may fold and let John win on a pat bluff. If either catches a strong hand and shows any betting strength, John folds with no additional cost. Also, neither will try to bluff into John's pat hand. And finally, if Sid and Ted do not improve, John Finn wins additional money if either one calls.

John Finn is the only good player in the Monday night game. He works hard, thinks objectively, and adapts to any situation. By applying the Advanced Concepts of Poker, he wins maximum money from the game.

To overcome mental laziness and restrictive thinking, he forces himself to think constantly and imaginatively about the game. That effort lets him make more profitable plays. For example, he breaks up a pat full house[9] to triple the size of the pot while

[9] *The opportunity to profitably break a full house by drawing to three of a kind rarely occurs. The above case results when several players with weak hands would fold if the full house were played pat, but would call if a draw were made. Also, the full house would be broken to draw to four of a kind if sufficient evidence existed that the full house was not the best hand.*

**decreasing his chances of winning only slightly (from 98 percent down to 85 percent). But that play increases his estimated investment odds from**

$$\frac{(\$100)\ (.98)}{\$20} = 4.9 \qquad \text{up to} \quad \frac{(300)\ (.85)}{\$40} = 6.4.$$

**John wins consistently, but still his opponents refuse to realize that they are paying him thousands of dollars every year to play in their game.**

*3. Edge Odds or Edge Percentages (12)*

Edge odds indicate the relative performance of a player in a poker game. These odds are calculated by the following formula:

$$\frac{\text{average winnings (or losses) of player, \$}}{\text{average winnings of the biggest winner, \$}} \times 100\% = \text{Edge Odds }\%^{10}$$

For example, if the biggest winner of each game averages plus \$150, and if a player averages plus \$75 per game, then the edge odds for this player are +75/150 x 100% = +50%. The more games used to calculate edge odds, the more significant they become. Edge odds based on ten or more games should reflect the relative performance of a player fairly accurately. The good poker player usually maintains edge odds ranging from 25 percent to 65 percent, depending on the game and abilities of the other players. An approximate performance grading of poker players based on the edge odds is tabulated in Table 5.

[10] *If you are not mathematically inclined and do not understand this or other formulas and ratios presented in this chapter, do not worry. Just skip over the formulas and read on. for these formulas are not necessary to understand and utilize the concepts identified in this book.*

*Poker: A Guaranteed Income For Life*

## TABLE 5
## EDGE ODDS

| Grading | Edge Odds in Games without a Good Player | Edge Odds in Games with a Good Player |
|---|---|---|
| Good player | N/A | 25 — 65 |
| Sound player | 10 — 25 | 5 — 20 |
| Average player | 0 — 15 | (-5) — 10 |
| Weak player | (-10) — 5 | (-15) — 0 |
| Poor player | (-20) — (-5) | (-65) — (-10) |

Edge odds are estimated for an average seven-man game.

The good player is a very expensive person to have in a poker game, as indicated by the sharp decreases in everyone's edge odds when he plays.

**In a black leather notebook, John Finn keeps records of every player. After each game, he estimates their winnings and losses. After every ten games, he calculates their edge odds, as shown below:**

*Ten-Game Average Edge Odds, %*

| Player | Estimated Average Win or Loss per Game, $ | Edge Odds* % | Grading |
|---|---|---|---|
| **John Finn** | + 262 | + 59 | **Good** |
| **Quintin Merck** | + 45 | + 10 | **Sound** |
| **Scotty Nichols** | - 10 | - 2 | **Average** |
| **Sid Bennett** | - 95 | - 21 | **Poor** |
| **Ted Fehr** | - 100 | - 22 | **Poor** |
| **Other Players** | - 135 | - 30 | **Poor** |

*\* The biggest winner for each game averaged +$445.*

**By reviewing his long-term edge-odds data (shown below), John notices slow changes in the players: Quintin is gradually improving, Scotty and Ted are deteriorating. while Sid remains stable.**

48

*Ten-Game-Average Edge Odds, %*

| Ten-game period # | 1 | 2 | 3 | 4 | 5 | 6 | 7 |
|---|---|---|---|---|---|---|---|
| John Finn | + 61 | + 53 | + 62 | + 59 | + 55 | + 60 | + 56 |
| Quintin Merck | - 2 | + 2 | - 5 | + 10 | + 8 | + 12 | + 15 |
| Scotty Nichols | + 4 | + 7 | + 6 | - 2 | + 1 | - 10 | - 18 |
| Sid Bennett | - 22 | - 20 | - 23 | - 21 | - 20 | - 18 | - 12 |
| Ted Fehr | - 18 | - 20 | - 19 | - 22 | - 28 | - 30 | - 31 |
| Other Players | - 23 | - 24 | - 26 | - 30 | - 25 | - 22 | - 20 |
| Average biggest winner, +$ | 295 | 315 | 430 | 445 | 570 | 650 | 630 |

**The steady increase in profit for the biggest winner also reflects John Finn's progress in driving up the betting stakes and pace.**

# VI
# BETTING (13)

Few players differentiate between the betting stakes and the betting pace. The betting stakes are the size of bets and raises permitted. The stakes are established by the house rules. The betting pace is the tempo or frequency of bets and raises. The pace depends on the games played and the willingness of players to bet. Both the stakes and pace determine how expensive the game is . . . or how much money can be won or lost.

The good player is seldom characterized as a tight player. His betting pattern is generally (but not always) aggressive[11] and often lopsidedly aggressive. Pushing hard whenever he has an advantage (i.e., at favorable investment odds) and quickly dropping against stronger hands let him maximize his wins and minimize his losses.

When the good player bets, he generally bets aggressively. For the good player, increased aggressiveness advantageously

---

[11] *Good players are confident in their betting and generally play aggressively, Poor players are either too loose or too tight in their betting and seldom play aggressively.*

quickens the betting pace, while lopsided aggressiveness advantageously creates confusion and fear in his opponents.

As the stakes increase with each round of betting, the losses of the poor players will increase faster than the potential losses of the good player. Indeed, the investment-odds formula in Concept 11 suggests that a steeper and steeper betting progression within a hand (causing the numerator to increase more rapidly than the denominator) permits greater and greater betting aggressiveness, which in turn allows the good player to bet with poorer and poorer hands. In other words, the good player not only tries to drive up the betting stakes and betting pace within a game, but also tries to create a steeper betting progression within a hand.

### 1. Betting Stakes (14)

Most players think only of the betting stakes when they consider the size of the game.

**The betting stakes in John Finn's Monday night games are as follows: In draw, $25 is the maximum bet or raise on the first round of betting. This maximum increases to $50 in subsequent rounds of betting. In stud, the maximum bet is $5 on the first up card. The bet then increases in $5 increments on each subsequent round of betting to $10, $15, $20, and so on. Only three raises are allowed except when only two players remain, and then raises are unlimited. Check raising is permitted.**

### 2. Betting Pace(15)

The betting pace is often more significant than the betting stakes in determining the size of the game. The good player knows the betting pace of both the game and of each individual hand. The betting pace of the game (game pace) is determined by comparing the betting done on various hands to the betting normally done on these hands. The pace may differ markedly in different poker games. In a fast-paced game, for example, two pair after the draw may be worth two raises. In a slow-paced game, those same two pair may be worth not even a single bet.

50

## Part One: Definitions

The betting pace of each hand (hand pace) is determined by comparing the extent of betting, calling, raising, and bluffing to the size of the pot. Often the pace is too slow during certain phases of a hand and too fast during other phases. The good player controls his offensive and defensive game by altering his betting pace at various phases of a poker hand. The ratios shown in Table 6 reflect the betting pace during the various phases of a poker hand.

### TABLE 6
### BETTING PACES

| *Phase* | *Ratio* | *Increasing Ratio* → |
|---|---|---|
| Open | $\dfrac{\text{(opening bet, \$) (\# callers)}}{\text{pot, \$}}$ | Slow pace → Fast pace |
| Raise | $\dfrac{\text{(raise bet, \$) (\# callers)}}{\text{pot, \$}}$ | Slow pace → Fast pace |
| Final bet | $\dfrac{\text{(last bet, \$) (\# callers)}}{\text{pot, \$}}$ | Slow pace → Fast pace |
| Bluff | $\dfrac{\text{(\# bluffs) (average \# final callers)}}{\text{\#hands played}}$ | Slow pace → Fast pace |

Few hands are played at the optimum betting pace. And if, for example, the betting pace is relatively slow, the optimum pace will be somewhat faster. A person increases his investment and edge odds by playing closer to the optimum pace.

**In the Monday night game, John realizes that the betting in seven-card stud moves at a fast pace during the early rounds, but slows considerably in the late rounds of big bets. He takes advantage of that imbalance by laying back during the early rounds as players get drawn in and disclose their betting**

51

tendencies. Then in the later rounds, he quickens the pace by betting aggressively. But while playing closer to the optimum pace himself, John is careful not to correct the imbalanced pace of other players.

The following ratios illustrate how John Finn estimates and influences the hand pace of the Monday night, seven-card stud game.

| Phase | *Without John Finn* | | *Pace* | *With John Finn* | |
|---|---|---|---|---|---|
| | *Estimated Ratios* | | | *Estimated Ratios* | |
| **Open** | $\dfrac{\$4 \times 4}{\$23}$ | =.70 | **Too fast** | $\dfrac{\$3 \times 5}{\$22}$ | =.68 |
| **Raise (first round)** | $\dfrac{\$5 \times 3}{\$38}$ | =.40 | | $\dfrac{\$5 \times 4}{\$42}$ | =.48 |
| **Final bet** | $\dfrac{\$20 \times 2}{\$198}$ | =.20 | **Too slow** | $\dfrac{\$25 \times 3}{\$297}$ | =.25 |
| **Final raise** | **Best hand should raise, but often does not** | | | **John Finn often makes final raise** | |

The techniques for applying the Advanced Concepts of Poker are described in Part Two of this book.

# PART TWO

---

# TECHNIQUES
## (DTC METHOD)

Discipline, Thought, and Control are the techniques of good poker. The DTC method is the application of these three techniques.

# VII
## DISCIPLINE (16)

Discipline is the mechanism of good poker. Discipline leads to self-control, which is necessary to—

- prevent emotions from affecting actions

- allow total concentration to focus on the game

- permit continuous objective thinking in order to analyze past action, carry out present action, and plan future action.

Self-control develops by practicing during the game the disciplines listed in Table 7:

53

## TABLE 7
### DISCIPLINES

| *Discipline Practiced* | *Self-Control Developed* |
|---|---|
| Consume no food or beverage | Awareness |
| Do not swear or display feelings | Emotional control |
| Maintain good posture—sit straight and keep both feet flat on the floor | Alertness |
| Memorize important hands played and performance of each opponent | Concentration |
| Mentally Review and criticize each play | Objectivity |

The good player increases his advantage as the game grinds into late hours. His disciplines become more nagging and thus more effective for maintaining self-control. At the same time, the concentration and playing ability of his tired opponents decrease. Also as his opponents develop into big winners or big losers for the evening, they become less objective and respond more to their feelings.

A decrease in discipline has a cumulative effect that can cause even a sound player to deteriorate into a poor player. For example, if a loss in discipline generates a breakdown in self-control, then a process of deterioration starts. Deterioration may be only temporary . . . but it can be permanent, especially with compulsive gamblers.

Deterioration can start spontaneously or can be induced by—

• a long losing or winning streak

- entering a higher-stake or a lower-stake game

- a close loss of a big hand

- a bad play or bet

- an upsetting remark

- boredom or weariness

- a personal problem

The good player recognizes any loss of discipline during the game. He adopts the following attitudes to prevent deterioration of his own discipline and play:

– Actual winning or losing of a pot is not important.

– Each well-played hand, won or lost, is a victory.

– Each poorly played hand is a defeat (even if the pot is won).

– Each move or action lacking discipline can eventually cost much more money than there is in any pot.

Consistent, tight discipline can build momentum toward a continuous string of flawless plays. If a bad play spoils this momentum, the resulting loss of self-control can lead to poorer-quality poker. A bad play to a good poker player can be as a cigarette is to an ex-smoker . . . one slip (betrayal of one's self) breaks the momentum of discipline and can bring disaster.[12]

A few minutes of postgame discipline are necessary to record valuable information and data about the game. In addition to his

---

[12] *The good player does not consider an honest error in judgment a flaw. To him a flaw is the failure to think and act rationally. The flawless play, therefore, is not based on omniscience or perfect judgment, but rather on full rational thought.*

notes written after each game, the good player periodically reevaluates the game and its players. These evaluations point out slow changes occurring in the game and often suggest changes in strategy necessary to maintain optimum edge odds.

**John Finn uses convenient photocopied outlines, as shown in Tables 8, 10, and 12, and periodically fills them out as shown in Tables 9,11, and 13. Those outlines provide him with consistent up-to-date information on the game and its players.**

A few minutes of pregame discipline is needed to review past notes. Also, a nap before the game improves discipline and thought. A bath and a shave help restore the freshness necessary to sustain peak performance throughout an all-night session.

TABLE 8
**WEEKLY GAME NOTES**[13]
**GAME—**
**DATE—**

**Highlights—**
**Evaluation of game—**
**Evaluation of own performance—**

| | |
|---|---|
| **(a) errors—** | **(b) unusual plays—** |
| **(c) number of wins—** | **(d) calculated edge odds—** |

**Information on opponents**

| | |
|---|---|
| **(a) observations** | **(b) performance** |
| **(c) winnings, losses, and debts, $** | **(d) bluffs, tried/called—** |

**Statistics**

| | |
|---|---|
| **(a) number of hands played—** | **(b) starting and quitting time—** |
| **(c) maximum win—** | **(d) maximum loss—** |

**Miscellaneous—**

[13] *Collecting and remembering the data for these Weekly Game Notes require discipline and concentration. Indeed, the chief value in acquiring these notes is not the data themselves, but the forced mental attention to the game that is required to collect the data.*

## TABLE 9
## WEEKLY GAME NOTES
### GAME—*Monday, weekly*
### DATE—*9/10*

**Highlights—**
*Sid cheats Quintin out of $700 pot Have talk with Quintin. Everything okay.... New player Jeff Klien is a good addition. Will be permanent loser.... Ted absent. Broke from playing horses. . . . Sid played wildly and poorly, but won big.*

**Evaluation of game—**
*Continues at fast pace. Near optimum stakes for now. Only Charlie appears in financial trouble. Scotty is starting to hurt.*

**Evaluation of own performance—***$550 win*

**(a)  errors —2**
   *(details in black book, p. 52)*

**(b)  unusual plays—3**
   *(details in black book, p. 78)*

**(c)  number of wins—12**
   *(7 full, 5 split)*

**(d)  calculated edge odds—**
   *550/650x100=85%*

**Information on opponents**
**(a)  observations**
*Jeff blinks eyes when a bet is made against his weak hand. Keeps eyes open wide when he has a strong hand.*

**(b)  performance**
*Aaron-fair; Quintin-good to fair; Scotty-fair to poor; Charlie- very poor; Jeff-fair; Mike- fair; Sid-poor; John-good*

**(c)  winnings, losses, and debts, $**

| | |
|---|---|
| *Sid +650* | *Aaron -250* |
| *John +550* | *Scotty -300* |
| *Mike +400* | *Quintin -350* |
| *Jeff +200* | *Charlie -900* |
| | *(borrows 300)* |

**(d)  bluffs, tried/ called—***30/19*

| | |
|---|---|
| *Aaron-3/2* | *Jeff-1/1* |
| *Quintin-1/10* | *Mike-0* |
| *Scotty-0* | *Sid-15/10* |
| *Charlie-6/15* | *John-4/1* |

Book 3

Poker: A Guaranteed Income For Life

**Statistics**

(a) **number of hands**
**played**—*108*
      *(% won=12/108=11%)*

(b) **starting and quitting**
**time**—
      *8:15 p.m.-5:00 a.m.*

(c) **maximum win**—
      *+$650 (Sid)*

(d) **maximum loss**—
      *-$900 (Charlie)*

**Miscellaneous—**

- *Need another regular player.*

- *Everyone absorbing losses okay, except Charlie, who is getting desperate.*

- *Problem about Ted's debts and bounced checks.*

TABLE 10
**SEMIANNUAL GAME PROFILE**
**GAME—**
**PERIOD—**

**Face and stakes—**

**Average maximum win—**

**Average maximum loss—**

**Performance of opponents—**

**Regular players—**

**New or occasional players—**

**Games played—**

**Ante per player—**

**Betting—**

**Raising—**

**Attitudes—**

**Personal performance—**

**Miscellaneous—**

## TABLE 11
## SEMIANNUAL GAME PROFILE
### GAME—*Monday, weekly*
### PERIOD—*1/8 -6/4*

**Pace and stakes**— *Fast pace is near maximum..Pressure for higher stakes.*

**Average maximum win: +$550**

**Average maximum loss: -$450**

**Performance of opponents**— *Average and fairly stable. Quintin is improving. Scotty, Aaron, and Ted are deteriorating.*

**Regular players**— *John Finn, Quintin Merck, Sid Bennett, Ted Fehr, Scotty Nichols.*

**New or occasional players**— *Aaron Smith, Mike Bell, Charlie Holland, Mac Zimmerman, Jim Todd, Jake Fehr, Lee Pennock, Jeff Klien.*

**Games played**— *Draw and stud with twists, high-low, and qualifiers. Occasionally use wild cards and the Bug.*

**Ante per player**— *$1 for stud. $5 for draw.*

**Betting**— *In draw, $25 opens, then $50 in subsequent rounds. In stud, $5 first card, then increase by $5 for each additional card. Twists are free....80% of bets are at the maximum.*

**Raising**— *Right-to-bet rule. Normally three raises. With only two players, raises are unlimited. Check raises okay.*

Book 3
Poker: A Guaranteed Income For Life

*Poker: A Guaranteed Income For Life*

**Attitudes—** *Generally good. Sid continues to cheat without problems. No one resentful or in danger of quitting.*

**Personal performance—** *Good, but leveling off in effort. Areas to improve—Increase focus on broader aspects of the game. Increase flexibility in style during early rounds.*

**Miscellaneous—** *Stakes are ready to move up to next level. Try doubling stakes for the last round in the next few games.*

## TABLE 12
## SEMIANNUAL PLAYER PROFILE
### NAME—
### PERIOD—

**Classification—**

**Motive—**

**Attitude—**

**Performance—**

**Average won or lost/game—**

**Edge odds—**

**Behavior—**

    **Open—**

    **Bet—**

    **Call—**

    **Raise—**

    **Last bet—**

    **Bluff—**

    **Fold—**

**Weaknesses—**

**Strengths—**

**Changes—**

**Miscellaneous—**

60

## TABLE 13
## SEMIANNUAL PLAYER PROFILE
### NAME—*Quintin Merck*
### PERIOD—*l/8-6/4*

**Classification** — *Sound player and improving.*

**Motive** — *Pass time. Satisfy ego....Shifting to motive of making money.*

**Attitude** — *Grouchy but Improving.*

**Performance** — *Above average.*

**Average won or lost/game** — *+$50 and increasing.*

**Edge odds** — *+10% and increasing.*

**Behavior—**

**Open** —*When under the gun, he holds back good hands When dealing, he will almost always open*

**Bet** — *Bets too lightly in early rounds. Same giveaway habits (listed in black book. p. 17)*

**Call** — *Calls with much weaker hands than he is willing to bet.*

**Raise** —*Too conservative. Seldom raises a good winning hand if it is of low value.*

**Last bet** — *Bets only when sure, but calls with weak hands.*

**Bluff** — *Seldom. Averages once every two sessions. Same giveaway habits (listed in black book, p. 17).*

**Fold** — *Folds too easily early in hand and too hard late in hand*

**Weaknesses** — *Play deteriorates when he gets angry from personal insults or from humiliating losses. Betting is out of proportion. Too conservative, but tires in late hours, then plays too loose.*

**Strengths** — *Fairly objective. Conservative. Tries to concentrate.*

**Changes** — *Improving and becoming more objective. Making conscious effort to improve. Better control over emotions.*

**Miscellaneous** — *He becomes less valuable as he improves. If improvement and winnings continue, he will be a liability. May have to eliminate him from the game.*

How valuable is discipline? Obviously it is important in poker. But how valuable is discipline when it comes to refreshments? Did you ever eat a $600 sandwich? Well, such costly sandwiches are sometimes eaten in John Finn's game.

Consider Scotty Nichols, who tries hard to play a good game.... Sid deals draw poker. Scotty seems nervous, as if desperate to win a pot. He opens for $25 with a pair of aces. Sid raises to $50. Now Scotty is sucked in and calls. Nervous hunger seizes him. He rushes to the food table and rapidly piles many slabs of ham and cheese into a giant sandwich. In the meantime, Ted Fehr draws a card and carelessly flashes it—the ace of diamonds. Then the dealer, waving the deck around, exposes the bottom card for all to see—except Scotty, who is laying pickles on his sandwich. The bottom card? It is the ace of clubs.

Now it is Scotty's turn to draw. Hurrying back to the table, he smiles at his sandwich. Then his teeth chomp into the pile of food. Beads of mustard ooze over the crust and drip onto his tight slacks. With mustard-covered fingers, Scotty picks up his cards. John Finn watches him play. Yes, the pair of aces are still there.

But wait—he also has four spades. Scotty wonders what to do. Staring at his sandwich, he continues to eat.

"Come on," Quintin grunts. "Speed up the game."

"Got to go with my best hand," Scotty finally blurts. He draws three cards to his pair of aces and then jams the rest of the sandwich into his mouth. The first card off the deck is the king of spades... his flush card. So what—he still catches another king to give him two pair, aces and kings... a pretty good hand.

That pretty good hand is enough to keep him in for a $50 bet plus a $50 raise. Quintin Merck wins with a queen high flush.

"What rotten luck," Scotty whines as he grabs an overflowing handful of potato chips. His words are followed by a slobbering crunch.

Rotten luck? If Scotty had stayed at the table, he would have seen the two flashed aces and drawn to his four flush to win the $600 pot. Instead he loses $150. That ham and cheese sandwich cost him $600!

Also, John Finn uses the mustard stains on Scotty's cards to identify them in future hands.

# VIII
# THOUGHT (17)

Thought is the labor of good poker. Objectivity and steady concentration are needed to think properly. Thinking requires discipline. *Analytical* thinking is necessary to understand and predict the actions of opponents. *Objective* thinking is necessary to plan the proper action.

The good player continually thinks about poker during the game. He looks at his cards quickly to allow maximum time for observation and thought. He never wastes precious time by slowly looking at or squeezing open his cards. When involved in a hand, his thoughts concentrate on strategy. The good player gains a major advantage over other players by thinking ahead and forming several strategic plans based on anticipated hands. When an anticipated hand develops, he can make quicker and more accurate playing decisions.

When not involved in a hand, the good player studies the game, gathers data, and plans future strategy. Between hands, he analyzes the action of each concluded hand.

Intensive thought and concentration also help to overcome nervousness, which even a good player may experience when playing in a strange, an unfriendly, or a high-stake game.

Since thinking is the labor of poker, maximum thinking effort should yield maximum returns. How much is this effort worth in dollars? When a player wins an average of $40 per game, his winning rate is equivalent to a job paying $15,200 a year.[14] Average winnings of $150 per game is equivalent to a $57,000 per year job.

Compare the effort in poker to the effort required in a job yielding similar earnings. For example, a winning rate of $5 per game is equivalent to a job paying only $1,900 per year; such pay would not be worth the effort needed to play good poker.

**Let us see how thinking pays off. John Finn is under the gun in draw poker. He has a four flush in hearts and checks. Next is Sid Bennett, who opens for $25. John check-raises to $50. Sid and Scotty call the raise. Now John draws and immediately looks at his card. He misses his flush. Does he give up? No... by paying attention and thinking, he still has a chance to win that $250 pot. John stays alert. and this is what he sees and hears:**

**Sid Bennett draws one card, sticks it in the center of his hand, then quickly looks at it. Is he drawing a flush, a straight, or two pair? Probably two pair because when Sid draws one card to the flush or straight he places the draw card at the back end of his hand and then looks at the card very slowly. That, along with his betting pattern (opens, then reluctantly calls a raise), suggests that Sid has two pair.**

[14] *This and the following figures calculated for a five-hour weekly game . . . and 1900 hours of actual work per year (estimated from data in the U. S. Government Bulletin, Employment, Earnings and Monthly Report on the Labor Force. vol. 12, no. 10).*

Ted Fehr flashes a black picture card when dealing Scotty's draw card. While ruffling the cards through his chubby fingers, Scotty exposes the deuce of hearts. Therefore, if he were going for the flush or straight, he missed it. Scotty slowly squeezes his cards open to look at his new card, then gives a blowing exhale. He usually inhales when he sees a good draw card.

Now John has a good view of the situation. The opener (Sid with two pair) looks weak with respect to the two one-card draw hands behind him... especially after John raised the first-round bet. Knowing that Scotty has a busted hand, John sits in a position of strength, despite his worthless hand. He has the last bet, and the other players respect his hand because of his first-round raise followed by his single-card draw. John has an excellent chance of buying the $250 pot with a bluff.

If Sid and Scotty check and John bets $50, Sid will probably drop his winning hand because he would have to contend with Scotty's one-card draw as well as John's one-card draw. If Sid folds, Scotty will then fold his busted hand, leaving John the pot. John figures his chances of a successful bluff under the circumstances are better than 1 to 2. The return for winning the pot would be about 5 to 1. He estimates his investment odds at $250 x 0.3/$0 = 1.5... those are good odds.

What if Sid bets his two pair? Does John fold his hand or does he still bluff by raising back? He would probably fold for the following reasons:

- After already betting $0, Sid would probably call John's raise—out of pseudo pride if for no other reason.
- Sid's bet would drive out Scotty, thus eliminating the key player needed to bluff Sid out. John's chances of a successful bluff would decrease sharply.
- John would have to risk $100 for a $300 pot — 3 to 1 return on his bluff play rather than the 5 to

65

**1 return if Sid does not bet. His investment odds would fall to $450 x 0.1/100 = 0.45... a very unfavorable level.**

**What actually happens? Well, things turn out better than John hoped. Sid checks. Scotty hesitates and then suddenly bets $50. This is his normal pattern when bluffing—hesitate and then bet fast. Scotty's obvious bluff attempt makes John's bluff even easier. He casually raises to $100. Sid and Scotty fold immediately.... John wins a $300 pot with a worthless hand plus a little thinking.**

**Incidentally, John Finn earns $42,000 per year by playing 400 hours in the Monday night game. This equals $105 per hour, which is equivalent to a job yielding $200,000 per year.... A job paying that much is worth a concentrated thinking effort.**

# IX
# CONTROL (18)

The result of good poker is control—control of self, opponents, and the game. When the good player achieves self-control through discipline and understands his opponents through thinking, he can seize control of his opponents and the game. When in control, he becomes the center of attention. His opponents spend a major portion of their time and effort trying to figure out his moves and then adjusting to them ... they play according to his moves and actions. From this controlling position he can—

- influence the betting, raising, and bluffing of his opponents

- force opponents into traps and wrong moves

- dilute opponents' attention toward one another so he can play them off against each other.

The player who continually strives for maximum *investment*

66

odds cannot control the game. Always making the play that yields the maximum return reduces the flexibility needed to control the players and to achieve maximum *edge* odds. The good player, therefore, chooses from a wide variety of plays available at slightly less favorable odds. For example, by backing away from the maximum investment odds, the good player can bet more aggressively and increase his flexibility in play-making so much that he can produce almost any desired effect. Also, by underbetting a hand and then overbetting a subsequent similar hand (with only occasional bets made at maximum investment odds), he makes his betting unpredictable. That flexibility and unpredictability let him control the betting.

Money flows toward the player who controls the betting. The best time to get that control is early in the hand while the bets are still small. The good player often gains control by unexpected or unusual bets (such as a raise into obvious strength of an opponent), by larger than usual first-round bets, or by weird bets (such as a $4 bet instead of the usual $5 bet). He then makes subsequent offensive or defensive betting manipulations designed to influence the big last-round bets and raises.

*Offensive* manipulations, designed to maximize a potential win, are done by altering (increasing or decreasing) the betting pace in order to—

- build pots

- encourage players to stay for the large last-round bets

- set up bluffs

- induce opponents to bluff.

*Defensive* manipulations, designed to minimize a potential loss, are done by altering (increasing or decreasing) the betting pace in order to—

- suppress bets or raises

- prevent bluffs

- drive out or keep in players in order to create favorable odds for drawing to a potential hand, such as a four flush or two pair.

Confusion and fear decrease the ability of players to think objectively and to play their hands properly. Most players fear the confusing play and unpredictable betting of the good player. By making spectacular shock plays, he further increases their fear of him. Many opportunities occur in which investment odds actually favor spectacular maneuvers such as—

- holding a high pair pat in draw poker

- breaking up a full house to draw to three of a kind

- raising and then dropping out on the next bet

- making a colorful bluff such as holding pat and betting four kings in a lowball game

- raising a weak-looking stud hand in the face of strong-appearing opposition

- dropping a strong-looking stud hand in the face of weak-appearing opposition.

**John Finn has a big psychological advantage over his opponents. He confuses, shocks, bullies, frightens, and worries them into focusing their attention on him. They react strongly to his actions. Their moves and bets are often distorted because they base them on trivial moves by John, while ignoring significant moves by other players. Knowing how they will react to his moves, John can often make them do what he wants, while he alone retains a balanced view of the game. The results? He controls the game.... This is how that control works:**

**Immediately after bluffing Sid Bennett (in the previous chapter), John spreads his cards face-up**

across the table. Seeing John's four hearts with a big black club right in the middle, Sid moans and groans as the other players laugh at him. With his face blushing red, he mutters, "I'll sleep in the street before you bluff me out again."

The players are still talking about John's bluff as Scotty Nichols starts the next deal. Ted opens for $25. Sid fumbles with his money ... an indication that he wants to raise. John has a pair of aces that could be played with good investment odds if he can gain an offensive betting position and prevent Sid's raise. That is an easy problem for John. He just throws some confusion at the players by making a weird $3 raise.

Sid drops the money he was fingering. "What's Finn up to?" he says, wrinkling his nose. "He's either got nothing or a powerhouse. Uh... probably hoping for a raise."

Perfect. That is exactly the reaction John wanted. The silent players stare at him as they try to figure out his bet. The result? Everyone just calls and then anxiously awaits John's next move. With that $3 bet, John prevents any raising, gets everyone's attention, and assumes the offensive betting position.

Now the draw. John Finn takes three cards—Sid frowns at him. Immediately John looks at his draw. He catches a pair of jacks to give him aces-up two pair. His expression remains unchanged. Sid draws one card, glances at it, and then grunts, "I had John beat all the time. Should've raised him out of his seat."

A convenient statement for John ... it verifies that Sid still has two pair. Scotty also draws one card. By knowing his betting and playing habits, John reads him for two pair also. Ted draws one card; his freckled face stiffens as he slowly squeezes his cards apart. Then with a burst of swear words, he flings the cards across the table.

"Miss your flush?" Quintin Merck asks, smiling with a fluttering mustache. Ted just pouts his lip and looks at the ceiling.

John makes a nominal $1 bet. Sid, still mumbling about being bluffed out of the previous hand and then being tricked out of the first-round raise, reacts emotionally, "You ain't getting off cheap this time," he snorts. "I raise fifty bucks."

Scotty Nichols hesitates a long time before calling. That confirms he has two pair. If Scotty had three of a kind or better, he would have called without hesitation. Now John is in a strong fundamental position with his aces-up; he raises to $100. Both Sid and Scotty, having already bet their hands heavily, feel compelled to call. So they do.... John's aces-up wins the $400 pot.

So with a normally unfavorable hand and position, John controls the betting and wins the pot. Also because he knows how to control the players, he builds a potential $100 pot into a $400 pot by tickling Sid's emotions.

John Finn is a good player because he disciplines himself, thinks objectively, and then takes control of the game. Discipline, thought, and then control—the DTC method—is his technique for good poker.

Parts Three, Four, and Five of this book show how the good player with the DTC method achieves—

- improved edge odds (increased advantage)

- faster money flow (increased income)

- more players and games (increased future earnings).

# PART THREE

# STRATEGIES

With discipline and objective thinking, the good player takes control of poker games. With the proper strategy, he molds those games to his maximum advantage. His prime strategical tool is deception.

# X
# INGREDIENTS OF STRATEGY (19)

Proper strategy depends on the game, opponents, and situation. Certain phases of poker remain more or less constant; other phases change from bet to bet, hand to hand, or game to game. The good player bases his long-term strategy on the more constant phases of poker and his short-term strategy on the variable phases. Good strategy contains the ingredients shown in Table 14.

### TABLE 14
### INGREDIENTS OF STRATEGY

| *Strategy* | *Principal Ingredient* |
|---|---|
| Long-range | Understanding of game (a constant) |
| Short-range | Knowledge of opponents (a variable) |
| Immediate action | Awareness of situation (a variable) |

71

*Poker: A Guaranteed Income For Life*

*1. Understanding Game (2O)*

The mechanics of poker are simple and can be learned in a few minutes. Yet the strategy of poker has limitless possibilities. Strategy depends more on proper technique than on experience. Even a novice can acquire an immediate strategic advantage over seasoned opponents by applying the DTC technique (discipline, thought, and then control).

Long-range (general) strategy develops from an understanding of the game. The good player understands the game by knowing the—

- quality of players

- betting pace

- availability of cash

- credit situation

- general attitude and friendliness

- areas of resistance and resentment

- bluffing attitudes

- reasons for player turnover.

When a player fails to appraise a game accurately, he experiences—

- decreased edge odds

- errors and missed opportunities

- less effective strategy.

The good player continually evaluates the game in order to detect changes and inaccurate appraisals.

72

**All sorts of game and player information are in John Finn's black leather notebook. Every month he summarizes his observations in a section labeled "General Appraisal of Game and Players." Here is a typical summary:**

**"Monday—7/9. The players have stabilized over the past month, except for the gradual disintegration of Scotty, who gets desperate when losing heavily and then makes poor bets and bluffs. The betting pace is increasing as wild modifications are added. The betting stakes remain stable. The cash situation is good despite heavy losses by Sid, Ted, and Scotty. But Ted is in financial trouble; he runs up large debts and then pays them off with borrowed money. He may soon go broke.**

**"Resentment is building between Quintin and Sid. Quintin sarcastically questions Sid's honesty. Sid shouts back angry insults about Quintin's stinginess. This quarrel must end before it hurts the game.**

**"The game is in good shape and yields a reliable and substantial income. No one seems about to quit, except Ted if he goes bankrupt. But the game needs one or two new players... Aaron Smith would be a profitable addition."**

*2. Knowing Opponents (21)*
Short-range strategy develops from knowledge of opponents. The good player knows his opponents by appraising their—

- personalities

- weaknesses and strengths

- behavior patterns

- motives for playing

- financial status

- betting and raising tendencies

73

- dropping and bluffing tendencies

- areas of confusion and errors

Classification of opponents is a major step toward understanding them. Poker players usually can be put into one of the eleven classes shown in Table 15A.

### TABLE 15A
### CLASSES OF PLAYERS

| Class of Player | Ability to Control | Ability to Read | Performance |
|---|---|---|---|
| Good | Hardest | Very difficult | Biggest winner |
| Sound | | Difficult | |
| Daring and unconventional | | Medium | |
| Loose winner | | Medium | |
| Tight winner | | Medium | |
| Tight loser | | Easy | Loser |
| Loose loser | | Easy | |
| Very tight | | Easy | |
| Wild | | Medium | |
| Desperate | | Medium | Biggest loser |
| Suicidal | Easiest | Medium | |

(Vertical annotations: "Increase ease to control" down the Ability to Control column; "Decrease winnings" and "Increase losings" down the Performance column.)

Some players are a mixture of two classes. Also, the class of a player can change from moment to moment or over the long term, as shown in Table 15B.

TABLE 15B
CHANGES IN PLAYERS

| *Time Span for Change* | *Reasons for Change* |
|---|---|
| Over long term | Increased experience, personality changes |
| From game to game | Feelings, emotions, stakes, financial condition |
| From one type of game to another | Differences in understanding various games |
| From hand to hand | Winning, losing, tired, upset |
| During play of a hand | Erroneous perspective on different phases of betting |

The players in this Monday night game are classified as follows:

| Player | Class | Ability to Control and Read | Performance | Changes |
|---|---|---|---|---|
| John Finn | Good | Very difficult | Big winner | Stable. General long-term improvement. |
| Quintin Merck | Sound | Hard | Winner | General long-term improvement. Some deterioration when tired or insulted. |
| Scotty Nichols | Very tight | Easy | Loser | Deteriorates when losing heavily or on a long losing streak, then plays loose and poorly. |
| Sid Bennett | Wild | Medium | Big loser | Plays wild when winning. Tightens up if feelings are hurt. |
| Ted Fehr | Suicidal | Easy | Big loser | Plays tight early in game and then disintegrates, especially if losing. His playing becomes even worse when on a horse-betting spree. |

*Part Three: Strategies*

*3. Situation and Position (22)*

Action strategy depends on the immediate situation and involves decisions about calling, opening, betting, raising, dropping, and bluffing. In making those decisions, the good player correlates the following poker variables to the immediate situation.

1. *Estimated strength*[15] and *statistical value*[16] of his own hand

2. Game
   pace
   temperament
   atmosphere
   time (such as first hand, a late hour, last hand)
   size of pot
   potential size of pot

3. Opponents
   indicated strength
   attitude
   attentiveness
   win or loss status
   effect of previous bet

4. Position
   fundamental
   technical

The good player appraises his situation from both a fundamental and a technical position. His *fundamental position* is the *estimated strength* and *statistical value* of his hand relative to other players. His *technical position* is the strategic and psychological advantage he holds over his opponents at a given moment. An important strategical consideration is *seat position*.

[15] *Estimated strength of a hand is relative to the estimated strengths of opponents' hands.*

[16] *Statistical value of a hand is relative to the number of opponents. The statistical value of a hand decreases with increasing number of opponents.*

Seat position is important in nearly every decision. The good player adjusts his strategy according to his seat position relative to the dealer, opener, bettor, raiser, and the strong and weak hands. He considers his seat position in decisions about—

- bluffing
- betting or raising
- declaring hand (in split-pot games)
- calling or dropping
- playing of cards
- influencing opponents to call or drop
- inducing opponents to bet or raise
- planning long-range strategy.

*Increasing importance of seat position*

The best seat position depends on where the other players sit. The next anecdote about John Finn shows why the good player likes to position himself as shown in Table 16.

## TABLE 16
### SEAT POSITIONS

| *Good player prefers to bet before these types of players—* | *Good player prefers to bet after these types of players—* |
| --- | --- |
| Weak | Strong |
| Wild, but readable | Impulsive, erratic, not readable or predictable |
| Loose, but predictable | Tight |
| Plays dealer-advantage games (such as twist and draw games) | Plays conventional stud games |
| Fast | Slow |

The good player usually gets a desirable seat at the start of a game because his opponents seldom care where they sit. If an opponent is conscious of position, he generally tries to sit behind (bet after) the loosest or wildest player—the opposite position sought by the good player. A player can often pick a good position by arriving after the players are seated and then squeezing into the best seat position. (But continuous late arrival can hurt a game.) The good player can also use the excuse of "changing his luck" to swap seats with a player in a better seat position. That ploy also gives his opponents the erroneous but advantageous impression that he is superstitious.

The dealer has an advantage in hold'em, draw, or any form of closed-hand poker in which he bets last. When the same person always deals (e.g., a house dealer), that advantage is evenly distributed by using a marker, a button, or a buck that passes in turn to each player. Usually the player with the marker bets first, and the player to the right of marker bets last, as would a dealer.

**Most regular players get into a habit of sitting in the same position. In the Monday night game, John quietly arranges the seating to his advantage, and then game after game the players sit approximately in the same positions. He maintains this arrangement by preventing the players from realizing that they keep sitting in positions favorable to him.**

**Ted Fehr's betting is wild, and impulsive. While John can usually read Ted's hands, he can seldom predict his betting actions. By positioning himself so Ted bets first, John can adjust his strategy according to Ted's play. Sid Bennett's betting is even wilder, but is predictable. By betting before him, John can often check his strong hands and let Sid do the betting for him. It makes less difference to John where Quintin (a sound player) or Scotty (a tight player) sit. The ideal seating arrangement for John is illustrated below:**

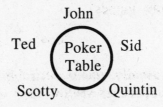

79

Book 3
Poker: A Guaranteed Income For Life

# XI
# TAILOR-MADE GAME (23)

The good player designs poker games to his maximum advantage by increasing the betting pace, the betting stakes, and his edge odds. A major step in this direction is to complicate the game by orienting the action around stud or hold'em variations of poker rather than draw poker. Stud variations offer the following advantages to the good player:

- More skill and effort are needed to assimilate the additional information and variables offered by the exposed cards.[17]

- Added rounds of progressively higher bets effectively increase the betting stakes.

- Faster and more rounds of bets effectively increase the betting pace.

## 1. Increasing the Betting Pace (24)

The good player increases the money flow in a poker game to increase his profits. But opposition to higher stakes exists in most games. Often a more subtle and effective way to increase the money flow is to increase the betting pace (rather than the betting stakes). A faster pace usually increases excitement in a way that is appealing to most players, especially weak players.

The betting pace is increased by adding modifications to the game such as those listed in Table 17.

---

[17] *The good player often adds another variable by inconspicuously altering the order of his face-up cards.*

## TABLE 17
## GAME MODIFICATIONS

| *Modification* | *Advantageous Effects* |
| --- | --- |
| Twists (extra cards) | Provides additional large last-round bets. Induces players to stay for twist cards. Increases confusion. Amplifies players' weaknesses. |
| Split pots (high-low) | Allows more bets and raises. Provides more playing and betting opportunities. Creates dynamic betting situations. Increases confusion. Amplifies players' weaknesses. |
| Check raises | Allows more and larger raises. |
| Pick-up checks | Permits larger bets. |
| Right to bet | Allows more raises. |
| Early bet | Early buildup of pot. Keeps more players in for large last-round bets. |
| Bet or get, blind bets | Produces more betting. Early buildup of pot. Keeps more players in for larger bets. |
| Additional cards | Produces more calls. |
| Novel games | Increases confusion. Amplifies players' weaknesses. |
| Wild cards, freak hands | May or may not increase betting pace. Increases confusion. |

Book 3
Poker: A Guaranteed Income For Life

| Table stakes: pot limit or no limit | Allows direct control over the betting stakes. Permits more aggressive betting and bluffing. |
| --- | --- |

The good player can usually work many advantageous modifications into most games — even into games that are not dealer's choice. The following paragraphs describe some of those advantageous pace-increasing modifications.

*a. Twist (25)*

The twist increases the betting pace. At the normal conclusion of a poker hand, a card or cards may be exchanged (twisted) for a new card or cards. An additional round of betting follows each twist. As players grow accustomed to that modification, they usually become addicted to it and make the twist a permanent part of the game.

A single twist played with five-card stud is the gentlest way to introduce this modification. Most players will accept a twist as a good way to convert normally dull five-card stud into a more lively "six-card" stud game. As players become accustomed to the twist, the good player can further quicken the pace by adding other twist modifications such as—

- twist in seven-card stud

- twist in draw poker

- pay for each twist (for example, an amount equal to the ante)

- double twists

- giant twist in stud (as many cards as the player desires are exchanged on each twist)

- progressive paying for unlimited twists (second twist costs twice the first twist, third twist costs twice the second, and so on).

*Faster betting pace*

82

## b. Split pot, high-low (26)

Because of the dynamic betting action between high hands and low hands, the betting pace increases markedly when pots are split between the highest hand and the lowest hand (high-low poker). Many players are initially hostile to high-low poker. Seven-card stud high-low is probably the easiest way to introduce split-pot games. With patience and persistence, the good player can usually generate great interest in high-low poker. Again, the good player can further quicken the pace by adding other high-low modifications such as—

- high-low five-card stud

- high-low draw

- High-low with qualifiers (minimum hands required to win, such as two pair for high and nine for low)

- high-low with a twist

- high-low with qualifiers and twists

*(left margin, vertical: Faster betting pace)*

## c. Check raise and pick-up checks (27)

Player A checks; player B bets; now player A raises... that is called check raising. Player A checks; player B checks; player C makes a bet three times larger than the maximum bet by making A's bet, B's raise, and then his own raise... that is called picking up checks. Check raising and picking up checks increase the betting flexibility as well as the number of large bets and raises. But if those modifications cause a defensive attitude among players, a decrease in the betting pace can occur. Also, house rules of many games prohibit check raising and picking up checks.

## d. Right to bet (28)

Every player has a chance to bet or raise during each round of betting. With this rule, a player holding a strong hand cannot be shut out of his bet or raise by three minimal raises made in front of him. Right to bet increases the betting pace, particularly in split-pot games. Players seldom object to this seemingly equitable modification.

83

### e. Early bet (29)

An indirect method to increase the ante is to permit a small bet after dealing the first hole card in stud or the second card in draw. The early bet usually holds more players in the game for the later rounds of more expensive betting. But if most players stay or drop on the strength of their early cards rather than on the size of the pot, this modification can drive out potential players and thus decrease the betting pace.

### f. Bet or get and blind bets (30)

No checking is permitted with the bet-or-get rule... each player must either bet or drop. This modification gets players involved early and keeps them in for the big last-round bets. Most players are unaccustomed to this modification and may object vigorously to it. A similar modification is blind betting (and raising) in which the first player after the dealer is forced to bet (and if called for, the next player is forced to raise). Blind betting and blind raising are common in public poker and are very effective for increasing the betting action.

### g. Additional cards (31)

An additional sixth card is dealt to each draw hand. The hands are then reduced to five cards during the draw. That additional card keeps more players in the hand, particularly in lowball draw. Players seldom object when this simple modification is introduced.

### h. Novel games (32)

Poorer playing normally results when new or novel games are introduced because most players do not understand the changes in play and odds that occur. Novel games may range from simple lowball draw or hold'em stud to a complex game such as "place-and-show-tickets split-pot-with-twist-your-neighbor." (That game is played as follows: At the conclusion of a stud or draw game, each player draws for use in his own hand a card from the hand of an adjacent player. The pot is then split between the second and third best hands.)

A decreased betting pace may result, however, if players become frightened or excessively confused by wild games or modifications that are too extreme or are introduced too rapidly.

*i. Wild cards and freak hands (33)*

Wild cards can increase the betting pace and loosen up certain games. As players become accustomed to wild cards, their fear of very strong hands usually dissipates. But if so many wild cards are used that hands such as five-of-a-kind and straight flushes become common and any betting strength suggests those maximum-value hands, the betting will dry up.

The bug card (the joker—used in low hands as a wild card, and in high hands as an ace or as a wild card for completing straights and flushes) can increase the betting pace without causing fear of maximum-value hands.

The good player rarely encourages the use of freak hands such as blazes, tigers, dogs, kilters, and skeets. While such hands could temporarily increase his edge odds by adding confusion, the use of freak hands may deter players from accepting other more profitable modifications such as twists and split pots.

*j. No-limit table stakes and pot limit (34)*

No-limit table stakes and pot-limit betting allow more aggressive betting and bluffing, giving the good player direct control over the betting. But such open-ended stakes can slow down the betting pace and normally cannot be used with split-pot games. In many games, therefore, no-limit table stakes or pot-limit betting (versus high-limit games) would actually decrease the financial opportunities for the good player.

**Six years ago, Sid Bennett insisted that good poker players liked only straight draw and stud games. He claimed five-card was the greatest gambling game of all. As John Finn gradually increased the betting pace by adding one modification after another, Sid went to the other extreme:**

**Sid is winning; his pale lips are smiling. He grabs the deck, shoves his face over the table, and announces, "New game!" He then deals two separate hole cards to everyone.**

"What's this?" Quintin says, frowning sourly.

"Seven-stud high-low. Everyone plays two hands. You can even raise yourself," Sid says with a snorting laugh. "And the hand to the left of the highest hand wins high and the hand to the right of the lowest hand wins low."

"I'm going home," Quintin says as he grabs his ante from the pot and stands up to leave.

"Sit down; we aren't going to play that," John Finn says. He then turns to Sid and explains gently, "I know its dealer's choice, but that's no poker game. You can't have hands next to the winners as winners."

"Bunch of ribbon clerks," Sid whines. "Okay, straight high-low ... play your left hand for high and right hand for low. And you can still raise yourself."

"That's more like it." John says.

Sid's toothy grin stretches wider as he continues to deal.

## 2. Increasing the Betting Stakes (35)

After increasing the betting pace, the good player can often increase the betting stakes sharply. Most games can withstand a tenfold to hundred fold increase in the betting stakes. Even when the big losers seem to be at their financial limits, the stakes can usually be increased significantly.

The good player increases the stakes in carefully planned steps. Several temporary increases may be necessary before higher stakes become permanent. But in some games, stakes can be increased immediately and rapidly. Opportunities to increase the stakes occur when players want—

- a chance to get even by increasing the ante or stakes in the late hours or during the last round

- a more equitable relationship to the ante by increasing the first-round or opening bets

- a chance to protect a hand by increasing the middle-round bets

86

- an opportunity to bet a good hand by increasing the last-round bets.

The stakes are normally easier to increase after the betting pace increases. Opposition to higher stakes and game modifications often diminishes when the resisting player is—

- tired

- losing heavily or winning big for the evening

- on a losing or a winning streak

- upset by some occurrence during the game

- affected by personal problems

- drinking.

A good way to increase the stakes is to let those players who want to double the stakes, for example, play at double stakes whenever they are the only players left in the hand.

**When John Finn started playing in the Monday night game, it was already seven years old and the stakes had been stabilized for five years. A dollar was the maximum bet, and only straight draw and stud games were allowed. The chart on page 67 shows how both the betting pace and stakes steadily increased after John took control of the game:**

| Months after First Game | Pace | Stakes, $ | Money Flow | | |
| --- | --- | --- | --- | --- | --- |
| | | | Average Big Winner, $ | John Finn's Average Winnings, $ | John Finn's Edge Odds, % |
| 0 | Straight stud and draw | 0.50—1 | 25 | 8 | 30 |
| 1 | Add twist | 1—2 | 40 | 14 | 35 |
| 2 | | —4 | 70 | 32 | 45 |
| 3 | | 2— | 100 | 40 | 40 |
| 7 | Add high-low | 5—10 | 170 | 94 | 55 |
| 8 | | 10—20 | 210 | 105 | 50 |
| 13 | | — | 260 | 130 | 50 |
| 18 | Add qualifiers | 25—50 | 360 | 234 | 65 |
| 19 | | 50—100 | 450 | 270 | 60 |
| 26 | | 25—50 | 600 | 210 | 35 |
| 27 | | 50—100 | 550 | 358 | 65 |
| 46 | | 50—100 | 700 | 350 | 50 |
| 61 | Add complex and wild modifications | | 1400 | 840 | 60 |

The data in the chart on page 86 show three interesting phenomena:

1. When the stakes increase, there is not a proportional increase in the average winnings or money flow because most players initially play tighter at higher stakes. But an increase in the pace causes looser play and a relatively large increase in the money flow.

2. John's edge odds go up when the pace increases and down when the stakes increase. This is because his opponents play more poorly as the pace increases, but more cautiously at higher stakes.

3. An increase in the pace eventually leads to higher stakes.

The data also show how the increases in stakes and pace affect John's profits. The doubling of stakes after twenty-six months causes his edge odds to drop sharply— from 60 percent to 35 percent. At those higher stakes, he must spend a greater portion of his income to hold valuable losers in the game. On realizing that, John drops the stakes back to the previous level and brings his edge odds up to a healthy 65 percent. Why the big increase in John's edge odds when he lowers the stakes? After getting a taste of higher stakes, the players bet more loosely and play more carelessly when the stakes are lowered to the old level. Nineteen months later, John doubles the stakes again... and this time the increase is profitable and permanent.

John usually tries raising the stakes soon after increasing the betting pace. Under the pretense of giving the losers a break, he often increases the stakes during the last round of the game. The following dialogue shows how he advantageously manipulates that last round.

"You're getting blasted again," Sid Bennett says to Ted Fehr. "Must be losing a grand."

"That's only four thousand hamburgers at my drive-in," Ted says, smiling weakly. "Wait till I get the deal. I'm doubling the stakes like we did last week. Got to make a big comeback."

"No sir, none of that," Quintin Merck interrupts as his cigarette falls from his mouth. "Next thing you know, we'll be playing the whole game at double stakes."

"Quintin's right," John says, trying hard to sound sincere. "If anything, we should ban double stakes even for the last round . . . it's too expensive."

"Yeah," Scotty Nichols says while counting his winnings.

Two hours later, John announces the last round.

"Hey, double the stakes for the last round," Ted cries.

"We made a rule against it," John says with a shrug. He then turns to the other players and continues, "We gave the losers a break last week. Ted is stuck bad. Let's double the ante and play a round of high-low draw—for Ted's sake."

"Yeah!" Scotty says as he checks his freshly emptied wallet.

"I'm in," Ted says, throwing his double ante into the pot.

"High-low draw? That's a stiff game," Quintin grumbles while anteing slowly. "That's worse than doubling the stakes."

What does John accomplish with that manipulation? He introduces the fast-pace, high-low draw game. He doubles the ante, which will make the stakes easier to increase at a later date. He creates the impression that he is both helping a loser and opposing higher stakes, while actually setting up conditions for both higher stakes and a faster pace.

*3. Increasing the Edge Odds (36)*

The good player designs a game to yield maximum edge odds. The theoretical maximum edge odds occur only when the perfect player is in the most complex game, under the most confusing circumstances, against the poorest players. While the conditions for theoretical maximum edge odds can never be achieved, the good player strives to approach them. The perfect situation is represented by the completion of the Diamond shown on the next page. The Diamond measures the idealness of a poker game for the good player.

**How far does John Finn go toward completing the Diamond? How much further could he increase his edge odds in the Monday night game? He makes the following estimations:**

| *Side of Diamond* | *% Completed* | *Maximum Possible %* | *Limitation* |
|---|---|---|---|
| **Increase skill of good player** | **95** | **100** | **None** |
| **Increase weakness in opponents** | **45** | **65** | **Availability of weak players capable of large losses** |
| **Increase confusion in game** | **70** | **80** | **Human tolerance** |
| **Increase complexity of game** | **90** | **95** | **Opponents' capacity to comprehend** |
| **Total (average), %** | **75** | **85** | |

**Playing with the Diamond 75 percent complete, John's edge odds are about 65 percent. He estimates that under the best conditions, the Diamond would be 85 percent complete, and thus his edge odds could improve to a maximum of 74 percent. That estimation of maximum edge odds establishes a goal toward which John Finn can strive.**

## THE DIAMOND

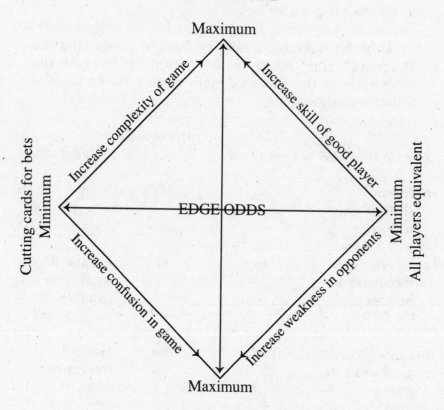

# XII
# BEHAVIOR (37)

The good poker player directs his actions toward achieving maximum advantages while preventing his opponents from realizing that he is motivated entirely by profit. He is a winner acting like a loser.

## 1. Systemization and Blandness (38)

To prevent opponents from reading his hand or sensing his strategy, the good player systemizes his—

- procedures for observing opponents

- physical movements

- verbal expressions

- vocal tones.

While playing his hand, the good player is seldom an actor. Instead he practices a bland behavior that—

- minimizes his readable patterns or tells

- frustrates and confuses his opponents

- allows greater concentration.

A good player never loses interest in his hand until the moment he folds. If opponents can sense his intention to fold before his turn, they will become more defensive when he does hold a playable hand, thus decreasing his edge odds.

Improvised acting while playing a hand is usually ineffective because the act does not develop from a well-planned basis. Yet when not involved in the action, the good player has many opportunities to act effectively on a carefully planned basis. Occasionally while playing in a hand, he deviates from his

93

systemized behavior when he knows a certain behavior will cause an opponent to make a desired move (call, drop, bet, or raise).

"What's John doing now?" Scotty Nichols whines. He rubs his whiskered face while wondering if he should call John's $50 raise. "Can't ever read him."

"That's 'cause he sits like a tree stump," Quintin Merck says. "Gives you nothing to grab. You guys that act are easy to read."

John Finn will act, however, when he is reasonably certain of his opponents' reactions. Consider that hand in which he is supposedly sitting like the tree stump:

Wanting Scotty to call, John lets his fingers creep into the pot and spread out the money. He pulls out the big bills and lays them on top. Scotty stares at the money; he is a loser, and winning that pot would make him even... he licks his lips and calls.

Poor Scotty never should have called. His kings-up two pair were no match for John's full house. Was John acting? Yes, because Scotty was undecided and John varied his own behavior to make him call. John also did some long-range acting toward Quintin Merck. How was that? Quintin observed John's maneuver to make Scotty call. John heard Quintin snort when Scotty fell into the trap.

The following week, John and Quintin are battling for a large pot. John raises... Quintin scratches his head and then starts to call. John's fingers creep into the pot and spread out the money. He pulls out the big bills and lays them on top. Quintin snorts, shows his three deuces to everyone, and then folds with a prissy smile. His smile snaps into a frown when John throws his hand face up on the table. His hand this time? A four flush.

Why did Quintin fall into that trap? He forgot that John would not apply the same tactic toward a poor player like Scotty as he would toward a sound player

**like Quintin. John plays against the individual as well as the situation.**

### 2. *Personality (39)*

The good player varies his personality to obtain the best advantage. Typical poker personalities he adopts are described below.

### a. Unfriendly or Intimidating (40)

In public (club or casino) games or in games consisting mostly of professionals or strangers, tough or unfriendly and intimidating behavior may be best. Such behavior disorients opponents ... and disoriented players are easier to control. Unfriendly behavior irritates opponents, causing them to act more emotionally and to play poorer poker.

The following unfriendly and intimidating behavior can be advantageously practiced by the good player:

— Silently throw bets and raises into the pot. Give ill-tempered replies when asked about those bets or raises. Make disagreeable remarks when other players err because of your silent bets.

— At the conclusion of a hand, throw cards face-up on the table without comment. Make opponents figure out the hand. Capitalize on their errors that favor you.

— Stage displays of bad temper.

— Delay anteing and making good on lights (money owed to the pot).

— When dealing new games, give inadequate explanations. When asked for further explanation, give details grudgingly and unpleasantly.

— Push rules and ethics to the limit. For example, fake moves to make the next player believe that you have dropped, called, or raised... then when he reveals his move (a drop, bet, or raise), remake your play accordingly.

95

Planned unfriendly or intimidating behavior can be effective for increasing edge odds and for controlling opponents. Still, the good player uses caution when being unfriendly. He analyzes the game and evaluates the effects of any behavior on both his short-term and long-term profits.

In some games, intimidating behavior is tolerated if a little humor or congenial behavior is blended in. Also, the good player may adopt a split personality or may be unfriendly to certain players and congenial to others ... whatever is most advantageous.

### b. Congenial (41)

Unfriendly and intimidating behavior is undesirable for most friendly or regular private games. Unpleasant behavior could break up the game, result in expulsion from the game, or cause valuable losers to quit. Congenial behavior is often necessary in such games. But most friendly traditions are disadvantageous to the good player, such as—

- no betting when only two remain in a hand

- no betting a lock hand (a sure winner)

- no squeeze raising when only three players are in a split-pot game.

Occasional but dramatic displays of friendly traditions will usually satisfy the other players.

**Sometimes John Finn is the most congenial player in the game. At other times, he is not so congenial. He always behaves in a way that offers him the greatest advantages.**

**How can John switch his personality to fit the game? He keeps himself free from emotional ties to the game and the players. That allows him to think objectively and define what behavior offers the most advantage. For example, he will drive a good player out of the game with unfriendly behavior (see Concept 108). Why will he do that? Another good player would**

**increase the financial strain on the losers, which in turn would cost John some of his profits to keep those losers in the game. In other words, a good player would cost John money . . . so why let him play? Why not replace him with a more profitable, poor player?**

### c. Introvert and extrovert (42)

The good player usually behaves oppositely to the general behavior of his opponents. For example, in a quiet game with serious players, an extroverted personality may be advantageous. In a wild or boisterous game, an introverted personality is often the most advantageous.

**The extent of introverted or extroverted behavior that John Finn assumes depends on the game, as shown below:**

| Game | Players' Behavior | Advantageous Behavior (John Finn 's Behavior) |
|---|---|---|
| **Monday** | **Mixed** | **Ambiverted** |
| **Tuesday** | **Introverted** | **Extroverted** |
| **Thursday** | **Ambiverted** | **Ambiverted** |
| **Friday** | **Extroverted** | **Introverted** |

### 3. Practicing Deceit (43)

Only in poker can a man lie and practice any form of deceit, except cheating, and still remain a gentleman ... and an honest person. The good player makes extensive use of his right to deceive. He conceals facts and lies about anything that offers him an advantage.

### a. Concealing desires (44)

To keep his opponents off guard, the good player conceals his desires, as shown in Table 18.

## TABLE 18
## CONCEALING DESIRES

| *Desire* | *Method to Conceal* |
|---|---|
| **More weak players** | Never discuss weaknesses of players. |
| **Faster betting pace** | Increase betting pace without verbally expressing a desire for a faster betting pace. Occasionally complain about the fast pace and wild modifications. |
| **Higher stakes** | Never suggest higher stakes unless chances for an increase are nearly certain, then suggest higher stakes as a way to give losers a break or to make the betting more equitable. |
| **More games** | Never reveal activities in other games. Organize games without expressing an eagerness to play. |

b. *Concealing facts(45)*

The good player conceals facts to avoid arousing unfavorable suspicions, as shown in Table 19.

## TABLE 19
## CONCEALING FACTS

| *Facts* | *Methods to Conceal* |
|---|---|
| **Easiness of game** | Never mention the poor quality of poker played in any game. Praise "skills" of opponents, especially of poor players. |
| **Winnings** | Never discuss personal winnings. After each game, report less than |

98

actual winnings or more than actual losses. But exaggerate only to a believable extent. Never reveal long-term winnings. Conceal affluence by driving an old car to the game.

| | |
|---|---|
| **Tight play** | Fold cards without comment or excuses. Make loose-appearing or wild plays whenever investment odds are favorable. |
| **Good play** | Never explain the true strategy behind a play. Instead, give erroneous reasoning for strategy. Never brag... downgrade own performance. |
| **Control over game** | Assume a humble but assertive attitude. |

To turn attention away from his poker success, the good player praises and exaggerates the poker ability of other winners. In a verbal smoke screen, he discusses and magnifies everyone's winnings except his own. When losing, the good player complains about the tough game and exaggerates his losses. But he never mentions the losses of other players.

*c. Lying (46)*

Lying is a key tool of strategy. For example, when asked about his folded cards, the good player lies about them to create the impression that he plays loosely or poorly. To lie effectively, he must always lie within believable boundaries to keep others from automatically doubting him.

**With careful lying and calculated deceit, John Finn builds his image as a kind-hearted, loose player who is an asset to the game. Here is an example of how he builds this advantageous image:**

The game is highball draw with a twist. John begins with a pair of aces, draws three cards, and ends up with two pair. During the betting, he notices Ted Fehr putting $25 too much into the pot. John says nothing and plays his two pair pat on the twist. Sid Bennett misses his flush and folds out of turn . . . that out-of-turn fold is very helpful to John.

Now with only two remaining in the hand, Ted bets $25. John reads him for trips and reasons Ted's bet like this: Ted thinks his three of a kind are beat by John's pat hand. So if he checks, John will bet the $50 maximum, and he will have to call. By making a smaller bet, he hopes that John will only call, thus saving him $25. Ted's strategy backfires . . . John raises to $75.

"How many cards did you draw in the first round?" Ted asks.

"One," John quickly lies.

"A one-card draw, then pat on the twist ... I can't call that," Ted sighs while folding his cards.

John places his cards face-down next to Sid's dead hand.

"What'd you have, the straight or flush?" Ted asks.

John pulls in the pot. He then picks up Sid's cards, gives them to Ted, and says in a low voice, "Don't tell anyone my hand."

"What!" Ted cries on seeing the cards. "You play a four flush pat to win a three-hundred-dollar pot?" John smiles and nods. Ted slumps in his chair.

"That's what I like," Sid says. "His wild playing beats all you tight players.... You're great, John."

John shrugs his shoulders and then throws $25 to Ted.

"What's this for?" Ted asks.

"Your last bet," John says "I don't feel right about taking it."

"Merciful guy." Ted smiles. Then, counting the money, he continues, "You might win all my money, but you're still a gentleman."

100

**"That's no gift,"** Quintin Merck mumbles, **"Ted put...**

**"Whose deal?"** John interrupts.... **So besides winning a $300 pot, he did a lot of favorable image-building with that hand.**

### 4. Creating an Atmosphere (47)

Carefree, relaxed, and pleasant poker atmospheres are advantageous to the good player. He creates those atmospheres in the following ways.

### a. Carefree(48)

A carefree atmosphere stimulates a careless attitude about money and causes opponents to play poorer poker. A carefree atmosphere is developed by—

- increasing the betting pace

- complicating the game

- using poker chips instead of money

- appearing careless with money.

The good player himself is never carefree about poker or careless with money ... he always respects money. His careless behavior is a planned act.

### b. Relaxed (49)

A relaxed atmosphere lulls opponents into decreased concentration, which diminishes their playing abilities and increases their readability. Contributing to a relaxed atmosphere are—

- a suitable location.

- good food and beverages

- a comfortable setting with proper table, chairs, and lighting.

*Poker: A Guaranteed Income For Life*

To maintain peak concentration, the good player denies himself the effects of comfort and relaxation.

### c. Pleasant (50)

A pleasant atmosphere holds weak players in the game and attracts new players. The good player creates a pleasant atmosphere by—

- being congenial (when advantageous)

- preventing unpleasant remarks and unfriendliness among players

- displaying a sympathetic attitude toward losers.

Most players gain pleasure from feeling accepted and belonging to the group. But the good player gains pleasure from his ability to win money and control the game.

**Whenever the Monday night game gets serious, the players think more clearly and make fewer mistakes. When serious, everyone plays tighter and is less prone to John Finn's influence. So he keeps the game carefree and careless by behavior such as described below:**

**A newcomer, playing in the high-stake Monday game for the first time, is nervous and is playing very tight. He shuffles... the cards spray from his trembling hands and scatter all over the floor. Finally he deals five-card stud. John gets a pair of aces on his first two up cards. Everyone drops out except big loser Scotty Nichols. "Haven't won a pot all night," he says and then gulps. "I... I gotta win one." John makes a few small bets. Scotty stays to the end and loses with his wired pair of queens. The pot is small, containing perhaps $35.**

**With quivering lips, Scotty slowly turns his cards over. Suddenly John shoves the whole pot across the table and into Scotty's lap while laughing, "Don't be so miserable. It's only money... Take it all."**

102

**The newcomer's mouth snaps open. "What a crazy game!" he exclaims. "I've never seen anything like that!"**

**Scotty grims and mumbles something about John's generous act.**

**"Help thy neighbor, help thy luck," John tells everyone. "Nothing is cheaper than money."**

**That move will be remembered and discussed for a long time. The cost to John: about $35. The return to John: certainly many times that.**

## 5. Observation (51)

The good player depends on his observations to plan his strategy. Observation of opponents requires an analytical technique. Observation of the cards requires a trained eye. And knowing what his opponents observe and know will also affect his strategy.

### a. Reading opponents (52)

All players have repeating habits and nervous patterns that give away their hands. The task of the good player is to find and interpret those patterns. Most poker players offer readable patterns (tells) in their—

- initial reaction to looking at cards (freshly dealt hands, draw cards, hole cards, up cards, opponents' up cards, flop cards)

- behaviors on making calls, bets, and raises

- reactions to calls, bets, and folds of opponents

- ways of handling and looking at cards

- ways of handling money before and during each bet

- extents and directions of interest during the action

- behaviors and remarks during each phase of action

- mumbling and spoken thoughts

- tones of voice

- reactions to comments

- responses to questions.

Questions are potent tools for reading opponents' hands. Often players reveal their hands by impulsive responses to seemingly innocuous questions as—

- How many cards did you draw?

- Who made the last bet?

- How much was the last bet?

- Is it your bet? (when it really is not)

- Did you call the last bet?

- Are you light?

Ways of looking at opponents are also important: The good player controls the position of his head and eyes to avoid a direct stare at those opponents who become cautious and less readable when feeling observed. He will, however, stare directly at those players who get nervous and more readable when feeling observed. In some games, especially public games, the good player may wear dark glasses to conceal his eye actions.

When involved in action, the good player reads his opponents and then makes his play accordingly. When not involved in the action, he analyzes all players for readable patterns. At the conclusion of each pot, he correlates all revealed hands to his observations. By that technique, he can discover and build an inventory of readable patterns for each opponent.

**The most valuable pages in John's black leather notebook describe the readable patterns of his opponents. For example, consider his notes about Scotty Nichols:**

**Before hand**—When winning, breaking even, or losing slightly, he plays very tight and never bluffs. Stays to end only when holding a strong hand. When losing heavily, he panics—he plays wildly while trying to bluff far too often. Once hooked in a hand, he stays to the end.

**Receiving cards**—Grabs for each dealt card when a good hand is developing. Casually looks at new cards when holding a poor-potential hand.

**Dealing**—Usually flashes bottom card when picking up the deck. Often flashes cards he deals to himself.

**Looking at cards**—When planning to play, he looks to his right. When planning to raise, he looks to his left. When planning to drop, he looks blankly into space.

**Handling cards**—Leaves cards on table when he intends to fold. If holding a playable pair, two pair, trips, a bobtail straight, or a full house, he arranges his cards and then does not disturb them. If holding a lowball hand or a four flush, he continuously ruffles the cards through his fingers.

**Before bet**—Touches his money lightly when going to call. His thumb lifts edge of money when going to raise. Picks up money when going to bluff. Does not touch money when going to fold.

**Betting**—Puts money in pot with a deliberate motion when not confident, with a flicking motion when confident, and with a hesitation followed by a flicking motion when sandbagging.

**Raising**—Cheek muscles flex when holding a certain winner. A stiffness develops around his upper lip when worried. Breathes through mouth when bluffing.

**Drawing**—Inserts cards randomly into his hand and then ruffles cards when drawing to a four flush or a pair. Puts cards on one end with no ruffling when drawing to a four straight or trips. Puts card second from the end when drawing to trips with a kicker. Puts card in center of hand when drawing to two pair. With two pair, he looks at draw quickly. With all other hands, he slowly squeezes cards open. Squeezes very slowly when drawing to lowball, flush, or straight hands. Jerks hand when he misses.

**Looking at draw**—Exhales when he misses, and his eyes stare blankly at the table. Inhales when he catches, and his eyes glance at his opponents and then at the pot.

**Stud up cards**—After catching a good card, he touches it first and then reorganizes his cards. Confirms catch by looking several times at his hole cards.

**Stud hole cards**—When hole cards are good, he keeps them neatly organized and touches them periodically. Does not bother to organize or touch poor cards. If one fakes a move to grab his hole cards, he impulsively jumps and grabs the cards if they are good . . . does nothing if they are poor.

**Last-round bet**—A quick call means he will call a raise. Picking up all his money when calling means he will not call a raise. Watching the next caller without looking directly at him means he is hoping for a raise.

**Questions**—"Do you have three tens beat?" Scotty blinks his eyes if his hand does not beat three tens ... no blinking if it does. "How many cards did you draw?" Scotty hesitates and turns eyes up in thought if he is bluffing. Gives a casual answer if holding a normal hand. Hesitates and stares at the pot if holding a powerful hand.

**After hand**—He will play carelessly when sulking over losses. He will play extra tight when winning and counting his money.

With so many readable patterns, Scotty has little chance against John Finn. By putting together several of those patterns, John reads him with consistent

106

accuracy. And Scotty's low awareness level keeps him from recognizing the habits that reveal his cards and intentions.

John also has similar dossiers on the other players and can usually read them accurately... even a sound player like Quintin Merck. Because of Quintin's greater awareness, he occasionally recognizes and eliminates a habit that reveals his hand. But John uses several habits to cross-check readable patterns and can quickly detect when anyone changes or eliminates a habit. After each game, he records in his notebook any new or changed habits... John Finn knows that all players have telling habits and readable patterns that give away their hands and intentions. The task of the good player is to identify and interpret those habits and patterns so he can accurately read the hands and intentions of every opponent. Reading opponents' hands is much more effective than using marked cards and it is honest.

The question-type giveaways or tells are quite reliable and are particularly useful for pinpointing the exact value of an opponent's hand. For example, if John holds trips and reads his opponent for trips, he might use questions to find out who has the best hand. Excessive use of questions, however, can rouse suspicion and decrease the usefulness of question-and-answer tells.

### b. Remembering exposed cards and ghost hands (53)

By remembering all exposed cards, a player increases his accuracy in estimating investment and card odds. In games with many players (eight or more), discarded and folded cards are often redealt. Knowledge of those cards can be crucial for estimating meaningful investment odds. In some games, discarded and folded cards are actually placed on the bottom of the deck without shuffling. (The good player encourages that practice.) If those cards are redealt during the late rounds, the good player will know what cards are to be dealt to whom... a huge advantage for the later rounds of big bets.

With disciplined concentration and practice, any player can learn to memorize all exposed cards. For the discipline value alone, remembering exposed cards is always a worthwhile effort. But many players excuse themselves from this chore by rationalizing that memorization of cards dissipates their concentration on the other aspects of the game. That may be true when a player first tries to memorize cards, but a disciplined training effort toward memorizing all exposed cards will ultimately increase his concentration powers in every area of poker.

Remembering the exposed draw hands or the order of exposed stud cards from the previous deal can bring financial rewards. Old hands often reappear on the next deal (ghost hands), especially when the shuffling is in complete (the good player encourages sloppy and incomplete shuffling). For example, a good player is sitting under the gun (on the dealer's left) and needs a king to fill his inside straight in five-card stud. But the last card dealt in that round (the dealer's card) is a king. The good player, rather than being discouraged, recalls that the winner of the previous hand held three kings. Since the deck had been poorly shuffled. the chances of the next card (his card) also being a king are good. Knowing this, he now has a strong betting advantage.

**John Finn memorizes all exposed and flashed cards He mentally organizes every exposed stud card into one of the four following categories by saying to himself, for example, Sid's two of hearts would help—**
- **my hand**
- **his (Sid's) hand**
- **another opponent's (e.g., Quintin's) hand**
- **no one's hand.**

**That association of each card with a definite hand not only organizes John's thoughts but also aids his memory.**

**Now if Sid folds and his two of hearts is the first card to go on the bottom of the deck, John will remember that the fifty-third card is the two of hearts. Then by mentally counting the dealt cards, John will know when and to whom the two of hearts will be**

108

**redealt. By that procedure, he often knows several cards that will be redealt. For example, he may know the fifty-third, fifty-fourth, fifty-seventh, sixtieth, and sixty-first card.... The cards he knows depends on how the folded cards are put on the bottom of the deck.**

## c. Seeing flashed cards (54)

Many important cards are flashed during a game. Players who see flashed cards are not cheating. Cheating occurs only through a deliberate physical action to see unexposed cards. For example, a player who is dealing and purposely turns the deck to look at the bottom card is cheating. But a player who sees cards flashed by someone else violates no rule or ethic. To see the maximum number of flashed cards. one must know when and where to expect them. When the mind is alert to flashing cards, the eye can be trained to spot and identify them. Cards often flash when—

- they are dealt

- a player picks up his hand or draw cards

- a player looks at his cards or ruffles them through his fingers

- a kibitzer or peeker picks up the cards of another player (peekers are often careless about flashing other players' cards)

- a player throws in his discards or folds his hand

- cards reflect in a player's eyeglasses.

The good player occasionally tells a player to hold back his cards or warns a dealer that he is flashing cards. He does that to create an image of honesty, which keeps opponents from suspecting his constant use of flashed cards. He knows his warnings have little permanent effect on stopping players from flashing cards. In fact, warned players often become more careless about flashing because of their increased confidence in the "honesty" of the game.

Book 3
Poker: A Guaranteed Income For Life

**Using data from one hundred games, John Finn compiles the following chart, which illustrates the number of flashed cards he sees in the Monday night game:**

*Flashed by*

*Average Number of Flashed Cards Identified per Hand (adjusted for a seven-man game)*

| | Draw | 7-Stud |
|---|---|---|
| **Dealer*** | 6 | 2 |
| **Active players** | 7 | 1 |
| **Kibitzers and peekers** | 2 | 1 |
| **Folded players** | 9 | 3 |
| **Total** | 24 | 7 |

*\*Also, the bottom card of the deck is exposed 75 percent of the time.*

These data show that in addition to seeing his own cards, John sees over half the deck in an average game of draw poker—just by keeping his eyes open. The limit he goes to see flashed cards is illustrated below:

Mike Bell is a new player. John does not yet know his habits and must rely on other tools to read him—such as seeing flashed cards.

The game is lowball draw with one twist. The betting is heavy, and the pot grows large. John has a fairly good hand (a seven low) and does not twist. Mike bets heavily and then draws one card. John figures he is drawing to a very good low hand, perhaps to a six low.

John bets. Ted Fehr pretends to have a good hand, but just calls—John reads him for a poor nine low. Everyone else folds except Mike Bell, who holds his cards close to his face and slowly squeezes them open; John studies Mike's face very closely. Actually he is not looking at his face, but is watching the reflection

110

in his eyeglasses. When Mike opens his hand, John sees the scattered dots of low cards plus the massive design of a picture card reflecting in the glasses. (You never knew that?... Try it, especially if your bespectacled victim has a strong light directly over or behind his head. Occasionally a crucial card can even be identified in a player's bare eyeball.)

In trying to lure a bluff from the new player, John simply checks. Having already put $100 into the pot, Mike falls into the trap by making a $50 bluff bet. If John had not seen the reflection of a picture card in Mike's glasses, he might have folded. But now he not only calls the bluff bet with confidence, but tries a little experiment—he raises $1. Ted folds; and Mike, biting his lip after his bluff failure, falls into the trap again— he tries a desperate double bluff by raising $50. His error? He refuses to accept his first mistake and repeats his error... Also, he holds cards too close to his glasses.

John calmly calls and raises another $1. Mike folds by ripping up his cards and throwing them all over the floor. His playing then disintegrates. What a valuable reflection, John says to himself.

*[Note: Luring or eliciting bluffs and double bluffs from opponents is a major money-making strategy of the good player. In fact, in most games, he purposely lures other players into bluffing more often than he bluffs himself.]*

## d. Intentional flashing (55)

The good player intentionally flashes cards in his hand to cause opponents to drop, call, bet, raise, or bluff. But he uses the intentional flash with caution. If suspected, intentional flashes are less effective and can cause resentment among players.

**After the final card of a seven-card stud game, John Finn holds a partly hidden flush—three clubs showing and two clubs in the hole. He also has a pair of jacks showing and a pair of sevens in the hole. Ted**

Fehr has the other pair of sevens showing, and John reads him for two pair— queens over sevens. Sid Bennett has aces up and makes a $1 bet. Ted, betting strong from the start, raises $25. John just calls.

"I should raise," Sid thinks out loud as he strokes his chin. "John is weak... probably has jacks up. But Ted might have three sevens... no other sevens are showing."

John picks up his hole cards, shifts his position and crosses his legs. Accidentally-on-purpose he turns his hand so Sid can see two of his hole cards—the pair of sevens.

"I'll raise to fifty dollars," Sid says and chuckles. He knows that John has two pair and that Ted cannot have three sevens. Never thinking that John might also have a flush, Sid looks pleased with his sharpness in spotting John's hole cards.

After Ted folds, John raises back. Sid calls and then slaps his hand against his massive forehead when John shows him a flush. He grumbles something about bad luck, never realizing the trap he was sucked into.

### e. Peekers (56)

Spectators and players who have folded often peek at undealt cards or at hands of active players. Most peekers exhibit readable behavior patterns that give away the value of every card and every hand they look at. Those patterns are found in their—

- levels of and changes in interest toward peeked-at hands

- timing of peeks and repeeks

- reactions (after folding) to peeking at hands of ex-opponents

- eye movements and areas of interest immediately after peeking at cards to be dealt.

*Part Three: Strategies*

Players who allow others to peek at their hands encounter problems of—

- readable patterns given to opponents

- flashed cards

- upset strategy

- disturbed concentration

- more frequent, unsolicited peeking.

The good player carefully selects those whom he lets look at his hand. He lets certain players peek at his cards in order to—

- convey certain information to the peeker or to the other players

- advertise plays that encourage loose or poor playing by others

- create a more carefree and careless atmosphere

- upset certain players by not allowing them to peek

- encourage peekers to look at hands of other players.

The good player controls peeking by the following methods:

- He never peeks at cards of other players. That avoids any obligation to let other players peek at his cards. After dropping out of a hand, he concentrates on observation and planning strategy rather than wasting his time on peeking.

- He develops a consistent way of holding his cards to prevent unwanted peeking.

113

- When players ask to look at his cards, he refuses gently by a remark such as, "I'll show you later."

- Whenever possible, he buries his folded hands before anyone can look at them. He can then advantageously lie about them.

**A new player, Charlie Holland, sits next to John Finn. Playing in his first big-stake game, Charlie is nervous and impressionable. John takes full advantage of this by using his peeking strategy to throw Charlie into permanent confusion:**

**In a hand of lowball draw, John discards a king and draws a seven low. Charlie holds a pat nine low. John has lured him into calling a large first-round bet and two raises. In the last round, Sid makes a defensive $25 bet; Charlie calls. John raises to $75 and everyone folds. John throws his cards on top of his discarded king and then pulls in the pot.**

**"What'd you have?" Charlie asks.**

**"A fat king," John says, smiling as he picks up the cards and shows him the king.**

**Charlie Holland groans. With a drooping face, he stares at the large pot. "I should've called," he moans as John slowly pulls in the pot while laying the larger bills on top for better viewing.**

**What does this have to do with peeking? Nothing yet.... The next hand is seven-card stud. Charlie drops out early to study John's technique. He stretches his neck to peek at John's hole cards. With an air of friendship, John Finn loops his arm around Charlie's shoulder and shows him the hole cards—John has an ace-king diamond flush.**

**"We'll kill 'em with this ace-king diamond flush," John says loudly.**

**Surprised that John announced his exact hand, Charlie looks at the cards again, then replies, "Yeah, man!"**

114

But actually, John is not confident of his flush because he reads both Ted and Quintin for two pair, and all eight of their full-house cards are alive. He figures the odds are about 1 in 2 that one of them will catch a full house. He also knows that they fear his flush and will not bet unless they catch the full house.

Scotty Nichols, who folded early, is sitting between Quintin and Ted. With his head bobbing back and forth, he peeks at their hands as they catch new cards. Now, the last hole card is dealt. John watches Scotty: First his plump head points toward the highest hand—Ted's queens over jacks. He peeks at Ted's new hole card; immediately his head snaps over to check Quintin's cards. Obviously Ted's new card is not very interesting ... he failed to catch his full house, John figures.

Now Scotty looks at Quintin's new card. He looks again and then glances at Quintin's up cards ... then checks the hole cards once again. Scotty does not say a word, but he may as well be yelling, "Interesting! A very interesting catch for the full house!"

Adjusting his thick glasses, Scotty next looks at John's up cards; his eyes then dart back and forth between Quintin and John while ignoring Ted's hand.

What happens? Ted foolishly bets $25. Quintin raises $1. Scotty covers his smiling mouth with his hand. Expecting some lively action, he waits for John to get sucked into Quintin's great trap. And across the table, Charlie Holland smiles; he waits for John to blast Quintin with a big raise. John Finn folds.

Charlie rises halfway out of his seat while making gurgling noises. "You .. you know what you dropped?" he stammers

"Yeah, a busted hand," John says, shrugging.

"A busted hand." Charlie bellows. His hand shoots to the table and grabs John's folded cards. "Look, you had an ace-king diamond flush. You even announced it!"

"Oh, no! I thought it was a four flush," John lies.

**Quintin glowers at John's flush and then shows his winning full house... Charlie sits down talking to himself.**

**Alert playing not only saves John money, but confuses everyone and sets up Charlie for future control.**

*6. Nongame Behavior (57)*

Table 20 shows ways the good player behaves toward nongame contacts that could influence his poker activities.

### TABLE 20
### NONGAME BEHAVIOR

| *Nongame Contact* | *Behavior* |
| --- | --- |
| Friend of a player | Praise the player and his performance in poker. Stress the merits of the game. |
| Potential player | Suggest the easiness of winning money in the game. Stress the social and pleasant aspects of the game. |
| Player from another game | Indicate a desire to play in his game. Extend an invitation to your own game. Create an image of being a loose, sociable player. |
| Family of a player | Flatter poker skill of the player. If they complain about his losses, suggest that his bad luck is due to change. |
| Other acquaintances | Indicate a desire to play poker. Downgrade personal performance in poker... talk about losses. |

116

*Part Three: Strategies*

Sometimes the good player practices contrasting *game* and *nongame* behavior. For example, if during the game he practices unfriendly behavior toward a certain opponent, he may find it advantageous to be congenial toward this same person outside the game.

**Although all poker players in the Monday night game view themselves as independent men, some of their wives retain various degrees of control over them. John plans his behavior toward their wives according to the following notations in his notebook:**

*Wife Summary*

**Betty Nichols**          **Concerned about Scotty's losses. To calm her, recall his past winnings. She will not make him quit if reminded that poker keeps him from drinking.**

**Florence Merck**          **Supports Quintin's playing, especially since he is winning.**

**Stephanie Bennett**          **Thinks Sid is foolish for playing. Realizes he will never win and wants him to quit, but also realizes she has little control over him. Besides, having plenty of money, she is not too worried about his losses.**

**Rita Fehr**          **Does not care and makes no attempt to influence Ted, despite his suicidal losses.**

# XIII
# POLICIES (58)

The good player forms policies about money, credit, and rules. These policies are his guidelines for strategy and are planned to yield both short-term and long-term advantages. Proper policies result in fewer mistakes and better decisions.

### 1. Money (59)

Poker is based on money. To win money is the only rational reason for investing time and effort in poker.

### a. Maintaining proper attitude (60)

Since poker is based on money, the proper attitude about money is crucial. What is the good player's attitude about money? Realizing that each dollar represents an irreplaceable segment of life (the time required to earn that dollar), he respects money out of respect for himself.

### b. Stimulating poor attitude in opponents (61)

A poor money attitude in opponents increases the edge odds for the good player. Since most players are influenced by the opinions of the good player, he uses that influence to stimulate poor money attitudes by advancing erroneous ideas such as—

* one must be dealt good cards to win

* luck is required to win

* streaks of luck run hot and cold, and cards should be played accordingly

* betting should depend on how much one is winning or losing.

The good player often encourages the use of poker chips instead of money in order to—

118

- decrease the sense of value for money

- stimulate looser play and a faster betting pace

- speed up the game.

In certain games, however, players will play for higher stakes when cash (rather than chips) is used.

### c. Increasing money in game (62)

The good player tries to increase the cash brought to the game because more cash—

- allows the betting pace and stakes to increase more rapidly

- decreases opponents' respect for money

- makes more money available for loans.

An effective way to increase money brought to the game is to increase the money needed to play by limiting the use of credit.

**Ted Fehr has been losing heavily on the horses. His cash position is low; he is borrowing excessively to stay in the action. John is worried because now Ted brings less than $100 to the game, loses his stake promptly, and then borrows for the rest of the game. John figures that each player should bring at least $300 to keep the game healthy at its current stakes. So he puts pressure on Ted to increase his cash position:**

**"Lend me a hundred," Ted says, turning to John after losing a pot.**

**"It's only the third hand and you're broke?" John growls and makes no move to lend him money. "I can't lend my cash right off ... what'll I play on?" The other players nod in agreement.**

**"Who'll lend me a hundred?" Ted asks as he looks around the table with his mouth smiling. When no one**

119

replies, his mouth droops.

Noticing Ted's sweaty forehead, John finally says, "Write out a check and put it in the game. Next time bring five or six hundred like everyone else does. Then if you run out, there'll be enough cash in the game to lend."

Ted's freckled face wrinkles as he pulls a blank check from his wallet. "I've lost thousands in this game," he says in a choking voice. "Can't even borrow a hundred. Isn't my credit any good?"

"Sure your credit is good," John explains as he cashes the check. "That's not the point. It's for your own protection. How can you possibly win without money to back you up? Got to have money to make money." . . . John knows this meaningless platitude will be swallowed as the truth by most players, especially gamblers like Ted.

"Got to have money to make money," Ted mumbles. "I'll bring plenty next week and overpower everyone."

During that week, Ted wins at the racetrack. Remembering John's advice and blaming his poker losses to a lack of cash, he brings over $1000 to the next game. The excess cash clouds his sense of value for money—he tries to overpower everyone. His overpowering play is an exhibition of wild, reckless poker. By two in the morning, Ted is writing a check; John Finn is a very big winner.


## 2. *Credit(63)*

Credit policies can determine the health of a poker game. The proper use of credit allows a faster betting pace and higher stakes. Since the good player is the most consistent winner, he is the prime source of credit and, therefore, exercises a major influence on the credit policies. He applies the following *credit rule* to poker games:

*All debts must be paid by the start of each game.*
*No one may play while owing money from a previous game.*

120

The above rule is effective in preventing bad debts that can damage or destroy a game. The credit rule also prevents a valuable loser from accumulating such a large poker debt that he quits the game and never plays again just to avoid paying the debt. When a loser is temporarily forced out of the game by the credit rule, he usually recovers financially, repays his debts, and then returns for more losses.

Enforcing the credit rule offers the following additional advantages:

- Provides a clear rule that forces prompt payment of poker debts.

- Forces more cash into the game, which means more cash available for the good player to win.

- Increases the willingness of players to lend money, which provides more cash for the losers.

- Detects players headed for financial trouble.

- Forces bankrupt players out of the game before serious damage is done.

The good player is flexible and alters any policy when beneficial. For example, he may ignore the credit rule to prevent a wealthy, heavily losing player from quitting the game. But he carefully weighs the advantages against the long-range disadvantages before making any exception to the credit rule.

By not borrowing money himself, the good player avoids obligations that could reduce his influence over the credit policies. If the good player loses his cash, he writes a check. A check puts more money into the game and sets a good example for using checks instead of credit. If the good player must borrow, he does so from a player who rarely borrows himself and thus would seldom demand a reciprocating loan.

*a. Extending credit (64)*

The good player extends credit only for personal financial

121

gain. He selectively extends credit for the following reasons:

- Available credit keeps big losers in the game. Steady losers who must constantly beg to borrow may quit the game out of humiliation or injured pride. But if big losers can borrow gracefully, they usually continue playing and losing.

- Opponents often play poorer poker after they have borrowed money.

- The good player can exercise greater influence and control over players who are in debt to him.

To obtain maximum benefits when lending money, the good player creates impressions that he—

- is extending a favor

- gives losers a break

- lends only to his friends

- lends only when winning and then on a limited basis

- expects other players, particularly winners, to lend money.

*b. Refusing credit (65)*

Easy credit automatically extended by a winning player will make him the target for most or all loans. Automatic credit decreases the money brought to the game, which in turn decreases the betting pace. Ironically, losers often feel ungrateful, resentful, and often suspicious toward overly willing lenders.

Refusal of credit is an important tool for controlling credit policies. The good player selectively refuses credit in order to—

- prod players into bringing more money

- force other players to lend money

122

- make borrowers feel more obligated and grateful

- avoid being taken for granted as an easy lender

- enhance an image of being tough (when advantageous)

- avoid poor credit risks

- upset certain players.

### c. Cashing checks (66)

In most poker games, checks are as good as cash. The threat of legal action forces fast payment of most bounced checks. The good player likes to cash losers' checks, because —

- money in the game is increased

- losers get cash without using credit

- his cash position is decreased, which puts pressure on other winners to supply credit

- losers are encouraged to write checks, particularly if resistance is offered to their borrowing, while no resistance is offered to cashing their checks.

### d. Bad debts (67)

A bad poker debt is rare. Losing players are gamblers, and most gamblers maintain good gambling credit. Some players go bankrupt, but almost all eventually pay their poker debts. When a loser stops gambling to recover financially, the best policy usually is to avoid pressuring him into paying his poker debt. Such pressure can cause increasing resentment to the point where he may never pay... or even worse, never return to the game to lose more money.

A house rule that allows bad debts to be absorbed by all players (e.g., by cutting the pot) has two advantages:

1. Lenders are protected; therefore, all players are more willing to lend money.

2. A debtor is less likely to welch against all the players than against an individual player.

Establishing a maximum bad debt that will be reimbursed by cutting pots is a wise addition to that house rule. Limiting this bad-debt insurance will—

- restrain excessive or careless lending

- provide a good excuse for not lending cash to a loser beyond this insurance level

- discourage collusion between a lender and a potential welcher

- avoid any large liability against future pots that could keep players away from the game until a large bad debt is paid by cutting the pot.

A gambling debt has no legal recourse (except debts represented by bad checks). A welcher, however, will often pay if threatened with a tattletale campaign. If he still does not pay, a few telephone calls to his wife, friends, and business associates will often force payment. The good player openly discusses any bad poker debt as a deterrent to others who might consider welching.

**Handling credit is an important and delicate matter for John Finn. He must make credit available to keep the game going, but must limit the use of credit to keep cash plentiful. He must appear generous in lending his winnings, while appearing tough against players abusing the use of credit. John pressures other winners into lending their money and pressures losers into writing checks. He must prevent hurt feelings on the part of losers as he enforces the *credit rule* (described**

124

in Concept 63).... All this requires careful thought and delicate maneuvering.

Sid Bennett is wealthy and loses many thousands of dollars every year. John takes special care of him. Usually Sid brings plenty of cash to the game, maybe $500 or $600. When he loses that, John gently pressures him into writing checks. Occasionally, Sid gets upset and refuses to write any more checks. He then borrows with gusto. Sometimes when he runs out of money, he scans the table for the biggest pile of money. Then, smash, his big fist descends without warning . . . he grabs the whole pile of money and peels off a couple hundred dollars. If the victim objects, Sid just grunts and looks the other way, but keeps the money. Most players grant him that liberty because they know he is rich and will always repay them.

Occasionally, Sid becomes bitter when suffering big consecutive losses and refuses to pay off his debts by the next game. John realizes that Sid might quit the game if the credit rule were applied to him. So if Sid owes him money under those conditions, John says nothing and lets the debt ride until the following week. But if Sid refuses to pay money he owes to another player, John pays off the debt while reminding everyone that debts cannot be carried over. Sid usually pays John later the same night or the following week. With his tantrums appeased, Sid happily goes on to lose many thousands more.

While lax with Sid, John Finn rigidly enforces the credit rule against other players. He is particularly tight about extending credit to Ted Fehr because of his poor financial condition. John often refuses him credit and makes him write checks That tough policy forces Ted to quit when he is broke. Then when he accumulates enough money, he returns to the game, pays off his debts, and loses more money.

When Ted quits for several weeks to recover financially, a losing player occasionally complains about holding one of Ted's debts or bounced checks. John

125

offers to buy the debt or check at a 25 percent discount. Such transactions keep everyone happy: they give the losers more cash to lose, and John acquires extra profits from the stronger players.

At times, John Finn refuses to lend money to anyone. Such action forces others to lend their cash. At other times, he puts on subtle displays of generosity. For example, if players with good credit run low on money, John advantageously reduces his cash position by handing them money before they even ask for a loan. Everyone is favorably impressed with his acts of fake generosity.

In John's notebook is the following list:

*Credit Rating*

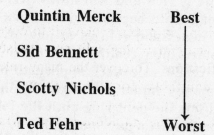

**Quintin Merck**          Best

**Sid Bennett**

**Scotty Nichols**

**Ted Fehr**          Worst

When a player writes a check, John usually makes a quick move to cash it. To him, checks are often better to hold than money because cash winnings are more obvious targets for loans than are check winnings.


## 3. Rules (68)

The good player shuns fixed poker rules. He does, however, provide equitable and consistent solutions to poker problems because such a policy—

- decreases rule problems and arguments

- increases acceptance of complex games and modifications

- increases his control over the game

126

- improves his image as a fair and desirable player

- increases his invitations to other games

- establishes him as judge and arbiter of all poker problems

- increases his ability to control the house rules.

Poker, unlike other card games, is not subject to rigid rules. Published rules and the various "Hoyles" on poker are merely descriptions of conventions. Strict adherence to any set of poker rules produces an array of contradictions and inequities. By avoiding reference to Hoyle or to any fixed rules, and by consistently interpreting poker situations and equitably resolving poker problems, the good player can gain control of the rules.

## a. Modified rules (69)

The rules found in poker books fail to cover many situations, especially in games involving split pots, twists, and other, more complex modifications. To cover the many ruleless situations, the good player equitably formulates new rules (actually, he formulates flexible guidelines rather than rules). He will then consistently follow the guidelines, even when that costs him money. Why would he do something that costs him money? Because in the long run, such a policy delivers major financial benefits by giving him control of the rules. Furthermore, he can from time to time remind everyone of the money he has lost because of his "fairness," which reinforces everyone's confidence in him as the controller of the rules.

## b. Disputed plays (70)

Because the good player interprets the rules consistently and fairly, his opponents implicitly trust him and depend on him to resolve disputed plays and technical problems about poker. Typical approaches he uses in settling commonly disputed plays are summarized in Table 21.

Book 3
Poker: A Guaranteed Income For Life

## TABLE 21
## DISPUTED PLAYS

| *Disputed Play* | *Consistent Approach* |
|---|---|
| Misdeal | Cards are never redealt because of a misdeal. Each player is responsible for his own cards. Any misdealt hand having an uncorrectable advantage must be folded. Any misdealt hand that is correctable or left at a disadvantage can be played. |
| Exposed card during the deal | An exposed card can never be exchanged for a new one—all cards must be accepted. |
| Exposed card before the deal | All cards must come off in order. No one can ask for a reshuffle, a cut, or a different card. |
| Out-of-turn betting, calling, raising, or checking | Any play made out of turn (except folding) is meaningless and can be remade or changed during the player's proper turn. |

*Note: These approaches are for private games. Approaches for public games (casino and club poker) may be entirely different. See Part six for information on public poker.*

The approaches in Table 21 provide clear and consistent solutions to disputes that commonly occur, especially in complex games involving split pots and twists.

### c. Inequitable rules (71)

The good player may favor a chronic loser with an inequitable rule interpretation in order to keep him in the game (to everyone's benefit). Yet, he interprets and applies a rule with favorable bias toward a loser only if the financial value of that loser outweighs the financial value of interpreting all rules consistently and equitably.

### d. House rules(72)

House rules are very important to the good player. They concern betting and playing procedures plus any other rules the players wish to adopt. The house rules determine not only the game stakes but also the game pace.

Since most players fail to differentiate between the house rules and poker rules, they often let the good player control the house rules because of his fairness in interpreting poker rules. Important house rules that the good player seeks to control and manipulate concern—

- stakes and antes

- games permitted

- rules for betting (e.g., betting limits for each round, table stakes, pot limit)

- rules for raising (e.g., pick-up checks, check raising)

- treatment of discards to be redealt (such as placing unshuffled discards on the bottom of the deck)

- courtesies (such as showing noncalled hands and hole cards).

The good player avoids well-defined or written rules to retain the flexibility needed to change the rules when advantageous.

**In the Monday night game, John Finn verbally insists on adhering to the rules, but he carefully avoids any reference to specific rules. Instead, he mediates all disputes fairly, even when it costs him the pot. In his black notebook, he records his rule interpretations and dispute settlements. As a book of law, he refers to those entries in settling future problems. The entries in which**

129

he loses money are marked by big stars and recorded in accurate detail. He remembers those entries, and at every appropriate opportunity he reminds everyone how his honest rule interpretations cost him money. Of course, he never mentions the interpretations that favored him.

With his consistent policy of "integrity", John wins the confidence of the players. They know he is fair—everyone trusts him. They ask him to settle disputes, and they abide by his decisions. They accept him as the controller of the rules. Failing to realize that the poker rules bear no relationship to the house rules, they let John's influence spill into the house rules, thereby giving him a key tool for controlling the game.

Using his influence over the rules, John slowly alters and then obliterates the original house rules. In the Monday night game, the original house rules allowed a maximum bet of $1 and permitted only straight draw and stud games . . . $50 winners were rare. Now $100 bets are made in draw. Wild and split-pot games with twists prevail. Thousand-dollar winners are common. After six years of controlling the rules, John increased his edge odds from 35 percent to 65 percent, and his profits soared from $2,500 to $42,000 per year.

### 4. Arguments and Emotional Situations (73)

The good player avoids involvement in emotional situations such as—

- personal disputes and arguments

- personal problems

- exposing cheaters.

He avoids involvement by outwardly ignoring the situation. The good player will, however, study an emotional situation in order to exploit it. He intervenes only in those situations that could cost him money. For example, he steps in to prevent a loser from quitting the game because of a personal argument.

When the good player faces a potential argument, he controls the situation either by yielding quickly or by standing firm. He avoids taking positions that he may have to compromise or yield. He takes a firm position only when financially profitable. When in doubt about yielding or holding firm, he usually yields before a confrontation occurs.

**Sid's loud mouth constantly bellows good-natured insults at the players. Professor Merck does not like Sid to tease him about his mustache, his tight playing, or his beret. He tells Sid to stop. But Sid Bennett grins and rides him even harder by calling him a dirty old man. Quintin accuses Sid of running a-dishonest road-paving business and calls him a pasty-faced crook. Sid shouts back louder insults. Since their bickering hurts their poker playing, John increases his winnings from the upset men... But their animosity increases each week and John begins to worry. Blows are nearly exchanged when Quintin threatens to expose Sid's payola on city paving contracts. Sid threatens to sue him for slander and then calls him a queer. Squinting his green eyes, Quintin cracks the edge of his hand on the table and threatens Sid with a karate blow. Sid vibrates his big fist close to Quintin's nose, calls him a queer again, and then storms out of the house while shouting that either he or Quintin must quit the game.**

**Fearing that Sid may quit, John telephones both men the next day and settles their argument. He explains how their feud is hurting their playing and is costing them money. They both agree and thank him for straightening out their problem.**

**John made extra money from their feuding. But when the feud almost caused the loss of the biggest loser, John stepped in and eliminated their argument in a way that improved his image as a desirable player.**

131

# XIV
# CHEATERS (74)[18]

The good player never cheats—he never needs to.

In friendly and private poker games, most players consider a cheater less honorable than a thief because a thief robs from strangers, but a poker cheat robs from his friends. The normal emotional impulse is to banish the cheater from the game... or worse.[19] The good poker player, however, resists acting on emotions. He views any cheating situation objectively and then acts in his best long-range financial interest.

## 1. Cheating (75)

Cheating involves the following manipulations of cards, money, or betting:

- Cards are covertly switched to alter the value of a hand. Cards are purposely flashed to see undealt or unexposed cards. The deck is culled and stacked to change the sequence of cards to be dealt.

- Money is stolen from the pot or from other players. Wrong change is purposely taken from the pot. Lights are purposely not paid.

- Mechanical devices such as marked cards, strippers, mirrors, and hold-out equipment, and techniques to smudge, nick, or mar cards for future identification, are used.

- Secret betting agreements or partnerships are made; the colluding partners signal each other when to bet or raise.

[18] *For more details and information about amateur and professional cheating see Chapters XXIX-XXXI.*

[19] *Stronger emotional reactions against cheaters are common. Some reactions can result in physical violence, even mayhem or homicide.*

Honest poker allows any behavior or manipulation, no matter how deceptive, except cheating. Cheating is the only dishonest, illegal, or unethical behavior in poker. But where does deception end and cheating begin? Actually, a sharp distinction exists between the two. Poker cheating is the conjuring up of advantages unavailable to others. Poker deception is the taking advantage of situations available to all. For example, all cards are marked. A sharp-eyed player can find printing imperfections in honest decks of cards. Some common printing imperfections are ink spots, inkless dots, and slightly off-centered designs on the back side of the cards. Also, the normal use of cards produces identifying smudges, nicks, scratches, and creases on their backs. (Purposely marring cards for identification would, of course, be cheating.) Those natural imperfections and markings that identify unexposed cards are available to any player willing to train his eye and discipline his mind. The good player willingly exerts the effort to learn and then use these natural markings. He may even increase that advantage by providing the game with cheaper (but honest) cards with less perfect printing patterns.

**Sid Bennett cheats. While it is quite obvious, only John Finn fully realizes that he cheats. Quintin Merck suspects it, but never makes any direct accusations. The other players watch Sid's cheating, but refuse to suspect him. His crude cheating techniques include—**

- **looking through the discards to select cards for use in his hand**

- **culling or sorting cards prior to dealing**

- **peeking at cards to be dealt, especially twist cards**

- **stealing money from the pot when going light**

- **slipping a good card into the hand of a losing player (Robin Hood cheating).**

**John estimates that Sid cheats once in every eight or ten hands.**

*2. Accepting Cheaters (76)*

The good player quietly accepts cheaters if they are losers. In fact, he often welcomes their cheating because they generally lose more money when cheating, particularly when cheating in complex games involving split pots and twists... A player usually increases his losses when cheating because he—

- dilutes his attention toward the game by worrying about and concentrating on his cheating

- overestimates the benefits of cheating and thus plays looser and poorer poker

- makes his cards more readable.

Why does a player cheat if his cheating increases his losses? Some players cheat to satisfy emotional needs. Other players cheat out of financial desperation.

**Sid cheats for emotional rather than financial reasons. His cheating costs him thousands of extra dollars every year, as shown by the data below. The data include a three-month period when Sid stopped his cheating because he was worried about getting caught.**

| Period | Cheating Frequency | Edge Odds for Sid Bennett Average Edge Odds, % |
|---|---|---|
| 1st year | Seldom | —10 |
| 2nd and 3rd year | Regular | —23 |
| 3 months in 3rd year | Seldom | —12 |

**The data indicate that Sid doubles his losses when cheating. With his current losses in the Monday night game totaling $20,000 per year, his cheating costs him about $10,000 per year.**

*3. Rejecting Cheaters (77)*
Under certain conditions, cheating by others can financially hurt the good player. For example, valuable losers might quit the game if they detected cheating. Or the game itself could be destroyed by cheating. If necessary, therefore, the good player can eliminate the cheater or his cheating in one or more of the ways shown in Table 22.

### TABLE 22
### REJECTING CHEATERS

| Time of Action | Form of Action | Results |
|---|---|---|
| Indirectly, during game | Make the cheater feel that he is suspected and is being watched. | Cheating stops. |
| Privately, outside of game | Tell the cheater that if he cheats again, he will be publicly exposed. | Cheating stops. |
| Privately, outside of game | Tell suspicious players about the cheater. Point out that he is a loser and the best way to penalize him is to let him play. | Cheating continues, and the players are satisfied. |
| Privately, outside of game | Form a conspiracy with other players to collude in order to bankrupt the cheater. | Cheater is driven from game. |

| Publicly,<br>during game | Expose the cheater during<br>the game in front<br>of everyone | Cheater quits<br>or is<br>expelled<br>from the<br>game. |

The best action against a cheater depends not only on the situation, but on the attitudes of the other players as well. If a cheater must be eliminated, the good player assumes a righteous hero's role by exposing the "nefarious cheater." That righteous role enhances the good player's image of being the most honest and trustworthy player in the game— an ideal image for manipulating opponents.

What about stealing money from the pot? If the good player does not win the pot, he keeps quiet when losers shortchange the pot or fail to pay their lights (money owed to the pot). But if chronic stealing upsets other players enough to hurt the game, the good player stops the stealing by taking one of the actions listed in Table 22.

**Scotty Nichols barely beats Ted Fehr to win a $900 pot. While everyone's attention is focused on the action, Sid Bennett casually takes the $100 that he was light and slips it into his shirt pocket for a quick $200 profit. John notices Sid's theft, but says nothing. With saliva drooling over his lip, Scotty rakes in the huge pot; his breathing quickens as his fingers sort the money... he forgets about Sid's lights. Since Sid is a big loser and Scotty a big winner for the night, the theft has an equalizing effect that benefits John.**

**Several hands later, Sid pulls the same trick by pocketing his $40 lights for an $80 profit. John wins the pot and says nothing. As the next hand is dealt, he quietly gives Sid $20 and says, "You owe me another hundred."... Sid blushes and then nods in agreement.**

## *4. Robin Hood Cheater (78)*

Some players cheat for others without benefiting themselves. The beneficiary is usually a poor player or a big loser. That kind of Robin Hood cheating is relatively common and benefits the good player by—

• distributing losses more evenly among players

• decreasing losses of big losers

• making the hands of both the Robin Hood cheater and his beneficiary more readable.

**Sid Bennett often cheats for big losers like Ted Fehr. For example, Sid folds, then looks at Ted Fehr's hand and sees a four-card heart flush. Quickly he grabs Ted's draw card—it is a club. Sid then rummages through the discards. Finding a heart, he switches it with Ted's club.... Ted smiles and wins the pot with a heart flush.**

**While Sid's card switch is crude and obvious, no one except John lets himself fully realize what happened. Later in the same game, Sid attempts a partnership with John. This is what happens:**

**The pot is large. Five players are in for the last bet— including John and Sid, who are sitting next to each other. Sid bets and then his knee nudges John's leg. John promptly folds his three queens. Sid wins with a full house.**

**"Remember that," Sid whispers to John while pulling in the pot.**

**A few hands later, Sid Bennett is dealt a pat straight. Again he nudges John, who folds immediately. Sid grins and winks a faded-blue eye at John.**

**Later that evening, John draws to a lowball hand that he has bet heavily during the first round. But he catches a pair of fives to ruin his lowball hand. Still**

137

**John bets the maximum in trying to bluff out his two remaining opponents.... Ted Fehr folds because Sid is sitting behind him with a pat hand. John's knee nudges Sid's leg. Sid smiles and then shows everyone his eight low as he folds. "Thanks," he whispers to John. Promptly John Finn spreads his hand face-up on the table to win the $600 lowball pot with a pair of fives.... Sid looks at the ceiling and sputters dirty words.**

**Instead of simply saying no to Sid's collusion-cheating offer, John earns a good profit while making his answer clear.**

## 5. Detection (79)

Most cheaters in private games use crude techniques that are easily detectable.[20] Yet most players ignore even obvious cheating to avoid arousing unpleasant emotions. When a player detects someone cheating, he often rationalizes it as a rule violation or a mistake. But the good player identifies cheating quickly and can detect even highly skilled cheaters without even seeing a dishonest move. How does he do that? Cheaters betray themselves by violations of logic and probability. The good player, with his sharply focused concentration on his opponents, the game, and the odds, has an acute awareness of any improbable playing and betting patterns. That awareness enables him to promptly detect cheating, even without seeing a suspicious move.

**Professor Merck suspects Sid of cheating. One night, Sid cheats him out of a $700 pot. After sitting in silence for several hands, Quintin abruptly leaves without a word and slams the front door. Knowing that Quintin detected Sid's cheating and fearful that he will tell others, John pursues him out the door. Quintin stops under the street lamp when he sees John approaching. For a moment, neither says a word.**

**"You saw it too?" Quintin asks, squinting his green eyes.**

[20] *See Chapters XXIX-XXXI for details about undetectable, professional cheating.*

138

"I see it in every game."

"So why haven't you said something!" the professor half shouts. "He should've been bounced from the game long ago."

"Look, who's the biggest loser in the game?" John quickly replies. "It's Sid. And you're a big winner. In the past couple of years, you've taken Sid for thousands of dollars. Sure he's cheated you, me, and everyone else out of pots. But what if we'd thrown him out two years ago? We'd have done him a $40,000 favor."

Quintin's mouth opens. He rubs his chin.

"Sid's a cheater and deserves to be penalized," John continues. "But the best way to penalize him is to let him play. We only hurt ourselves by bouncing him from the game."

"Never thought about it that way," Quintin says, scratching his head. "Maybe you're right.... Who else knows about his cheating?"

"No one who'll admit it. Cheating is a strange thing. Most players have strong feelings against acknowledging it.... Everyone subconsciously knows that Sid cheats. But no one wants an unpleasant emotional experience, so no one sees him cheat."

"Someday, someone will accuse him."

"Perhaps," John continues, "but visible suspicion will occur first. Take yourself—he cheated you out of $700 tonight. Yet, still you didn't accuse him. You passed it off till next time. The next time you may accuse Sid, or you may pass it off again."

"But what happens when someone does accuse him outright... what then?"

"If he's accused outright, we not only lose Sid, but other players might quit. The game might even fold. We must convince any seriously suspecting players that the best action is to let him play. If they won't accept this, then we must either stop the cheating or eliminate Sid from the game."

"So for now, we leave everything as is?"

"Right," John replies with a nod. "And when Sid

steals your pot, just remember he'll pay you back many times."

"But why is he a big loser if he cheats?"

"A cheater, like a thief, is unrealistic. He overestimates the value of cheating and plays a poorer game. In fiction, the cheater may be a winner. But in reality, he's a loser, and usually a big one. The good player—the winner—never needs to cheat."

"True, true," Quintin mumbles.

"See you next week," John says as he walks away.

What does John accomplish by his discussion with Quintin? He keeps the game intact by pacifying Quintin, and keeps Sid in the game to continue his cheating and losing.

The good player can lose to cheaters in certain situations. Two or more professional cheaters, for example, can gang up on a good player to reduce his edge odds to a losing level. The good player, however, quickly detects team or gang cheating and either beats it or eliminates it or quits the game (see Chapter XXXI).

# XV
# TAXES AND LAWS (80)

For federal tax purposes, net annual poker winnings must be declared as *income*.[21] Poker income can be listed under the heading of "Other" on Federal Income Tax Form 1040. In most states, net poker gains can also be declared as income. Gambling losses can be deducted (on Schedule A) from poker income, but net gambling losses cannot be deducted from taxable income.

---

[21] *Carmack v. Commissioner of Internal Revenue. 183 E 2d l (5th Cir. 1950).*

Poker players' winnings are not subject to the federal excise taxes on gambling.[22] Apparently the federal government does not classify poker players as gamblers (even though poker income is treated as gambling gains by the IRS).

A survey by the author (summarized in Table 23) shows that poker games are technically illegal in most states. Nevertheless, few if any states apply their anti-gambling laws to private poker games. But house games (in which pots are cut or raked for a profit or during which players pay collection fees) are vulnerable to legal action in most states.

Table 23 gives information about the legal and tax status of poker in each state.

### TABLE 23
### STATE LAWS ABOUT POKER
*\*Opinion for private poker games (for guideline use only).*

| State— Is Poker Legal?* | Source of Information— Legal Reference | State Income Tax 1980 |
|---|---|---|
| Alabama No | NAACP of Montgomery, Alabama— Alabama State Statutes | Yes |
| Alaska No | Bar Association Section 11.60.140 | Yes |
| Arizona No | Bar Association— Revised Statutes 13.431 | Yes |
| Arkansas No | Assistant Attorney General— Statutes Annotated 41-2011 and 3809 (Repl. 1964) | Yes |

[22] *According to the United states Excise Tax Regulation 4401 (paragraphs 4020-4032) poker winnings are not subject to the 10 percent excise wagering tax. And according to Regulation 4411 (paragraphs 4075-4083) poker players, even professional players, are not required to register and purchase the wagering Occupational Tax stamp.*

## Poker: A Guaranteed Income For Life

| State— Is Poker Legal?* | Source of Information— Legal Reference | State Income Tax 1980 |
|---|---|---|
| California No | Deputy Attorney General— Penal Code 330: Refers only to stud poker as illegal | Yes |
| Colorado No | Bar Association— Revised Statutes, Section 40-10-9 | Yes |
| Connecticut No | State Police— Sections 53-272-277 | No |
| Delaware Yes | Assistant Attorney General— Title II Code of 1953. Section 665 | Yes |
| Florida No | Attorney General— Section 849.08 | No |
| Georgia No | Assistant Attorney General— Georgia Code, Section 26-6404 and 6401 | Yes |
| Hawaii No | Bar Association— No specific reference given | Yes |
| Idaho No | Assistant Attorney General— Section 18-3801, Idaho Code | Yes |
| Illinois No | Legislative Reference Bureau— Criminal Law, Chapter 38, Section 28-1 | Yes |
| Indiana No | Bar Association— Act of 1905, Chapter 169, Statute 10-2307 | Yes |

| State—<br>Is Poker<br>Legal?* | Source of Information—<br>Legal Reference | State<br>Income Tax<br>1980 |
|---|---|---|
| Iowa<br>No | Solicitor General—<br>Chapter 726, 1966 Code | Yes |
| Kansas<br>No | Bar Association—<br>No specific reference given | Yes |
| Kentucky<br>No | Bar Association—<br>No specific reference given | Yes |
| Louisiana<br>Yes | Republican Party of Louisiana—<br>No specific reference given | Yes |
| Maine<br>No | Assistant Attorney General—<br>Revised Statute 1964 | Yes |
| Maryland<br>No | Assistant Attorney General—<br>Maryland Article 27, Section<br>237-264 | Yes |
| Massachusetts<br>No | Bar Association—<br>Section 1, Chapter 37, General<br>Laws | Yes |
| Michigan<br>No | Democratic State Central<br>Committee of Michigan—<br>Penal Code, 1945, Sections<br>750.314 and 750-315 | Yes |
| Minnesota<br>Yes | Attorney—<br>Statutes 609, 75 | Yes |
| Mississippi<br>No | Bar Association—<br>Code of 1942, Section 2190 | Yes |

## Poker: A Guaranteed Income For Life

| State—<br>Is Poker<br>Legal?* | Source of Information—<br>Legal Reference | State<br>Income Tax<br>1980 |
|---|---|---|
| Missouri<br>No | Governor—<br>State Statute | Yes |
| Montana<br>No | Attorney General—<br>Section 94-2401, R.C.M., 1947:<br>Licensed poker clubs only | Yes |
| Nebraska<br>Yes | Bar Association—<br>No specific reference given | Yes |
| Nevada<br>Yes | Bar Association—<br>No specific reference given | No |
| New Hampshire<br>No | Bar Association—<br>577.7 Gaming | No |
| New Jersey<br>No | Deputy Attorney General—<br>Statutes 2A:112-a and 218:85-7 | Yes |
| New Mexico<br>No | Assistant Attorney General—<br>Section 40A-19-1 to 3, N.M.<br>Statutes Annotated, 1953<br>Compilation (P.S.) | Yes |
| New York<br>No | Assistant Council to Governor—<br>Article 1, Section 9 of N.Y. State<br>Constitution, and Sections<br>970-998 of N.Y. State Penal Law | Yes |
| North Carolina<br>No | Bar Association—<br>No specific reference given | Yes |
| North Dakota<br>No | Bar Association—<br>Chapter 12-23-01 | Yes |

| State— Is Poker Legal?* | Source of Information— Legal Reference | State Income Tax 1980 |
|---|---|---|
| Ohio No | Bar Association— Section 2915.06, Revised Code | Yes |
| Oklahoma No | Oklahoma State University— Title 21 of Oklahoma Statutes, 1961, Section 941 | Yes |
| Oregon No | Attorney General— ORS 167.25 and 167.510 Licensed poker clubs only | Yes |
| Pennsylvania No | Deputy Attorney General— No specific reference given3 | Yes |
| Rhode Island No | Attorney General's office— No specific reference given | Yes |
| South Carolina No | Research Clerk— Sections 16-804, 505 | Yes |
| South Dakota No | Bar Association— No specific reference given | No |
| Tennessee No | Attorney General— Section 39-2001, Tennessee Code Annotated | No |
| Texas Yes | Governor— Texas Jurisprudence, 2nd volume 26 | No |
| Utah No | Attorney General— Section 76-27-1 to 3, Utah Code Annotated, 1953 | Yes |

*Poker: A Guaranteed Income For Life*

| State—<br>Is Poker<br>Legal?* | Source of Information—<br>Legal Reference | State<br>Income Tax<br>1980 |
|---|---|---|
| Vermont<br>No | Bar Association—<br>Section 2132 and 13,<br>VSA 2133 | Yes |
| Virginia<br>No | Attorney General—<br>Section 18.1-316 | Yes |
| Washington<br>No | Assistant Attorney General—<br>Revised Code<br>9.47.010-9.47.030:<br>Licensed poker clubs only | No |
| West Virginia<br>No | Bar Association—<br>No specific reference given | Yes |
| Wisconsin<br>No | Bar Association—<br>Chapter 945 | Yes |
| Wyoming<br>No | Attorney—<br>Statute 6-203, 1957 | No |
| District of<br>Columbia<br>? (not clear) | United States Attorney—<br>Title 22, D.C. Code,<br>Sections 1501-1515 | Yes |
| Puerto Rico<br>No | Bar Association—<br>No specific reference given | Yes |
| Virgin Islands<br>No | Attorney—<br>Sections 1221-1226, Chapter 61,<br>Title 14 | — |
| United States<br>Government<br>Yes | Deputy Attorney General—<br>Legality is up to individual states.<br>Winnings are taxable income. | — |

This section of the 1040 Federal Tax form shows how John Finn declared his **$54,000 poker income** over a decade ago.[23]

**Form 1040  U.S. Individual Income Tax Return  1965**

for the year January 1–December 31, 1965 or other taxable year beginning_____ 19___US Treasury Department—Internal Revenue Service 1965, ending_____

| | | |
|---|---|---|
| 4 Pensions and annuities, rents and royalties, partnerships, & estates or trusts (Schedule B) | | |
| 5 Business income (Schedule C) ▶ | | |
| 6 Sale or exchange of property (Schedule D) ▶ | 3,450 | 00 |
| 7 Farm income (Schedule F) ▶ | | |
| 8 Other sources (state nature) | | |
|    Monday Poker Games | 42,000 | 00 |
|    Other Poker Games | 12,000 | 00 |
|    Total other sources ▶▲▶▲▶▲ | 54,000 | 00 |
| 9 Add lines 2 through 8. Enter here and on page 1 line 6, ▶▲▶▲▶▲ | 57,450 | 00 |

[23] *1965 is the last year John Finn's poker records and tax returns were made available. With inflation and expanded poker action, John Finn's annual poker income is estimated at $200,000 for 1980.*

Book 3
Poker: A Guaranteed Income For Life

147

# PART FOUR

# OPPONENTS

In poker, all opponents are potential financial assets. The good poker player first gets his opponents involved in the game, then he exploits them to win their money.

## XVI
## INVOLVEMENT (81)

As players become emotionally and financially involved in a poker game, they become easier to exploit and their chances of quitting the game decrease.

## Poker: A Guaranteed Income For Life

### 1. Emotional (82)

Emotional involvement can result from gambling impulses... and most poker players are gamblers.[24] When a gambler loses, he keeps on playing in an attempt to recover his losses. When a gambler wins, he forgets his losses and concludes that he has finally learned how to win. The gambler's subconscious desire to punish or destroy himself emerges as an abiding, irrational optimism. The good player exploits that optimism in gamblers to generate a continuous income for himself.

Some players use poker as a narcotic-like diversion to escape reality. Others develop soul-mate friendships with other players. Such involvement can be emotionally soothing and pleasant—sufficiently so to compensate those losers for many large losses.

[24] *Gambling is defined in this book as "The wagering of money at unfavorable odds." In poker, the good player with favorable edge odds is not gambling, but players with unfavorable edge odds are. Horse players, casino patrons, and losing poker players are gamblers. That definition is consistent with definitions given in: (1) Webster's Third New International Dictionary—"To wager money or stakes on an uncertain outcome." The good player's outcome is certain; therefore, he is not gambling; (2) Funk and Wagnall's Standard Dictionary— 'To lose, squander, or dispose of by gaming." By that definition, the good player is not gambling, but losing players are; and (3) The Random House Dictionary—"Any matter or thing involving risk or hazardous uncertainty." The good player's situation is essentially riskless and, therefore, is not a gambling situation.*

*A gambling situation yields a statistically minus return on money wagered, while a nongambling (investment) situation yields a statistically plus return on money invested.... The intensity of the situation (rate of loss or rate of return) is determined both by the time span of the wager or investment and by the percent loss or the percent return. The intensity of' gambling and nongambling (investment) situations is illustrated by Tables 24 and 25. The tables, compare the Monday night poker players to other investment and gambling situations: The good poker player is in by far the best investment situation. By contrast, the poor poker player is in one of the worst gambling situations.*

150

## TABLE 24
## INTENSITY OF INVESTMENT SITUATIONS

| Investment Situation | *Estimated per Investment* | | Investment Intensity* |
|---|---|---|---|
| | Average Return Rate,% | Time Span | |
| Good poker player **(John Finn)** | +25 | 6 minutes | +2,000,000 |
| Sound poker player **(Quintin Merck)** | + 5 | 6 minutes | +400,000 |
| Bonds | +14 | 1 year | +14 |
| Banks | + 8 | 1 year | +8 |
| Stocks | +6 | 1 year | +6 |
| Business | + 6 | 1 year | +6 |

* *Investment-intensity values are average-return values calculated on an annual basis.*

## TABLE 25
## INTENSITY OF GAMBLING SITUATIONS

| Gambling Situation | *Estimated per Gamble* | | Gambling Intensity* |
|---|---|---|---|
| | Average Loss Rate,% | Time Span | |
| Lottery | -50 | 1 week | -$2,500 |
| Numbers | -40 | 1 day | -15,000 |
| Average poker player **(Scotty Nichols)** | - 1 | 6 minutes | -90,000 |
| Casino poker | varies according to casino rake+ | | |
| Carp shooting | - 1 | 1 minute | -500,000 |
| Horse racing | -15 | 12 minutes | -700,000 |

151

*Poker: A Guaranteed Income For Life*

| | | | |
|---|---|---|---|
| Poor poker player<br>**(Sid Bennett)** | -10 | 6 minutes | -900,000 |
| Poor poker player<br>**(Ted Fehr)** | -10 | 6 minutes | -900,000 |
| Roulette | - 3 | 30 seconds | -3,300,000 |
| Slot machines | -20 | 5 seconds | -130,000,000 |

* *Gambling-intensity values are the average-loss values calculated on an annual basis.*

+ *Poker can be a gambling situation even for the good player if the pots are regularly cut or raked by the house, as they are in public casinos. A large arbitrary cut can reduce or eliminate the profitable edge odds of a good player. And while the good player can retain a great advantage over the other players in a casino poker game, he cannot stop that house cut. Also, he cannot take control of the public game and its players as he can in the private game. Still, the good player can earn a guaranteed income from public poker (Nevada-type casino poker or Gardena-type club poker) if he adjusts his game to a public-professional style of poker (see Part Six).*

### 2. Financial (83)

For a losing player, financial involvement is a form of emotional involvement. When losses force him to use his savings or to borrow money, he keeps playing in a vain attempt to recover his losses. An occasional win gives him enough encouragement to hold him in the game.

Ironically, a winning player can also get financially involved and entrapped if he becomes too dependent on his poker income. He can even turn into a chronic loser if a series of losses disrupts his income. How does that happen? If his temporary loss of poker income causes a loss of objectivity, then the quality of his play will deteriorate. If that cycle of decreased objectivity and increased deterioration continues, his future losses will be assured. Memories of past winnings will then sustain him through heavy losses.

**John Finn and Quintin Merck bet only when they judge the odds to be in their favor; they are not gamblers. But the other players in the Monday night**

152

**game are gamblers.... Each one is emotionally and financially involved as shown in the following chart:**

|  | *Emotional Involvement* | *Financial Involvement* |
|---|---|---|
| John Finn | (minimum involvement) | Receives substantial income. |
| Quintin Merck | Supports ego; finds companionship; relieves boredom. | Receives moderate income useful for boasting about his poker skill. |
| Scotty Nichols | Avoids drinking problems; escapes business disappointments. | Tries to regain his past winning form. |
| Sid Bennett | Hides insecurities; finds companionship; releases tensions. | Seeks hot streak to recover past losses. |
| Ted Fehr | Satisfies gambling compulsion to hurt himself; escapes domestic problems. | Hopes for big win to parlay on the horses. |

# XVII
# EXPLOITATION (84)

Once players are involved in the game, the good player can take greater advantage of them through—

- their personal weaknesses

- their play of cards

- their betting and raising

- hypnosis

*Poker: A Guaranteed Income For Life*

- distractions

- agreements.

## 1. Personal Weaknesses, Favors, and Bribes (85)

Most poor poker players become hooked on or involved in games through their personal weaknesses. The good player exploits those weaknesses. He knows that almost all players have one or more of the following weaknesses:

| | | |
|---|---|---|
| altruism | ignorance | nervousness |
| capriciousness | impulsiveness | parasitism |
| carelessness | inattentiveness | preoccupation |
| compulsiveness | inconsistency | self-pity |
| dishonesty | inexperience | stubbornness |
| exhibitionism | instability | subjectiveness |
| faith | irrationality | superstitiousness |
| fear | laziness | timidity |
| greed | mysticism | worry |

Each personal weakness grows out of a player's resistance to objective thinking, discipline, and rational behavior.

The good player identifies and records the personal weaknesses of each opponent in his notebook. He then uses those weaknesses to influence their playing decisions, to read their hands, and to manipulate them into faster betting paces, higher stakes, and poorer-quality poker. He regularly reviews and revises his notes on their weaknesses in order to—

- refresh his memory

- devise new and better ways to manipulate his opponents

- better understand each opponent

- detect changes in opponents.

**John Finn identifies and lists the personal weaknesses of his poker opponents as shown in the above chart. Indeed, the following incident shows how**

**John uses his opponents' personal weaknesses to win extra money:**

Missing his flush in draw poker, John finds himself in a good position to bluff, so he bets $50. Scotty and Sid fold immediately. Ted Fehr holds two pair and thinks he should drop, but is desperate and considers calling. John must prevent him from calling.

Everyone knows that Ted is superstitious about pennies and never keeps any... especially when gambling. So when Ted leans over and shows Sid his hand, John takes a penny from his pocket and slips the coin onto the edge of Ted's money.

"Call!" Sid bellows as he gazes blankly at Ted's two pair. "He's got nothing."

"Yeah," Ted says and then grins as he picks up his pile of money to call. "What!" His grin fades as the penny tumbles from the money. "No wonder I'm losing!" he yells while picking up the coin and throwing it across the room. As the penny bounces off the wall and rolls around the floor, Ted folds his hand and says, "At least that penny made me fold. I saved fifty bucks..." His voice fades when John shows his winning hand... a four flush. Ted's eyes water. His superstition cost him a $200 pot.

Consider another example of John's exploitation of an opponent's weakness:

Sid Bennett injures his foot and cannot leave the house. At the last moment, John switches the game to Sid's house so the injured loser can play. Knowing Sid's house will lack a good supply of food, John stops at a delicatessen and invests in a gigantic Italian submarine sandwich nicely wrapped in cellophane.

At three in the morning, Scotty Nichols grips his stomach. He rummages through Sid's bare kitchen and finds a couple handfuls of dry cereal to eat.

*Personal Weaknesses*

| John Finn | Sid Bennett | Scotty Nichols | Ted Fehr |
|---|---|---|---|
| greed* | capriciousness | carelessness | capriciousness |
| | carelessness | faith | compulsiveness |
| | dishonesty | fear | faith |
| | exhibitionism | greed (uncontrolled) | fear |
| | impulsiveness | inattentiveness | impulsiveness |
| | inattentiveness | laziness | instability |
| | irrationality | mysticism | irrationality |
| | laziness | preoccupation | laziness |
| | stubbornness | self-pity | preoccupation |
| | | subjectiveness | self-pity |
| | | timidity | subjectiveness |
| | | worry | superstitiousness |
| | | | worry |

Quintin Merck
greed*
laziness
stubbornness
superstitiousness

\* *Greed can be a personal strength if rationally controlled.*

156

The next hand is seven-card stud, high-low with two twists. John's hole cards are the ace and the joker[25] ; he has another ace face-up... the best possible start for high-low poker. He wants the maximum number of callers. Now is the time to use his investment. He reaches under the chair and pulls the huge sandwich from a brown paper bag. All eyes turn toward the juicy submarine. Scotty moans as his tongue laps his puffy lips.

John lays the elongated sandwich across the pot. "The winners split it," he declares... Scotty's face is sweating, and his stomach is growling.

With eyes fixed on the sandwich, everyone calls the first bet. John aggressively bets his strong hand. Many players keep calling. The final bets are large. Scotty keeps calling with a poor hand. "Should fold," he says, catching his breath. "But that sub ... yum." The red-faced man spends over $100 on calls. Three other players also call as their eyes remain fixed on the sandwich. The pot is the largest of the night—over $700. John wins both high and low with an ace-high full house and a six-five low. He also wins back the sandwich, which he later used to build another pot.

**With a small investment, John Finn exploits opponents' lack of discipline to win may extra hundreds of dollars.**

The good player continually exploits man's most pervasive weakness—laziness. Laziness foments desires to gain values without effort. That, in turn, leads to seeking unearned approval, respect, and money. The good player uses those desires to manipulate his opponents with "favors" that symbolize (and falsely promise) approval, respect, and money. His victims bend to his will in seeking those pseudo favors.

[25] *The joker (also called the bug) is a wild card for low, an ace for high, and good for filling straights and flushes. In high-low games the joker can be used as both a high card and a low card in the same hand.*

"Favors and bribes that the good player extends and withdraws for his personal profit include—

- loans
- advice
- compliments
- sympathy
- showing of cards.

Out of the loser's desire for "favors" and approval from a respected winner, the good player can often get, for example, a loser's support for changes in house rules that further benefit the good player at the loser's expense (e.g., faster-paced games and higher stakes).

## 2. Play of Cards and Betting (86)

The good player constantly exploits his opponents as they play their cards. He repeatedly lures them into playing poorer and poorer poker. With the proper strategy, he causes them to—

- make mistakes
- improperly estimate the value of their hands
- play a looser game
- play hands that should be dropped
- drop hands that should be called.

**An exploitation ploy that John Finn uses (especially in split-pot games) involves the following maneuver to make a hesitant player call a bet:**

**The game is high-low, five-card stud with two twists. John has a winner—a lock on low. Quintin and Ted are playing for high. Quintin bets $20. Ted has a four flush and wants to call, but is afraid that John**

**will raise and Quintin will reraise, thus costing him $40
more. He starts to fold. John picks up a $20 bill and
holds it over the pot. Now, knowing that John will only
call and not raise, Ted calls. He then catches a flush
on the twist. After more betting and raising, Ted ends
up beating Quintin for high. John wins low and makes
an extra $50 by not letting Ted fold.**

**John seldom fakes that maneuver. So when players
see him holding the call money, they know with
confidence that he will not raise. But he will often fake
the reverse maneuver of not holding the call money
and then not raising.**

The good player also exploits his opponents through betting.
When holding a strong hand, he can build much larger pots by
getting other players to do his betting and raising. Successful
*indirect* betting requires accurate reading of opponents' hands and
knowledge of their betting habits. Miscalculation of indirect
betting can result in smaller pots. Thus, when uncertain about
his opponents' intentions, the good player will bet aggressively
rather than check his strong hand.

*Disproportionate* betting can throw opponents into more
vulnerable and exploitable betting positions. For example, by
making a bet or a raise completely out of proportion to the
normal or expected bet, the good player can confuse opponents
into making the desired bet, raise, call, or drop. Disproportionate
betting is useful as both an offensive and a defensive tool.

**Scotty deals draw poker with one twist. John Finn
gets a four-card straight flush. For his best investment
odds, John wants the maximum players calling a bet
big enough to keep them in for the large last-round
bets. He also wants to avoid raises that would make
players fold. So John opens for $14 instead of the
normal $25. Noses wrinkle. Players with poor hands
smile and call at this bargain price. Potential raisers,
suspicious of the weird bet and fearing a sandbag, only
call. The results are perfect for John ... everyone calls
and no one raises. John's estimated investment odds**

159

**soar to a highly favorable—**

$$\frac{(\$600)\,(.4)}{\$80} = 3.0.$$

**But if John had bet the normal $25 and only two players called, his estimated investment odds would have tumbled to—**

$$\frac{(\$250)\,(.5)}{\$75} = 1.7.$$

**Now suppose John had bet $25, someone raised to $50, and everyone else folded. If John had called the raise (which he probably would not have), his estimated investment odds would have fallen to an unfavorable—**

$$\frac{(\$222)\,(.4)}{\$100} = 0.8.$$

**By making the disproportionate $14 bet, John sets up the hand for maximum profits while gaining control of the betting. Moreover, if he checks his bet on the next round, usually one or more players will feel deprived of a full opening-round bet and thus bet aggressively. John can then passively let them do the betting and raising for him. On the other hand, if John bets on the next round, the other players will probably remain defensive and avoid betting or raising.**

**So with that disproportionate S14 bet, John increases his investment odds and leaves himself in a flexible betting position. John's checking will induce his opponents to bet aggressively; his betting will cause them to remain defensive. Thus he can conveniently turn the betting into either an offensive tempo (by checking) or a defensive tempo (by betting)... whichever is more advantageous to him.**

*Part Four: Opponents*

### 3. Hypnosis (87)

Because the good player is able to intensely study and closely scrutinize each poker opponent, he quickly gets to know their minds and psyches. With planned experiments, he can discover subconscious responses in many players and then actually hypnotize certain players—particularly the dull, emotional, or mystical ones. Typical hypnotic stimuli are—

- staring into the subject's eyes (psychological)

- moving a finger through the pot (visual and motion)

- breathing audibly during a tense silence (sound)

- tapping fingers on the table (sound and motion)

- repeating sub audible chant-like commands (e.g., "fold—fold—fold," or "raise—raise—raise").

Various repeated motions, sounds, or muffled voices can subconsciously instruct or signal vacillating opponents to make specific folds, calls, bets, or raises. The alert player can discover subconscious or hypnotic signals that will trigger automatic or trained reactions in his opponents.

While the good player can get certain opponents to bet, call, or fold by hypnosis, he uses hypnotizing actions cautiously to avoid revealing his own hands and intentions to alert opponents.

**After the draw, John Finn takes the final raise for $100. He has Scotty Nichols beat and wants him to call. Scotty groans. Looking at the huge pot, he sees John's finger slowly stirring the pile of money—stirring slowly and smoothly. Ten and twenty-dollar bills are moving in circles. Scotty's floating brown eyes start rotating with the money. His chubby hand slowly picks up a $100 bill. He calls the bet.**

**Scotty tries to smile as John pulls in the pot. Eventually he may become aware of that hypnotic trick. But then John will simply use another trick.**

161

Book 3 Poker: A Guaranteed Income For Life

**John estimates his earnings per life of hypnotic trick range from several hundred to several thousand dollars.**

### 4. Distractions (88)

The good player can exploit his opponents more easily when they are distracted. A radio or television for sporting events has excellent distraction value. A late newspaper is usually good for several hands of distracted play from opponents checking horse-race results, the stock market, and the news. Pornographic literature offers an absorbing distraction. Good spreads of food and assorted drinks provide steady and effective distractions.

Availability of beer and liquor usually benefits the good player. One drink takes the sharpness off a player's ability to think and concentrate. Even a single beer will reduce the effectiveness of a superior player. That is why the good player never drinks before or during the game. And that is why the good player is glad to see superior-playing opponents take a drink.

Moderate amounts of alcohol have less effect on poor players because their concentrations are already at reduced levels. The poor player must drink enough to become intoxicated before his edge odds are reduced to even lower levels. But the advantages of having intoxicated opponents are sometimes canceled by disadvantages such as slowing down the game and causing drinking problems that may drive profitable opponents from the game.

**Each week, John Finn is a good fellow and brings beer to the game, along with the late evening paper containing the complete stock-market closings and horse-race results. Ted and Sid read this paper while playing their hands. Every now and then they lose a pot to John because of that distraction.**

**Those newspapers cost John less than $15 per year, but are worth about a $1000 a year in distractions— or about $20 per newspaper.**

**By encouraging and creating distractions, John Finn increases everyone's confusion. At the same time, he keeps the action moving. In the Monday night game, however, he discovers his opponents will play for**

significantly higher stakes when using cash rather than faster-moving poker chips. (In most games, the reverse is true, and thus the good player normally prefers using poker chips.) To offset this, John speeds up the game by alternating two decks of cards between each shuffle and deal.

By using an array of distractions, John increases his edge odds by about 20 percent. That means $8000 additional income per year at his current winning rate. He estimates that while playing their hands, his opponents are distracted 35 percent of the time. And they are distracted a much higher percentage of the time when they are not involved in the action. The chart on page 161 estimates the in-action distractions of each player:

*5. Agreements (89)*

The good player sometimes makes profitable agreements with other players. Occasionally, he can make an agreement with a loose player whereby each time either one wins a pot he will pay the other, for example, $5. Such an agreement will give the good player a guaranteed side income. Even when the loose player is a big loser, he will usually win more pots than the good player. Many poor players will gladly make such an agreement because they erroneously believe that a winner must win more pots than a loser. Also, most losers desire an association with a winner (the good player); such an association boosts their self-esteem by making them feel they are on the same level as the winner. Often a loose player happily maintains such an agreement indefinitely without ever admitting or even realizing that he is providing the good player with a steady side income.

Compared to John Finn, Sid Bennett plays more then twice as many hands, wins about 50 percent more pots, but loses nearly three times as often. He eagerly accepts John's suggestion that they pay each other $5 every time one of them wins a pot. Two years later, Sid is still pleased with this arrangement as indicated by his comments:

**Time Distracted, %**
**(when in action)**

| | Eating | Gossiping | Daydreaming | Radio, TV, Newspaper | Miscellaneous | Total |
|---|---|---|---|---|---|---|
| **Quintin Merck** | 2 | 5 | 10 | 5 | 2 | 24 |
| **Scotty Nichols** | 10 | 2 | 15 | 2 | 5 | 34 |
| **Sid Bennett** | 2 | 25 | 5 | 10 | 5 | 47 |
| **Ted Fehr** | slight | slight | 25 | 15 | 2 | 43 |
| **John Finn** | 0 | 1 | slight | slight | 2 | 4 |

"At least I keep collecting these side bets," he says with a broad smile as John wins a huge pot and gives him $5. "Don't understand why you made such a stupid bet."

"Ha!" Quintin Merck snorts. He knows John makes money from the agreement. John knows it too, and his notebook data prove it:

*The Sid Bennett Agreement*

| | # of Plus Weeks, Average Gain | # of Minus Weeks, Average Loss | Net Income |
|---|---|---|---|
| 1st year | 40, +$30 | 10,—$10 | +1100 |
| 2nd year | 40, +$35 | 8,—$10 | +1320 |

So far, Sid has lost $2,420 on John's "stupid bet," and is very happy about it—an ideal arrangement for John.

# XVIII
# MONEY EXTRACTION (90)

The good poker player is involved in a long-term process of extracting maximum money from the game as well as from each individual player.

## 1. Winning Too Fast (91)

Money extraction at the maximum rate is not always in the best long-term financial interest of the good player. Uncontrolled maximum money extraction can cause the following problems:

- Players who would be long-term sources of important income may quit the game.

- Stakes or rules may be disadvantageously changed.

- Unfavorable attitudes may develop.

• Game may break up.

To extract maximum money, the good player often decreases his winning rate in order to control the flow of money. In other words, maximum-money extraction over the long term may require a slower winning rate.

## 2. Uncontrolled Money Flow(92)

Over a period of many games, uncontrolled money flows in a pattern similar to that illustrated by the top diagram on the Money-Flow Pattern chart shown after Table 26. As the good player accumulates performance data on each player, these money-movement patterns become increasingly obvious.

Data for uncontrolled money flow are tabulated in Table 26. Notice the heavy losses absorbed by poor players A and B compared to players C and D. In that game, the good player, E, is extracting winnings through a natural, uncontrolled money flow. But poor player A may quit, for example, because continuous losses hurt his pride. And poor player B may insist on lower stakes because his sharp losses are causing him financial problems. The good player may be risking his future earnings unless he alters the money flow to a controlled pattern similar to that illustrated by the *bottom* diagram of that Money-Flow Pattern chart (page 168).

The ideal money-flow pattern for the good player occurs when he wins at the maximum rate each player can tolerate. That usually means winning less from the poorest players and more from the better players.

## 3. Controlled Money Flow (93)

The good player evaluates the money-extraction patterns on both a short-term and a long-term basis. If a controlled pattern seems desirable, he then determines how the money flow should be altered (extent and direction). In a controlled pattern, he usually extracts money more evenly from his opponents ... he extracts less from the poorer players and more from the better players. Controlled money flow shifts everyone's performance, as shown in Table 27.

## TABLE 26
## UNCONTROLLED MONEY FLOW FOR TEN GAMES
### Dollars Won (+) or Lost (-), $

| Player—Rating— | A Poor | B Poor | C Weak | D Sound | E Good | Irregular Players* |
|---|---|---|---|---|---|---|
| 12/4 | +200 | -200 | +100 | +200 | -220 | -100 |
| 12/11 | -200 | +300 | -100 | +50 | -80 | +50 |
| 12/18 | -100 | -200 | -150 | +50 | +440 | -50 |
| 1/8 | -150 | -400 | -200 | -250 | +860 | +100 |
| 1/15 | -350 | Absent | Absent | +200 | +260 | -100 |
| 1/22 | -400 | -100 | +550 | 0 | -100 | +50 |
| 1/29 | Absent | -300 | +250 | +150 | +240 | 350 |
| 2/5 | -200 | +100 | -250 | -150 | +680 | -200 |
| 2/12 | +400 | +50 | -200 | +100 | +20 | -350 |
| 2/19 | -100 | Absent | -100 | +100 | +520 | -400 |
| Totals | -900 | -750 | -100 | +450 | +2620 | -1350 |
| Average+ | -100 | -95 | -10 | +45 | +262 | -135 |
| Edge Odds, %++ | -22 | -21 | -2 | +10 | +59 | -30 |

* Average winnings or losses for all the irregular players combined.
+ Averages are calculated by dividing the number of games attended by each player into the net winnings or losses of that player.
++ The biggest winner for each of the ten games averages plus $445 per game. Edge odds of the good player E, for example, are calculated as $262/$445 X 100 = 59%.

167

*Poker: A Guaranteed Income For Life*
*MONEY-FLOW PATTERNS*

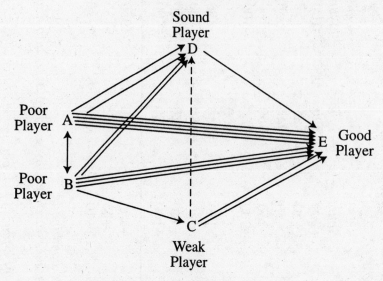

Normal, uncontrolled money flow

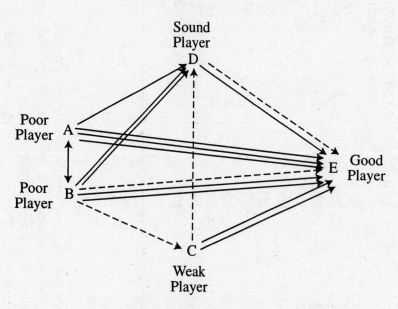

C ontrolled money flow

*Broken arrow represents half the money flow of a solid arrow.*

168

## TABLE 27
## PERFORMANCE DATA
### (Averages for 100 games)

| Player—Rating— | A Poor | B Poor | C Weak | D Sound | E Good | Irregular Players* |
|---|---|---|---|---|---|---|
| Uncontrolled money flow, $/game | -102 | -85 | -22 | +54 | +196 | -41 |
| Controlled money flow, $/game | -58 | -52 | -35 | +6 | +174 | -35 |

* Average values for the irregular players.

169

That controlled pattern costs the good player an average of $22 per game. But if the money flow were not controlled, the continued heavy losses of poor players A and B could destroy the game, costing the good player his $17,400 winnings over those one hundred sessions. That $22 per session is his insurance premium for keeping the game going at high-profit conditions. The good player keeps performance records to determine the cost, value, and effectiveness of his control over the money flow. Money-flow control normally costs him 10-15 percent of his net winnings.

The good player usually takes control of the money flow during the early rounds, when his betting influence can be the greatest at the lowest cost. He alters the money-flow patterns by the following methods:

- He helps and favors the poorest players at the expense of the better players whenever practical.

- He drives the poor players out with first-round bets when a better player holds a strong hand. And conversely. he uses first-round bets to keep the better players in when a poor player holds a strong hand.

- He avoids, when practical, playing against a poor player after everyone else has folded in order to decrease his advantage over the poor player at a minimum cost. He also tries to make his least favorable plays (e.g., his experimental, image-building, and long-term strategy plays) against the poorest players.

**John Finn spends some of his winnings to hold big losers like Sid Bennett and Ted Fehr in the game. The following data from John's records indicate that his insurance costs are profitable investments.**

*Part Four: Opponents*

*Breakdown of Poker Income and Insurance Costs*

| For One Year Source of Income | Estimated Net Income, $ | Estimated Insurance Costs, $ (calculated losses) |
|---|---|---|
| Quintin Merck | 2,500 | 100 |
| Scotty Nichols | 5,500 | 500 |
| Sid Bennett | 13,000 | 2,000 |
| Ted Fehr | 9,000 | 700 |
| Others | 12,000 | 1,200 |
| Total | 42,000 | 4,500 |

Without paying that insurance, John theoretically could have won $4500 more during that year. Yet without the insurance, the greater psychological and financial pressures on the big losers might have forced them to quit . . . and each big loser is worth much more than the entire $4500 insurance cost. Also, if several big losers had quit, the poker game could have been destroyed. John, therefore, considers the insurance cost an important and profitable investment.

How does he spend this $4500? The money buys him the valve that controls the money flow. He watches the losers closely. When they are in psychological or financial trouble and on the verge of quitting, he opens the valve and feeds them morale-boosting money until they are steady again.

Winning players are of little value to John. Since there is no need to help them or boost their morale, he keeps the valve closed tight on them. He may even spend money to drive them out of the game if they hurt his financial best interests.

John Finn never spends money on any player except to gain eventual profits.

171

# PART FIVE

---

# GAMES

More players and more games mean more income for the good player. He increases his poker activity by—

- finding other games

- organizing games

- expanding current games

- maintaining or reviving games

- starting new games.

## XIX
## OTHER GAMES (94)

Other poker games offer new sources of income. Even if the stakes are not financially worthwhile, the good player enters new games in order to—

- take control of them and then increase their betting paces and stakes to worthwhile levels

173

- evaluate the losers—some may be good candidates for higher-stake games

- . make contacts with new players that may lead to still other poker games and other new players.

**When John Finn first entered the Monday night game, the stakes were not worth the effort required to play winning poker. But he took control of the game, reorganized it and then steadily increased the pace and stakes. The chart shown in Concept 35 tabulates John's progress during five years as his profits climbed from $200 to $42,000.**

*1. Finding a Game (95)*

Practically every regular poker game needs, at times, additional players. Likewise, most games need more permanent players. When a "desirable" player spreads word of his poker interest, he usually gets invitations to other games. Most poker players consider a player desirable if he—

- plays a clean game

- arrives on time

- is cooperative and congenial

- acts respectful toward other players

- plays to the end regardless of his winnings or losses

- keeps the game organized.

The good player by design has those "desirable" traits, but considers such traits in his opponents as neither important nor desirable. Since he is interested only in extracting maximum money from the game, his desirable opponents are—

- poor players

- steady players

- players with plenty of excess

- money players who will not harm the game.

Ironically, most players will invite the costly good poker player to their game in preference to a profitable poor player.

**The players in the Monday night game consider John Finn a desirable player and an asset to the game. They refuse to realize that he is their biggest liability— staggering liability of $42,000 per year. They are glad John is in the game because he is cooperative, congenial. and respectful. He plays a clean game, always arrives on time, and plays until the end. They are grateful that he keeps the game organized. He is a pleasant, soothing, comfortable player. Everyone appreciates him.**

**John works hard to keep his opponents satisfied and happy. His fee for the effort — $42,000 per year.**

### 2. Becoming a Permanent Player (96)

Once in a game, the good player gets a repeat invitation by making the other players feel favorable and obligated toward him. He does that with "thoughtful" gestures such as—

- lending money at the first opportunity

- offering his own cigars, candy, and gum to the players (even if he does not smoke, eat candy, or chew gum)

- helping to pick up the cards between deals

- sympathizing with losers

- praising winners

- complimenting good plays of his opponents

- helping to clean up after the game

- offering to bring refreshments (especially beer) to the next game.

If the new game is financially worthwhile, the good player plans his behavior to get a permanent invitation by—

- avoiding the image of being a tight or a tough player

- keeping quiet about his activities in other poker games.

The good player generally will not press for maximum edge odds until he becomes a permanent player. Once a permanent player, he concentrates on taking control of the game. He builds the ego of key players (those with important influence over the game) in order to gain their friendship and confidence. With the support of key players, he is in a strong position to take control of the game.

**The first time John Finn played in the Monday night game, he was a nice fellow—humble, quiet, even timid— and very considerate in passing out his cigars and admiring everyone's poker skill. Best of all, he lost money and played loose. And he never slowed down the game or irritated anyone.**

**A fish, an ideal player, a nice guy—so everyone thought. How about those nutty plays he makes? Raising, then drawing four or five cards. Loosest player I've ever seen. Did you see how he lent Sid $50 even though Sid never even asked him for it? He even offered to pick up the refreshments for the next game. Sure hope he becomes a regular player. At least he'll come back next week to collect Sid's loan.**

**Over the next few sessions, John put zest into the game. He played wild, exciting poker. Everyone knew he was bound to be a big loser. His popularity grew; his friendships deepened. He established himself with supporters, and no one had an excuse to get rid of him. As soon as John became a permanent player, he began taking control of the game. Five years later, he had**

**taken $90,000 from the game, but was just as popular. John Finn never gave anyone a reason to dislike him.**

In public games (casino or club poker) or in other one-shot games, especially those with strangers, the good player will press for immediate and maximum advantages over his opponents. Many of his tactics are opposite to those he would use in regular games: His behavior in one-time games may be almost unbearably tough, unfriendly, and aggressive. He concentrates on extracting money at a maximum rate from the weakest players. He is not concerned about being a nice fellow if his opponents have no future value to him.

### 3. Quitting a Game (97)

The good player quits a game that is not financially worthwhile or that conflicts with a more profitable game. He normally quits under the best possible circumstances and retains good relationships with its players. Even after quitting, he may occasionally play in the game to renew his contacts and to recruit players for bigger games.

**John Finn quit the Thursday night game because it was not profitable enough to consume another weekday night on poker. He quit under congenial circumstances and occasionally returns to play and recruit new players for the bigger games. In the past two years, he has recruited four players from that game for the higher-stake Monday and Friday night games. He won an estimated $10,000 from those four players in one year.**

### 4. Breaking up a Game (98)

The good player sometimes breaks up a game to free its players for more profitable games. If he controls the game by keeping it organized, he can usually destroy the game simply by not organizing it. He can then feed its players to other games.

**Besides the Monday night game, John Finn regularly plays in a Friday night game and occasionally**

177

in Tuesday and Thursday night games. The low-stake Tuesday game has the least profit potential, but one of its players would be a good addition to the high-stake Monday game. John estimates that his entire income from the Tuesday game is less than the money he could win from that one player if he were shifted to the Monday night game. So John breaks up the Tuesday game by focusing his aggression on the two worst players, causing them to suffer consecutive, morale-damaging losses. After three weeks, those two losers quit and the game collapses when John makes no effort to reorganize the players.

By destroying that game, John gains a free night, along with a new player for the high-stake Monday night game. Also, he can now feed the other players from the defunct Tuesday game into the Friday and Thursday games.

# XX
# ORGANIZATION (99)

The financial potential of a game depends on how well it is organized. The good player organizes a game by—

- scheduling it on a regular basis at a time and place best for maximum attendance

- establishing a firm starting time

- contacting players before each game to get commitments to play.

## 1. Regular Game (100)

Compared to the occasional game, the regular weekly game is easier to organize because players can plan for it in advance. A regular weekly game also provides more frequent opportunities for money extraction. But most important, poker players get more emotionally and financially involved in games that are regular and frequent.

If a game is about to collapse because certain players are losing at rates beyond their financial limits, the good player may temporarily reduce the betting pace or stakes. Or, occasionally, he may temporarily reschedule the game on a biweekly or monthly basis instead of reducing the betting pace or stakes.

**To keep the Monday night game going on a weekly basis, John Finn increases the stakes until some players are losing at rates beyond their financial limits; he then lowers the stakes. He may raise and lower the stakes several times before permanently establishing them at a higher level.**

**In going to higher stakes, the losing tolerances of players increase as they adjust and get accustomed to their greater losses. When John lowers the stakes, the big losers are usually the first to insist on returning to higher stakes.**

**Sometimes John stabilizes a shaky game by bringing in new players. Those new players not only contribute to his income, but they also help hold the game at higher stakes. By controlling the betting pace and stakes and by adding new players, John has kept the highly profitable Monday game going on a regular weekly basis for the past six years.**

### 2. Starting Time (101)

An indefinite starting time can eventually destroy a game. If players must wait for others to arrive before starting the game, then the early-arriving players may come later the next week to avoid waiting—thus causing progressively later starting times and a subsequent loss of disgruntled players. The following methods encourage players to arrive on time:

- Make a firm starting time clear to all players.

- Emphasize the reason and importance of being on time.

- Admonish late-arriving players.

179

- Establish fines or penalties for late arrivals.

- Fill the game early so late-arriving players will not get a seat.

**The Monday night game is supposed to start at eight o'clock. As more and more players arrive late, the game starts later and later. Eventually players start arriving at ten and eleven o'clock. Attendance begins to drop, so John Finn takes action. He suggests a $5 fine for anyone arriving after the game starts. The players, disgusted with the late starting times, all agree.**

**The following week, six players arrive by eight o'clock and the game starts at eight fifteen—the earliest start in months. At nine o'clock, Quintin Merck wanders in.**

**"Get it up!" Sid roars.**

**"Uh, what ya mean?" Quintin grumbles as he seats himself at the table.**

**"You're late," Sid says, grinning. "Five-buck fine, buddy."**

**"Ah, don't give me that kid stuff. Deal the cards," Quintin says. He then puffs hard on his cigarette.**

**Sid deals Quintin out.**

**"Hey!" Quintin slaps his hand on the table. "What about my hand?"**

**"You ain't playing till you pay your fine," Sid says. The other players nod in agreement.**

**"We play for thousands of dollars and you boy scouts hound me for five bucks," Quintin growls while throwing a $5 bill at Sid.**

**The following week, all the players are at Scotty's house by eight o'clock. Since the fine was put into effect, the game never starts later than eight fifteen.**

**It's amazing, John thinks to himself. They'll casually lose thousands through lack of effort, but they'll make a big effort to avoid a $5 fine.**

### 3. Quitting Time (102)

As a game continues through the night and into the morning, most players tire and their ability to concentrate on poker decreases. That increases the good player's edge odds. He therefore encourages an indefinite or late quitting time. But if players start avoiding the game because the late hours are interfering with their jobs or harming their health. the good player may enforce an early quitting time (at least temporarily) to keep the losers playing and to preserve the game. He will also quit early in lower-stake games that are not worth staying up all night for. The good player often breaks up a game when he leaves in order to keep the poorer players from losing their money to the better players after he is gone. He breaks up the game so he can win this money for himself in future games.

Making players quit early is easier when the last round is played at higher stakes. Higher stakes not only benefit the good player, but serve as a psychological climax to the game as well. If the good player wants to enforce an agreed-upon quitting time, he plans the final round so the last deal ends with him. He then gathers the cards after he deals the last hand, cashes in his chips, and leaves before anyone can start a new deal.

But the need for a definite or an early quitting time decreases if any player, winner or loser, feels free to leave whenever he wishes. Furthermore, the game becomes more relaxed under those conditions and more profitable for the good player.

**John Finn plays all night on Mondays because the additional profits he garners after midnight are worth his time. In one year, he played about 400 hours of Monday night poker and won $42,000. Of that amount, $23,000 was won after midnight at the rate of $115 per hour, while $19,000 was made before midnight at the rate of $95 per hour. The following data show another important reason why John plays all night in this high-stake game.**

*Estimated Edge Odds, %*

|  | P.M.<br>8:00-12:00 | A.M.<br>12:00-4:00 | Change |
|---|---|---|---|
| John Finn | +56 | +62 | + 8 |
| Quintin Merck | +15 | +5 | -10 |
| Scotty Nichols | -2 | -8 | - 6 |
| Sid Bennett | -24 | -16 | + 8 |
| Ted Fehr | -24 | -18 | + 6 |
| Others | -27 | -31 | - 4 |

The data show that John's edge odds increase by 6 percent after midnight. Also, the losing rates of poorer players (Sid and Ted) decrease at the expense of better players (Quintin and Scotty); that advantageous shift in money flow is accomplished without costing John money. In other words, John controls the money flow at lower costs during the late hours.

In determining the value of playing all night, John considers the effects of his job, health, and personal life. He evaluates each game, and then enforces an earlier quitting time in games of lesser value.

### 4. Contacting Players (103)

A list of players and a telephone are two important tools for organizing a game. The good player usually asks other players to help him organize the game. (Eager players and recent winners will normally help.) To conceal his eagerness for losers to play, the good player asks other players to call the big losers. If negative feelings develop about his organizing efforts, he simply stops telephoning anyone for a few games. His "strike" quickly makes the other players appreciate and support his organizing efforts.

The best time for telephoning players is late in the afternoon before the game. This is early enough so everyone can plan for the game and late enough so those available will seldom have a subsequent excuse for not playing. The good player then knows who his opponents will be for that evening.

An important and convenient tool is a photocopied form (as

The data in the following chart indicate that personal considerations outweigh the additional $28,000 per year that John could have earned by playing as late and as often in the lower-stake games as he does in the high-stake Monday night game.

| Game | Quitting Time | One-Year Income (# games) | Estimated Income for 50 Games Played until 4:00 am. |
|---|---|---|---|
| Monday | None (4-5 a.m.) | $42,000 (50) | $42,000 (d=0) |
| Tuesday and Thursday | 12:30 a.m. | $2,500 (17) | $17,600 (d=$15,100) |
| Friday | 1:00 a.m. | $9,500 (48) | $22,400 (d=$12,900) |
| Totals | | $54,000 | $82,000 (d=$28,000) |

*d = The difference between columns 3 and 4.*

183

**Book 3**
**Poker: A Guaranteed Income For Life**

shown in Table 28) that lists the players' names and telephone numbers along with a column for their responses. By filling out those forms (as shown in Table 29) and periodically reviewing them, the good player obtains valuable information about the—

- health of the game

- attendance patterns

- character of his opponents and their motives for playing

- losers with declining attendance records who may need special treatment to bring them back as regular players

- ways to keep the game organized and players interested.

In some games, players do not expect telephone calls. The game is played on a regular basis, and everyone just shows up. While such a game is convenient, the good player generally prefers to organize each game because his telephone calls provide opportunities to—

- get or provide "confidential" information

- increase his control over the game

- propagandize players and talk to them about their problems

- obtain definite commitments that make the game less vulnerable to collapse from a lack of players.

**John Finn telephones the players each Monday afternoon and fills out the telephone-response form as shown in Table 29.**

## 5. A Place to Play (104)

A game kept in one location is easier to organize, which benefits the good player. Usually, at least one player is willing to establish the game at his house permanently. The good player

184

## TABLE 28
## TELEPHONE CALLS

**MONDAY GAME**

DATE _____

| Player | Phone # | Called by (Time) | Response | Comments |
|---|---|---|---|---|
| Quintin Merck | 568-7295 (O) | | | |
| | 564-1467 (H) | | | |
| Scotty Nichols | 966-3460 (O) | | | |
| | 837-0446 (H) | | | |
| Sid Bennett | 964-8391 (O) | | | |
| | 548-7382 (H) | | | |
| Ted Fehr | 389-5267 (O) | | | |
| | 732-8793 (H) | | | |
| Charlie Holland | 964-9006 (O) | | | |
| | 548-3388 (H) | | | |
| Aaron Smith | 964-1147 (O) | | | |
| | 732-5493 (H) | | | |

*Others*
Mike Bell    ?

*(O) = office phone, (H) = home phone*

185

## TABLE 29
## TELEPHONE CALLS

*MONDAY GAME*      DATE___ Monday 6/4

| Player | Phone # (*) | Called by (Time) | Response | Comments |
|---|---|---|---|---|
| Quintin Merck | 568-7295 (O) 564-1467 (H) | John (3:30) | Yes | Quintin will call Sid and Charlie |
| Scotty Nichols | 966-3460 (O) | John | Yes | Seems shaky and upset, but eager to play. Must be a personal problem. |
| Sid Bennett | 964-8391 (O) 548-7382 (H) | Quintin (5:30) (6:30) | – Yes | Check—not contacted Check-OK |
| Ted Fehr | 389-5267 (O) 732-8793 (H) | John (3:45) (5:30) (7:00) | – – Yes | Not contacted. Must be at the races. Not contacted. OK, 30-minute discussion about the game, finances, and credit. Sounds like he's in bad shape. |
| Charlie Holland | 964-9006 (O) 548-3388 (H) | Quintin (5:30) | No | Stunned and disgusted by heavy loss last week, but probably will play next week. |
| Aaron Smith | 964-1147 (O) 732-5493 (H) | John (3:35) | Yes | Check — OK, excited about winning last week. |
| *Others* Mike Bell | ? | Scotty (5:40) | Yes | Check — OK, concerned about recent losses. |

*(O) = office phone, (H) = home phone

186

seldom plays in his own house in order to avoid the impression that it is "his game." If necessary, a player is induced to keep the game permanently at his house by, for example, cutting the pot for weekly cleaning expenses.

Playing at the same location each week offers the following advantages:

- The game is more stable.

- The burden of locating suitable places to play is eliminated.

- Players not contacted always know where the game is.

Still a game played at a different location each week offers advantages:

• There is closer control over who is invited (e.g., undesirable players, such as other good players, cannot drop in and play if they do not know where the game is located).

• There is more flexibility because the game can easily be changed to locations offering the greatest advantage.

• The possibility of a robbery (particularly in a high-stakes game) is decreased.

# XXI
# EXPANSION (105)

The good player gains the following advantages by filling a poker game to capacity:

- The game becomes more stable.

- More sources of income (players) are available.

- Choices for selecting profitable opponents (losers) increase.

- Losses are spread more evenly among losers.

- Confusion increases.

- Greater control over the game is possible.

- Betting pace and stakes are easier to increase.

- If tight play offers better edge odds, any such tight play is less obvious and less resented in a full game.

A poker game is expanded by adding new players and by improving the attendance of current players.

### 1. New Players(106)

The good player mentions poker to all potential losers. He gauges his comments to bring out their poker interests. The more he mentions poker, the more potential players are revealed. He hunts for losers, and evaluates all potential players with respect to the maximum income that could be extracted from them.

**John Finn tries to fill the Monday night game with at least eight players. He has a nucleus of five players (Sid, Ted, Scotty, Quintin, and himself) who have played regularly over the years. Two or three other players regularly circulate in and out of the game; they usually survive three to twelve**

188

months, sometimes longer. Also eight or nine different men play sporadically or when coaxed. Those irregular players provide important income and are valuable for filling and stabilizing the game.

About half of the new players are introduced to the Monday game by John. His major source of new players is other, lower-stake poker games. Mentioning poker to social and business acquaintances generates a few players, especially for the smaller games. Some of those players later graduate to the big game.

*a. Keeping players (107)*

If a new player is a financial asset, the good player keeps him in the game by—

• being friendly and helpful to him (especially if the new player is timid or nervous)
• making him feel that the game is relaxed and enjoyable
• countering other players' remarks and actions that may upset him (probably more players quit poker because of hurt feelings than because of hurt finances)
• avoiding overpowering or scaring him
• not taking full advantage of his weaknesses
• making him feel that he is a welcome member of the group
• favoring him whenever possible
• flattering him when he wins and offering him sympathy when he loses
• giving him encouragement and advice about the game.

John Finn brings a new player, Aaron Smith, to the big Monday night game. Although Aaron plays in the lower-stake Friday night game, he is timid and nervous. Knowing that Aaron will lose many thousands of dollars if he becomes a permanent player, John sits next to him and helps him whenever possible. He protects Aaron from upsetting losses that could scare him out of the game. He shields him from derogatory remarks that could insult him out of the game. John

189

**knows that Aaron will absorb large losses and take insults gracefully once he gets accustomed to the game and its players.**

**Whenever John folds, he studies Aaron's hand and gives him sound advice; John helps him to a winning night. Aaron is excited ... his confidence increases and his fear decreases. Whenever Sid throws an insulting remark at Aaron, John counters with an ego-boosting comment. By his third game, Aaron Smith is hooked; he loves the Monday night game and its players. At that point, John withdraws his help and Aaron is on his own.**

**When Aaron Smith (or any big loser) gets discouraged and contemplates quitting, John Finn extends his protection to hold the loser in the game through the crisis.**

### b. Rejecting players (108)

If a new player is a financial liability, the good player gets him out of the game. The simplest way to eliminate an undesirable player is not to invite him to the next game. If this is not possible, the good player forces him out by—

- instigating unpleasant and unfriendly incidents toward him

- insulting him

- hurting his feelings

- refusing him credit

- telling him not to play again.

**Scotty Nichols brings a new player, Boris Klien, to the Monday night game. John Finn quickly realizes that Boris is a winning player who will drain money from the game. Boris's winning will increase the financial strain on the losers, which in turn will force John to reduce his winnings in order to keep those losers in the game. Boris is a financial liability and therefore an undesirable player. John wants him out of the game, quickly and permanently:**

190

"Highball draw with a twist," Quintin Merck announces. John notices how Boris carefully watches the deck for flashed cards during the deal.

John checks. Boris opens for $5.

"Five bucks? We ain't playing penny-ante," Sid says while raising to $30. "You've gotta bet something in this game."

"I'll just call; now you can reraise to fifty," Quintin adds as he winks at Boris.

"I'll raise... fifty-five dollars," Boris responds in a clipped voice.

"Hey, he knows what he's doing," Sid says. "He sandbagged us!"

On the draw, Boris raps his knuckles on the table. "Pat!" he says sharply and then bets $50. Sid folds and Quintin calls.

On the twist, Quintin draws one card. Boris again plays pat and then holds a $50 bill over the pot.

"Put your money in if you're betting," John Finn snaps and then turns to Quintin and continues, "That's an old bluff trick..."

Boris scowls at John.

"Forget it," Quintin says, folding his hand without realizing what John is telling him. "I just had two little pair."

Boris grabs the pot and shouts, "Looky here!" He then spreads his cards face-up across the table to reveal a worthless hand.

"He's got nothing!" Ted Fehr rasps "He pulls a pat bluff on his first hand and wins a three-hundred-dollar pot!"

"Wise guy," Quintin says while scowling at Boris' worthless cards. The other players sit in frowning silence.

Over the next hour, Boris Klien plays very tight. He avoids all action until a lowball hand with John Finn. The pot is large; and after the last bet, only Boris and John remain. Boris turns his cards face-up and declares his hand. John says nothing, so Boris reaches for the pot.

"Keep your hands off my money," John snarls.

"Uh? What do ya mean?" Boris asks. "I won, didn't

"Can't you read?" John says while turning his winning hand face-up on the table. He then snatches the pot from under Boris' stiffened fingers.

"Why didn't you declare your hand?" Boris asks.

"Why didn't you look at my cards?" John growls out of the twisted corner of his mouth. "This is a poker game, buddy boy. Cards speak for themselves, remember?"

"Wish I hadn't come to this game," Boris mumbles to Scotty Nichols. "I'm not only losing, but I'm getting a bad time."

"Wish I hadn't come myself," Scotty whines. "Lost all my money I won last week."

"Yeah, but I..."

"Listen," John says, shaking his finger close to Boris' face, "no one made you play. If you don't like our game... get out!"

Three hours later Boris Klien is winning over $400.

"He's taking all our money," Sid Bennett remarks.

"I started out losing four hundred," Boris says, trying not to smile. "I'm still stuck a hundred."

"Liar!" John snaps. "You're up four hundred bucks... Scotty, where'd you dig up this clod?"

"At this point, I don't know or care," Scotty groans. "I'm losing plenty, and Boris won most of it."

"This is my last round," Boris says. "I've..."

"The bore is even a hit-and-run artist!" John cries while snapping his hand on the table. "Plan on this being your last round—permanently!"

Boris frowns. Then, looking at his pile of money, his frown disappears.

"Seven-card stud, high-low with qualifiers and one twist," John announces as he deals. "Trips-eight,"[26] he adds in a whispering voice.

[26] *Trips-eight means that three of a kind are needed to qualify for high, and an eight low is needed to qualify for low.*

192

After the sixth card, John raises on his low hand and drives out the other low hands. By the last card, only Boris remains; he calls John's final $30 bet.... John wins low.

"Don't know why you were wasting our time by betting," Boris says, while showing his two pair. "We just split the pot. Obviously you're low and I'm high."

"Look at that hand!" John hoots as he points to Boris' cards. "The sucker calls all my big bets and doesn't even qualify for high. I get the whole pot!"

"What do ya mean I don't qualify?" Boris sputters. "I got two pair."

"Three of a kind qualifies for high, you creep," John says as he shoves Boris' cards into the deck.

"Trips for qualifiers!" Boris shouts. "They've been two pair all night."

"I announced trips-eight," John says with a laugh. "You'd better clean your ears, clod."

"I heard him announce it," Ted Fehr mutters weakly.

"Yeah?... Well, then it'd be impossible for me to call," Boris says, reaching for the pot. "I'm taking back my last bet."

"It stays in the pot," John growls, slapping his hand over the money. "When you make a stupid play, buster, you pay for it."

"I've had enough," Boris says, getting up to leave.

"You're winning," Scotty whines. "Sit down and play awhile."

"Let the rock go. We'll play longer without him bothering us," John says. Then, turning to Boris, he makes a sharp hitchhiking motion toward the door. "So long, sucker, hope we never see you again."

"I won't be back," Boris huffs.

"Good!" John yells. Boris grabs his coat and leaves, slamming the front door.

"He'll never come back," Scotty Nichols says while scratching his head. "Why so rough on him? He's an honest player."

193

"He's a milker," John explains gently. "He hangs back and waits for a big hand to kill you with. Look how he hurt you tonight. Why should we let a stranger in our game to leech money from the regular players? Not only that, he cries when he wins, tries to take back bets, lies about his winnings, and leaves early when he's ahead."

"Don't understand it," Scotty says. "Seemed like a nice guy outside of the game. Maybe we should give him another chance."

"Don't ask him back," John replies. "He'd ruin our game."

"You're probably right," Scotty says, nodding his head. "I'll tell him to stay away."

"Besides, he's a good player," Sid Bennett adds. "We need more fish with lots of money."

"More players like Sid," Quintin says as his leathery face breaks into a smile.

## c. Women Players (109)

The mind and character are neuter. Rationality, competence, and objectivity are human traits, not sexual traits. Poker, therefore, is an activity in which women not only can compete with men, but can regularly beat them by applying the Advanced Concepts of Poker.

Moreover, women have basic advantages over men players. For example, because women represent only a small minority of players in serious or high-stake poker games, they can gain more experience against male opponents than men can gain against female opponents. That advantage is similar to the advantage held by left-handed pitchers, boxers, and tennis players who can gain more experience against right-handed opponents than their right-handed counterparts can gain against left-handed opponents.

A woman's greatest advantage, however, comes from exploiting her opponents' misconceptions about women lacking the "killer instinct" to compete against tough players in high-stake poker. As shown by the Advanced Concepts, winning poker requires discipline, thought, and control—not the so-called killer instinct. Winning poker demands objective attitudes and clear conceptions of reality. The "inferior-player" view of women is a nonobjective, flawed view. So the woman player who is not inferior can profitably exploit all opponents who stereotype her as an innately inferior player and thus misplay her.

Still, the woman player will encounter stubborn machismo attitudes, especially when she tries to organize and control high-stake, male-dominated games. But by using the Advanced Concepts, she can exploit any erroneous attitude in her opponents to beat them.

Since the Advanced Concepts have been published, the near-total male dominance of professional poker has been crumbling. Today, about 10 percent of the public professional poker players are women using the Advanced Concepts. And in private poker, perhaps 1 percent of the professionals are women. As the Advanced Concepts of Poker become more widely known, the percentage of women poker players (both amateur and professional) should increase, especially in private games.

The Advanced Concepts provide women with the tools needed not only to compete against men, but to beat them. Increasingly, women are discovering that they can exploit the erroneous and machismo attitudes imbued in most male poker players. And because of the subtle but real advantages women players hold over men, women could eventually dominate public poker and regularly win the major tournaments.

As with all opponents, the good poker player considers female players only from a financial viewpoint. If a woman player is an overall financial asset, she is a welcome player. A woman player can cause men to be less objective, thereby increasing the good player's edge odds. But, on the other hand, if she is a good player and a steady winner, she is a financial liability and unwelcomed. Also, control over men players and attempts to increase the betting stakes can be more difficult when a woman is present.[27] For that reason, the good player more often than not tries to keep women out of the game.

---

[27] *Women players often bring out and amplify the dominant or macho characteristics in men players, making those men players more difficult to manipulate and control.*

As the game starts, Scotty informs the players that Sid is bringing his wife, Stephanie Bennett, to play poker. All object to having a woman, particularly the wife of a player, in the game. Quintin even threatens to quit if she plays.

"I don't want her playing either," John says. "But she's already expecting to play... Let her play tonight; we'll keep her from playing again."

Just as the players finish their first hand, Sid and Stephanie arrive. She is wearing a tight dress with a hemline well above the knees. All the players stand up to greet her.

"Just treat me like one of the boys says the woman while touching her hair which sweeps up in a French twist with curls on top; she sits down and crosses her long, curving legs.

"Impossible," Quintin rasps as his nose sniffs the air.

The game becomes erratic; eyes keep focusing on the woman. When Stephanie is in a hand, the betting becomes subdued; the players are reluctant to bet into her. When she is not in a hand, the betting and raising become heavier than usual as the men show off in front of the perfumed woman. John Finn takes full advantage of their distorted betting to increase his edge odds.

After two hours of playing, Stephanie is winning about $50 and her husband, Sid, is losing $300. Some players begin to fidget and grumble under the strain of her presence. John gets involved with Stephanie in a game of five-card stud with two twists. On the third up card, she has a pair of aces showing and bets $15. Sid raises to $30 with his pair of kings showing; Stephanie raises back. Quintin folds while mumbling that Sid is raising to build the pot for his wife.

"Aye," Sid snorts. "Greed is a many-splendor thing."

Abruptly John raises to $60. Sid emits a gagging cough.

After the next card, John has a king, queen, jack, and the ten of diamonds showing—a four-card straight flush. On the twist, Stephanie pairs her fives to give her two pair showing—aces and fives. John stays pat.

"Pat!" Sid exclaims. "He's got to have the flush or straight."

John bets $25, and Sid folds. Stephanie calls and then twists her hole card. John plays pat again and bets S30. - - Sid advises his wife to drop.

"He might be bluffing," she says while starting to call.

"Naw!" Sid shouts. "Not after staying pat with all that betting and raising. Any fool can figure that out."

"Sid's right. I can't take your money," John says, waving his hand. "I've got the diamond flush."

"Thanks for saving me money," Stephanie replies as she throws away her cards.

John Finn peeks at his hole card—the jack of clubs. He then quickly mixes his worthless cards into the deck. Handing Stephanie $25, he says. "Here's your last bet. Guess I'm not a good gambler. Can't take money from a woman. So I'll quit while you're playing."

"No, no," Stephanie says, handing the money back and standing up. "I lost it fairly. And you already lost money by not letting me call that last bet. Now you keep on playing. I'm tired and going home now.... I've had my fling at poker."

Sid Bennett drives his wife home and then hurries back to the game.

"Stephanie should play instead of you," Quintin says when Sid returns. "She'd win if you'd..."

"That lovely woman doesn't belong in this tough game," John interrupts. "Don't let her play again."

"You're right," Sid sighs as he counts his money. "I'll never let her play again."

## 2. *Improving Attendance (110)*

Players are attracted to a full game. In fact, they become eager to play in games that are completely filled. So an effective way to expand a game is to fill it. For example, if eight players are the maximum for a game, the good player may make sufficient telephone calls to invite nine or ten players—or more. When the game is so crowded that some players cannot be seated, an interesting phenomenon occurs... irregular players become regular players, and the scheduled starting time becomes rigidly adhered to. Good attendance is also encouraged by keeping the game well organized and by maintaining the proper atmosphere. Excess attendance means excess players who can be shifted to other games.

**John tries to keep the Monday night game filled. The full game helps draw the big losers back each week. The crowded table and fast action excite the players, especially poor players like Sid and Ted who feel they are missing something if left out of the action.**

**A packed game increases John's flexibility. With excess players, he can increase the stakes and pace more quickly since the loss of one or two players would not seriously hurt the game. Excess players also lessen the need for him to reduce his earnings in order to keep losers from quitting.**

# XXII
# MAINTENANCE (111)

Maintenance of a poker game determines its health. The good player keeps losers in the game by protecting them, lifting their morale, and by making the game attractive.

## 1. *Making the Game Attractive (112)*

A player often tolerates heavy financial losses if he enjoys the game. Also, an attractive game will draw new players... The good player makes the game more attractive by—

- encouraging a carefree and relaxed atmosphere

- keeping players out of serious arguments or feuds

- preventing or ameliorating complaints about the game

- selecting the more pleasant and weaker players for the game, especially when available players are abundant

- keeping the game well organized

- keeping the action exciting

- providing good refreshments and new cards.

**John Finn makes certain that at least a dozen new decks of cards are available for every Monday night game. Although the pots are cut to pay for these cards, the players appreciate the luxury. Losers like Sid feel important when they can call for a new deck of cards at their whim, just like big gamblers in a big game. And big gamblers in a big game bet more money.**

**Other small deeds by John also help make the Monday night game relaxed and carefree. For example, he spends a few dollars on a dozen green plastic eye shades. At three in the morning, when most players are glumly reflecting on their losses, John pulls the eye shades from a brown bag and hands one to each player. Everyone appreciates John's sudden "thoughtful" gift. When Scotty suggests they cut the pot for the eye shades, John refuses with a shaking head and a waving hand. All players smile as they don their green shades and laughingly make remarks about gambling at Vegas and on Mississippi riverboats. John Finn smiles too as he silently surveys the money still in front of each player.**

## 2. Helping Losers(113)

Poor players are valuable assets to the good player. He keeps them in the game by shielding them from—

- personal comments that could hurt their feelings

- arguments

- unpleasant players

- personal problems of other players

- bad credit.

Poor players and big losers are usually grateful for the good player's "protection." They don't allow themselves to realize that he is the one who sets them up for their heavy losses. Still, if big losers never win, they will lose interest and may quit the game long before they are broke. So occasionally the good player helps them to a winning night. He helps poor players (relative to better players) by—

- increasing the ante

- increasing the betting pace for early bets

- decreasing the betting pace for late bets

- interpreting the rules to favor the poorest players and biggest losers

- assisting the poorest players and biggest losers whenever possible.

But the good player helps others only to the extent that he can profit himself.

**Big losers like Ted Fehr think that John is helping them when indeed he is bankrupting them. Consider**

**the following incident with Ted Fehr**

Ted is losing over $1000. It is four in the morning; Quintin and Sid get up to leave.

"Hey! Play a little longer," Ted says in a shaky voice. "Don't quit now. I'm stuck a fortune. I... I never quit when you're hooked."

"You never quit 'cause you never win." Sid laughs.

"I'm going," Quintin grumbles. "You can win it back next week."

Ted turns his sweaty face toward John and rasps, "We can't quit now."

"Look," John says, raising his hand, "Ted is way down. Give him a break. Everyone play another hour at double stakes. We'll all quit at five o'clock sharp."

"Yeah," Ted says, now smiling. "Everyone play another hour at double stakes."

Quintin Merck objects to the higher stakes. Sid, who is winning nearly $1000, objects to playing another hour. But they both sit down to resume playing.

"Thanks," Ted says, leaning over and patting John on the shoulder. "You're the one guy who always gives losers a break."

At five in the morning the game ends. In that extra hour, Ted loses another $800. He is pale and staggers around the room with unfocused eyes. In that extra hour, John wins another $1000. He leaves quietly.

After a few days, Ted forgets his losses; but he always remembers the favors his friend John does for him... such as keeping the game going when he is losing.

## 3. Raising the Morale of Losers (114)

The good player raises the morale of losers whenever possible. Sympathy and understanding properly offered can keep losers in the game indefinitely—or until they are bankrupt. Yet, after suffering sharp losses, some players develop attitudes that could decrease the good player's profits, such as demanding a slower betting pace or lower stakes. A good player can often change those attitudes by talking to the losers in private about their troubles. Private "little talks" usually have comforting and therapeutic effects on big losers.

**New player Mike Bell is a valuable financial asset to John Finn. After losing several weeks in a row, Mike becomes discouraged. Fearful that he may quit, John moves to boost his morale. By leading him into several winning pots, he carries Mike to a winning night. Then with the following dialogue, he further boosts Mike's morale:**

"The way you're winning, you'll break the game," John says. "How much you ahead?"

"A few big bills," Mike says as he splits a high-low pot with Quintin. Suddenly he looks up at John and grins while adding, "I've been lucky."

"Lucky? The way you caught that full house—I call that skill," John remarks while adjusting his voice to a deeper tone. "Why'd you throw your ace and keep the ten kicker?"

"The other three players drew one and two cards," Mike replies in a gloating tone. "They probably were going for low hands—so they'd be holding aces rather than tens. My chances were best for drawing another ten." Mike Bell then glances around. Bored expressions cover all faces except John's—he listens with an open mouth while slowly nodding his head up and down. Mike leans toward him and says in a low voice, "I drew the ten to catch the full house, didn't I?"

"Right," John replies. "Pretty smart thinking."

"Ban Mike from the game!" Sid cries. "Smart thinking is illegal in this game."

"Don't listen to him," John says as he puts his hand on Mike's shoulder. "We respect a man who plays good poker."

"Look who's talking about good poker!" Sid cries again. "You win lowball games with full houses. You hear about that one, Mike?"

"Sure did. Scotty told me all about it," Mike

answers. He then shakes his finger at John. "Don't ever pull that on me. I'd call you from my grave."

"At least John plays more than two hands a night," Sid says. "If we all played tight like Quintin, the game would die from boredom."

Mike Bell counts his winnings, smiles, and then says to John, "Guess I'll be playing permanently in this game."

### 4. Off-Days (115)

When a good player has an off-day or is not feeling well, he may skip the game to avoid a breakdown in his concentration or discipline. Or he may play on an off-day (knowing he may not be playing at his best) in order to—

- alter the consistency of his play

- make money with decreased but still favorable edge odds

- maintain the continuity of the game (even when he misses a game, he helps organize it whenever possible.).

John Finn seldom misses the Monday night game. Even when feeling below par, he still makes an effort to play. Consider the following Monday night game:

"Where's John?" Mike Bell asks.
"Recovering from the flu," Scotty replies.
"But he called me this afternoon about playing," Mike says with a wrinkling forehead.
"He'll organize the game even if he's sick."
"Mighty thoughtful guy."
"He's also mighty thoughtful about taking all your money," Quintin grumbles. "He's won a fortune in this game."
"Still he takes your money pleasantly . . . hardly mind losing to him," Mike says. "He's always fair."
"But he's tough on anyone who's wrong," Sid adds. "Remember how he tore apart that Boris jerk?"

About midnight, John walks in and says with a weak smile, "I'm never too sick for a poker game."

"Good!" Sid cheers. "We need your money."

"I took a nap after dinner," John replies as he sits next to Sid. "Woke up about eleven feeling pretty good. I'm ready for action."

After two hours, John Finn is losing over $600.

"You're playing a lousy game," Sid remarks. "You're losing almost as much as me."

"When my luck turns bad, I lose big," John says while forcing a sigh. "Losing over a thousand—going for the all-time record loss."

"Great act," Quintin Merck mumbles. "Great act."

### 5. Leaving the Game Early (116)

When a good player must leave early and wants the game to continue, he minimizes any disturbance and resentment over his leaving by—

- announcing before the game starts that he must leave early

- announcing his last round before going, then quietly leaving without breaking up the game.

The Monday night game usually breaks up about four or five in the morning. Occasionally it continues into the next day. John Finn seldom leaves before the end... The longest Monday night game on record is twenty-seven hours (from eight thirty Monday night until eleven thirty Tuesday night). This is how John leaves after twenty-two hours:

At seven in the morning, Scotty's wife chases the players from the house. Heavy loser Ted Fehr is playing with money from the second mortgage on his restaurant. He has $1000 left and begs everyone to continue playing at his place. The five players eat breakfast at a diner and then go to Ted's barren apartment.

Ted continues to lose—slowly at first, then at an

204

increasing rate. By eleven in the morning, most of his cash is gone. He plays carelessly and is involved in nearly every hand. He no longer seems to care... he even smiles when he loses a pot.

John Finn is a big winner, but avoids getting involved in hands with Ted. Yet, Sid and Scotty continue to beat Ted and win most of his money. By now, all of Ted's cash is gone; he asks John for a loan.

"They've won all your money," John says, nodding toward Sid and Scotty. "They'll lend it back."

By five-thirty in the afternoon, Ted's bloodshot eyes gaze into space. He has lost all his cash and has borrowed over $2000. Now Sid and Scotty are running out of cash, even though they are winning.

"We broke the record—over twenty-one hours of poker," John announces. "You guys keep playing, I'm leaving at six."

After another round and in the middle of a big hand, John Finn silently leaves. He has most of the cash in the game and escapes without lending money to Ted.

At six-thirty, Ted asks for another loan. Sid and Scotty are out of money. The only person with cash is Quintin, and he refuses to lend Ted any more money. Then with trembling fingers, Ted writes another check. When Quintin refuses to cash it, the freckle-faced man sits in a stupor and stares blankly at him with his mouth open. After a moment of eerie silence, Quintin stands up and says, "I'm going home." After another moment of silence, Sid and Scotty stand up to leave.

"No, you can't leave!" Ted suddenly screams, rising from his chair. The players start rushing toward the door. "You took all my money! Please don't quit! I'm due for a comeback! I gotta win my mortgage money back!...I gotta!" Ted sinks back into his chair with his arms falling to his side as everyone runs out the door. Continuing down the hallway, the players hear him calling out, "Please, give me a break... give me a break like John always does . . . like my friend John!"

No one ever saw Ted Fehr again.

# XXIII
# MAJOR-LEAGUE AND
# MINOR-LEAGUE GAMES (117)

For continuous and expanding income, the good player organizes several regular games at different stakes. He runs those games as major-league and minor-league games with a sort of baseball farm-system relationship among them.

### 1. Major League (118)

A major-league game is the highest-stake game; it is the most valuable game to the good player. He tries to populate that game with (1) players having the most money to lose, (2) compulsive gamblers, and (3) players "trying their luck" in the big game. In that game, the good player continually pushes the pace and stakes to the maximum. The size and health of the big game depend on the availability of poor players and their financial resources.

The minor-league or smaller-stake games are a major source of poor players for major-league games.

### 2. Minor League (119)

The good player can garner worthwhile income from lower-stake games. But more importantly, he uses the lower-stake or minor-league game as—

• a pool for selecting new players for higher-stake games

• a place to break in new players (many players who never intended to play in a higher-stake game will gradually accept such a game after becoming accustomed to or bored with the lower-stake game)

• a proving ground to test and develop new plays, concepts, and modifications before deploying them in higher-stake games

- a game in which poor players who will never play in the higher-stake games can conveniently lose their money to the good player

- a resting place for players dropping out of higher stake games. (Lower-stake games provide a place to hold valuable losers who are driven out of the big game. Without a lower-stake game to fall back on, those losers might quit poker completely. With a lower-stake game, they can continue to play and, in time, they usually recover their confidence, nerve, or finances and return to the big game.)

When playing in several different games, the good player must carefully plan his schedule in order to budget and invest his limited time into the most profitable situations.

### 3. Farm System (120)

The good player controls both the major-league and minor-league games. He directs advantageous transitions of players from one game to another. That system allows him to make the best use of his resources (poker players). He promotes players to higher-stake games when they appear ready to move up. Conditions that indicate when a player is ready for higher-stake games are—

- an increase in financial resources

- a winning streak that provides capital and courage

- development of experience and confidence

- a personal situation or problem that makes the player want to play in higher-stake games.

An obvious sign that a player is ready to drop back to a lower-stake game occurs when he quits playing poker. In approaching him about a smaller game, the good player must be tactful to avoid injuring his pride. The proper approach depends

207

on his reason for quitting. Reasons that a player quits a high-stake game include—

- going broke

- discouragement from a losing streak

- loss of too much money

- hurt feelings or pride

- personality conflicts

- personal problems

- time conflict

- health reasons.

If the reason for his quitting is identified and if the approach is proper, that player will usually welcome the opportunity to continue playing in a lower-stake game (or even to return to the higher-stake game).

**The following chart summarizes John Finn's system of poker games for one year and his earnings from each game (for the final year for which his records were made available).**

**John Finn guarantees himself a substantial income by applying the Advanced Concepts of Poker. By continuing to work his system of games and allowing for escalating inflation, he will earn over $1,000,000 from poker in the next five to ten years ... or much more if inflation occurs.**

## Weekly Poker Games

| Game<br>League,<br>Purpose | Games Played in a Year<br>Annual Earnings<br>(average $ per game) | Regular<br>Players, # | Irregular<br>Players, # | Major-League<br>Candidates, # |
|---|---|---|---|---|
| Monday<br>**Major,<br>Income** | **50**<br>**$42,000 (840)** | **5** | **12** | **—** |
| Tuesday<br>Minor,<br>New contacts | **7**<br>**$ 1,100 (160)** | **4** | **7** | **1** |
| Thursday<br>Minor,<br>New contacts | **10**<br>**$ 1,400 (140)** | **6** | **8** | **2** |
| Friday<br>Intermediate,<br>Farm team,<br>Income | **48**<br>**$ 9,500 (200)** | **6** | **8** | **4** |
| **Totals** | **115**<br>**$54,000 (470)** | **21** | **35** | **7** |

# PART SIX

## PROFESSIONAL AND PUBLIC POKER

### XXIV
### A GUARANTEED INCOME FROM PUBLIC POKER

Any man or woman using the Advanced Concepts of Poker can earn a guaranteed income by playing public poker (i.e., poker in casinos and in commercial card clubs). But first this person must understand the difference between *private* poker, as discussed in Parts One through Five of this book, and *public* poker, as discussed in Part Six.

The two major differences (or problems) of public poker are (1) the house cut that permanently extracts large amounts of money from every player in every game, and (2) the professional cheating that pervades the higher-stake games.

With the information in Part Six, the good player not only can win in most club and casino poker games, but also can identify those games in which he cannot win. In addition, Part Six provides the information needed to accept or reject public poker as a source of income.

# XXV
# PRIVATE POKER VS. PUBLIC POKER

Over 95 percent of all poker played in the United States and throughout the world is private poker. Generally, the good poker player can make much more money from private games than from public (club or casino) games. That is why over three-quarters of this book is devoted to explaining concepts for extracting money from private poker games.

Nevertheless, many private-game players will try public poker sometime during their lives. And almost all private-game players will wonder at times:

- What is it like to play poker in public clubs and casinos? How do those games compare with the games I play in?

- How well would I do in public poker? Could I win consistently? Could I make a living by playing poker in clubs and casinos?

- The constant availability of games, players, and money in clubs and casinos seems attractive, but how much would the house cut and professional competition decrease my odds? Could I beat the professional players? Would I encounter cheaters? Could I beat the cheaters?

Part Six answers those questions.

To win consistently in public club and casino poker (such as played in the California card clubs and in the Nevada casinos), the good player must use the Advanced Concepts of Poker that are relevant to public poker.

To compete in public poker, a new player must first understand the differences between private and public poker. Table 30 summarizes the major differences. By understanding them, the good player will know which of the Advanced Concepts of Poker are applicable to public poker.

212

In addition to the differences listed in Table 30, public poker differs from private poker in minor and subtle ways that influence the good player's strategy. Part Six identifies many of those subtle differences, and the good player will discover others as he plays public poker.

# XXVI
# THE HOUSE CUT

For the good player, the most negative feature of public poker is the damage that the house cut (time collection or casino rake) does to his profit potential. Card clubs and casinos, through their continuous collections and raking, gradually but permanently remove most of the available cash from all public games. In private games, the bulk of that house-removed cash would have ended up in the good player's pocket. Tables 31 and 32 illustrate the draining effect that the house cut has on the earnings of the good player. If the house cut is sufficiently high (e.g., 15 percent or more), the good player may be unable to win over the long term, no matter how great his advantage is over the other players.

The far-right-hand columns of Tables 31 and 32 show that the house cut diminishes the good player's earnings much more than the amount actually collected from him. That is because the house cut relentlessly drains cash away from every opponent, steadily shrinking the amount of money available for extraction from poor players by the good player. Because of the constantly draining house cut, the poorest players (the good player's most valuable assets) are driven from the game more quickly than are the tougher players. That phenomenon results in higher concentrations of tough or superior players than would occur in comparable games without a house cut. Also, the house cut produces more losers who, in turn, will play tighter poker, thus further diminishing the good player's advantage and edge odds.

Adding to the cash drain in casino poker is the toking (tipping) of the house dealer by the winner of each pot. Because of the arbitrary raking power of most casino dealers, toking is necessary to avoid extra-heavy rakes from future pots that the player may win. Toking increases by as much as 20 percent the

213

## TABLE 30
## DIFFERENCES BETWEEN PRIVATE POKER
## AND PUBLIC (CLUB AND CASINO) POKER
*(All data are estimates based on author's direct experience)*

|  | *Private Poker* (Worldwide) | *Casino Poker* (Las Vegas, Nevada) | *Commercial Club Poker* (Gardena, California) |
|---|---|---|---|
| **Availability** | Whenever and wherever game can be organized. | 24 hours, 365 days. | 24 hours (20 hours on Sundays), 365 days. (On separate days, each club is closed one day a week.) |
| **Game stakes** | Any agreed-upon stakes. Usually controlled by the good player. Most flexible. | $1-$2 up to no limit. Established by each casino according to player and market demands. Flexible. | $1-$2 up to $200 maximum bet. Established by law. Least flexible. |
| **Speed of play** | Very slow to fast. | Fast. | Very fast. |

214

|  | | | |
| --- | --- | --- | --- |
| **Betting pace** | Controlled by good player. Betting pace increased by introducing game modifications such as twists, wild cards, bizarre games. | Controlled by dealer and all players collectively. Generally fast paced within limits of games permitted. | Controlled by all players collectively. Some influence by strongest players. Generally fast paced within limits of games permitted. |
| **Poker games played** | All types of poker. Generally controlled by good player. | Mostly seven-card stud and hold 'em. Also highball or lowball draw and stud. A few split-pot games. No wild cards, except jokers in lowball. | Only draw poker, high and low. No oddball games, twists, or wild cards, except jokers in lowball. Stud or open-hand poker prohibited by law. |
| **Profitability for good players** | Most profitable. | Varies, depending on house cut or rake. High % rakes (e.g., 20%) eliminates profits for good players. Highest-stake games have lowest % cut. | Generally better than casino poker because of smaller % house cut - an advantage partly offset by the higher percentage of better players in Gardena and recent increases in collection fees. |
| **Skill of average player** | Least. | Intermediate. | Most. |

215

|  | | | |
|---|---|---|---|
| **Quality of average professional** | Best—the most independent, secretive, honest, and successful of the professionals. | Most dependent on cheating and collusion with dealers, shills, and fellow professionals. | Better than casino professionals, but many are dependent on the professional establishment and cheating. |
| **Professionals in high-stake games, %** | 2-5 | 10-40 | 5-30 |
| **Extent of cheating** | Least. | Most. | Intermediate. |
| **Professionals who cheat, %** | 10 | 60 | 40 |
| **Average winnings of top professional players Without cheating** | Unlimited. | $20,000-$100,000. | $20,000-$50,000. |

216

| | | | |
|---|---|---|---|
| **Average winnings of top professional players With cheating** | Winning potential decreases with cheating. | $20,000-$200,000 with cheating in high table-stake games. | $20,000-$70,000 with cheating in highest-stake lowball games. |
| **Cheating techniques most commonly used** | Crude culling, stacking, collusion and peeking by amateurs and losers. Cheating by professionals or good players is rare. | Undetectable collusion between professionals and house dealers who know hole cards in high-stake stud and hold 'em poker. | Signaling and card flashing between professional partners in highest-stake lowball games. Occasional opportunities for card manipulation. |
| **Neocheating** | Just beginning. | Spreading. | Spreading. |
| **Danger of violence or robbery** | Some risk, depending on players, game, and location. | Essentially none. | Almost none. |

217

> Book 3
> Poker: A Guaranteed Income For Life

\* *In any given year, the earnings of a top professional player could significantly exceed these average amounts.*

## TABLE 31
## EFFECT OF CHEATING AND HOUSE CUTS —
## GARDENA CLUB POKER

*(For 3000 hours of poker per year. All data are estimates based on author's direct experience.)*

| | Professional Cheating (estimates) | Earnings of Best Professionals* (with cheating) | Earnings of Good Players (noncheating) | House Cut+ per Player | Earnings of Good Players in Equivalent Private Games |
|---|---|---|---|---|---|
| **High Draw** | | | | | |
| $ 5-$10 | Little | $ 10,000 | $20,000 | $15,000 | $ 30,000+ |
| $20-$40 | Some | $ 25,000 | $30,000 | $30,000 | $ 80,000+ |
| $30-$60 | Considerable | $ 40,000 | $50,000 | $42,000 | $100,000+ |
| **Low Draw** | | | | | |
| $ 5 blind | Some | $ 10,000 | $15,000 | $15,000 | $ 35,000+ |
| $ 20 blind | Considerable | $ 30,000 | Uncertain | $30,000 | $ 90,000+ |
| $100 blind | Extensive | $100,000 | Possible loss | $60,000 | $250,000+ |

* *Earnings are estimated for the best professional players observed in Gardena. The average professional in Gardena (including house shills and proposition players who are paid by the club for staring and maintaining poker games probably nets less than $15,000 per year. The net average earnings of all the professional poker players in Gardena are estimated at $15,000 per year per professional player.*

+ *The average Gardena table extracts an estimated $109,000 per year from its players, as shown in Table 34. The house-collection schedule is shown in Table 33.*

218

## TABLE 32
### EFFECT OF CHEATING AND HOUSE CUTS— LAS VEGAS CASINO POKER

(For 3000 hours of poker per year. All data are estimates based on author's direct experience.)

| | *Professional Cheating (estimates)* | *Earnings of Best Professionals\* (with cheating)* | *Earnings of Good Players (noncheating)* | *House Cut+ per Player* | *Earnings of Good Players in Equivalent Private Games* |
|---|---|---|---|---|---|
| **High Stud and Draw** | | | | | |
| $ 5-$10 | Little | $ 5,000 | $15,000 | $15,000 | $ 40,000+ |
| $10-$20 | Some | $10,000 | $20,000 | $20,000 | $ 75,000+ |
| $20-$40 | Considerable | $15,000 | $25,000 | $25,000 | $100,000+ |
| $40-$80 | Extensive | $20,000 | $30,000 | $30,000 | $125,000+ |
| $100+ | Extensive | $25,000 | $30,000 | $35,000 | $150,000+ |
| Table Stakes | Extensive | $35,000 | Possible loss | $35,000 | No limit |
| **Low Stud and Draw** | | | | | |
| $ 5-$10 | Little | $10,000 | $20,000 | $15,000 | $ 45,000+ |
| $10-$20 | Considerable | $15,000 | Uncertain | $20,000 | $ 85,000+ |
| $20-$40 | Extensive | $20,000 | Probable loss | $30,000 | $125,000+ |
| $40-$80 | Extensive | $30,000 | Probable loss | $35,000 | $150,000+ |
| $100+ | Extensive | $35,000 | Probable loss | $35,000 | $175,000+ |

219

*Poker: A Guaranteed Income For Life*

\* *Earnings are estimated for the best professional players observed in Las Vegas. The average professional in Las Vegas (including house-shills who are paid by the casino for starting and maintaining poker games) probably nets less than $18,000 per year. The net average earnings of all the professional poker players in Las Vegas are estimated at $18,000 per year per professional player.*

\+ *While most Nevada casinos have a harsh percentage rake averaging about 10 percent, some have a $2-$3 maximum rake per hand for higher-stake games. (For high-stake games, some casinos have a lower-percentage Gardena-type time collection.) Even with a $2-$3 maximum cut per hand, casinos can remove $1400-$2000 per day per table, which is $500,000-$700,000 per year per table. Accounting for low-stake games and slack periods, the average casino poker table extracts an estimated $300,000 per year from its players (see footnote in the survey of Casino Poker, Table 39). Additional money lost to house dealers in tokes or tips can exceed 10 percent of the house-cut total.*

220

money removed from the game by casinos. Since public card clubs have no house dealers, their customers are spared that additional drain (although toking of floormen does occur in some high-stake club games).

The house cut (rake) in poker is actually higher than the house cut in most major gambling games such as blackjack, craps, and roulette. The primary difference between gambling and playing public poker is that in gambling, individuals play directly against the house (the casino) and have no way to overcome the house cut or house percentage.[28] But in poker, individuals play against one another, not against the house or casino. The good poker player can, therefore, consistently extract money from all inferior players. He will win in casino and club poker if his money extraction from the other players is greater than the amount the house extracts from him. Conversely, the loser or the inferior player takes a double loss in public poker—the loss to the winners and the loss to the house.

In calculating his edge odds, the good player must include the house as the biggest winner. As indicated by Tables 31-34, the house will be the biggest winner in almost every game, with the good player averaging a distant second. In private poker, the good player tries to eliminate any competing big winner as quickly as possible (or he quits that game and finds a more

---

[28] *The single exception to the unbeatability of casino games occurs when a Thorpe-type counting system is properly used in blackjack. The validity of blackjack counting systems is limited and provides at best a theoretical advantage of less than 1 percent (or investment odds of less than 1.01). Furthermore, such systems are mainly mechanical and inflexible—they are difficult and boring to apply and basically impractical for accumulating any significant or reliable income. Casinos can eliminate any player advantage in blackjack whenever they want to or need to (which is seldom) simply by increasing the frequency of shuffles until counting becomes impractical or unprofitable. Moreover, by publicizing their feigned dislike and fear of counting systems, casino managements surreptitiously promote and encourage the use of blackjack counting systems. The burgeoning interest in those systems has caused major increases both in blackjack activity and in profits for the casinos. (Technically the game with a house dealer as played in all casinos is "21"; not blackjack in which the deal constantly changes or rotates.)*

221

profitable game without a competing big winner). But in public poker, the good player can never escape from or eliminate the biggest winner (the club or casino). By playing only in private games and avoiding the house cut, the good player makes *himself* the biggest winner.[29]

The time collections of public poker clubs (e.g., Gardena, California poker club[30]) are generally less expensive and less harmful to the good player's earnings than are the percentage rakes of Nevada casinos.[31] Still, the Gardena-type time collections

---

[29] *In private poker, the good player can sponsor a game with pleasant distractions and discipline-breaking amenities (e.g., "free" gourmet buffets, rich desserts, expensive liquors). But if the good player acts as the house (with profitable collections or rakes), he could cause his opponents to believe that he is sponsoring the games solely for profit (which, of course, would and should be true). Such a belief would make his opponents more defensive and harder to manipulate, and thus harder to control and extract money from. Besides, the good player can win by finesse all available money without having to compete against himself by mechanically collecting money through a house cut. Also, most states consider running a profitable game with regular house cuts an illegal gambling operation. Such activity could leave the sponsoring player vulnerable to a criminal complaint filed, for example, by an unhappy loser ... or by the loser's wife.*

[30] *California has 400 legal poker clubs. A few other states such as Montana, Washington and Oregon also have legal poker clubs. But by far the most important area for public club poker is Gardena, California, where legalized poker began in 1936. Today, Gardena has six of the most prosperous poker clubs in the country and is the mecca for both amateur and professional public-club poker players.*

[31] *Some Nevada casinos are switching from harsh percentage rakes to milder, Gardena-type time collections, especially for their higher-stake games. Increasing competition for poker players is causing this trend toward milder house cuts as more and more Nevada casinos, attracted by the profitability of public poker, are adding poker to their operations or are expanding their existing poker facilities. In fact, the maximum rake for some high-stake casino games has fallen below $2.00 per hand, reducing the house cut to well below 5%. But the competition in those games is much stiffer since the best players and professionals gravitate to the low-cut games. But countering the trend toward lower rakes in Nevada casinos, the California card clubs are raising their collection fees as shown in Table 34.*

222

## TABLE 33
## MONEY EXTRACTED BY GARDENA POKER CLUBS VIA
## TIME COLLECTIONS

| | Minimum Collection $1/half hour (for $1-$2 game) | Average Collection $2/half hour (Average for all games) | Maximum Collection $12/half hour (for $100-$200 games) |
|---|---|---|---|
| Each hour/seat | $2 | $4 | $20 |
| Each day/seat (22-hour day) | $44 | $88 | $440 |
| Each year/seat (310-day year) | $13,640 | $27,280 | $136,400 |
| Each year/filled table (8 seats/table) | $109,120 | $218,240 | $1,091,200 |
| Each year/average table (50% filled) | $54,560 | $109,120 | $545,600 |
| Each year/club (35 tables) | — | $3,819,200 | — |
| Each year/Gardena (6 clubs) | — | $22,915,200 | — |
| Estimated money extracted per year by professional poker players | — | $1,500,000 to $3,000,000 | — |

223

## TABLE 34
## HOUSE-COLLECTION SCHEDULE
(Public Card Clubs in Gardena, California)

| Stakes, $ | Approximate Half-Hour Collections $/PIayer* | Average Hourly Rates, $/Player |
|-----------|---------------------------------------------|--------------------------------|
| 1-2       | 1.00                                        | 2.00                           |
| 2-4       | 1.25                                        | 2.50                           |
| 3-6       | 1.50                                        | 3.00                           |
| 5-10      | 2.50                                        | 5.00                           |
| 10-20     | 3.00                                        | 6.00                           |
| 20-40     | 5.00                                        | 10.00                          |
| 30-60     | 6.00-7.00                                   | 13.00                          |
| 40-80     | 8.00                                        | 16.00                          |
| 50-100    | 9.00                                        | 18.00                          |
| 100-200   | 10.00-12.00                                 | 22.00                          |

*\* An extra $1-$2 is added to collections from lowball games with blind bets.*

---

relentlessly and permanently remove the major portion of available cash from every game. Table 33 shows that each year, the six Gardena clubs end up with more than ten times the cash that is won by all the professional poker players in Gardena combined. The table shows that the six Gardena poker clubs extract over $22,000,000 per year from their customers.

Poker generates substantial profits for the club owners—even after subtracting business expenses, high taxes, and an annual payroll of over $8,000,000 (according to the Gardena Chamber of Commerce). Who, then, are the smartest and most prosperous poker players in Gardena? The answer is the quiet, invisible club owners. Indeed, those club owners deserve admiration. What player could ever match their edge odds and consistent winnings from poker?

Still, how do the other poker players fare? If the average professional poker player in Gardena nets about $15,000 per year (estimated in footnote to Table 31), then the estimated 100 to

224

200 professionals in Gardena would extract $1,500,000 to $3,000,000 per year from all the other poker players. After allowing for those seats occupied by the professionals plus the empty seats and vacant tables during slack periods, the nonprofessional players occupy an estimated average of 800 seats in the six Gardena poker clubs. Those clubs, therefore, must extract $28,500 per year from each of these 800 seats to account for the $22,000,000 permanently removed each year. That means that the nonprofessional regular customer who plays forty hours per week must lose an average of $7000 per year if he plays better than half the other players in Gardena. (And, as a group, the Gardena players are the best and the toughest poker players in the world.) If he does not play better than half the players, he will lose more than $7000 per year by playing forty hours per week. If he is a much better player than the average Gardena player and can extract a net gain of $7000 per year from the other players, he will break even. And if he is good enough to extract a net gain of $22,000 per year from the other players by playing *sixty hours* every week, he will be in the same class with the average professional poker player by earning $15,000 per year. In other words, except for the few very best and toughest players, people pay dearly in both time and money for the privilege of playing poker regularly in Gardena. And as indicated in Table 32, players in the lower-stake games pay even more dearly for the privilege of playing poker regularly in Nevada casinos because of the higher percentage casino rake, but less dearly in most higher-stake games because of the lower percentage rake.

To earn a steady income from public poker requires an exceptionally tough player with poker abilities far superior to those of the average player. To be a professional poker player in the Gardena clubs or the Nevada casinos requires long, hard hours that yield relatively poor yearly incomes. So most professional casino or club players seem to be wasting their abilities in unrewarding careers. And most other public poker players (the losers) are throwing away their time and money with methodical certainty.

# XXVII
# LEARNING PUBLIC POKER

The good player can extract a steady income from the unlimited supply of players and money offered by public club and casino poker. But the house cut, the stiffer competition (resulting from the higher percentages of superior and professional players in public poker), and the rigid rules and betting limitations of public poker all serve to reduce the good player's edge odds, flexibility, and income. As a result, private poker is generally more profitable than public poker.

## 1. Club Poker

Public poker in the Gardena card clubs is tough, fast, and different. As a group, the Gardena poker players are the best in the world. Most newcomers to public club poker lose money not only because of the house collection and the superior competition, but also because of their own confusion, errors, and lack of knowledge. Even the experienced private-game player will be confused, perhaps shaken, the first time he plays public club poker—especially if the first time is in Gardena, California.

Unlike casino poker, in club poker there are no house dealers to protect, help, or guide new players. Also, club poker moves faster and is higher pressured than casino poker. The newcomer to Gardena poker often encounters harassment, intimidation, and pressure from other players. The nonprofessional regular players in the lower stake games especially try to press for advantages by intimidating newcomers into losing money through confusion and errors. Superior players and professionals in higher-stake games, on the other hand, usually do not harass new players because they want to hold them in the game for longer-term money extraction Thus, the newcomer can learn public poker more comfortably in the higher-stake games, but he will pay more for his lessons because he will be up against superior competition.

After twenty to forty hours of Gardena poker, the good player begins integrating the unique characteristics of club poker into his own poker experience and skills. The good player will then start to detect patterns among different games and players. As

226

he continues to play club poker, those patterns will become increasingly familiar. After a dozen or so games, the good player will start to recognize a sameness for each kind of club game (e.g., low-stake, high-stake, highball, lowball) and for each class of player (e.g., losers, winners, sporadic players, regular amateurs, regular professionals). Because of the rigid customs and rules in club poker, the playing and betting actions of club players fall into more predictable patterns than do similar actions by private-game players. Once familiar with club poker and its patrons, the good player can enter any club and after a few hands be able to read and predict most actions of both amateur and professional players with good accuracy.

The good player can reduce or even eliminate the cost of learning Gardena poker by rattling his opponents by switching the pressures and intimidation from him to them. The good player's normal technique for rattling and intimidating opponents requires a confidently bold and aggressive style. But, for the newcomer, such a style would be unconvincing and ineffective because of his weak, defensive position during his first few ventures into public poker.

Ironically, that temporary weakness places the good player in an ideal position to use unorthodox behavior or bizarre actions to confuse and frighten his opponents. By such actions, he can often nullify the disadvantage of his own initial confusion by throwing his opponents into even greater confusion. Being a stranger, he can effectively induce bewilderment and fear in others through the unknown. For example, feigning insanity can induce paralyzing fear in others. Who would not fear a deranged stranger? Few players would dare to pressure or intimidate a psychotic at their table. Indeed, most players would be rattled into making errors. Feigning a physical disorder such as a severe tic or emitting strange guttural sounds will also rattle opponents into errors. Feigning deafness, muteness, or severe handicaps usually eliminates harassment and provides peace.

**John Finn first experienced public poker in the Gardena, California, card clubs. He promptly canceled the disadvantages of being a newcomer by rattling his**

opponents into errors. He learned public poker at their expense.

After arriving in Gardena, John Finn parked his rented car in the self-park area behind the Eldorado Card Club. He entered the club through the automatic glass doors. He walked past the darkened lobby partly illuminated by a large gas-fed fireplace and abruptly stopped and stared into the brightly lit pitlike playing area filled with rising layers of white smoke. A low rumble of voices came from the cloudy pit. For an instant, John felt he was witnessing several hundred vagabonds huddling around tables in a cavernous Salvation Army hall. He moved to the observation rail that partly circled the poker pit and studied the scene. Some people were poorly dressed, which gave the entire crowd a tacky appearance. Everyone seemed to homogenize into a blend of middle-aged and elderly men and women. A few looked younger, but most looked pallid and wan... some looked cadaverous. About 25 percent of the players were women—some seemed slack and bored, others were tense and desperate. John observed more closely. Contrary to his first impression, many faces reflected an intelligence and a strength... or at least a faded intelligence and perhaps a surrendered strength, especially in the older people. He estimated that 70 percent of the players were addicted smokers... John Finn knew he could extract money from this crowd.

After watching from the rail for thirty minutes and reading through a house-rule booklet obtained in the lobby, John Finn went to the large chalkboard that listed the poker games in progress and the waiting list for each game. The lowest-stake game was $1-$2 high draw, jacks or better to open. John gave the boardman the false initials "J.R." to be listed for that low-stake game. In ten minutes, "J.R." was announced over the speaker system. Moments later, John was sitting in his first public poker game. ...His opening ploy was to rapidly cross himself several times in view of everyone.

228

After an hour, John was still winless and had forfeited two pots because of technical errors: On his first forfeited pot, he had turned up his pair of queens to show openers after no one called his final bet. When he tossed his other three cards face-down on the discards, a collective shout from the other players informed John that his hand was dead. (According to Gardena house rules, all five cards—not just openers—of the opening hand must be spread face-up before any of those cards touch the discards.) John forfeited the pot. Several hands later, he held three kings. His only opponent held two pair and stayed pat. John was the dealer. He drew one card, but forgot to burn a card (deal a card into the discards) before drawing. Again a collective shout informed John that his hand was dead. The player with two pair promptly spread his cards face-up, grinned, and yanked the pot into his pile of chips.

John decided he had learned enough from that game and wanted to establish a stronger psychological position in a higher-stake game. Looking at the game board, he noticed that a $3-$6 draw game had no waiting list. John played one more hand. He opened with three tens. Everyone folded. He promptly spread his hand face-up and pulled in the 40-cent ante—his first pot in public poker. As he stood up to leave, a wizened old woman sitting across from him looked up, stretched her skinny neck, and cackled. "Hey, buster, don't tell 'em where ya won all that money."

As he moved to the $3-$6 game, John already knew his strategy. He would nullify the disadvantages of his inexperience by rattling his opponents into yielding advantages to him.

After silently slipping into the empty seat, he put his chips on the table, anted for the next pot, touched his fingertips together in a praying position, bowed his head, and waited for the cards to be dealt. Someone asked him a question. John did not look up or even acknowledge the question. He looked at no one, said nothing, and moved with squared, mechanical-like motions. Between movements he sat with fingertips joined and stared silently at the "action spot" on the table. The conversation at the table diminished as the players began casting glances at him and then at one another. John knew they were worried about his behavior.

His total withdrawal gave John Finn a two-way advantage: First, it allowed him to shut out interference and distractions from the other players so that he could concentrate, learn, think, and plan strategy. Second, since the other players were reluctant to pressure or intimidate him because they were nervous about his behavior, John had the solitude and time to think and act deliberately, thereby decreasing his confusion and errors.

But this technique, being a short-range tool, needed constant reinforcement as new players entered the game and as other players became tired of John's behavior and began challenging it with intimidation. For example, after a profitable hour of this silent playing, John bowed his head as a portly player entered the game and sat beside him. The stout man began chatting with other players. After two hands, he noticed John's silent, mechanical-man behavior and jabbed John's shoulder several times while blurting, "Hey, man, you alive? You some kind of a robot? Say something so I know I'm not playing against a computer."

Without moving or looking at the man, John kept staring at the table while answering in low monotones, "Doctors at state hospital make me like this ... to control myself. They keep accusing me of being paranoid . . . they keep lying about me. They keep accusing me of being violent. This way I stay controlled and peaceful."

Several players shuddered. But the portly neighbor pressed on, "Hey, man, what hospital? Who's your shrink? I need someone to make me stay controlled and peaceful. I need someone to make me quit gambling and eating. Man, how do I get committed to that hospital?" He punched John's shoulder again.

John Finn jumped up, pointed a stiff finger at the man's face, and shouted, "Don't bug me! Don't bug me or I'll lose control!"

The stout man picked up his chips. "No ... no offense, sir," he said. "I'm leaving. See, I'm leaving." He stood up and left.

Everyone became silent. Another player abruptly stood up and left. John played two more hours in peace while winning $100. As other players left, new players entered the game. Gradually the players became hostile toward John because of his mechanical behavior. So he decided to reinforce his act again at their expense.

The opportunity came several hands later. Before the draw, John had the last bet and raised the maximum on his two pair—jacks and fours. He drew one card and caught the third jack for a full house. He knew his three opponents held weak hands; they would check and probably fold on any betting strength from him. After catching his full house, John had to change his strategy in order to build a larger pot for himself. So he used his abnormal behavior to elicit bluffing and betting action from his opponents: With a jerk, John rose from his seat and faced the player on his left. Lifting his upper lip to expose his teeth, he bowed and whispered, "Thank you, sir, for my straight flush." Turning clockwise, John bowed and uttered his thanks to every player. With each bow, he flashed the jack of hearts and the four of clubs in his carefully arranged hand that concealed his other three cards. He then slumped into his seat, closed his eyes, lowered his head to the table, and continued muttering words of thanks.

The first player snorted and bet the maximum. The second player raised. And the third player called. Without lifting his face from the table, John shoved all his chips toward the pot and said in a muffled

231

voice. "Reraise the maximum." After long pauses, each player called. Still pressing his forehead against the table, John spread his full house face-up against the table. All three players threw down their cards and promptly left the table. Another player stood up and left. The game had been broken. John grabbed the $110 pot, picked up his chips, and left.

Perhaps John Finn overacted in that last hand, causing the players to flee. But so what? Unlike private games, each public game is a one-shot combination of opponents. What they think, feel, or experience has little bearing on future games. So by acting abnormally, John rattled his opponents and won an extra-large pot on top of the $100 he had won earlier— all while learning to play club poker in Gardena. If John had not rattled his opponents, he probably would have lost money in that game—$100 or more. A little planned acting made at least a $300 difference. John exchanged his initial weakness for a bizarre aggressiveness that intimidated and confused his experienced opponents into making multiple errors. With careful planning and unorthodox action, he beat his opponents while learning their game.

## 2. Casino Poker

Casino poker is easier to learn (especially in the major casinos) than club poker because the nonplaying casino dealer controls the game and protects the new player by guiding him through unfamiliar rules and customs. That help from the dealer reduces the new player's technical errors and allows him more thinking room to analyze the game and execute strategy. The good player makes a wise investment by toking (tipping) dealers who provide him with pressure-relieving protection and helpful information. With the dealer's protection and help, the new player can win pots that he might otherwise have lost or forfeited because of his inexperience. But, in the faster-moving higher-stake games, dealers are more reluctant to help or protect the newcomer. Yet even here, the inexperienced good player can beat experienced professionals by rattling them with unorthodox actions.

**When he first moved up to higher-scale casino poker, John Finn twice assumed the role of a mute in order to play in peace and to gain the thinking time necessary to turn certain high-pressure situations into winning hands. On another occasion, he faked a severe tic to successfully bluff a professional player out of a $240 lowball pot.**

**Once John Finn had control of casino and club poker, he dropped most of his short-term ploys for the more profitable long-range strategy of tough, sound poker based on the Advanced Concepts of Poker.**

When to use unorthodox or bizarre acts and which act to use depend on the game and its players. Such acts benefit the good player when he is first adjusting to or learning a new game situation—such as casino or club poker. Once he has the new situation and its players under control, the good player will find his straight poker skills are more effective than unorthodox or bizarre behavior.

*3. Notes on Public Poker*

John Finn made the following notes while playing poker in the Gardena card clubs and in the various Nevada casinos:

1.  **Advantages of private poker over club and casino poker: (1) No house cut to drain away available cash and profits. (2) The same players are available week after week for the long-range manipulation necessary for increasing money extraction and a growing poker income. (3) Generally weaker players.**

2.  **Advantage of club and casino poker over private poker: The constant supply of fresh players allows maximum aggressiveness and ruthlessness without fear of destroying the game. If best strategy dictates, unrestrained action can be directed toward upsetting opponents. No need to mollify losers. Establish psychological dominance early. Only limitation — avoid excessively obnoxious tactics that**

might alienate club or casino management and result in banishment from their establishments.

3. The six card clubs in Gardena, California, provide simultaneous action for up to 1680 poker players. Over 400 licensed card clubs in California and more than 80 Nevada casinos continuously offer thousands of fresh poker players for money extraction, every hour of every day and night, all year round.

4. Major poker clubs and casinos always offer a selection of games and players. Carefully select the most advantageous game with the weakest players. Keep aware of the other games, and promptly abandon any game for a more advantageous game (e.g., more profitable stakes or weaker players).

5. Seek games with careless players, nervous players, women players, drinking players, players with tattoos or unkempt beards, and especially players wearing religious crosses or medals, good-luck charms, astrology symbols, or other mystical amulets. Avoid games with high ratios of calm, controlled, or intelligent-looking people.

6. Because of his initial confusion and inexperience when first learning public poker, the good player's statistical game (the mechanical aspects—the figuring of odds and money management) is weaker than his strategical game (the imaginative and thinking aspects—the strategy and bluffing). Conversely, the statistical game of most public-game professionals is stronger than their strategical game because of their greater dependence on mechanical routines and rules designed to yield statistically maximum investment odds on every play. Their more rigid consistency makes them more readable and predictable. The good player, on the other hand, does not strive for

234

maximum investment odds on every play; thus he is more flexible and unpredictable.

7. Collection fees or time cuts in public games range from $2 per hour per player for a $1-$2 game to about $24 per hour per player for games with blind bets and, raises of $100. The casino rake (from every pot) can range from a 5 percent maximum up to a 25 percent maximum—or even higher for snatch games designed for naive tourists. Maximum rakes in casinos are usually posted in the poker area. And in most snatch games, the casino dealer immediately drops the raked chips into the table slot rather than stacking them on the side for all to see until the hand is over.

8. House cuts are less harmful to the good player's profits in the faster-moving, higher-stake, time-cut games (versus the slower-moving, lower-stake, pot-raked games).

9. In public poker, lowball games are generally less flexible (more mechanical) than equivalent highball games. Therefore, the good player can usually use the Advanced Concepts of Poker more advantageously in highball games. But the faster betting pace of lowball can outweigh this advantage. Professional players, however, cheat more frequently and more effectively in high-stake lowball.

10. The narrow and fixed betting ratios (e.g., $10-$20) in all public club games and in most casino games diminish the effectiveness of the good player's poker abilities, especially in executing bluffs and power plays. Casino table-stake games usually offer the best profit opportunities for the good player experienced enough in public poker to be highly aggressive.

11. Most casino and club shills (house players) play

235

conservative and predictable poker (especially women shills), making them dependable decoys and unwitting partners for manipulating other players.

12. In public poker, women are generally weaker players than men. Many women lack the aggressiveness necessary for good poker. They play more mechanically and more predictably than men. In Gardena, during weekdays, up to 40 percent of the players are women. (The percentage of women players drops by half by nightfall.) Many are poor players—some are desperate players gambling with their Social Security checks and grocery money. Still, an estimated ten to twenty good, tough women professionals work the Gardena clubs. Successful women professionals are rarer in the Nevada casinos, but are increasing.

13. Opponents generally play looser and poorer poker on or immediately after paydays (e.g., on the first of the month and on Friday nights).

14. Best to enter games fresh and rested at 1:00 a.m.-5:00 a.m. (while faking tiredness, nervousness, or drunkenness) in order to work over groggy players, drunk players, loose winners, and desperate losers.

15. To conceal poker abilities and to throw good players off guard, wear a religious cross.

16. Rattle opponents through physical invasions of their "territories" (e.g., by using elbows or hands, by pushing poker chips or money around, by knocking over drinks). Foist feelings of outrage, guilt, inferiority, or fear onto opponents through personal verbal attacks. Temper bad-boy behavior only to avoid physical attacks or banishment from games.

17. Never give opponents a break. Make them sweat. Grant them no mercy.

18. In highball, elevate height with extra chair cushions to see more carelessly exposed hands. In lowball, diminish height and sit low in order to see more cards flash during the shuffle and on the deal and draw.

19. Highly visible and self-publicized professional poker players, including those who play in and have won the World Series of Poker, reveal a composite character (with individual exceptions) of a prematurely aged, physically unfit heavy smoker who is prone to boasting, gross exaggeration, and gambling. Yet he is a character who is basically intelligent and shrewd — though vulnerable to manipulation through his flaws. He is a character who can be exploited and beaten by the good player.

In six days, John Finn put both public club and casino poker under his profitable control — at least for the lower-stake and medium-stake games. For the higher-stake games, John had an additional major problem to deal with — the problem of professional cheating.

# XXVIII
# PROFESSIONAL POKER PLAYERS

Professional poker players generally fall into two classes: (1) those who extract money from private games, and (2) those who extract money from public games.

Successful private-game professionals explicitly or implicitly understand and use many of the Advanced Concepts of Poker. Private-game professionals are usually quiet, ostensibly self-effacing, independent loners who never need to join an establishment[32] or cheat to extract maximum money from their opponents. (Cheating would actually decrease both their investment odds and their long-range edge odds.) Private-game professionals generally prosper more and spend fewer hours playing poker than do public-game professionals.

While all public-game professionals explicitly or implicitly must understand and use enough of the Advanced Concepts of Poker to generate a regular income, many public-game professionals misunderstand or violate various key concepts. For example, many public-game professionals not only openly boast about their poker abilities, but compromise their independence by joining a tacit professional establishment. Because of their compromised independence, most of those public-game professionals limit both their potential winnings and their future. And more and more of those professionals are depending on cheating (at the expense of playing good poker) to extract money for their livelihood.

But some public professionals have considerable financial incentives for maintaining a braggadocio, flamboyant style. Those professionals are supreme hustlers who use their visibility to attract victims. By becoming famous and highly visible, they not only attract gamblers to back them to high-stake games, but they also attract wealthy challengers who want action against a big-name player. The better-known big-name players have won up to $1 million in a single session against such wealthy but foolish challengers. But some big-name professionals have also set themselves up for being cleaned out by shrewd, unknown Advanced-Concept players posing as foolish challengers.

---

[32] *Professionals who get involved with establishments or cliques usually limit their potentials and acquire rigid, stereo-typed characteristics that the good player can identify. Once he has identified the stereotyped characteristics of those professionals, the good player can predict their actions and consistently beat them—even when they cheat. The good player or superior professional, on the other hand, usually remains independent and avoids stereotyped characteristics. And often his opponents never realize that he is a good player who is winning all of their money.*

# XXIX
# PROFESSIONAL CHEATING

Perhaps the most profound difference between private poker and public poker (club or casino) is the collusion cheating practiced by many professional players in public poker. Few outsiders or victims detect or even suspect professional cheating in public poker because such cheating is visually undetectable. Public-game professionals execute their collusion so naturally and casually that upper management of major casinos and card clubs generally remain unaware of their cheating, even when it routinely occurs in their casinos and clubs. Many public-game professionals accept and practice collusion cheating without qualms. They consider their cheating a natural and legitimate trade tool that enables them to offset the draining effect of the house rake or collection.

The most important classical and modern professional cheating methods and devices are listed in Table 35.

## TABLE 35
## CHEATING METHODS AND DEVICES

| *Card Manipulations* | *Card Treatments* | *Other Devices* |
|---|---|---|
| * blind shuffling | * daubing (Golden | check copping |
| * crimping | Glow, nicotine | cold deck |
| * culling | stains, soiling) | * collusion |
| dealing seconds, | corner flash | partners |
| dealing bottoms, | denting and | * card flashing |
| dealing middles | rounders | * crossfiring |
| * false cutting | luminous readers | * signals |
| * false riffling | marking | * spread |
| foiling the cut | nailing (indexing) | holdouts |
| palming | punching | shiners |
| * peeking | sanding | |
| * pull through | slicked-aced deck | |
| * stacking | stripping | |
| * Las Vegas riffle | waving | |
| * overhand stack | | |

239

* riffle cull and stack      [See the Glossary in
* undercut stack           Appendix C for definitions
                                 of these terms.]

* *Professional cheating methods most commonly used today in public poker.*

To win consistently at high-stake casino or club poker, the good player has two choices: (1) join the professional establishment and become part of their collusion-cheating system,[33] or (2) develop and use techniques to profit from the cheating of others. But in certain games such as high-stake lowball, collusion cheating by professionals can prevent even a good player from winning. As identified in Chapter XXXI, professional collusion cheating in lowball poker can diminish the good player's investment odds so greatly that he cannot win, even with his superior alertness, poker skills, and strategy.

Table 36 summarizes some of the important cheating techniques that professional poker players use in public clubs and casinos. That table also includes the classical but crude cheating techniques occasionally used by amateurs.[34] Contrary to popular belief, almost any player can master effective, invisible cheating methods with only a few hours of practice. A book, *Neocheating — The Unbeatable Weapon in Poker, Blackjack, Bridge and Gin*, by Frank R. Wallace, Mark Hamilton, and William S., identifies and

---

[33] *Most public-game professionals admire and respect the good poker player and readily accept him into their establishment (especially in Gardena and Las Vegas). Their ready acceptance of the good player seems contradictory to their best interests since such acceptance increases competition for the losers' money. But those professionals both respect and fear the independent good player. He is a threat to their system. They eliminate that threat by making him a part of their system. By contrast, the private or non establishment good player tries to get rid of any competing player who is good enough to drain money from the game.*

[34] *Classical cheating (e.g., stacking specific hands, second dealing, holding out cards) seldom occurs in club or casino poker. Occasionally amateurs, strangers, or newcomers attempt classical cheating in public poker. But since their techniques are almost always crude, they are*

describes in detail those new and easy cheating techniques that professional players are using today in poker clubs and casinos.

In club poker, the alert player detects professional cheating most often in the highest-stake lowball games in which signaling systems and card-flashing collusion are devastatingly effective. In casino poker, the alert player detects collusion cheating most often in the highest-stake stud and hold 'em games.

Not all public-game professionals are cheaters or part of the professional establishment.[35] Not all high stake public games have cheaters, or even professionals, present. But any high-stake public game free of cheaters and professionals is ripe for exploitation and quickly attracts professionals and cheaters. Still, out of justice and fairness, the good player never considers anyone to be a cheater until he has adequate proof of cheating. Moreover, the good player strives to be just and fair in order to know more accurately what is going on and thus avoid costly errors. Being just and fair boosts his profits.

The good player resists the temptation to blame tough or painful losses on being cheated (rather than on coincidence or on his own errors). Because of the extra quick folds and the extra-aggressive bets used to beat cheaters, the good player can make an expensive error by misreading an opponent as a cheater.

Since cheating harms the long-range business interests of all public card clubs and casinos, management of the major clubs and casinos seriously oppose any form of cheating. They have always taken firm measures to eliminate and prevent cheating in their operations. For them, cheating means only bad publicity, lost business, lower profits, and potential legal problems. Without cheating, clubs and casinos can eventually extract all the money gamblers have to offer. With cheating, clubs and casinos could eventually go out of business.

Using tight controls and effective surveillance systems, the management of major casinos keeps all gaming operations (except poker) free of major, organized, or chronic cheating. All casino games, except poker, function between casino and player, allowing management to closely monitor and tightly control the

---

[35] *Likewise, not all private-game professionals are independent loners or above cheating.*

TABLE 36

## CHEATING TECHNIQUES USED IN PUBLIC (CLUB AND CASINO) AND PRIVATE POKER

| | Uses | Methods |
|---|---|---|
| **Manipulation Techniques—more common in private poker** | | |
| Classical and amateur manipulations (solo) | Least effective, most detectable. Shunned by today's professional establishment. Crudely used by amateurs in private games. Effectively used only by the rare, classic card-sharp who is highly skilled, dexterous, and experienced. | Classical deck stacking, holding out cards, palming, second and bottom dealing, shaved decks, shiners, marked cards, and various mechanical devices used to cheat opponents. |
| Full flashing of draw and hold 'em hole cards (dealer to partner) | More effective for stud and games. | With smooth, imperceptible motions, the dealer lifts or tilts cards just enough for his partner to see. Done only when others are not looking or are unaware. The dealer may also allow his partner to see cards during the riffle. |
| Modern and professional manipulations (solo) | Most effective, easiest to learn, usually undetectable. Used by professional players in both private and public poker. Neocheating. | Easy techniques of culling cards, blind shuffling, false riffling, false cutting, foiling cuts—especially the new and easy Neocheating techniques. |

242

## Collusion Techniques—more common in club poker

Partial flashing of draw and hole cards (dealer to partner) — Most effective for high-stake, lowball draw.

Player sits low enough to see shades of darkness, blur intensities, or the actual values of cards being dealt face-down—with or without the dealer's help.*

Collusion betting (partner to partner) — Most common in high-stake lowball and in bluff-dependent games.

Requires system of "strength of hand" and "when to bet, raise, or fold" signals between colluding partners.

## Combined Techniques—more common in casino poker

Collusion and manipulation (house dealer to partner) — Most effective and common in casinos with house dealers who manipulate cards and work in collusion with professional players.

The dealer culls or manipulates memorized cards to top of deck. He then knows everyone's hole cards and signals his partner when to bet, raise, or drop.

243

* *Good players train themselves to evaluate the shades of darkness or blur intensities of partially flashed cards (e.g., darker shades or more intense blurs indicate higher-value cards—valuable information for lowball). If a player sees flashed cards without dealer collusion, he is not cheating since the same advantage is available to all players who choose to be equally alert. Alert players also watch for flashed cards as the dealer riffles, shuffles, and cuts.*

action. But in poker, the game functions between player and player (not between casino and player), leaving the management unable to monitor and control the action. That uniquely uncontrollable situation combined with the undetectability of professional collusion cheating makes poker the only casino game in which management has no practical way to detect or eliminate such cheating. Also, casino management and its employees are less motivated to ferret out poker cheating because in poker, the players (not the casino) lose money to cheaters. But in other games, the casino (not the players) loses money to cheaters.

The public view of casino cheating differs markedly from the actual situation. Several years ago, for example, a major poker-cheating conspiracy was publicly exposed in the Las Vegas MGM Grand Hotel and Casino, the world's largest gambling establishment. The police arrested the cardroom manager, the floorman, two dealers, and five outside partners—all were charged with illegal conspiracy and felony swindling. That publicized incident coincides with the public view of professional cheating in casino poker. But the authorities caught those alleged "professional cheaters" only because they were amateurish and crude in their techniques of culling, stacking, and peeking. Allegedly, they even resorted to copping chips from pots. But the MGM cheating scandal did not involve or even touch on the real professional cheating that flourishes with casual finesse in higher-stake poker games, unchecked by casino management and unnoticed by the public.

Even if professional cheaters were eliminated from a high-stake game, a wave of new professionals and cheaters would fill the vacuum in order to exploit the "easy pickings" inherent in any new or clean public poker game. The financial incentive is too great to prevent professionals and cheaters from quickly moving into high-stake poker games filled with tourists, losers, and other easy amateurs.

What will happen when management and the public become increasingly aware of this uncontrollable professional cheating? Most casinos could simply drop poker from their operations (or at least eliminate cheater-prone high-stake poker) with little lasting effect on their profits. But how will commercial poker clubs handle undetectable professional cheating? Nearly their

244

entire business depends on poker, which, in turn, depends on the trust and confidence of their most important customers—the losers. Unless management can stop the spread of professional cheating (especially Neocheating), the commercial poker clubs could encounter business difficulties if the majority of their customers (the losers) began discovering and understanding the extent of professional cheating in their games.[36]

Since many professional poker players depend on collusion for a living and since their cheating is generally undetectable, management currently has no practical way to eliminate their cheating. One long-range solution might be tamper-proof mechanical or electronic shuffling and dealing devices that would not only eliminate undetectable dealer-player collusion, card flashing, and most card manipulations, but could also reduce operating costs by eliminating dealers, accelerating the action, and automating house collections. In turn, lower operating costs could result in lower-percentage house cuts. Also, elimination of competition from professional cheaters would further increase the profits of good players and independent professionals who win through their own skills rather than through cheating.

# XXX
# WHY PROFESSIONALS CHEAT

The canons of poker, as clearly understood and tacitly accepted by every player, allow unlimited deception to win maximum money from ownerless pots. Therefore, everyone can and should freely use unlimited deception in every poker game. But no one should use deception outside of poker. If a person "plays poker" outside of a poker game, he becomes a dishonest person. Even in poker, however, a person becomes dishonest if he violates the understood and accepted canons of poker by usurping money through cheating. (Cheating is any manipulation

---

[36] *Chronic or heavy losers might even sue those card clubs and casinos in which they had systematically lost money to professional cheaters. But those losers would probably need corroboration from several professional cheaters to support any serious litigation.*

of cards or any collusion that gives a player or players advantages not available to other players.)

Many poker players, including most professionals, do not fully distinguish between what is honest and what is dishonest, in and out of a poker game. For example, many professional players who day after day lie and practice deceit in poker ironically do not grasp the rightness of their poker deception. To them, lying and deception in poker become little different from cheating in poker. Their ethics become hazy and ill-defined. They feel the only barrier to crossing the line from lying and deception to cheating and stealing is the threat of being caught. By removing that threat (e.g., through undetectable Neocheating techniques), they cross over the line and begin cheating.

The failure to understand the black-and-white moral differences between deception in poker and cheating in poker is one reason why many players react so strongly (often violently, sometimes murderously) against a cheater. They fear that without strong anticheating reactions, everyone would easily cross over the line from deceiving them to cheating them. Sensing their own capacity to cheat, they assume the same capacity resides in everyone. Thus, even if they never cheat others, they fear that others will cheat them. Generally those who react most violently against cheaters are those who would most readily cheat others if their fear of being caught and evoking similarly violent reactions from their opponents did not restrain them.

Most amateur poker players hold the classical but misleading views about cheating. They perceive nearly all cheating as being done either by bumbling amateurs who are easily caught or by highly dexterous and invincible cardsharps who have perfected sleight-of-hand skills through years of laborious practice and dangerous experience. In holding those misleading classical views, most amateur poker players remain unsuspecting of the casual, natural-appearing collusion cheating and Neocheating practiced among the professional establishment.

As the stakes of public games increase, the percentage of professional players increases—as does their motivation to cheat. Every player should increasingly expect and look for cheating as he progresses to higher-stake club or casino games ... right up to the highest-stake games, including the finals (down to the last three

246

players) of the million-dollar world championship, freeze-out tournaments held in Las Vegas, Nevada. Most finalists in those tournaments are public-game professionals who have worked in the professional establishment for years. Few members of the professional cheating establishment would have qualms about making collusion arrangements in those tournaments or any high-stake game: Two of the three final players could safely and swiftly squeeze the third player out of the game with collusion betting to assure both the remaining players, for example, a several-hundred-thousand-dollar return on their original $10,000 stakes (their entry fees). By their collusion, the final two players would vastly improve their investment odds—they would eliminate any possibility of losing while guaranteeing themselves a large win.

When, how, and why does a public-game professional begin cheating? Imagine a lonely public-game player struggling against the house cut to become a full-time professional and suddenly discovering a friendly professional establishment with an ongoing cheating system readily available to him... an undetectable cheating system requiring no special skills and available for his immediate profit. Such a player, especially if he is a mediocre or marginal professional, will often embrace that opportunity by tacitly cooperating with the establishment professionals in perpetuating their system. He accepts their collusion cheating as a trade tool required for playing competitive, professional poker. As he blends in with those professionals and adopts their system, he becomes increasingly dependent not only on their establishment but on collusion cheating to survive. He loses his independence and becomes a stereotyped, public-game professional. With a sense of professional righteousness, he becomes a cheater.

# XXXI
# BEATING PROFESSIONAL CHEATERS

The alert player who is familiar with the basic professional cheating techniques can detect any cheating, even the most skilled and invisible cheating, without actually seeing the cheating. An alert player usually can tell who is cheating, what technique is being used, and exactly when the cheating is occurring by detecting patterns and combinations of illogical betting, raising, pace, and playing style by his opponents.[37]

Once a player has detected and confirmed cheating in public poker, he has five options:

1. Join the cheating.
2. Beat the cheaters through the poorer playing, greater readability, and greater predictability that result from their cheating.
3. Eliminate the cheating.
4. Expose the cheating.
5. Quit the game.

The good player rejects his or her first option as not only dishonest and unhealthy, but also as the least profitable option. Several of John Finn's encounters with professional cheating described next in this chapter illustrate the other four options.

---

[37] *To detect invisible cheating, a player must be involved in at least one hand and perhaps several hands in which cheating occurs in order to observe the illogical poker patterns and variables. For that reason, every player must be cautious about high-stake or no-limit games in which he could be lured into a single cheating setup and financially wiped out before detecting any cheating. A player must never relax his vigilance against being set up for a one-shot, big-hand play designed to wipe him out. Indeed, the wise player views with suspicion and is prepared to throw away without a bet any super-powerful hand (e.g., four of a kind or a straight flush) that he receives in high-stake games with strangers.*

*The alert and adroit player, nevertheless, can beat the one-shot, big-hand cheating setup by scalping the bait but not swallowing the hook when the setup hand finally appears. Being aware of a cheating setup, the shrewd player can sometimes extract sizable bait (e.g., $5000) by staging an illusory huge payoff (e.g., $100,000). After plucking the bait, he must fold without a bet on the first super-powerful hand dealt to him. Or better yet, he should leave the game before the big hand is sprung—in which case, he may even be able to return for more bait.... But the good player is also smart—he never tries conning unsavory players who might rob, assault, or even kill him for his counter-intrigue.*

*Part Six: Professional and Public Poker*

Although John Finn played mainly in private poker games because of their greater profitability, he did recently spend several months playing public poker in the Gardena, California, card clubs and in the Las Vegas, Nevada, casinos. In both the clubs and casinos, he discovered professional cheaters operating in the higher-stake games. John's public-game experiences uncovered six common cheating methods used in public poker (see A-F on the following pages). He also learned how the good player can routinely beat professional cheaters in public poker. More important, he learned to identify those situations in which he could not beat professional cheating.

*1. Gardena, California*
A. Collusion Cheating — Reciprocal Card Flashing

During his first two days in Gardena, John Finn played in each of its six poker clubs. After the second day, he became aware of a cliquish network of amateur players, professional players, floormen, and cardroom managers woven through those six clubs. The continuous circulation of poker players among the clubs allowed everyone in that network to effectively communicate (and gossip) with each other. While most of the habitual amateur players in Gardena recognized they were a part of a clique, few recognized that the professional establishment was using them as fodder.

In the lower-stake games, John Finn found mainly amateurs; the few professionals were usually shills. In those games, he detected no cheating. On the fourth day, he graduated to a $20 blind, lowball draw game. In that game, he discovered from their poker styles and conversations that players in seats 2 and 5 were professionals involved in collusion cheating. Even before identifying them as full-time professionals, he knew they were colluding. Their methods were simple, effective, and unnoticeable. Both players sat low in their seats... each slumping a little lower when the other dealt. On

249

dealing draw cards with smooth quicker-than-the-eye motions, the dealer would expose key cards as fleeting blurs perceptible only to his partner. The partner would return the favor on his deal. The cheaters accomplished their card flashing with out suspicion despite the great pressure on dealers in the Gardena card clubs not to flash cards. (Only once did John observe a collusion cheater being scolded for his "careless" dealing. Ironically, John observed on numerous occasions non cheating dealers being scolded for flashing cards.)

By knowing when his own lowball draw card had been flashed, John Finn could outmaneuver the cheating partners by more accurately predicting what they would do as the result of their knowing his draw card. The cheaters, therefore, were constantly misled by John's counter actions—they repeatedly misjudged what he would do. John Finn exploited and beat both collusion partners by using the cheating counteractions described in his notes on lowball cheating:

1. Save money by folding promptly against a cheater's more readable winning hand.

2. Lure the cheater into making an expensive bluff when he draws a picture card or a pair in low-ball and knows you have drawn a high card such as a ten or a jack. The cheater's overconfidence often encourages him to bluff excessively.

3. Set up the cheater for an easy bluff. For example, a strong lowball bluff position develops when the cheater knows you have drawn a good low card (e.g., a six or lower), but does not know you paired the low card.
4. When you draw a powerful low hand, the overconfident cheater can sometimes be misled into believing you did pair, causing him to call a final bet.

5. **When the readable cheater bluffs, use his aggressive betting to drive out other players who have you beat. When the other players are driven out, simply call the cheater's bluff. Or when necessary, bluff out the bluffing cheater with a final raise.**

In each of the above examples, the cheater would have either won more money or lost less money if he had concentrated on playing sound poker to gain broad information about his opponent (rather than on cheating to gain information only about his opponent's draw card).

Throughout the night, John Finn used those counteractions to exploit and beat both collusion cheaters. And on occasion, when positioned properly, John saw cards flash between the partners. He used what he saw to further improve his advantage. When the game ended at seven in the morning, the two professional players were big losers. They left the table cursing their "bad luck," never realizing that their own cheating had victimized them.

Over the next several days in Gardena, John Finn noticed five trends while moving from lower-stake to higher-stake games:

1. The ratio of professional players to amateur players increased. But the proportion of out-of-town losers decreased only slightly.

2. The skill of the professional players increased.

3. The incidence of collusion cheating increased.

4. Cheating became more dominant and profitable in lowball poker (compared to highball poker). Also, professional players became more dependent on cheating in lowball draw, but were more dependent on skill in highball draw.

251

**5. The edge odds for outside players generally decreased, especially in lowball draw. (In the highest-stake lowball games in which the best professional cheaters operate, the edge odds for the good player can drop to unprofitable levels.)**

**Because the best public-game professionals and cheaters concentrated on the highest-stake lowball games (in which professional cheating was most effective and profitable), John Finn found that he could often improve both his edge odds and his investment odds by dropping back a level or two from the highest-stake games. When he dropped to lower-stake games, competition lessened— money extraction was easier and often more profitable because of the decreased ratio of tough professionals and cheaters to easy losers and amateurs.**

In public poker, great pressure is on the dealer not to flash cards, especially in high-stake lowball. But these games offer professional collusion cheaters the greatest profit incentive to flash cards. Most card flashing, therefore, occurs in the high-stake lowball games. The flashing motions are usually so quick and smooth that very few outsiders ever notice or even suspect card flashing. And most professional collusion cheaters use cautious discretion and avoid flashing cards whenever they sense suspicion by others. If flashing is suspected, the colluding partners will usually switch to a less effective signaling system or move to another game.

Still, many professional cheaters in Gardena use only reciprocal signaling systems because they are not sufficiently knowledgeable about systematic card flashing. And while collusion *signaling* is more commonly used among cheaters, card *flashing* is more effective and flexible because the colluding partners need no prearrangements, no agreements, no payments, no splitting of loot, no secret signals, no collusion betting, no deck stacking, and not even card flashing on the initial deal: They need only to flash draw cards toward their fellow professionals— toward any fellow professional who will tacitly return the favor. Their flashing movements are usually so natural and guiltless that few if any opponents ever see them. And if they are suspected, neither the victims nor the poker club management can directly accuse the colluders of cheating because they have no concrete evidence. Furthermore, the cheaters can have different, unplanned collusion partners for every game so no fixed set of partners can ever be pinned down and accused of collusion cheating.

In any case, collusion cheating of all varieties among establishment professionals is becoming increasingly common as they silently extend to one another their mutual, professional "courtesies." In fact, some California card clubs have compiled lists of suspected collusion cheaters who are either barred from the club or are not permitted to play at the same table.

But whenever a poker player cheats, the quality of his play declines because his time, energy, and thought must shift from sound-poker actions to cheating actions. He usually becomes overconfident and careless about playing poker—his objectivity, concentration, and discipline diminish as his thinking efforts become diluted. His betting becomes distorted and usually overly aggressive. And most importantly, his hands become more readable and his actions become more predictable whenever he cheats.

**The classical card-manipulation type of cheating is rare among the Gardena professionals. John encountered that kind of cheating only once, and he made a quick profit from the cheater by pulling an old ploy against him—the torn-corner flash:**

**In his final lowball game at Gardena, John sat to the left of a collusion cheater who had switched a card with his partner to win a pot. After the hand, John saw the cheater ditch a face card on the floor. No one noticed the missing card. On the next hand, the cheater summoned the floorman for new cards. The cards were exchanged, but the ditched card remained on the floor. Two hands later, when the same cheater was involved in another pot, John leaned under the table to pick up some money he had purposely dropped. While under the table, he quickly tore the corner off the ditched**

253

card and slipped the corner into his jacket pocket.

Several hands later, John had a powerful six low. The cheater on his right had a callable low hand. John reached into his pocket, withdrew the torn face-card corner, and positioned it at the top edge of his cards. Then while concealing his other cards, he accidentally-on-purpose flashed his hand to the cheater, who immediately spotted the "picture card" in John's hand. John bet the $20 maximum. Now positive that John was bluffing a busted lowball hand, the cheater raised. John inconspicuously dropped the torn corner beneath the table and reraised. Since they were the only two players remaining in the hand, the number of raises was unlimited. They reraised each other the maximum $20 bet many times. Suddenly the cheater stopped betting. He choked, pushed back his chair, and looked on the floor. Dropping his hand face down on the table, the red-faced man promptly left the game without even calling John's last $20 raise. John pulled in the $460 pot.

John Finn left Gardena knowing that he could consistently beat both the professionals and the cheaters to earn a regular income from any club game, except possibly from the highest-stake lowball games that were dominated by the best professional players and cheaters.

2. *Las Vegas, Downtown*
   B. Collusion Cheating with House Dealer— Natural-Play Technique

John Finn first encountered professional casino cheating in a large poker room of a major hotel casino in downtown Las Vegas. The cheating involved the dealer, the cardroom manager, and his friend—and was unusual because management was involved.[38]

[38] *Normally even the lowest-level management in major casinos is unaware and innocent of professional cheating in their cardrooms.*

Initially, John Finn was not suspicious of or looking for cheating patterns because (1) the game was fairly low stakes $5-$10 high stud (although that was the highest-stake game in the cardroom at the time), and (2) the cardroom manager was not only playing, but was sitting next to the dealer. The game seemed safe from cheating.

Moving clockwise from the dealer's left sat (1) the cardroom manager, (2) a professional poker player, who was also a friend of the manager, (3) a poor-playing tourist, (4) a regular player, (5) [an empty seat], (6) an ex-poker dealer, (7) John Finn, and (8) a woman who was an off-duty blackjack dealer.

Within an hour, newcomer John Finn was the biggest winner. He was playing aggressively, winning heavily, and badly beating the other players—especially the woman player in seat 8, who was playing poorly.

The manager and several other players seemed annoyed and confused over John Finn's unorthodox and unpredictable play. After a shift change of dealers, the woman player switched to empty seat 5. Two hands later, another tourist sat in empty seat 8. He found a loose card beside John's elbow. The card apparently had slid under a napkin left by the woman player, and the dealer never noticed the missing card. (Some dealers can feel when one card is missing by the bulk and weight of the deck.) Several players glanced sharply at John as if they had discovered how he was beating them. The manager left the table and returned moments later.

Before the next hand, a floorman brought two fresh decks of cards to the dealer. John Finn became puzzled on noticing the cards were in a brown box bearing an orange-shield label from the Normandie Club in Gardena, California. Two hands later, John maneuvered into a strong position and was betting heavily. The manager beat him in a series of illogical but infallible calls and bets that did not coincide with

255

the manager's poker style or ability. Staring straight at John Finn, he pushed the large pot to the woman player—the heavily-losing, off-duty blackjack dealer in seat 5. She took the money without appearing grateful or surprised by the manager's "generous" action.

Several hands later, John Finn again maneuvered into a strong and favorable position; he bet heavily, but once more was beaten in a similar series of illogical calls and raises by the manager's friend—the professional player. John became alert and suspicious. At first he thought his hole cards were being flashed, especially since the professional player sat low in his seat. Trying to counter that possibility, John was unsuccessful as he lost two more large pots to the manager, who again won through a series of illogical but infallible moves. John then noticed a slight crimp in his cards—such as might occur if a dealer had crimped for a false cut and then failed to bend out the crimp. In addition, the dealer gripped the cards in a way to facilitate false cutting. Yet, John detected no evidence of card culling, discard sorting, or deck stacking. After certain hands, however, the dealer would periodically glance at face-down discards as he gathered cards for the next deal. Still he made no attempt to rearrange any cards.

John Finn lost another large hand to the manager's friend. While assuming that he was the victim of collusion cheating, John did not know how or when it was occurring. His counteractions not only failed, but increased his losses. He had lost his winnings and was losing over $200 before he realized how the cheating was occurring. The method was simple, essentially undetectable, yet devastatingly effective. After each hand, the dealer simply gathered the face-up stud cards in a natural way, making no attempt to cull, sort, or stack them ... he merely remembered the value and order of the exposed cards. If too few cards had been exposed, he would simply glance at some face-down cards. By remembering fourteen cards[39] and by keeping them in an unchanged order on top of the deck through blind shuffles, false riffles, and false cuts, the dealer would know everyone's hole cards—thus, he would know everyone's exact hand right up until the seventh and final card. From that omniscient position, the dealer would then make all the playing and betting decisions for his partner (or partners) by signaling when to fold, call, bet, or raise. The playing partner would never need to know anyone's hand, including his own; he would only need to follow the signals of the all-knowing dealer.

On losing his third large pot to the low-sitting professional, John Finn realized that he could not beat that kind of collusion cheating and that his only choice was to quit the game. In order to gain some benefit, in order to analyze player reactions, John decided to openly declare his suspicion of cheating without revealing how much he really knew. He wanted to leave himself in the most knowledgeable and strongest position should he decide to return to the game.

After losing the pot, John placed one of his crimped hole cards on the flat palm of his hand and lifted the card to eye level. The dealer was waiting for the card as everyone watched John Finn. "Are these cards marked?" he asked, knowing that except for the crimping they probably were not. At that moment, he yanked his hand from beneath the card. It fell in an irregular motion to the table. Everyone stared at John... everyone except the dealer, the manager, and the professional player—they kept glancing in different directions. John Finn picked up his chips and left. He had learned something.

An all-knowing collusion dealer greatly increases the

[39] *Rapid memorization of large groups of cards can be difficult. But, with practice, most players can learn to rapidly memorize fourteen or more cards (even the entire deck) by association, mnemonic, and grouping techniques. (Reference: Perfecting Your Card Memory by Charles Edwards, Gambler's Book Club, Las Vegas, Nevada, 1974.)*

investment odds for his playing partner while leaving the playing partner immune to errors and detection as well as to having his hands and intentions read by the good player. Furthermore, the cheater's cards always appear normal and above suspicion. No dramatic or improbable set-up hands occur. The cheater may fold at any time during the hand and sometimes is beaten on the last card... all normal in appearance and above suspicion— except for the cheater's illogical playing and betting patterns and his unnaturally improved investment and edge odds.

More important to the good player, such a cheating system is difficult if not impossible to beat. The good player has only the seventh and final down card with which to outmaneuver and beat the cheater. (That final card is the only unknown to the signaling collusion dealer.) But by the final bet, the good player's investment odds would be so diminished by the previous four bets controlled by an infallible pair of collusion cheaters that he probably could not beat them over the long term. If the cheating technique includes the dealer's knowing or peeking at the final down card or if the game is five-card or six-card stud with no final down card,[40] the good player then has no way to beat the dealer-player collusion cheaters, even if he could crack their signaling code.

The strength of their collusion system lies in its simplicity and natural-appearing play. By contrast, the classical cheating systems involve dramatic big-hand or certain-win setups. Such setups are not necessary or even desirable. The dealer-player collusion system quietly extracts money from its victims. Such a collusion system is ideal for casino poker because the house dealer[41] deals every hand, thus leaving the collusion partners in

---

[40] *Six-card stud with no final down card has nearly replaced seven-card stud in Reno and is beginning to appear in Las Vegas. Without an unknown final hole card, five-card and six-card stud give an unbeatable advantage to the dealer-player collusion cheaters.*

[41] *Not every house dealer cheats. In fact, most casino dealers never cheat and are probably unaware of any professional collusion cheating occurring around them. When a collusion dealer is temporarily relieved by a non cheating dealer, the collusion partner will sometimes leave, but will often continue playing while waiting for the collusion dealer to return. Agreements with and payments to collusion dealers are usually made off shift, away from the casino. Payments are by a flat rate, by a percentage of winnings, or by a combination of both.*

an ideal cheating position for every hand (unlike club or private poker in which each partner deals only once each round.) That constantly favorable cheating position allows a slower, more casual and natural method for extracting money from victims. Furthermore, no player touches or cuts the cards except the house dealer, thus greatly facilitating and simplifying the cheater's card manipulations and false cuts. But in club or private poker, a non dealing player usually cuts the cards, making card manipulations and deck stacking more difficult for the dealer.

C. Collusion Cheating with House Dealer —
Culling and Stacking

**On the following afternoon, John Finn entered a newly remodeled downtown casino that had introduced poker only a few weeks before. The card area was small and offered only $1-$3 stud games. Wanting to examine low-stake casino poker, John Finn sat in the open seat on the dealer's left. Again, he did not expect cheating in a low-stake game. He soon realized that the other four players were locals—they all knew one another and the dealer. But none of the players appeared to be professionals or good players. The players and the dealer chatted amicably among themselves. John Finn played the role of an inexperienced tourist by asking naive questions about the rules. The game was loose. On the third hand, all four players stayed until the final card. Sixteen face-up cards were exposed, including an exposed two pair of aces and queens. Another ace and another queen were also among the face-up cards. John Finn watched with narrowing eyes as the dealer picked up the cards—he scooped up a queen and an ace and then three other cards. His hand darted back to scoop up the second queen and ace and then three more random cards before scooping the final queen and ace. He then gathered the rest of the cards.**

**After carefully squaring the deck, the dealer made several false riffles and a false cut before dealing.**

John knew what was going to happen. He did not even look at his two hole cards. His first up card was a queen. The first up card of the player on his left was an ace. The player with the ace looked twice at his hole cards and then bet $1. Everyone folded to John. He paused and looked at each player and then at the dealer. Everyone was watching him and waiting. The dealer stopped smiling when John placed the edge of his right hand firmly over the lower half of his hole cards and tore them in half. He then turned over his two torn queens, placed them face-up alongside his third queen. John then quickly flipped over his opponent's hole cards, which were aces, and placed them face-up alongside that opponent's third ace. Everyone remained silent.

"Redeal." John ordered. The dealer glanced toward the mirrors in the ceiling over the blackjack tables and then quickly collected the cards—including the torn ones. He redealt from a new deck. Over the next dozen hands, John Finn aggressively manipulated his now tense and confused opponents. In twenty minutes, he ripped $50 from the low-stake game and left. As he walked down the aisle of blackjack tables, he glanced toward the poker area. The dealer and the players he left behind were still staring at him.

That was a mistake, John Finn thought to himself. I revealed too much about myself for only $50.

*3. Las Vegas, the Strip*
D. Collusion Cheating trough Partner Crossfire Betting
That evening, John Finn entered a major casino on the Strip. The casino had a large poker area. The action was heavy. In addition to many low-stake and intermediate-stake games, several high-stake stud games ($30-$60 games of high stud, low stud, and high-low stud) were in progress. John began in a $5-$10 game, moved up to a $10-$20 game and then graduated to a $15-$30 stud game before encountering professional cheating.

The cheating was simple collusion between two professionals who signaled the strengths of their hands to each other. The cheater with the strongest hand or position would indicate to his partner when to check, bet, or raise. Their collusion entrapped or drove out players and increased or decreased the betting pace— whatever was most advantageous to the cheaters at the moment. The collusion partners increased their investment odds by either sucking in or driving out players to improve their betting position and their odds for winning. They entrapped players and then generated bets and raises to build larger pots whenever either cheater held a strong hand. They consistently bilked the tourists and transient players... at least until John Finn entered their game.

He promptly detected collusion cheating by the illogical patterns of checks, bets, and raises between the partners. Since the dealer was not involved with card manipulations or flashing, John easily turned the collusion to his own advantage at the expense of the cheaters. He beat the cheaters because their collusion actions markedly improved his accuracy in reading their hands and intentions. When either partner held a strong hand, John read their strength more quickly and folded sooner—thus saving considerable money. Moreover, when the cheating partners revealed a strong hand and John held a stronger hand, he quietly let them suck him and other players into the pot. He let them build the pot for him with extra bets and raises. On the final bet, John would end his passivity with a maximum raise.

Also, the colluding partners doubled their losses to John whenever they bet as a team into pots that John won. If they had not colluded, normally only the player holding the strongest hand (rather than both players) would have been betting into John's winning hand.

To further increase his advantage, John Finn manipulated the readable hands and intentions of those cheaters against the other unsuspecting players. But

261

John reaped his most profitable advantages from the cheaters when they bluffed. (Most collusion cheaters are overconfident and often can be lured into bluffs.) John would keep calling with a mediocre or even a poor hand as the bluffing partners kept betting aggressively to drive out players who held superior hands. John would then simply call the final bluff to win the pot. Or when necessary, he himself would bluff by stepping in with a raise after the final bet to drive out the bluffer and any remaining players to win the pot with a busted or a poor hand.

In three hours, John Finn converted the two professional cheaters from substantial winners into the biggest losers at the table and drove them from the game. With a $600 profit, he left that table to explore other games. He sat down at a table where four professional players were operating as two separate teams of colluding partners, cheating each other as well as the other three players. John assumed the role of a slightly drunk, wild-playing tourist—an ideal fish. He promptly broke the game open by playing all four cheaters against one another and against the other three players. In an hour, John ripped $900 from the game and then abruptly left the table. As he walked away, some of the players mumbled about his "unbelievable hot streak" and his "dumb luck."

John walked over to the highest-stake game in the house—a fast-paced, $30-$60 lowball, seven-stud game (razz). As he studied the action, he wondered about the unusual house rule that allowed five raises instead of the standard three. The five raises greatly increased the flexibility and advantage of collusion cheaters over their victims. John also wondered about the much higher proportion of professional players and collusion cheaters he observed in this casino. Was the management aware of their collusion cheating, he wondered. Did the management establish the five-raise rule to accommodate the cheaters? Or were the professional collusion cheaters drawn to this casino because of a five-raise rule innocently established by management to increase the betting action?... John assumed the latter to be true.

Standing behind the dealer, John Finn continued to watch the high-stake game. For nearly an hour, he studied the two biggest winners. From their conversation and style, he knew they were professionals, yet neither seemed to be cheating or colluding. Still he noticed that in spite of the large pots, the dealer was not being toked (tipped) when either professional won a pot. John Finn studied the dealer more closely: Gathering the face-up cards in a routine left-to-right order, the dealer made no attempt to rearrange the cards. But as players folded, the dealer would make a pile with their face-down discards and then gather their face-up cards and flip them on top of the discard pile. He would then flip the later-round face-up cards directly on top of the discard pile while slipping dead hole or face-down cards beneath the pile. If the hand ended with fewer than fourteen up cards being exposed, the dealer would casually glance at several face-down discards and toss them on top of the discard pile.

Although John could not actually see any blind shuffles, false riffles, or false cuts (or verify any illogical cheating patterns[42]), he speculated that the dealer was memorizing everyone's hole card and then signaling the best moves to one or both of the professional players ... in a way similar to that used

---

[42] *The alert player detects and verifies illogical cheating patterns by evaluating the actions of cheaters relative to his own playing and betting actions. But without actually playing in the game, an outside observer, even an alertly suspicious and knowledgeable observer, cannot easily see or verify the illogical patterns of a competent cheater... at least not in a short period of time. (That is one reason why casino management is seldom aware of professional cheating in poker; few people can detect competent poker cheating without actually playing against the cheaters in order to notice and evaluate illogical cheating patterns.)*

by the dealer who was colluding with the casino manager and his friend two days earlier in the downtown casino. And, as in the downtown casino, John Finn concluded that with his current knowledge and experience, he could not beat that kind of dealer-collusion cheating. He therefore left the casino without playing in the $30-$60 game.

E. Amateurish Collusion Cheating with Sanction of House Dealer

Traveling south on the Strip, John Finn came to another major casino with a large cardroom. He observed the various poker games for thirty minutes. After considering the higher-stake games, he sat in a medium-stake ($10-$20) seven-card stud game because more of its players looked like losers. All were out-of-town gamblers and tourists, except for two women players sitting together across from John. Although their conversation revealed they were experienced local players, both women played poorly. Nevertheless, they were winning moderately because of their collusion cheating, which was crude and obvious. They blatantly showed their live hole cards to each other and then coordinated their betting to produce a collective advantage. The other players either did not notice their collusion or were too indifferent or timid to object. By quietly taking advantage of their much more readable hands, John converted the two women from winners to losers.

John then lost a fairly large pot to the women cheaters. During the hand, they had flashed their hole cards to each other. Then in a crude and visible manner, they actually swapped their final hole cards during the last round of betting, allowing one woman to win with a full house. After she turned her hole cards face-up, John Finn stuck his arm over the pot when the dealer started pushing it toward the woman. John then silently removed all the chips he had put into the pot. "Any objections?" he asked, looking at the two women and then the dealer. No one objected. John had his information. He picked up his chips and left for a higher-stake game.

F. Unbeatable Collusion Cheating through Dealer-Player Partnerships

John Finn entered the casino farther south on the Strip that normally offered the highest-stake poker games in Las Vegas. For twenty minutes, he watched six players in a $100-$200 seven-card stud game. He detected two professional players in the game and studied them (one was apparently losing slightly, the other was winning heavily). They were working over four out-of-town gamblers, all of whom were losing. While the two professionals did not seem to be in direct collusion with each other, when winning a pot neither player toked (tipped) the dealer. And while the dealer never glanced at face-down cards when gathering cards for the next deal, he did riffle and shuffle the cards several extra times whenever the previous hand produced fewer than twelve face-up cards. Without seeing anything else, John speculated that when the dealer was riffling the cards he was also memorizing the hole cards of every player. As before, John knew he could not beat collusion cheating involving a house dealer who knew everyone's hole cards. So he left without playing.

After three days in Las Vegas, John Finn realized that professional collusion cheating was well ensconced in higher-stake casino poker. He also knew that the alert good player could subvert and beat most forms of professional cheating in public poker. And most important, he identified those collusion situations that he could not beat.

In theory, even collusion cheating involving all-knowing house dealers can be beaten by the good player with superior strategy and better money management. Yet to beat such cheaters, the

265

good player needs to know what the cheaters know ... he needs to know the concealed or hole cards of every opponent through near perfect card reading. But few if any players can achieve such perfection. Therefore, essentially all players, no matter how good, will lose money in games dominated by well-executed dealer-collusion cheating.

In any case, justice prevails in poker. The honest good player will generally win more money from poker than will the professional cheater. Furthermore, as a professional player becomes increasingly dependent on cheating for his support, he will become increasingly entrapped in an unproductive career and a limited future. The honest player, on the other hand, retains his independence and freedom to seek more creative and profitable opportunities, both inside and outside of poker.

Nevertheless, because of the cosmopolitan and dynamic nature of public poker, it is often a harbinger or indicator of what will eventually occur in private poker. Indeed, today the new and subtle, yet simple and invisible, cheating techniques (Neocheating) that are spreading throughout public poker are already infiltrating private home games.

# XXXII
# SURVEY OF CLUBS AND CASINOS

Six commercial poker clubs in Gardena, California, are surveyed in Table 37. Those six clubs provide 210 poker and pan tables with 1680 seats. Throughout California, 400 licensed poker clubs have a potential capacity of 14,000 tables and 112,000 seats. State licensed poker parlors are also found in Montana, Oregon, Washington, and other states.

Thirty-three major casinos in Las Vegas, Nevada, are surveyed in Tables 38 and 39. The growing interest in public poker and the attractive profit margins possible from a well-run poker operation have caused sharp increases over the past few years in the number of poker tables in Nevada casinos. In addition to the more than thirty major poker rooms in Las Vegas, at least forty additional casino poker rooms exist in other cities and towns in Nevada. And major casino poker rooms are found in Reno at Cal Nev, Circus Circus, Harold's Club Harrah's, Horseshoe Club, MGM Grand, and Sahara Reno: and in Lake Tahoe at Park-Tahoe and Sahara Tahoe.

*Notes on draw games*

- By law, only draw games are allowed in California card clubs

- High draw is played with fifty-two cards. Low draw is played with fifty-three cards using the joker as a wild card.

- Jacks is draw poker that requires a pair of jacks or better to open. California is draw poker that can be opened on anything.

- High low is not a split-pot game, but is high draw with aces to open. If the pot is not opened, the game switches to low draw.

- Blind open means the player on the dealer's left must bet. Blind raise means the player to the left of the blind opener must raise.

- Razz played in Gardena poker clubs is not lowball stud, but is a blind, lowball draw game in which the winner of the previous pot bets last and may be required to double the blind bet

- Pan (Panguingue) is not poker, but a form of rummy that requires less skill than poker. Pan is of little interest to good poker players.

267

## TABLE 37
### SURVEY OF CLUB POKER IN GARDENA, CALIFORNIA
*(Clubs open 24 hours Monday through Saturday, open 20 hours on Sunday)*
*(Games subject to change)*

| Card Club | # of Tables | Draw Games* | Stakes, $ | Comments |
|---|---|---|---|---|
| **Eldorado Club** 15411 South Vermont Avenue Gardena, California (213) 323-2800 (Closed Thursdays) | 35 | High Jacks Low Blind Blind raise Pan | 1-2 to 50-100 1-2 to 100-200 | More emphasis on high-stake lowball. Attracts toughest lowball professionals. Rough on beginners and amateurs. |
| **Horseshoe Club** 14305 South Vermont Avenue Gardena, California (213) 323-7520 (Closed Wednesdays) | 35 | High Jacks California High-low Low Straight Blind open Blind raise Razz | 1-2 to 50-100 2-4 to 100-200 | Most crowded. Greatest variety of poker. More higher-stake games. Highest percentage of tough professionals. Roughest on beginners and amateurs. |

268

TABLE 37 Continued....
SURVEY OF CLUB POKER IN GARDENA, CALIFORNIA
(Clubs open 24 hours Monday through Saturday, open 20 hours on Sunday)
(Games subject to change)

| Card Club | # of Tables | Draw Games* | Stakes, $ | Comments |
|---|---|---|---|---|
| **Monterey Club** 13927 South Vermont Avenue Gardena, California (213) 329-7524 (Closed Tuesdays) | 35 | High Jacks Low Straight Blind Pan | 1-2 to 40-80 2-4 to 50-100 | Same management as next-door Rainbow Club. Some of the best professionals work these two clubs. |
| **Rainbow Club** 13915 South Vermont Avenue Gardena, California (213) 323-8150 (Closed Tuesdays) | 35 | High Jacks Blind Low Straight Blind Pan | 1-2 to 50-100 2-4 to 100-200 | Same comments as Monterey Club. More emphasis on pan. |

269

TABLE 37 Continued....

SURVEY OF CLUB POKER IN GARDENA, CALIFORNIA

(Clubs open 24 hours Monday through Saturday, open 20 hours on Sunday)

(Games subject to change)

| Card Club | # of Tables | Draw Games* | Stakes, $ | Comments |
|---|---|---|---|---|
| **Normandie Club** 1045 West Rosecrans Boulevard Gardena, California (213) 323-2424 (Closed Thursdays) | 35 | High Jacks High-low Low Straight Blind Razz Pan | 1-2 to 10-20s  1-2 to 20-40 | Tendency toward lower stakes. Fewer professionals. Generally less crowded than other clubs. Good club to learn in. |
| **Gardena Club** 15446 South Western Avenue Gardena, California (213) 323-7301 (Closed Wednesdays) | 35 | High Jacks Low Straight Blind Pan | 1-2 to 20-40  1-2 to 20-40 | Same management as Horseshoe Club. More relaxed atmosphere. More regular players, but fewer professional players. More low-stake action than other clubs. Best club to learn in. |

## TABLE 38
## CASINO POKER ON THE STRIP
## IN LAS VEGAS, NEVADA
*(Starting south on the strip and moving north)*
*—22 casinos. 167 tables with 24-hour poker—*

| Casino | # of Tables | Games Played | Stakes, $* |
|---|---|---|---|
| Hacienda (739-8911) | 4 | 7 Stud | 1-3 |
| Tropicana (739-2222) | 6 | 7 Stud<br>Razz | 1-2 to 3-6<br>1-4 |
| Treasury (739-1000) | 3 | 7 Stud<br>Razz<br>Hold 'em | 1-3<br>1-3<br>2-4 |
| Marina (739-1500) | 4 | 7 Stud<br>Hold 'em | 1-4, 5-10<br>2-4 |
| Aladdin (736 0111) | 9 | 7 Stud<br>Hold 'em | 1-3 to 5-10<br>3-6, 5-10 |
| Dunes (734-4110) | 10 | 7 Stud<br>Hi Lo Stud<br>Hold 'em<br>Razz<br>2-7 Lowball | 1-4 to 500-1000<br>15-30 to 50-100<br>3-6 to 500-1000<br>1-3 to 30-60<br>100-200 to 1500-3000 |
| MGM Grand (739-4111) | 16 | 7 Stud | 1-3 to 5-10 |
| Caesar's Palace (731-7110) | 9 | 7 Stud | 1-3 to 5-10 |
| Barbary Coast (737-7111) | 5 | 7 Stud | 1-3, 3-6 |

271

*Poker: A Guaranteed Income For Life*

TABLE 38 Continued...
CASINO POKER ON THE STRIP
IN LAS VEGAS, NEVADA
*(Starting south on the strip and moving north)*
—22 casinos. 167 tables with 24-hour poker—

| Casino | # of Tables | Games Played | Stakes, $* |
|---|---|---|---|
| Castaways (731-5252) | 2 | 7 Stud | 1-3 |
| Holiday Casino (732-2411) | 8 | 7 Stud | 1-2, 3-6 |
| Imperial Palace (731-3311) | 6 | 7 Stud<br>Draw Low | 1-2 to 5-10<br>2-5 to 2-10 |
| Desert Inn (733-4444) | 7 | 7 Stud<br>Hold 'em | 1-3, 3-6<br>1-5 |
| Silver Slipper (734-1212) | 6 | 7 Stud<br>Hold 'em | 1-3, 3-6<br>3-6 |
| Stardust (732-6111) | 20 | 7 Stud<br>Razz<br>Hold 'em | 1-3 to 15-30<br>15-30 to 50-100<br>3-6 |
| Landmark (733-1110) | 4 | 7 Stud<br>Hold 'em<br>Razz | 1-2 to 3-6<br>2-4 to pot limit<br>1-3 |
| Silver City (732-4152) | 6 | 7 Stud<br>Hold 'em | .50-1 to 1-6<br>pot limit |
| Circus Circus (734-0960) | 13 | 7 Stud<br>6 Stud<br>Hold 'em | 1-3, 3-6<br>2-4, 4-8<br>1-5 |

TABLE 38 Continued...
CASINO POKER ON THE STRIP
IN LAS VEGAS, NEVADA
*(Starting south on the strip and moving north)*
*—22 casinos. 167 tables with 24-hour poker—*

| Casino | # of Tables | Games Played | Stakes, $* |
|---|---|---|---|
| Riveria (732-0960) | 14 | 7 Stud | 1-3 to 500-1000 |
| | | Hold 'em | 3-6 to no limit |
| | | 2-7 Lowball | no limit |
| Sahara (737-2111) | 8 | 7 Stud | 1-4 to 15-30 |
| | | Hi Lo Stud | 10-20, 15-30 |
| | | Razz | 3-6 to 5-10 |
| Bingo Palace (876-8223) | 3 | 7 Stud | 1-3 |
| | | Hold 'em | 2-4 to pot limit |
| Vegas World (382-2000) | 4 | 7 Stud | 1-2, 1-3 |
| | | Hold 'em | 1-5 |
| | | Draw | 1-3 |

\* See footnote to Table 39.

Book 3
Poker: A Guaranteed Income For Life

273

*Poker: A Guaranteed Income For Life*
## TABLE 39
## CASINO POKER
## IN DOWNTOWN LAS VEGAS, NEVADA
*(Starting at Fremont Street and moving east)*
*—12 casinos, 79 tables with 24-hour poker—*

| Casino | # of Tables | Games Played | Stakes, $* |
|---|---|---|---|
| Union Plaza (386-2110) | 7 | 7 Stud | 1-3 |
| | | Hi Lo Stud | 3-6 |
| | | Razz | 3-6 |
| | | Hold 'em | 1-3, 1-6 |
| Holiday International (385-2181) | 6 | 7 Stud | 1-2, 1-6 |
| | | Razz | 1-3 |
| | | Hold 'em | 2-4 |
| Las Vegas Club (385-1874) | 4 | 7 Stud | 1-2, 1-6 |
| | | Razz | 1-3, 3-6 |
| Mint (385-7440) | 10 | 7 Stud | 1-2, 1-3 |
| | | Hold 'em | 1-2, 2-4 |
| | | Draw (low) | 3-6 |
| Golden Nugget (385-9086) | 12 | 7 Stud | 1-2, 1-3 |
| | | Razz | 3-6 |
| | | Hold 'em | 1-2 to 20-40 |
| | | Draw (low) | 3-6 |
| Horseshoe (382-1600) | 0 | No poker, except the annual World Series of Poker in May. | — |
| Fremont (385-3232) | 16 | 7 Stud | 1-3 to 3-6 |
| | | Razz | 3-6, 5-10 |
| | | Hold 'em | 2-4, 3-6 |
| | | Draw (low) | 2-5 |

## TABLE 39 Continued...
## CASINO POKER
## IN DOWNTOWN LAS VEGAS, NEVADA
*(Starting at Fremont Street and moving east)*
*—12 casinos, 79 tables with 24-hour poker—*

| Casino | # of Tables | Games Played | | Stakes, $* |
|---|---|---|---|---|
| Four Queens (385-4011) | 9 | 7 Stud | 1-3 | |
| | | Hold'em | 1-4 | |
| | | Draw (low) | 1-5 | |
| Lady Luck (384-4680) | 4 | 7 Stud | 1-3 | |
| | | Draw | 1-3 | |
| | | Draw (low) | 2-4 | |
| El Cortez (385-5200) | 4 | 7 Stud | 1-2, 1-3 | |
| | | Hi Lo Stud | 3-6 | |
| Sam's Town (456-7777) | 4 | 7 Stud | 1-3 | |
| | | Hold 'em | 2-4 | |
| | | Dealer's Choice | 1-4 | |
| Nevada Palace (458-8810) | 3 | 7 Stud | 1-3, 3-6 | |
| | | Razz | 1-3 | |
| | | Hold 'em | 1-3, 2-4 | |

* Maximum rake at some casinos is as low as $1.50-$2.00 per pot (ask the cardroom manager or floorman for information on game rules and house cut). With thirty to forty hands played per hour, even that low rake permanently removes $45-$80 per hour or about $1000-$2000 per table per day. Allowing for lower cuts and slack periods, the amounts removed from a low-rake table with four or five players averages $500-$1000 per twenty-four-hour day. The average casino poker table extracts from its players an estimated $850 per day or about $300,000 per year. (Also see the second footnote to Table 32.)

The buy-in (the minimum cash value of chips a player must buy to enter the game) is usually ten times the limit of the first bet.

# XXXIII
# THE BILLION-DOLLAR POKER INDUSTRY

Public poker is a billion-dollar-a-year industry involving 400 California card clubs, scores of card clubs in other states, and about 100 Nevada casinos.

The public poker industry could collapse if a majority of its customers — the losers — ever fully realize the amount of money that they will lose with automatic certainty to the winners (good players, professionals, and professional cheaters) and to the casinos or card clubs (through automatic rakes or time collections). Once they clearly understand their inevitable and inescapable loser's role, some public players might quit poker to save their time and money. Others might switch to private poker to eliminate their automatic losses to the house, the professionals, and the cheaters. Still others might switch to other gambling or casino games to eliminate their losses to the good players, the professionals, and the cheaters. Or would they quit or switch? Would the losers abandon public poker despite knowing the inescapable multiple tributes they must pay to the house, the good players, the professionals, and the cheaters?

All other legalized games have a sound and honest operating base that mechanically extracts fixed percentages from all players. Professional players and widespread cheating do not exist for any casino game (except poker) because in those other games, players cannot extract money from other players — and no player can extract money from the house or casino over the long term. Therefore, no true professional player can exist for any casino game (except in poker and perhaps rare cases in blackjack) because no player can support himself by gambling against immutable odds that favor the house or casino.

The public poker industry, on the other hand, is built on a unique establishment of genuine professional players who make a living by applying superior poker abilities, collusion cheating, or a combination of both to consistently extract money from the other public players — the losers.

276

*Part Six: Professional and Public Poker*

Could the billion-dollar public poker industry survive if the losers clearly understood their role of being permanent milch cows to the house, the professionals, and the cheaters? Perhaps... perhaps not... depending on how many public players would continue to accept their role as suckers and losers.

If the losers ever began rejecting their sucker's role by quitting public poker, the public poker industry would collapse.[43] Indeed, the entire gambling industry would collapse if customers ever became imbued with rational self-interest and began rejecting their loser's role.

[43] *The demise of public poker could benefit good players in private games by causing an influx of losers into their private games, especially in Nevada, California, and other areas in which public poker now exists. But a disadvantageous influx of public-game professionals and cheaters into their private games could also occur.*

PART SEVEN

# POKER NOTES

## XXXIV
## POKER NOTES —1968 TO 1980

This chapter compiles and summarizes some poker ideas and concepts accumulated since the Advanced Concepts of Poker were first published.

*1. Who Is Buying the Poker Manual?*

More winners than losers are buying this book. The most profitable advertising for the Poker Manual comes from successful-oriented publications such as *Forbes*, *Fortune*, and *The Wall Street Journal*. A scanning of letterheads from orders confirms that the majority of Poker Manual buyers are successful individuals. In other words, winners are more interested than losers in improving their performance.... That is logical.

The Poker Manual exposes the rationalizations and self-deceptions of chronic losers. It strips away their excuses and facades. Many losers resentfully reject the identifications made throughout the Manual. As long as they reject the identifications, they will remain losers. Yet, any loser who owns the Manual can become a winner if he chooses to apply the Advanced Concepts of Poker.

279

*2. What Will Happen When All Players Own the Poker Manual?*

As sales of the Poker Manual increase, more and more players ask, "What will happen when all poker players own the Manual? Will the advantage gap between good players and poor players narrow? Will the potential earnings for those players applying the Advanced Concepts of Poker diminish?"

The answer to the last two questions is no. The potential earnings of good players should increase as the circulation of the Poker Manual increases. This paradox is explained by examining the nature of the game, the good player, and the poor player, in the following four paragraphs:

Thousands of players around the world already own the Poker Manual. By clearly identifying the total nature of poker, the Manual is gradually but permanently changing the game and its players. The Advanced Concepts of Poker are dispelling the myths that have always worked against the good player in his efforts to create faster-paced, higher-profit games. The Manual eliminates most objections to profitable poker innovations such as hold 'em, split pots, twist cards, and lowball variations by disproving the myth that such pace-increasing variations change poker from a game of skill to a game of luck. As the distribution of the Poker Manual continues, the more profitable, fast-paced games will become increasingly acceptable and easier to introduce — thus allowing the good player to increase his profits at faster rates and to higher levels.

But will the dispelling of other poker myths (e.g., the validity of luck) improve the performances of poor players and chronic losers, thus decreasing the edge odds for the good player? On the whole, the answer would be no. A few poor players (those who would work to steadily improve their game even without the Manual) will benefit from the Manual. But most poor players are static players who will not use the Advanced Concepts of Poker or do anything to improve their game. Why? Consider the nature of chronic losers: Most chronic losers have deeply entrenched habits that militate against the ingredients of good poker — *discipline*, *thought*, and then *control*. The Advanced Concepts of Poker demand intensive discipline and continuous thought — the very efforts that chronic losers seek to avoid. In fact, they build elaborate rationalizations or excuses to avoid any

280

such discipline and thought. They play poker to "relax" their minds. Applying the Advanced Concepts of Poker would contradict and threaten their rationalized excuses for losing.

Revealing the Advanced Concepts of Poker to chronic losers is similar to revealing the logical advantages of being sober to chronic alcoholics, or revealing the unbeatable casino odds to inveterate gamblers. Few chronic losers will change their self-destructive habits when confronted with their errors.... On reading the Advanced Concepts of Poker, some chronic losers temporarily become wary of the good player and alert to some of his techniques. But in most cases, their alertness soon fades and their awareness sinks even lower because of a tranquil confidence that develops from now "knowing" the good player's techniques and from "being savvy" to his tricks. They quickly let themselves forget that his techniques and deceptions continue to extract money from them.

Yet any loser at any time can choose to use his mind[44] to make himself a winner. The mind is the instrument required to use the Advanced Concepts of Poker Winners make themselves winners by choosing to effectively use their minds. And losers make themselves losers by choosing to default on the effective use of their minds. Responsibility for the results of poker rests squarely and solely on the individual.

### 3. Why Does the Author Reveal the Advanced Concepts of Poker?

In addition to the answer above (that revealing the Advanced Concepts of Poker will not diminish the good player's profits), the author gives two additional answers:

1. Compared to playing poker and extracting money from a limited number of players, the potential profit is greater for selling the Advanced Concepts of Poker to 47,000,000 poker players domestically and to an estimated 75,000,000 poker players worldwide.

---

[44] *The effective use of the mind is not related to intelligence. A genius can (and often does) default on the effective use of his mind to make himself a loser. Conversely, a man with mediocre intelligence can elect to use his mind effectively—to beat competitors of superior intelligence.*

281

2. After writing the Manual and identifying the nature of winning poker as a highly profitable but time-consuming, nonproductive activity that requires bringing out the worst in opponents, the author stopped playing poker.

Poker can work against the good player's self-esteem and happiness no matter how much money he wins since the source of self-esteem and happiness lies in being productive,[45] and poker is a nonproductive activity. Also, in the long run, a person will almost always earn more money by pursuing productive routes rather than nonproductive or destructive routes.

Furthermore, in poker, the good player must strive to surround himself with losers — with people who are constantly defaulting on the use of their minds — the opposite kind of people whom the good player could respect and enjoy. That poker is not a very satisfying or rewarding way for him to consume large, irreplaceable portions of his life... The good player, therefore, may be the biggest loser in the game.

And the superior professional player is perhaps the biggest loser in poker, especially in public poker. Constantly surrounded by losers, he consumes his intelligence and time in a situation that provides a guaranteed income, but offers neither an interesting nor a productive future.

### 4. John Finn's Notes on Private Poker
*(See Chapter XXVII for John Finn's notes on public poker.)*

1. Beat opponents through their personal weaknesses — through their irrationalities. Smoking, for example, is a self-destructive irrationality that represents a vulnerability — a lack of discipline and control. If an opponent constantly hurts himself through irrationalities such as smoking (or drinking excessively, chronic gambling, mysticism, dishonesty, or physical unfitness), he can

---

[45] *Productivity is defined as adding to the sum total of mankind's material, intellectual, physiological. psychological, or aesthetic well-being. Humans earn genuine self-esteem and happiness through the pursuit of productive goals.*

certainly be manipulated into hurting himself through a much more subtle irrationality such as poker.

2. Probe all opponents for weaknesses that can be manipulated in order to extract maximum money from them. Also identify and eliminate your own weaknesses (or at least guard against losing money through your weaknesses). Constantly strive to identify and correct your errors — and then capitalize on corrected errors (i.e., by springing traps on those alert opponents who were capitalizing on your past errors).

3. Be alert to changes. Opponents can undergo drastic changes during a poker session. In a few minutes, an opponent can change from a tight, careful player to a loose, reckless player — or vice versa. To maintain the best investment odds, constantly monitor and adjust to all changes in all opponents.

4. To evaluate more accurately the quality of poker played by any individual, analyze his game in two separate segments — his statistical game and his strategical game. The statistical game is the shorter-range card-playing and money-management aspects (the mechanical aspects) that depend on an understanding of the odds or probabilities and on discipline and control. The strategical game is the longer-range imaginative aspect that depends on alertness and on independent and objective thinking effort. The good player usually beats professional players and cheaters with a superior strategical game.

5. Concentrate on areas that provide maximum advantages. For example, in a game with weak players, concentrate more on opponents' play and do more manipulating. In a game with strong players, concentrate more on your own play and do less manipulating (which can give away your hand and intentions). Better yet, avoid playing with strong players.

6. Breathe deeply to release tensions, especially in the neck, shoulders, and buttocks. Tension-free relaxation makes a player more effective for extracting money from opponents. Also, being physically fit (especially being aerobically fit via regular roadwork) can make a significant contribution not only to your stamina, but also to your ability to concentrate and implement the Advanced Concepts of Poker.

7. Use hypnotic motions and whispered chants to condition and train players to react favorably — to "obey commands" (e.g., to fold, bet, or raise).

8. Often you can profitably check strong hands from deeper positions than most players realize (e.g., you can profitably check four sevens from a deeper position than two high pair). Not too serious if no one opens after checking a strong hand, since opening against all non-bettors would normally result in a small pot with few, if any callers — and they would be weak callers. The rewards of winning larger pots by check raising are greater than the risks of losing smaller, passed-out pots. But also avoid underbetting hands — especially strong hands.

9. Opponents holding openers or good hands tend to be more alert. Players who suddenly start policing the game usually have at least openers. Players glumly staring at their cards will seldom open. Players who are tense and not looking at their cards (but are alertly looking at the pot or other players) will usually open.

10. By learning to read opponents' hands accurately, the card odds become less important as the manipulation of opponents and bluffing become easier and more important.

11. Predicting cards and odds becomes increasingly accurate — especially in stud games — as the hand progresses. For the more dealt cards a player knows, the more accurately he can predict what cards remain in the deck

— or how rich or lean the remaining deck is for any particular card. (The good poker card-counter has a much greater winning advantage than the good blackjack card-counter, whose maximum advantage is less than 1 percent.)

12. By knowing how rich or lean the remaining deck is in various cards, a player can predict with increasing accuracy both his own and his opponents' probabilities for drawing specific cards as the deck diminishes. Furthermore, the observant player can often discover the actual value of cards being dealt in two ways: First, he can often see the cards flash while being dealt or while being picked up and handled by opponents. And second, he can discover the value of cards about to be dealt from markings on their backs that occur during normal play — such as spots, creases, nicks, folds, and stains.

13. Since neither total inconsistency nor total consistency is possible, all hands of all opponents potentially can be read by the observant player.

14. Usually the more an opponent tries to hide the strength or weakness of his hand, the easier and more accurately his hand can be read The player who never looks at his cards until his turn to bet is often the hardest player to read, but he leaves himself with less time to plan strategy relative to his cards.

15. Evoke giveaway reactions from opponents by hesitating before betting. Pretend the pot is light and then count the chips to induce giveaway reactions. Also evoke card-reading or giveaway reactions with surprise moves, unusual acts, or point-blank questions. To extract useful information or reactions, ask opponents point-blank questions about their hand, their bet, or what they plan to do... Be careful not to give away your own hands or intentions through those tactics.

285

16. Most losers look hard for excuses to bet or bluff. When holding winning hands, provide those excuses for them.

17. Reading bluffs of opponents offers major moneymaking opportunities. Players often reveal pat-hand bluffs by not looking at their cards long enough to assure themselves of pat hands. When bluffing, many players try to project confidence and strength with fast bets or by feigning relaxation or cheerfulness. Also, players who back out of bluffs early in a hand will often try to bluff again within the next few hands.

18. The purpose of every bluff should be to win the pot. The advertising value of a bluff is only a secondary benefit.

19. In early developed bluffs, make players believe that they must improve their hands to win. In general, cancel bluff plans if opponents do improve their hands.

20. To reinforce a loose-player image, never admit to folding good hands and generally show weak hands that win. Never reveal poker skills or the ability to read opponents' hands by betting too confidently, by folding too quickly, by giving "lessons," or by explaining strategy.

21. Fiction and movies like The Cincinnati Kid offer cliched and misleading views of poker, cheating, and good players. In reality, prosperous good players are not flamboyant "big-man" types. Instead, they strive to appear mundane. They are nonfamous. They are Clark Kents. They are stealthy and clandestine. Moreover, they play wide-open, fast-paced games — not five-card stud. And they never need to look under tables or examine overhead lamps to protect themselves from cheating. The stereotyped, fictionalized, and romanticized views of poker and good players provide helpful covers for the real-life good players as they surreptitiously extract all available money from all opponents.

22. Usually the good player benefits more by focusing his concentration on playing sound poker than by diluting his concentration on acting. But in games with several good players or world class professionals (games that the good player would normally avoid), the faking of carefully planned tells (behavior patterns that give away a player's hands or intentions) can make a good player essentially unbeatable against superior competition. In fact, the better his opponents are, the more easily they can be drawn into traps by subtle, preplanned tells. Because both good players and experienced professionals look for, detect, and use tells projected by each opponent, they are vulnerable to fake or set-up tells. A variety of effective set-up tells also distracts observant opponents from detecting unintentional tells projected by the good player. Indeed, a good player can beat other good players and dramatically win major professional poker tournaments with a series of preplanned, well-executed tells that "give away" good hands, poor hands, and bluffs. The good player beats superior competition by systematically training his observant opponents to react to his set-up tells and then reversing or faking those tells for the crucial, big pots... But again, such faking or acting is generally not worthwhile against poor or average poker players.

23. Poker is actually a game of discipline and effort — not luck or skill. Almost any novice armed with the Advanced Concepts of Poker and a few weeks practice can with sheer discipline and effort beat experienced poker experts. By contrast, activities requiring skill such as tennis, violin playing, and brain surgery take years to develop the skills and experience needed to compete with the experts. Once those skills are developed, however, the effort required to properly execute them diminishes. But in poker, no matter how much experience a player gains, the discipline and effort required to execute good poker never diminishes.

24. No-limit, table-stake games offer the most advantage to the good player. In such games, his tools of

287

aggressiveness, manipulation, psychology, and bluffing become much more effective for outplaying opponents. On the other hand, the most lucrative losers often stay away or are quickly driven from such no-limit games. So ironically, the best long-term profit opportunities for the good player usually exist within limit stake games that he can control. In such limit games, the good player can extract increasing amounts of money from his opponents, game after game, year after year.

## 5. Neocheating — The Rising Menace to Poker, Blackjack, Bridge, and Gin

Neocheating is the ultimate evolution of cheating. It is a new kind of cheating — an invisible, incredibly easy kind of cheating. Once a person understands Neocheating, he can quietly beat all his opponents in poker, blackjack, bridge, or gin.

The maneuvers of Neocheating are so subtle and the mechanics so easy that they can be invisibly executed with relaxed confidence. Guaranteed winning hands such as four aces can be routinely obtained. And more than one powerful hand can be dealt at a time to ensure a big score (e.g., in poker: four aces to the Neocheater and four jacks to the victim). Yet, the Neocheater seldom arranges such powerful hands or goes for big scores (although he easily can). Instead, he casually uses just enough of his power to give him constant, unbeatable advantages. His steady, hidden attack lets him win consistently and comfortably in poker, blackjack, bridge, and gin.[46]

Neocheating is not like classical or traditional cardsharping that requires years of practice or a dangerous reliance on aids such as marked cards and hold-out devices. Neocheating requires no special skills, gall, or devices; it requires only a special knowledge and a few hours of practice.

Many card players would cheat if not for (1) their fear of being caught, or for (2) the time and effort required to learn how

46 Reference *Neocheating—The Unbeatable Weapon in Poker, Blackjack, Bridge, and Gin,* by Frank R. Wallace, Mark Hamilton, and William S., 192 pages, Neo-Tech Publishing Company, Las Vegas, Nevada (1980).

to cheat effectively. But Neocheating eliminates both deterrents. And as this easy, invisible form of cheating spreads, it will not only increasingly menace players of poker, blackjack, bridge, and gin, but also tempt players to Neocheat in all games played for money or prestige.

This is what John Finn says about the Neocheater:

*For the first tine, good players need to worry about getting wiped out . A new breed of player is invading the card tables. He is the Neocheater. And the Neocheater does not lose.*

*Neocheating is invisible. How can it be stopped? The Neocheater is impossible to catch in the act and hard to get rid of. In fact, all honest players unaware of Neocheating are in financial danger. The Neocheater is the most dangerous threat to ever invade the card tables.*

What can stop Neocheating from spreading? Publicly revealing the techniques of Neocheating may initially cause a cheating spree that could create chaos at the card table. But ironically, that same knowledge, as it becomes widely known, will begin to expose and nullify Neocheating. Players no longer need to be helpless or doomed when confronted with Neocheating. Instead, they will be able to counter and eliminate that menace.

# CONCLUSION

Poker is merciless.

Poker is a game of money and deception. The consequences are always deserved. The penalties go to the weak — the rewards go to the strong. The loser dissipates his time and money. The winner earns satisfaction and money. But what is the net result of poker? Is it merely time consumed and money exchanged with nothing positive produced? Is the net result a negative activity?

Poker exposes character ... poker is a character catalyst that forces players to reality. Those who evade thinking and act on whims cannot escape the penalties. Those who use their minds and act on logic are rewarded. The results are clear and true: The lazy evader loses — he can never fake success. The thinking performer wins — he is always rewarded.

The good poker player functions rationally. He views all situations realistically. With objective thinking, he directs his actions toward winning maximum money. He pits the full use of his mind against the unwillingness of his opponents to think. Thus, the good player cannot lose.

In poker, a person is on his own. He must act as an individual. No one will help him. Success depends on the rational use of his mind. Success depends on exercising his positive qualities and overcoming his negative qualities. Success depends on him alone. In poker, a person can function entirely for his own sake. The results are his own. The loser makes himself a loser. The winner makes himself a winner.

Poker is sheer justice.

291

# Appendix A

## HISTORY

The memoirs of an English actor (Joseph Crowell) touring America in 1829 described a game being played in New Orleans in which each player received five cards and made bets — then whoever held the highest combination of cards won all bets. Mr. Crowell was probably describing the earliest form of poker or its immediate predecessor, the Persian game of Âs.

The first direct reference to poker was found in Jonathan H. Green's book, An Exposure of the Arts and Miseries of Gambling (G. B. Zieber, Philadelphia, 1843). Green described poker games on a steamer running between New Orleans and Louisville. His book indicated that poker began in New Orleans about 1830.

Research on the evolution of poker (outlined on p. 296) revealed that poker descended directly from the Persian game of Âs Nâs and not, as commonly believed, from the French game of Poque, the German game of Pochen, or the English game of Bragg. But those and other European games soon exerted their influence on the original game of poker, as shown in the following two diagrams on the derivation and evolution of poker.

Sailors from Persia taught the French settlers in New Orleans the gambling card game Âs, which was derived from the ancient Persian game of Âs Nâs. The Frenchmen would bet by saying, for example, "I poque for a dollar," and would call by saying, "I poque against you for two dollars." Those were the betting expressions used in their game of Poque, a three-card game first played by commoners in France and then by Frenchmen in America as early as 1803. Poque was similar to Bouillotte, a card

293

game popular with the aristocrats in France just prior to the French Revolution of 1789.

Combining the words "Âs" and "Poque," the game became known as "Poqas." Then, influenced by the German bluff game of Pochen and the southern accent, the pronunciation of "Poqas" became "Pokah." Under Yankee influence, the pronunciation finally became "Poker."

Poker moved from New Orleans by steamboat up the Mississippi and Ohio rivers. From the river towns, the game spread east by the new railroad and west by covered wagons. Between 1834 and 1837, the full fifty-two-card deck replaced the original twenty-card deck. Soon after that, the flush was introduced. During the Civil War, modifications such as open cards (stud poker), the draw, and the straight became popular. When the joker was introduced as a wild card in 1875, the European influence of poker ended. Further development of the game was essentially American.

Jackpot poker (draw poker requiring both an ante and a pair of jacks or better to open) began about 1875. Split-pot and lowball poker started around 1903. Two Missouri assemblymen (Coran and Lyles) introduced a bill to the state legislature in 1909 to control and license poker players in order to prevent "millions of dollars lost annually by incompetent and foolish persons who do not know the value of a poker hand." In 1911, California's attorney general (Harold Sigel Webb) ruled that closed poker (draw poker) was skill and beyond antigambling laws . . . but open poker (stud poker) was luck and therefore illegal. That stimulated the development of new draw games and the use of wild cards. The variety of poker games grew steadily, particularly during the First and Second World Wars. In the 1960s, poker variations further developed with innovations such as twists (extra draws) and qualifiers (minimum hands to win).

In 1968, Wallace's Advanced Concepts of Poker was first published. By 1972, the publication had become the largest-selling poker book in the world. The Advanced Concepts of Poker fully identified for the first time the potentially ruthless, manipulative, but highly profitable nature of poker. In addition, the characteristics of consistent winners, and chronic losers were identified. Also identified for the first time were three different kinds of odds, the effects of the betting pace versus the betting stakes, the advantages of aggressive betting, and the advantages gained by the good player when complex and fast-paced games were played. And most important, the Advanced Concepts of Poker clearly identified the differences between the financially profitable good poker and financially destructive gambling as well as the differences between winners and losers.

## DERIVATION OF POKER

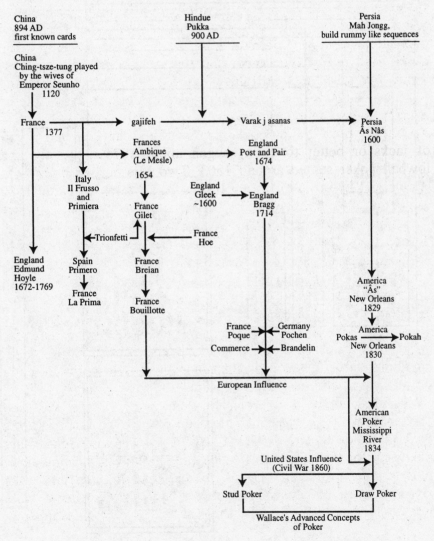

# EVOLUTION OF POKER

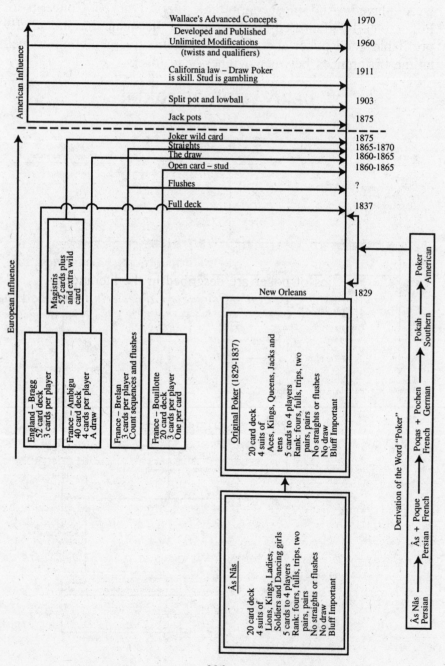

# Appendix B

## BIBLIOGRAPHY

Early poker literature tried to establish firm rules for the game. Unlike other card games in being a uniquely dynamic game (a competitive money-management game rather than a routine card game), poker could never be bound in rigid rules. Continuously changing within a loose framework of traditions, poker remained a versatile, living game always subject to modifications and variations (over 150 varieties of poker are described in the literature).

As early as 1674, *Cotton's Complete Gamester's* (published in England) described a card game called Post and Pair, a predecessor to Bragg, which, in turn, was a predecessor to poker with a full deck. Bragg and the art of bluffing were first described in Cotton's 1721 edition. Poque, a French card game that directly influenced the development of poker, was described in the eighteenth-century editions of Acadence Universelle des Jeux.

Until 1850, there were no printed rules for poker.[47] Neither of the two American Hoyles then in print (George Long, New York, 1825, and G. Cowperthwait, Philadelphia, 1838) mentioned poker. The English Hoyle (*Bohn's Handbook of Games*) made

[47] *The common reference "poker according to Hoyle" is curious because the English writer and lawyer, Edmund Hoyle (1672-1769), never heard of poker: he died sixty years before the game originated. Hoyle was a famous whist player. His original book described three card games—whist, piquete and quadrille. But his authority for card-game rules grew until all card and board game rules became known as "Hoyles." Since many different "Hoyles" now exist, "poker according to Hoyle" depends on the editor and publisher of that particular Hoyle.*

no reference to poker in either its 1850 or its 1887 edition. But the 1850 American reprint of Bohn's book mentioned poker in an addendum. Also in 1850, *Hoyles' Games* (H. F. Anners, Philadelphia) had a brief note about poker that described a full deck, ten players (therefore, no draw), and a bonus paid for any hand of trips or better. In 1857, Thomas Frere's *Hoyle* (T. W. Story, New York) described poker without referring to a draw.

The first mention of draw poker appeared in the 1867 edition of *Hoyles* (Dick and Fitzgerald, New York). Also, that edition was the first book to mention an ante, a straight (which beat two pair, but not trips), and the straight flush (which beat four of a kind). The 1875 edition of *Hoyles* (Dick and Fitzgerald, New York) mentioned jackpot poker and the joker used as a wild card.

The first printed poker rules in England were written by General Robert E. Schenck, the United States minister to England. He introduced poker to the guests at a country house in Somersetshire. The hostess, a prominent duchess, persuaded him to write down the rules. In 1872, the duchess privately printed those rules for her court. The game caught Queen Victoria's fancy, and the popularity of poker spread through Great Britain. Poker in England soon became known as "Schenck poker,"

In 1875, a description of poker appeared in Cavendish's *Round Games of Cards* (De La Rue & Co.).

After 1875, books about poker appeared regularly in America, England, and Continental Europe. Data on all poker books (whose locations and dates of publication are known) published in the one hundred years between 1875 and 1975 have been tabulated below.

| Number of Books | % | Country Where Published |
|---|---|---|
| 93 | 72.6 | United States |
| 22 | 17.2 | England |
| 8 | 6.2 | France |
| 2 | 1.6 | Italy |
| 1 | 0.8 | Germany |
| 1 | 0.8 | Holland |
| 1 | 0.8 | India |
| | | (for 1875-1965) |
| 128 | 100.0 | |

| Years<br>*(in 10-year intervals)* | Number of<br>*Poker Books Published* |
|---|---|
| Up to 1875 | 2 |
| 1876-1885 | 13 |
| 1886-1895 | 18 |
| 1896-1905 | 13 |
| 1906-1915 | 11 |
| 1916-1925 | 9 |
| 1926-1935 | 9 |
| 1936-1945 | 4 |
| 1946-1955 | 11 |
| 1956-1965 | 17 |
| 1966-1975 | 20 |
| | 127 |

*[Note: From 1976 to 1980. an additional 20 poker books were published.]*

The Addendum Bibliography at the end of this Appendix B reviews each poker book published since 1968.

A bibliography of all known poker books is tabulated below:

## Books on Poker in The Library of Congress

| Catalog<br>Number | Subject Heading "Poker"<br>Library of Congress Card Information<br>*(verbatim)* |
|---|---|
| 1. GV1251<br>A15 | Abbott, Jack. A treatise on Jack pot poker, with the game of sancho pedro, when played for stakes. New Orleans, Clark & Hofeline, printers, 1881. 64 pages |
| 2. GV1258<br>A43 | Allen, George W. Poker rules in rhyme, with chances to improve the hand by drawing. St. Louis, Mo., 1895. 74 pages |

3.  GV1251    Blackbridge, John. The complete poker player.
    B6       A practical guidebook to the American national
    (other     game: containing mathematical and experimental
    editions)   analysis of the probabilities at draw poker. New
               York, Dick & Fitzgerald, 1880. 142 pages

4.  GV1253    Brown, Garrett. The autocrat of the poker table,
    B8       or, How to play the game to win. 3rd ed.,
    1916      Boston, R.G. Badger, 1916. 105 pages
    (other editions)

5.  GV1251    Cady, Alice Howard. Poker: the modern game.
    C15      With passing description of its origin. New
               York, American Sports Publishing Company,
               1895. 37 pages

6.  GV1251    Coffin, George Sturgis. Fortune poker: a world
    C65      wide roundup of the traditional American game.
               Complete with new laws according to Hoyle.
               With a forward by Ely Culbertson. Philadelphia,
               D. McKay Co., 1949. 198 pages

|  | *Catalog Number* | *Subject Heading "Poker"*<br>*Library of Congress Card Information*<br>*(verbatim)* |
|---|---|---|

7.  GV1251    Coffin, George Sturgis. The official laws of
    C67      poker. Baltimore, Ottenheimer, 1956. 64 pages

8.  GV1251    Coffin, George Sturgis. Pocket guide to the play
    C68      of poker. Baltimore, Ottenheimer, 1956. 64 pages

9.  GV1251    Curtis, David A. The science of draw poker; a
    C95      treatise comprising the analysis of principles,
               calculation of chances, codification of rules,
               study of situations, glossary of poker terms
               necessary to a complete understanding of the
               great American game. New York, D. A. Curtis,
               1901. 216 pages

10. GV1253
D62
Dowling, Allen Nicholas. Confessions of a poker player by Jack King (pseud.). New York, I. Washburn, Inc., 1940. 209 pages

11. GV1253
D62
Dowling, Allen Nicholas. Under the round table by Jack King (pseud.). Philadelphia, Dorrance, 1960. 219 pages

12. ?
Edel, Edmund. Poker ein spieler—roman. Charlottenburg, E. Beyer, 1912. 176 pages

13. GV1253
E26
Edwards, Eugene. Jack pots; stories of the great American game. With over fifty original pen and ink illustrations. Chicago, Jamieson-Higgins Co., 1900. 342 pages

*Subject Heading "Poker"*
Catalog
Number
*Library of Congress Card Information*
*(verbatim)*

14. GV1251
F5
Fisher, George Henry. How to win at stud poker... instruction for the novice, principles of strategy, problem hands, hand valuation, card probabilities, complete set of rules, history of the game, etc. Los Angeles, The Stud Poker Press, 1933. 111 pages

15. GV1251
F83
Florence, William Jermyn. The gentleman's handbook on poker. New York, London, G. Routledge Sons, Ltd., 1892. 195 pages

16. GV1251
Foster, Robert Frederick. Practical poker. New York, Brentano's 1905. 253 pages

17. GV1251
G47
Gilkie, Robert J. Experimental drawing at poker from five thousand hands. Dorchester, Mass., 1886. 13 pages

18. GV1251  Girardet, Philippe. Philosophie et mathematique
    G5    du poker. Paris, M. Senac, 1929. 160 pages

19. GV1251  Gray, E. Archer. Hints on poker. Washington,
    G77   D.C., 1886. 16 pages
    (other editions)

20. GV1251  Hardison, Theodore. Poker: a work exposing the
    H2    various methods of shuffling up hands, as
          well as other ways of cheating that are
          resorted to by professional gamblers, also
          embracing the cardinal principles by which
          every sleight-of-hand trick known with cards
          may be played. St. Louis, Hardison Publishing
          Co., 1914. 120 pages

|                    | *Subject Heading "Poker"* |
| *Catalog*          | *Library of Congress Card Information* |
| *Number*           | *(verbatim)* |

21. GV1251  Heineman, Walter Raleigh. Draw poker, a
    H4    compilation of rules governing the game of
          "Jack pots," by Jack Pot (pseud.). New York,
          Chrisholm Printing Co., 1923. 48 pages

22. GV1251  Henry R. J. Poker boiled down... the latest
    H52   authentic rules... on the great national game...
    (other editions) 1st edition. Boston, Massachusetts, Tourist
          Publishing Company, 1890. 13 pages

23. GV1233  History and anecdotes of card games (especially
    H8    poker). 43 cuttings from newspapers, etc...
    (temporary entry) bibliographical notes in ms... Gift of Prof.
          Brander Matthews

24. GV1251  Jacoby, Oswald. Oswald Jacoby on poker, with
    J2    a forward by Grantland Rice, and an

| 1947<br>(other editions) | introduction by William E. McKenney. Rev. ed. Garden City, New York, Doubleday & Company, Inc., 1947. 175 pages |
| --- | --- |
| 25. GV1251<br>J22 | Jacoby, Oswald. Winning poker. New York, Permabooks, 1949. 189 pages |
| 26. GV1251<br>K59 | Keller, John William. The game of draw poker. Including the treatise by R.C. Schenck and rules for the new game of progressive poker... New York, White, Stokes & Allen, 1887 84 pages |
| 27. GV1251<br>M15 | MacKenzie, Collins. Jack pots. A collection of poker stories. By A. Pair (pseud.). Chicago, the Illustrated Publishing Co., 1887. 160 pages |

|  | *Subject Heading "Poker"* |
| --- | --- |
| *Catalog<br>Number* | *Library of Congress Card Information<br>(verbatim)* |
| 28. GV1251<br>P32 | Patton, F. Jarvis. How to win at draw poker. Showing all the chances of the game. New York, Dick & Fitzgerald, 1896. 45 pages |
| 29. GV1253<br>P6<br>(Office) | Unknown. Poker as it was played in Deadwood in the fifties. Palo Alto, California, Wheatstalk Press, 1928. 5 pages (A reprint from an article in Hutching's California magazine in August, 1858-Vol. III, pg. 85) |
| 30. GV1253<br>P77<br>(Houdini<br>Collection)<br>(other editions) | Poker: how to play it. A sketch of the great American game with its laws and rules, and some of its amusing incidents. By one of its victims. London, Griffith & Farran, 1882. 109 pages |
| 31. QA/273<br>P96 | Proctor, Richard Anthony. Chance and luck: a discussion of the laws of luck, coincidences, wagers, lotteries, and fallacies of gambling; with |

notes on poker and martingales. London, Longmans, Green & Co., 1887. 263 pages

32. GV1251
R3
(other editions)

Radner, Sidney H. The key to playing poker and winning. Owing Mills, Maryland, Ottenheimer Publishers, 1964. 189 pages

33. GV1251
R37

Reese, Terence. Secrets of modern poker. New York, Sterling Publishing Co., 1964. 148 pages

34. GV1251
R4

Renaudet, G. Le poker; regles completes et commentaires, L'art de gagner au poker, poker a 52 cartes; a 48, 44, 40, 3 et 32 cartes; freeze out; la partie a la cave; calud des probabilities; le blugg, physiologie du jeu. Paris, S. Bornemann, 1922. 31 pages

|  | *Subject Heading "Poker"* |
| --- | --- |
| *Catalog* | *Library of Congress Card Information* |
| *Number* | *(verbatim)* |

35. GV1253
R47

Rhoades, William Morston. Poker, smoke, and other things; fun and pictures. Rules of poker, recipes, toasts, mixed drinks. Chicago, the Reilly & Britton Co., 1907. 69 pages

36. BF21
A7
(other editions)

Riddle, Ethel Maris. Aggressive behavior in a small social group; bluffing, risking, and the desire to beat... studied by the use of a poker game as an experimental technique. New York, 1925. 19 pages (Also published as a Ph.D. thesis in psychology, Columbia University)

37. GV1251
R65

Rottenberg, Irving. Friday night poker, or, Penny poker to millions, by Irv Roddy (pseud.). New York, Simon Schuster, 1961. 222 pages

38. GV1251
S32

Schenick, Robert Cummings. Rules for playing poker. Brooklyn, New York, Private printing,

1880. 17 pages (1st edition, 1872)

39. GV1251    Schenick, Robert Cummings. Draw poker.
    S32      Published for the trade, 1880. 8 pages
    1881
    (Toner Collection. Office)

40. GV1251    Smith, Russell A. Poker to win. El Paso, Texas,
    S5       1925. 110 pages

41. GV1251    Seig, Irwin. Common sense in poker. New
    S68      York, Cornerstone Library, 1963. 188 pages

42. GV1251    Steig, Irwin. Poker for fun and profit. New
    7        York, McDowell, Obelensky, 1959. 181 pages

*Subject Heading "Poker"*
Catalog          *Library of Congress Card Information*
Number                        *(verbatim)*

43. GV1251    Talk of Uncle George (pseud.) to his nephew
    T2       about draw poker. Containing valuable
             suggestions in connection with this great
             American game. New York, Dick & Fitzgerald,
             1883. 50 pages

44. GV1251    United States Playing Card Co. Poker official
    U55      rules and suggestions, endorsed by Association
             of American playing card manufacturers.
             Cincinnati, Ohio, The United States Playing
             Card Company, 1941. 64 pages

45. GV1251    Walter & Philip (pseud.) Il poker familiare,
    W3       come si giuoca in Italia. 2nd edition, Milano,
             U. Hoepli, 1945. 81 pages

46. GV1253    Webster, Harold Tucker. Webster's poker book
    W4       glorifying America's favorite game; a handy

volume for the hearthside consisting of fifty portraits; informative and diverting text on the joys, rules, love and pitfalls of poker; sideline suggestions and interpolations; authoritative data on the history and technique of poker; including hints from Hoyle and a forward by George Ade; together with a compartment containing a set of poker chips and a pad of I.O.U. forms ready for instant use. New York, Simon & Schuster, 1925. 126 pages

47. GV1251
    W5
    1944
(other editions)

Wickstead, James M. How to win at stud poker. Louisville, Kentucky, Stud Poker Publishing Co., 1944. 115 pages

|  | *Subject Heading "Poker"* |
|---|---|
| *Catalog* | *Library of Congress Card Information* |
| *Number* | *(verbatim)* |

48. GV1251
    W55

Winterblossom, Henry T. The game of draw poker, mathematically illustrated; being a complete treatise of the game, giving the prospective value of each hand before and after the draw, and the true method of discarding and drawing with a thorough analysis and insight of the game as played at the present day by gentlemen. New York, W.H. Murphy, 1875. 72 pages

49. GV1251
    X3

Xavier, Francois. Le poker, sa technique, sa psychologie, suivi d'une etude sur le stud poker. Paris, B. Grasset, 1955. 222 pages

50. GV1251
    Y3

Yardley, Herbert Osborn. The education of a poker player, including where and how one learns to win. New York, Simon & Schuster, 1957. 129 pages

51. GV1243
C8

Culbertson, Ely. Morehead, Albert H. and Goeffrey, Matt Smith. Culbertson's Hoyle: the new encyclopedia of games, with official rules. New York, Gray stone Press, 1950. 656 pages

52. Reference

Encyclopedia Britannica. Poker. Volume 10, pg. 128, Chicago, William Benton, 1965. 4 pages

53. GV1251
F79

Fox, Richard K. Poker, how to win, together with the official rules. New York 1905. 90 pages

54. GV1243
F85

Frey, Richard L., ed. The new complete Hoyle: an encyclopedia of rules, procedures, manners, and strategy of games played with cards, dice, counters, boards, words, and numbers. Philadelphia, D. McKay Co., 1947. 740 pages

*Subject Heading "Poker"*

Catalog Number

*Library of Congress Card Information (verbatim)*

55. GV1239
J3

Jacoby, O., et al. The fireside book of cards. New York, Simon & Schuster, 1957. 364 pages

56. PZ3
L628P

Lillard, John F. B., ed. Poker stories, as told by statesmen, soldiers, lawyers, commercial travelers, bankers, actors, editors, millionaires, members of the Ananias club and the talent, embracing the most remarkable games, 1845-95. New York, F. P. Harper, 1896. 251 pages

57. GV1243
D8

Ostrow, A. A. The complete card player. New York, McGraw-Hill Book Company, Inc., 1945. 771 pages

58 GV1291
P6

Poker-bridge; een nieuw kaartspel. Amsterdam. A. J. G. Strengholt, 1954. 32 pages

59. AP2    *Poker Chips*, a monthly magazine devoted to
    W64    stories of the great American game. New York,
           F. Tousey, June-Nov. 1896. 243 pages
           (continued as the White Elephant magazine)

60. GV1247  Scarne, John. Scarne on cards. Including a
    S37     photographic section on cheating at cards.
            Revised, New York, Crown Publishers, 1965.
            435 pages

[Note: The Library of Congress does not catalog books about poker under the subject of "Gambling." The 375 books listed under "Gambling" include books on blackjack, boule, cards (nonpoker), cardsharping, craps, fero, horse-race betting, parimutuel betting, probabilities, raffles, roulette, speculation, trente-et-quarante, and wagers . . . but none on poker. Apparently, the Library of Congress does not consider (classify) poker as gambling.]

Seventy-two other poker books not found in the Library of Congress are listed below:

61. Allan, L., *The Laws of Poker*, Mudie, 1929.
62. Ankeny, Nesmith, *Scientific Poker*, Harper, 1967.
63. *Ante—I Raise You Ten*, Jamieson-Higgans.
64. Arnold, F. and Johnston, H., *Poker*, Routledge, 1929.
65. Bergholt, E. G. B., *Poker*, De La Rue.
66. Browning, H. S., *Royal Auction Bridge and Poker*, Routledge, 1920.
67. Carcini, Nick, *A Course in Professional Poker Playing*, Memphis, Tennessee, Edall Publishing Co., 1965.
68. Carleton, Henry Guy, *Thompson Street Poker Club*, Dick & Fitzgerald, 1888.
69. Coffin, G. S., *Poker Game Complete*, Faber and Faber, 1950.
70. Coffin, G. S., *Complete Poker Game*, Wehman.
71. Crafton, A., *Poker: Its Laws and Principles*, Wyeil, 1915.
72. Crawford, John R., *How to be a Consistent Winner Most Popular Card Games*, New York, Doubleday, 1953.
73. Curtis, D. H., *Queer Luck*, New York, Brentano's, 1900.

74. Dalton, W., *Pocket Guide to Poker Patience*, De La Rue, 1909.
75. Davis, A. D., *An Analysis of Five and Seven Card Poker*, Philadelphia, 1959 (Mimeographed Master's Thesis).
76. Debebian, D., *Game of Poker*, New York, 1889.
77. *Decisions on Moot Points of Draw Poker*, New York.
78. Diehl, Charles Vidol, *Poker Patience and Progressive Poker Patience*, London, The Advanced Publishing Co., 1909.
79. *Draw Poker*, Dick.
80. *Draw Poker*, Fitzgerald Publishing Corporation.
81. *Draw Poker*, London, i884,63 pages.
82. *Draw Poker and Spoil Five*, London, Routledge & Sons, 1884.
83. Ellinger, M., *Poker*, Faber, 1934.
84. Erdnase, S. W., *The Expert at the Card Table*, London, Stationers' Hall, 1902.
85. Fisher, G. G., *Stud Poker Blue Book*, Los Angeles, Stud Poker Press, 1934.
86. *Football Poker*, Brentano's.
87. Foster, J. H., *Traite de Jeu de Poker*, Paris, 1889.
88. Foster, R. F., *Pocket Laws of Poker*, De La Rue, 1910.
89. Gilbert, Kenneth, Alaskan Poker Stories, Seattle, R. D. Seal, 1958.
90. Guerndale, Richard, *Draw Poker without a Master*, Dillingham.
91. Guerndale, Richard, *The Poker Book*, London, I. Upcott Gill, 1889.
92. Habeythe, *Jeu de Poker*, Paris, 1886
93. Hirst, E. deF., *Poker as Played by Skilled Professional Gamblers*, 2nd ed., 1902.
94. Hoffman, W., *Draw Poker, the Standard Game*. Dutton, 1913.
95. *How to Play Poker*, Wehman Bros.
96. *How to Win at Draw Poker*, Dick.
97. *How to Win at Draw Poker*, Westbrook.
98. Hoyle (pseud.), *How to Play Poker*, Ogilvie, 1916.
99. Jackpot, *Poker-Patience*, International Card Co., 1909.
100. Lamenti, C. E., *Il Poker*, Milano, A. Corticelli, 1929.
101. La Shelle, Kirbe, *Poker Rubaiyat*, Phoenix, Arizona, Bunder

Log Press, 1903.

102. Laugher, A. B., *Poker*, C. Goodall, 1913.

103. Laugher, A. B., *Poker*, London, 1889.

104. Laun, *Jeu de Poker*, Paris, Watilliaux, 1897.

105. Major, *The Poker Primer*, New York, 1886.

106. Matthews, J. B., *"Poker Talk"* (p. 187 of Penn and Ink), New York, Longmans, Green & Co., 1888.

107. Meehan, C. H. W., *The Rules for Playing Draw Poker* (Game of Euchre), Philadelphia, T. B. Peterson, 1877.

108. Morehead, Albert Hodges, *New Complete Hoyle*, Toronto, Doubleday, 1956.

109. Morehead, Albert Hodges, *My Secret: How to Play Winning Poker*, Los Angeles, W.R. Mathews and Sons, 1957.

110. Morehead, Albert Hodges, *The Complete Guide to Winning Poker*, New York, Simon and Schuster, 1967.

111. Moss, John (pseud. for Jack Potter), *How to Win at Poker*, Doubleday, 1955.

112. Mott, *Street Poker Club*, Dick.

113. Nabot, *Jeu de Poker*, Paris, Henri Gautier, 1893 (contains many probability tables).

114. Pardon, C.F. (Raudon Crawley), *Poker*, London, Chas. Goodhall & Sons, 1889.

115. Percy, Alfred, *Poker: Its Laws and Practice*, Allahabad, India, Pioneer Press, 1879.

116. Phillips, Hubert, *Profitable Poker*, Arco Publications, 1960.

117. Philpots, E. P., *A Treatise on Poker*, London, 1904.

118. *Poker: The Nation's Most Fascinating Card Game*, Cincinnati, United States Playing Card Company, 1950.

119. *Poker*, Heines Publishing Co., Inc., Minneapolis, Minnesota.

120. *Poker, How to Play It*, London, 1882.

121. *Poker Primer*, Platt & Nourse.

122. Potter, Jack, *How to Win at Poker*, Garden City Books, 1955.

123. *Primer*, Excelsior.

124. Proctor, R. A., *Poker Principles and Chance Laws*, New York, Dick & Fitzgerald, 1883.

125. Rander, S. H., *How to Play Poker and Win* (Key), Assoc. Booksellers, 19B5.

126. Reese, Terence, and Watkins, Anthony, *Poker: Game of*

*Skill*, Wehman, 1962.

127. Reynolds, A., *Poker Probabilities Calculated*, Sheffield, 1901.

128. *Rules of Poker*, London, 1882.

129. Sinclair, E., *Poker*, Arco Publications, Ambassador, 1964.

130. Strong, Julian, *How to Play Poker*, London, New York, W. Foulsham, 1928.

131. "Templar," *Poker Manual*, Warne.

132. Welsh, Charles, *Poker: How to Play It*, London, Griffith & Farren, 1882.

133. Virt, L. H., *Traite' Complet du Jeu de Poker*, Paris, 1913 (contains only rules).

## Addendum Bibliography
## of Poker Books Published
### *since 1968*
### *(through 1980)*

134. Anno, James N., *An Encyclopedia of Draw Poker*, New York, Exposition, 1973. Shows mathematical calculations of various poker odds and probabilities. Some errors. Not much value. Interesting history of poker.

135. Anthony, Ross, *Get Rich Playing Poker*, Birmingham, Alabama, RAM Enterprises, 1975. Author is objective and honest. Valid advice for low-stake games with poor players. Good tips for running profitable house games.

136. Brunson, Doyle, *How I Made Over $1,000,000 Playing Poker*, Las Vegas, Nevada, B & G Publishing Co., 1978. A monumental work on public professional poker. Reveals not only the strengths and secrets of the best traditional professionals in public poker, but their flaws and weaknesses that will allow any Advanced-Concept player to beat them.

137. Caro, Mike, *Bobby Baldwin's Winning Poker Secrets*, Las Vegas, Nevada. B & G Publishing Co., 1979. Mainly a fictionalized, biography that is embarrassingly personal and rather ludicrous, but provides a useful list of poker tips for various games.

138. Castle, J. L.. *How Not to Lose at Poker*, Boston, Little,

Brown and Company, 1970. Perpetuates many of the erroneous clichés about poker. Goes deep into probability mathematics. Little value.

139. Dangel, Philip N., *Poker Poker*, Las Vegas, Nevada, Gambler's Book Club, 1977. Little new information. Mainly theoretical and mathematical. An unrealistic approach to poker.

140. Dowling, Allan ("Jack King"), *Play Winning Poker*, Las Vegas, Nevada, Gambler's Book Club, 1974. Good history of poker. Some interesting observations about opponents and table-stake games. But littered with fallacies.

141. Fox, John, *Play Poker, Quit Work, and Sleep Till Noon*, Seal Beach, California, Bacchus Press, 1977. Poorly written. Borrows, uses, and distorts various Advanced Concepts of Poker. Contains some original and useful ideas about draw poker in public card clubs. Worthwhile for serious players who can sort the useful information from the misleading material.

142. Gibson, Walter, *Poker Is the Name of the Game*, New York, Barnes & Noble, 1974. Instructions and "rules" for eighteen basic variations of poker. Little new or useful information. Some erroneous concepts.

143. Hamilton, Mark, *Poker Answers*, Las Vegas, Nevada, I & O Publishing Company, 1978. An exclusive interview with Frank R. Wallace. 250 new questions about poker are answered.

144. Jacoby, Oswald, *Penny-Ante and Up*, Garden City, New York, Doubleday & Company, Inc., 1979. Mostly rules for various poker games. Reveals such a naive and faulty understanding of poker that one wonders if someone other than Oswald Jacoby wrote this book.

145. Livingston, A. D., *Poker Strategy and Winning Play*, Philadelphia, J. B. Lippincott Company, 1971. Little new information except for two tables of odds for hold 'em poker.

146. Montgomery, John, *How to Play and Win at Poker*, Santa Barbara, California, Cameron and Cameron Publishers, 1978. Little valuable information. Many erroneous concepts.

147. Percy, George, *7-Card Stud, The Waiting Game*, Las Vegas, Nevada, Gambler's Book Club, 1979. Best primer available for seven-card stud. Well written and adopts many Advanced Concepts that apply to stud. A few errors. Helpful section on casino poker.

148. Preston, Thomas Austin ("Amarillo Slim"), *Play Poker to Win*, New York, Grosset & Dunlap, 1973. Interesting poker anecdotes. Some useful tips about hold 'em and lowball.

149. Rubins, J., *Win at Poker*, New York, Funk & Wagnalls, 1968. Well written, but based on many of the fallacious concepts advanced by other poker books.

150. Scarne, John, *Scarne's Guide to Modern Poker*, New York Simon & Schuster, 1979. Nothing new. Repeats old errors, but still useful to read.

151. Silberstang, Edwin, *Winning Poker Strategy*, New York, David McKay Co., Inc., 1978. The best primer on poker. Few errors. Recommended for all beginners and losers.

152. Sklansky, David, *Hold 'em Poker*, Las Vegas, Nevada, Gambler's Book Club, 1978. The first book to offer detailed information about hold 'em poker. Some errors.

153. Sklansky, David, *Poker Theory*, Las Vegas, Nevada, Gambler's Book Club, 1978. A recasting of certain Advanced Concepts into theoretical forms that are often impractical or flawed. Some value. Interesting game-theory chapter.

154. Sklansky, David, *Sklansky on Razz*, Las Vegas, Nevada, Gambler's Book Club, 1980. Some new and useful information on Razz (seven-card-stud lowball) that is not covered in other books.

155. Smith, Al, *Poker to Win*, Las Vegas, Nevada, Gambler's Book Club, 1975. Good outline of cheating techniques used in poker. But presents many erroneous views about poker.

156. Smith, Brian, *Pineapple Hold 'em*, Las Vegas, Nevada, Gambler's Book Club, 1979. The only book dealing with pineapple hold 'em (players receive three hole cards and then discard one). A valuable book that reflects a good

Book 3
Poker: A Guaranteed Income For Life

understanding of poker.

157. Spanier, David, *Total Poker*, New York, Simon and Schuster, 1977. Mainly history and anecdotes about poker. Devotes a dozen pages to the Advanced Concepts of Poker. Interesting reading, but not a how-to-play book.

158. Taetazsch, L., *Winning Methods of Bluffing and Betting in Poker*, New York, Drake Publishers, 1976. Limited value. Uses some of the Advanced Concepts of Poker.

159. Thackrey, Ted, Jr., *Dealer's Choice*, Chicago, Henry Regnery Co. 1971. Fairly well organized. Some valid ideas about elementary poker strategy. Other ideas are in error.

160. Wagner, W., *To Gamble or Not to Gamble*, New York, World Publishing, 1972. Interesting anecdotes and facts about casino, club, and private poker. Spoiled by unsubstantiated assertions and false conclusions.

161. Wallace. F. R., Hamilton, M. and William S., *Neocheating— The Unbeatable Weapon in Poker, Blackjack, Bridge, and Gin*, Las Vegas, I & O Publishing Company, Inc., 1980. A definitive treatment of Neocheating in poker.

162. Wallace, Frank R., Poker, *A Guaranteed Income for Life by Using the Advanced Concepts of Poker*, Las Vegas, I & O Publishing Company, Inc., 1968-1976. New York, Crown Publishers, Inc., 1977. Warner Books, 1980, paperback.

163. Wallace, Frank R., *An Obituary for the Public Professional Poker Player*, Las Vegas, Nevada, I & O Publishing Company, Inc., 1979. A special report showing how the Advanced-Concept player can bankrupt today's public poker professionals.

164. Wallace, Frank R., *Poker Power*. To be published in 1981.

165. Wallace, Frank R., and Savage, Eric, *Poker Troubleshooting Guide and Answer Book*. To be published in 1980.

166. Winfield, T. D., *If You Are Going to Play Poker . . . Win*, McLean, Virginia, the Kingsway Company, 1971. Some practical information, but laced with fallacious clichÈ's about poker.

167. Zachary, Hugh, *Wild-Card Poker*, Brattleboro, Vermont, Stephen Greene Press, 1975. Recognizes the added skill needed to play wild-card games. Little new information.

Contains erroneous concepts.

168. Zadek, Norman, *Winning Poker Systems*, Englewood Cliffs, New Jersey, Prentice-Hall, 1974. Heavily oriented to a mathematical approach. Interesting and moderately useful, but not a valid approach to poker.
169. Zahrobsky, Robert F., *The Computer Guide to Hold 'em Poker*, Las Vegas, 1979. A misleading emphasis on mathematics. Still worthwhile—some unique and interesting tables of data for hold 'em percentages. Almost nothing on strategy and other crucial aspects of poker.

Notes:

1. The most complete source of poker and gambling books (both in and out of print) is Gambler's Book Club, 630 South 11th Street, Dept. PB, Las Vegas, Nevada 89101. A free catalog listing over 700 titles on poker and gambling is available.

2. The University of Nevada (Las Vegas) library has a special collection of nearly 2000 gaming books, including more than 83 different titles on poker. Many historic poker books were donated by I&O Publishing Company.

Book 3
Poker: A Guaranteed Income For Life

# Appendix C

## GLOSSARY

Over a thousand words and phrases used in poker literature and heard in poker games are defined below. While this is the most comprehensive glossary ever compiled, it provides something much more than a long list of colorful jargon: Reading through the glossary provides unique insights into poker, available nowhere else.

### - A -

A-C Player—The Advanced Concept Player.

Aces Up—A pair of aces with one other pair.

Action—The betting.

Action Spot—The table area where the betting is BAD Agent—A confederate or collusion partner in cheating.

Alien Card—A card not belonging to the deck in play.

Alive Card—See Live Card.

All Blue, or All Pink—A flush.

All-In—The betting by a player of all his money on the table.

All the Way—Cincinnati with a progressive bet.

Alternate Straight—A sequence of every other card, such as two, four, six, eight, ten (Dutch Straight, Skipper, Skip Straight).

Ambique—A French card game that influenced the draw variation of poker.

American Brag—A game where the raiser shows the first caller his hand and the worst hand folds.

Anaconda—A seven-card game with bets made on five rolled-up cards.

317

Announce—To declare high, low, or the moon in high-low poker.

Announced Bet—A verbal bet made by a player before putting his money in the pot.

Ante—Money put in the pot before dealing.

A Priori Odds—The probability that an event will occur.

Arkansas Flush—A four flush.

Around the Comer Straight— A sequence running from the highest to the lowest values, such as queen, king, ace, two, three.

Âs Nâs—A Persian card game from which poker was directly derived.

Assigned Bettor—The player who bets first.

Australian Poker—Draw poker with a blind opening.

Automatic Bluff—A lowball situation that almost always requires a bluff.

## - B -

Baby—A small card, usually a five or less.

Back-in—To win by default or unexpectedly.

Backer—A nonplayer who finances an active player.

Backraise—A reraise. To make a minimum raise to avoid a larger raise.

Back-to-back—A pair on the first two cards dealt in stud (Backed Up).

Bait—A small bet that encourages a raise.

Bank—Where the money from purchased chips is kept.

Banker—The person responsible for selling and cashing chips.

Bank Night—High-low five-card stud with two twists.

Barn—A full house.

Barracuda—A tough player.

Baseball—A stud game involving nines and threes as wild cards.

Beans—Chips.

Bear—A tight player.

Beat the Board (Table)—To have a hand better than all others showing.

Beat Your Neighbor—A five-card game that requires each player in turn to expose his cards until his hand beats the board.

Bedsprings—Similar to Cincinnati except ten cards are dealt face-up for use in everyone's hand.

Belly-Buster Straight—An inside straight.

Belly Hit—When a draw fills an inside straight (Gut Shot).

Belly Strippers—Cards with slightly trimmed edges that taper from a wider center to the ends (Humps).

Best Flush—A game in which only flushes win the pot.

Bet Into—To bet before another player who apparently has a better hand.

Bet or Get—A rule that one must either bet or fold with no checking allowed (Bet or Drop, Passout).

Bet the Limit—To bet the maximum amount allowed.

Bet the Pot—To bet an amount equal to the pot.

Bet the Raise—The maximum bet being twice that of the previous bet or raise.

Betting Interval—The period from the first bet to the last call in any given round.

Betting Pace—The degree, extent, and aggressiveness of bets and raises.

Betting Stakes—The dollar limits of all bets and raises permitted.

Betting Ratios—The differences in maximum bets allowed with each round of betting.

Betty Hutton—Seven-card stud with nines and fives wild.

Bicycle—A straight to the five . . . ace, two, three, four, five (Wheel).

Bid—To declare for high or low in split-pot poker.

Big Bill—A hundred dollars or a thousand dollars.

Big Blind—The final and largest blind bet.

Big Bobtail—A four-card straight flush.

Big Cat—Five unpaired cards from the king to the eight.

Big Dog—(1) Five unpaired cards from ace to nine. (2) A big underdog.

Big Full—The highest possible full house.

Big One—A thousand dollars.

Big Squeeze—Six-card high-low stud with one twist.

Big Tiger—See Big Cat.

Bill—A dollar or a hundred dollars.

Bird Dog—One who gets players for a game.

Blaze—A five-card hand containing five picture cards.

Blaze Full—A full house in picture cards.

Bleed—To slowly bleed money from a game or a player.

Bleeder—A tight, winning player.

Blind—A mandatory or forced bet before the deal by the first player to the dealer's left.

Blind Bet—To bet before looking at one's hand,

Blind Low—Five-card stud bet blind all the way to the last bet.

Blind Open—An opening bet made without looking at one's cards.

Blind Shuffle—A cheater's shuffle used to stack cards or to leave stacked cards undisturbed after shuffling (False Shuffle).

Blind Tiger—Draw poker with a blind open and a blind raise (Open Blind and Straddle).

Block System—An ante, open, and first raise automatically done in the blind by the dealer.

Blood Poker—A higher-stake poker game played primarily for money rather than for social reasons.

Blow Back—A raise after previously calling or checking.

Bluff—The attempt to win a pot by making better hands fold.

Blur Intensity—The lightness or darkness of printing visible on partially flashed cards, indicating a high or a low card.

Board—(1) The poker table. (2) All face-up cards in stud or hold 'em.

Bobtail Flush or Straight—A four-card flush or a four-card, open-end straight.

Bolt—To fold.

Bone—A white chip, the lowest denomination chip.

Bonus—A fixed sum established by house rules that is paid by each player to the holder of a very high-value hand

such as a straight flush (Premium, Royalty, Penalties).

Book—A three-card draw.

Boost—To raise.

Border Work—Markings added by cheaters to the printed borderlines of cards to identify their value.

Bottom Deal—To deal cards off the bottom of the deck when cheating.

Bouillotte—A French card game that influenced the open-card stud variation in poker.

Boxed Card—A card turned the wrong way in a deck.

Boy—A jack.

Brag—The betting expression in the English game of Bragg.

Bragg—An English three-card game that influenced the use of the full fifty-two-card deck in poker.

Braggers—Jacks and nines as wild cards. Or the ace of diamonds, the jack of clubs, and the nine of diamonds as wild cards.

Brandeln—A card game similar to Commerce.

Breakers—Openers.

Breathe—To pass the first opportunities to bet.

Brelen—(1) A French card game that influenced the use of straights and flushes in poker. (2) Three of a kind.

Brelen Carre—Four of a kind.

Brief—A single stripper card in a deck used to facilitate illegal cuts.

Buck—(1) A marker used to designate the dealer. (2) A marker or a knife used to designate the player permitted to deal a special hand, usually a hand with a dealer advantage such as draw. (3) A dollar.

Buddy Poker—To avoid betting against a friend or a partner.

Buffalo—To fool opponents.

Bug—(1) The joker used in high-hand poker as an ace or as a wild card for filling straights and flushes. A wild card in lowball. Can be used in high-low as both a high card and a low card in the same hand (Joker). (2) A device fastened beneath the poker table by a cheater to hold out a card or cards.

Bull—A player who raises frequently.

Bull or Bullet—An ace.

Bull Montana—Five-card stud with betting, then jacks required to open the final bet.

Bull the Game—To bluff or bet aggressively.

Bump—A raise.

Buried Card—A card randomly inserted in the deck.

Burn—(1) A full house. (2) To lose a hand. (3) Deal a burn card.

Burned, Burnt, or Burn Card—(1) An exposed card put face-up on the bottom of the deck (2) A card dealt face down into the discards.

Busted Hand—(1) A worthless hand (Bust). (2) A hand that failed to fill a straight or a flush on the draw.

Busy Card—Any card that completes a hand.

Butcher Boy—An open-hand form of poker where four of a kind is needed to win.

Button—(1) A marker used to signify a theoretical dealer when there is a house dealer. (2) A second or third pair.

Buy—(1) To call bets in order to draw cards. (2) To bluff someone out.

Buy In—The stack of chips that a player buys at the start of a game.

By Me—An expression meaning to pass or check.

# - C -

California—Draw poker, open on anything.

California Lowball—Low-ball in which ace, two, three, four, five is the best hand.

Call—Money put in the pot to match a bet or raise.

321

Calling Station—A player who calls almost any bet (Telephone Booth).

Carding—Noting of exposed cards during a hand.

Card Odds—The probabilities of being dealt or drawing to various hands

Cardsharp—A cheater.

Cards Speak—A rule that the value of a hand is based on what the cards are rather than on what a player declares.

Case Card—The last available card of a particular value or suit.

Cash In—To exchange poker chips for cash and then to quit (Cash Out).

Casino Poker—Public poker played in gambling casinos.

Cat—Any big or little tiger or cat hand.

Catbird Seat—A position in high-low poker that assures a player at least half the pot.

Catch—To be dealt a certain card or hand ... usually a desirable card or hand.

Chalk Hand—An almost certain winner.

Chase—To stay against a better hand.

Cheater—A player who intentionally violates the rules to gain advantage unavailable to others.

Check—To pass without betting.

Check Blind (Check in the Dark)—To check without looking at one's own cards.

Check Cop—A paste palmed in a cheater's hand and used to steal poker chips or to hold out cards.

Check Copping—To steal poker chips.

Check Raise—To check and then subsequently raise in the same round of betting.

Chicago—Seven-card stud in which the hand with the highest spade wins half the pot.

Chicago Pelter—A kilter.

Chicken Picken—A game with eleven cards—two cards in hand and nine on the table in rows of three.

Chink Ink—A special ink used by cheaters to mark the edge of cards.

Chip—Money represented by a plastic disc.

Chip Along—To bet the smallest amount possible.

Chip Declaration—To use chips in declaring for high or low.

Chip In—To call a small bet.

Chipping—Betting.

Choice Pots—Dealer's choice.

Cinch Hand—A certain winner (A Lock, an Immortal).

Cincinnati—A ten-card game with five in each hand and five face-up for everyone's use (Lame Brains).

322

Cincinnati Liz—Like Cincinnati, except the lowest face-up card is wild.

Clam—A dollar.

Class—Rank of a poker hand.

Closed Card—A concealed card in one's hand.

Closed Game—A game barred to newcomers or outsiders.

Closed Hand—The concealed cards in one's hand as in draw poker.

Closed Poker—Any form of poker in which all cards are dealt face-down.

Close to the Chest—To play tight (Close to the Belly).

Club Poker—Poker played in public card clubs. (See Gardena, California.)

C-Note—A hundred-dollar bill.

Coffee Housing—To act oppositely to one's emotions or situation.

Cold Deck—(1) A deck from which poor hands are being dealt. (2) A prestacked deck.

Cold Feet—A description for a player wanting to quit the game early.

Cold Hands—(1) Showdown hands. (2) A run of poor hands.

Cold Turkey—A pair of kings, back to back, on the first two cards in five-card stud.

Collection or Axe—See Time Cut.

Collusion—Two or more players working together to cheat other players.

Come—See On the Come.

Come In—To call.

Come Off—To break up a lower-value hand to draw for a higher-value hand.

Commerce—A three-card game with three cards in the widow.

Common Card (Communal Card)—An exposed card for use in every player's hand.

Consecutive Declaration—A rule for declaring high-low hands in consecutive order.

Contract—To declare for high or low at the conclusion of split-pot poker.

Contract Poker—High-low split-pot poker with oral declarations.

Cop—To steal chips from the pot.

Corner Card—An eight-card game—five cards in hand and three on the table, with the last card up and all like it as wild.

Corner Flash—To tear off a corner of a foreign card and to flash it as a real card in one's hand.

Cosmetics—Preparations such as ashes, waxes, abrasives, aniline pencils, and luminous inks used by cheaters for marking cards (Daub).

Counter—(1) One chip. (2) A

323

player who continuously counts his chips.

Count Cards—The jack, king, and queen (Court Cards, Face Cards, Picture Cards).

Coup—A brilliant play.

Cowboy—A king.

Crank—To deal.

Crazy Otto—Five-card stud with the lowest card as wild.

Crimp (Bridge)—To bend and hump the upper or lower section of the deck to make a false or an illegal cut. (See Debone)

Crisscross—Same as Southern Cross except five cards are laid out with the center one wild.

Crooked-Honest System (C-H System)—The system of two cheaters in partnership: One catches a strong hand, and he signals the other to raise, thus squeezing all callers (Cross Life, Crossfire).

Cross (The Cross)—Like Cincinnati, except the five cards are in a cross formation with the center card and all similar cards as wild.

Crosscards—A ten-hand poker solitaire game (Patience Poker).

Crossfire—See Crooked-Honest System.

Crossover—A combination of draw and stud poker involving wild cards.

Cull—To arrange or cluster good cards together for cheating.

Curfew—The agreed-upon quitting lime.

Curse of Mexico—The deuce of spades.

Curse of Scotland—The nine of diamonds.

Customer—An opponent who calls.

Cut the Cards—Putting the bottom cards of a deck on top of the deck.

Cut the Pot—Money withdrawn from pots for a purpose, such as to pay for refreshments.

- **D** -

Dame—A queen.

Daub—See Cosmetics (Golden Glow brand).

Dark Bet—A blind bet.

Dead Cards—Discarded or folded cards.

Dead Hand—A foul hand that cannot be played.

Dead Man's Hand—Usually aces and eights, two pair. Sometimes aces and eights, full house ... or jacks and eights, two pair.

Deadwood—Dead cards.

Deal—To distribute cards to the players.

Dealer—(1) A person who deals

324

the cards. (2) The operator of a gambling game in a casino.

Dealer-Advantage Game— Any game where the dealer has an advantage.

Dealer's Choice—The selection by dealer of game to be played.

Dealer's Percentage—Any game offering the dealer a significant advantage (Dealer's Game, Dealer's Advantage).

Deal Off—To deal the final hand of the game.

Deal Out—To omit a player from a hand.

Debone—A card or portion of a deck that has been crimped lengthwise or crosswise.

Deception—An important and accepted tool of poker.

Deck—All the cards used in the game (Pack)

Declare—To announce if going for high or low.

Deep Low—The lowest hand for any card (i.e., a deep seven is an ace, two, three, four, seven).

Defensive Bet—A bet designed to decrease one's potential loss.

Dent—To mark cards by creasing their corners (Rounding).

Deuce—A two.

Deuces Wild—Playing all deuces as wild cards.

Devil's Bedposts—A four of clubs.

Diamond—See Poker Diamond.

Dig—To replenish one's stake or money while playing a hand.

Discard—To exchange old cards for new cards during the draw or twist.

Disproportionate Bet—A peculiar bet or a bet much larger or smaller than the normal bet.

Doctor Pepper—Seven-card stud with deuces, fours, and tens wild.

Dog—(1) Any big-dog or little-dog hand. (2) An underdog.

Doghouse Cut—Any cut that divides the deck into more than two stacks.

Double—To raise.

Double-Barreled Shotgun— High-low draw with four rounds of betting after the draw as each card is turned face-up (Texas Tech).

Double Bluff—A bluff made by making a bluff bet on the final round and then reraising a subsequent raise.

Double-End Straight—See Bobtail.

Double Header—(1) A pot not won that passes to the next deal. (2) A second game that follows an earlier one.

Doubling Up—Betting twice as much as the previous bet.

Down and Dirty—The final hole card dealt in seven-card stud.

Down Cards—Cards dealt face-down.

Down the Chute—To take a heavy loss.

Down the River—Seven-card stud.

Drag (Snatch)—Money separated from a pot to signify the amount owed by a player (Light).

Draw—The exchange of a card or cards for new ones.

Draw Out—To catch the winning hand with the last card or with draw cards.

Draw Poker—One of the two basic forms of poker (the other is stud). Played as a closed five-card hand with a closed draw.

Drawing Dead—Drawing a hand that cannot win.

Drib—An inferior player.

Driller—A loose player. A player who bets and raises frequently.

Driver's Seat—The player holding the best advantage.

Drop or Drop Out—To retire from a hand by not calling a bet or raise (Fold).

Drum—To play tight.

Drummer or Drummer Boy— A tight player.

Dry—To be out of money (Broke).

DTC Method—The technique of good poker . . . Discipline, Thought. and then Control.

Duck—A deuce.

Duffer—An inexperienced or poor player.

Duke—A hand of cards.

Dutch Straight—See Alternate Straight.

Dynamite—A two-card poker game.

## - E -

Eagles—The cards of a fifth suit in a sixty-five-card deck.

Early Bet—A small bet after the first card in stud or the first two cards in draw.

Edge—(1) An advantageous position. (2) The dealer or sometimes the Age.

Edge Odds—The advantage or disadvantage of a player relative to all other players.

Edge Shot—A bet made from an advantageous position.

Eldest Hand—The first player to the dealer's left.

Elimination—Like Cincinnati, but cards matched with table cards are discarded (Weary Willie).

End Bet—The last bet of an interval.

End Bets—Last-round bets.

326

End Strippers—Cards tapered along the ends for cheating.

English Poker—Draw played with a blind opening.

English Stud—A stud game with a draw.

Ethics or Etiquette—The understandings and courtesies of which violations do not constitute cheating.

Exposed Cards—Cards purposely dealt face-up as in stud.

## - F -

Face Card—Any picture card.

Faced—(1) A face-up card. (2) To receive a face card.

Fall of the Cards—The order in which cards are dealt.

False Cut—A cheater's cut in which the stacked portion of the deck remains intact on top of the deck.

False Openers—A hand that has been opened improperly.

False Riffle—A cheater's riffle used to keep stacked cards undisturbed after riffling.

False Shuffle—See Blind Shuffle.

Family Pot—A pot in which everyone calls the bet.

Farm System—Several poker games at different stakes under control of a good player.

Fast Game—A game with a fast betting pace.

Fatten—To increase the money in the pot (Sweeten).

Feeble Phoebe—Like Hollywood, except table cards are turned over two at a time and played for high and low.

Feed the Pot—To bet or raise foolishly.

Feeler Bet—A small or nominal bet made to seek out strength or raising tendencies of opponents.

Fever—A five.

Filling—Drawing and then catching a full house, flush, or straight.

Fin—Five dollars.

Finger Poker—A game run on credit.

Finn Poker—To play poker with the objective of winning maximum money.

First Jack Deals—A method to determine who has the first deal.

First Hand—The first player allowed to bet a hand.

Fish—An easy or a poor player.

Fish Hook—A seven or a jack.

Five and Dime—A hand containing a five and a ten with three unpaired cards in between.

Five-Card Stud—Stud poker played with one hole card and four exposed cards.

Five of a Kind—Five cards of the same value.

Fix—To prearrange the cards or stack the deck.

Fixed Limit—Betting with agreed-upon limits or maximums.

Flash—(1) To expose concealed cards (2) To turn up a common card for everyone's use when insufficient cards are available to complete a stud game. (3) Five cards, one of each suit plus the joker.

Flat Limit—A game in which only one consistent amount is allowed for all bets and raises.

Flat Poker—Poker with a blind open.

Flicker Flicker—Five-card, high-low stud.

Flinger—A wild or crazy player.

Flip Stud—Five-card stud in which the optional hole card and matching hole cards are wild.

Floorman—(1) A cardroom manager. (2) Shift boss in a casino.

Flop—The first three exposed cards in hold 'em poker.

Flush—Five cards of the same suit.

Fluss (Flux]—A flush.

Foiling the Cut—A cheater's method of returning cards to their original position after a cut.

Fold—To drop out of a hand by not calling the bet or raise (Drop).

Football—A stud game similar to baseball involving sixes and threes as wild cards.

Force-in—A mandatory blind bet, usually with an option to raise.

Foul Hand—A hand containing the wrong number of cards.

Four Flush—Four cards of the same suit.

Four-Flusher—(1) A cheater. (2) One who tries to win pots by purposely miscalling his hand.

Four Forty Four—Eight-card stud with fours wild.

Four of a Kind—Four cards of the same value (Fours).

Fox—an expert player.

Freak—A joker or a wild card.

Freak Hands—Nonstandard poker hands such as Blazers, Dutch Straights, Kilters, and Skeets.

Free Ride—Playing without paying.

Free Roll—A lock on half the pot with a chance to win the whole pot.

Free Wheeler—A bankrupt player allowed to play free until he wins a pot.

Freeze Out—A rule requiring player to leave the game after losing a certain amount of cash.

Freezer—A call for less than the amount of the bet in table stakes (Short Call).

Friend—A card that improves a hand.

Full House, Full Barn, or Full Tub—Three of a kind with another pair (Full Hand).

Fundamental Position—The value of a player's hand relative to the other player's hands.

Fuzzing—Mixing the cards by continuously stripping off the top and bottom cards (Milking, Snowing Cards).

# - G -

Gaff—A cheater's device or technique.

Gallery—Nonplaying spectators.

Gambler—A player who wagers money at unfavorable edge odds.

Gambler's Last Charge—A game played with five hand cards and five table cards with the last card turned up being wild when matched in one's hand (If).

Gambling—Betting money at unfavorable investment and edge odds.

Game Behavior—Artificial behavior used in a poker game.

Game Pace—Betting done on various hands compared to betting normally done on those hands.

Gang Cheating—Two or more players cheating in collusion.

Gap—The missing space (card) required to fill a straight.

Garbage—The discards.

Gardena, California—The Mecca for public club poker.

Gardena Razz—See Razz (2).

Ge—A pair.

Ghost Hand—A hand that reappears on the next deal because of inadequate shuffling.

Giant Twist—A twist allowing the exchange of up to all of one's cards.

Gilet (Gillet or Gile)—An old French card game that was the predecessor of Brelan.

Gimmick—See Gaff.

Girl—A queen.

Gi-Till-Satisfy—Unlimited giant twisting with progressively increasing costs for new cards.

Gleek—{1) Three of a kind. (2) An early English card game.

Go—To start dealing.

Go All In—To bet all of one's money in table stakes.

Going Better—A raise.

Going In—A call.

Golden Chairs—Player with four held cards and three table cards with one's low card sometimes played as wild.

Golden Glow—A superior brand of daub. (See Cosmetics.)

Good Hand—A winning hand.

Good Player—A player who extracts maximum money from the game.

Go Out—To drop.

Grand—A thousand dollars.

Gravy—One's winnings.

Greek—A cardsharp (Grec).

Greek Bottom—The second card from the bottom dealt by a dishonest player.

Grifter—A cheater.

Gut Shot—See Belly Hit.

Guts to Open—To allow any value hand to open.

## - H -

Half-Pot Limit—A betting limit equal to half the size of the pot.

Hand—The cards dealt to a player.

Hand Cards—Concealed cards that are dealt face-down.

Hand Pace—The extent of betting, calling, raising, and bluffing compared to the size of the pot.

Head to Head—Two people playing poker.

Heavy—A pot with too much money.

Hedge Bet—A side bet to limit possible losses.

Heeler—A kicker.

Heinz—Seven-card stud with fives and sevens wild and also penalty cards.

Help—To improve a hand on receiving additional cards in stud or draw poker.

Hidden Declarations—A rule for declaring high-low hands by concealing different color chips in one's hand.

Highball—Poker in which the highest hand wins.

High-Low—A game in which the highest and lowest hands split the pot.

High Spade in Hole—Seven-card stud in which the hand with the high spade in the hole divides the pot with the high hand.

Hilo Pocalo—Five-card stud in which the up cards can be refused and passed to the player on the left (Take It or Leave It).

Hit—A draw or catch that improves one's hand.

Hokum—A stud variation providing an option to receive cards face-up or face-down.

Hold 'em (Hold Me Darling)—A seven-card game with two face-down cards for each player and five face-up cards for everyone's use (Tennessee Hold Me, Texas Hold 'em).

Hold Out—To cheat by concealing a card or cards for future use.

Hold Out Device—A mechanical device used by cheaters to hold out a card or cards (See Bug, Lizard, Spider).

Hole Cards—Cards dealt face-down in stud.

Hole-Card Stud—Five-card stud in which betting starts on the first hole card.

Hollywood—Fifteen-card Cincinnati with five in each hand and ten table cards.

Holy City—A big hand, usually with aces and picture cards.

Honest Readers—The normal marks or irregularities on any deck of cards.

Honor Card—A ten or higher value card.

Hook—A jack.

Hot Deck—A deck from which good hands are being dealt.

Hot Hands—A run of high-value hands.

Hot Pot—A special pot, usually played for higher stakes (Pistol Stud).

Hot Streak—A run of good "luck" or winning hands (Spinner).

House—A person or organization running a poker game for profit.

House Cut—The amount cut from pots for the house, club, or casino.

House Game—A poker game in which admission is charged or the pots are cut for the

host's profit. Considered illegal in most states.

House Rules—Rules, especially betting, agreed upon by the players.

Hoyles—Any accepted rules for card games.

Humps—See Belly Strippers.

Hurricane—Two-card poker.

# - I -

Ice—A cold deck.

Ideal Edge Odds—The theoretical maximum edge odds, which are impossible to achieve.

Idle Card—A card that adds no value to a hand.

"If"—See Gambler's Last Charge.

Ignorant End of a Straight—The lowest end of a straight, especially in Hold 'em.

Immortal—(1) The best possible hand. (2) A certain winner.

Improve—To draw cards that improve one's hand.

In—To remain in the pot.

In Action—The time when a player is involved in playing his hand.

In a Row (Line)—A sequence or a straight.

Index—(1) The number or letter printed on the corners of cards. (2) The marks a cheater puts on the edge of cards.

Indirect Bet—An opponent betting or raising for a player sandbagging a strong hand.

Inside Straight—A broken sequence of four cards, such as three, five, six, seven.

Insurance—A side bet to ensure winning some money in a large pot.

Intentional Flashing—Purposely flashing or showing one's closed cards to an opponent.

In the Hole—Cards dealt face-down in stud poker.

In the Middle—The position of the players calling bets between two raising players (Middle Man).

Investment Odds—The estimated returns on betting investments.

Iron Duke—An unbeatable hand (Ironclad Hand).

# - J -

Jack and Back—Jackpot poker that reverts to low-ball if no one opens (Jack and Reverse, Jacks Back, Jackson).

Jackpots—See Jacks to Open.

Jacks to Open—Draw poker in which jacks or better are required to open (Jackpots).

Jack Up—To raise.

Jam—A hand in which several players are raising each other.

Jinx—A curse of bad luck.

Jog—An unevenly stacked deck used by a cheater to mark where his partner should cut the deck (Step).

John, Jake, J-Boy—A jack.

Joker—The 53rd card added to a deck (See Bug).

Joker Poker—Poker played with the joker as wild.

Jonah—An unlucky player.

# - K -

Kankakee—Seven-card stud with the joker as wild.

K-Boy—A king.

Key Card—An important card needed to complete a hand.

Key Player—A player with important influence over the game.

Kibitzer—A commenting spectator.

Kicker—An extra card held with a pair, trips, or four of a kind during the draw or twist.

Kick-it—To bump or raise the pot.

Killing It—Taking the final raise allowed.

Kilter—A five-card hand starting with the ace and alternating values to the nine.

King without the Mustache—The king of hearts as wild.

Kitty—Money cut from pots.

Knave—A jack.

Knock—To check or pass by rapping the table.

Knock Poker—Draw poker with rummy drawing.

Ku Klux Klan—Three kings.

# - L -

Laddie—A fellow poker player.

Lady—A queen.

Lalapolooze—A freak hand allowed to win only once a night.

Lame Brain Pete—Same as Cincinnati, except the lowest exposed card and all cards like it are wild.

Lame Brains—See Cincinnati.

Las Vegas Riffle—A faster, more concealed method of riffling cards. At times used for cheating.

Lay Down—The revealing of hands after the last bet.

Lay Odds—To offer a larger bet against a smaller bet.

Lead—To make the first bet.

Leader—The player who is betting first.

Lid—The top card or the card of a single-card draw.

Light—Money separated from a pot to signify the amount owed by a player.

Limit—The maximum bet or raise allowed.

Limit Stakes—Poker with maximum bets and raises established by the house rules.

Limp In—The calling of a bet.

Little Blind—The first and smallest blind bet.

Little Bobtail—A three-card straight flush.

Little Cat—Five unpaired cards from the eight to the three.

Little Dog—Five unpaired cards from the seven to the two.

Little Squeeze—Five-card high-low stud with a twist.

Little Tiger—See Little Cat.

Little Virginia—Six-card stud with one's low hole card as wild.

Live Blind—A blind bettor with an option to raise.

Live Card—A card that has not been dealt or exposed.

Live Hand—A hand with a good chance to improve.

Lizard—A hold-out device that works up and down a cheater's sleeve.

Lock—A hand that cannot lose.

Long Studs—Stud poker with more than five cards dealt to each player.

Look—To call.

Looking Down One's Throat—Having an unbeatable hand against an opponent.

Lowball—Poker in which the lowest hand wins, and five, four, three, two, ace is the perfect low.

Low Hole—A stud game in which one's lowest hole card and all matching cards are wild.

Low Poker—Poker in which the lowest hand wins, and seven, five, four, three, two is the perfect low.

Luck—An illusion of winning or losing beyond statistical reality.

Luck Out—To outdraw and beat a good hand.

Luminous Readers—Cards marked by cheaters with a special ink so the markings can be seen through special lenses or glasses (See Pink Eye).

# - M -

Ma Ferguson—Five-card stud with the low card on board and all like cards as wild.

Main Pot—The first pot apart from side pots.

Major Hand—A straight or better.

Major-League Game—The largest-stake game of several poker games.

Make Good—To pay money owed to the pot.

Make the Pack—To shuffle and prepare the cards for dealing.

Marked Cards—Cards with inconspicuous markings that enable cheaters to read them from the back side.

Marker—(1) See Buck. (2) A promissory note.

Matching Card—A card of the same value or suit as another card.

Match It—Five-card stud with one's hole card becoming wild if matched by an up card.

Match the Pot—To put in the pot an amount equal to that already there.

Mate—A card that matches or pairs another card.

Maximum-Win Approach—A playing strategy that directs all effort toward winning maximum money.

Mechanic—A dishonest dealer who cheats by manipulating the cards.

Mechanic's Grip—A special way to hold a deck for dishonest dealing.

Meet a Bet—To call the full bet.

Mexican Stud—Five-card stud in which cards are dealt down, and the player has an option to choose his hole card.

Mickey Mouse—A worthless hand.

Middle Dealer—A cheater who can deal cards from the middle of the deck.

Middle Man—See In the Middle.

Milker—A tight player.

Milking the Cards—See Fuzzing.

Milking the Game—The slow draining of money from the

game by tight playing.

Minnie—The perfect low hand.

Minor-League Game—A smaller-stake game.

Misdeal—A faulty deal resulting in a redeal.

MisÈre—The English name for low.

Miss—The failure to draw a helpful card.

Mistigris—A wild joker.

Money Flow—The direction, amount, and pattern that money passes among players in a game. Measures the money that can be won or lost per unit of time.

Monkey Flush—A three-card flush.

Monte—A three-card poker game.

Moon—(1) To win both halves of a split-pot game. [2] To declare for both high and low.

Moon Hand—A hand of good high and low value.

Mortgage—Seven-card stud requiring a player to win twice before winning the pot.

Mouth Bet—A bet not backed by money.

Murder—A two-card or a six-card high-low game with several twists.

Mystical Attitude—An irrational, unreasoned attitude.

# - N -

Nailing (Blistering, Indexing, Jagging, Pegging, Punctuating, Pricking)—A cheater's technique to mark cards with his fingernail or a device.

Natural—A hand without wild cards.

Neocheater—A player who wins by Neocheating.

Neocheating—Simple, invisible, highly effective cheating techniques.

New-Breed Player—An Advanced-Concept player in public or casino poker.

New Guinea Stud—Seven-card stud starting with four down cards, followed by turning up or rolling any two cards.

New York Stud—Five-card stud in which a four flush beats a pair.

Nickel-Dime—A small-stake game.

Nigger Bet—An unusual bet such as a $9 bet instead of the normal $10 bet.

Nigger Mike—Six-card draw with a bet on each dealt card.

Nits and Lice—(1) Two pair or a full house of deuces and threes (Mites and Lice). (2) Deuces and threes as wild cards.

No Limit—The allowing of any size bet or raise (Sky's the Limit).

Northern Flight—Seven-card stud with all hearts wild, unless a spade is in the hand.

Nucleus Players—The dependable, regular players.

Nursing—Fondling cards.

Nut—The winnings needed to survive as a professional.

Nuts—A hand that is a certain winner.

## - O -

Objective Attitude—A rational attitude based on reality.

Odds—The chances of getting various hands or cards.

Odds Against—The number of failures per success.

Odds For—The number of attempts per success.

Odds On—Odds at less than even money.

Offensive Bet—A bet designed to build the pot.

Office Hours—A straight from a five to a nine, or from a four to an eight.

Omaha—Seven-card stud with two hole cards in one's hand and five table cards that are rolled up one at a time.

One-End or One-Way Straight— A four-card straight open only on one end, such as

jack, queen, king, ace.

One-Eye Jacks—The jack of hearts and jack of spades as wild cards.

One Eyes—Picture cards with profiles showing only one eye (Jack of Hearts, Jack of Spades, and the King of Diamonds).

On the Come—To bet before one has made a good hand.

On Tilt—Playing very poorly or wildly, usually after losing badly or winning big.

Open—The first bet of the first round.

Open at Both Ends or Open End—A four-card sequence that can be made a straight by two different value cards.

Open Blind—(1) To open without looking at one's cards. (2) A forced open.

Open Blind and Straddle—A forced opening bet followed by a forced raise.

Open Cards—Face-up cards in stud (Up Cards).

Opener—The player who opens the pot.

Openers—A hand with which the betting can be started.

Open Game—A game in which anyone can play.

Open Pair—An exposed pair in stud.

Open Poker—Stud poker.

Open Seat—A chair available

for another player.

Option—Five-card, high-low stud with a twist.

Option Card—(1) A card that may be either kept or exchanged (Twist). (2) A stud card that may be either kept in the hole or exposed.

Original Hand—The cards dealt to a player before the draw.

Outs—A poor hand that can win on the draw.

Overcall—The calling of a big bet after others have called.

Overcard—A card that is higher than any card showing.

Overcards—Cards that rank higher than a pair.

Overhand Shuffle—A shuffle made by sliding cards from the top of the deck into the other hand.

Overhand Stack—An overhand shuffling technique for stacking cards.

## - P -

Pace—See Betting Pace, Game Pace, and Hand Pace.

Pack—The deck of cards.

Packet—A portion of the pack.

Pa Ferguson—Five-card stud with high card on board and all cards like it as wild.

Paint—A face card in a lowball hand.

Pair—Two cards of the same value.

Palmed Card—A card concealed for future use by a cheater.

Pan or Panguingue—A form of rummy played in some Nevada casinos and California poker clubs.

Paperwork—Markings added to cards by cheaters.

Partners—Collusion cheaters.

Pass—To check or drop out instead of betting.

Pass and Out—A game in which checking is not allowed on the first round.

Passed Pot—When no one opens the pot.

Pass-Out—To fold when a bet or a fold is required.

Pass the Deal—To relinquish one's turn to deal.

Pass the Trash (Garbage)—A high-low stud game involving the exchanging of cards among players.

Pasteboard—A card.

Pat Hand—A hand in which the player keeps all his cards without drawing or twisting new cards.

Patience Poker—See Crosscards.

Peeker or Peeper—(1) One who looks at an active player's hand (2) A cheater who peeks at cards yet to be dealt.

Peek Poker—Seven-card stud.

Peep and Turn—See Mexican

Stud.

Pelter (Bracket)—A five-card hand containing a two, five, nine, and one card either a three or a four, and the other card either a six, seven or eight (Skeet).

Penalties—See Bonus.

Penny Ante—A very low-stake game.

Penultimate Card—The next to the last card in the deck.

Percentage—(1) The house cut. (2) Probabilities expressed as percentages.

Perdue—Cards turned down.

Perfect Low—An unbeatable lowball hand, such as ace, two, three, four, five; or ace, two, three, four, six, or two, three, four, five, seven depending on the game.

Philosopher—A cardsharp.

Pick Up Checks—To allow a player to bet or raise the limit for every check made before his play.

Picture Card—A jack, queen, or king.

Pigeon—(1) An easy player or a sucker. (2) A valuable card for a hand.

Pig in the Poke—See Wild Widow.

Pile—A player's money.

Pinch—Five dollars.

Pineapple Hold 'em—A hold 'em variation involving three hole cards and discarding one.

Pink Eye (Red Eye)—A pink-tinted contact lens worn by a cheater to identify marked cards or luminous readers. (See Luminous Readers)

Pips—The spots or marks on the face of a card.

Piranha—An aggressive bettor.

Pistol Stud—See Hole-Card Stud.

Place and Show Tickets Split Pot with Twist Your Neighbor—A game in which cards are drawn from hands of other players and the pot is split between the second and third best hands.

Place Tickets—(1) The second best hand. (2) Draw poker in which the second best hand wins.

Play—To call or stay in

Play Back—To declare a false stake in table stakes.

Played Card—A card dealt to a hand.

Poch—The best pair, three of a kind, or four of a kind.

Pochen—A German card game from which the name poker was partly derived.

Point—The value of a card.

Poker—A money-management game that uses cards for manipulation and deception for winning.

Poker Diamond—A diagram that measures the idealness of a

338

game.

Poker Dice—Cubical dice, each with a nine, ten, jack, queen, king, and ace on its six faces.

Poker Face—A face not showing any emotion or change in expression.

Poker Rules—A loose, flexible framework of traditions for playing poker.

Poker Solitaire—See Crosscards.

Pone—The player on the dealer's right.

Pool—A pot.

Poque—(1) A French card game from which the name of poker was partly derived. (2) A French betting expression.

Position—The relative situation of a player to the other players (Fundamental Position, Seat Position, Technical Position).

Pot—The area in which antes, bets, and raises are placed.

Pothooks—Nines.

Pot Limit—Poker stakes in which the maximum permitted bet is the size of the pot.

Pot-Limit Dig—Pot-Limit poker with no table-stake restrictions.

Poverty Poker—A game in which a player can lose only a predetermined amount, after which he can play with the winners' money.

Powerhouse—A very strong hand.

Premium—See Bonus.

Primero—An old, betting card game of Spanish origin.

Private Poker—Poker played without money being cut for the house or for the host's profit.

Proctor and Gamble—A game with four cards in each hand and three rolled table cards with the last card and all like it as wild.

Progression of Bets—The increase in betting limits for each round of betting.

Progressive Poker—A game in which the ante, bets, and opener requirements increase after a passed pot.

Public Poker—Poker played in gambling casinos or in public card clubs in which the pots are cut for profit.

Pull Through—A false shuffling technique used by cheaters.

Punching—Marking cards with pinpricks.

Punters—Those who gamble against the banker.

Puppy Feet—Clubs.

Puppy Foot—The ace of clubs.

Push—Passing unwanted cards to players on one's left.

Put Up—To pay money owed to the pot.

339

# - Q -

Quadruplets—Four of a kind.

Qualifier—The minimum value hand allowed to win the pot.

Quart—A four-card straight flush.

Quint—A straight flush.

Quint Major—A royal straight flush.

Quitting Time—An agreed-upon time to end a poker game (Curfew).

Quorum—The minimum number of players needed to start a poker game.

# - R -

Rabbit—A weak player.

Rabbit Hunting—Looking through the undealt deck of cards.

Rags—Worthless cards.

Raise—To increase the bet.

Raise Blind—(1) To raise without looking at one's cards. (2) A forced raise.

Rake-Off—Money taken from the pot by the house or casino (Rake).

Rangdoodles—A game in which the betting limit is increased after a very good hand such as four of a kind.

Rank—The relative value of hands.

Rat Holer—A player who pockets his money or winnings during the game.

Razz—(1) Seven-card lowball stud. (2) Draw poker in which the winner of the previous pot bets last (Gardena Razz).

Readable Pattern—A behavior pattern that reveals the value of a player's hand.

Readers—Marked cards.

Redeal—A new deal after a misdeal.

Redskin—A face card.

Rembrandt—Any game in which all face cards are wild.

Reraise—A raise after having been raised.

Rest Farm—An expression for the whereabouts of a player driven from a game because of heavy losses.

Restraddle—The third blind bet that is twice as much as the straddle or the second blind bet.

Restricted Pot—A rule requiring a minimum-value hand to win the pot (Qualifier).

Ribbon Clerk—(1) A player unwilling to play poker at higher stakes or at a faster pace. (2) A small-time gambler.

Rickey de Laet—A form of Mexican Stud in which the player's hole cards and all like them are wild for him.

Ride Along—To remain in a hand because no bets are

340

made.

Ride the Pot—To go light.

Riffle—To flip with the thumb through the edge of a deck.

Riffle Cull—A technique for arranging cards in preparation for stacking the deck.

Riffle Shuffle—To shuffle by riffling the cards together.

Riffle Stack—A technique for stacking the deck.

Right to Bet—A rule allowing every player the right to bet or raise at least once per round regardless of the number of raises during that round.

Ring Game—A full game.

Ring In—Slipping an unfair or stacked deck into play.

Robin Hood Cheater—One who cheats for someone else without benefiting himself.

Roll or Rolled Card (Rolling, Rolling Up)—A face-down table card or cards turned up one at a time, usually with a round of betting after each exposure.

Rolled Up—The first three cards being three of a kind.

Roll Your Own Baseball—Same as baseball, except one of three original hole cards is turned up, and the low hole card and all like it are wild.

Roodles—A round of play at increased stakes

(Wangdoodle).

Rotation—Movement in the direction of the deal ... clockwise.

Rough—The highest lowball hand of a given value, such as seven, six, five, four, three.

Round of Betting—The action sequence in which each player is allowed to check, open, bet, raise, or drop.

Round of Play—The action sequence in which every player deals a poker hand.

Round the World—The same as Cincinnati, except four cards are dealt to each player and four cards are dealt to the widow.

Rounding—See Dent.

Routine—A straight flush.

Rover—One unable to play because the game is full.

Royal—The best possible lowball hand.

Royal Flush—A straight flush to the ace.

Royals—See Eagles.

Royalties—See Bonus.

Rub the Spots Off—To excessively shuffle the cards.

Run—A sequence or a straight.

Run One—An attempt to bluff.

Runt—A hand of mixed suits and no pairs.

Run Up a Hand—To stack a deck during the day, often by culling discards.

Rush—A winning streak.

341

# - S -

Sandbag—(1) To check and then raise the opener. (2) To check or hold back raising to get more money in the pot (Check Raising).

Sanding—A system of marking cards by sanding the edges or ends of cards.

Sawbuck—Ten dollars.

Say—The turn of a player to declare what to do.

Scarne Cut—To cut by pulling cards from the center of the deck and placing them on top of the deck.

Schenck's Rules—First known rules of poker printed in England in 1872.

Schoolboy Draw—An unsound draw.

Scooping—See Shoot the Moon.

Screwy Louie—Similar to Anaconda, except discards are passed to the player on one's left.

Seat Position—The position of a player relative to the other players.

Seat Shot—A bet or raise made from an advantageous seat position.

Second—The second card from the top of the deck being dealt.

Second Best—The best losing hand.

Second Deal—To deal the second card from the top of the deck when cheating.

See—To call in the final round of betting.

Seed—An ace.

Selling a Hand—A strategy to get opponents to call.

Sequence—Cards of consecutive value as in a straight (e.g., four, five, six, seven, eight).

Sequential Declaration—The last bettor or raiser being required to declare his hand in high-low poker.

Session—The period in which a poker game is held.

Set—Three or four of a kind.

Seven-Card Flip—Seven-card stud in which the first four cards are dealt down and then the player turns any two up.

Seven-Card Pete—Seven-card stud with all sevens as wild ... or one's low-hole card (or one's last card) and all like it as wild.

Seven-Card Stud or Seven-Toed Pete—Stud poker played with three hole cards and four exposed cards.

Sevens Rule—A rule in low-ball in which anyone with seven low or better must bet or forfeit further profits from the pot.

Seven-Toed Pete—Seven-card stud.

Sharp, Sharper, or Sharker— A

342

cheater (Cardsharp).

Sharp Top—An ace.

Shifting Sands—The same as Mexican stud except one's hole card and all matching cards are wild.

Shill—A house man or woman who actively plays in the game for the house, club, or casino.

Shiner—A tiny mirror or any reflecting device used by a cheater to see unexposed cards.

Shoe—A device from which cards are dealt.

Shoot the Moon—To declare both high and low in an attempt to win both halves of a high-low pot (Moon, Scooping, Swinging).

Short—Insufficient money or cards (Shy).

Short Call—To call part of a bet in table stakes with all the money one has on the table.

Short Pair—A pair lower than openers, such as a pair of tens in jackpots.

Short Stud—Five-card stud.

Shotgun—Draw poker with extra rounds of betting that start after the third card is dealt.

Shove Them Along—Five-card stud in which each player has the choice to keep his first up card dealt to him or to pass it to the player on his left (Take It or Leave It).

Show—To expose one's cards.

Show Cards—The exposed cards in stud.

Showdown—(1) The showing of cards at the end of a hand. (2) An open hand played for a predetermined amount.

Show Tickets—(1) The third best hand. (2) Draw poker in which the third best hand wins.

Shuffle—To mix the cards prior to dealing.

Shy—See Short.

Side Arms—The second pair of two pair.

Side Bet—Any bet made outside the pot.

Side Cards—Cards that do not influence the value rank of a hand.

Side Money or Side Pot—The amount set aside from the main pot in table stakes.

Side Strippers—Cards tapered along the Sides for cheating.

Sight—To call for a show of hands after tapping out.

Signals—The system that collusion cheaters use to secretly exchange information about their cards and instructions about betting and raising.

Silent Partner—An innocent player used by a cheater as an unwitting partner.

Simultaneous Declaration—

High-low poker in which everyone declares his hand at the same time.

Sixty-six—Six-card stud with sixes wild.

Skeet—See Pelter.

Skeet Flush—A skeet in one suit.

Skin—A dollar.

Skin Game—A game having two or more collusion cheaters.

Skinning the Hand—A cheater's technique to get rid of extra cards.

Skip Straight or Skipper—See Alternate Straight.

Skoon—A dollar.

Sky's the Limit—A game in which no maximum is placed on any bets or raises.

Slicked-Aced Deck—A deck with chemically treated slippery aces that allows a cheater to locate the aces from within a deck.

Slow Play—Passively allowing opponents to bet while holding a strong hand.

Smooth—The lowest lowball hand of a given value, such as seven, four, three, two, ace, for a seven low.

Smooth Call—Making a call with a raising hand.

Snarker—A player who wins a pot and then ridicules the loser.

Snatch Game—A casino or house game in which pots are excessively cut or raked, often covertly.

Snow—To fake or bluff.

Snowing Cards—See Fuzzing.

Sorts—A deck of cards made up of irregular or imperfect cards sorted from many normal decks of cards.

Southern Cross—A variation of Cincinnati with nine up cards arranged in a cross.

Spider—A hold-out device attached to the cheater's coat or vest.

Spike—(1) An ace. (2) A pair in lowball.

Spinner—A winning streak (Hot Streak).

Spit Card—A card turned up that is used in every player's hand.

Spit in the Ocean—A draw game in which an exposed card and all matching cards are wild.

Split Openers—To break up the hand required to open.

Split Pair—A pair in stud with one card in the hole and the other exposed.

Split Pot—A pot equally divided between two winners.

Spot—An ace.

Spot Card—Any card from the deuce to the tell.

Spots—The printed marks on the face side of a card.

Spread—(1) A hand. (2) An

344

illegal exchange of cards between two collusion cheaters.

Squared Deck—An evenly stacked deck ready for cutting or dealing.

Squeeze—To look at cards by slowly spreading them apart (Sweat).

Squeeze Bet or Raise—To bet or raise against another strong hand in order to extract more money from a third player holding a weaker hand.

Squeezed Player—A caller who is being bet into and raised by players on both sides of him (Whipsaw).

Squeezers—Cards with suit and value indicators printed at the corners.

Stack—(1) A pile of chips. (2) To cheat by prearranging cards to be dealt.

Stacked Deck—A deck with prearranged cards for a dishonest deal.

Stake—The money with which a player enters a game.

Stand—To decline a draw.

Stand Pat—To play the original hand without drawing.

Stand-off—A tie.

Stay—To remain in the hand by calling the bet or raise.

Stenographers—Four queens.

Step—See Jog.

Still Pack—The deck not in play

when two decks are used.

Stinger—A sequence.

Stock—(1) The cards remaining in the deck after dealing. (2) The stacked portion of a deck.

Stonewall—One who calls to the end with a poor hand.

Stormy Weather—Similar to Spit in the Ocean, except three cards are dealt in the center.

Straddle—(1) A forced or a compulsory raise (Blind Raise). (2) The right to buy the last-bettor position.

Straight—Five cards in sequence, such as three, four, five, six, seven.

Straight Draw—Draw poker not requiring openers.

Straight Flush—Five cards of the same suit in sequence.

Stranger—A new or unfamiliar card in a hand after the draw.

Streak—A run of winning or losing hands.

String Bet—A hesitating bet made in segments to lure giveaway reactions from other players, especially those on one's left—not allowed in most casinos and poker clubs.

Stringer—A straight.

Stripped Deck—A deck used with certain cards purposely removed, such as the deuces.

Stripper Deck—A dishonest

deck with slightly wedge-shaped cards (usually one thirty-second of an inch tripped off the card's edge or side) allowing the cheater to pull certain cards from the deck. (See Belly Strippers, Side Strippers, End Strippers, Brief.)

Strip Poker—A game in which the loser of each pot must remove an article of clothing.

Stud Poker—One of the two basic forms of poker (the other is draw) and played with open or exposed cards (up cards) and with one or more concealed hole cards (down cards).

Substitution—An exchange of a card for one from the deck (Twist).

Suck—To call when the proper play is to fold.

Sudden Death—High-low five-card stud.

Suicide King—The king of hearts ... the king with a sword pointed at its head.

Suit—Any of the four sets (clubs, diamonds, hearts, and spades) in a deck of cards.

Super Seven-Card Stud—A game starting with five cards to each player; then after discarding two, the game proceeds as in seven-card stud.

Sweeten—To add more money to a pot such as an extra ante.

Swinging—See Shoot the Moon.

## - T -

Table—See Board.

Table Cards—Cards turned face-up on the table for use in everyone's hand, such as used in Cincinnati.

Table Stakes—Stakes in which the betting and raising is limited to the amount of money a player has in front of him.

Take It or Leave It—See Shove Them Along.

Take Out—The number of chips a player starts with in table stakes.

Take the Lead—To make a bet or raise.

Talon—The remainder of the deck after the deal.

Tap—To bet all one's money in table stakes.

Tap City—A player having gone broke in a game.

Tap Out—To bet and lose all one's cash, forcing one to leave the game.

Tap You—(1) An expression for a player betting an amount equal to all the money his opponent has on the table in table stakes. (2) A raise.

Technical Position—The strategic and psychological advantage of a player

346

relative to the other players.

Telephone Booth—A very loose player (Calling Station).

Tells—Characteristics, habits, or actions of a player that give away his hand or intentions.

Tennessee—Draw poker in which a bet is made after each round of cards is dealt.

Tennessee Hold Me—See Hold 'em.

Tens High—Poker in which no hand higher than a pair of tens can win.

Ten Ten—High-low five-card stud with ten for low and a pair of tens for high as qualifiers. Usually played with two twists.

Texas Hold 'em—See Hold 'em.

Texas Special or Texas Tech— See Double-Barreled Shotgun.

The Diamond—A measurement of the idealness of a poker game for the good player.

Thirty Days or Thirty Miles— Three tens.

Thirty Three—Six-card stud with threes wild.

Three-Card Monte—A three-card game similar to Bragg.

Three of a Kind—Three cards of the same value (Treys, Triplets, Trips).

Three-Toed Pete—Three-card poker.

Throat Shot—An expression for a player barely losing a big

pot.

Throw Off—To discard.

Throw Up a Hand—To fold.

Ticket—A card.

Tie—Two hands of equal value. The pot is usually divided between tied hands that win.

Tierce—A three-card straight flush.

Tiger—A low hand from the two to the seven.

Tight Player—A player who seldom bets unless he has a strong hand.

Time Cut—Money charged each player on a time basis by a casino or poker club. Charge is usually on a 3 minute or an hourly basis (Axe, Collection).

Time Game—Poker game in which players are charged by the house, club, or casino a specified amount each hour or half hour for playing privileges.

Toke—A tip, especially to a dealer in a gambling casino.

Top—To beat an opponent.

Tough Player—A superior poker player.

Trey—A three.

Tricon—Three of a kind.

Trio, Triplets, or Trips—Three of a kind.

Trips Eight—Stud or draw split-pot poker with an eight for low and trips for high as qualifiers. Often played with

347

one or two twists.

Tulsa—See Omaha.

Turn—A player's chance to deal, receive cards, or bet.

Turn Down—To fold.

Turnie-Turnie—See Mexican Stud.

Twenty-Deck Poker—Poker played with twenty cards. All cards lower than tens are removed.

Twin Beds—A high-low game involving five cards in each hand and ten turned up on the table.

Twist—A draw in stud or an extra draw in draw poker.

Twist Your Neighbor—To draw cards from the hands of other players.

Two-Card Poker—Any poker game in which the best two cards win.

Two Pair—Two separate pairs of different values in a hand.

Two Pair Nine—Stud or draw split-pot poker with a nine for low and two pair for high as qualifiers. Often played with one or two twists.

Two-Way Hand—A hand having possibilities of winning both high and low halves of a split-pot game.

## - U -

Uncle Doc—Five-card stud with a single spit or table card and all like it as wild.

Undercut—(1) The final down card being the lowest hole card in low-hole stud. (2) A shuffling technique for preparing a stacked deck. Especially useful for preparing two stacked hands simultaneously.

Under the Gun—The position of the first bettor.

Unlimited Poker—Poker in which no limit is placed on bets or raises.

Up—(1) The ace of anteing. (2) The higher of two pair—e.g., queens and tens is queens up.

Up Cards—The face-up cards in stud (Open Cards).

Up the Creek—A game in which split-whiskered kings are wild.

Utah—See Cincinnati.

## - V -

Valet—A jack.

V8 Ford Special—Thirteen-card stud with five cards to each player and eight table cards in a V formation, with one side of the V played for high and the other side played for low.

Vigorish—The amount taken by the house for running a game.

# - W -

Walk the Table—The automatic winning of the entire pot with a certain specific card or hand.

Wash—To Shuffle.

Waving—Coiling or crimping cards by a cheater so the wavy card can be spotted in an opponent's hand or in the deck.

Weary Willie—See Elimination.

Wedges—Certain tapered or shaved cards that can be pulled from a deck when needed by the cheater.

Welcher—A player who fails to pay a debt.

Whangedoodle—A round of jackpots played after a big hand such as four of a kind.

Wheel—See Bicycle.

Whipsaw—To bet and raise aggressively on both sides of a calling player. (Squeezed Player).

Whiskey Poker—Draw poker with widow cards that can be exchanged from one's hand.

Whore—A queen.

Widow—(1) A card or cards common to all hands (Spit Card). (2) The money cut from pots (Kitty).

Wild Annie—See Double-Barreled Shotgun.

Wild Card—A card changeable to any value or suit desired by its holder.

Wild Game—(1) A game using wild cards. (2) A highly spirited or fast-paced game.

Wild Widow—A card turned up for use as a wild card (with all similar cards being wild) in every player's hand (Spit Card).

Window—The card exposed or flashed at the end of a player's closed hand.

Window Dressing—A card purposely flashed from one's closed hand.

Wing—To have a winning streak.

Wired (Back-to-Back)—A pair, trips, or four of a kind dealt consecutively or back-to-back in a hand ... usually in a stud hand starting with the first card.

Woolworth—A game in which all fives and tens are wild.

World Series of Poker—A Hold 'em tournament with a $10,000 buy-in held every May at Binion's Horseshoe Casino in Las Vegas.

# - X -

X Marks the Spot—See Crisscross.

# - Y -

You Roll Two—See New
Guinea Stud.

# - Z -

Z-Game—The lowest-stake
game in the house.

# Appendix D

## POKER ODDS

Appendix D compiles the following card odds:

1. Rank of Hands with Odds
2. Draw Odds
3. Pat-Hand Odds
4. Lowball Odds
5. Hold 'em and Stud Odds

6. Seven-Stud Odds
7. Seven-Stud Catch Odds
8. Two-Pair Odds
9. Wild-Card Odds
10. Comparison of Odds.

Card odds can be calculated and expressed as shown on page 352.

To calculate, for example, the number of three-of-a-kind hands possible *on the deal*, simply divide the deals per pat hand (47) into the total number of hands possible with a 52-card deck (2,598,960). That calculation gives a rounded-off answer of 55,300 possible hands of three of a kind on the deal. The precise answer (as shown in odds table #1 is 54,913 possible hands, which is calculated by using exact figures and not rounding off numbers.

But in calculating the card odds for *drawing* various poker hands (such as tabulated in odds table #2), a special problem arises that makes draw odds reported in all other poker books either inaccurate or imprecise. Furthermore, no practical way exists to give precise draw odds for certain hands. As a result, all the odds in this Appendix were defined and then calculated

## Example of Three-of-a-Kind Odds

| | Deals Per Pat Hand | (52-card deck) Before the Draw | Lower Value Hands per Pat Hand | Odds Against |
|---|---|---|---|---|
| Odds For | 47 | (Starting with 5 cards) | 46 | 46 to 1 |
| 1 in 47 | | | | |

| | Draws per Catch | After the Draw | Misses per Catch | Odds Against |
|---|---|---|---|---|
| Odds For | 8.7 | (Draw 3 cards to a pair) | 7.7 | 7.7 to 1 |
| 1 in 8.7 | | | | |

*Note: All values are rounded at two figures.*

on IBM computers at the University of Delaware. Those calculations provided the only accurately defined and consistently calculated odds in the literature. While certain draw odds are not precise for every situation, all odds provided in this Appendix can be used with confidence since the additional knowledge of the slightly different, precise draw odds would probably never make a meaningful difference for any poker decision.

For those interested in a more detailed explanation of the draw-odds calculations, see the footnote for Poker-Odds Table #2.

Book 3
Poker: A Guaranteed Income For Life

# 1. RANK OF HANDS WITH ODDS
*(highest to lowest)*

| Rank | Hand | Example | Number of Hands Possible |
|---|---|---|---|
| * | Five Aces (with Bug ) | AAAAB | 1+ |
| * | Five of a Kind | 8888W (joker wild) | 13+ |
| * | Five of a Kind (with Wild Card) (deuces wild) | | 672 |
| * | Skeet Flush | 2S 4S 5S 8S 3S | 24 |
| 1 | Royal Straight Flush | 10H JH QH KH AH | 4 |
| 1 | Straight Flush | 4C 5C 6C 7C 8C | 40 |
| 2 | Four Aces | XAAAA | 48 |
| 2 | Four of a Kind | X7777 | 624 |
| * | Big Bobtail | X 8D 9D JD QD | 144 |
| * | Blaze Full | QQKKK | 144 |
| 3 | Full House | 66JJJ | 3,744 |
| 4 | Flush | DDDDD | 5,108 (n.s.) |
| * | Big Tiger (Big Cat) | 8 - - - K | 4,096 (i.f.) |
| * | Little Tiger (Little Cat) | 3 - - - 8 | 4,096 (i.f.) |
| * | Big Dog | 9 - - - A | 4.096 (i.f.) |
| * | Little Dog | 2- - -7 | 4,096 (i.f.) |
| 5 | Straight | 78910J | 10,200 (n.f.) |
| * | Round the Corner Straight | 32AKQ | 3,060 (n.f.) |
| * | Skip Straight (Dutch Straight) | 579JK | 8,120 (n-f.) |
| * | Kilter | A - - - 9 | 35,840 (i.f.) |
| * | Five and Dime | 5 - - -10 | 4,096 |
| * | Skeet (Pelter, Bracket) | 2 - 5 - 9 | 6,144 (i.f.) |
| 6 | Three of a Kind | XX10 10 10 | 54,912 |
| * | Little Bobtail | XX6C 7C 8C | 3,120 |
| * | Flash | HDSCB | 685,464 + |
| * | Blaze | PPPPP | 792 |
| 7 | Two Pair | X3399 | 123,552 |
| * | Four Flush with a Pair | DDD 5D 5 | 34,320 |
| * | Four Flush | XHHH | 111,540 |
| 8 | Pair | XXX88 | 1,098,240 |
| 9 | No Pair (+) | XXXXX | 1,302,540 |
| 9 | Ace High (+) | - - - - A | 502,860 |

| Rank | Hand | Example | Number of Hands Possible |
|------|------|---------|--------------------------|
| 9 | King High (+) | - - - - K | 335,580 |
| 9 | Queen High (+) | - - - - Q | 213,180 |
| 9 | Jack High (+) | - - - - J | 177,500 |
| 9 | Ten High (+) | - - - - 10 | 70,360 |
| 10 | Nine Low (+ +) | - - - - 9 | 71,860 |
| 10 | Eight Low (+ +) | - - - - 8 | 35.840 |
| 10 | Seven Low (+ +) | - - - - 7 | 15,360 |
| 10 | Six Low (+ +) | - - - - 6 | 5,120 |
| 10 | Five Low (+ +) | A2345 | 1,024 |

Total hands possible with a 52-card deck     2,598,960

+ Total hands possible with a 53-card

deck (with a joker)     2,869,685

Code:

    * = Not a normal hand (freak hand)

    B = Bug card (joker)

    W = Wild card

    P = Any picture card

    H = Heart

    D = Diamond

    S = Spade

    C = Club

    A = Ace

    K = King

    Q = Queen

    J = Jack

    X = Any nonpaired side card

    - = A specific nonpaired side card

  (+) = No straights or flushes, ace is high

(+ +) = Including straights and flushes, ace is low

  i.f. = Including flushes,

  n.f. = no flushes,

  n.s. = no straights

Book 3
Poker: A Guaranteed Income For Life

## 2. DRAW ODDS

| Original Hand | Cards Drawn | Final Hand | Approximate* Draws per Catch |
|---|---|---|---|
| Ace | 4 | Two pair or better | 14 |
| Ace-King, same suit | 3 | Two pair or better | 14 |
| Pair | 3 | Any improvement | 4 |
| — | 3 | Two pair | 6 |
| — | 3 | Trips | 9 |
| — | 3 | Full | 100 |
| — | 3 | Four | 380 |
| Two-card flush | 3 | Flush | 100 |
| Pair + kicker | 2 | Any improvement | 4 |
| — | 2 | Two pair | 6 |
| — | 2 | Trips | 13 |
| — | 2 | Full | 125 |
| — | 2 | Four | 1100 |
| Pair + ace | 2 | Aces up | 9 |
| — | 2 | Two pair (lower) | 18 |
| Trips | 2 | Any improvement | 10 |
| — | 2 | Full | 16 |
| — | 2 | Four | 24 |
| Three-card straight flush, double open | 2 | Straight or better | 12 |
| — | 2 | Straight flush | 1100 |
| Three-card straight flush, KQJ or 432 | 2 | Straight or better | 14 |
| Three-card straight flush, AKQ or 32A | 2 | Straight or better | 21 |
| Three-card straight, double open | 2 | Straight | 24 |
| Three-card flush | 2 | Flush | 25 |
| Two pair | 1 | Full | 12 |
| Trips + kicker | 1 | Any improvement | 12 |
| — | 1 | Full | 16 |
| — | 1 | Four | 48 |

| | | | |
|---|---|---|---|
| Four-card straight, open both ends | 1 | Straight | 6 |
| Four-card straight, inside or one end | 1 | Straight | 12 |
| Four-card flush | 1 | Flush | 5 |
| Four-card straight flush, open both ends | 1 | Straight or better | 3 |
| — | 1 | Straight flush | 24 |
| Four-card straight flush, inside or one end | 1 | Straight or better | 4 |
| — | 1 | Straight flush | 48 |

*\* Approximate values rather than precise values must be reported for the following reason: Consider an extreme example — the odds on a four-card draw to an ace. Does one assume a blind draw into a forty-seven-card deck that would give a precise value of 12.8 draws per catch of two pair or better? Or does one assume a draw into a fifty-one-card deck (a deck with one ace missing) that would give a precise value of 15.6 draws per catch of two pair or better? Now a 20 percent difference exists between those two precise values with no basis for selecting one assumption over the other (forty-seven-card deck versus fifty-one-card deck). Furthermore, neither assumption represents the actual situation: The draw is not blind from a forty-seven-card deck, and the draw is not from a fifty-one-card deck. An accurate and precise value is obtained only by defining each of the four discarded cards and then drawing from a forty-seven-card deck. But that would not be practical because a complete table of draw odds to the ace alone would consist of hundreds of thousands of values. All those values do, however, lie somewhere between the values for a blind draw into the forty-seven-card deck and a draw into the fifty-one-card deck. So where necessary, draw odds are calculated at the midway value between the two extreme precise values and then rounded off to a whole number. That is the most practical way to report such draw odds in a consistent and accurately defined manner.*

### 3. PAT-HAND ODDS

#### A. Various Hands

| Hand | Hands Possible | Pat Hands per 200,000 Deals | Deals per Pat Hand | Deals per Pat Hand or Better |
|---|---|---|---|---|
| Royal straight flush | 4 | .15 | 649,740 | 649,740 |
| Straight flush | 36 | 1.4 | 72,193 | 64,974 |
| Four of a kind | 624 | 22 | 4,165 | 3,914 |
| Full house | 3,744 | 144 | 694 | 590 |
| Flush | 5,108 | 196 | 509 | 273 |
| Straight | 10,200 | 392 | 255 | 132 |
| Three of a kind | 54,912 | 2,113 | 47 | 35 |
| Two pair | 123,552 | 4,754 | 21 | 13 |
| One pair | 1,098,240 | 42,257 | 2.4 | 2 |
| No pair | 1,302,540 | 50,118 | 2 | 1 |
| Total | 2,598,960 | 100,000 | — | — |

#### B. High Pairs

| Hand | Hands Possible | Pat Hands per 200,000 Deals | Deals per Pat Hand | Deals per Pat Hand or Better |
|---|---|---|---|---|
| Aces | 84,480 | 3,250 | 31 | 9 |
| Kings | 84,480 | 3,250 | 31 | 7 |
| Queens | 84,480 | 3,250 | 31 | 6 |
| Jacks | 84,480 | 3,250 | 31 | 5 |

358

*Appendices*

## C. Draw Hands to Straights and Flushes

*(Compiled for the Advanced Concepts of Poker
by Michael J. Caro, a leading authority
on draw poker and poker mathematics.)*

| Hand | Hands Possible | Pat Hands per 200,000 Deals | Deals per Pat Hand | Deals per Pat Hand or Better |
|------|------|------|------|------|
| Four-card straight,* any | 325,008 | 12,505 | 8 | — |
| Four-card straight,* inside | 251,136 | 9,663 | 10 | — |
| Four-card straight,* outside | 73,872 | 2,842 | 35 | — |
| Four-card flush* | 105,744 | 4,068 | 25 | — |
| Four-card straight flush* | 5,796 | 223 | 448 | — |
| Three-card straight flush* | 8,064 | 310 | 322 | — |

* Excludes pat hands and higher-value draws.

359

## 4. LOWBALL ODDS

### A. Pat Card Odds on the Deal
*(52-card deck — no joker\*)*

| Highest Card in five cards | Including Straights and Flushes, Ace is Low | No Straights and Flushes, Ace is Low | No Straights and Flushes, Ace is High |
|---|---|---|---|
| | *Pairless Hands Possible* | | |
| Ace | 0 | 0 | 502,860 |
| King | 508,880 | 502,860 | 335,580 |
| Queen | 337,920 | 335,580 | 213,180 |
| Jack | 215,040 | 213,180 | 127,500 |
| Ten | 129,024 | 127,500 | 70,360 |
| Nine | 71,680 | 70,360 | 34,680 |
| Eight | 35,840 | 34,680 | 14,280 |
| Seven | 15,360 | 14,280 | 4,080 |
| Six | 5,120 | 4,080 | 0 |
| Five | 1,024 | 0 | 0 |

### B. Draw Odds
*(52-card deck — no joker\*)*

| Highest Card in four cards | five cards | Including Straights and Flushes, Ace is Low | No Straights and Flushes, Ace is Low | No Straights and Flushes, Ace is High |
|---|---|---|---|---|
| | | *One-Card Draws per Catch* | | |
| Ten | Ten | 2 | 2.03 | 2.45 |
| Nine | Nine | 2.4 | 2.45 | 3.10 |
| Eight | Eight | 3 | 3.10 | 4.30 |
| Seven | Seven | 4 | 4.30 | 7.53 |
| Six | Six | 6 | 7.53 | — |
| Five | Five | 12 | — | — |

360

| Highest Card in | | Including Straights and Flushes, Ace is Low | No Straights and Flushes, Ace is Low | No Straights and Flushes, Ace is High |
|---|---|---|---|---|
| three cards | five cards | Two-Card Draws per Catch | | |
| Eight | Eight | 7.35 | 7.59 | 13.44 |
| Seven | Seven | 12.50 | 13.44 | 30.75 |
| Six | Six | 24.50 | 30.75 | — |
| Five | Five | 73.50 | — | — |

| Highest Card in | | | | |
|---|---|---|---|---|
| two cards | five cards | Three-Card Draws per Catch | | |
| Seven | Seven | 30.63 | 31.91 | 95.15 |
| Six | Six | 76.56 | 95.15 | — |
| Five | Five | 306.25 | — | — |

| Highest Card in | | | | |
|---|---|---|---|---|
| one card | five cards | Four-Card Draws per Catch | | |
| Seven | Seven | 65.08 | 70.02 | 244.96 |
| Six | Six | 195.24 | 244.96 | — |
| Five | Five | 976.17 | — | — |

* For a fifty-three-card deck with a joker, the number of pat hands possible increases by a few percent to several hundred percent, depending on the hand.

## 5. HOLD 'EM AND STUD ODDS

### First Two Cards

| (stud and hold 'em) | Deals per Catch |
|---|---|
| 2 aces | 221 |
| 2 kings, etc. | 221 |
| Any pair | 17 |
| Any hand with a pair or an ace | 5 |
| Ace-king suited | 332 |
| Ace-king not suited | 111 |
| Any two cards suited | 4 |

### First Three Cards (High)

| (7 stud & pineapple hold 'em) | Deals per Catch |
|---|---|
| 3 aces | 5525 |
| 3 kings, etc. | 5525 |
| Any trips | 425 |
| Three straight flush | 86 |
| Three flush | 25 |
| 2 aces | 77 |
| Any pair | 6 |

### First Three Cards (Low)

| (Razz) | Deals per Catch |
|---|---|
| A-2-3 (lowest) | 345 |
| 4 and lower | 86 |
| 5 and lower | 34 |
| 6 and lower | 17 |
| 7 and lower | 10 |
| 8 and lower | 6 |
| 9 and lower | 4 |

## 6. SEVEN-STUD ODDS

| Hand | Hands Possible | Approximate Hands per 100,000 Deals |
|---|---|---|
| Straight flush | 37,444 | 28 |
| Four of a kind | 224,848 | 168 |
| Full house | 3,473,184 | 2,590 |
| Flush | 4,051,784 | 3,030 |
| Straight | 8,466,876 | 6,330 |
| Three of a kind | 6,374,520 | 4,760 |
| Two pair | 30,834,000 | 23,050 |
| One pair | 56,851,296 | 42,500 |
| No pair | 23,470,608 | 17,500 |
| Total Hands | 133,784,560 | |

## 7. SEVEN-STUD CATCH ODDS

*Misses per Catch of a*

| Start With | Straight (outside) | Flush | Full House or Fours |
|---|---|---|---|
| FFX | 66 | 31 | 13 |
| FFXX | 106 | 275 | 19 |
| FFXXX | — | — | 38 |
| FFGG | 53 | 137 | 4 |
| FFGGX | — | — | 7 |
| FFGGXX | — | — | 11 |
| FFF | 4 | 4.5 | 1.5 (11 for fours) |
| FFFX | 8 | 9 | 1.7 |
| FFFXX | 22 | 23 | 2 |
| FFFXXX | — | — | 4 |
| FFFF | 1.5 | 1 | — |
| FFFFX | 2 | 2 | — |
| FFFFXX | 5 | 4 | — |

F or G = a flush, straight (outside) or a paired card.

X = a nonhelping card.

## 8. TWO-PAIR ODDS

| Hand | Hands Possible | Hands Higher | Hands Lower |
|---|---|---|---|
| Aces up | 19,008 | 0 | 104,544 |
| Kings up | 17,424 | 19,008 | 87,120 |
| Queens up | 15,840 | 36,432 | 71,280 |
| Jacks up | 14,256 | 52,272 | 57,024 |
| | | | ...........50% |
| Tens up | 12,672 | 86,528 | 44,352 |
| Nines up | 11,088 | 79,200 | 33,264 |
| Eights up | 9,504 | 90,288 | 23,760 |
| Sevens up | 7,920 | 99,792 | 15,840 |
| Sixes up | 6,336 | 107,712 | 9,504 |
| Fives up | 4,752 | 114,048 | 4,752 |
| Fours up | 3,168 | 118,800 | 1,582 |
| Threes up | 1,584 | 121,968 | 0 |
| Total | 123,552 | — | — |

## 9. WILD-CARD ODDS
*Various Hands*

*Deals to Get on First Five Cards*

| Hand | No Wild Cards | Joker Wild | Deuces Wild | Deuces Wild, Hands Possible |
|---|---|---|---|---|
| Five of a kind | — | 220,745 | 3,868* | 672 |
| Royal straight flush | 649,740 | 119,570 | 5,370 | 484 |
| Straight flush | 72,193 | 14,666 | 575 | 4,072 |
| Four of a kind | 4,165 | 920 | 81* | 30,816 |
| Full house | 694 | 438 | 205 | 12,672 |
| Flush | 509 | 362 | 159 | 13,204 |
| Straight | 255 | 221 | 38 | 66,236 |
| Trips | 47 | 21* | 8* | 355,056 |
| Two pair | 21 | 23 | 27 | 95,040 |

*Deals to Get on First Five Cards*

| Hand | No Wild Cards | Joker Wild | Deuces Wild | Deuces Wild, Hands Possible |
|---|---|---|---|---|
| One pair | 2.4 | 2.4 | 2.4 | 1,222,048 |
| No pair | 2 | 2.2 | 3.4 | 798,660 |
| Total | — | — | — | 2,598,960 |

*\* With deuces wild, five of a kind is easier to get than a straight flush, four of a kind is much easier to get than a flush or a full house, and three of a kind is easier to get than two pair.*

# 10. COMPARISON OF ODDS
## *Various Hands*

No Wild Cards         Joker Wild         Dueces Wild

1,000,000

royal straight flush

five of a kind
royal straight flush

straight flush       100,000

straight flush

royal straight flush     10,000
five of a kind

four of a kind

1,000

full house      four of a kind
flush           straight flush
full house
flush
straight        straight

full house
flush
four of a kind     100

trips                 straight
two pairs    two pairs    two pairs
trips

10

trips

no pair
pair          pair         pair
no pair       no pair

1

*Deals per Pat Hand*

Book Four

# Neocheating

## The Unbeatable Weapon for Poker, Blackjack, Bridge, and Gin

# NEO-TECH I
## The Pre-Discovery

### AN IMPORTANT NOTICE

Do not be concerned or upset by the focus on cards and cheating. Both cards and cheating are used as metaphors to understand the nature of Neocheaters and Neo-Tech.

You are not expected to be knowledgeable or even interested in cards, much less cheating, to make full use of the Neocheating Discovery. In fact, interest in cards and cheating is a time-wasting (although quickly profitable) diversion that prevents full prosperity from Neo-Tech.

If you, as most owners of Neo-Tech, are not interested in cards or cheating, then read only Chapters XII and XIII, Appendix A ("Cheating as a Metaphor"), and Table 5 ("Neocheating Beyond Cards") at the end of the book.

### SYNOPSIS OF THE NEO-TECH DISCOVERY

The Neo-Tech Discovery allows ordinary people to live much more prosperous lives. Anyone can immediately benefit from Neo-Tech. Moreover, the Neo-Tech Discovery debunks "positive thinking," mystical, and other such approaches that lead to nothing.

The uses of the Neo-Tech Discovery range from making anyone unbeatable at cards (even wealthy, if he chooses, as shown in this book), to much more important uses such as gaining power and advantages where it really counts... in business, financial transactions, social relationships (as shown in Neo-Tech Decoded, Book 2), to breaking free of external authorities to gain the greatest possible rewards.

Equally important, Neo-Tech not only protects one from those who cheat others out of the happy, prosperous life they earn, but Neo-Tech transfers the power from external authorities (government, religion, neocheaters, mystics) to one's own self— where the power belongs.

3

# NEOCHEATING
# THE RISING MENACE

*Neocheating—The Unbeatable Weapon
and the
Neo-Tech Discovery
Beyond Cards*

by
Frank R. Wallace

Mark Hamilton

William S.

Neocheating exists as (1) specific techniques and (2) general concepts. The specific *techniques* are based on the safe and invisible Neocheating maneuvers first uncovered by Frank R. Wallace. Those techniques that apply to card games are identified and taught in Part One of this book. The Neocheating techniques are selected for their effectiveness, safety, and subtlety. They have obsoleted all other techniques, such as those described by S.W. Ernase, Scarne, and others. But far more important have been the discovery, development, and understanding of the Neocheating *concepts*. Those concepts unfold in the latter chapters. And with those totally new concepts, the reader can both profitably apply and effectively counter invisible Neocheating not only in card games but in *all* areas of life including business, politics, and social relationships.

5

# THE BAD NEWS

This book reveals something new — something dangerous. This book reveals the lethal techniques of Neocheating.

With Neocheating, the average cardplayer can bankrupt all his opponents. He can safely drain money from any card game, from the easiest Friday-night game to the toughest professional game. And no one will ever see him cheat.

Neocheating is not like classical or traditional cardsharping that requires years of practice or a dangerous reliance on aids such as marked cards and hold-out devices. Neocheating requires no special skills or devices; it requires only the knowledge in this book and a few hours of practice. With less than a day's practice, a player can wipe out his opponents with invisible Neocheating. And with less than a week's practice, he can quit his job to become a full-time professional Neocheater.

Honest players should realize that many cardplayers would cheat if not for (1) their fear of being caught, or for (2) the time and effort required to learn how to cheat effectively. But Neocheating eliminates both deterrents. And as this easy, invisible Neocheating spreads, it will increasingly menace players of poker, blackjack, badge, gin, and all other card games played for money or prestige. ... That is the bad news.

# THE GOOD NEWS

But this book reveals something more — something extraordinary. This book reveals simple defenses and easy counterattacks that nullify or beat all forms of cheating, including Neocheating. The counterattacks are unique, ingenious, and honest. They can be executed in peace and without the knowledge of others.

While cheaters will find a temporary gold mine in this book, honest players with this new knowledge can identify and easily eliminate (without any hassle) all cheaters. Furthermore, this book shows how any player can now, for the first time, casually beat all cheaters from crude amateurs to highly skilled cardsharps — even invisible Neocheaters. And those cheaters will never know what hit them.

As this knowledge spreads, it will increasingly nullify and eventually eliminate cheating not only in poker but in all card games played for money or prestige.... That is the good news.

# PREFACE
# THE NEOCHEATING REVOLUTION

Imagine if simple techniques were available that would enable anyone — after only a few hours of practice — to invisibly relieve cardplayers of all their money. Now imagine if those techniques were available to everyone. What would happen to poker? And what about other card games played for money such as blackjack, bridge, and gin? Would poker and other card games break up and vanish as this effortless and invisible cheating spreads?

Effortless and invisible cheating? Is that only a dream of those seeking easy money and prestige? Well, that dream has come true. The dream is called Neocheating. And this book identifies, illustrates, and teaches Neocheating — clearly and completely.

Neocheating will eventually become known around the world. Cardplayers from the Las Vegas professional to the neighborhood amateur will increasingly use Neocheating. It is contagious and will spread like an epidemic. Yet by simply reading this book, you will have armed yourself with the knowledge needed both to profit from Neocheating and to turn back all threats of the Neocheating revolution.

# FOREWORD BY JOHN FINN

For the first time, good players need to worry about getting wiped out. A new breed of cheater is invading the card tables. He is the Neocheater. And the Neocheater does not lose.

Neocheating is quietly spreading. What will happen when hoards of people using Neocheating invade card games throughout the world? Those people could drain all available money from all players and games. The resulting paranoia and chaos could

7

eventually destroy most card games played for money.

Neocheating is invisible. How can it be stopped? The Neocheater is impossible to catch in the act and hard to get rid of. Indeed, all honest players unaware of Neocheating are in financial danger. Only the readers of this book can prepare themselves for the Neocheating revolution.

# THE 1986 INTERVIEW WITH DR. FRANK R. WALLACE ABOUT NEO-TECH VERSUS NEOCHEATING

A new field of knowledge was discovered by Dr. Frank R. Wallace. For two decades, Dr. Wallace developed a powerful array of integrated knowledge called Neo-Tech. In 1986, Dr. Wallace was interviewed about Neo-Tech. Below is a condensed, edited portion of that interview which explains his early discoveries:

*Q: What is Neo-Tech? How can I benefit from it?*

WALLACE: Neo-Tech is a new, integrated method for capturing major business and personal advantages everywhere. Neo-Tech has nothing to do with positive thinking, religion, or anything mystical. Once a person is exposed to Neo-Tech, he can quietly profit from any situation — anywhere, anytime. He can prosper almost anywhere on earth and succeed under almost any economic or political condition. Neo-Tech applies to all money and power gathering techniques — to all situations involving the transfer of money, business, power, or love

Ironically, I first sensed Neo-Tech through poker — the money game, the international strategy game. Strange how a discovery so important as Neo-Tech started with something so minor and restricted as poker. Indeed, poker is just one rather minute and insignificant area involving the transfer of money in which a person can profit through Neo-Tech.

8

Subsequently, I pursued Neo-Tech beyond cards to uncover far greater advantages in competitive situations involving work, investments, speculating, business, politics, and personal relationships. Neo-Tech applies to all competitive situations: It is a new, quiet approach for collecting unbeatable advantages everywhere.

Neo-Tech has its roots in the constant financial pressures and incentives to develop the easiest, most profitable methods of gaining advantages. Over the decades, successful salesmen, businessmen, politicians, writers, lawyers, entrepreneurs, investors, speculators, gamers, and Casanovas have secretly searched for shortcuts that require little skill yet contain the invisible effectiveness of the most advanced techniques. I identified those shortcuts and honed them into practical formats called Neo-Tech.

*Q: Is Neo-Tech like cheating; is it a metaphor for cardsharps, Don Juans, con artists, dishonest merchants, destructive politicians?*

WALLACE: Definitely not. Neo-Tech is totally honest and ethical; it is not based on fraud, collusion, gall, hustling or swindling as are most cheating techniques and con jobs. Indeed, Neo-Tech requires no special skill, devices, or nerve. Neo-Tech requires no risk or changes in life style — only a new integrated knowledge that generates advantages and power. Moreover, Neo-Tech renders deception and cheating ploys so obsolete that they are no longer an important threat. ...Someday Neo-Tech will dominate all competitive situations as it spreads into business and personal relationships.

*Q: Who exactly is the Neo-Tech person?*

WALLACE: He's a person of quiet power — a person who cannot lose. He can control not only every competitive situation, but can vanquish every threatening situation.

*Q: What actually makes him so effective?*

WALLACE: Neo-Tech is totally natural. Thus, it can be executed anytime, anywhere with casual confidence. The

9

techniques let a person gain unbeatable advantages consistently and comfortably — year after year, decade after decade. Eventually, Neo-Tech men and women will quietly control all.

*Q: In the real world, how quickly can I benefit from Neo-Tech?*

WALLACE: A person can use Neo-Tech immediately to gain advantages needed to prosper in business and in personal relationships. Additionally, that person can never be taken advantage of again in any business transaction, investment, or personal contact. His Neo-Tech knowledge protects him. It arms him with a sword and shield. Neo-Tech knowledge is the best insurance policy anyone could own: Within days, a person with Neo-Tech can gain more power than most people without Neo-Tech can gain in a lifetime.

*Q: Specifically, what does Neo-Tech mean to the ordinary person?*

WALLACE: Well, to be specific, the most potent shortcuts prior to Neo-Tech were beyond the reach of ordinary people as only the money/power giants developed the combinations to unlock and use those shortcuts. Moreover, those potent but customized or highly specialized shortcuts in specific fields could not help most people even if they had access to those shortcuts. In addition, the nature of those potent shortcuts limited the money/power giants to their particular fields. Still, genuine power lies beneath all those customized shortcuts. Neo-Tech not only captures that power but brings everything down to earth and removes all limitations. That, in turn, yields a still greater power that even the money/power giants were denied. More important, today, most ordinary men and women will only flounder through life until they discover Neo-Tech.

*Q: Beyond the immediate financial advantages and quick profits available from Neo-Tech, how will the Neo-Tech Discovery affect you and me in the real world...in society?*

WALLACE: Neo-Tech meets the criteria: certain and safe —

10

but powerful. Therefore, more and more people will increasingly use Neo-Tech in all areas. And the lives of those people will grow richer. Of those, some will choose to use Neo-Tech concepts to gain enormous power and wealth. But, equally important, people knowledgeable about Neo-Tech cannot be drained by others. The ordinary person, no matter how low on the power scale, can reverse the situation. With Neo-Tech, a person can take away the power from those Neocheaters who have drained that person for years or decades. That capturing of personal power through Neo-Tech is crucial. For, all major Neocheaters today extract money and power from the masses of unknowledgeable people. How? Through the subtly camouflaged usurpation and destruction of values created, built, or earned by others. In fact, those value destroyers use Neocheating without fear of being caught, without suspicion. ...And they are successful to the extent they use Neocheating.

Consider how many of the most successful politicians have for years destructively regulated and harmfully controlled the value producers. They have neocheated the public for unearned personal power. Their power ploys have created jungles of destructive regulations and inefficiencies. They hassle busy individuals, cripple creative scientists, and prevent private enterprise from fully developing its productive and technological capacities. That arrogated authority not only diminishes everyone's spirit, but diminishes everyone's standard of living and even prevents the development of cures for scourges such as heart disease, cancer, and AIDS.

*Q: You know, "60 Minutes" recently dealt with something like that. And I hear about that kind of thing more and more these days. How can it be stopped?*

WALLACE: Today, as Neo-Tech spreads, people in steadily increasing numbers can, for the first time, avoid the harmful ploys of those external authorities. As people become informed about Neo-Tech, they will identify and circumvent those master Neocheaters who have previously drained them. Now, ordinary people will fill their own pockets with profits rather than lining the pockets of Neocheaters. As more and more people learn about

11

Neo-Tech, they will increasingly understand that professional mystics, pragmatic politicians, bogus-job bureaucrats, and other such false authorities are destructive drains on value producers and society.

I have two charts that demonstrate how most people have unknowingly let their lives be drained by those external authorities. This information also shows how the informed will financially and emotionally benefit by breaking free from those master Neocheaters. Indeed, everyone informed of Neo-Tech will have the tools not only to break free but to profit from the decline of external authority. Furthermore, this information shows exactly how the average person can turn into a Neo-Tech person...a person who can acquire far greater advantages than any Neocheater — even a master Neocheater.

*Q: Your charts uncover things I was never aware of. It's bad enough that those Neocheaters conceal their ripped-off power, but it's rotten how they're doing it by draining me, you, and everyone else....*

WALLACE: Yet, we're the ones who hold the power on this planet. Most people have never been aware of that fact. Now, with Neo-Tech, we can totally control our future. That's why the Neocheaters never told us their secret. For, we would take away their power that is rightfully ours. You, like everyone else, could never really know the facts behind external authorities without understanding Neo-Tech. The actions of such external authorities usually depend on Neocheating — on undetectable routes to easy money or power at the expense of others. They seemingly benefit their victims by giving them guidance, leadership, or doctrines to follow — making those victims easy to control. Fortunately, however, publicly revealing Neo-Tech exposes the Neocheater's essence. That will lead to the eventual demise of external authority.

Indeed, today, you as the Neo-Tech person never again have to feel helpless. You never again have to be on the defense. You never again have to depend on anyone or anything of the past. You can enter a new world and control your own future. You can become a Clark Kent — a quiet superman. You can gain the real power — the real advantages and profits that few ever knew existed.

*Q: Now I know why the Neo-Tech Discovery will immediately....*

WALLACE: Also, consider another benefit from understanding Neo-Tech: the stopping of the pain and harm caused by certain everyday acquaintances straight up to the authoritarian bureaucrats who surround everyone in almost every area of life. Neo-Tech can abruptly stop the pain and harm caused by being beaten by destructive authorities, cheated or exploited by one's spouse, manipulated by parents, drained by bosses, gypped by merchants, intimidated by pushy or monied people, misled by professional people, stunted by dishonest and incompetent educators, used by friends, abused by strangers, fouled up by bureaucrats, fooled by mystics, and hurt by government.

Neo-Tech puts an end to all those hurts and diminishments that have constantly kept you from becoming the person you've always dreamed of — the person you were meant to be.

And there are other side benefits. For example, when viewing network TV with the knowledge of Neo-Tech, a person becomes acutely aware of the steady stream of Neocheaters — TV commentators, news editors, journalists, sociologists, faddists, mystical gurus, and religious proselytizers. Those fake authorities constantly gain destructive advantages from their followers in countless subtle ways. Neo-Tech concepts allow people to identify and nullify Neocheaters who drain everyone's life daily.

With the concepts of Neo-Tech, a person nullifies those Neocheaters while transferring their power from them to himself. He no longer needs to bow to or idolize the man on the hill. With Neo-Tech, a person knows with fearless certainty that he, himself, is the most important person — and everyone will sense that he is the most powerful person.

*Q: Can you restate what you're saying to bring me back to earth?*

WALLACE: The Neo-Tech concepts are practical tools for

13

integrated thinking. Neo-Tech really puts one on the right track. No longer do people have to suffer in silent frustration watching their lives and dreams be quietly drained away.

*Q: Yes. Who hasn't felt that distant, lonely sadness....*

WALLACE: The Neo-Tech concepts are the most powerful thinking tools for profits. Those concepts are the cutting edge for prosperity...for making the grandest dreams come to reality. Neo-Tech can rekindle the sparks that flickered out long ago.

*Q: Is all that really true? I mean, does all that really apply to us — to us who work for a living?*

WALLACE: You are the good, the innocent, the powerful, you are the Clark Kents. Over are the days of your being defrauded of wealth, pleasure, and happiness. Over are the days of being victimized by the politicians, bureaucrats, mystics, and pseudo intellectuals. In your innocence, you have unknowingly been drained by Neocheaters. Now, at last, you can break free and take what all productive human beings rightfully earn but seldom take...a guiltless life of power, pleasure, and wealth. But even more, you can now become a Neo-Tech person and command your own future.

*Q: That's pretty profound. I'll have to give that some deep thought.*

WALLACE: You should. For the more one thinks about Neo-Tech, the more one profits from it.

*Q: What if I want to profit more and more? What if I get a little greedy? What if I want to become the man on the hill now — through Neo-Tech?*

WALLACE: Look again at the charts. Contrary to what some people might initially think, the highest profits of Neo-Tech come not from destroying advantages of others, although anyone can do that with Neocheating to gain tremendous power

14

and profits. But the highest profits come from creating honest advantages for oneself by delivering maximum competitive values to others and society. Indeed, to any chosen extent, you can apply Neo-Tech to personally gain both immediate and long-range advantages in business, personal life, and social situations...the applications are endless.

Back to your question about becoming a little greedy. As the first step, anyone can immediately profit by collecting the Neocheating advantages available in any competitive situation. Moreover, anyone can use Neocheating to outflank all competition — control even the sharpest, most-alert people. Master Neocheaters use undetectable techniques to gain maximum advantage from every situation to acquire extreme power and wealth. And anyone can use Neocheating to gain easy advantages or profits to any chosen degree. But who needs that? The Neocheater, yes, he can easily do all of that. But the Neo-Tech person...he needs none of that. For him, Neocheating is limiting and obsolete.

Just acquiring the knowledge of Neo-Tech will show you how to reach you goals quickly, directly, easily. You will experience a mounting sense of power and excitement while learning about Neo-Tech. Indeed, through the Neo-Tech Discovery, you too can achieve great strength in your career or field of interest by becoming a quiet Neo-Tech person. In addition, you will forever be immune to Neocheaters...immune to most harmful situations.

*Q: How quickly will Neo-Tech spread?*

WALLACE: As people gain this knowledge, they will begin using its techniques because they are irresistibly logical and overwhelmingly practical. Thus, as people discover the unbeatable advantages of Neo-Tech, those advantages will spread throughout the world as the most potent discovery since the Industrial Revolution.

# Introduction

The following fifteen questions and answers about Neocheating provide the background for this book:

## 1. What is Neocheating?

Neocheating is the ultimate evolution of cheating. Neocheating is *not* based on sleight-of-hand or magician's skills as are many classical and traditional cheating techniques. Neocheating is a new, scientific kind of cheating — an invisible, incredibly easy kind of cheating based on simplicity and low skill. Once a person understands Neocheating, he can use its techniques to quietly beat opponents, anytime — anywhere on earth. But also, he can use that knowledge to defend against and defeat all cheating, including Neocheating.

## 2. How did Neocheating evolve?

Neocheating evolved from constant financial pressures and incentives to develop the easiest, safest, and most profitable methods of winning. Over the decades, the smartest profiteers have searched for shortcuts that require little skill, but contain the invisible effectiveness of the most advanced cardsharping techniques. Those shortcuts are identified in this book and then honed into practical-attack formats called Neocheating.

## 3. How is Neocheating so easy?

Neocheating is insidiously easy because it has been distilled by short-cut seekers over the years to the simplest essentials upon which all effective cheating depends. If a person understands those essentials, he will understand all cheating, allowing him to defend against any cheating, including Neocheating. But at the same time, any player with larceny in his heart can now easily and safely beat any card game played for money.

## 4. How is Neocheating so safe?

Neocheating is so subtle that no one can ever prove a person is Neocheating. Even if others were certain someone was Neocheating, no evidence would exist to accuse the Neocheater because his maneuvers are invisible.

## 5. How can Neocheating be so easy and safe, yet still be the most potent form of cheating?

The simpler and subtler the cheating technique, the easier and safer and, therefore, the more effective it will be (as will become evident throughout the book). Indeed, the Neocheater's confident characteristics result from his exclusive use of simple, effective, and invisible techniques.

## 6. What are the characteristics of a Neocheater?

Neocheaters generally display characteristics opposite to those of traditional cheaters as shown in the chart below. In fact, the closer people observe a Neocheater, the more assured they become that no cheating is occurring. And ironically, as shown in the final chapter of this book, the Neocheater is often the most trusted person in the game.

### CONTRASTING CHARACTERISTICS

| *The Traditional Cheater* | *The Neocheater* |
| --- | --- |
| Nervous | Confident |
| Stiff | Relaxed |
| "When should I do it" feeling — cheats at every opportunity | Knows exactly when to Neocheat — Neocheats selectively |
| Keeps players from watching him closely with distractions and concealments | Lets players watch him "thoroughly shuffle" without distractions or concealments |
| Uses distractions constantly; they often interfere with the difficult and dangerous maneuvers of conventional cheating | Uses distractions rarely; they seldom interfere with the simple and safe maneuvers of Neocheating |
| Causes suspicion with his cheating moves — fears all opponents | Eliminates suspicion with Neocheating moves — fears no one |

17

# CONTRASTING CHARACTERISTICS

| The Traditional Cheater | The Neocheater |
| --- | --- |
| Makes opponents unhappy | Makes opponents happy |
| Worries that his cheating will be seen | Knows that Neocheating cannot be seen |
| Worries about the consequences of being caught in the act | Knows he cannot be caught in the act |

Why the difference in characteristics? Alert or knowledgeable opponents can usually detect traditional cheating — unless the cheater has acquired great classical skill through years of laborious practice and experience. Even then, the cardsharp must execute each cheating maneuver perfectly, every time, putting him under great pressure. Moreover, the traditional cheater becomes obviously guilty once caught, leaving him to face the consequences. That fear of being caught haunts most traditional cheaters and overwhelms countless potential cheaters.

By contrast, Neocheating is invisible, routine, and requires little skill. The Neocheater's tactics are so subtle that, even if accused, his cheating cannot be proven. Indeed, he can always avoid the consequences because he can never be caught *flagrante delicto* or "in the act".

The traditional cheater fears his telltale characteristics. But the Neocheater works in harmony with his deceptive characteristics, preventing people unknowledgeable about Neocheating from ever suspecting him. As a result, the Neocheater flourishes.

## 7. Where is Neocheating going?

Simple and effective Neocheating is today spreading throughout poker games in Nevada casinos and California card clubs. Indeed, Neocheating is already infiltrating private games of poker, blackjack, bridge, and gin. And Neocheating will keep on spreading, leaving no game or player immune from attack.

## 8. What can stop Neocheating from spreading?

Publicly revealing the techniques of Neocheating may initially cause a cheating spree that could create chaos at the card table. But ironically, that knowledge, as it becomes widely known, will begin to expose and nullify Neocheating. Players no longer need to be helpless or doomed when confronted with Neocheating. Instead, they will be able to counter and eliminate Neocheating.

## 9. If Neocheating is invisible, how can it be detected and stopped?

Neocheating cannot be detected directly, and the Neocheater can never be accused or caught outright. But with the knowledge of Neocheating, a player can sense Neocheating —know when it is occurring. And then with special countermeasures (taught in this book), he can win in the presence of a Neocheater... or, if he chooses, easily cause the Neocheater to leave the game.

## 10. How can you prevent Neocheating from ruining your game?

Simply use the counterattack techniques described in this book to beat or drive Neocheaters from your game.

Or tell your opponents about this book. If an opponent knows that you have read this book, he will never dare cheat in your presence. Moreover, if your fellow players know about the information in this book, they too could detect any cheater. Indeed, your fellow players would thank you for awakening them to knowledge that will always protect them. Also, with other players in your game knowledgeable about Neocheating, you will never face a cheater alone.

Or give a cheater in your game this book and watch him stop cheating —watch him leave your game to cheat elsewhere. In fact, if every cardplayer in the world had the information in this book, no one would dare cheat.

## 11. Who is the Neocheater?

He is a player who cannot lose. He can drain everyone's money at will. He may be in your game now. . . or next week. Or he may be you. The Neocheater will inevitably threaten every card game played for money. Moreover, he considers Neocheating no more wrong than bluffing or normal card deception.

19

## 12. How does the Neocheater differ from the cardsharp?

The Neocheater is *not* a cardsharp. He is a new breed of player who may soon rule the card table.

The cardsharp has existed since the invention of cards. He cheats without the knowledge of Neocheating. Still, he may unknowingly use various Neocheating techniques. But generally his cheating relies on skill and gall.

The Neocheater, on the other hand, relies on neither skill nor gall. He relies on simple, invisible maneuvers. For him to use any other means of cheating (such as palming cards or using marked cards) would be unnecessary and foolish since Neocheating is not only safe, but so much easier and more effective.

## 13. What makes the Neocheater unbeatable?

The maneuvers of Neocheating are so subtle and the mechanics so easy that they can be executed with relaxed confidence. Guaranteed winning hands such as four aces can be routinely obtained. And more than one powerful hand can be dealt at a time to ensure a big score (e.g., in poker: four aces to the Neocheater and four jacks to the victim). Yet, unlike the cardsharp, the Neocheater seldom stacks powerful hands or goes for big scores (although he easily can). Instead, he casually uses just enough of his power to give him constant, unbeatable advantages. In fact, he may never even Neocheat for himself, but instead simply use Neocheating to shift money from the strongest players to the weakest players and then win legitimately from those weak players. His steady, hidden attack lets him win consistently and comfortably in poker, blackjack, bridge, and gin — week after week, year after year.

This book shows not only how the Neocheater can easily create spectacular advantages for himself, but how he can create smarter, unsuspicious, casino-like advantages to safely extract maximum money from all games. With those invisible advantages, he keeps his opponents happy while comfortably controlling the game, even a network of games. ... Neocheating is that easy.

### 14. How does Neocheating apply to games such as blackjack, bridge, and gin?

The Neocheating techniques in this book apply to all card games. Most techniques, however, are presented with a poker slant because most card cheating has traditionally been centered around poker - the money game. Also Neocheating techniques are more easily illustrated through poker examples. But Neocheating will become increasingly common in all card games played for money or prestige.

In bridge, cheating occurs frequently in private, home games. And cheating scandals are not uncommon in major tournaments. Dishonest bridge players, however, have traditionally relied on signaling since that was easier and generally more practical than manipulating cards. But Neocheating, because it is so safe and effective, will increasingly penetrate bridge, especially private games played for money. In fact, bridge today is especially vulnerable to Neocheating because its players generally look for and suspect only signal-type cheaters. (Signaling requires the collusion of two players. But Neocheating can be performed alone, without anyone else's knowledge.)

Blackjack is particularly vulnerable to Neocheating. Undetectable maneuvers executed through Neocheating techniques offer unbeatable advantages to any dealer or partner.

And Neocheating in gin routinely produces winning hands and a constant influx of money.

While this book reveals techniques specific to poker, bridge, blackjack, and gin, Neocheating in general can be applied to those or any other card game played for money or prestige.

Today, anyone could leave any card game a consistent loser, read this book, and return the following week never to lose again.

### 15. Is revealing Neocheating immoral?

Can revealing the truth ever be immoral? Only by revealing Neocheating fully can honest players defend and protect themselves completely.

\* \* \*

Although this book gives step-by-step instructions for Neocheating, an honest player needs only to read through this book to gain the special knowledge needed fully to defend himself against all cheating, including Neocheating. But, if the honest player invests a little time in actually executing the various Neocheating maneuvers, he will gain an enjoyable sense of power while learning to subject any deck of cards to his will.

So why not read this book while sitting at a cleared table with a deck of cards beside you? As you read each step, actually do it. The steps themselves are really much simpler than their detailed descriptions. And unlike the more difficult traditional and classical cheating techniques, Neocheating maneuvers are fun and easy to learn.

Hopefully most people who read this book will choose not to neocheat. Still, everyone will experience a mounting sense of control and power as they read "Neocheating". After all, how many people can invisibly deal themselves four aces after only an hour's practice? Moreover, each reader will gain the knowledge needed to protect himself in any card game (private, public, tournament, or casino), against any opponent (friend or stranger), and against any form of cheating (amateur or professional). But most importantly, this book will save the reader from being drained by Neocheaters, not only in cards but in all areas of life.

# NEOCHEATING
## The Unbeatable Weapon for
## Poker, Blackjack, Bridge, and Gin

### TABLE OF CONTENTS

### PART ONE
### NEOCHEATING — SOMETHING NEW AND EASY
### SOMETHING LETHAL

## PART TWO
### *DEFENSES AND COUNTERATTACKS*

## PART THREE
### *BECOMING THE NEOCHEATER*

### APPENDICES

# PART ONE

## NEOCHEATING — SOMETHING NEW AND EASY SOMETHING LETHAL

27

# Chapter I
# The Nature Of Cheating

To gain full benefit from this book, the reader must understand the nature of cheating. This chapter explains the nature of amateur cheating, professional cheating, and Neocheating in poker and in all other card games played for money.

## 1. Defining Cheating.

To properly define cheating, the nature of poker as opposed to other card games must first be understood. Poker is unique to other card games or situations in that honest poker explicitly permits any behavior or manipulation, no matter how deceptive, except cheating. In fact, the ethical basis of poker *is* lying and deception. Indeed, the only unethical behavior in poker is cheating.

But where does deception end and cheating begin? Actually a sharp distinction exists. Poker *cheating* is the conjuring up of advantages unavailable to opponents. Poker *deception*, however, involves exploiting advantages that are available to all players. When cheating, a player initiates one or more of the abnormal, physical manipulations listed at the bottom of this page. But when deceiving, a player is simply taking advantage of situations *already available* to his opponents. For example, the normal use of cards produces smudges, nicks, scratches, and creases on their backs. Such natural markings that identify unexposed cards are equally available to all players willing to train their eyes and discipline their minds. The good player willingly exerts that effort to spot, remember, and then deceptively use those natural markings on cards to gain advantages over his opponents. Such

29

actions do not constitute cheating in poker. On the other hand, *deliberately* soiling, marring, or marking cards for identification would constitute cheating in poker or in any other card game.

Still many deceptive actions that are honest and proper in poker are considered in other games as cheating or dishonest (such as lying, deceit, and other violations of specific ethics or rules). Yet anything considered as cheating in poker would be considered as cheating in any other card game. Cheating in poker or in any card game can, therefore, be defined as initiating any one of the following abnormal manipulations of cards, signals, or money:

- Cards are covertly switched to change the value of a hand.
- Cards are purposely flashed to see the value of undealt or unexposed cards.
- Cards are culled or stacked to change their natural sequence.
- Cards are purposely soiled, smudged, nicked, marred, or marked for future identification.
- Mechanical devices are used such as marked cards, strippers, mirrors, and hold-out equipment.
- Secret betting agreements or partnerships are made so that colluding partners can signal each other the value of their hands . . . or when to fold, bet, or raise.
- Money is stolen from bets being made, from the pot, or from other players. Extra change is purposely taken from the pot. Lights are purposely not paid. (These last items are direct theft in contrast to the indirect theft of card and signal cheating.)

And definitions for the different styles of card cheating are—

*Classical:* A smooth, mechanical style of cheating developed in the 19th century requiring high skill for stacking, palming, and manipulating cards.

*Cardsharping:* A skilled style of card cheating executed through card manipulations.

*Invisible:* Cheating moves that are not discernible or visible to the human eye — previously associated only with classical or highly skilled cheating. The essence of Neocheating.

*Gaffing:* A dangerous-to-use, non-skill cheating style that

30

utilizes marked cards, shiners, and other external or mechanical devices.

*Colluding:* A non-skill cheating style involving two or more partners covertly signaling information or instructions to one another.

*Traditional:*

a) *Skilled* — A cheating style occasionally used today. Requires extensive practice and experience. Invisible in its ultimate form.

b) *Unskilled* — A common cheating style that relies on outside help such as marked cards, holdouts, shiners, and collusion. Sometimes involves crude or low-skill card manipulations, or even stealing.

*Neocheating:* "The New Cheating" — A low-skill, highly effective and invisible style of cheating that is easily and quickly learned. Neocheating is smart, safe, short-cut cheating that is spreading from public to private poker and will eventually dominate all cheating.

## 2. Accepting Cheaters.

Most players fear cheaters. But the good player quietly accepts them if they are losers. In fact, he often welcomes their cheating because, as explained in the next paragraph, they generally lose more money while cheating, particularly in complex games involving split pots and twists. The good player can even convert expert cheaters into financial assets by nullifying their cheating or by beating them with the defenses and counteractions described in later chapters.

Indeed, contrary to popular belief, most players actually increase their losses while cheating because they

— dilute their attention toward the game by worrying about and concentrating on their cheating.

— overestimate the benefits of cheating and thus play looser or poorer poker.

— overlook or miss vital information about their opponents and the poker action.

— make their hands and intentions much more readable.

— use ineffective techniques that do not deliver net financial benefits.

A good player can take profitable advantage of the above weaknesses in cheaters as demonstrated by the anecdotes at the end of this chapter.

So why do players cheat if their cheating increases their losses? Some cheat out of financial desperation, others cheat out of neurotic desires to swindle their opponents, but many cheat simply out of naiveness or stupidity. Neocheaters, however, cheat "smartly" with the sole motive to extract maximum money from their opponents. And Neocheaters do not lose; they must be rejected.

### 3. Rejecting Cheaters.

If a cheater consistently wins money, he is a financial liability to both the good player and the game. Also under certain conditions, a cheater can financially harm the good player, even if the cheater is a loser. For example, other more profitable losers may become upset and quit the game if they detected someone cheating. Or cheating can cause a profitable game to break up. In such situations, a good player either stops the cheating or eliminates the cheater by using one or more of the nine methods listed in Table 1.

### 4. Detecting Cheaters.

Invisible Neocheating will eventually menace all players in public and private card games throughout the world. But much of today's cheating in private games is still done by amateurs using crude, visible techniques that are easily detectable and beatable by methods described in this book. Yet most players ignore even obvious cheating to avoid arousing unpleasant or perhaps violent emotions. When a player detects cheating, he often rationalizes it as a rule violation or a mistake rather than cheating.

Any player, however, can detect all cheating quickly, without ever seeing a dishonest move, even highly skilled professional cheating and highly knowledgeable Neocheating. How can he do that? All cheating and cheaters are betrayed by violations of logic and probability. Cheating is an unnatural injection of distorted action that perceptively jolts the otherwise logically connected occurrences in poker. So if a player monitors and compares the

## TABLE 1
## METHODS TO ELIMINATE CHEATING

| Time of Action | Form of Action | Results |
|---|---|---|
| Indirectly, during game | Make the cheater feel that he is suspected and is being watched. | Cheating stops. |
| Privately, outside of game | Tell the cheater that if he cheats again, he will be publicly exposed. | Cheating stops. |
| Privately, outside of game | Tell suspicious players about the cheater. Point out that he is a loser and the best way to penalize him is to let him play. | Cheating continues, but the suspicious players are satisfied as the cheater continues to lose. |
| Privately, outside of game | Form a conspiracy with other players to collude collectively in order to bankrupt the cheater. | Cheater is driven from the game. |
| Privately, during game | Use Neocheating defenses and counterattacks to bankrupt the cheater. | Cheater is driven from the game. |
| Publicly, during game | Expose the cheater during the game in front of everyone. | Cheater quits or is drummed out of the game. |

## TABLE 1
## METHODS TO ELIMINATE CHEATING

| *Time of Action* | *Form of Action* | *Results* |
| --- | --- | --- |
| Publicly, during game | Inform all players including the cheater about this book and Neocheating. | Cheating stops. |
| Privately, outside of game | Give the cheater a copy of this book. | Cheating stops or the cheater leaves for another game. |
| Privately, during game | White-hat Neocheating. (Described in Chapter X.) | Cheater is driven from the game. |

actions of his opponents to the most logical actions according to the situation and odds, he will quickly detect the distorted playing and betting patterns that always arise from cheating. That awareness enables him to sense cheating without ever seeing a suspicious move as demonstrated by the anecdotes at the end of this chapter.

## 5. Professional and Amateur Cheating.

One of the major differences between private poker and public (club and casino) poker is the collusion cheating routinely practiced by cliques of professional players in public poker. Few outsiders or victims ever suspect professional cheating in public poker because the techniques used are subtle and hard to observe visually. Most public-game professionals execute their collusion so naturally and casually that the management of major casinos and card clubs remain unaware of their cheating, even when it routinely occurs in their own card rooms. Moreover, many public-game professionals practice collusion cheating without qualms. They consider their cheating as a legitimate trade tool that enables them to offset the draining effect of the house rake or collection.

*Part One: Neocheating — Something Lethal*

The chart on the next page lists the most important classical and traditional, professional and amateur cheating methods used in public and private card games.

## PROFESSIONAL AND AMATEUR CHEATING METHODS

| *Card Manipulations* | *Card Treatments* | *Other Devices* |
|---|---|---|
| *blind shuffling | *daubing (Golden | *colluding partners |
| *crimping | Glow, nicotine | *card flashing |
| *culling | stains, soiling) | *crossfire betting |
| dealing seconds, | corner flash | *signals |
| bottoms, | denting and | *spread |
| middles | rounders | *marked decks |
| *false cutting | luminous readers | cold decks |
| *false riffling | marking | chip copping |
| foiling the cut | nailing (indexing) | holdouts |
| palming | punching | shiners |
| *peeking | sanding | stripper decks |
| *pull through | slicked-aced deck | |
| *stacking | stripping | |
| * Las Vegas riffle | waving | |
| * overhand stack | | |
| * riffle cull | | |
| and stack | | |
| * undercut stack | | |

*\* Professional cheating methods most commonly used today.*

Table 2 on the next page summarizes the most important cheating techniques used in private games as well as in public clubs and casinos. Table 2 also summarizes both the crude cheating techniques used by amateurs and the skilled techniques used by professionals.

Not all professional cardplayers are cheaters. And not all high-stake games have cheaters or professionals present. But any high-stake game, public or private, is vulnerable for exploitation and will tend to attract professionals and cheaters. Yet a player must vigilantly avoid considering anyone a cheater without

35

Book 4
Neocheating: The Unbeatable Weapon

## Table 2
## CHEATING TECHNIQUES USED IN PRIVATE, CLUB, AND CASINO POKER

| | Uses | Methods |
|---|---|---|
| **Manipulation Techniques (more common in private poker)** | | |
| Classical and amateur manipulations (solo) | Least effective, most detectable. Effectively used only by the rare, classic cardsharp who is highly skilled, dexterous, and experienced. Shunned by today's professional establishment. Crudely used by amateurs in private games. | Classical deck stacking, holding-out cards, palming, second and bottom dealing, shaved decks, shiners, marked cards, and various mechanical devices used to cheat opponents. |
| Full flashing of draw cards and hole cards (dealer to partner) | More effective for stud and hold-'em games | With smooth, imperceptible motions, the dealer lifts or tilts cards just enough for his partner to see. Done only when others are not looking or are unaware. |
| Modern and professional manipulations (solo) | Most effective, easiest to learn, usually undetectable. Used by professional players in both private and public poker. | New concepts of culling cards, stacking, blind shuffling, false riffling, false cutting, and foiling cuts as described in this book. |

36

## Table 2
## CHEATING TECHNIQUES USED IN PRIVATE, CLUB, AND CASINO POKER

| Uses | Methods |
|---|---|

### Collusion Techniques (more common in club and casino poker)

| Uses | Methods |
|---|---|
| Partial flashing of draw cards and draw. hole cards (dealer to partner) | Most effective for high-stake, lowball Player sits low enough to see shades of darkness blur intensities, or the actual values of cards being dealt facedown.* |
| Collusion betting (partner to partner) | Most common in high-stake lowball, stud, and hold 'em. Requires system of signals between colluding partners that indicates "strength of hands" or "when to bet, raise, or fold". |

### Combined Techniques (more common in casino poker)

| Uses | Methods |
|---|---|
| Collusion and manipulation (house dealer to partner) | Most effective and common in casinos with house dealers who manipulate cards and work in collusion with professional Players. The dealer manipulates memorized cards to top of deck. Then knowing everyone's hole cards, he signals his partner when to bet or fold. |

\* *Observing flashed cards without the dealer's help or collusion is not cheating. For example, good players train themselves to evaluate the shades of darkness or blur intensities of partially flashed cards (e.g., darker shades or more intense blurs indicate higher value cards - valuable information, especially for lowball). If a player sees flashed cards without dealer collusion, he is not cheating since the same advantage is available to all players who choose to be equally alert. Alert players also watch for flashed cards as the dealer riffles, shuffles, and cuts.*

37

objective indications of cheating. A player must resist the temptation of blaming tough or painful losses on being cheated (rather than on coincidence or his own errors). Assuming cheating exists when there is none can lead to costly errors. For example, misreading or rationalizing an opponent as a cheater and then implementing the distorted playing techniques used to nullify or counterattack cheaters (e.g., quick folds, extra-aggressive betting, and other techniques explained in later chapters) will result in costly errors.

## 6. Why Poker Players are Prone to Cheating.

The nature of poker — as generally understood and accepted by every player — allows unlimited deception to win maximum money from ownerless pots. Therefore, anyone can freely use deception in any poker game and remain honest. But no one can use deception outside of poker and remain honest. Likewise, if a person "plays poker" outside of the game, he becomes a dishonest person. But in poker, a person can be dishonest only by usurping money through cheating.

Many poker players, including most professionals, do not clearly distinguish between what is honest and what is dishonest in and out of poker. For example, many professional players who day after day, year after year, lie and practice deceit in poker ironically do not grasp the rightness of their poker deception. In fact, many professionals and regular players never grasp the sharp difference between poker deception and cheating. Their ethics, therefore, become hazy and ill-defined. The major barrier in crossing the line from deception to cheating is the fear and threat of being caught. By removing that threat (i.e., by using undetectable Neocheating), many easily slip across that line and begin cheating with fearless ease.

Failure to fully distinguish between poker deception and poker cheating is one reason why certain players react so strongly (often violently, sometimes murderously) against a cheater. Without strong anticheating reactions, they believe opponents would step across that line and begin cheating them. Sensing their own capacity to cheat (checked only by the fear of being caught), they assume the same capacity lurks in everyone. Thus, even if they never cheat others, they fear others will cheat them. So, ironically, those who would react most violently against cheaters are often those who would most readily cheat others if not for their fear of being caught and evoking similarly violent reactions from others.

## 7. Beating All Cheaters.

Most amateur poker players hold the classical but misleading view about cheating. They perceive cheating as being done either by bumbling amateurs who are easily caught or by highly dexterous and invincible cardsharps who have perfected sleight-of-hand skills through years of laborious practice and experience. In holding that misleading classical view, most poker players remain oblivious to the cheating and collusion practiced by professional cheaters, especially those in public casino games. In fact, most players remain oblivious even to the crude and routine cheating of private-game amateurs. So without the information in this book, players today have no chance of detecting the Neocheater.

The alert player familiar both with the traditional cheating techniques and with Neocheating can detect any cheating. He can even detect the most skilled and invisible cheating without ever seeing a dishonest move as demonstrated in the anecdotes at the end of this chapter. Furthermore, the alert player familiar with Neocheating can usually tell who is cheating, what technique is being used, and exactly when the cheating is occurring. He garners that information by detecting patterns and combinations of illogical betting, raising, and playing styles of particular opponents.

But normally to detect invisible cheating, a player must be involved in at least one hand and perhaps several hands in which cheating occurs in order to sense the illogical playing and betting patterns. For that reason, every player must be cautious about high-stake or no-limit games in which he could be wiped out in a big, one-shot cheating setup before detecting any cheating. Indeed, the wise player views with suspicion and is prepared to throw away without a bet any super-powerful hand (e.g., four of a kind, a straight flush) dealt to him in high-stake games with strangers.

Also, as the stakes for card games increase, the motivation for cheating increases. Every cardplayer should increasingly expect and look for cheating as he progresses to higher-stake games.

In any case, when poker players cheat, the quality of their play declines as their time, energy, and thought shifts from analyzing poker actions to executing cheating actions. Also their objectivity, concentration, and discipline diminish as they rely more and more on cheating to win. Their betting becomes distorted and often overly loose. And most importantly, their hands become more readable and their actions become more predictable whenever they cheat. For those reasons, a good player usually has little trouble beating cheaters, especially after detecting their cheating.

**8. Protection from Public-Casino Cheating.**

The examples on the next eight pages for detecting and countering public-casino cheating provide insights into the nature of all cheating. While occurring two years before Neocheating was identified and isolated, some of the anecdotes illustrate the seeds of Neocheating being sown in public poker. And because of the cosmopolitan and dynamic nature of public poker, it is often an indicator of what will eventually occur in private poker. Indeed, Neocheating is today not only spreading throughout public poker, but is already infiltrating private, home games.

## SIX KINDS OF PUBLIC-CASINO CHEATING

**Although John Finn[1] played almost exclusively in private poker games because of their greater profitability, he did spend the summer of 1976 playing public poker in the Gardena, California, card clubs and in the Las Vegas, Nevada, casinos. In both the clubs and casinos, he discovered professional cheaters operating in the higher-stake games. John's public-game experiences uncovered six common cheating methods used in public poker. He also learned how to protect himself from professional cheaters in public poker.**

[1] *John Finn, a retired professional poker player, was the original Advanced-Concept player. His poker experiences are described in Frank R. Wallace's book, "Poker, A Guaranteed Income for Life by Using the Advanced Concepts of Poker", Crown (hardbound), Warner Books, New York, 1980 (revised and expanded edition).*

More importantly, he learned to identify and thus avoid those cheating situations that he could not beat — the beginnings of Neocheating that would soon invade private poker.

### A. Collusion Cheating — Reciprocal Card Flashing

During his first two days in Gardena, John Finn played in each of its six poker clubs. After the second day, he became aware of a cliquish network of habitual amateur players, professional players, floormen, and cardroom managers woven through those six clubs. The continuous circulation of poker players among the clubs allowed everyone in that network to constantly and effectively communicate (and gossip) among themselves. While most of the habitual amateur players in Gardena recognized they were a part of a clique, few recognized that the professional establishment was using them as fodder.

In the lower-stake games, John Finn found mainly amateurs; the few professionals were usually shills. In those games, he detected no cheating. On the fourth day, he graduated to a $20 blind, lowball draw game. In that game, he discovered from their poker styles and conversations that players in seats 2 and 5 were professionals involved in collusion cheating. Even before identifying them as full-time professionals, he knew they were colluding. Their methods were simple, effective, and unnoticeable. Both players sat low in their seats... each slumping a little lower when the other dealt. On dealing draw cards with smooth quicker-than-the-eye motions, the dealer would expose key cards as fleeting blurs perceptible only to his partner. The partner would return the favor on his deal. The cheaters accomplished their card flashing without suspicion despite the great pressure on dealers in the Gardena card clubs not to flash cards. Only once did John observe a collusion cheater being scolded for his "careless" dealing. Ironically, John observed on numerous occasions noncheating dealers being scolded for flashing cards.

By knowing when his own lowball draw card had been flashed, John Finn could outmaneuver the cheating partners by more accurately predicting what they would do as the result of their knowing his draw card. The cheaters, therefore, were constantly misled by John's counteractions — they repeatedly misjudged what he would do. John Finn exploited and beat both collusion partners by using the cheating counteractions taken from his notes about lowball cheating:

1. Save money by folding sooner against a cheater's more readable winning hand.

2. Lure the cheater into making an expensive bluff when he draws a picture card or a pair in lowball and knows you have drawn a high card such as a ten or a jack. The cheater's overconfidence often encourages him to bluff.

3. Set up the cheater for an easy bluff. For example, a strong lowball bluff position develops when the cheater knows you have drawn a good low card (e.g., a six or lower), but does not know you paired the low card.

4. When you do draw a powerful low hand, the overconfident cheater can sometimes be misled into believing you did pair, causing him to bet into your winning hand, to call your final bet, or to try a bold bluff, especially if the pot is large and if other bluffable players (whose draw cards the cheater also knows) are still in the pot.

5. When the readable cheater bluffs, use his aggressive betting to drive out other players who have you beat. When the other players are driven out, simply call the cheater's bluff. Or when necessary, bluff out the bluffing cheater with a final raise.

Throughout the night, John Finn used those five approaches to exploit and beat both collusion cheaters in lowball. And on occasion, when positioned properly, John saw cards flash between the partners to further improve his advantage. When the game ended at seven in the morning, the two professional players were big losers. They left the table cursing their "bad luck", never realizing that they had been victimized by their own cheating.

### B. Collusion Cheating with House Dealer — Natural-Play Technique

*Part One: Neocheating — Something Lethal*

John Finn first encountered professional casino cheating in a large poker room of a major hotel-casino in downtown Las Vegas. The cheating involved the dealer, the cardroom manager, and his friend. The collusion setup was unusual because management was involved.[2]

Initially off guard, John Finn was not suspicious of or looking for cheating patterns because (a) the game was at fairly low stakes — $5-10 seven-card stud (although that was the highest-stake game in the cardroom at the time), and (b) the cardroom manager was not only playing, but was sitting next to the dealer. ... The game seemed safe from cheating.

Moving clockwise from the dealer's left sat (1) the cardroom manager, (2) a professional poker player, who was also a friend of the manager, (3) a poor-playing tourist, (4) a regular player, (5) [an empty seat], (6) an ex-poker dealer, (7) John Finn, and (8) a woman who was an off-duty blackjack dealer.

Within an hour, newcomer John Finn was the biggest winner. He was playing aggressively, winning heavily, and soundly beating the other players -especially the woman player in seat 8, who was playing poorly.

The manager and several other players seemed annoyed and confused over John Finn's unorthodox and unpredictable play. After a shift change of dealers, the woman player switched to empty seat 5. Two hands later, another tourist sat in empty seat 8. He found a loose card beside John's elbow. The card apparently had slid under a napkin left by the woman player, and the dealer never noticed the missing card. (Some dealers can feel when one card is missing by the bulk and weight of the deck.) Several players glanced sharply at John as if they had discovered how he was beating them. The manager left the table and returned moments later.

Before the next hand, a floorman brought two fresh decks of cards to the dealer. John Finn became puzzled on noticing the cards were in a brown box bearing an orange-shield label from the Normandie Club in Gardena, California. Two hands later, John maneuvered into a strong position and was betting

---

[2] *Since cheating harms the long-range business interests of all public card clubs and casinos, the management of major clubs and casinos always strongly opposes any form of cheating.*

43

heavily. The manager beat him in a series of illogical but infallible calls and bets that did not coincide with the manager's poker style or ability. Staring straight at John Finn, he pushed the large pot to the woman player — the heavily-losing, off-duty blackjack dealer in seat 5. She took the money without appearing grateful or surprised by the manager's "generous" action.

Several hands later, John Finn again maneuvered into a strong and favorable position; he bet heavily, but once more was beaten in a similar series of illogical calls and raises by the manager's friend — the professional player. John became alert and suspicious. At first he thought his hole cards were being flashed, especially since the professional player sat low in his seat. Trying to counter that possibility, John was unsuccessful as he lost two more large pots to the manager, who again won through a series of illogical but infallible moves. John then noticed a slight crimp in his cards — such as might occur if a dealer had crimped for a blind shuffle and then failed to bend out the crimp. In addition, the dealer gripped the cards in a way to facilitate false cutting. Yet John detected no evidence of card culling, discard sorting, or deck stacking. After certain hands, however, the dealer would periodically glance at face-down discards as he gathered cards for the next deal. Still he made no attempt to rearrange any cards.

John Finn lost another large hand to the manager's friend. While assuming that collusion cheating was occurring, John did not know how or when it was occurring. His counteractions not only failed, but they increased his losses. He had lost his winnings and was losing over two-hundred dollars before realizing how the cheating was occurring. The method was simple, essentially undetectable, yet devastatingly effective. After each hand, the dealer simply gathered the face-up stud cards in a natural way, making no attempt to cull, sort, or stack them... he merely remembered the value and order of the exposed cards. If too few cards had been exposed, he would simply glance at some face-

---

[3] *With practice, most players can learn to rapidly memorize fourteen or more cards (even the entire deck) by association, mnemonic, and grouping techniques. [Reference: "Perfecting Your Card Memory" by Charles Edwards, Gambler's Book Club, 1974 ($2.00).]*

down cards. By remembering fourteen cards[3] and by positioning them in an unchanged order on top of the deck through blind shuffles, false riffles, and false cuts, the dealer would know everyone's hole cards — thus, he would know everyone's exact hand right up to the seventh and final card. From that omniscient position, the dealer would then make all of the playing and betting decisions for his partner (or partners) by signaling when to fold, call, bet, or raise. The playing partner would never need to know anyone's hand, including his own; he would only need to follow the signals of the all-knowing dealer.

On losing his third large pot to the low-sitting professional, John Finn realized that he did not immediately know how to beat that kind of collusion cheating. Therefore, his only choice was to quit the game. So he picked up his chips and left.

## C. Collusion Cheating with House Dealer — Culling and Stacking

On the following afternoon, John Finn entered a newly remodeled downtown casino that had introduced poker only a few weeks before. The card area was small and offered only $1-3 stud games. Wanting to examine low-stake casino poker, John Finn sat in the open seat on the dealer's left. Again, he did not expect cheating in a low-stake game. He soon realized that the other four players were locals — they all knew one another and the dealer. But none of the players appeared to be professionals or good players. The players and the dealer chatted amicably among themselves. John Finn played the role of an inexperienced tourist by asking naive questions about the rules. But he knew that low-stake, local amateurs usually played very tight in trying to survive at casino poker. Yet this game seemed rather loose. On the third hand, all four players stayed until the final card. Sixteen face-up cards were exposed, including a pair of aces and a pair of queens. Another ace and another queen were also among the face-up cards. John Finn watched with narrowing eyes as the dealer picked up the cards — he picked up an ace and a queen and then three other cards. His hand darted back to pick up the second ace and queen and then three more random cards before grabbing the final ace and queen.

45

He then gathered the rest of the cards.

After carefully squaring the deck, the dealer made several false riffles and a false cut before dealing. John knew what was going to happen. He did not even look at his two hole cards. His first up card was a queen. The first up card of the player on his left was an ace. The player with the ace looked twice at his hole cards and then bet a dollar. Everyone folded to John. He paused and looked at each player and then at the dealer. Everyone was watching him and waiting. The dealer stopped smiling when John placed the edge of his right hand firmly over the lower half of his hole cards and tore them in half. Turning over the two torn queens, he placed them faceup alongside his third queen. John then quickly flipped over his opponent's hole cards, which were aces, and placed them alongside his opponent's third ace. Everyone remained silent.

"Redeal." John ordered. The dealer glanced toward the mirrors in the ceiling over the blackjack tables and then quickly collected the cards — including the torn ones. He redealt from a new deck. Over the next dozen hands, John Finn aggressively manipulated his now tense and confused opponents. In twenty minutes, he ripped fifty dollars from that low-stake game and left. As he walked down the aisle of blackjack tables, he glanced back toward the poker area. The dealer and the players he left behind were still staring at him.

That was a mistake, John Finn thought to himself. I revealed too much about myself for only fifty dollars.

### D. Collusion Cheating through Partner Crossfire Betting

That evening John Finn entered a major casino on the Strip. The casino had a large poker area. The action was heavy. In addition to many low-stake and intermediate-stake games, several high-stake stud games ($30-60 games of high stud, low stud, and high-low stud) were in progress. John began in a $5-10 game, moved up to a $10-20 game and then graduated to a $15-30 stud game before encountering professional cheating.

The cheating was simple collusion between two

professionals who signaled the strengths of their hands to each other. The cheater with the strongest hand or position would indicate to his partner when to check, bet, or raise. Their collusion entrapped or drove out players while increasing or decreasing the betting pace — whatever was most advantageous to the cheaters at the moment. The collusion partners increased their advantages by either sucking in or driving out players to improve their betting positions. They entrapped players and then generated bets and raises to build larger pots whenever either cheater held a strong hand. They lived by constantly bilking tourists and transient players... at least until John Finn entered their game.

He promptly detected collusion cheating by the illogical patterns of checks, bets, and raises between the partners. Since the dealer was not involved with card manipulations or flashing, John easily turned the collusion to his own advantage at the expense of the cheaters. He beat the cheaters because their collusion actions markedly improved his accuracy in reading their hands and intentions. When either partner held a strong hand, John read their strength more quickly and folded sooner — thus saving considerable money. Moreover, when the cheating partners revealed a strong hand and John held a stronger hand, he quietly let them suck him and other players into the pot. He let them build the pot for him with extra bets and raises. On the final bet, John would end his passiveness with a maximum raise.

Also, the colluding partners doubled their losses to John whenever they bet as a team into pots that John won. If they had not colluded, normally only the player holding the strongest hand (rather than both players) would have been betting into John's winning hand.

To further increase his advantage, John Finn manipulated the readable hands and intentions of the colluding cheaters against the other unsuspecting players. But John reaped his most profitable advantages from the cheaters when they bluffed. (Most collusion cheaters are overconfident and can often be lured into bluffing.) John would keep calling with mediocre or even poor hands as the bluffing partners kept betting aggressively to drive out players who held superior

47

hands. John would then simply call the final bluff bet to win the pot. Or when necessary, he himself would bluff by raising after the final bet to drive out the bluffer and any remaining players to win the pot with a busted or a poor hand.

In three hours, John Finn converted the two professional cheaters from substantial winners into the biggest losers at the table and drove them from the game. With a $600 profit, he left that table to explore other games.

Eventually he sat down at a table where four professional players were operating as two separate teams of colluding partners, each team cheating the other team as well as the other three players. John assumed the role of a slightly drunk, wild-playing tourist — an ideal fish. He not only took advantage of the more easily readable hands of all four cheaters, but promptly played the two teams of collusion cheaters against one another and against the other three players. In an hour, John ripped $900 from the game and then abruptly left the table. As he walked away, some of the players mumbled things about his "unbelievable hot streak" and his "dumb luck."

John walked over to the highest-stake game in the house — a fast-paced, $30-60 lowball, seven-stud game (razz). As he studied the action, he wondered about the unusual house rule that allowed five raises instead of the standard three. The five raises greatly increased the flexibility and advantage of collusion cheaters over their victims. John also wondered about the much higher proportion of professional players and collusion cheaters he observed in this casino. Was the management aware of their collusion cheating? he wondered. Did the management establish the five-raise rule to accommodate the cheaters? Or were the professional collusion cheaters drawn to this casino because of a five-raise rule innocently established by management to increase the betting action? . . . John assumed the latter to be true.

Standing behind the dealer, John Finn continued to watch the high-stake game. For nearly an hour, he studied the two biggest winners. From their conversation and style, he knew they were professionals. Yet neither seemed to be cheating or colluding. Still he noticed that in spite of the large pots,

48

the dealer was not being toked (tipped) when either professional won a pot. John Finn studied the dealer more closely: Gathering the face-up cards in a routine left-to-right order, the dealer made no attempt to rearrange the cards. But as players folded, the dealer would make a pile with their face-down discards and toss their face-up cards on top of that discard pile. He would also toss the later-round face-up cards on top of the discard pile while slipping dead hole or face-down cards beneath the pile. If the hand ended with fewer than fourteen up cards being exposed (when seven players were seated), the dealer would casually glance at several face-down discards and toss them on top of the discard pile.

Although John could not actually see any blind shuffles, false riffles, or false cuts (or verify any illogical cheating patterns[4]), he speculated that the dealer was memorizing everyone's hole card and then signaling the best moves to one or both of the professional players... in a similar way that the dealer was colluding with the cardroom manager and his friend two days earlier in the downtown casino. And, as in the downtown casino, John Finn concluded that he could not beat that kind of dealer-collusion cheating with his current knowledge and experience. He, therefore, left the casino without playing in the $30-60 game.

### E. Amateurish Collusion Cheating with Sanction of House Dealer

Traveling south on the Strip, John Finn entered another major casino also with a large cardroom. He observed the various poker games for thirty minutes. After considering the higher-stake games, he sat in a medium-stake ($10-20) seven-

---

[4] *The alert player detects and verifies illogical cheating patterns by evaluating the actions of cheaters relative to his own playing and betting actions. Without actually playing in the game, an outside observer, even an alertly suspicious and knowledgeable observer, cannot easily see or verify the illogical patterns of a competent cheater... at least not quickly. (That is one reason why casino management is seldom aware of professional cheating in poker; few people can detect competent poker cheating without actually playing against the cheaters in order to notice and evaluate illogical cheating patterns.)*

stud game because more of its players looked like losers. All were out-of-town gamblers and tourists, except for two women players sitting together across from John. Although their conversation revealed they were experienced local players, both women played poorly. Nevertheless, they were winning moderately because of their collusion cheating, which was crude and obvious. While playing, they would blatantly show their hole cards to each other and then coordinate their betting to produce a collective advantage. The other players either did not notice their collusion or were too indifferent or timid to object. But by quietly taking advantage of their much more readable hands and poorer poker resulting from their cheating, John converted the two women from winners to losers.

John then lost a fairly large pot to the women cheaters. During the hand, they had flashed their hole cards to each other. Then in a crudely visible manner, they actually swapped their final hole cards during the last round of betting, allowing one woman to win with a full house. After she turned her hole cards faceup, John Finn stuck his arm over the pot when the dealer started pushing it toward the woman. John then silently removed all the chips he had put into the pot. "Any objections?" he asked looking at the two women and then the dealer. No one objected. John picked up his chips and left for a higher-stake game.

## F. Unbeatable Collusion Cheating through Dealer-Player Partnerships

Moving farther south on the Strip, John Finn entered a casino that normally offered the highest-stake poker games in Las Vegas. For twenty minutes, he watched six players in a $100-200, seven-card stud game. Two professional players were squeezing money from four out-of-town gamblers who were losing heavily. While the two professionals did not seem to be in direct collusion with each other, when winning a pot neither player toked (tipped) the dealer. And while the dealer never glanced at face-down cards when gathering cards for the next deal, he did riffle and shuffle the cards several extra times whenever the previous hand produced fewer than twelve

**face-up cards. Not seeing any other suspicious moves, John speculated that when the dealer riffled the cards he was also memorizing the hole cards of every player. John knew he could not beat collusion cheating involving a house dealer who knew everyone's hole cards. So he left without playing.**

**After three days in Las Vegas, John Finn realized that professional collusion cheating was well ensconced in higher-stake casino poker. He also knew that the alert, good player could subvert and beat most forms of professional cheating in public poker, especially collusion cheating. And most important, he identified those dealer-partner collusion situations that he could not beat.**

* * *

For the first time, good players must worry about getting wiped out by cheaters. In theory, even collusion cheating involving an all-knowing house dealer can be beaten by the good player who uses superior strategy and better money management. Yet to beat such cheaters, the good player needs to know what the cheaters know... he needs to know the concealed or hole cards of every opponent through near-perfect card reading. But few if any players can achieve such perfection. Therefore, most players, no matter how skillful, will lose money in games dominated by well-executed, dealer-partner Neocheating such as described in the previous anecdotes. That unbeatable Neocheating, however, is rare or nonexistent in private poker and occurs mainly in higher-stake casino poker that uses house dealers to shuffle, cut, and deal every hand (i.e., no one except the dealer ever cuts or touches the cards before the deal).

51

# Chapter II
# The First Move — Cutting Aces

When you finish reading the next nine chapters, you will have a complete working knowledge of not only Neocheating but of every other important technique used by professional and amateur cheaters. And more importantly, after a few hours of practice, you will be executing undetectable Neocheating... you will be controlling the cards in ways that would confound and beat your opponents — even if they are experienced and alert cardplayers. And most importantly, you will have the knowledge needed to identify and protect yourself from all cheating, including Neocheating.

\* \* \*

If your fingers possess ordinary dexterity — that is if you can shuffle cards without dropping them all over the table or without brutally bending them out of shape — then by the time you finish reading this chapter, you will be able to—
   a) pick up any deck of cards, shuffle it thoroughly,
   b) cut the deck, place it on the table, and then
   c) cut an ace for high card — even *after* another person cuts first.

By the end of the fourth chapter, you will be able to thoroughly shuffle any deck of cards, place them on a table, turn your head away, shut your eyes, and flawlessly read the cards by "feeling their backs" with your fingertips.

Impossible? Before you finish the next chapter, you will be able to stack four of a kind or a straight flush for yourself in a six-handed poker game — taking fifteen seconds or less... Almost nothing is impossible with Neocheating as you will soon discover.

Now, a popular maxim states: "You can't cheat an honest man." But this book demonstrates how false that maxim is. Actually, that maxim serves as a convenient cover for cheaters who constantly fleece unsuspecting, honest men. And with this book —with Neocheating — a person not only can cheat honest men, but can fleece them so smoothly and thoroughly that they

52

*Part One: Neocheating — Something Lethal*

will leave the card table broke and in a daze... and not the slightest bit wiser.

Why are most honest players so vulnerable? They are vulnerable because they are honest — they are not cheaters and do not know what is really involved in cheating. In fact, many believe they can spot cheaters. And most believe it takes years of intensive practice to become an effective, professional card cheater. But today, with Neocheating, both of those beliefs have become flatly untrue. In fact, modern, professional cheaters neither possess nor need much skill or dexterity.[5] Today, the most effective professional cheaters operate on a basis of minimum skill but maximum knowledge (presented in this book); they operate on a system of Neocheating... And when considering professional expertise, think of the following irony:

You can go to college for four years, spend thousands of hours in intensive study, and invest thousands of dollars to get a degree. Yet even that is no guarantee of profit and hardly makes you an expert or a professional in your chosen field. But ironically, with this book, you can become a professional Neocheater in less than fifty hours while spending no more than a few dollars for fresh decks of cards.

You can, in fact, gain enough knowledge and skill by studying this book a day or two to pass for a professional cardsharp among your peers. After a few hours, you will be effortlessly cutting aces and stacking four of a kind. And after a dozen hours with this book, the only thing that will separate you from a professional cardsharp is that he makes his living by cheating whereas you could make a living by cheating.

Throughout history, cheaters have made fortunes by fleecing honest men. Honesty does not imply knowledge. Indeed, this book provides the knowledge that can quickly convert any ordinary cardplayer into an effective, professional Neocheater. But more importantly, this book will provide the knowledge to protect

[5] *If the reader thinks any special skill or dexterity is required for Neocheating, he can peruse the next chapter on Preliminary Stacking right now; and after thirty minutes of practice, he will be stacking aces back-to-back in stud or three of a kind in draw as effectively as many professional cardsharps. But the reader will still have to return to this chapter to learn two indispensable maneuvers.*

53

Book 4
Neocheating: The Unbeatable Weapon

you from cheaters. When you know how modern professional cheating (Neocheating) is done, when you understand its seeming mysteries, you can then approach the subject of cheating with knowledge and confidence instead of gullibility and awe. What may have seemed fantastically impressive and skillful before you picked up this book will become routine and easy if you simply follow the text and illustrations.

\* \* \*

Now you are ready to learn Neocheating in the comfort of your own home and without anyone's knowledge. The Neocheating method of cutting aces is easy and far less complicated than its detailed description. See for yourself how quickly and easily you can learn Neocheating. And experience both the fun and the power of Neocheating. After all, how many people can cut aces at will or invisibly stack four of a kind in seconds?

But first you must know four important terms that are used throughout the book:

1. *Culling:* locating desired cards while shuffling, riffling, or gathering discards and then maneuvering those cards to the top or bottom of the deck.
2. *Stacking:* arranging the sequence of cards, usually while shuffling, riffling, or gathering discards.
3. *Crimping:* bending cards to produce a slight gap in the deck that can be felt when cutting.
4. *Blind Shuffling:* shuffling the cards — seemingly all the cards — while keeping the stacked portion of the deck intact.

Proceeding now to the first Neocheating technique — cutting aces: this chapter shows how to cut aces (or any desired card) at will. That knowledge will be the building block for the devastating cheating techniques described in later chapters.

## 1. Step One — Locating an Ace in Seconds.

With a deck of cards, sit at a table with a cleared surface. Cardboard cards are preferred when learning the Neocheating techniques. If you use a brand-new cardboard deck, the cards may

54

be too slippery to manipulate properly; so shuffle them several times to reduce the slickness. Plastic-coated cards are more durable, but do not respond to manipulation as well once they begin to wear. And plastic (not plastic-coated) cards are extremely resilient and durable, but require much more pressure to crimp. (Crimping will be explained shortly.) Actually any deck will do, provided it is not heavily worn.

Your hands are your tools. If they are too dry, rub some hand lotion into your palms and fingers to sensitize your touch. If your hands feel too moist (which is preferable to dryness), use a little talcum powder. Incidentally, if you smell hand lotion during a high-stake card game — beware.

Now pick up the deck of cards and give it an ordinary riffle shuffle. The difference between a riffle shuffle and an overhand shuffle is described below:

To *overhand shuffle*, hold the deck in the left hand, thumb on top, fingers underneath, hand tilted slightly. (If you are lefthanded, follow the same instructions throughout the book, but use the opposite hand.) With your right hand, remove the lower half of the deck. Then raise your left thumb and toss the cards, a few at a time, from your right hand onto those in your left hand.

To *riffle shuffle*, hold the deck in the right hand while at the same time resting the deck on your left hand. Now riffle the cards with your right thumb, but stop about halfway and part the deck as shown in Figure 1A. Pass the lower portion of the deck to your left hand, which then grips that lower portion between the thumb and fingers at opposite ends. Knuckle the forefingers down on the tops of the separated deck halves to hold them firmly in place. Next, using both thumbs, interlace the cards with a riffling action as shown in Figure 2A. Then push the cards together and square them into a full deck.

Riffles and shuffles are simple. Yet they are key maneuvers for the Neocheater. He uses those two elementary maneuvers to accomplish most of his "miracles".

The riffle, for example, is used to locate and control an ace (or any other desired card): As shown in Figure 1A, hold the deck with your right thumb and fingers, forefinger knuckled down on top, thumb and midfingers at opposite ends of the deck. Tilt the deck slightly upward from the table, keeping the ends of the

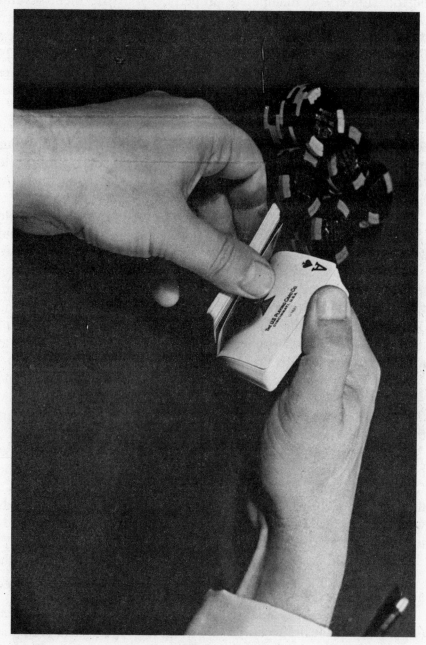

Figure 1
A. Riffle Shuffle: Parting the Deck
B. Spotting the Ace While Riffling

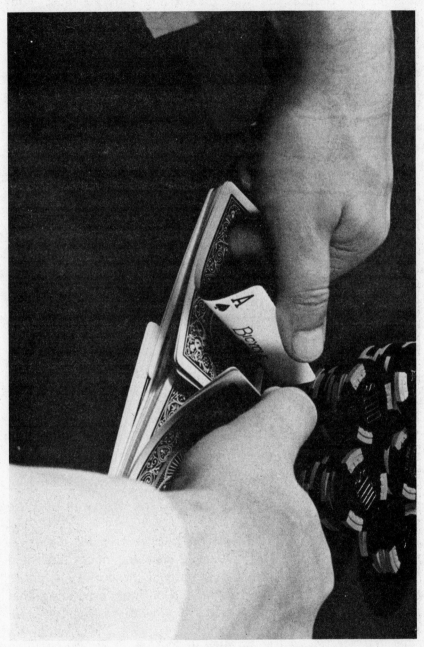

Figure 2
A. Riffle Shuffle: Interlacing
B. Letting the Ace Fall on Top of the Deck

deck squared. Before you start the riffling motion, place your index and middle finger of the left hand beneath the bottom card with the left thumb centered beneath the end of the deck. That steadies the deck as the cards are parted with the right thumb. The left thumb catches the parted cards as they fall and facilitates their transfer to the left hand.

Now to locate the ace, begin riffling the deck with your right thumb. Observe the faces of the rapidly passing cards. (The Neocheater does not stare, but glances casually at them.) Now repeat the process, but riffle more slowly. Stop immediately when you see an ace as shown in Figure 1B. (Figure 1B deliberately exposes the ace to show its position. The Neocheater, of course, does not expose the ace to others.) At first, you will probably pass the ace by two or three cards. So try again. Riffle the cards with a casual rhythm — not too fast, not too slow. Stop the moment you spot an ace. Do this for five minutes. You may feel clumsy at first, but speed and smoothness come rapidly. Soon only the ace will slip by, leaving it the top card on the lower portion of the deck. And that is where you want the ace.[6]

Now part the deck, passing the portion with the ace on top to your left hand. Then riffle shuffle all the cards together with both hands. But either riffle the left-handed portion of the deck more slowly or retain the ace with your left thumb until the deck is riffled together, dropping the ace last as shown in Figure 2B.

Remember, as you actually try these moves and steps, you will find they are much simpler than they appear in their detailed descriptions.

## 2. Step Two — Getting the Ace to the Bottom in One Overhand Shuffle.

As explained above, riffle the deck to an ace, let it fall on top of the lower section of the deck, part the deck, and then riffle shuffle so that the ace lands on top of the deck. The entire procedure takes only a few seconds. Continue practicing that move until you can do it smoothly. If you miss stopping at an

---

[6] *If the first ace you spot is too high or too low in the deck (within the top or bottom ten cards or so), pass that ace. Try stopping at an ace closer to the middle. But aces only a third of the way from the top or bottom of the deck are also perfectly workable.*

ace and your thumb has already parted two-thirds of the deck, complete a normal riffle shuffle. Repeat the riffle until you have located an ace. Extra riffle shuffles produce the illusion that the deck is being thoroughly shuffled. (Be cautious of thorough shufflers in a card game.) Using this method to cull an ace or any other card, the Neocheater appears to be riffle shuffling the deck and nothing more. With just ten minutes of practice, anyone can invisibly cull an ace that way.

To proceed, you now have an ace on top of the deck after riffle shuffling. But you want the ace on the bottom for the next move. So place the deck in your left hand for one overhand shuffle. Keep your left thumb firmly on the top card as you lift the entire deck with your right hand. The ace will remain in your left hand. Smoothly and without hurry, overhand shuffle the other cards on top of the ace. That maneuver happens instantaneously and looks perfectly normal.

### 3. Step Three — Positioning the Ace by Crimping.

The ace is now on the bottom after one overhand shuffle. Naturally, Neocheaters do not flash the ace or peek to make certain it is there.

Next, you are going to cut the deck without disturbing that bottom ace. As you finish your overhand shuffle, place the deck face down in the palm of your left hand. Pull fifteen or twenty cards from the center of the deck with your right hand as shown in Figure 3 and gently slap those cards on top of the deck. When done three or four times in rapid succession, such center cuts look very convincing, but the culled ace remains intact.

Now, as shown in Figure 4, grip the lower deck with your left thumb on one side, three fingers on the opposite side, and your left forefinger knuckled beneath the bottom card. Next, grip the upper deck with your right hand, four fingers on top, thumb pressed against lower left corner. At that moment, your right hand completely shields the deck. In a rapid "squaring" motion, press the lower left corner of the deck firmly down and inward with your right thumb to crimp that lower portion of the deck as shown in Figure 4. The thumb presses against and crimps one third to one half of the lower deck — or roughly fifteen to twenty-five cards. That crimping move takes only a second and

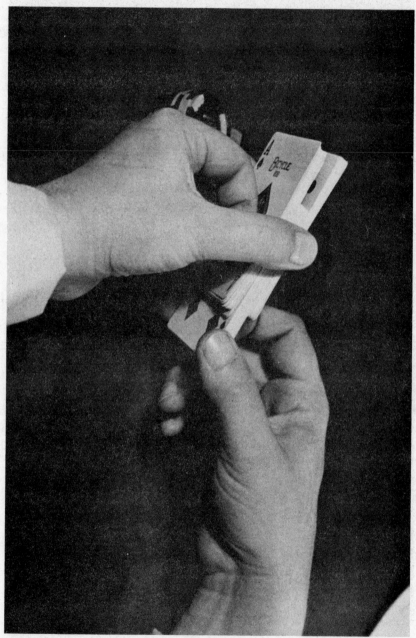

Figure 3
Removing Center Portion of Deck During Center Cut

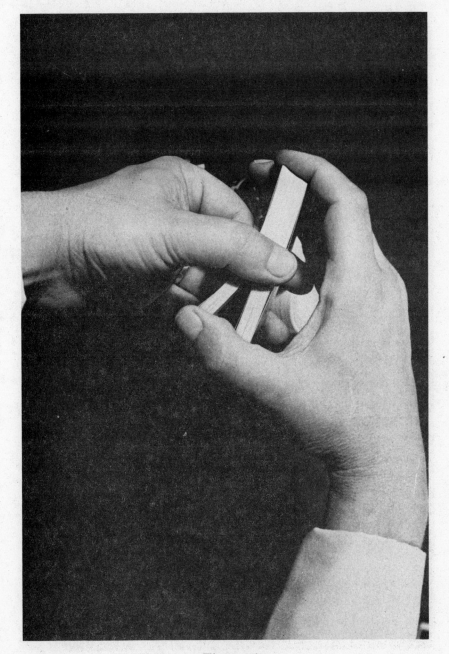

Figure 4
Making a Side Crimp by Pushing Down Corner of Deck

Figure 5
Deck with an Exaggerated Side Crimp

Figure 6
Flexing Cards Outward to Remove Crimp After Cutting

is undetectable.

After the lower inside part of the deck has been crimped by your right thumb, shift your right hand to grip the rear lower edges of the deck between your thumb and fingers. Then make an undercut by pulling about half the deck from the bottom and slap those cards on top in a final cut. As you put the deck on the table, quickly square the sides with your fingers.

The Neocheater places the deck with the crimp facing him. Thus, the sides facing his opponents have no visible gaps. Ideally, the crimp should not be visible, only felt. Good crimps leave gaps so slight that they are essentially invisible — a sixty-fourth of an inch is good. And the gap should never be more than a thirty-second of an inch. (See Figure 5 in which the gap is just slightly larger than a thirty second of an inch for illustrative purposes.) Too much pressure leaves a glaring gap, which, although facing only the cheater, makes the deck look awkwardly tilted.

### 4. Step Four — Cutting the Ace.

The deck is now crimped at the ace located in the middle of the deck. The sides of the deck are squared. If you lightly grasp the cards while cutting at about the halfway mark, your thumb will naturally cut at the crimp. Simply lift the upper part of the deck and you will have cut the ace. After the cut, flex the cards outward with your thumb and fingers to remove the crimp as shown in Figure 6.

Missing your crimp can be caused by (a) not crimping forcefully enough — a rarity with cardboard cards, (b) not squaring the sides of the deck just before you cut, or (c) gripping the deck too tightly as you cut.

### The End Crimp

A second method of crimping — the end crimp — requires pressure on the lower half of the deck while pulling it out to place on top during the final cut as shown in Figure 7. The pressure is exerted quickly with the thumb and fingers of the right hand while tilting the deck and using the left hand to shield the crimping motion from players on the left. Note that the forefinger of the left hand is knuckled underneath the deck, holding it firmly as the lower half of the deck is pushed down and inward by the right thumb and fingers.

Neocheaters often prefer another method of end crimping — a deck-squaring method involving the right hand as a cover to shield the crimping motion from all directions: With the left forefinger knuckled beneath the bottom card to hold the deck firmly, the left thumb and middle fingers crimp by pulling both lower corners of the deck sharply downward and inward under the protective cover of the right hand that is seemingly squaring the deck.

Figure 8 shows an end crimp with a gap slightly exaggerated for illustrative purposes. A few minutes of practice will reveal how much pressure[7] is necessary to produce a crimp that is barely visible but easily felt.

Because most players habitually cut at the sides of decks, end crimps reduce their chance of mistakenly hitting the crimp. Also, end crimps require much less pressure than side crimps and are easier to remove.

## 5. Letting Others Cut First.

If another player is to cut first, the Neocheater crimps as usual, but then pulls at least three-quarters of the deck from the bottom and slaps it on top. (The gentle slapping gives the cut an air of finality and conviction, as though he had really mixed the cards thoroughly.) The crimp would then lie quite low in the deck. And since the victim will seldom cut as deep as three-quarters of the deck, the ace is almost always left for the Neocheater.

## 6. Forcing Others to Cut Deuces or Treys.

As an alternative approach when other players cut first, the Neocheater simply reverses his procedure: Instead of culling an ace, he culls a deuce or trey, crimps it, and places the crimp near the middle or slightly higher in the deck. The victim will often cut that deuce or trey at the crimp, leaving the Neocheater with very favorable odds for cutting a higher card.

## 7. Putting it All Together — Quickly and Easily.

Fortunes can be won and lost on card cutting. After a

---

[7] *Different cards (cardboard, plastic, and plastic-coated cards) require different pressures to crimp.*

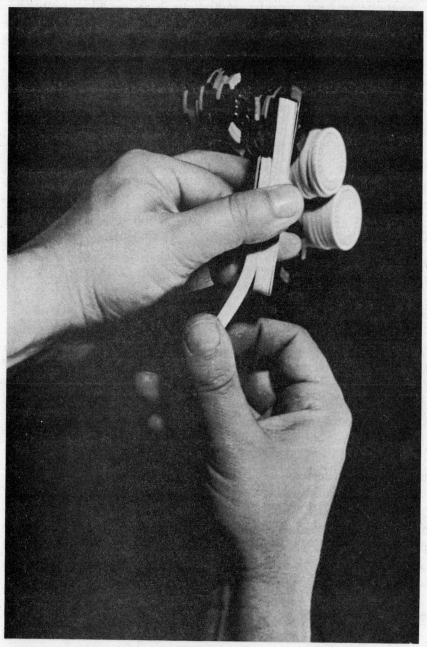

Figure 7
Another Way to Crimp — The End Crimp

Figure 8
Deck with an Exaggerated End Crimp

strenuous night of card playing, players will sometimes risk all their cash or winnings in a final rash or weary decision to "get it over with" on the cut of a single card. The Neocheater makes sure that the cash from cutting cards ends up in his pocket.

The complete ace-cutting procedure — riffling, locating the ace, shuffling, crimping, and cutting, including two or three center cuts, takes no more than fifteen seconds. With one hour of practice, you can do the entire procedure rapidly and smoothly.

The success of the ace-cutting technique hinges on two basic maneuvers — culling the ace (bringing it to the bottom of the deck) and then crimping the deck in a natural motion... The key steps in cutting aces with some added tips are reviewed below:

First, riffle the deck to locate an ace. No matter how fast you stop when you see an ace, it usually slips past your thumb by one card, which necessitates the overhand shuffle to position that ace on the bottom. But suppose you stop dead on the ace. Simply complete the riffle, letting the ace —the bottom card of the deck-half in your right hand— fall first so it is on the bottom. Then crimp and cut (an undercut) the deck to position the crimped ace within the deck. Gently square the sides of the deck before cutting to the crimp. Do not fumble or feel around for the crimp; just naturally grip the deck at about the crimp and the ace will be there waiting.

Practice slowly at first. Strive for naturalness. When riffling, avoid having the cards directly facing you. Instead, hold them at a slight angle so you see just the corners flashing. And if you miss the aces on the first riffle or two, simply riffle shuffle again until you locate an ace — riffle shuffles are reassuring to victims.

After perhaps a center cut or two, crimp the deck in one quick movement. Remember, the Neocheater's hands and fingers shield the deck while crimping. Practice various pressures with your thumb. Strive to make the crimp nearly invisible. But if a slight gap exists, that is generally acceptable so long as it is not too obvious. Ideally, the gap should be felt, but not seen.

If suspicion develops during a sloppy crimp procedure, several quick center cuts after crimping instead of before can eliminate that suspicion. The undercut (which positions the crimped ace within the deck) looks reassuring immediately after a few center cuts. The center cuts must be pulled from the upper center portion of the deck to avoid disturbing the crimped portion of the deck.

Now, after positioning the crimped ace in the deck with the undercut, square the deck, cut with a gentle grip, and you will not miss the ace. Practice cutting with your eyes closed to get the feel of the crimp.

After cutting the ace, always flex the cards outward to remove the crimp. And if possible, give the edge of the deck a final riffle with your thumb to eliminate any remnants of the crimp.

A good routine for practicing the entire ace-cutting procedure is to cull for ten minutes, crimp for five minutes, and repeat. Then perform the entire procedure from beginning to end for ten minutes. You can master the complete ace-cutting maneuver in an hour.

\* \* \*

In the next chapter, you will learn some shortcuts for culling and stacking. Neocheaters never disdain shortcuts or easy advantages in a card game. Indeed, they constantly seek them.

The culling and stacking methods in the next chapter are fast and easy shortcuts routinely used by Neocheaters. After an hour of practice, you will be stacking yourself winning hands in fifteen seconds. You will be invisibly stacking yourself four of a kind in draw, a wheel[8] in lowball, and aces back-to-back in five-card stud while also knowing every opponent's hole card.... And if you have ever wondered if professional cheaters really can stack themselves four of a kind with what appears to be two or three rapid shuffles and a cut, the next chapter will open your eyes.

---

[8] A "wheel" or "bicycle" is an A,2,3,4,5 of any suit — the best possible hand in most lowball poker games played today.

## 8. Detection and Defense.

### Detection of Neocheating During Card Cutting[9]

*Neocheating Tells*

Suspicion
Begins

Suspicion
Grows

Suspicion
High

- The dealer looks at the cards while parting and riffling the deck. (Unreliable indicator since most card players do that.)
- The dealer drops the top card in his left hand on top of the riffled deck. In subsequent shuffles, the dealer keeps that card on top.
- The dealer holds the cards with a finger knuckled underneath deck.
- The dealer's right hand and forearm suddenly flexes while holding or "squaring" the cards — could be the application of a crimp.
- Neocheating nearly confirmed when:
  1. The dealer uses center cuts concluded with one undercut.
  2. The dealer neatly squares the deck after placing it on table prior to cutting.
  3. The dealer flexes cards outward after cutting himself an ace or king. The dealer gives the cards a final riffle after his cut.
- A crimp on the side or end of deck facing the dealer is observed or felt. Expert crimps, however, are nearly invisible.

### *Defense Against Neocheating During Card Cutting*
- Let the Neocheater cull and crimp.
- Watch the final cut to know approximately where crimp lies.

[9] *Rarely can Neocheating be confirmed by observing just one of the above tells. Since any Neocheating is natural appearing or invisible, it can be confirmed only by observing repeating sequences of tells. While various tells can be used to confirm personal suspicion, they are not grounds to prove cheating to others.*

- Decide if the Neocheater has crimped a low card or a high card by who is going to cut first and by the depth of the final undercut.
- Now you are in a cannot-lose situation.
- Insist on cutting first. The Neocheater usually places a high-card crimp low in the deck — well below the point where opponents generally cut. Thus he will seldom object to your cutting first. Besides, a cheater will normally obey such requests by his "victim" to avoid suspicion. But if the cheater insists that he cuts first, tell him the bet is off. He will probably be relieved to drop it.
- When the Neocheater has prepared the deck for him to cut last, cut his ace at the low crimp (or avoid the high crimp at which he may have positioned a low-value card for you to cut).
- Remove the crimp after you cut with outward flex of the cards.

# Chapter III
# The Second Move —
# Stacking Four Of A Kind

In a later chapter, you will learn how to cull a desired hand and then stack it in the "normal" course of riffling, shuffling and cutting. But in this chapter, you will learn methods of discard stacking[10] — simple, effective shortcuts commonly used by Neocheaters.

## 1. Three Techniques for Stacking Without Shuffling.

The use of discards for either culling or stacking is fast, easy and, when done correctly, undetectable. The three basic methods of discard stacking are—
1) stacking while gathering discards,
2) stacking from discards tossed to the dealer face down, and
3) stacking from discards already piled on top of the deck.

When you finish this chapter, you will be able to execute all three methods of discard stacking.

## 2. Stacking Aces Back-to-Back in Stud.

Deal a five-handed game of five-card stud as shown in Figure 9. Note the face-up cards in the various hands. You will usually find two or three aces or kings showing. For the moment, however, confine yourself to stacking a pair of aces. As naturally and as quickly as possible, pick up two aces in a sequence that for a five-handed game will place four cards on top of each ace. (The number of cards placed on top of each card stacked for yourself must always be one less than the number of hands or players; an error in counting will cause the stacked hand to go awry.)

After thirty minutes of practice, you can execute discard stacking with smoothness and speed. Want proof? Set up five hands as shown in Figure 9. Now scoop up and stack yourself

---

[10] *Everything in this chapter that applies to stacking also applies to culling (bringing desired cards to the top or bottom of the deck). Culling is easier and quicker than stacking, but culling is useless until you learn the simple stacking techniques described in Chapter V.*

Figure 9
Scooping the First Ace While Discard Stacking

Figure 10
Scooping the Second Ace While Discard Stacking

two aces in sequence for a five-handed game as shown in Figures 9 and 10: First, using the hole card in the fifth hand, scoop in that hand and turn it face down, leaving four cards on top of the ace. That ace is now stacked for your next hand. Next, pick the ten and jack off the ace in the third hand and slip those cards beneath the turned hole card (a three) as shown in Figure 10. Now scoop in that hand, leaving the ace on the bottom with four cards on top. By tossing those five cards face down on top of the first five cards stacked and throwing the combined stack on top of the deck, you have stacked yourself aces back to back.[11]

Breaking the sequence of a hand when gathering discards as done in Figure 10, or gathering part of one hand and then part of another, looks completely natural when done smoothly and without hesitation. ... Now you have two options for the remaining cards:

1) Gather the remaining hands, turn them face down, and place the stacked deck on top of those cards. That option is the simplest procedure.
2) Gather the remaining hands, square those discards face down, lift half of the stacked portion of the deck and insert those discards. (Lift enough cards to protect your stack.) That option gives the appearance of a preliminary cut.

With a little practice, you can effectively stack discards without thinking about it. And often desired cards will lay practically pre-stacked, particularly in games with five or more players.

The Neocheater's motions are natural, his pace unhesitating. Using blocks of cards to scoop up other cards is natural. (Some players gather their hands and toss them to the dealer face down before he can stack them. That contingency will be explained later in this chapter.) Practice scooping up high pairs while stacking them in the process. The faster that is done, the

---

[11] *A discard stacker will alter his scooping sequences to prevent suspicion. For example, he may gather eight cards with an ace being the third card from the top after throwing them face down on the deck; and then he may gather six cards with another ace being the fifth card from the top after tossing those cards on the deck. He has now stacked himself aces back to back. Moreover, a good discard stacker can quickly gather discards with both hands simultaneously making his stacking moves impossible to follow.*

75

smoother it looks. No one can see a dishonest move in the Neocheater who performs smoothly. He first chooses the order of gathering cards in his mind and then promptly gathers the cards in that order. ... The following practice exercise will quickly make you an expert at discard stacking:

Deal out a six-handed game of five-card stud. Choose your desired cards quickly. Then see how rapidly you can stack three or four of a kind for yourself by gathering the discards without hesitation. With six hands to select from, you will almost always have three of a kind available, and often four of a kind. (Do not bother with straights or flushes; they are not worth the effort of stacking a full five cards. Besides, stacking four or five cards is done more quickly and easily by the methods taught in Chapter V.) If you find a pair in one hand and two matching cards in two other hands, experiment with splitting that pair to stack four of a kind.

Paired discards may be troublesome at first if they are to be part of your intended hand. But pairs are actually easy to handle. For example, if one hand contains a pair of aces, and the other two aces lie in different hands, attack the pair first. Scoop up a hand of five cards that does not have an ace and use that hand to split the pair of aces by scooping up the ace nearest you along with the cards after it and toss those cards on the deck. One ace is now stacked for six-handed poker. Suppose the other ace has two cards above it. Grab three cards from another hand, scoop up the two cards with that ace, and toss those six cards on top of the deck. You now have split and stacked that pair and can attack the other aces in order to stack yourself four aces. Incidentally, stacking wheels for lowball by discard gathering is almost as easy.

After practicing discard stacking for an hour or so, you can stack yourself four of a kind in a few seconds while scooping up the discards. And after a few convincing blind shuffles (taught in the next chapter) and a false cut, you can deal yourself four of a kind with dazzling nonchalance. You eliminate any suspicion that might arise while discard stacking with blind shuffling, which when executed with any degree of smoothness, is undetectable from genuine shuffling. Combined with a false riffle or two and a false cut, the effect is so superb that those unfamiliar with

76

Neocheating would never believe that a stacked deck could survive such thorough mixing. In fact, they would never have the faintest glimmer of what is happening.

### 3. Knowing Everyone's Hole Cards.

While stacking aces back-to-back in five-card stud, the Neocheater can also know every opponent's hole card. How? He simply memorizes the sequence — numbers only — of those cards on top of the last ace he stacks (that last ace will be his hole card). A Neocheater always memorizes everyone's hole card — not to do so would be an extravagant waste of an enormous advantage.[12]

The Neocheater stacks his first ace while starting to gather the discards. As he scoops up his second ace, which will be his hole card on the next hand, he notes with a glance that the discards being scooped read, top down: 10-J-3-7-A.[13] After some blind shuffles and false cuts, and if necessary, successfully foiling an opponent's cut (taught in a later chapter), he recalls while dealing that the first player to his left has a ten in the hole, the second player has a jack, the third a three, the fourth a seven, and he an ace... Mentally repeating the card sequence (i.e., 10-J-3-7-A) while shuffling and dealing aids the memory.

The advantage of knowing everyone's hole card in stud is overwhelming, particularly while holding aces or kings back-to-back. In fact, the Neocheater can often make more money over the long run by not stacking the deck at all, but by simply knowing everyone's hole card and then playing accordingly. Indeed, consistently creating innocent, small advantages (rather than dramatic, huge advantages) is the key to a Neocheater's extracting maximum money from his opponents as demonstrated in the last chapter of this book.

---

[12] *Likewise, the Neocheater can easily know both hole cards of every opponent in seven-card stud or hold 'em poker by memorizing the appropriate number of cards stacked on top of the deck.*

[13] *In both describing and memorizing hands, it is easier to refer to an ace as A, a king as K, a queen as Q, a jack as J, the joker or bug as B, and all other cards by their numerical values.*

Suits of opponents' hole cards are of little importance in five stud and do not have to be memorized. The chances of catching a flush are minimal. In any case, the Neocheater with aces wired can either drive out opponents with flush possibilities or make them pay dearly to chase their flush. In addition, the Neocheater knows the refinements of peeking (described later) and can easily know the final card to be dealt to any opponent.

## 4. Stacking Face-Down Discards.

As soon as the dealer for the next hand folds, impatient players often toss him their discards face down so he can without delay begin organizing the cards for the next deal. (Other players may keep their discards until the pot is won, or toss the cards to the side of the pot[14], or toss them to the current dealer, depending on whether he is in or out of play. Those situations are handled by a third technique of discard stacking taught later in this chapter.) To facilitate his setting up the next hand, the Neocheater usually drops out early when his deal is next, unless he has a strong possibility of winning that hand. And if stud poker is being played, he watches the cards closely to organize his upcoming scooping motions.

Informal, private games constitute over 95% of all poker played. In those games, players after folding often glance at discards out of curiosity, usually without objection from others. But the Neocheater glances at discards only as he gathers them for dealing and then only when necessary. Moreover, his glancing action is completely natural and inconspicuous. For example, in a six-handed game of five stud, the Neocheater (his deal is next, so he is hereafter called the dealer) folds during the first round and turns his two cards face down. Player A folds during the second round of betting and tosses his three discards to the dealer. The dealer casually glances at the cards as he gathers them. An ace or king is not among them, so he puts those three cards face down on his own two cards. He now has a pile of five discards. Player C folds and tosses his three cards toward

---

[14] *If the discards are tossed to the side of the pot, the dealer of the next round can usually begin gathering them immediately after he drops out of the current hand.*

the dealer. Gathering them, the dealer casually glances at the cards to notice the hole card (a king) on top. So he places his pile of five discards on top of those three discards to stack himself a king for a six-handed game.

During the next round, Player E folds and tosses the dealer his four discards, which contain a king. The dealer glances at the cards while quickly memorizing their sequence from hole card to top card as Q-9-K-3. He must now inconspicuously get the king on the bottom to help his stack. He can do that in several ways: For instance, with cards face down, he can casually slip the trey to the top while squaring the cards, giving him 3-Q-9-K. Or he can spread the cards face down on the table and casually slide the third card— the king — beneath the others as he picks them up. Or he can, as many players have a nervous habit of doing, especially while waiting for other players to bet, slip the cards one by one from top to bottom while holding them face down in his fingers. In that case, he will pass only the Q-9-K, leaving the king on bottom. And, of course, he remembers the altered sequence (3-Q-9-K) in order to know everyone's hole card.

After tossing the four rearranged cards on his stacked discard pile, he still needs two more cards on top to complete his stack; their values do not matter as long as he knows them. So he simply glances at two other discards, tosses them on top of his stacked pile, and puts that pile on top of the remaining discards. He has now stacked a pair of kings for himself and knows everyone's hole card for the next hand.

To gain adroitness in discard stacking, deal random hands and toss yourself discards as players would. See how easily and quickly you can stack a deck by using those cards. You will soon be stacking three or four of a kind.

## 5. Stacking Four of a Kind and Wheels.

In five-card stud, the dealer concerns himself only with stacking his first two cards and knowing the other players' hole cards. In seven-card stud, the dealer can easily stack himself three of a kind. (But stacking three of a kind in five-card stud does not work because someone usually folds the first round of betting and the third stacked card will go astray. Besides, the strength of three of a kind is seldom needed to win in five-card stud.) In draw, the dealer can stack himself three or four of a kind (or a wheel in lowball). After folding on the hand prior to his deal, he immediately begins collecting discards for his deal, glancing briefly at them when necessary, and proceeds with his culling or stacking:

The Neocheater can stack three or four of a kind in draw quite easily. Remember, he scans the cards with a glance, never staring at them and always turning them face down as quickly as possible. His movements are natural — casual and unhurried. Even for lowball, he can usually stack at least a four-card low combination, striving to include the joker if it is used. And he can frequently stack a wheel. Generally, however, the Neocheater avoids such powerful hands as they would be too suspicious to deal to himself hand after hand. Also, as explained in the final chapter, winning too often with powerful hands can actually work against winning maximum money.

Now to proceed to the third method of discard stacking: Suppose the Neocheater has a good hand and prefers to play it out, although his deal is next. Or suppose the discards are tossed to the current dealer, and the Neocheater has no easy access to them. In those cases, all the discards or the entire deck may come to him in a flood, all at once face down, when the play is over. The technique described next is a rapid and effective method for stacking or culling[15] in such situations.

The Neocheater gathers the mess of discards, keeping the pile uneven with edges and corners of cards protruding at all angles. He holds the cards vertically and facing him as shown in Figure 11. In such situations, cards facing the dealer are quite natural and unsuspicious. To others, the dealer is simply shielding the card faces from the other players as he squares the deck before shuffling.

---

[15] *As mentioned earlier, what applies to stacking discards also applies to culling. Culling simply involves maneuvering desired cards to the top or bottom of the deck without stacking them. Discard culling is especially important in Chapter V, which describes and teaches other simple but highly effective stacking techniques involving culled cards.*

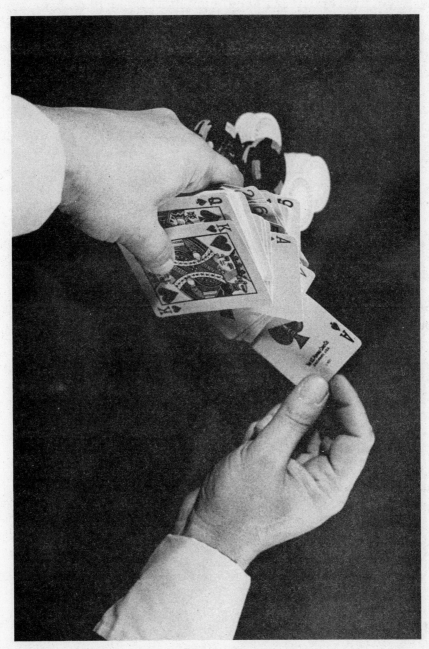

Figure 11
Bringing Aces to the Top Through Discard Culling

81

Figure 12
Bringing Aces to the Bottom Through Discard Culling

## Part One: Neocheating — Something Lethal

What the Neocheater strives for is a virtual mess of cards that will completely conceal his culling. To the other players — who see only the backs of the cards — his culling is simply an attempt to square the deck by smoothing out awkwardly tilted cards. Done rapidly and casually, the entire process appears innocuous and normal to others.

Quickly and smoothly, while straightening the sides of the deck and squaring the cards from their vertical angles to a horizontal position, he culls aces or kings (or unpaired low cards for lowball); he passes them to the top or bottom of the deck as shown in Figures 11 and 12. Once passed to the top or bottom, those cards are available for rapid stacking by several simple techniques described in Chapter V.

You can quickly and easily cull aces or kings from the discards. For example, spot an ace, pass it to the top; spot another, pass that quickly to the top; then repeat the process once or twice more. Three or four aces can be culled in a few seconds. While passing cards to the top (or bottom), use your fingers to alternate the passing movements with brief squaring motions on the sides of the deck. Or periodically take an awkwardly tilted card and pass it to the opposite end of the deck from your culled cards. The point is, never hesitate and keep your fingers in constant motion. When you cannot immediately locate a second or third ace, or other desired card, use your thumb to fan small batches of cards that may stick together. The fanning motion is shielded by other cards sticking out at various angles and, therefore, cannot be seen by other players. Such fanning not only spreads the cards for a better selection, but also keeps the deck from being squared too quickly.

With a little practice, anyone not only can cull, but also can discard stack by the above method. For example, stack a pair of aces for stud: First find an ace in the mass of discards and pass it to the top. Next seize two or three cards and pass those above the ace. Then while keeping count, pass two or three more cards to the top, depending on the number of cards you are trying to stack above the ace. Alternate the culling movements with brief but deceptive squaring motions on the sides of the deck. Now find and pass your second ace to the top, fanning cards with your thumb if necessary to locate that ace. Then again pass the

83

necessary number of cards above that ace so both aces are stacked to end up in-your hand. ... And as always, memorize the top cards of the stack in order to know everyone's hole card.

But since several easier and quicker stacking techniques are taught in Chapter V, the above discard-squaring method is usually reserved for rapid culling. In any case, the Neocheater never spends more than eight or ten seconds with the deck facing him. Practice seizing and quickly passing desired cards to the top or bottom of the deck. And the more uneven the discards are, the more selection and time you will have for culling cards. (In Figure 12, the culled cards have been passed to the bottom and the deck has been squared.)

When practicing this method of discard stacking, start by dropping the deck face down from a height of six inches onto the table. Use a sharp twisting motion with your wrist to unevenly spread the corners of the cards. Or actually deal out hands and then gather them as discards, deliberately effecting sloppiness while tossing those cards on top of the deck so they will require more time to square. In either case, pick up the mess of cards all at once and commence with culling or stacking. Fan small batches of cards with your thumb to expose their corners. Glance at the cards, but never stare. Keep your eyes in motion, glancing from the cards, to where a player would be, back to the cards, to where the ante would be - all in an unhurried pattern... When done without hesitation, discard culling and stacking look quite natural. Try discard culling in front of a mirror to see the moves from the victims' viewpoint.

\* \* \*

Now that the Neocheater has stacked himself a winning hand, how does he thoroughly shuffle and cut the deck without destroying his stack?... The answer lies in the next chapter.

## 6. Detection and Defense.

### *Detection of Neocheating During Discard Stacking[ 16 ]*

#### *Neocheating Tells*

Suspicion
Begins

- A player regularly folds early on hands just prior to his deal.
- The dealer effects sloppiness while gathering and picking up all the discards at once.
- The dealer keeps the discards facing him while squaring them.
- The dealer fans the discards (sometimes noticeable when looking for that maneuver).
- The dealer gathers the discards in sections rather than all at once.
- The dealer glances at discards.
- The dealer juggles separate stacks of discards before combining them.
- The dealer runs some cards one by one from top to bottom of the discard pile just before his deal.

Suspicion
Grows

- The dealer moves cards to top or bottom of the deck while squaring them.
- The dealer places a pile of discards on top of the deck and inserts another pile either under or between the deck.
- The dealer gathers discards, especially in stud, with scooping motions. While the cheating moves of a good discard stacker quickly gathering cards with both hands are invisible, his scooping motions can indicate stacking.
- The dealer bets in an abnormal manner unless he knew his opponents' hole cards.

Suspicion
High

- The dealer wins more frequently when dealing, especially with wired high pairs in five stud, wired trips in seven stud, or three of a kind or better in draw.

**Defenses Against Discard Stacking**

• Whenever the suspect is to deal, take charge of
  gathering discards and present them to the
  suspected dealer in a neatly squared pile.
• Fold early whenever the suspect deals.
• Just as the suspect is about to deal, politely — or
  somewhat suspiciously — excuse yourself from the
  hand and have him deal you out. His stacked hand
  will be scattered among the other players. Do that
  once or twice and the prudent cheater will stop
  cheating.
• Ask to cut the deck and complete the cut yourself.
  Introduce and enforce a house rule that prohibits
  the dealer from looking at discards.
• Use other defense methods described in later
  chapters and applicable after learning about blind
  shuffling stacked decks. You will even learn how
  to make cheaters work against themselves and for
  you, which eventually halts their cheating or
  bankrupts them while enriching you.

---

[16] *Rarely can Neocheating be confirmed by observing just one of the
above tells. Since any Neocheating is natural appearing or invisible,
it can be confirmed only by observing repeating sequences of tells.
While various tells can be used to confirm personal suspicion, they
are not grounds to prove cheating to others. ... Anyone, however, can
without ever seeing a dishonest move detect cheating by perceiving
illogical and improbable bets as demonstrated in the anecdotes in
Chapter I.*

# Chapter IV
# The Third Move — Controlling Hands

Many traditional cheaters use flagrant ploys to deal themselves good hands. As crude as their ploys may be, however, they often work when blended with basic Neocheating maneuvers of blind shuffling and false riffling. For example, some amateurs pretend to count the cards face up to make sure the deck is complete (e.g., "This deck doesn't feel complete", or "Are you sure the cards are all here?" are common signals). During their ploy, they casually cull aces to the top or bottom of the deck and proceed to center cut and crimp. Then a few blind shuffles and a false cut or two make their ploy effective.

Essentially all effective cheaters today mix at least some Neocheating into their techniques. Indeed, the Neocheating portion of their techniques makes them workable. The pure Neocheater, however, uses only the simple and invisible techniques described in this book. Crass ploys such as described in the above paragraph are never used or needed by the pure Neocheater.

## 1. Controlling Hands While Shuffling.

### Blind Shuffling

Blind shuffling is crucial to the Neocheater. He automatically and constantly blind shuffles — with deadly effects. Blind shuffling is easy. With about two hours of practice, anyone can appear to thoroughly shuffle a deck of cards while actually leaving the upper half or two thirds of the deck (the stack) undisturbed.

Blind shuffling is a key tool for Neocheaters. Any suspicion aroused by awkward or hesitant movements in the process of stacking is dissipated after a few blind shuffles and a false cut. In fact, in many games, a player could simply spread cards on a poker table and laboriously stack them one by one as other players watch, but as long as he thoroughly blind shuffles the deck afterward, no one will accuse him of cheating.

So effective is the blind shuffle that a person can stack a number of cards, blind shuffle and then convince opponents that their cards are marked by reading the values of the cards prior to turning them over one by one. Or he can convince players that he is a "psychic", able to read the backs of cards with his eyes tightly shut while his fingertips "feel the vibes". He can fool anyone — not only mystics, but scientists, businessmen, poker professionals — anyone except another Neocheater or the reader of this book.

Ironically, intelligent men can spend thousands of hours playing cards, but know nothing about manipulating them. And almost all honest cardplayers are ignorant of Neocheating maneuvers. "I can spot a crook anytime," is one indicator of an easy target for the Neocheater. The Neocheater loves to encounter the closed mind. He knows how easy it is to empty the wallet of the man who thinks he knows everything.

Professional cheaters generally disdain tricks such as "proving" cards are marked or "reading" them with their fingertips. Professionals call those tricks cheap flash, but such tricks demonstrate the seemingly miraculous effects of blind shuffling.

Commencing with the blind shuffle:

**Step One:** Assume that you have stacked the deck using either discard stacking or methods described later. You now need to produce the illusion of thoroughly shuffling the deck before dealing. So begin by preparing for what appears to be a normal overhand shuffle by placing the deck in your left hand as shown in Figure 13. Note the position of the fingers on the deck: Thumb on top, forefinger placed against the front edge, two middle fingers on bottom, and the little finger curled around the rear edge. Hold the deck so it feels comfortable and natural. (Neocheaters generally use those finger positions when shuffling blind or otherwise.) Tilt the upper end slightly downward toward the table to facilitate faster shuffling and to keep the cards from flashing. With your right hand, pull half the deck or less from the bottom using the two right center fingers and right thumb on opposite ends. The right forefinger should rest on top of the deck portion just pulled out by your right hand.

Now, using your left thumb, slide the top card from the deck portion in your right hand onto the deck portion retained in your left hand. But jut this top card toward you about an eighth of an inch (or slightly more) so that it protrudes a little from the rear of the deck in your left hand. Your curled left little finger will rest against this jutting card on top. Now casually overhand shuffle the remaining cards in the right hand, a few at a time, onto the top jutting card in the left hand. The jutting card is now located near the middle of the deck, and your cards should look approximately like those shown in Figure 13. The jutting card, hereafter called the break card, creates a break in the deck not visible to others. The half of the deck beneath the break-card is the stack. That portion of the deck will remain intact.

**Step Two:** Withdraw the lower part of the deck, the stack, with your right hand, up to but not including the jutting break card, and throw this entire portion on top of the cards in your left hand, briefly squaring the deck with your right fingers. Now the stack sits again undisturbed on the top; yet, the deck appears to be shuffled.

Repeat steps one and two for ten minutes, doing the steps as relaxed and smoothly as you can. Do not worry about speed; simply get the feel of that jutting break-card. Your left little finger should be brushing the break-card, and your right thumb should easily feel the break-card as you pull out the stack. Try for a natural rhythm, a casual pace. After the first ten minutes of practice, you should not have to look at the cards.

The Neocheater does not worry about others being conscious of the jutting break-card; the deck is in constant motion and looks perfectly normal. For anyone to see the break-card, they would have to stand directly behind the dealer. Even then the deck would look normal, for no one shuffles cards with the edges of the deck precisely squared at all times. Ideally, the break-card should protrude no more than an eighth of an inch, although protrusion varies from time to time up to a quarter of an inch.

Now, prepare to repeat the overhand shuffle in Step One by placing the deck in the left hand as shown in Figure 13. The stack is on the top. As before, with your right hand, pull half the deck or less from the bottom using the two right center fingers and right thumb on opposite ends of the deck. Then using your left thumb, slide the top card of the deck portion just pulled out by your right hand onto the deck portion retained in your left hand. Jut this top card toward you about an eighth of an inch, protruding slightly from the rear of the deck. Your curled

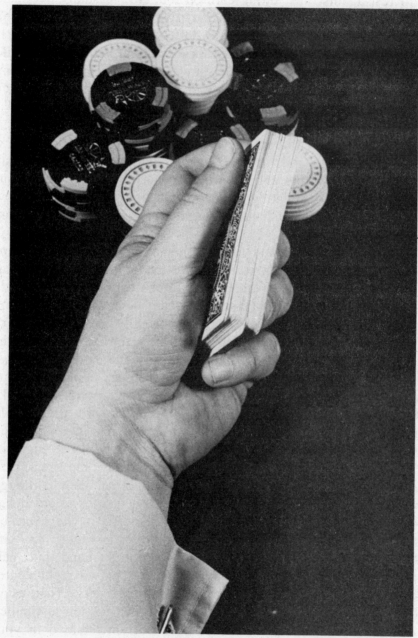

Figure 13
Holding the Deck During the Blind Shuffle

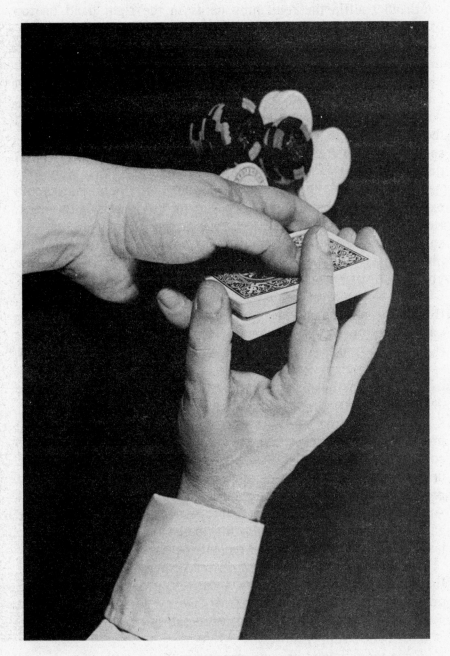

Figure 14
The Gap During the Blind Shuffle

91

left little finger will rest against this protruding break-card. Now overhand shuffle the remaining cards in the right hand on top of the jutting break-card in the left hand.

**Step Three:** Next, with your right hand, lift the entire deck from your left hand to prepare to overhand shuffle back into the left hand. But first press your right thumb against the jutting break-card (now located approximately in the middle of the deck) with an upward pressure while squaring that break-card against the rear of the deck. You will create a slight gap (about a thirty-second of an inch wide) at the rear of the deck. Figure 14 shows that gap slightly exaggerated for illustrative purposes.

The gap will appear only at the rear of the deck and should extend no more than an inch or so along the length of the deck. Be sure your right forefinger extends across the top of the deck shielding the gap from opponents as shown in Figure 14 (in the photograph, the deck is angled for illustrative purposes so that you can view the otherwise hidden gap).

**Step Four:** Now overhand shuffle the cards, a few at a time, from your right hand into your left hand, but only up to the gap. When you reach the gap (you will feel the gap with your right thumb), throw the remaining block of cards — your stack — in a single toss on top of the shuffled cards in your left hand. You now have your undisturbed stack back on top of the deck once again.

Practice that move for ten or fifteen minutes. Your gap will probably be too wide at first, so strive to narrow it. Practice the complete blind shuffle slowly at first, trying to develop a natural, unhesitating rhythm. During the first twenty minutes or so of practice, you will tend to hesitate while shuffling up to the gap. And you will probably stare at the cards, afraid of missing the gap and shuffling some cards off the stack. The right thumb, however, will quickly get the feel of the gap.

If during practice your fingers tend toward dryness and you find the cards slipping as you shuffle, try using a moistening preparation such as Sortkwik or Tacky Finger, which are inexpensive preparations used for billcounting and are available at most office supply stores.

Once your fingers become familiar with the jutting break-card and the gap, you will rarely have to look at the deck. Although glancing at the cards while shuffling is perfectly natural and does not cause suspicion, Neocheaters make the gap as small as possible, but allow enough of a gap to work smoothly. A thirty-second of an inch or less is good. To help determine how small you can make your gap and still work smoothly, turn the top card of the deck face up as you practice, and make certain that the same top card of your stack reappears each time the shuffle is completed.

When practicing the blind shuffle, do not gap the deck during the first twenty minutes of practice. After you get the feel of the break-card, start using the gap. Then begin gapping the deck every time. For variety, however, during every three or four blind shuffles you might use the jutting break-card only (without the gap) during the blind shuffle. Practice keeping at least half the deck intact by overhand shuffling only about half to a third of the deck from the bottom onto the jutting break-card.

Practice doing the blind shuffle strictly by feel when you are watching television or at other idle times. Rhythm is more important than speed; you will gain speed naturally with practice. This shuffle can be done slowly, and it will look convincing as long as it is done smoothly and without hesitation, especially when creating the gap.

After an hour of practice, this maneuver becomes so easy and routine that you will be blind shuffling with fair smoothness and steadiness. In two to three hours, blind shuffling becomes second nature. It is that simple. Done correctly, the deck appears to be thoroughly shuffled. And when the blind shuffle is done in conjunction with the false riffle and false cut (described later in this chapter), you can convince even the most alert players that the deck has been thoroughly mixed.

Using that basic blind shuffle and a simple false cut (described later), even neophytes can shuffle their cards and then deal themselves prestacked four aces or straight flushes to everyone's astonishment. No one questions that the cards have been thoroughly shuffled. And no one can imagine how a prestacked deck could survive such shuffling.

Even a beginner can cull four aces or four kings using the simple discard-culling technique described in the previous chapter. He can then give the deck several rapid blind shuffles, a false cut, and triumphantly toss four aces off the top of the deck to the astonishment of all observers. Moreover, beginners need to master nothing more than a preliminary discard-stacking technique and the blind shuffle, plus have some knowledge about Neocheating to win in almost any game.

Let us assume you have spent at least an hour or two practicing the blind shuffle and can now perform it fairly easily. To test its effectiveness, pick up someone else's deck. Fan the first three or four cards, face down, and pretend to study the designs on their backs for about ten seconds. Frown as you study the cards, as though something were suspicious. Then turn the cards face up and glance at them to quickly memorize the cards in their proper sequence before turning them face down again. Forget the suits; they are unimportant. Square the cards together in your right hand and then fan the next three or four cards face down. Again, study their designs for a few moments and then, in a quick glance, memorize those cards in sequence. During this ruse, glance at the cards as briefly as possible — as if confirming something you have seen in the designs on their backs. Rapidly square this next batch of memorized cards beneath the first memorized batch in your right hand.

You might be able to fan and memorize another batch of cards. Many people, however, have trouble memorizing more than six or seven digits. But after a little practice, most people can learn to easily remember nine or ten digits. Still, no more than six or seven memorized cards are necessary to make this ruse convincing. Constantly repeat in your mind the numbers in groups of three or four at a time as you shuffle. Now put the memorized cards back on top of the deck in your left hand. The memorized top cards may be, for example, Q-6-2-A-5-10-J — you need to memorize only their initials. Next proceed to blind shuffle several times, explaining as you shuffle that imperfections in the manufacturer's design exist as tiny flaws that are consistent in every deck of that particular brand. Talk also serves as a minor distraction from the shuffle; although if you can blind shuffle with even minimum competence, you can perform in total silence in a filled amphitheatre without anyone knowing that you are blind shuffling.

If you think experienced cardplayers will not believe a story about visible imperfections on the backs of cards, proceed as follows: When you have finished your blind shuffles, slap the deck gently onto the table (creating an air of finality; rarely will anyone ask to cut the cards when you do that, especially if you do not hesitate and proceed immediately), lean close to the cards and "read" them from their backs, one by one. Take your time before calling and turning each card — four or five seconds is about right. Peer intently at the backs of the cards before calling them, and then note your viewers' reactions. By the time you have "read" the fifth or sixth card, your audience will be studying the backs of the called cards. You can send experienced cardplayers on long searches for "legal" marks on cards. Ironically, they will often find such marks and imperfections, especially in cheaper brands of cards, that will actually let them read the backs of certain cards.

Professional cheaters scoff at such pointless ruses. (If no profit exists, why bother?) But those ruses demonstrate the power of the blind shuffle. And beginners can use ruses for practice and to build confidence before actually Neocheating for money. Be certain your blind shuffles are smooth before you attempt such demonstrations. Combined with the false cut described later in this chapter, the effect is spectacular.

You must always be aware of the number of cards in the stack. If a Neocheater stacks aces back-to-back for stud poker in a six-handed game, he worries only about keeping the top twelve cards of the deck intact. If he has stacked four of a kind in a six-handed game, then he must keep twenty-four cards unshuffled. And if he has stacked a pat hand or a wheel in lowball, he then has thirty cards in his stack — more than half the deck for a six-handed game.... Professionals seldom stack straights or flushes in draw because of the number of cards involved. Why stack five-card pat hands when four of a kind is easier to stack.[17]

In any case, when stacking pat hands, you must keep up to two-thirds of the deck intact. That is, you actually shuffle only the bottom third or so of the deck. Do not worry about

---

[17] *In any case, a Neocheater will seldom stack such powerful sure-thing hands because they are less profitable in the long run, as explained in Chapter XI.*

appearances; if your blind shuffle is smooth, the cards will seem mixed beyond suspicion.

### a. Detecting Blind Shuffling
- Observe the dealer's grip on the deck when shuffling. Beware if the grip resembles that shown in Figure 13.
- Watch for an initial one-card pass from one hand to the other during the overhand shuffle (indicates a break-card).
- Watch for the dealer who consistently tosses an unshuffled portion of the deck over the shuffled portion. (Must be alert to see that.)

### b. Defending Against Blind Shuffling
- Review the nine methods on page 6 to eliminate cheating or cheaters.
- Insist on cutting the deck whenever the Neocheater deals and then ruin his stack with deliberate center cuts.
- Sit to the Neocheater's right and carefully cut at the crimp *plus* cut one extra card. You will then receive the hand stacked for the dealer.

## 2. Controlling Hands While Riffling.

### False Riffling

The false riffle shuffle is nearly as effective as the blind shuffle and is necessary for certain kinds of culling and stacking taught in the next chapter. Moreover, the false riffle is easy to learn:

The deck is stacked. Now, handle the deck in the same way described for culling an ace in Chapter II. That is, place the thumb and two center fingers of the right hand at opposite ends of the deck while knuckling the forefinger down on top. Riffle-part the end of the deck with your thumb as shown in Figure 1A on page 25. But before reaching the halfway mark, stop riffling and pass the lower portion of the parted deck to your left hand. Now begin a riffle interlacing of the cards, but riffle the cards in your left hand much more rapidly than those in your right hand, and retain the top card in your left hand with your left thumb. At that stage you should still have a block of about fifteen or so cards in your right hand that are unshuffled (your stack). Smoothly and rapidly

96

drop that entire block on top of the interlaced portion and then, without hesitation, drop the card retained by your left thumb on top of your intact stack as shown in Figure 15. (The retained card — the ace — is deliberately flashed for illustrative purposes... Neocheaters normally do not flash cards.) Immediately push the halves together and square the deck.

Practice this riffle shuffle repeatedly, getting the feel of that single card retained by your left thumb, and quickly dropping that card at the last moment to complete the riffle. Later, you will learn a refined version of the false riffle that looks considerably smoother,[18] but you must first perform this basic false riffle with ease.

After each riffle shuffle, you will have one extra card on top of the deck — on top of the unshuffled block of cards that is your stack. (Eventually, you will be able to leave at least half the deck unshuffled this way, but do not attempt manipulating large stacks at this stage.) Treatment of those extra cards accumulated on top by false riffling will be discussed shortly.

Perform the riffle shuffle with rapidity. Unlike the blind shuffle, never try the riffle shuffle slowly. And although the movements may feel awkward at first, the shuffle does not appear awkward to other players. After only a few minutes of practice you will develop enough speed to increase the number of unshuffled cards until you can keep half the deck or more intact while riffle shuffling.

To preserve, for example, a four-of-a-kind stack in a seven-handed game, part and then pass only about a third of the deck to your left hand for riffle shuffling. Then interlace all but the top card in your left hand with only the bottom third or so of the cards in your right hand. Now drop the entire batch of cards retained in your right hand (which contains your undisturbed stack) on top of the interlaced cards and then immediately drop the final, single card retained by your left thumb. You will now have your stack preserved one card below the top of the deck.

Suppose you do the false riffle shuffle four times. You will

---

[18] *That version of riffle shuffling is called the Las Vegas Variation (it is the shuffle used by dealers in the Las Vegas casinos). As described in Chapter V, the deck in the Las Vegas Variation is completely shielded by the hands during the riffle shuffle.*

then have four extra cards to remove from the top of your stack. The simplest method to remove those cards is to blind shuffle. So proceed with the blind shuffle (as described earlier in this chapter) by placing the squared, riffle-shuffled deck in your left hand and pulling out about a third of the cards from the lower portion of the deck with your right hand. Now with your left thumb, pull the top card from your right hand back onto the left-hand portion and jut that top card slightly. Next, overhand shuffle all the other cards in your right hand onto the cards in your left hand. The break-card is jutting out from the rear of the deck four cards above your stack. With your right hand, pull out all the cards up to the break-card and then with your left thumb, slide off (overhand shuffle) those four extra cards from the top of your stack very rapidly, one by one, back into your left hand. Then toss in a single block all the remaining cards in your right hand on top of the deck portion in your left hand and quickly follow with another complete blind shuffle.

To facilitate running the cards one by one, spend five minutes running through the entire deck with your left thumb slipping the cards off one at a time as quickly as possible.

In many games, the blind shuffle and the false cut are sufficient tools for the Neocheater. But the false riffle is indispensable to the Neocheater using the stacking techniques described in the next chapter.

### a. Detecting False Riffling
- The cards move too fast for even an alert player to see a good false riffle. But closely watch left thumb of dealer for retaining the top card and consistently dropping that card last.

### b. Defending Against False Riffling
- Same defenses as against blind shuffling described on page 96.

* * *

98

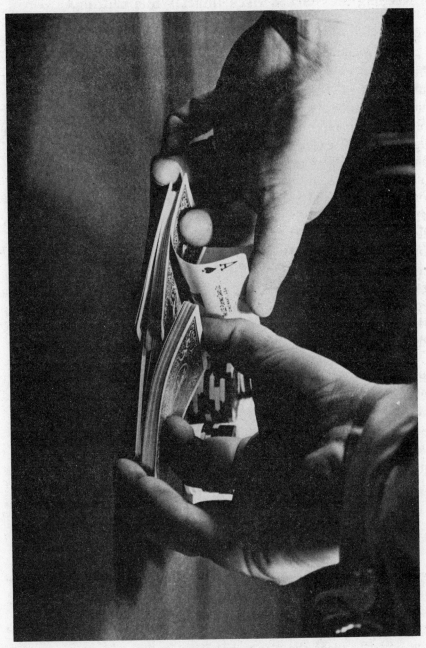

Figure 15
Retaining the Top Card
with the Left Thumb During the False Riffle

99

## 3. Keeping the Stacked Deck Intact While Cutting.

### <u>False Cutting</u>

With your undisturbed stack resting on top of a "thoroughly shuffled" deck, you then want to execute a legitimate-appearing cut that leaves your stack intact. To accomplish that, grasp the deck with both hands at opposite ends with the thumbs and index fingers (or middle fingers) as shown in Figure 16. Now while looking at Figures 16-18, execute this false cut by first pulling out about a third of the deck from the bottom with your right thumb and index finger and place those cards on top of the deck portion held by your left thumb and index finger (but retain your grip on the block of cards in your right hand). Then as shown in Figure 17, grasp the upper half of the cards held by your left hand with part of your right thumb and right middle finger while simultaneously releasing your left thumb and index finger from that same block of cards. At that brief moment, the deck will be split into three separate blocks, your right thumb and index and middle fingers gripping the two upper blocks while the left thumb and middle finger grips the bottom portion as shown in Figure 17.

Instantly release the uppermost block from your right index finger and thumb, at the same time pulling outward and slightly upward the two other blocks beneath held by your right and left hands. Each hand will be grasping about a third of the deck as you do this, and the top portion will now fall through the other two blocks of cards onto the table. You may use your right index finger to help guide the right-hand portion of loose cards as they fall to the table.

Next, with a slow smooth motion, slap the portion of the deck in your left hand onto those loose cards now on the table as shown in Figure 18. Then place the remaining cards (your stack) in your right hand on top of those cards and square the deck. Again, your stack sits undisturbed on top. Executed with any degree of smoothness, the cut looks very thorough and legitimate.

A mirror to view your motions is helpful for practice. For the best effect, you should perform the cut fairly rapidly, but slow down to place the two remaining blocks of cards from your left and right hands on top of the portion that falls to the table. Your stack will end up intact on top of the deck.

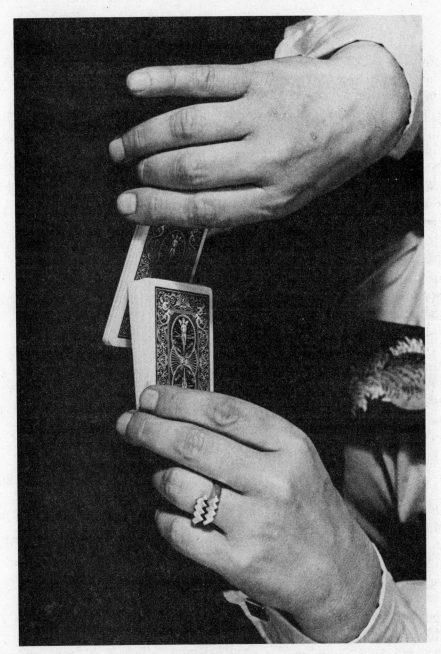

Figure 16
Starting the False Cut

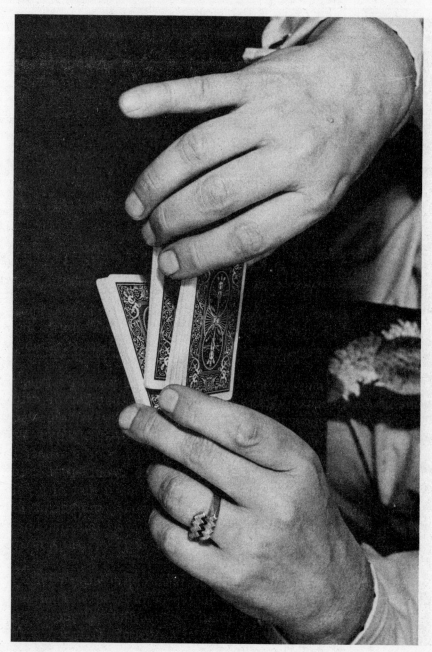

Figure 17
Breaking the Deck into Thirds

102

Figure 18
Placing the Stack on Top

103

After thirty minutes of practice, you can execute this cut fairly smoothly. Remember to angle the card-blocks in your right and left hands in a slight upward sweeping motion as the top block falls between them. Strive for gracefulness. Again, the first phase of this cut, including dropping the top block between the other two portions in your hands, should be done fairly fast. But the final phase, which completes the cut by placing the other two blocks of cards on top, should be done more slowly.

More false cuts are described later in this book. But learn this basic standby cut first. The cut need not be done perfectly to be effective. And even if the cards tend to spread somewhat when they are dropped, do the cut without hesitation.

### a. Detecting False Cutting
• Watch for the same block of cards consistently ending on top of the deck.
• Be suspicious of fancy cuts, extra thorough-looking cuts, and quick three-way cuts. Also, watch for simple crimp cuts (described next in this chapter).

### b. Defending Against False Cutting
• Same defenses as against blind shuffling described on page 96.

* * *

The three basic techniques in this chapter — blind shuffling, false riffling, and false cutting — are invaluable to the Neocheater. He uses those techniques constantly. With only a few hours practice, each technique quickly becomes habit, performed routinely without groping or thinking.

The blind shuffle will usually dispel any suspicion of cheating or stacking. For example, when cutting an ace for high card, a Neocheater culls an ace to the top of the deck in one riffle shuffle; he then blind shuffles the deck four or five times, runs the ace to the bottom in one overhand shuffle, crimps the lower deck, gives it two or three rapid center cuts and then a final bottom cut before slapping the deck on the table... The deck now appears thoroughly shuffled and cut.

The blind shuffle is more convincing than the false riffle. And when the blind shuffle is combined with the false cut, the illusion is deadly. In certain games, Neocheaters will not even need to offer the deck for a cut, and rarely will anyone request a cut if the Neocheater executes the blind shuffle and false cut with any degree of smoothness.

## 4. Controlling Hands as Other Players Cut.

### Foiling the Cut

The Neocheater discard stacks himself aces back-to-back for stud poker, knows everyone's hole card, thoroughly blind shuffles and false cuts the deck, and is ready to deal. But what if an opponent demands a cut? An easy and simple method often used by Neocheaters to foil an opponent's cut is described below. Other more sophisticated techniques for negating any cut are described in later chapters.

Before offering the deck for a cut, the Neocheater rapidly crimps the deck as he would for cutting an ace as described in Chapter II and illustrated in Figures 4 and 5. He crimps by pushing downward and inward the bottom corner of the deck with his right thumb. Now with the stack on top, he quickly cuts the deck and then extends the crimped and squared deck to the player on his right for his cut. If that player cuts at the crimp, the stacked cards will end up right back on top of the deck, ready for dealing.

Most players will cut at any crimp near the middle of the deck eighty per cent of the time. Their thumb and fingers automatically go to the crimp four out of five times, even though they are unaware of the gap. The crimp is slight, and it is extremely unlikely that anyone would notice the gap. Even if the gap were noticed, few would consider it unusual since many players, especially chronic losers, bend and punish cards violently during the course of play as though the cards were mortal enemies.

The player on the right will occasionally miss the crimp, although the odds are well in the Neocheater's favor. But the professional accepts this vicissitude. Or he can use one of the advanced techniques (taught in Chapter VI) for foiling the cut. Those techniques do not depend on opponents cutting at the crimp. In any case, the professional makes a habit of noticing at what position the player on his right habitually cuts the deck — near the top, middle, or roughly the three-quarter mark. He then places the crimp accordingly. Most players unthinkingly cut the deck at the approximate center. If the player on the right consistently cuts at the ends of the deck instead of the sides, the Neocheater simply crimps at the ends, using the end-crimping technique described in Chapter II and illustrated in Figures 7 and 8.

The crimp used for high-card cutting (as described in Chapter II) is gapped on only one side of the deck. In the course of a game, however, as opposed to high-card cutting, players are less alert to the cutting process, and your crimp will usually be more effective if it exists on both sides of the deck. Crimping both sides of the deck is described below:

First, crimp as you would when cutting for an ace, but instead of bending the lower left corner of the deck with your right thumb as described in Chapter II, push down with your right thumb at the center of the lower rear end of the deck. That will cause both sides of the deck to gap. Too much pressure from the thumb, however, will create a glaring crimp.

Some professionals use "agents" (other players working in collusion) who sit to their right. They will cut at the dealer's crimp every time or use a convincing false cut (such as the three-way false cut described on pages 100-105) that leaves the stack intact. The colluding partners also use a variety of other techniques to drain opponents of their money; those tactics will be covered in Chapter VII. This book, however, primarily teaches the lethal techniques of Neocheating — techniques increasingly used by ordinary people who walk into games on their own and walk away with stuffed wallets, without ever using confederates, marked cards, or artificial and dangerous devices. But for the sake of comprehensiveness, all cheating methods and contrivances will be identified in later chapters.

A Neocheater's effectiveness and margin of safety lies in his own ten fingers. Anyone who can perform the maneuvers described up to this point with a degree of smoothness is already on par with most working professionals. Now you are ready for the stacking techniques covered in the next chapter. None are exceptionally difficult, two are relatively easy, and all are based primarily on techniques you already know.

# Chapter V
# Culling And Stacking —
# The Invisible Way

## 1. Culling and Stacking the Neocheating Way.

Neocheaters extensively use the discard-culling and discard-stacking techniques described in Chapter III because easy opportunities to cull from the discards exist almost every time they deal. But also, with only a few hours' practice, anyone can pick up any deck without knowing the whereabouts of a single card and then cull and stack a hand in the "normal" course of riffling and shuffling. Indeed, the Neocheater will frequently cull and stack during the shuffle *in conjunction* with his discard stacking. Assume, for example, he has stacked only one ace using the discards. He can easily add a second and a third ace to his stack during the shuffle by using the techniques taught in this chapter.

This chapter will progress from the easiest to the somewhat more difficult stacking techniques executed while shuffling. Every stacking technique has its advantages and disadvantages. The first technique described is the undercut shuffle. It is the easiest and fastest way to stack a deck during the shuffle. With a little practice, you can stack any hand with any number of players in any game *in one undercut shuffle* — you can stack yourself a pair, three of a kind, full house, four of a kind, straight flush, royal flush, or in lowball, a pat wheel.[19] In fact, you can execute undercut stacking with some degree of skill in ten minutes. In thirty minutes, you will be competent at stacking. And in an hour or two, you will stack with professional ease.

While the undercut shuffle is less subtle than other techniques, Neocheaters execute the undercut with speed and confidence to dissipate any suspicion. Moreover, undercut stacking is safe in neighborhood games and informal sessions, especially in low-stake to medium-stake games. But Neocheaters would not use the technique in knowledgeable company, and

[19] *As identified in Chapter XI, the Neocheater can easily, but will seldom, stack himself powerful, sure-thing hands. He makes much more money over the long term by creating more modest but consistent advantages that do not arouse suspicions or resentments*

almost never in professional high-stake games. Yet, the undercut is often used with great success in high-stake games with naive or unalert players and is a powerful money pump in the average Friday-night poker game.

The first step in undercut stacking requires culling. You already know two culling methods: Culling from discards described in Chapter III, and riffle culling described in Chapter II. Riffle culling is the only practical technique to stack a deck cold (i.e., when no discards are available such as with a new deck, a deck just put into play, or when alternating decks are used for every other hand). With a few hours of practice, you can control any cold deck through riffle culling. If you can cull one ace in one riffle, you can cull four aces in four riffles. Riffle culling is taught in more detail later in this chapter.

But for now, assume you have culled a winning hand by using one of the discard-gathering methods. For example, someone tosses you his folded two pair, kings over sixes, while someone else folds a hand with a pair of kings. You then maneuver those four kings on top of the deck by using the discard-squaring method described in Chapter III. You are now ready to execute the undercut.

### a. Undercut Stacking

Your four culled kings, however, must be on the bottom of the deck to execute the undercut. You can cull discards to the bottom instead of the top of the deck, but culling to the top is usually smoother and more natural appearing. Moreover, the technique that switches culled cards from the top of the deck to the bottom is very easy and takes only a few seconds: Lift the deck in your right hand for an overhand shuffle and rapidly slide off your four culled kings, one by one, with your left thumb into your left hand. Then overhand shuffle the rest of the deck from the right hand onto those four cards in your left hand. Now your four kings are on the bottom of the deck ready for the undercut.

In the previous chapter, you practiced running cards one by one off the deck with your left thumb. The undercut depends on running off cards rapidly and smoothly. The maneuver is easy if your thumb and fingers are not too dry. Some professional stackers keep in their pocket a thin, small diameter container of a moistening conditioner such as Sortkwik or Tacky Finger used for bill-counting. As their deal approaches, they moisten their fingertips to make the undercut easier. But such conditioners must be used sparingly so as not to leave any residue on the cards and are generally avoided by Neocheaters.

Now, returning to undercut stacking: Your four kings are on the bottom, and you must deal six hands. So grasp the deck in the right hand for an overhand shuffle. With your left thumb and left two center fingers, simultaneously grasp both the top and bottom cards of the deck and pull them together into your left hand as illustrated in Figure 19. That move is called the undercut and is used here to place bottom cards (i.e., your four culled kings) in the desired stacked position. Now, with your left thumb, rapidly run off four cards from the top of the deck in your right hand onto the two cards in your left hand. Repeat the process: Top card and bottom card from the right hand are pulled together into the left hand, then four successive cards are pulled from the top of the right-hand portion of the deck onto the cards in your left hand. Repeat the same process twice more to finish stacking your four kings for a six-handed game.

Then pull one more card onto the left-hand cards; jut that card towards you about one eighth of an inch.[20] Next, overhand shuffle the remaining deck from the right hand onto that jutting break-card in your left hand. Now complete your blind shuffle by pulling out all the cards beneath the break-card with your right hand and tossing them in a single block back on top of the deck portion still in your left hand. That move puts your stack on top of the deck.

After a little practice, you can stack by using the undercut an entire five-card pat hand in fifteen seconds, complete with a concluding series of blind shuffles. The effectiveness of the undercut depends upon speed and rhythm. Your left thumb and fingers should not be too dry, and the cards cannot be too worn or they will tend to stick together and slide off the deck in blocks of two rather than one by one.

You will soon be doing the undercut so rapidly that removal

[20] *A moment before you jut the break-card, you may need to square the stacked cards in your left hand by quickly tapping the rear of those cards with your right little finger.*

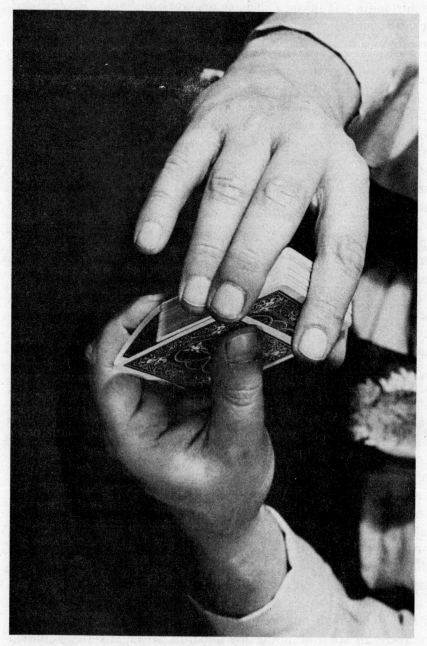

Figure 19
Pulling Cards from the
Deck During the Undercut

of the bottom cards becomes an invisible blur, giving the appearance of a legitimate overhand shuffle. But you can then slow down the subsequent blind shuffles for a reassuring effect.

The mathematics of stacking hands for any number of players is simple: After getting the culled cards to the bottom of the deck and after simultaneously slipping off the top and bottom card from the deck, run off two less cards than the number of players from the top of the right hand portion of the deck onto the cards being stacked in the left hand. Repeat that process the same number of times as cards to be in your stacked hand. For example, repeat the process twice for a pair, three times for three of a kind, four times for four of a kind, and five times for a full house or other pat hands.

When stacking for gin rummy or any two-handed game, simply continue to slip off the top and bottom cards together into the left hand, as many times as the number of cards to be stacked in your hand. Then pull off one more card, jut it, and blind shuffle. In all cases, however, begin with your culled hand on the bottom of the deck, stack the cards with the undercut, and conclude with convincing blind shuffles.

### b. Undercut Stacking Two Hands Simultaneously

Besides its simplicity, the undercut has another powerful advantage: Two hands can be stacked at the same time — one for the Neocheater and one for his victim. Again the first step is culling. The dealer can, for example, use *discard culling* and the undercut to deal his victim — preferably a heavily-winning or well-monied opponent — a six-four low in lowball while dealing himself a five low. (*Riffle culling* two hands simultaneously is generally too cumbersome and time consuming.) And in high draw, the dealer may cull four jacks for his victim and four kings for himself while gathering discards. In such a case, the dealer maneuvers his four kings to the bottom of the deck and his opponent's four jacks to the top while culling. Or he may put both hands on top of the deck. In that case, his hand should lie above his opponent's hand, (e.g., the four kings above the four jacks[21]). Now to get his own hand to the bottom of the deck while avoiding excessive blind-shuffling maneuvers, he simply overhand shuffles his four kings, one by one in quick succession, off the top of the deck and slides them to the bottom of the deck. He now has the losing four jacks on the top of the deck and his winning four kings on the bottom of the deck.

For two-handed poker, he holds the deck in his right hand for an overhand shuffle and simply pulls with the left thumb and middle finger the top card and the bottom card together simultaneously into his left hand, four times in succession. He then slides one more card from the deck onto the cards stacked in his left hand and juts that top card, completes a blind shuffle, and ends up with the two hands stacked on top of the deck. He can then false cut or foil the cut and proceed to annihilate his opponent: On being dealt four jacks, the victim will lick his lips in anticipation of draining every penny from his opponent, but instead he will be cleaned by the Neocheater.

The undercut stacking maneuver is ideal for gin rummy and other two-handed games. If the Neocheater stacks two hands and if the deck is cut at the crimp, the victim is doomed.

Now assume the Neocheater is playing seven-handed poker and has run four aces to the bottom of the deck and four queens to the top of the deck. How does he arrange his stack so he will get the four aces and, say, the third player from his left (a big winner or a monied fat-cat) will get the four queens? First, he simultaneously runs together with his left thumb and fingers the top card and the bottom card four times in a row from the deck in his right hand, just as if he were stacking for a two-handed game. Then he overhand shuffles the rest of the deck on top of those eight cards in the left hand. The interlaced aces and queens are now on the bottom of the deck ready for the final stack.

Putting the deck back into his right hand and selecting his monied victim as the third player from his left, the Neocheater executes a two-step maneuver — **Step One:** he again pulls off the top card and the bottom card of the deck together into the left hand, but then pulls two extra cards from the top of the deck

[21] *If during the culling, the four jacks end above the four kings, the dealer reverses their order by simply overhand shuffling those eight cards one by one off the top, then pulling off one more card, jutting it, and blind shuffling to leave those eight cards back on top with his four kings now above his victim's four jacks*

onto those two cards. **Step Two:** he repeats the process of pulling the top and bottom cards from the deck plus an extra- card from the top and letting those three cards fall on top of the first four cards pulled from the deck in step one.

Each such shuffling maneuver moves seven cards and stacks the cards for one round of dealing to seven players with the stacked cards going to the dealer and the third player from his left. He executes that two-step shuffling maneuver a total of four times (the number of cards to be stacked in his hand) and slides the final extra card *plus* a break-card from his right hand onto the stack in his left hand. The break-card is jutted and used to execute a concluding blind shuffle. The third player will now receive the four queens and be relieved of his bankroll by the dealer who will receive the four aces.[22]

Two limitations exist for the undercut when stacking two hands simultaneously: (1) In games with more than two players, the hand stacked for the victim cannot be dealt to the player directly on the dealer's left or right, regardless of how many players are in the game. And (2) the undercut cannot be used to stack two hands when only three players are in a game... Except for two-handed games, undercut stacking always results in at least one non-stacked hand between any two stacked hands.

---

[22] *To deal the four queens to the second (instead of the third) player on his left, the dealer pulls off the top and bottom cards plus three extra cards for the first half of the stacking maneuver; he then pulls off the top and bottom cards with no extra cards to complete the stacking for the first round of dealing. After all the cards are stacked, he pulls off only a break-card for blind shuffling. Now, if the victim is the fourth player from his left, the dealer pulls off one extra card for the first step of the maneuver and two extra cards for the second step. The formula for figuring the extra cards pulled off for step one is: [# of players] - [# of players from dealer's left + 2]. And for step two: [# of players] - [# of extra cards in step one + 4].*

*Realizing that cards pulled from the deck during stacking are in reverse order than when they are dealt will help you visualize exactly how the undercut works. ...And do not fret if the mathematics of stacking seem complicated. It is simple arithmetic. When practicing the stacking maneuvers, continually try different combinations for various numbers of players in various positions and the arithmetic of stacking will quickly become routine.*

Discard squaring described in Chapter III is the most convenient method to cull cards for the undercut. But any method or combination of methods for culling is practical as long as the Neocheater gets the hand he wants without being suspect. A Neocheater, of course, avoids suspicion by never using four of a kind, a full house, or even trips just played. Instead he would use, for example, a pair from one discarded hand and matching single cards from other hands to cull three or four of a kind.

The undercut is ideal for lowball since hands previously played can be used directly because no one will remember the exact hands or suits of previously played hands. The Neocheater, however, will generally not use the undercut for stud-type games since faster and more efficient culling and stacking techniques exist for those games (such as the discard culling and stacking techniques described in Chapter III).

Neocheaters always conclude undercut stacking (or any other stacking technique) with a series of blind shuffles or false riffles, often topped off with a false cut.[23]

## Detecting the Undercut

• Suspect any dealer who repeatedly runs single cards off the deck just prior to overhand shuffling.

• By detection methods described in Chapter IV, look for blind shuffles, false riffles, or false cuts that must follow any undercut-stacking maneuver.

• The undercut can be done so swiftly that no one can see the top and bottom cards being pulled off individually, but the alert player can sometimes detect the snapping sound of cards being pulled together from the top and bottom of the deck.

\* \* \*

[23] *Table 3 on page 115 shows the number of cards involved in culling and stacking various hands according to the number of players in the game. As Table 3 indicates, when stacking more than three cards in games with over six players, the stack becomes rather unwieldy for convenient manipulation.*

# TABLE 3
## CARDS REQUIRED FOR CULLING AND STACKING

| # Cards Stacked per Stacked Hand | One Hand Stacked —for Dealer— | | Two Hands Stacked —for Dealer plus Victim— | |
| --- | --- | --- | --- | --- |
| | # Cards Culled | # Cards in Stack | # Cards Culled | # Cards in Stack |
| *2 players in game* | | | | |
| 1 | 1 | 2 | 2 | 2 |
| 2 | 2 | 4 | 4 | 4 |
| 3 | 3 | 6 | 6 | 6 |
| 4 | 4 | 8 | 8 | 8 |
| 5 | 5 | 10 | 10 | 10 |
| *3 players in game* | | | | |
| 1 | 1 | 3 | 2 | 3 |
| 2 | 2 | 6 | 4 | 6 |
| 3 | 2 | 9 | 6 | 9 |
| 4 | 4 | 12 | 8 | 12 |
| 5 | 5 | 15 | 10 | 15 |
| *4 players in game* | | | | |
| 1 | 1 | 4 | 2 | 4 |
| 2 | 2 | 8 | 4 | 8 |
| 3 | 3 | 12 | 6 | 12 |
| 4 | 4 | 16 | 8 | 16 |
| 5 | 5 | 20 | 10 | 20 |
| *5 players in game* | | | | |
| 1 | 1 | 5 | 2 | 5 |
| 2 | 2 | 10 | 4 | 10 |
| 3 | 3 | 15 | 6 | 15 |
| 4 | 4 | 20 | 8 | 20 |
| 5 | 5 | 25 | 10 | 25 |
| *6 players in game* | | | | |
| 1 | 1 | 6 | 2 | 6 |
| 2 | 2 | 12 | 4 | 12 |
| 3 | 3 | 18 | 6 | 18 |
| 4 | 4 | 24 | 8 | 24 |
| 5 | 5 | 30 | 10 | 30 |
| *7 players in game* | | | | |
| 1 | 1 | 7 | 2 | 7 |
| 2 | 2 | 14 | 4 | 14 |
| 3 | 3 | 21 | 6 | 21 |
| 4 | 4 | 28 | 8 | 28 |
| 5 | 5 | 35 | 10 | 35 |

115

## TABLE 3
## CARDS REQUIRED FOR CULLING AND STACKING

| # Cards Stacked per Stacked Hand | One Hand Stacked —for Dealer— | | Two Hands Stacked —for Dealer plus Victim— | |
|---|---|---|---|---|
| | # Cards Culled | # Cards in Stack | # Cards Culled | # Cards in Stack |
| *8 players in game* | | | | |
| 1 | 1 | 8 | 2 | 8 |
| 2 | 2 | 16 | 4 | 16 |
| 3 | 3 | 24 | 6 | 24 |
| 4 | 4 | 32 | 8 | 32 |
| 5 | 5 | 40 | 10 | 40 |

Before proceeding to the next stacking technique, riffle culling must be examined in more detail:

### c. Riffle Culling

Even in the strictest games with alert or fussy players, the Neocheater can usually cull a high pair and often three of a kind using one of the discard-gathering techniques taught in Chapter III. But assume he has been unable to cull a single card from the discards or no discards are available such as occurs when a new or different deck is brought into play. He must then work the deck cold in order to cull a favorable hand. One easy and effective method to cull directly from the deck is to use the riffle cull described below.

As in the technique described in Chapter II for cutting aces, pick up the deck, and begin parting the deck by riffling through the cards with your thumb. Stop the moment you spot an ace, and let that ace drop. Now separate the deck so that the ace becomes the top card of the deck-portion in your left hand. Then riffle shuffle the two deck halves together, but retain the top ace with your left thumb and drop that ace last on top of the shuffled deck. Now riffle again and locate a second ace — or other desired card — and place it on top of the first culled ace with another false-riffle shuffle, controlling the deck halves with your thumbs so the second culled ace falls on top of the first ace without any unwanted cards falling between them. Repeat the process for the third and fourth card, or until you have culled

116

your desired hand to the top of the deck, ready for stacking.

With practice, you can riffle cull four aces to the top of the deck in less than twenty seconds. Four aces are merely an example. Actually you can riffle cull any desired cards or hands.

A Neocheater, however, seldom relies solely on riffle culling for stacking full or big hands, although he could. Instead, he usually uses riffle culling as an auxiliary to discard culling. For example, if he is able to cull only one ace to the top of the deck while squaring the discards, he can then quite easily riffle cull a second and third ace on top of that first ace. Whether he tries to cull the fourth ace depends on how long he took to cull the previous two cards, on the location of the final ace (it may be too close to the top or bottom of the deck), and especially on his objective. (Neocheaters can but seldom need to stack themselves blatantly powerful hands.)

After culling your desired cards to the top of the deck, run those cards quickly to the bottom of the deck in one overhand shuffle and stack them with the undercut or one of the other stacking techniques described later in this chapter.

A high pair can almost always be culled using discard squaring. One quick riffle cull should produce a third matching card in less than five seconds. After an hour's practice, you should be fairly adept at riffle culling. Remember always to keep the deck squared when riffle parting the deck so that the cards pass by individually, smoothly, and at the proper speed for quick selection.

When working a deck cold, you should be able to cull a pair of aces to the top with two riffles. And starting with a pair of aces provides an enormous advantage in draw poker and an even greater advantage in stud games.

A problem you will encounter when first practicing the riffle cull is flipping past your selected card by an extra card to leave an unwanted stranger on top of the culled card. If that happens, you have three options:

First, when interlacing the parted deck portions, retain both top cards (your culled card and the unwanted card) with your left thumb and drop those two cards last on top of the deck. Then execute a quick, single card overhand shuffle to get rid of the extra card by simply pulling it off the top with your left

117

thumb and slipping it beneath the deck. And against alert or sophisticated opponents, the removal of that top card can be camouflaged by a subsequent blind shuffle.

Second, assume you have a pair of aces already culled on top of the deck and you have passed your third ace by one card while riffling through the deck. Just riffle shuffle that third ace right back into the deck, making certain the two aces in your right hand still fall last — on top of the deck. Then make another attempt to cull that third ace during your next riffle.

Or, third, as you will learn in Chapter VI, use a split-second cut that instantly gets rid of any extra cards on top of your stack.

Spend thirty minutes practicing the riffle cull. See how fast you can get a pair and then three of a kind to the top of the deck. The riffle cull is a potent ally when used with discard culling. Also, riffle culling is the most practical method for culling a deck cold (or when discards are unavailable). But remember, Neocheaters keep their eyes in natural motion, glancing but never staring at the cards being riffled.

Used with or without other culling techniques, the riffle cull is a valuable asset in the Neocheater's repertoire. With even a minimal mastery of the riffle cull, he can control cards in any deck under most circumstances.

## Detecting the Riffle Cull

• A good riffle culler is almost impossible to detect. A person usually must detect Neocheating in earlier stages such as during discard manipulation or in later stages such as during the blind shuffle or false cut. Watch for the dealer who habitually glances at the passing cards while riffle parting the deck. (Most players do that, but if a dealer never looks at the riffling cards, you can rule out the riffle cull.) Also watch for the dealer who extensively uses riffle shuffles while consistently dropping one, two, or three cards last on the deck from his left thumb.

Continuing now with the next stacking technique:

### d. Overhand Stacking

The Neocheater regularly uses the overhand stack to stack pairs and three of a kind with ease; but he seldom uses this technique to stack four of a kind, a full house, or other pat hands, unless he has already used discard stacking (described later) or the undercut to initially stack part of the hand — such as a pair or three of a kind.

Like many stacking methods, this technique is particularly effective when used in conjunction with other stacking techniques to build the desired stack. All Neocheating knowledge and skill is cumulative; the more the Neocheater knows, the more effective and resourceful he will be at the card table. If a Neocheater stacks a high pair using discard-stacking, he can easily overhand stack or riffle stack the third matching card and probably the fourth, if he wishes. Or, say someone tosses him discards that contain a pair that matches his stacked pair. He may use the overhand stack to add that pair to his stack, giving him four of a kind.

In any case, suppose you begin with a culled pair of aces on top of the deck and want to stack the cards so those aces are dealt to you in a six-handed game. You can accomplish that in three quick moves by using the overhand stack:

Move 1 — Hold the deck in the left hand. From the lower portion, pull out about half the deck with the right hand. Then using your left thumb, rapidly slide five cards, one by one, from the right-hand portion onto the two culled aces in your left hand. (You are stacking for a six-handed game.) Then with your left thumb pull off one more card from the right-hand deck portion onto the left-hand deck portion and jut that card so it sticks out an eighth of an inch or so from the back end of the deck. That card is your break-card needed to blind shuffle. Next, overhand shuffle the rest of the right-hand portion on top of that break-card. Then complete your blind shuffle by pulling out all the cards below the break-card with the right hand and throwing them in a single block back on top of those cards still in your left hand. You now have *five cards* above your two aces on top of the deck.

Move 2 — Now transfer the entire deck to your right hand for an overhand shuffle. Rapidly pull off six cards, one by one, from the top of the deck with your left thumb and then, without hesitation, slide those cards back on top of the deck. Or more precisely: the right hand which holds the bulk of the deck simply moves forward, sliding the deck behind those six cards in the left hand and repositioning those six cards (now in reverse order) back on top of the deck. The hardest part is now done: you have stacked your second ace. Next, allowing the deck to rest in the left hand with the right hand remaining around the deck, immediately make the next move to stack your first ace.

Move 3 — With your right hand, remove the lower half of the deck leaving the top half of the deck in your left hand. Then using your left thumb, rapidly slide (run off) five cards, one by one, from the cards in your right hand onto the top of the deck portion in your left hand. Immediately follow with a blind shuffle by sliding off one more card, jut it as your break-card, and overhand shuffle the rest of the right-hand portion of the deck onto the left-hand portion. Now complete the blind shuffle by pulling all the cards from beneath the break-card with the right hand and tossing them in a single block back on top of the cards still in your left hand. The pair of aces is now stacked to be dealt to you.

With practice, the overhand stack becomes so rapid that the Neocheater often must execute a few extra blind shuffles or false riffles to make the deck appear thoroughly shuffled.

The overhand stack is ideal for adding one card to a pair or three of a kind already stacked by either discard stacking or undercut stacking. For example, assuming the Neocheater has discard stacked a pair of queens for draw poker and has managed to get a third queen to the top of the deck, either through discard culling or riffle culling.[24] To stack that third queen, he removes the bottom half of the deck with his right hand for an overhand shuffle and simply runs off one card less than the number of players from the right-hand deck portion onto the cards in his left hand. He then runs off one more card, juts it, and completes a blind shuffle. He now has stacked three queens for himself.

As you practice this technique, pause at each step to review the progressive journeys of the cards you are stacking so you can understand precisely what is happening to them.

One drawback of the overhand stack is running the stacked

---

[24] *When riffle culling a partially stacked deck, the dealer must consciously protect that stacked portion by not culling a card too high in the deck. He must also protect his stack when false riffling the deck halves together.*

120

cards off the top of the deck and then sliding them right back on top of the deck. But that move is camouflaged by promptly executing an overhand blind shuffle. And when your stack is complete, crown it with a few extra blind shuffles and a false cut to completely dissipate any suspicion.

If you have practiced running the cards one at a time off the deck for the undercut, you will have little trouble with the overhand stack. When executed properly, both the undercut and the riffle stack (described later) are generally superior to the overhand technique. Yet, in some situations, the overhand stack is ideal. Most Neocheaters learn the overhand stack because of its simplicity. And they often use the technique to add one card or a pair to their stack. With only an hour or two of practice, the overhand stack can be executed with relative ease and rapidity.

While it is possible to stack three or four of a kind using the overhand stack, Neocheaters seldom do. Stacking such hands is usually more effectively done by combining the overhand stack with either the undercut or the riffle stack. Neocheating stacking techniques rely on flexibility and improvisation. Indeed, Neocheaters usually combine or overlap various techniques for the easiest, safest, and most effective results. So the more familiar the Neocheater is with the different techniques, the more effectively will he drain opponents.

Most Neocheaters master the overhand technique for stacking at least a pair, especially since the technique is so convenient when combined with discard stacking or riffle stacking (described later). And the overhand technique is particularly effective for stacking two or three of a kind when combined with riffle culling. Still at times, the Neocheater finds it easier to simply discard stack his entire hand, thus avoiding all shuffle-stacking techniques.

## Detecting the Overhand Stack

• Watch for the dealer who runs individual cards off the deck after parting it or prior to overhand shuffles.

• Especially watch for the dealer who runs a few cards off the top of a deck and then slides the deck behind those cards. That is a big giveaway.

• Watch for blind-shuffle and false-cut maneuvers following an overhand shuffle.

121

### e. Knowing Everyone's Hole Card

What if you are playing five-card stud and want to use either the undercut stack or the overhand stack to deal yourself kings back-to-back, *plus* you want to know everyone's hole card? As explained in Chapter III, that is easy to accomplish when using discard stacking. But neither undercut stacking nor overhand stacking offers opportunities to glance at the cards as they are being stacked. So, how do you get to know everyone's hole card without discard stacking?

Assume you have stacked yourself a pair of kings for a six-handed game of five-card stud by using either undercut stacking or overhand stacking. Now to learn everyone's hole cards, simply execute a false riffle in the following manner: Part the stacked deck for a riffle shuffle. Now execute a false riffle, remembering to protect your stack as an undisturbed block of fifteen cards or so by riffling the left-hand portion more rapidly than those cards in the right hand, dropping the stack in a single block just prior to dropping the last card — the single card retained by your left thumb. But, as you finish the riffle, instead of dropping your stack in a single block, riffle those cards with your right thumb. Then slow the riffling motion for the last six or seven cards while bending those cards with your thumb just far enough to read their values as they fall in succession.[25] Remember the values of the last five cards above your stacked king. (That slow riffling action is easy to control and takes only a few minutes of practice to learn.) You then drop the single card retained by your left thumb last, having memorized the sequence of those five cards above your first stacked king. To get rid of that extra top card, you can simply slip it to the bottom of the deck and avoid suspicion with a subsequent blind shuffle.

Now the top five memorized cards will be your opponents' hole cards. If, for example, when you spotted your king during

---

[25] *While interlacing the cards, hold the two deck portions in a sharp V formation in order to see the value of the cards flash at their outer corners as they riffle from the right thumb. Or still better, whenever you want to read the cards, reverse the parting procedure so the left hand removes the top portion of the deck containing the stack. Then the stack win be riffled by the left thumb with the corner designs directly facing you. From that position, the values of the cards are more visible, easier to read, and can be flashed with less suspicion.*

the riffle and then memorized the next five cards as say 4-Q-9-J-7, then the player to your right will receive the 4 and, counterclockwise, the next player will receive the Queen, the next player a 9 and so on. ...You will have given yourself a tremendous advantage, not only by dealing yourself a wired pair of kings, but by knowing everyone's hole cards.

### f. Riffle Stacking

If you have practiced riffle culling and can perform the false riffle with any degree of smoothness, then you already know the moves required for riffle stacking. For example, look again at Figure 2 on page 57. Notice that four cards are retained by the right thumb while the single ace is retained by the left thumb. That picture suggests a shortcut method for stacking your first ace: Instead of dropping that ace last, drop it first and then drop the four cards from the right thumb on top of the ace and, presto, that ace is stacked for you in a five-handed game. In other words, the first ace has been culled in one riffle and the right thumb simply retains and then releases four cards on top of the ace in order to stack it for a five-handed game. Each additional ace or card to be stacked for the dealer's hand must be culled and singly passed to the top. Then as explained in Step 1 below, the left thumb subsequently builds the stack by releasing the required number of cards on top of each card culled to the top of the deck.

Beginning with a completely shuffled deck, you can riffle stack aces back-to-back for yourself in stud poker while knowing what every opponent has in the hole by taking the following two steps:

**Step 1** —Place the deck in your right hand. Using your right thumb, riffle the deck until you spot an ace. Let that ace drop and immediately stop riffling. Then pass that lower portion of the deck with the ace on top into your left hand; and as in Chapter II when culling an ace, riffle shuffle the left and right hand cards together, but retain the ace with the left thumb in order to drop that card last on top of the deck. Again part the deck by taking the top portion into your right hand and passing the lower portion into your left hand for another riffle shuffle. But do not cull another ace yet. Instead, execute a false riffle; and with your left thumb retain and drop at least two, preferably three or four cards on top of your ace. Begin practice by retaining

123

and dropping only two cards at a time from your left thumb. Practice until you can easily drop with accurate control four or more cards on top of your ace.

Suppose you cull an ace. Execute two false riffles while each time dropping on that ace two cards retained by your left thumb. You then will have four cards on top of your first ace. If you are playing in a five-handed game, your first card is stacked. If more than five are playing, you must drop the required number of additional cards on top of the ace so that it will be dealt to you.

Although your first riffle-stacking attempts may be awkward, you can with an hour or two of practice do the riffle stack with relative speed and ease. Keep in mind that you are essentially executing a false riffle but striving to get more than one card on top of the stack with each riffle shuffle. Quickly square the edges of the deck with your thumbs and fingers before each riffle for better control.

**Step 2** — Cull your second ace exactly as you did your first, retaining it in your left thumb while protecting your stack with a false riffle. Drop that second ace on top of your stack as the last card. Should you fail to cull a second ace during that riffle, simply execute a false riffle which will leave an extra card on top of your stack. For now, remove that card with a blind shuffle. In the next chapter, you will learn an easier method to remove extra cards accumulated during false riffles.

After culling your second ace, you must riffle the required number of cards on top of that ace to stack it while protecting your first stacked ace. Proceed with the same method used to stack your first ace by riffle shuffling the proper number of cards onto that second ace while protecting the stack. But when playing stud, remember to bend the top cards upward with your left thumb[26] in order to briefly glance at and remember their sequence while riffling them onto the stack above your second ace. By remembering those cards, you will know everyone's hole card

---

[26] *Whenever possible, arrange for your left hand and thumb to riffle cards to be glanced at and memorized. When riffled from the left hand, the designs on the card corners are on the inside facing the dealer and are, therefore, easier to see and read. If riffled from the right thumb, you must position the two deck halves in a V formation in order to see the card designs flashing by on the outside corners.*

in addition to dealing yourself a pair of aces.

Remembering opponents' hole cards is easy: Assume a six-handed game of five-card stud in which you have already stacked your first ace and culled your second ace on top of those stacked cards. Now with your next riffle, say you drop two cards on top of your stack while bending those cards slightly upward with your thumb and noticing they are, for example, a jack and a four. Your mind registers J-4. You riffle again dropping two more cards onto your stack while observing they are a king and a ten. Your mind registers K-10-J-4. Another riffle and you drop a single card, a nine, to complete your stack. Now you know the other players' hole cards will read clockwise 9-K-10-J-4 around the table, and you will be dealt aces back-to-back. ... For seven-card stud or hold'em, execute the riffling process twice while remembering both sets of cards stacked above each ace. You will then know both hole cards of each opponent.

Your thumb will gradually become accustomed to retaining and controlling batches of three and four cards to be dropped on your stack while mentally counting them (and, when advantageous, remembering them). Your goal is to smoothly cull and accurately stack with a minimum number of riffle shuffles.

You can cull and stack four of a kind or pat hands with riffle stacking. But usually stacking such hands is easier done by combining the riffle stack with other stacking techniques. For example, the riffle stack is especially convenient for adding the third or the fourth-of-a-kind card to a pair or three of a kind already culled and stacked from the discards.

Still, the riffle stack alone is often ideal for five-card stud, seven-card stud, and hold'em since you can cull and stack a high pair for yourself while knowing everyone's hole card (or cards) in fifteen seconds or less. In draw poker, however, using the riffle stack alone to stack four of a kind or a pat hand is generally not as easy or practical as using a combination of other stacking techniques.

Another stacking variation consists of initially culling all your cards in consecutive riffles. This method gets the culling out of the way first. For example, cull two kings, then proceed to stack them by retaining the top king with your right thumb and injecting the required number of cards between the top and second king with a couple of riffles. When that move is completed, riffle shuffle the required number of cards on top of your second king to complete the stack.

Neocheaters normally avoid the repetition and time required to riffle stack three or more cards by combining two or more culling and stacking techniques. (See Combination Stacking later in this chapter.) Various combinations can provide safer, easier, and faster routes to stacking four or five cards. As pointed out in Chapter XI, however, the pure Neocheater finds maximum advantages in the simplest and easiest maneuvers — he seldom has to stack more than one or two cards for himself. And often he does not stack any cards for himself, but simply remembers his opponents' hole cards while riffling (or he simply follows what-to-do signals from a colluding dealer, especially from a colluding house dealer in a casino) to gain unbeatable advantages.

### Detecting the Riffle Stack

• Watch for the symptoms of false riffles as described in Chapter IV.

• Watch for the dealer who consistently uses his left thumb to retain one to five cards that are dropped on the deck last after interlacing all the other cards.

• Watch for the dealer who squares the deck before each riffle.

### g. The Las Vegas Variation

As a refinement of the riffle stack, the Las Vegas variation uses the same principles learned so far, but the position of the hands while culling and riffling is different. For culling, the thumbs riffle and split the deck along the sides of the cards, as shown in Figure 20, instead of at their ends. This method of culling has the advantage of concealing all the moves from opponents with your hands and fingers. Also, after several hours of practice, the Las Vegas variation cull becomes faster and smoother than the regular riffle cull. Note the position of both thumbs in Figure 20; the moment the culled ace drops to the top of the lower deck half the left thumb is ready to split the deck. Then the two deck portions can be promptly riffle shuffled together while keeping the culled ace on top.

126

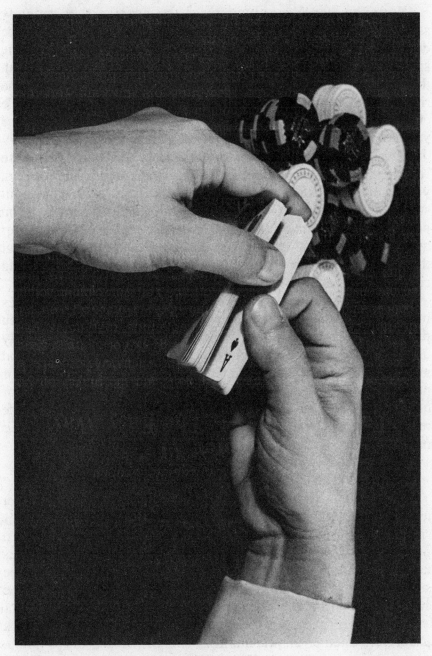

Figure 20
Riffling and Splitting the Deck at the Sides
in the Las Vegas Variation

127

With the Las Vegas variation, the cards are completely shielded by the fingers of both hands while being stacked as the deck lies flat on the table (see Figure 21). After interlacing, the split deck portions are then pushed together and squared with the palms of both hands. Because the cards are shielded, the riffling process can be slowed not only for greater accuracy while culling and stacking but for greater ease while memorizing the value and sequence of everyone's hole cards.

The Las Vegas variation works especially well for false riffling. Because of the shield created by the hands and fingers, you can easily keep two-thirds of the deck intact without suspicion. Experiment for awhile with this variation to see if you prefer it to the regular riffle stack and false riffle. Switching over to the Las Vegas variation requires several hours of practice, but the technique will look smoother and offers more flexibility and control over the deck.

The advantage of the Las Vegas variation ironically produces its only disadvantage: ostensibly the cards are shielded to keep them from flashing — that is why dealers in casinos commonly use this variation. In naive company, however, or in neighborhood games, the Las Vegas variation may appear too expert or professional, and the shielding may appear to be done for questionable purposes. (Which it is!) Against such opponents, the regular false riffle and riffle stack may be preferable because their maneuvers appear more amateurish, open, and natural.

## Detecting the Las Vegas Variation

• Culling and stacking by the Las Vegas variation is harder to detect than other culling and stacking methods. But, while this riffling method is extensively used by honest casino dealers, private players rarely hold and riffle the cards by their sides unless they are manipulating or peeking at the cards. So be suspicious of dealers (even certain casino dealers) who shield the cards and riffle them along their sides instead of at their ends.

• Be suspicious of a dealer who squares the side of a deck just before another player cuts it.

• Be especially suspicious of any dealer offering a crimped or gapped deck.

• Watch for other suspicious moves by any dealer who

128

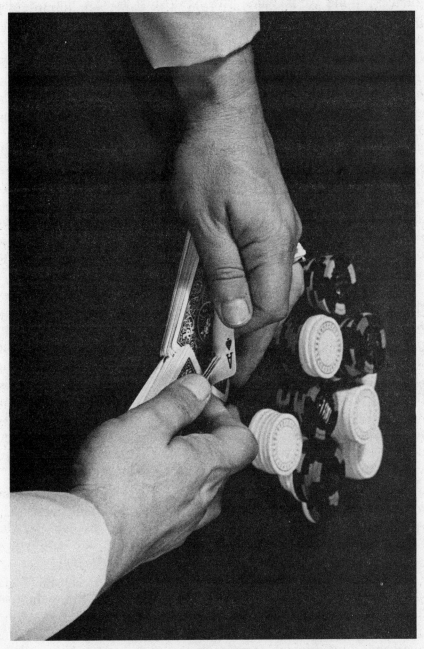

Figure 21
Shielding the Deck from Opponents
with the Las Vegas Variation

glances at the cards when riffling. (Most honest players also glance at the cards while riffling and shuffling; so if a dealer never glances at the riffling cards, he is neither cheating nor Neocheating—at least while riffling.)

### h. The Intermediate-Stacking Variation

The intermediate-stacking variation is an abbreviated, faster version of the Las Vegas variation used for both false riffling and stacking. In both variations, the cards are culled along their sides as shown in Figure 20. But instead of placing the two deck halves flat on the table for riffling, the dealer holds the cards in his hands above the table and riffles them at an angle as shown in Figure 22. Otherwise, the stacking movements are the same as in the Las Vegas variation. And after the riffle shuffle by either variation, the deck halves are pushed together and squared with the palms of both hands.

While the shielding is less than in the Las Vegas variation, the advantage of the intermediate variation is its increased speed for culling and stacking cards. With a dozen or so hours of practice, rapid culling and stacking can be executed by using the intermediate variation. The action is fast, but remember that the sides of the deck must be smoothly squared after each riffle so the thumbs can effectively control individual cards when culling and stacking. Some Neocheaters prefer this variation, especially for stacking high pairs in stud or hold'em. And, of course, casino dealers who collusion cheat almost always use one of the two variations when manipulating or peeking at the cards.

### Detecting the Intermediate-Stacking Variation
• Use the same methods for detecting the Las Vegas variation as described on page 128.

### i. Combination Stacking

Combination stacking involves switching from one technique to another while stacking the deck. For example, if someone discards two pair, you can get them to the bottom in one overhand shuffle, stack them with the undercut, and then riffle cull another matching card to the top of the already stacked cards. Next, you can use either the riffle stack or an overhand blind

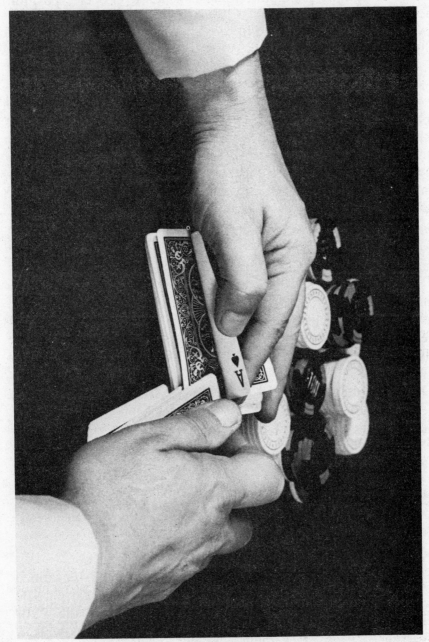

Figure 22
Shuffling Cards at an Angle for Speed
in the Intermediate-Stacking Variation

131

shuffle to add the required number of cards to properly position that fifth card into the stack. Then, after a false cut or foiling your opponent's cut, you will automatically deal yourself a pat full house.

Or, if you have managed to stack an ace, deuce, and trey for lowball from the discards, you can riffle cull a four and a five or a joker in two consecutive riffle shuffles and use the overhand stack to position those two final cards so your stack will provide you with a pat wheel.

The stacking combinations are limitless. But even if you can perform nothing more than the preliminary stacking techniques described in Chapter III plus the blind shuffle, the false riffle, and the false cut described in Chapter IV, you will possess formidable power for draining money from almost any game or opponent.

## Detecting Combination Stacking

•   Review the detection methods described for each culling and stacking technique in this chapter. In order to detect or even suspect a Neocheater, you must be aware of one or more of his specific techniques (e.g., discard stacking, crimping, false riffling, blind shuffling, false cutting, foiling the cut).

### j. Stacking for Blackjack (or Twenty-One)

Any simple culling or stacking technique that applies to stud poker, applies nicely to blackjack. The requirements for blackjack — an ace with any picture card or ten — are simple to stack. Blackjack is, in fact, the easiest card game to stack. Remember to add one extra card to your stack for "burying" or "burning" (discarding the top card or placing the top card of the deck face up on the bottom of the deck before dealing).

### k. Neocheating for Bridge

A technique for dealing grand slams in bridge is described in Chapter VIII. The technique involves a unique false riffle (called the Complete False Riffle, also known as the Pull-Through) that is used in poker and other card games as well as in bridge. During that riffle, every card of the deck is kept intact while seemingly being shuffled with complete thoroughness.

## 2. Detecting and Defending Against All Stacking.

• Review detection techniques for blind shuffles, false riffles, and false cuts in Chapter IV, pages 96, 98, and 104.

• Review the nine methods listed in Table I on page 33 for methods to eliminate cheating or cheaters.

• Insist on cutting the deck whenever the cheater or Neocheater deals, and then ruin his stack with deliberately thorough cuts.

• Sit to the Neocheater's right and carefully cut at the crimp plus one extra card. You will then be dealt the stacked hand intended for the dealer. But beware of the extra alert Neocheater who will adjust the stack so when you cut one extra card you will set yourself up for a bankrupting loss.

# Chapter VI
# False Cutting — The Easy Way

Suppose you are playing stud poker, and the player on your left seems to be winning too consistently whenever he deals. But the deck seems free of marks or gaffs; he is not using a shiner; and after careful observation you conclude that he is using Neocheating techniques to stack the deck. Moreover, you have been unconsciously cutting at his crimp. Yet, you cannot actually see him cheat. What should you do?

First, you could openly accuse him of cheating. But since you have no direct proof, accusing him may be the worst option. If, for example, you publicly revealed his subtle techniques, you could become suspect as being "too knowledgeable about cheating", thus tainting your reputation and perhaps even threatening your tenure in that game, especially if you are a consistent winner. Also, accusing the cheater could be risky, especially if you do not know how he will react. He may try to deflect the accusation by acrimoniously accusing you of cheating. Or he may try to bury the accusation by attacking you (even physically attacking you) for "questioning his honesty" or "besmirching his reputation". ...Accusing anyone of cheating without direct proof is risky business.

A player using Neocheating techniques to stack the deck is always safe —you cannot catch him in the act or prove his cheating. You may not like the way someone shuffles or riffles, or the way he cuts the deck, but that is his individual prerogative and cannot be the basis for an accusation. In fact, when it comes to shuffling and dealing, many innocent players look far more suspicious than most cheaters. A Neocheater's movements are natural; his methods are designed to allay suspicion. Moreover, many impeccably honest and experienced cardplayers know nothing about stacking or crimping, yet they shuffle and riffle the cards with very suspicious maneuvers: clumsily squaring the deck with the cards flat on the table facing them, shuffling the deck with mechanical and laborious motions, sifting awkwardly through discards, even riffling the cards face up.

A better move against the Neocheater is simply to miss his

crimp by inconsistently cutting the deck extremely high or low. (For defense or counterattack purposes, try to sit on the immediate right of a suspected cheater so you can control the cut.) That would ensure a fair game and cause mounting frustration for the cheater, who would sooner or later realize the futility of further stacking. You could also destroy his stack by pulling a block of cards from the center of the deck, placing those cards on top, and then executing a regular cut.

Missing the crimp by purposely cutting very high or very low has a cat-and-mouse effect since the cheater will not be certain that you suspect him. Initially at least, he will probably classify you as one of those annoyingly erratic types who cannot decide where to cut next. He may try to change seats. Or he may simply give up his stacking efforts as long as you remain seated on his right.

Leaving the game is another way of responding to cheating. In fact, most "authorities" on cheating advise that the best course is to promptly leave any game in which you suspect or detect cheating. Following that advice is generally the least profitable route. Although in a few situations such as identified in Chapter I and XI, leaving is the only choice. But usually such action is unnecessary since the cheater can almost always be foiled and often be soundly beaten.

The above example of foiling the cheater is the simplest way to counter him. Below is a more profitable way to counter him. And Part Two of this book (DEFENSES AND COUNTERATTACKS) presents a full array of techniques designed to nullify, counter, and beat all cheaters.

## 1. False Cutting the Neocheating Way.
### a. The Special Cut (The One-Card Cut)
With the special cut you can turn a cheater's stacking efforts to your advantage. Sit to the immediate right of the suspected cheater and deliberately cut at the crimp, restoring the deck to his stack. But then give the deck an additional, rapid single-card cut (the special cut), and you will get the dealer's stacked hand. The cheating dealer may not know exactly what you have done. And since the special cut looks like a normal center cut when executed swiftly, he will assume his stack was destroyed during

that extra cut. The cheater will then be surprised and confused when you get his stacked hand. But because he knows that you did originally cut at or near his crimp, he will probably doggedly stack the deck another time or two until he realizes that you are not only aware of his cheating, but are taking advantage of him. At that point, he may leave the game, frustrated and outsmarted.

But beware of the extra alert cheater who knows the special cut. If he anticipates a repeat of that one-card cut the next time he deals, he can simply set you up for a big loss by adjusting his stack so you will cut yourself powerful cards while leaving him or a collusion partner with even more powerful cards.

The special cut is easy and takes about an hour of practice to perform smoothly. The major function of the cut is to remove the top card from the stack, while leaving the rest of the stack intact on top of the deck. Thus if you are sitting to the right of the dealer and remove the top card from his stack, you will receive any hand that he has stacked for himself.

Also, the special cut is ideal for removing an extra card from your own stack — such as removing the extra card placed there by a false riffle (as described on page 123). Moreover, the special cut is an excellent follow-up to the false riffle and is much faster than blind shuffles that are normally used to remove extra cards.

To perform the special one-card cut, first pick up the deck with your left hand. Then referring to Figure 23, use both hands to grasp the deck. Grasp each end between the thumbs and middle and ring fingers. The forefingers (index fingers) of each hand are positioned on the top card, but the left finger presses *firmly* down, while the right forefinger rests *loosely*. Also the left ring finger grips the bottom half of the deck while the left middle finger is held loosely.

Now, grasping the upper half of the deck with the right middle finger and thumb, smoothly pull that portion of the deck out with a straight sliding motion as the left forefinger exerts pressure to hold back the top card as shown in Figure 23. Now drop the left-hand portion of the deck with that retained top card onto the table and complete the cut by slapping the right hand cards gently on top of those just dropped on the table. Then square the deck.

Rapidly executed, the special cut gives the appearance of a normal center cut. When practicing the special cut, note that the deck is gripped by the left hand at the bottom half mainly with

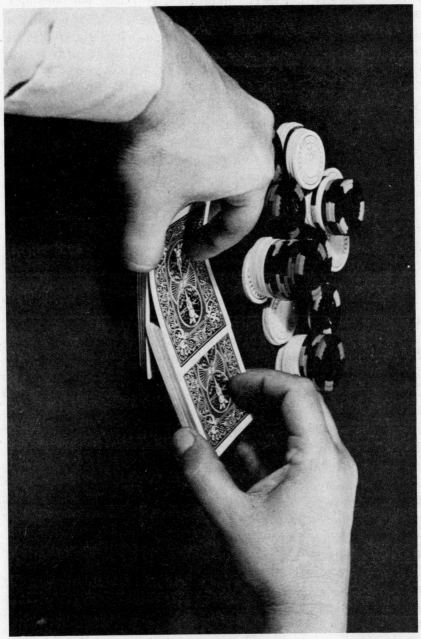

Figure 23
Getting Rid of the Extra Top Card
(The One-Card False Cut)

137

the thumb and left ring finger. With the right hand, tilt the block of cards slightly upward while pulling them from beneath the single top card retained by the left forefinger. The right forefinger should exert no pressure against the top card so as not to hinder its retention in the left hand.

When using this cut for your own stack (e.g., to get rid of an extra top card left there by a false riffle), keep in mind the number of cards in your stack. If, for example, you have stacked a pat hand in a six-handed game, you must then control the top thirty cards of the deck by pulling out at least thirty cards with your right hand (or else the top card of the deck retained by your left forefinger will end up in the stacked portion, damaging the stack). But normally, unless you are stacking pat hands, you can routinely pull out about half the deck without disturbing the stack when executing the special cut.

### b. The Four-Block Cut

The next false cut looks incredibly thorough, but leaves the stack completely intact and is nothing more than an elaborate extension of the basic false cut taught in Chapter IV.

To help visualize the finger positions for this cut, refer to Figure 24 which shows the four-block cut in its final stages. Begin practicing this cut by first holding the full deck with your left two center fingers and thumb along the sides, near the end. Hold the left forefinger out slightly, not touching the cards. Next, grasp about a fourth of the deck from the bottom with your right forefinger and thumb, pull out that block of cards and place it over the top of the deck — but continue holding the right-hand end of those cards about a quarter of an inch above the deck. Now separate (roughly in half) the lower block of cards in your left hand by parting your left middle and ring fingers about a half an inch. The side of the deck gripped by your left thumb will remain solidly together.

Then your right middle finger (or ring finger, if easier) and your right thumb dip down and seize about half of that bottom, split portion of the deck. But at the same time, your right thumb and index finger retain their grip on the topmost block of cards. As shown in Figure 24, the right thumb and middle finger then partially withdraw (about two inches) that lower block of cards along with the upper block. At that juncture, each hand holds

138

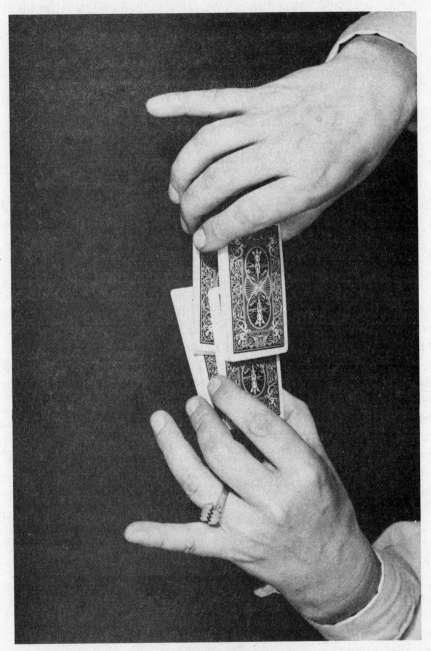

Figure 24
Separating Cards During
the Four-Block False Cut

two separate blocks of cards, parted but not completely separated from the deck (as shown in Figure 24).

Both hands now tilt upward slightly and the right index finger and thumb release only the top block of cards as both hands part to let that top block fall through to the table. (This upward V-angled parting motion is similar to that used in the basic three-block false cut described on page 100.)

Now drop the bottom block of cards in the left hand on top of those cards on the table. Then drop the remaining block of cards in the right hand, and finally drop the last block of cards still in the left hand as shown in Figure 25. ...Your stack remains on top, completely intact despite an incredibly thorough-looking cut.

Like many Neocheating maneuvers, the description seems much more intricate than the actual execution. The entire four-block false cut takes no more than five or six seconds to execute, even when done without haste. The moves are relatively easy to execute, especially if you have practiced the three-block cut described in Chapter IV. And, as in that three-block cut, the first step of bringing the bottom portion of cards to the top is performed faster than the subsequent card-dropping steps. After an hour or two of practice, you will be executing the four-block cut smoothly. And if you decide to master this cut, you will develop a nimbleness in your fingers that will be valuable for executing almost any card-manipulation technique.

The intricate-appearing, four-block false cut adds a convincing finality to any stacking procedure. But against certain opponents (e.g., against very naive or against very savvy opponents), extra thorough or elaborate cuts may actually increase suspicion. In such cases, a simpler or more straight forward cut is best.

The next false cut is neither as complex nor as flourishing as the one above. Instead, the cut has a crisp businesslike appearance and is worth mastering for both its simplicity and efficacy.

### c. The Basic Workhorse Cut

Lift the deck from the table and grasp the cards with both hands by placing the thumbs and middle fingers along the sides at each end and resting the forefingers lightly on top. Next, create a slender gap along the inner side of the deck (as shown in Figure 26-A) by pushing down (crimping) the right inside corners of the bottom

Figure 25
Completing the Four-Block False Cut

141

few cards with your right thumb; and then with your right thumb and middle finger pull out about half of the lower deck and place that crimped portion on top of the other deck half. The exposed side of the deck facing opponents should be even, with no visible gaps. The right fingers shield the gap on the right end, and the right forefinger pressing down on top of the deck keeps the gap from being visible along the inside edge and on the left end.

With the left thumb and middle finger, proceed with a series of shallow cuts by pulling small blocks of cards from the top and placing them one above the other on the table as shown in Figure 26-B. When you approach the gap let it open wider by releasing the pressure from your right forefinger (which has been pressing down on top of the deck) — with the wider gap you can more easily and accurately hit your crimp. Continue pulling off small blocks of cards up to that crimp. Then with an air of finality slap the remaining entire block of cards on top of those already on the table. ... Your stack now sits undisturbed on top. Square the deck on the table with your thumbs and fingers.

In thirty minutes to an hour, you should be able to execute this basic false cut with speed and smoothness. The series of small-block cuts should be fairly rapid and without hesitation, especially when you reach the gap.

The basic workhorse cut is popular among clever mechanics and, for the Neocheater, is well worth mastering. Also, this false cut can preserve a bottom cull or stack by making the first cut up to the gap, followed by a series of small-block cuts with the remainder of the deck.

## 2. Detecting and Defending Against False Cutting.

Detect false cuts by:

• Watching for the same block of cards consistently ending on top of the deck.

• Being suspicious of fancy cuts, extra thorough-looking cuts, and quick multi-way cuts. Also watch for simple crimp cuts.

Defend against false cuts by:

• Using the methods described at the beginning of this chapter to foil the cheater's cut or to get his stacked hand.

• Using the defenses against blind shuffling as described on page 96.

Figure 26
A. The Gap During the False Cut
B. Pulling Off Small Blocks of Cards

143

# Chapter VII
# Peeking And Colluding —
# The Safe Way

## 1. Peeking the Neocheating Way.

Peeking — seeing a card in the deck while dealing — without making any suspicious movements is easy to master and can be worth a fortune. In fact, certain peeking maneuvers are so easy and invisible that they are Neocheating. Peeking can be an especially useful Neocheating tool for stud poker and blackjack. And knowing (by an invisible peek) the last card dealt to an opponent in lowball offers a crushing advantage. Even in gin rummy, a Neocheater can through an invisible peek always know the next card to be drawn from the deck by his opponent.

### a. Stud and Blackjack Peek

The first peeking technique is particularly suited for stud and blackjack (but is also useful for draw poker, especially lowball). Suppose the Neocheater is dealing seven-card stud, and only he and one other player are left in the action. One face-down card remains to be dealt. The Neocheater's opponent has raised, probably on three fours plus a four-card flush. The Neocheater must now drop, call, or reraise. With three wired aces, he has his opponent beaten, but could be destroyed if that opponent improves on the next card.

To know the next card, the Neocheater simply grips the deck in his left hand as he normally would when dealing — his index finger curled across the top edge, his three fingers wrapped around the bottom, and his thumb across the top card. With understandable caution, the Neocheater then decides to "recheck his hole cards". To help camouflage his peek, he may check his two hole cards one at a time — not peeking while checking his first hole card.

But as he lifts his second hole card with his right thumb and index finger, his left hand moves in (ostensibly to prevent opponents from seeing his hole card). During that shielding process, the dealer inverts the deck in a casual and normal manner as shown in Figure 27. Now with the top of the deck

Figure 27
Stud and Blackjack, Top-Card Peek

concealed from everyone's view except the dealer's, his left thumb slides back slightly and then pushes forward on the top card to warp that card just enough to see its value in the upper corner. Immediately, his left thumb releases the pressure, and he casually brings the deck face down again while simultaneously releasing the hole card from his right thumb.

In private blackjack, the dealer follows the same procedure to peek at the hit card to be dealt to himself as he checks his hole card or cards. (This peek is not practical for casino 21 because the dealer hits himself according to fixed rules.)

The peek is done without hesitation or hurry. With both hands synchronized, it takes only a few minutes of practice to execute smoothly. When inverting the deck, arrange your finger and hand positions as shown in Figure 27 to completely shield the peek. Ironically, during this natural-appearing move, the most an opponent might object to or worry about is someone seeing the relatively insignificant bottom card flash (without ever realizing that the dealer is simultaneously peeking at the crucial top card). To avoid that objection, simply hold together your left fingers that are wrapped around the bottom card to completely conceal it. But the Neocheater may purposely expose that bottom card to the other players in order to diabolically distract them by letting them think that they are gaining a sneaky advantage over the dealer (since he cannot see the bottom card from his angle).

### b. Stud-Peek Variation #2
An alternative peeking technique designed for stud poker is illustrated in Figure 28. As the top card is turned over while being dealt, the dealer holds that card in his right hand momentarily over the top of the deck while announcing the card's value. As shown in Figure 28, that card provides a shield for the peek. And that peek is especially effective when only one opponent remains because that peeked-at card will be dealt to him on the next round.

### c. Stud-Peek Variation #3
This peek differs from the previous two peeking techniques in that the bottom corner rather than the top corner of the top card is read. Figure 29 shows the position of the deck for this

Figure 28
Stud Peek Variation #2

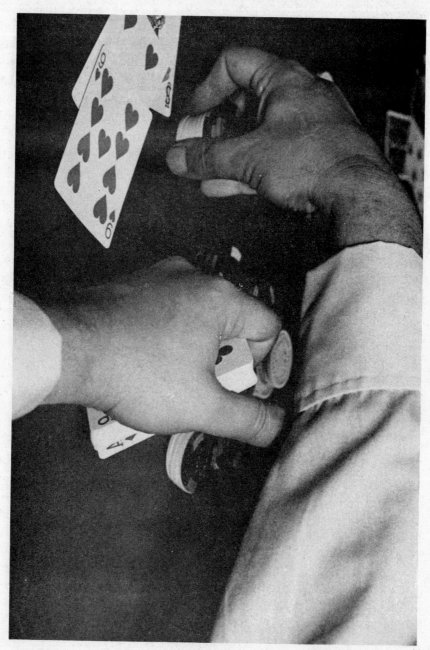

Figure 29
Stud Peek Variation #3

peek variation. The dealer holds the deck well down in the left palm with the middle finger meeting the right corner and with the left thumb resting parallel across the top. He wedges the upper left edge of the deck tightly against the fleshy base of the thumb. His left thumb then reaches slightly forward (across the top card) and slides back that top card so it can be read as shown in Figure 29. After the peek, a push with the base of the thumb quickly moves that top card back into normal position for dealing.

As with peek variation #2 the dealer does not have to feign looking at his hole cards to execute this peek. He peeks in conjunction with any natural movement that momentarily conceals the deck, such as when putting chips into the pot with the right hand while peeking with the left hand (as shown in Figure 29) or when counting chips or bills with the right hand. Some peekers keep an ashtray to the front and left of their chips and peek while using the right arm as a cover when putting out a cigarette or flicking ashes. ... Neocheaters always glance, never stare when peeking. And they expose only enough of the card to glimpse its value.

### d. Bottom-Card Peek

The bottom-card peek is easy. The deck is held in the left hand. The right hand then comes over to either square the deck or put it on the table. As the right fingers grip the top of the deck, the left index finger slips beneath the deck. The first joint of the left index finger then presses against the bottom card and slides it out about a half inch from the rear of the deck. Immediately the right thumb grips that bottom card and bends it up, flattening it against the rear of the deck (as shown in Figure 30) so the card can be quickly read. The entire move can be done in one or two seconds. The moment the card is read, it is released and the left index finger pulls the card forward, square against the deck again.

A player does not have to be a bottom dealer to take advantage of this peek. Simply knowing that bottom card can give him a slight edge and at times a very important edge, especially in stud poker.

149

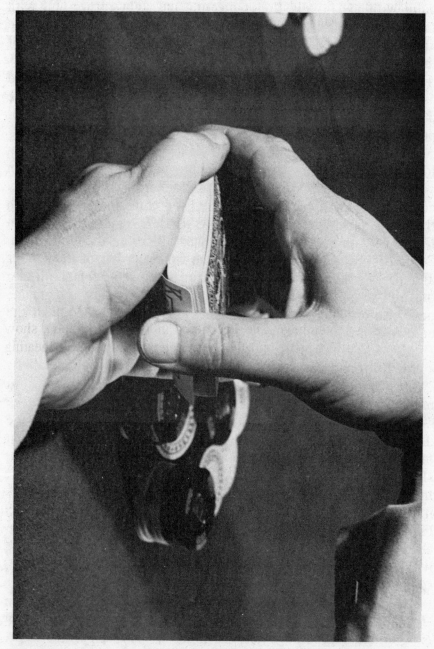

Figure 30
Bottom-Card Peek Variation

### e. Gin-Rummy Peek

The gin-rummy peek is used in rummy games or in any game in which cards are drawn off a deck that sits on the table. The dealer's right center finger slides the top card towards him with just enough pressure to drag the second card out slightly over the edge of the deck. The right thumb then lifts both cards at the same time as shown in Figure 31. Immediately after glimpsing at the second card, the forefinger quickly flattens both cards down again before removing the top card from the deck. With a little practice, this maneuver is invisible and undetectable.

## 2. Colluding the Neocheating Way.

Neocheating is a concept — a concept of safe and easy cheating. Actually, *any* cheating technique including any traditional or classical technique that is safe and easy is Neocheating. Even collusion cheating becomes Neocheating when it delivers safe and easy advantages. In fact, one of the ultimate Neocheating ploys involves collusion.[27]

That collusion ploy is one of the subtlest and most potent of all cheating techniques. The anecdotes in the first chapter show two examples in which John Finn encounters collusion Neocheating in stud and hold 'em poker in public casinos. Even with all his poker expertise, John cannot beat that kind of cheating.

Such collusion Neocheating involves a dealer who casually remembers the sequence of gathered cards. He then blind shuffles and false riffles those cards. Thus after dealing, he knows everyone's hole cards and proceeds to signal the appropriate moves (bets, raises, folds, calls) to his partner. With those instructions from an all-knowing dealer, the partner gains natural-appearing but unbeatable advantages. ... The dealer in effect makes his partner function as a super good player who plays flawlessly by "reading every hand perfectly". Moreover, by being totally indifferent to the fall of the cards, the Neocheating partner cannot be read. To beat that kind of collusion Neocheating, a player would have to know what the dealer knows (i.e., everyone's hole cards) through perfect reading of all opponents. But unfortunately, perfect reading of all opponents is not possible.

[27] *For details on that and other forms of collusion cheating, see Chapters 1, VII, and XI.*

151

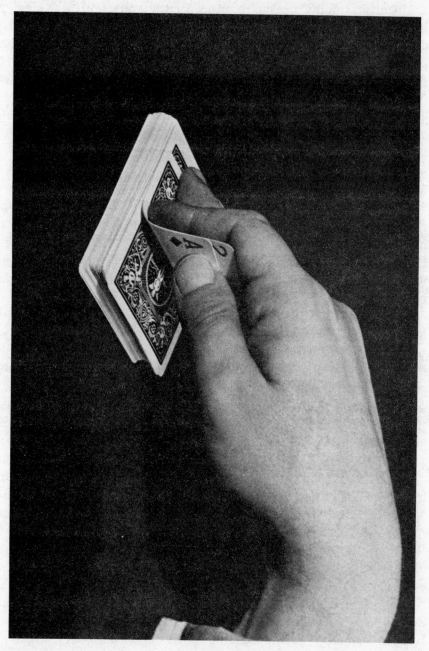

Figure 31
Gin-Rummy, Second-Card Peek

Collusion Neocheating flourishes in casino poker because the house dealer totally controls the cards and deals every hand — no player ever touches or cuts the deck. (Ironically, one reason casinos employ poker dealers is to prevent cheating.)

Recently, a similar form of potent Neocheating has begun penetrating private games. In private games, however, the Neocheater does not need a partner. He simply learns (by methods described in previous chapters) and remembers all opponents' hole cards during his deal. While unlike the casino dealer and his partner who have their collusion advantages available for every hand, the Neocheater's advantages in private poker are available only once every round —during his deal. Still, that advantage is sufficient to generate unbeatable long-range advantages in most games. And most importantly, that Neocheater cannot be caught because he not only never needs to use tell-tale devices or gaffs, but he never even needs to stack the cards. In fact, no direct evidence is ever available for accusing him of cheating.

## 3. Detecting and Defending Against Peeking and Colluding

Detect peeking by:

• Watching for the deck being turned sideways or inverted during any movement by the dealer.

• Watching for any unnecessary movement of the dealer's free hand toward the hand holding the deck.

• Watching for any suspicious movement of cards below the top card wherever a player draws from the deck in games such as rummy.

Defend against peeking by:

• Demanding an immediate cut of the deck on detecting any suspicious movement such as described above.

• Using the knowledge that the dealer has peeked at your card to bluff or beat him (must wait for the right setup or situation).

Detect and defend against colluding:

• See pages 40-54 and Chapters I, X, and XI.

# Chapter VIII
# Degrees Of Neocheating And Future Neocheating

## 1. Degrees of Neocheating—More Difficult Neocheating

An essence of all Neocheating is its simplicity and ease of execution. But the ease of execution for different Neocheating techniques varies somewhat. Some Neocheating maneuvers require more effort than others. But any maneuver must be safe, easy, and effective to qualify as Neocheating. And all Neocheating maneuvers are easier and safer than classical or traditional cheating.

An example of a difficult classical-cheating technique evolving into a relatively easy, invisible Neocheating maneuver is the complete false riffle. While that false riffle requires several hours of diligent practice and is one of the more difficult Neocheating maneuvers, it is still easy compared to classical techniques and safe compared to traditional techniques.

### a. The Complete False Riffle (the Pull-Through)

The complete false riffle is also called the pull-through. It is invisible and hinges on a unique false riffle that keeps the *entire* deck intact. The complete false riffle can be effectively used not only in poker but in any card game. The maneuver is executed as follows:

With the deck on the table, remove the top half of the cards with the right hand and proceed to riffle shuffle as you would in the Las Vegas variation (described on pages 126-128) with two exceptions — (1) riffle shuffle the deck legitimately, *without* keeping the upper right-hand deck portion intact, and (2) keep the right-hand portion of the deck angled as shown in Figure 32 (half the deck is turned face up to illustrate the moves more clearly).

For the Las Vegas variation, you continue shielding the cards with your hands and fingers while using your palms to push the deck halves together. But for the complete false riffle, you stop shielding the deck as your hands shift immediately after interlacing the deck halves and before pushing the halves together. Your hands shift so that the middle fingers and thumbs

154

Figure 32
Pull-Through, Step One
Angling the Deck Halves During the Riffle Shuffle
(face-up deck half for illustrative and practice purposes)

grip the sides of the deck halves near the ends and the ring fingers press against the deck ends as shown in Figure 32.

Keeping the deck angled, push the deck halves together as far as they will go so the angled halves move completely through each other and protrude at opposite ends as shown in Figure 33. Next, grip the protruding corners of the deck at their sides between the middle fingers and thumbs of both hands while keeping the outer fingers close together to shield *only* the deck ends. Now with your thumbs and fingers square the sides of the deck, *but not the ends*.

At that moment, the deck halves are no longer angled, but form a straight line as the interlaced halves protrude about a quarter to a half inch from each end. Those protruding ends are hidden by the fingers of both hands that are squaring the sides of the deck and *seemingly* squaring the ends as the little fingers caress the ends of the deck. The entire side-squaring maneuver should take no more than two or three seconds.

With the fingers still shielding the ends of the deck, the thumbs and middle fingers firmly grip both sides of the deck at the corners. Now with a tight grip, swing the far left edge of the deck toward you an inch or so with your left hand and pull those cards smoothly outward to extract the entire original right-hand portion of the deck (the original stacked, top portion) as shown in Figure 34. Press down with your left forefinger as you extract those cards— the entire block should slide out easily. Then simulating a cutting motion, slap that block of cards on top of the right-hand block and square the deck. All the cards, including the stacked cards, are now back in their original positions.

Done properly, the complete false riffle is undetectable. With practice, it can be done very rapidly and gives the appearance not only of thoroughly shuffling but of capping each shuffle with a solid cut. The key to executing that maneuver lies in lightly and *loosely* riffling the cards and then gently pushing the halves inward. After the side-squaring motion and without groping or fumbling, the original top block of cards is pulled out intact with the left hand.

Since the complete false riffle looks so reassuring, the maneuver is valuable to the Neocheater—especially when he is discard stacking. But the Neocheater must be willing to invest a

Figure 33
Pull-Through, Step Two
Pushing the Halves Together Until They Protrude at Opposite Ends
(face-up deck half for illustrative and practice purposes)

157

Figure 34
Pull-Through, Step Three
Completing the Pull-Through

few hours of practice to master the maneuver. Three or four rapid repetitions of the complete false riffle, followed by a crimp and a false cut is a perfect, invisible maneuver for the discard stacker.

Note particularly the difference in the position of the hands between the Las Vegas variation riffle and the complete false riffle: In the former maneuver, the deck remains completely shielded during the entire riffle shuffle. In the latter maneuver, everyone can clearly see that the dealer has thoroughly "shuffled" the deck when his fingers grasp the sides of the deck and push the interlaced card together. Only after that push-through does the dealer shield the deck to falsely square its ends. That allows him to pull the deck apart again with all the cards in their original positions.

When practicing the pull-through, go slowly at first and concentrate on accuracy — speed comes with practice. Also when practicing, invert one of the deck halves as shown in Figures 32-34 to ensure that the entire deck stays intact during each complete false riffle. Your stack can be ruined if a card or two from one block of cards get caught and end up in the other block of cards.

### b. Winning at Bridge

The complete false riffle is not only effective in poker, but is especially effective in bridge for dealing premium hands to you and your partner, even for arranging grand slams. Bridge seems tailored for discard stacking since players can handle and spread out tricks on the table in order to "check, think about, and memorize" the cards that have been played. The object is to discard stack a few extra honor cards or to concentrate suited cards for the next hand by casually placing the desired cards in the proper stacking order as the tricks are handled and gathered.

Assume you have easily discard-stacked aces, kings, and queens for yourself and your partner by placing them in the proper sequence as the tricks are spread and then collected. Now, after the hand is played and the cards are stacked and gathered, use the complete false riffle to "shuffle" the deck four or five times. Next, crimp and cut the stacked deck at about the middle and offer it to your opponent for a cut. Four out of five times he will cut at your crimp. Thus with the complete false riffle, you can regularly deal you and your partner cards with unbeatable advantages. ...And *your partner never needs to know what you are doing*. He along with everyone else will simply believe you are both lucky.

But suppose your opponent misses your crimp and cuts so that he and his partner will be dealt the premium hands. In that case, you can "accidentally" expose a card during the deal and insist on redealing.

## Detecting the Complete False Riffle

- Watch for the Las Vegas variation grip.
- Watch for the shuffling and pushing together of the deck halves at an angle that leaves the corners of both deck halves protruding at opposite ends.
- Watch for the dealer who squares the sides of the deck while shielding the ends so you cannot actually see him squaring the ends.
- After the dealer seemingly squares the deck and as he pulls it apart into split halves with both hands, look for the deck being pulled apart from an interlaced position.
- Notice if after each riffle shuffle, the dealer seemingly cuts the deck soundly.

## Defending Against the Complete False Riffle

- On suspicion, simply demand and make a cut that will destroy any possible stack — center cut several times and square the deck before the dealer picks up the cards to deal.

## 2. Future Possibilities.

Most Neocheating techniques have evolved from difficult or risky forms of classical or traditional cheating. If a safe and easy Neocheating maneuver presently does not exist for a particular function,[28] such a maneuver may possibly evolve in the future. For example, no Neocheating method presently exists for *very* rapidly stacking culled hands for two or more players. But a

---

[28] *Once the Neocheating maneuver fills a function, all other more difficult or detectable forms of cheating for that function become obsolete. That is why, as demonstrated in Appendices A and C, Neocheating has obsoleted essentially all classical and traditional cheating techniques.*

classical cheating maneuver called the interlace (also known as the faro shuffle) can stack culled hands for two, four, or eight players in less than five seconds. The interlace, however, is not Neocheating because it requires too much skill when used to stack cards, as described below:

### a. The Interlace Stack

Ironically, the basic interlace maneuver is innocently used by many honest players executing sloppy wedge or butt shuffles. But when the interlace is purposely executed with *precision*, it is far from innocent: The deck is split into two equal portions as it sits on the table. (The deck need not be split precisely in half.) Each half is then gripped at the ends along the sides between the thumbs and third fingers. With the edges of the deck halves perfectly squared —an absolute necessity — the ends are pressed *lightly* together as the halves are held at a slight V angle (i.e., the inner ends are pressing together while resting on the table-top as the outer ends are held about an inch above the table as shown in Figure 35). After some diligent practice, the cards will interlace perfectly one by one as the butted deck halves are lifted while being *lightly* pressed together. With light pressure, the alternating interlacing action commences from the top and works its way down. (The interlace is easier to execute with plastic cards than with cardboard ones.)

The interlace is effective for *quickly* stacking culled hands. The technique, however, is applicable only to two, four, or eight players. With the culled hands on top of the deck, one interlacing riffle stacks for two players, two interlacing riffles stack for four players, and three interlacing riffles stack for eight players. But since so many other easier and effective Neocheating techniques are available for stacking, the interlace is rarely used in poker.

The interlace, nevertheless, can be ideal for stacking gin rummy and bridge hands. But a player must be willing to invest much more time and effort in mastering interlace stacking than the easier Neocheating stacking techniques. And since so much practice is needed to achieve the required perfect alternation of the cards, chances of encountering an interlace stacker today are rare. Still, as with all stacking methods, any suspicious move can be countered simply by demanding and making deliberate center

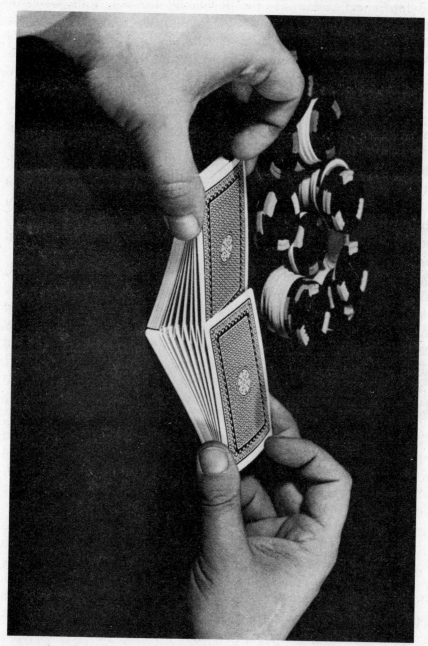

Figure 35
Holding the Cards for a Perfect Alternating Interlace

cuts that would destroy any possible stack. And to prevent the cut from being foiled by the dealer, always cut in noncrimped areas, complete the cuts, and square the deck before the dealer picks up the cards.

* * *

While interlace stacking is a safe and innocent-looking maneuver, its proper execution currently requires too much practice and skill to be classified as Neocheating. But if a *sufficient* need or advantage exists for very quickly stacking culled hands for two, four or eight players, interlace stacking could evolve into Neocheating. Shortcuts might evolve — perhaps just a certain angle of the cards or a turn of the wrist would make interlace stacking easy and nearly skill-free. The technique then would become Neocheating.

But if another maneuver were developed or evolved that could also *quickly* stack culled hands to several players, safely and easily, cheating techniques filling that function, including the interlace stack, would become obsolete. ...Thus as safe and easy Neocheating techniques evolve, all corresponding classical and traditional cheating techniques become obsolete.

# Chapter IX
# The Inevitable Spread Of Neocheating

While public poker differs from private poker in many respects, new developments in the more dynamic and cosmopolitan public-poker arena are almost always harbingers of future developments in private poker. Recently, the increasing spread of Neocheating throughout public poker suggests that such Neocheating will increasingly menace private poker and all other card games played for money or prestige. In fact, Neocheating is already spreading throughout private poker as well as into blackjack, bridge, and gin. And as in public poker, Neocheating will probably spread geometrically because it is so safe, easy, and effective to execute. In fact, all who have ever yearned to cheat but were afraid of being caught or were unwilling to spend the years of practice required to master the classical cheating techniques can now Neocheat safely, easily, and effectively.

But another reason that Neocheating is spreading — especially in public poker — is that the quality of poker itself is rapidly improving with the availability of several good poker books and with the advent of the Advanced-Concept player (described in Chapter XI). Because of the improving competition, more and more serious players are searching for ways to compensate for the diminishing supply of easy opponents. And professionals especially are seeking to bolster their sagging profit margins due to steadily increasing competition that threatens their livelihood. Also, escalating inflation puts increasing pressure and desires on all players to extract more money from their games. Neocheating offers a quick and easy solution to those problems and needs. Thus more and more serious players of blackjack, bridge, and gin are discovering and using Neocheating.

# PART TWO

## DEFENSES AND COUNTERATTACKS

165

# Chapter X
# White-Hat Neocheating
# And Other Defenses And
# Counterattacks
# Against Cheating

## 1. Understanding the Cheater's Philosophy and Psychology.

The following quoted paragraphs are the unedited, written words of a professional cheater. Although filled with overblown phrases and confused assertions, his statements unmistakably reveal his philosophy — his justification for cheating:

*Man is basically an aggressive creature. In spite of the high-sounding platitudes with which so-called 'leaders' have soothed mankind for so many generations, very often while manipulating and exploiting them for maximum profit, the simple truth is that it's going to take many eons of evolution to eradicate the instinct that provokes certain men to take advantage of others. The instinct may never be extinguished. In the meantime, there are two basic alternatives:*

*You can either try to escape the harsh realities of life by seeking spiritual solace in the here and now rather than the hereafter, thus detaching yourself from the inevitable grief and sorrows of human existence. You will also, however, detach yourself from the numerous pleasures and profits of the same existence. Anyone who wants absolute protection in any game, poker or otherwise, will only achieve it by refusing to play.*

*Or you can be a stark realist and accept man's folly and greed, and align yourself with those who decide to play for maximum enjoyment and profit. Whether or not you decide to exploit the flaws of others in the process is up to you. The term "cheating" is often inflicted on those individuals who refuse to abide by social rules which are very often rigid and repressive, deliberately stifling individual resourcefulness and imagination. Conscience is a social invention (in spite of the nonsense we're taught as infants), and it's necessary for the survival of society; without it chaos would be rampant. But, in the final analysis, if a man plays at all, he plays by his own rules or by the rules of others, with the choice of his life all too often made by others who dominate.*

*Your habitual style of playing poker reveals your habitual life-style, since it's only a miniature stage, which deceives many players; they think that by entering a sideshow they're escaping the main tent. This is self-deception on a grand scale. Nowhere does character ultimately display itself more clearly than in a man's poker game. Complainers will complain, even when they're winning heavily. Stoics will be philosophic and taciturn whether they win or lose. The rash and improvident are punished equally along with the timid. The bold are almost always the biggest winners, because nature favors the bold. Exploiters will milk every opportunity, creating their own if none exist, and losers will (and must, by their own unconscious preference) be victimized.*

*Whether you choose to be a victim or an opportunist is your decision. If a man develops his talents and potential, he is said to be exploiting himself, and he's viewed with admiration and acclaim for his achievements. If he exploits others, he's accused of being dishonest and immoral. The difference, you'll note, is in the label; the principle is the same.*

The above rationalization for cheating not only expresses the philosophy for that particular cheater, but expresses the philosophy of most professional cheaters who retain their self-esteem by justifying their cheating. By positing their cheating as superior knowledge, they project themselves as superior to honest players. In fact, only by justifying their cheating can they develop the calmness and gall needed to cheat professionally. And not only do professional cheaters justify their cheating, but they base their self-esteem on cheating: they begin to crave cheating — the more they cheat, the more superior they consider themselves.

*Part Two: Defenses And Counterattacks*

Understanding the psychology *as well as* the philosophy of cheaters is helpful for beating them: In public or casino poker, many professional players eventually involve themselves in surreptitious cheating cliques. How and why do they involve themselves in such cliques? Imagine a lonely public-game player struggling against the house cut to crack the nut — to become a full-time professional. He then suddenly discovers a friendly professional establishment with an ongoing cheating system — an undetectable cheating system requiring no special skills and available for his immediate profit. Such a player, especially if he is of mediocre ability struggling to survive as a professional, will often embrace that establishment. He begins tacitly cooperating with the cheating cliques. He accepts their collusion as a trade tool required for playing competitive, professional poker.

As he gains advantages from those professionals and adopts their system, he becomes increasingly dependent on their collusion to survive. He loses his independence and becomes a stereotype, public-game professional. Indeed, with a sense of professional righteousness, he becomes a collusion cheater.

In a sense, all chronic cheaters become entrapped with similar physical and psychological dependencies on cheating. Moreover, professional cheaters learn to feel little or no conscious guilt about their dishonesty. And only the honest player knowledgeable about cheating can stop them.

## 2. Stopping Cheating and the Cheater.

What to do when you encounter a cheater depends on (1) the type of cheater and, (2) your objectives:

As explained in Chapter I, most traditional cheaters are losers who often lose more money *because* of their cheating. For that reason, a good player usually tries to keep such cheaters in the game as sources of income. But the continued presence of a cheater can cause suspicion or resentment among other players, possibly jeopardizing the game and future profits by causing valuable losers to quit.... If the cheater adversely affects your game or profits, you must stop his cheating. And if the cheater is a steady winner or a Neocheater, you must get him out of the game quickly and permanently.

You can usually eliminate a cheater or stop his cheating by

169

using one of the nine methods in Table 1 on page 33. But you may instead want to profit from his cheating. To do that, follow John Finn's example of staying one step ahead of the cheater as John did in Anecdote A and D of Chapter I. That approach, however, requires much effort. An easier way to profit from cheaters is through white-hat Neocheating as described below.

## 3. White-Hat Neocheating.

Neocheating used to benefit all honest players is called white-hat Neocheating. For example, you can benefit honest players by bankrupting cheaters with Neocheating.

By bankrupting the cheater, you rid the game of a menace to benefit the other players. While you can win extra money directly from the cheater with Neocheating, a prerequisite of white-hat Neocheating is that no player (except the cheater) lose money because of the cheating.[29]

You can also benefit the other players with white-hat Neocheating by arranging for the cheater to lose directly to the other players, especially to the cheater's biggest victims and the game's weakest players (Robin Hood cheating). With no one realizing what you are doing, you can use white-hat Neocheating to assume a God-like role with the responsibility of keeping the game honest while temporarily helping the cheater's victims and weak players.[30]

Assume, for instance, you detect a player marking cards. You could use one of the several noncheating approaches listed on page 33 to stop his cheating or to break him. But why not bankrupt him with white-hat Neocheating? By breaking that cheater, everyone else not only becomes safe from his cheating, but benefits from his losses.

[29] *Neocheating is the best way to white-hat cheat. Classical or traditional cheating techniques could be used to beat cheaters, but those techniques require too much skill, effort, gall, or risk to be practical, especially since easier and safer Neocheating as well as noncheating methods (such as listed on page 33) are available to stop cheaters.*

[30] *After arranging for weak players to bankrupt the cheater through white-hat Neocheating, the good player can then proceed without cheating to win all the money from those weak players*

*Part Two: Defenses And Counterattacks*

Because you attack only the cheaters and especially when you arrange for other players to win, white-hat Neocheating need not be as subtle as dishonest or black-hat Neocheating. For that reason, white-hat Neocheating is especially effective for beating Neocheaters. Moreover, out of fear of having their own actions revealed, cheaters cannot effectively defend themselves against white-hat cheating. And few would dare accuse someone of cheating them.

Through white-hat Neocheating, you can fearlessly arrange powerful hands such as four aces to a loser and four queens to the cheater to drain that cheater. And if you are not the winner of those big hands, no one would suspect anything more than coincidence. In addition, most players root for losers and weak players to win big hands and are glad when they do because extra money in the hands of losers and weak players is easier to win.

## 4. Defending Against Neocheating.

By now you know the techniques of Neocheating. But that knowledge alone does not assure complete protection. You must also know what actions to take against cheaters. Directly detecting a properly executed blind shuffle, false riffle, or discard stack is essentially impossible, even if you can flawlessly execute those maneuvers yourself. In addition, as explained in the next chapter, the Neocheater selectively uses only a fraction of his power, making him even more difficult to detect. And unlike those cheaters using marked cards, shiners, strippers, cold decks, holdouts, punches, and daubs in gaffed games, the Neocheater leaves no direct evidence of cheating. The Neocheater provides nothing tangible — nothing that can be identified or proven.

Alert and knowledgeable players, however, can sense a Neocheater through the illogical playing and betting patterns inherent in any cheating. And usually that is the only way to detect or, more precisely, to sense the Neocheater. Even then, no one can actually prove his cheating. Still, with (1) knowledge of Neocheating and (2) knowing what defensive action to take against cheaters, anyone can protect himself against all cheating, including Neocheating. Those defensive actions could range from white-hat Neocheating to leaving the game.

As evident from the verbatim quote at the beginning of this

171

Book 4
Neocheating: The Unbeatable Weapon

chapter, the professional cheater feels no guilt or sympathy for his victims. In fact, he usually feels contempt for them. And most Neocheaters genuinely believe that they are rightfully exercising superior knowledge over their opponents. But this book has shown how to recognize, nullify, and even beat those Neocheaters. Other defenses and counterattacks that are effective against both cheaters and Neocheaters are listed below:

### a. Cutting Aces

If you practiced an hour or so cutting high cards as described in Chapter II, you can now cut aces at will. But if you merely read that chapter without actually trying the technique, you will still understand the nature of culling and crimping enough to sense and counter any cheating when cutting high cards for money:

(1) Insist on cutting your card first if you suspect Neocheating—but do not insist on cutting first until after the cheater has shuffled and placed the deck on the table. Indeed, he will probably inquire about your choice while shuffling in order to determine whether to crimp a high card for himself if he cuts first — or a low card for you at the approximate center (a high card for himself very low in the deck) if you cut first. Tell him he can cut first, but change your mind once he has placed the deck on the table.

(2) If he refuses to let you cut first, you can assume he has crimped himself a high card. In that case, simply refuse to cut. But if he agrees to let you cut first, which he usually will do to avoid suspicion, run your thumb or fingertips lightly from the bottom of the deck up until you locate the crimp. Then cut the high card he had crimped for himself to win the bet.

That counterattack can generally be used only once against the same cheater. If the bet was large enough to break the cheater, the action is over anyway. But if he wants another cut, he will probably switch tactics and crimp a low card near the center of the deck for you to hit, whether you cut first or last. When the cards are on the table ready for cutting, suddenly insist on cutting for low card (i.e., the lowest card wins). If he refuses, simply avoid cutting at the crimp . . . or refuse to cut altogether.

(3) If the Neocheater (or any cheater) does not ask who will

172

cut first while preparing the cards for cutting, he then is probably crimping a high card for himself very low or very high in the deck and assuming you will not cut that low or high. Or, he is crimping a low card near the center of the deck and assuming that you will cut at the crimp. In any case, be sure that *you* cut first. Then before cutting, slowly and lightly run your thumb or fingertips up the side of the deck to locate the crimp. If the crimp is very low or very high, you will probably get a high card by cutting at that crimp. If the crimp is near the center of the deck, move past that crimp to avoid cutting a low card.

(4) You also have other options to nullify or beat the Neocheater when cutting high cards:

(a) Riffle-shuffle the deck yourself and then white-hat Neocheat the cheater. You can use a foolproof Neocheating ploy by crimping a low card with a high card positioned directly behind that low card. Then offer your opponent the cut. If he is unsuspecting of your crimp, he may simply cut that low card at the crimp to lose. If he misses the crimp or is suspicious and purposely avoids your crimp, you can put your fingertips on the crimp during your cut, but leave the low card behind to cut the high card and win.

(b) Refuse to cut with him at all — *especially* if you suspect him of using the foolproof Neocheating ploy described above.

## b. Blind Shuffling, False Riffling, False Cutting, and Crimping

Blind shuffling, false riffling, false cutting, and crimping are key maneuvers for cheating, but by themselves they do not constitute cheating. They are *covers* — the tools and props for cheating maneuvers such as stacking. Three basic ways, therefore, exist to detect cheating: (1) detect the "covers" of cheating: blind shuffling, false riffling, false cutting, crimping. Those covers always indicate previous cheating moves, even if no cheating move can be detected; (2) detect or sense the cheating itself: stacking, peeking, memorizing opponents' hole cards, culling, collusion; and (3) detect or sense the *results* of cheating by observing illogical or omniscient betting and playing patterns that could occur only by gaining unnatural advantages through cheating as described in Chapter I.

Blind shuffling properly done is invisible and undetectable. But with alertness and with the right knowledge, cheating can be sensed without ever seeing an illegal move. Still, blind shuffling ineptly or awkwardly done is detectable by simply observing the portion of the deck that never gets shuffled. Any player, however, unfamiliar with the mechanics of blind shuffling will not suspect, much less detect, even a clumsy blind shuffler.

If a cheater is blind shuffling, he has already stacked the deck or perhaps has memorized everyone's hole cards *without* stacking. If he is using Neocheating techniques, you will probably never see his stacking. Nevertheless, you can indirectly sense the results of his stacking or memorizing hole cards by observing omniscient betting patterns that would be possible only if that player had stacked the deck or knew everyone's hole cards. Once his cheating moves are detected by, for example, the methods listed in Chapters III and IV, or are sensed as described in Chapter I, you can then use the defenses and counterattacks listed on the next page to protect yourself or beat the cheater.

False riffling can often be spotted if you are looking for it, *except* for the Las Vegas variation during which the deck is covered with both hands while riffling (as described in Chapter IV). Such false riffling cannot be detected with certainty, only suspected.

Spotting or sensing a false cut depends on the cut used. The standard, three-block false cut described in Chapter IV and its more elaborate four-block false variation described in Chapter VI can be detected, or at least suspected, once you know their basic movements. The shifting block cut in which small blocks of cards are moved rapidly from top to bottom (also described in Chapter VI) is a fairly common, legitimate cutting procedure. Still, be alert for cheating whenever a player uses such a cut. And finally, the cut used to remove one card from the top of the deck is hard to detect when done rapidly, but shifting that single card often makes a recognizable snapping sound.

Any time you can see an obvious crimp, you are playing against a careless or inept cheater (or an oafish player who innocently but brutely bends the deck when shuffling). An intended crimp always indicates a previous cheating maneuver,

174

usually stacking. On suspecting a crimp, you can defend yourself by taking one of the following steps:

## Defenses Against Stacking

(1) After the deck has been cut by the player on the dealer's right, request another cut whether you suspect the dealer of having an agent next to him or not.

(2) If you are sitting on the dealer's right, purposely hit his crimp but leave one card behind when you cut. Or cut at the crimp and give the deck an additional rapid cut to remove only the top card as described on pages 135-138. Those counterattack maneuvers will give you the dealer's stacked hand. And after the first or second time the cheater deals you his hand, he will not only realize that you know about his cheating, but that you are counterattacking him.

(3) If you are not sitting on the cheater's right, ask (or demand) to shuffle the deck after the cut. Such a move, however, is an indirect accusation of the dealer. But if you can get the deck and have mastered the basic Neocheating maneuvers, give the deck a quick blind shuffle. When you reach your gap, simply run off, one by one, the number of cards equal to the number of players *clockwise* from you to the dealer. For example, if you are the third player from the dealer's right, run off three cards. Then toss the rest of the deck on top of those cards, execute a false cut, and hand the deck back ready for dealing. The cheater will then deal you the hand he had stacked for himself.

(4) Maneuver yourself into the seat to the right of the cheater. You can then collect his stacked hands by using the one-card-removal cut after hitting his crimp. Or, of course, you can simply destroy his stacks with your cuts. With complaints about "luck" or other excuses, you can often exchange seats to position yourself on the cheater's right — unless that seat is held by his agent or collusion partner.

Be careful on repeating counterattacks that involve, for example, the one-card-removal cut. An alert cheater can set you up for a big loss by stacking two powerful hands and then placing an extra card at the crimp. Upon removing that extra card, you will be setting yourself up to receive, for example, four jacks to another player's four aces.

175

### c. Discard Stacking

Knowing about Neocheating lets you quickly learn effective discard-stacking techniques. But that knowledge will not make you infallible in detecting another discard-stacker, especially a Neocheater. Stacking hands with discards can be done as fast as the cards can be scooped up. The moves will appear completely natural.

When the cheater gathers face-up cards, especially in stud poker, you can often predict the hand or hands being stacked by seeing the bottom face-up card of each scoop. But as explained in Chapter III, Neocheaters will alter their scooping motions so the bottom face-up card of each scoop will not be one of the stacked cards. And discard-stackers using both hands can grab cards and turn them face down so fast that the scooped cards appear only as blurs and are impossible to follow. Moreover, if discard stacking is done in segments before the betting rounds are complete, you can at best only suspect but can never be certain that the dealer is stacking.

Nevertheless, you can detect or sense all such discard stacking by using the methods described on pages 85-86 in Chapter III. You can then counter the stacking by taking one of the four steps listed on page 175.

### d. Undercut Stacking

The undercut stack done by amateurs is easy to spot. But when done very rapidly and followed by a number of blind shuffles, false riffles and false cuts, the undercut is hard to follow. In any case, the review on page 80 in Chapter V shows how to detect the undercut. As with all stacking techniques, however, blind shuffling and false riffling are used as effective covers once the deck is stacked.

Professional cheaters generally reserve the undercut for naive company or when setting up two hands for a killing as described on pages 111-114 in Chapter V. Defenses and counterattacks against undercut stacking involve the same techniques listed on page 175 for all stacking techniques.

### e. Overhand Stacking

The tipoff for overhand stacking is the dealer pulling cards one by one rapidly off the deck during the shuffle and subsequently sliding those same cards back on top of the deck followed by a blind shuffle. But again, the maneuvers can be done so fast you must be alert to detect overhand stacking. You must know exactly what moves to look for — such as the moves listed on page 86.

### f. Riffle Stacking

Riffle stacking is essentially impossible to detect when done properly, especially when done with the Las Vegas variation. If you suspect expert riffle stacking, notice if the dealer wins too consistently when he deals or if his betting seems illogical or too omniscient (as explained in Chapter I). Indeed, because of its invisibility, the riffle stack is favored by many Neocheaters. Review pages 126, 128, 130, and 132 in Chapter V and page 175 in this chapter for detecting and defending against the riffle stack and other stacking variations.

### g. The Pull-Through

Technically, the pull-through is a false riffle, not a stack. But the pull-through always indicates a stack, often a discard stack. The tipoff for the pull-through occurs when the dealer cuts the deck into approximate halves for each riffle shuffle and then angles those halves as he riffles them together.

Some professional cheaters use nothing more than discard stacking and a pull-through to operate profitably. That routine is also very effective for bridge. For defending against the pull-through, follow the procedures listed on page 175.

### h. Collusion Cheating and Crossfire Betting

The anecdotes in Chapter I show how an alert player who understands cheating can soundly beat most collusion cheaters once he detects them. Still, even knowledgeable and alert players can be helpless against dealer-partner Neocheating collusion as revealed in Chapter I and further described in the next chapter.[31]

---

[31] *See Appendix B for information about efforts to find an effective way to counter and defeat "unbeatable " dealer-collusion Neocheating*

Recourses against such "unbeatable" Neocheating include simply getting out of the game as John Finn did in anecdote B of Chapter I; not playing in games suspect of dealer-partner Neocheating as John Finn did in anecdote F of Chapter I; making a secret arrangement with the dealer to trap his original collusion partner in a bankrupting loss; or, in private games, using white-hat Neocheating to drive colluding partners from the game.

In private games in which you deal, however, you can effectively counterattack even Neocheaters in dealer-partner collusion with white-hat Neocheating. Or you can drive those Neocheaters from your game with still other methods described later in this chapter and in the next chapter.

### i. Peeking

You can easily detect inept or careless peekers by simply noticing the awkward manner or unnatural angle in which they hold the deck when peeking (or while waiting to peek between dealing moves). But peeking by a professional or a Neocheater can be impossible to spot.

The effective peeker not only synchronizes his movements, but he acts with his body as well as with his face. His full attention, for example, focuses on the actions performed by his right hand as he peeks at a card in the deck resting in his left hand. Such misdirection is magnetically distracting as he rivets his entire body — his neck, arms, shoulders, spine — in the direction of his right hand. But his eyes will flick briefly to peek at a card in his left hand. ... For the amount of practice invested, peeking is one of the safest and most profitable cheating ruses.

If you can spot someone peeking, he is neither an expert nor a Neocheater. Effective responses on detecting or sensing a peeker include: (1) immediately demand a cut the moment you sense a peek. If necessary, you can announce as the reason for cutting is, for example, that the top card was flashed, and (2) politely or rudely (whatever the situation calls for) insist that the deck *stay* on the table whenever cards are not actually being dealt. For other detection and defense methods against peeking, see page 153 in Chapter VII.

When the peeker realizes someone suspects him of cheating, he usually stops peeking. If he persists, simply refuse to ante whenever he deals. Repeated refusals will not only protect you, but should soon stop his peeking.

In gin rummy, if you suspect someone of peeking, spread the deck slightly and carefully watch him draw his cards. With the deck slightly spread, you can more easily notice movement of the spread cards if anyone peeks at the second or any other card.

## 5. Stopping the Neocheater.

If you are playing against a consistent winner, he may be a complete Neocheater (as defined in the next chapter). If so, he will execute such mild, smart cheating — just enough to give him unbeatable long-range advantages — that you may never detect or even suspect him of cheating. In fact, you may never know for sure if he is a Neocheater or simply a good player.[32]

Regardless, you need not know if he is a cheater or simply a good player to get rid of him — you need only to know that he will be a steady winner, thus a financial liability. In fact, the defense against the unbeatable Neocheater is the same as the defense against the unbeatable good player: get him out of your game before he drains your opponents of their money — money that you could win.

The following anecdote is a final defense against both the Neocheater and the good or Advanced-Concept player. The anecdote was paraphrased from Wallace's "Advanced Concepts of Poker" and describes John Finn's encounter with a player who may have been either a Neocheater or a good player, but a certain winner in either case.

* * *

[32] *Even if a Neocheater's attack is so subtle you can never defect his cheating, his playing will still be distorted by his cheating. If constantly alert to his performance versus his quality and style of play, you can sense if he is cheating by illogical and inconsistent betting patterns that would result only if he were omniscient or had gained unnatural advantages through Neocheating. Still, you can never accuse him because you can never prove his cheating - he leaves no trace or evidence of cheating*

In one of his private games several years ago, John Finn encountered what may have been a Neocheater. At that time, however, Neocheating had not been identified. But while John Finn did not know about Neocheating, he knew that a particular player — a newcomer to the game — would be a consistent winner who could steadily drain money from the game. John, therefore, realized that the new player would be a financial liability and wanted him out of the game promptly and permanently:

Throughout the evening, Boris Klien played tightly, but strangely loosened up on his deal. And when he dealt, he won about twice as often as he would when other players dealt. Moreover, he was the game's biggest winner — up nearly five-hundred dollars. He then engaged John Finn in a lowball hand. The pot was large. By the last bet, only Boris and John remained. Boris turned his cards face up and declared his hand. John said nothing, so Boris reached for the pot.

"Keep your hands off my money," John snapped.

"Uh? What do ya mean?" Boris asked. "I won, didn't I?"

John snorted, turned his winning hand face up on the table, and snatched the pot from under Boris' stiffened fingers.

"Why didn't you declare your hand?" Boris complained.

"This is a poker game, buddy boy," John growled out of the twisted corner of his mouth. "Cards speak for themselves, remember?"

"I'm getting a bad time," Boris mumbled.

"Listen," John said shaking his finger close to Boris' face, "No one made you play. If you don't like our game... get out!"

"No, don't leave!" a big loser cried. "You're winning all our money."

"I started out losing three hundred," Boris said, "I'm still stuck a hundred."

"Liar!" John shouted. "You're up over four-hundred bucks!"

"This is my last round," Boris said. "I've..."

"The bore's even a hit-and-run artist!" John yelled while slapping his hand on the table. "Plan on this being your last round... permanently!"

Boris frowned and glanced toward the door. John had

been riding Boris that way all evening. Boris did not like his treatment. But he was still the big winner.

"Seven-card stud, high-low with qualifiers and one twist," John announced as he dealt. "Trips-eight,"[33] he added in a whispering voice.

After the sixth card, John raised on his low hand and drove out the other low hands. By the last card, only John and Boris remained. He shrugged and called John's final $30 bet.

"Don't know why you wasted our time betting," he said showing his two pair. "We split the pot. Obviously you're low and I'm high."

"Look at that hand!" John hooted while pointing at Boris' cards. "The sucker calls all my big bets and doesn't even qualify for high. I get the whole pot!"

"What do ya mean I don't qualify?" Boris sputtered. "I got two pair."

"Three of a kind qualifies for high, you creep," John said shoving Boris' cards into the deck.

"Trips for qualifiers!" Boris cried. "They've been two pair all night."

"I announced trips-eight," John said laughing. "Clean your ears, clod."

"I heard him announce it," one of the players said weakly.

"Yeah? . . . Well, then it'd be impossible for me to call," Boris said reaching for the pot. "I'm taking back my last bet

"It stays in the pot," John said slapping his hand on the money. "You make a stupid play, buster, you pay for it."

"I've had enough," Boris said getting up to leave.

"You're winning big," a losing player whined. "Sit down and play awhile."

"Let the rock go," John said. "We'll play longer without him bothering us." Then turning to Boris, John made a sharp hitchhiking motion toward the door. "So long, sucker, hope we never see you again."

"I won't be back," Boris huffed.

"Good!" John yelled. Boris grabbed his coat and left, slamming the door. ...John was somewhat surprised at how

---

[33] *Trips-eight means that three of a kind or better are needed to win for high, and an eight low or lower is needed to win for low.*

**little harassment was needed to drive Boris from a game in which he could have won a fortune.**

\* \* \*

The above anecdote describes an overtly harsh defense against good players who are steady winners. That approach is even more effective for getting rid of Neocheaters. The Neocheater is basically lazy and works entirely by the policy of easy money through smart but easy cheating. Thus if you make his job difficult or make him work hard for his money, he will quickly leave for an easier game. The good player, on the other hand, being guilt free and willing to work harder, will fight more tenaciously for his rights in a game. He cannot be driven from a game as easily as a Neocheater.

In a private game, the alert player can eventually determine if a consistent winner is a Neocheater rather than a good player by detecting illogical playing and betting actions that win too consistently. In other words, a Neocheater wins too consistently—his quality of cardplaying is not commensurate with his frequency and amount of winnings. A good player, however, can legitimately beat cheaters even Neocheaters by knowing their moves and staying one step ahead of them. For example, against a cheater, the good player can—

(1) save money by quickly folding against the cheater's winning hands made more readable by his cheating.

(2) lure the cheater into making expensive bluffs and double bluffs.

(3) use the cheater's aggressive but readable bluffs to drive out the players with better hands. With the other players out, the good player can then simply call the cheater's bluff or, when necessary, double bluff the cheater with a final raise.

## 6. Counterattacking with White-Hat Neocheating.

A powerful counterattack weapon against cheaters and Neocheaters is white-hat Neocheating (honest cheating). The white-hat approach ranges from directly wiping out cheaters to neutralizing the Neocheater's advantages and then winning simply by playing better poker when the honest players deal.

*Part Two: Defenses And Counterattacks*

The Neocheater, by nature, is lazy and relies on his cheating to win. If you neutralize his cheating advantage, then, in a sense, you make the game "honest" again, allowing the better players to win all the money over the long term.

A white-hat Neocheater can quickly drain cheaters including Neocheaters with big-hand traps that dishonest or black-hat Neocheaters would rarely if ever dare attempt. The white-hat Neocheater does not always win for himself when he cheats. And he eliminates suspicion when he arranges for the cheater's victims or big losers to beat the cheaters (Robin Hood cheating). So even if the white-hat Neocheater were discovered, he would be hailed by everyone, except the cheater, as a hero.

As you counterattack, however, the Neocheater may turn on you with all his power and cunning. Still, by being aware of his techniques, he cannot really harm you. And you can always avoid his cheating by simply not anteing during his deal. In any case, the Neocheater will usually give up and quit the game on realizing he has been discovered — especially on realizing he is being beaten by white-hat Neocheating. ...The black-hat (dishonest) Neocheater normally quits easily because he can usually find safer and easier games to drain.

## 7. Electronic Cards.

Someday, electronic cards will eliminate most cheating and Neocheating. Players will hold small devices showing images of their electronically shuffled and dealt cards transmitted from a tabletop micro computer. Without physical cards for manipulation, essentially all cheating will disappear (except for collusion signals, which can be easily detected and countered). ... Moreover, electronic cards will accelerate the action, remove everyone's fear of cheating, and lower the costs of public and casino games by eliminating the dealer and automating the house collection.

The advantages of electronic cards will overwhelm any nostalgic desire to physically handle cards as low-cost, tamper-proof devices begin replacing cards and dealers. And further in the future, electronic checkbook betting will reduce the need for physical cash (also reduce armed robberies of high-stake games).

183

# PART THREE

## BECOMING THE NEOCHEATER

185

# Chapter XI
# The Unbeatable Neocheater
# And Black-Hat Neocheating

Black-hat Neocheating is the use of Neocheating for personal gain of money or prestige — or both — at the expense of honest players. And with the information in this book, anyone can easily black-hat neocheat his opponents. Thus, all cardplayers are vulnerable to financial injury by black-hat Neocheaters.

## 1. Understanding the Neocheater.

Up until now, this book has revealed *Neocheating*, but not necessarily the *Neocheater*. An important distinction exists:

Properly revealing Neocheating requires exposing the full extent it can be applied. Chapter III, for example, explains how anyone can quickly learn to stack four aces. But the Neocheater operates with quiet subtleness and rarely needs to stack powerful hands. In fact, stacking such hands is seldom desirable and often works against his extracting maximum money from card games.

The complete Neocheater operates on the principle that only small but consistent, casino-like advantages are needed to extract all available money from all opponents. But traditional and classical cheaters usually strive for overwhelming short-term advantages —often far beyond the point of diminishing returns.

The complete Neocheater creates advantages that safely deliver maximum long-range profits. He applies his Neocheating power in small doses so his opponents keep losing money to him game after game without ever suspecting him of cheating.

The Neocheater has the following characteristics:

- Works in harmony with his characteristics or symptoms as explained in the Introduction on page vii.
- Knows all the subtle, invisible maneuvers of Neocheating, but uses only a fraction of his power to safely extract maximum, long-range money from all opponents.
- Operates on concepts of maximum smartness and minimum skill.
- Plays against opponents who are naive about Neocheating.

The earlier chapters in this book show how to detect

## Part Three: Becoming The Neocheater

*Neocheating.* But detecting the Neocheater may be more difficult — his strategy of subtly using Neocheating makes his moves appear natural and completely normal.

The Introduction to this book speculates that many card games will be damaged or even destroyed as Neocheating spreads. The Introduction also speculates that the information in this book will eventually eliminate most card cheating. But perhaps a third alternative exists: While most card cheating techniques, including most Neocheating, may eventually be eliminated, the low-profile Neocheater might never be caught or even suspected. Indeed, he could quietly rule the card tables without creating any paranoia or suspicion among his opponents. And most dangerously, he considers Neocheating no more wrong than bluffing or normal card deception.

Concepts for winning maximum money in poker <u>without cheating</u> are identified and developed in Wallace's book, *Poker, A Guaranteed Income for Life by Using the Advanced Concepts of Poker.* That book develops 120 Advanced Concepts along with a concept called the Maximum-Win Approach. All Advanced-Concept (A-C) players[34] use the Maximum-Win Approach, but so does the Neocheater. While the following paragraph quoted from Wallace's Poker Manual describes the Advanced-Concept player using the Advanced Concepts, that same paragraph could also describe the Neocheater using Neocheating:

*The Advanced-Concept player plays solely for his own benefit. He is not a gambler because he bets only when the odds favor him. By contrast, gamblers bet money at unfavorable odds and eventually lose all the money they risk. The Advanced-Concept player cannot lose because he functions like a casino; he fixes the odds permanently in his favor by using the Advanced Concepts and eventually wins all the money that all the gamblers risk.*

With constant <u>hard effort</u> in applying the Advanced Concepts, anyone can consistently win money in poker. But with <u>little effort</u> in applying Neocheating, anyone can consistently win money in any card game. The Advanced-Concept (A-C) player, however, is honest; the Neocheater is dishonest. Nevertheless, neither player can be beaten over the long term because they both fix the odds in their favor.

[34] *The Advanced-Concept player is also referred to as the A-C player.*

187

*Neocheating: The Unbeatable Weapon*

In addition to both being certain winners, The Advanced-Concept player and the Neocheater have other similar characteristics. Both maintain low profiles. Neither uses the full force of his winning power. And by operating below full power, each gradually extracts maximum money from all opponents.

Furthermore, the Neocheater can enhance his profits by actually using various Advanced-Concepts for —

- increasing the betting stakes and pace
- planting the desired emotions in opponents
- developing congenial relationships with valuable losers
- creating attractive atmospheres in profitable games
- controlling money situations (e.g., credit, cash flow)
- influencing and controlling the house rules
- encouraging loose and poor play
- creating nonthreatening images and concealing winnings
- forcing winners out of the game
- holding losers in the game
- detecting and exposing other cheaters.

While adopting many characteristics of the Advanced-Concept player, the Neocheater differs markedly from other cheaters. For example, traditional or common cheaters must constantly worry about and concentrate on their cheating techniques as they press for maximum advantages. They usually strive for big killings. By contrast, the Neocheater casually and easily gives himself lesser but safe, casino-like advantages that let him gradually extract maximum money from everyone.

Consider the differences among the following three cheaters:

*Stan Smith is a municipal property inspector for a large midwestern city. He is also a crude, **traditional cheater** who struggles to cheat in almost every hand he plays. He constantly executes blatant and dangerous cheating ploys, such as switching cards and using marked cards. Much gall is needed to pull those crude ploys, and Stan feels the pressure. In fact, he worries so much about getting caught that he often feels relief when he loses a big pot in which he has cheated. Moreover, Stan cannot concentrate on his cardplaying as he is constantly consumed with worry about being caught and publicly castigated — perhaps even physically assaulted — because of his cheating. ... Stan is a loser* *and his cheating makes him lose even more.*

*Jim Butler is a full-time **classical cheater** from El Paso, Texas. He possesses much skill that took years to master. He is forty-two years old, but looks sixty. Although maintaining a dignified and prosperous appearance, Jim endures great pressure while performing at high stakes. He constantly presses for big killings to survive. Indeed, his whole life is centered around cheating and finding victims. He cannot settle down; instead he must constantly run from games and victims he has fleeced and then travel to find new high-stake games for more quick killings. He cannot find games often enough and constantly worries about hustling enough new opponents. And he worries about seeing the same face twice. Indeed, he has become somewhat paranoid. Also, traveling and living expenses add to Jim's worries. Aside from his strenuous, worrisome life and belying his prosperous appearance, Jim is far from being financially secure. In fact, he lives with constant anxiety, feeling at times he is only one step from being a hobo.*

*Professor Arthur G. Gallbreath teaches consumer economics at a prestigious Eastern university. He has been mentioned as a possible Nobel laureate. He is also a **Neocheater**. Once a week he plays in a local, high-stake poker game. His winnings average $1200 per game. Yet, Professor Gallbreath could easily rip $10,000 from the game in one night with big-score, cheating setups that he is perfectly capable of executing. But unlike Jim Butler who always tries for maximum kills, Dr. Gallbreath never does. Big killings would quickly eliminate his opponents and destroy his game. Instead, the Professor devotes a few easy hours each week to collect sure and consistent profits. In the long run, he garners higher net profits from poker than does Mr. Butler. He has no expenses and apparently leads a relaxed, normal life. And everyone in his game likes him. Moreover, he is a respected member of his community. Professor Gallbreath does, however, spend thousands of dollars a year on visits to his psychiatrist and increasingly disappears on drinking benders.*

## 2. The Advanced-Concept Player Versus the Neocheater.

The Advanced-Concept (A-C) player achieves his unbeatable advantages through hard work. The Neocheater achieves his unbeatable advantages through easy Neocheating. The Advanced-Concept player represents the ultimate evolution of honest poker. The Neocheater represents the ultimate evolution of dishonest cheating. Thus, in a sense, the Advanced Concepts and Neocheating are opposites. Still they both result in extracting maximum money from opponents and are linked by the same basic principle — the Maximum-Win approach.

Until recently, only the Advanced-Concept player would incorporate and apply the Maximum-Win approach. And only the Advanced-Concept player could win a steadily increasing income from poker. But the evolution of cheating has produced the Neocheater. By using easy and invisible Neocheating techniques, the cheater can now base his poker strategy on the Maximum-Win approach to win as consistently as the Advanced-Concept player.

The diverted concentration involved in using traditional cheating techniques and the extraordinary skill involved in using classical cheating techniques simply do not allow most traditional or classical cheaters enough capacity or time to think about winning long term, game after game. But the Neocheater with his easy, subtle attack has both the capacity and time to think and act long term.

Past cheaters have sweated and worked for their gains, but the Neocheater collects his gains with ease and relaxation. And the long-range, more subtle Maximum-Win approach makes his cheating even easier and safer to execute. Indeed, Neocheating becomes a simple, invisible tool for garnering money from opponents.... From the smallest penny-ante game to the largest table-stake game, all money eventually flows to the Neocheater. His key weapon is Neocheating.

Both the Advanced-Concept player and the Neocheater strive to maintain their long-term advantages; they never compromise their advantages for the sake of others. They share their advantages with no one; both play solely for their own benefit. They are not gamblers; both set the odds in their favor.

Gamblers bet money at unfavorable odds and eventually lose all the money they risk. Poor players and most traditional cheaters are gamblers who eventually lose everything they risk. The Advanced-Concept player and the Neocheater are not gamblers;

190

they eventually win everything that the gambling players risk.

Both the Advanced-Concept player and the Neocheater direct all their actions toward winning maximum money. They never give anything away or help others without the motive of eventual profit. But they treat their opponents with care and respect; their opponents are their sole sources of income — their sole assets.

### a. Exploiting Emotions of Opponents

The Advanced-Concept player and the Neocheater direct their reactions and actions to the same principle — to win maximum money. The only difference is that one extracts money honestly while the other extracts money by cheating. But both the Advanced-Concept player and the Neocheater purposely evoke emotions in opponents that cause those opponents to play a looser, happier, and poorer game. Each also strives to evoke carefree and pleasant emotions in opponents to keep them less concerned and less aware of their losses.

But at times the Advanced-Concept player may evoke negative emotions in a *financially* undesirable player (e.g., a steady winner) to upset him, causing him to play poorly or even to leave the game. The Neocheater, on the other hand, seldom if ever needs to evoke negative emotions in opponents. Against good players he simply extracts their money by neocheating them while striving to keep all opponents happy and unsuspicious.

The Advanced-Concept player and the Neocheater recognize and exploit the misguided attitudes and erroneous actions of their opponents. Some of those exploitable attitudes and actions are summarized in the table on page 192. That table also contrasts the attitudes of ordinary players and cheaters to Advanced-Concept players and Neocheaters.

### b. Controlling Winnings

The Neocheater, like the Advanced-Concept player, designs games to his maximum advantage by controlling the game, its players, and the money flow. The Neocheater wants to win maximum money; and like the Advanced-Concept player, he must be careful not to win too much too quickly. Uncontrolled winning can arouse angry suspicion, drive out valuable losers, or even destroy the game. The Neocheater, like the Advanced-Concept player, thinks

## TABLE 4
## GENERAL ATTITUDES OF PLAYERS AND CHEATERS

| Situation | Poor Player (loser) | A-C Player (winner) | Crude Cheater (loser) | Neocheater (winner) |
|---|---|---|---|---|
| Poker game | A relaxing mental diversion to escape reality. | A mental discipline requiring full focus on reality. | A situation to establish big-win cheating setups. | A situation to establish favorable casino-like odds for steady, long-term winning. |
| Evaluation of a play | Winning the pot is most important. | Playing the hand properly is most important. | Winning when cheating is most important. | Making odds favorable is most important. |
| Winner or loser | Play according to winnings or losses. | Never be influenced by winnings or losses. | Cheat more frequently (and more carelessly) when losing. | Neocheat consistently if winning or losing. |
| Streaks of luck | Chances or odds are influenced by previous events. Luck runs in cycles. | Past means nothing, except for the psychological effects it has on opponents. | Believes bad luck, not poor poker concentration causes losses. | Does not consider luck. Considers only his advantages from Neocheating. |

192

## TABLE 4
## GENERAL ATTITUDES OF PLAYERS AND CHEATERS

| Situation | Poor Player (loser) | A-C Player (winner) | Crude Cheater (loser) | Neocheater (winner) |
|---|---|---|---|---|
| **Wild games** | Such games require less skill and are scorned by "good" players. | Wild or complex games require more skill and benefit good players. | Cheating is less effective in wild or complex games. | Wild and complex games increase opportunities to neocheat at improved odds. |
| **Play past quitting time** | Chances of winning decrease. | Advantages for good player increase as opponents get careless and think less. | Burned out from worry and pressures. Chances of winning decrease in late hours. | Relaxed and confident — remains fresh and alert during late hours. |
| **Rule violations by opponents** | Enforce rules equally. | Interpret rules equitably, but enforce less rigidly against weak players. | Carefully abides by decisions about rules to avoid suspicion. | Encourages rule violations that help obscure his Neocheating distortions. |

193

# TABLE 4
## GENERAL ATTITUDES OF PLAYERS AND CHEATERS

| Situation | Poor Player (loser) | A-C Player (winner) | Crude Cheater (loser) | Neocheater (winner) |
|---|---|---|---|---|
| Opponents' e r r o r s such as betting out of turn | Scold or penalize the culprit. | Benefits the good player. Encourages sloppy play. | Becomes upset by any action that interferes with his plans. | Does not faze the relaxed Neocheater. |
| Cheaters | Throw any cheater out of game. | If a cheater is a loser, say nothing and let him play. | Upset by any competition. | Drains cheaters by neocheating them. |
| Neocheaters | Unaware of his existence. | Get him out of the game. | Unaware of his existence. | Get him out of the game. |

194

long range. Consider, for instance, the following two examples:

Example A: Opponent loses $1000 to the Neocheater during one big night, becomes angry and permanently quits the game. Net worth to Neocheater = $1000.

Example B: Opponent loses to the Neocheater an average of $300 each week throughout the year. Net worth to Neocheater = $15,000 per year.

Example B demonstrates the Maximum-Win approach, which is not only more profitable but is generally an easier, more pleasant way to extract money from opponents. To use the Maximum-Win approach, the Neocheater shifts the odds only slightly in his favor by using the easiest, safest, and most subtle Neocheating techniques (e.g., perhaps by knowing the opponents hole cards each time he deals).[35] The Neocheater's Maximum-Win, high-frequency, low-intensity approach is opposite to that of the traditional cheater's low-frequency, high-intensity approach.

### c. Handling Winners and Losers

Unlike the Advanced-Concept player who tries to drive steady winners from his game, the Neocheater often welcomes winning players as they can help balance and camouflage the Neocheater's attack. He can, for example, neocheat to drain money from those steady winners without directly attacking the big losers, thus helping to balance the money flow and stabilize the game.

But like the Advanced-Concept player, the Neocheater tries to keep his losing opponents happy while extracting their money. He may at times stack morale-boosting winning hands for valuable losers to keep them from quitting the game. Or he may stack winning hands for players who are getting upset over his steady winnings and perhaps even suspecting him of cheating. Dealing a few winning powerhouses to suspicious players usually makes them forget their suspicions.

[35] *The Neocheater may use his full power as in Example A if the game is a one-time affair, or if he is facing a one-time opponent, or if the game is destined to permanently disband anyway. In such cases, the Neocheater would choose to win maximum money — the $1000 — in one night rather than, for example, $300 per session for only one or two sessions. Or he may selectively use his full Neocheating power to drive potential troublemakers, cheaters, or even another Neocheater from the game.*

### d. Keeping a Low Profile

Like the Advanced-Concept player, the Neocheater tries to conceal or deemphasize his winning position by projecting a low profile. When possible, he even tries to appear as a loser. Also, like the Advanced-Concept player, the Neocheater conceals the following facts to avoid arousing unfavorable feelings or suspicions:

| *Facts* | *Methods to Conceal* |
|---|---|
| Easiness of game | Never mention the poor quality of poker played in any game. Praise skills of opponents. |
| Winnings | Never discuss personal winnings. After each game, report less than actual winnings or more than actual losses. But exaggerate only to believable extents. Never reveal long-term winnings. Conceal affluence by driving an old car to the game. |
| Tight play | Fold cards without comment or excuses. Make wild or loose-appearing plays whenever the investment odds are favorable. |
| Good play | Never explain the true strategy behind a play. Instead, give erroneous reasoning for strategy. Never brag— downgrade own performance. |
| Control over game | Assume a humble but assertive attitude. |

### e. Controlling the Money Flow

The Neocheater, like the Advanced-Concept player, works to increase his opponents' willingness to lose money while increasing the money flow without damaging or breaking up the game. In most games, the majority of players will initially oppose higher stakes. The Neocheater, therefore, may use more subtle ways to increase the money flow. Increasing the betting pace rather than the betting stakes, for example, will subtly but effectively increase the money flow. And a faster betting pace usually increases excitement in a way that appeals to most players. In poker, the Neocheater may increase the pace by introducing game and betting modifications such as twists (extra draw cards), split pots (high-low), early bets, additional cards, novel games, wild cards, table stakes or pot limit. Not only can he easily work such modifications into games by using various Advanced Concepts described in Wallace's Poker Manual, but he can also control the money flow by using other Advanced Concepts.

### f. Using the Advanced Concepts

The Neocheater may choose to apply any number of the 120 Advanced Concepts taught in Wallace's Poker Manual. By contrast, the techniques of the traditional or classical cheater are too distracting or difficult to allow effective use of the Advanced Concepts to play a good game. That inability to play a good game is why most cheaters end up losers. Neocheating, on the other hand, is so safe and easy that a player can concentrate on executing good card strategy while simultaneously Neocheating. And interestingly, the better the Neocheater plays, the less he needs to neocheat.

Neocheating requires little effort, whereas good poker strategy requires concentrated effort. In either case, simultaneously neocheating and executing various Advanced Concepts in any ratio will deliver consistent winnings.

Other Advanced Concepts that can enhance the Neocheater's advantage are, for example, keeping a friendly attitude towards players, maintaining a healthy game, keeping notes and charts on opponents' reactions to various situations and hands. And most importantly, the Neocheater can use the Advanced Concepts to markedly increase the money size of his game, often by 100 times or more from its initial levels.

In many ways, the Neocheater acts like the Advanced-Concept player: The Neocheater keeps a low profile and disguises his actions to prevent suspicion. When profitable, he is promiscuously friendly. He conceals facts about his poker income, drives old cars to the game, lies about his performance, minimizes or conceals his winnings. He is scrupuously fair in settling all disputes while using the Advanced Concepts to become the most trusted person in the game. He acts in a carefree, pleasant, and relaxed manner to loosen up opponents. And at times, he might even accept other cheaters in his game (if they are not too obvious or are not Neocheaters), because they can be good sources of income and can deflect suspicion away from him. By contrast, traditional cheaters fear other cheaters and are often paranoid about being cheated themselves. But the Neocheater has no fear of traditional cheaters or their cheating. He can wipe them out whenever he chooses.

A Neocheater can apply *any* of the 120 Advanced Concepts to any degree. Some of the Advanced Concepts are easy to apply. Others, however, require hard work that demand concentrated discipline, thought, and control — the essence of good playing. But the essence of Neocheating is its easiness. Most Neocheaters, therefore, are not interested in hard work and apply only the easiest of the Advanced Concepts — those concepts that most easily enhance their style and Maximum-Win approach.

In any case, the Neocheater usually tries to extract maximum long-range money from his opponents. He avoids winning too fast by Neocheating in small, subtle doses to win quietly and safely, game after game.

The Neocheater tries to keep everyone as happy as possible while gradually extracting money. To minimize resentments from losers, he extracts more of his winnings from the content players, the better players, and the winners. He may even neocheat for the benefit of losers (Robin Hood cheating) to more evenly distribute his opponents' losses and to keep the game financially stable. At the same time, if an opponent is a financial liability or harmful to the game, the Neocheater can repeatedly attack him until he is broke and driven from the game.

Moreover, the Neocheater is cunning. He may play for hours and not win a single hand. But all the while, he will be neocheating for others — transfering money from harmful players (other cheaters, big winners, good players) to big losers and poor players. Then, when the time is right, he will quietly extract his share of winnings for the evening. ...Neocheating is the easiest and safest way to extract maximum money from any game.

And finally, the Neocheater may control several games or even a network of games. ...Neocheating is that easy.

### g. Combining the Advanced Concepts with Neocheating

Only two certain winning techniques exist: (1) using the Advanced Concepts and (2) using Neocheating. Any honest player wins in proportion to the extent he applies the Advanced Concepts. Likewise, any cheater wins in proportion to the extent he applies Neocheating. But a cheater applying Neocheating is not a *Neo*cheater until he grasps and uses certain Advanced Concepts, namely those concepts involving the long-range, Maximum-Win approach as described in this chapter.

The ultimate evolution of good playing *without* cheating is the Advanced Concepts. The ultimate evolution of cheating is Neocheating. A blend of those two ultimate evolutions creates a terrifying player called the Neocheater — the most dangerous threat ever to invade the card tables.

### 3. The Ultimate Neocheater.

Most Neocheaters will not cheat when they are on a hot streak or winning naturally. They may play the entire evening without cheating. Most will neocheat only when needed to assure that their cardplaying sessions are financially worthwhile. But the *ultimate* Neocheater *never* cheats for himself. Instead, he neocheats only to transfer money from strong, good players to weak, poor players. During his deal, the ultimate Neocheater will, in a sense, Robin Hood cheat for the poor players, using them to drain the good players. After transferring money from strong players to weak players, the ultimate Neocheater then plays legitimate but superior poker to easily win that money from those weak players.

That indirect method of cheating is the shrewdest of all ways for a cheater to extract money from opponents. And as with white-hat Neocheating (described in the previous chapter), he need not be overly subtle when cheating for the benefit of losers. Unlike other Neocheaters, however, he must be a relatively good player to legitimately extract the money once he has transferred it to the poor players.

Often the only way to discover Neocheating is to observe that when a particular player deals he seemingly makes omniscient or illogical bets that uncannily turn to his advantage. And those advantages cause him to win too frequently and too much when he deals. But how can anyone discover the *ultimate* Neocheater? When cheating, he is actually losing. Moreover, when cheating, he is not gaining any direct advantages for himself as he delivers unbeatable advantages to weak players and losers. And weak players winning from strong players is almost always a "crowd-pleasing" event.

Those good players extract money from the weak players game after game. So almost everyone likes to see weak players win from strong players. That way, those weak or easy players will remain in the game with extra money to lose. In addition, the weak players themselves will gain euphoric satisfactions from beating strong players. Of course, the ultimate Neocheater eventually ends up with all the money. But ironically, when he cheats, his opponents are the happiest as he builds the weak players' hopes and egos. Only after he stops cheating does the ultimate Neocheater begin winning for himself.

By "helping" the losers, the ultimate Neocheater creates a perfect rationalization to justify his cheating: he never wins when he cheats. Still, he is *not* a white-hat Neocheater (who ironically will win at times when he is cheating while the ultimate Neocheater will never win while cheating). The white-hat Neocheater is honest since he cheats *only* cheaters. And when cheating, he never seizes advantages for himself at the expense of honest players. The ultimate Neocheater, on the other hand, is a dishonest (black-hat) cheater because he cheats honest players in order to gain unnatural advantages for himself — albeit indirect advantages through the poor players and losers.

By driving the good players from the game while temporarily enriching the poor players, the ultimate Neocheater eliminates his competition and thus his need to cheat. He then extracts money from those weak players — his "regular" players — simply by playing good poker. The ultimate Neocheater works to populate his game with weak players. He uses Neocheating only to drain good players that may enter his game. After driving them from the game, he has no reason to cheat. Still, at times, he may welcome good players in order to drain their money with Neocheating.

The ultimate Neocheater creates an illusion of removing himself from cheating by never winning when he cheats. Instead he

200

arranges for poor players to win from good players so that later he can legitimately drain that money from those poor players.

Neocheating is the ultimate concept of cheating. And the ultimate Neocheater is the ultimate application of that concept. Yet, even the ultimate Neocheater can be detected: First you must be aware of his indirect attack and then sense that weak players too often win big hands from good players when that ultimate Neocheater deals. One certain defense against the ultimate Neocheater is simply refuse to ante whenever he deals. You can then win from the Neocheater's retinue of weak players when he is not dealing. By continuing such action, you embarrass the ultimate Neocheater and leave him unable to attack you. And by remaining in the game, you reduce or eliminate his profits. That tactic will sooner or later make him leave and seek other easier, more profitable games.

## 4. The Forbidden Question.

The contents of this book mandate the asking of the forbidden question: Why not allow cheating in card games as a new dimension of skill and strategy? Is not cheating simply another variation of the deceptive strategies that are accepted as integral parts of most card games played for money and prestige? Why not allow deceptive cheating? Why not allow it just as bluffing and other deceptive ploys are allowed?

Actually, anything is allowable if mutually agreed upon. Deception is a universally agreed upon feature of many games, especially poker. So why not agree to allow cheating? The only reason that cheating cannot be allowed is that it has an open-ended nature — it has no limits. Bluffing and deception, for example, are limited by the effectiveness of ingenuity and guile. Likewise, *illegal* cheating is also limited by the effectiveness of ingenuity and guile. But *legal* cheating would be boundless because the need for skilled, subtle cheating would be gone . . . all kinds of crude cheating and blatant stealing would escalate rapidly to destroy any card game.

Openly accepted cheating would cause such chaos and anarchy in card games that they would rapidly become unmanageable and unplayable. *Every* game needs a limitation, a cutoff point. For instance, a polevaulter cannot wear miniature rockets on his back

—a limitation to keep that sport playable. The football player cannot wear steel-spiked shoulder pads — a limitation to keep football playable. The cardplayer cannot cheat — a limitation to keep card games playable.

## 5. The Final Showdown.

In the past few years, the quality of poker players has improved markedly, especially in public casino poker. But the Advanced-Concept (A-C) player is still very rare. And although more Advanced-Concept players are developing, they probably will always be rare because full application of the Advanced Concepts requires hard work and constant discipline (but actually, little skill). In private games, the Advanced-Concept player patiently develops control over the game, the rules, and his opponents. He invests many hours in studying, analyzing, and taking notes about his opponents. He develops his games over long periods of time, even years, to steadily increase their pace and stakes while striving to reach the full profit potential of each game. He works hard for his winnings. ... Most poker players, however, would rather take their chances with more luck and less work. *Who wants to work that hard to win when it's time to relax?* most players subconsciously rationalize. That is why Advanced-Concept players are rare.

The Neocheater, on the other hand, will become increasingly common because Neocheating is easy and requires little sustained effort. Moreover, the Neocheater can move into any private game of any size and start winning immediately. Neocheating is a comfortable, fast, and easy way to make money or gain prestige. Many cardplayers, therefore, will prefer to use Neocheating to extract money rather than to put forth the effort required to play well enough to win equivalent money.

Thus in private games, players will encounter Neocheaters with increasing frequency. And Neocheaters will multiply so extensively that they may eventually link together in collusion pacts among private games as they are already doing in public poker. On the other hand, players will seldom if ever encounter the rare Advanced-Concept player. Nevertheless, if a Neocheater did run across an Advanced-Concept player in a private game, he would find that the game belongs to that Advanced-Concept player who usually has a substantial investment of time and effort in tailoring that game to his maximum advantage. Indeed, the Advanced-Concept player will strenuously protect his game as his most valuable asset.

Neocheaters are the *only* cheaters the Advanced-Concept player fears. He fears Neocheaters because, if they choose, they can quickly drain money to break valuable players and destroy the game. In addition, the Advanced-Concept player cannot beat certain Neocheaters. He will, therefore, try to drive them from his game using white-hat Neocheating or the harassment methods described in Chapter X.

Most Neocheaters will quickly leave private games in which an Advanced-Concept player is pressuring them because playing under constant stress contradicts their nature of seeking easy money. Instead of taking the abuses and pressures applied by the Advanced-Concept player, most Neocheaters will simply find other games that have no Advanced-Concept player to interfere with their easy-going money extraction.

But what happens when the Advanced-Concept player encounters the Neocheater in high-stake public poker? Consider the following situation in a world-class poker tournament played in a Las Vegas casino:

**Forty-two players have entered the freeze-out hold 'em tournament, each paying a $15,000 entry fee. The last surviving player wins all the money — over one-half million dollars.**

**After three days, only two players remain in the tournament — an Advanced-Concept player (John Finn) and a well-known professional poker player. That professional player is also a Neocheater who has made a colluding arrangement with one of the dealers involving an unbeatable form of Neocheating (as described in anecdote B of Chapter I). Through memorized cards, invisible blind shuffles, false riffles, and false cuts, the dealer always knows the nine cards to come off the deck for each round of play. During the play, John can sense their collusion, but cannot accuse them because their cheating is invisible and appears completely natural. Moreover, John realizes that even if he could crack their collusion code, he would still lose because unlike most**

R 4

collusion codes that are one dimensional (codes that indicate only present values of hands), their code is two dimensional in that the dealer not only knows both the Neocheater's hand and John's hand at every moment, but he knows all the cards yet to be dealt. Thus that dealer can plan ahead with perfect knowledge and guide the Neocheater with flawless strategy.

Without knowing the cards to be dealt, John has no way to read or forecast the dealer's strategy. Indeed, in such collusion situations, the Neocheater becomes a more-than-perfect player because his moves are perfect through the dealer's knowing every hole card, and his strategy is flawless through the dealer's knowing all the cards still to be dealt. To beat that kind of cheating, a player must not only read everyone's hole cards perfectly, but he must also precisely foretell all the cards to be dealt. And no one can precisely foretell cards without cheating. Thus, John concludes that against such Neocheating collusion, he cannot win. And how can he accuse his adversaries of invisible cheating? No evidence exists. The only possibilities that John has of winning are to (1) refuse to play when that dealer takes his turn, insist on another dealer, and hope that the new dealer will not collude with the Neocheater, (2) meet privately with the dealer during a break and ask him to stop colluding, or (3) find the dealer's price to flash false signals at crucial moments to bankrupt (tap out) the Neocheater. In other words, neocheat the Neocheater. ...John Finn selected option 2 and lost the tournament. He resolved to use option 3 next time.

Neocheating begets Neocheating, and Neocheaters beget Neocheaters. Where will it end?

204

*Part Three: Becoming The Neocheater*
# Chapter XII
# The Neo-Tech Discovery

The Neo-Tech discovery evolved from the earlier discovery of Neocheating. In a sense, Neocheating was not a discovery but an identification of elegantly sophisticated techniques of card cheating that met two criteria: *(1) required little effort or skill, and (2) were undetectable or unassailable as dishonest.*

The effects of Wallace's identification of Neocheating are similar to the effects his earlier identification of the Advanced Concepts of Poker had on the poker world during the 1970s: Like Neocheating, various Advanced Concepts of Poker had been unknowingly used not only by winning poker players but by unbeatable strategists beyond the card tables. And the extent that they randomly used the various Advanced Concepts was the extent that they won. With the 1968 publication of Wallace's book, "Poker, A Guaranteed Income for Life", the Advanced Concepts (a total of 120 advantage levers) were identified for the first time and systematically gathered into one source. That gathering and publishing of all the Advanced Concepts into one book produced big profit increases for those players who had acquired Wallace's book. As a result, the number of professional players, competitive players, successful women players, as well as high-stake games and tournament games escalated dramatically since the Advanced Concepts of Poker were first published.

And now, the 1980 publication of "Neo-Tech" (Neocheating) is having an even more profound impact on poker (and other card games), especially on high-stake casino and public-card-club games. Moreover, the effects are spreading into private poker, particularly into high-stake games. But, at the same time, a counterbalancing phenomenon is occurring: Everyone who learns about Neocheating automatically learns how to effectively nullify *all* cheating. Thus, the continued distribution of Neocheating information will at first greatly increase undetectable cheating, but eventually will ironically eliminate all cheating.

After identifying the Neocheating concepts, Frank Wallace made an even more important discovery by extending those concepts beyond cards — *into business, politics, social*

Book 4
Neocheating: The Unbeatable Weapon

205

relationships, and other areas of life. His discovery is called the Neo-Tech discovery. Once the concepts of Neocheating are fully understood, their application beyond cards becomes limitless. And more importantly, all Neo-Tech practitioners (who abound with impunity in most areas of life) become fully visible to those who understand Neocheating. Moreover, anyone understanding the concepts of Neocheating can render Neocheaters harmless.

Neocheating concepts used in business and other areas of life are so exquisitely subtle that the initial effect is shocking on realizing the enormous advantages one gains by using those concepts beyond cards.

## Neocheating
## Beyond Cards

Neocheating beyond cards involves gaining easy advantages and power over others through combinations of techniques that meet two criteria: *(1) easy to execute, and (2) not vulnerable to detection or assailable as dishonest.* Once those two criteria are established, Neocheating formats can then be established in any area of life. With such formats, a person not only gleans unbeatable advantages over others, but commands easy shortcuts to profits and power.... Those who use Neocheating formats to achieve wealth or power are called Neo-Tech practitioners.

Examples of master Neo-Tech practitioners are illustrated on page 191 and in Appendix A on page 211. Other examples are summarized in table 5 on page 215.

Master Neo-Tech practitioners who use subtle, invisible Neocheating concepts to maximum effectiveness can gain enormous power and wealth. Such practitioners range from the President of the United States to the presidents of international banking conglomerates. But anyone can use the Neocheating concepts to gain profits to any chosen degree, ranging from business people neocheating customers (e.g., selling unneeded or fraudulent insurance policies), professional people neocheating clients (e.g., doctors promoting unneeded surgery), husbands neocheating wives (e.g., psychologically or physically abusing spouses into dependence, then into submission and subservience), women neocheating men (e.g., deceiving for entrapment and wealth extraction), teachers neocheating students (e.g., dishonestly attacking value producers to usurp unearned power); parents neocheating children (e.g., destructive manipulation for social images).

One major benefit of understanding Neocheating beyond cards is the rapid identification of Neo-Tech practitioners who surround everyone in almost every area of life. Once identified, Neocheaters can be prevented from diminishing one's own well-being.

Perhaps the most startling benefit of understanding Neocheating occurs when viewing network TV news. With knowledge of Neo-Tech, a person becomes acutely aware of the steady stream of Neocheaters (TV commentators, news editors, sociologists, politicians, educators, nutritionists, faddists, mystical gurus, and religious proselytizers) who constantly diminish everyone's life. With the concepts of Neocheating, however, a person not only can nullify those Neocheaters, but can transfer their usurped power from them to himself with honest effective Neo-Tech techniques. For example, manipulating the ego of a Neocheating politician or bureaucrat to remove coercive government regulations that are damaging a company's productive capacity is one example of using the Neo-Tech discovery honestly — of using White-Hat Neocheating.

The three possible approaches for using the Neo-Tech Discovery are the low-power approach, the high-power approach, and the Neothink/Neopower approach:

## THE THREE APPROACHES

1. The Low-Power Approach: Neo-Tech is used defensively to avoid loses to Neocheaters. The "Neo-Tech Discovery" reveals (in Parts Two and Three) detailed, specific techniques for the low-power approach, including the original White-Hat Techniques that are effective, ethical, and honest.

2. The High-Power Approach: Neo-Tech is used offensively to gain advantages and profits — in cards or beyond. The "Neo-Tech Discovery" also reveals (in Part One) detailed techniques for the high-power approach, including the Black-Hat Techniques that are unethical but ravagingly effective. Yet, with Neo-Tech information, a person can safely defend himself against Black-Hat Neocheating and all other forms of cheating.

3. The Neothink/Neopower Approach: The Neo-Tech Discovery is used not only to identify and nullify Neocheaters,

but to gain honest profits *as a result* of Neocheaters. The following table summarizes various Neo-Tech formats that profitably counter Neocheaters:

| NEOCHEATING AREA | NEO-TECH FORMAT |
|---|---|
| Business | Identifying Neocheaters and understanding their techniques provide valuable knowledge that delivers larger profits and decreased losses through more beneficially accurate decisions. |
| Media | Rapid identification of Neocheaters allows an accurate evaluation of literature, TV shows, news programming, media events, movies... permitting more accurate and profitable decisions. Understanding Neocheating lets one quickly identify the 180 degree inversion of crucial values by devious business practices, political or social demagoguery, religious doctrines, and mystical illusions. |
| Politics and Education | Knowing the Neocheating techniques of all politicians and many educators provides a powerful tool not only for protection, but for profiting from the machinations of politicians, governments, and educators. |
| Religion and Mysticism | Understanding Neocheating provides startling realizations of how Neocheating is the essence of mysticism... and how most religious and mystical leaders are expert Neocheaters. That understanding is necessary not |

only for avoiding the life-consuming influences of religion and mysticism, but for gaining maximum happiness, well-being, and profits from life.

Personal Relations — The Neo-Tech Discovery provides a rapid sorting mechanism for discarding destructive relationships and for winning beneficial relationships that deliver profits and happiness.

Science — Knowledge of Neo-Tech allows one to reject, for example, most warnings by government "scientists" of cancer risks with their accompanying regulations (e.g., the banning of cyclamates). Neocheating with science damages the productive segments of life and diminishes everyone's well-being.... Knowledge of Neo-Tech permits valid value judgments and delivers peace of mind that Neocheaters constantly seek to undermine.

The Neocheating concepts are not only easy, practical tools for profits, but are crucial tools for thinking. Those concepts allow a person to identify and nullify Neocheaters who have beguiled human life for three-thousand years. Without understanding Neocheating, a person has no way of thinking about Neocheaters or of realizing how they constantly extract values from unknowledgeable people. Without those thinking tools to identify Neocheaters people can only suffer in silent frustration as their lives and dreams are drained by Neocheaters.

But the supreme value of the Neocheating concepts is that those new thinking tools will be the cutting edge for rejecting and eventually eliminating the power of government bureaucrats, religious leaders, political leaders, dishonest businessmen, external authorities, and all other Neocheaters.

The concepts of Neocheating as revealed by the Neo-Tech Discovery are among the most powerful thinking tools for future prosperity.

# Chapter XIII
# Neocheating Beyond Cards

## Neocheating in Business, Politics, Religion and Social Relationships

The first two thirds of this book teach the techniques of Neocheating specific to cards while identifying the differences between Neocheating and all other cheating. The specific Neocheating techniques for cards provide the concrete base needed to understand the *concepts behind* Neocheating. By understanding those concepts, the wider applications of Neocheating become obvious in the last four chapters.

Also, as becomes obvious toward the end of this book, the concepts of Neocheating can be used in any area of life to usurp money, power, respect, or love. But in the long run, people who extract values by Neocheating become dependent on cheating as they undermine their competence and self-esteem by embezzling rather than earning their values. The careful observer will recognize that by far the highest percentage of people involved in building false self-esteems to justify their existences are those pursuing careers in politics and religion. Such careers are by nature anti-productive and depend on Neocheating the public to extract money, respect, and power.

# Appendix A

## CHEATING AS A METAPHOR

What positive value can be found in card cheating? One magnificent value: Card cheating is a superb metaphor for identifying and classifying dishonest people . . .

The traditional cheater is, for example, the crude sneak thief. He is also the small-time bureaucrat or politician on the take. He needs little skill and much gall to extract his living. But he lives in constant danger of being caught in the act and subjected to the consequences.

The classical cheater is, for example, the elegant con-artist thief. He is also the respected technocrat who, for example, helps develop weapons for a repressive government. Application of his skills (that took years to polish or develop) lets him extract a "good" living. His dishonesty usually remains unseen and uncalled by those who surround him as he cheats countless people out of their assets and lives.

The Neocheater is, for example, the subtle executive thief who climbs to a high-paid corporate position by deceptive machinations rather than by productive efforts. He is also the religious leader who gleans a glorious living by promoting self-sacrifice among the multitudes. And the ultimate Neocheater is the politician gracing the highest office. He usurps a sumptuous living, enormous power, and a hugh ego trip by converting productive assets of the earners into nonproductive waste for the "public good" through the invisible manipulations of government force (e.g., taxes and regulations). His techniques require neither skill nor effort: he is simply shrewd and subtle enough to keep most people from realizing that he is constantly neocheating them — constantly draining their lives and assets. And most dangerously, he considers his neocheating as necessary for the "good of all".

Neocheaters are by far the deadliest menace to honest and productive people, everywhere.

# Appendix B

## AN OBITUARY FOR TRADITIONAL AND CLASSICAL CHEATERS

Neocheating renders all forms of classical and traditional cheating. Once the safe and easy techniques of Neocheating become widely known, difficult classical cheating and risky traditional cheating will cease to exist. As knowledge of Neocheating spreads, cardsharps will abandon their inferior forms of cheating and switch to the more potent yet safer and easier Neocheating. Many will become Neocheaters. Then, in turn, those Neocheaters will wipe out the remaining traditional and classical cheaters.

Neocheaters abhor the traditional cheater's crude or less-than-smart techniques. They also scorn the classical cheater's unnecessary big-win setups that generate suspicion, drain money too fast from valuable opponents, and jeopardize the game. Neocheaters, therefore, will often use their superior techniques to bankrupt those bothersome cheaters still using traditional or classical techniques. Besides, a Neocheater wants opponents to lose only to him in a relaxed, happy atmosphere — without the rush, trauma, or suspicion inherent in the old-style cheating techniques.

All forms of classical and traditional cheating will eventually die as the use of Neocheating accelerates. Many professional cardplayers will adopt Neocheating techniques — so will every player who ever yearned to cheat but was unwilling to spend the time to learn or was afraid of being caught.

# Appendix C

## A $1000 REWARD
## <u>TO SEAL THE COFFIN ON ALL CHEATERS</u>

This book shows how to discover and stop all cheating, including Neocheating. And hopefully this information will eventually stop that new frightening player called the Neocheater. Certainly as more and more honest players read this book, the lid will close on all cheaters. Toward that end, a $1000 cash reward awaits the first person who can discover a practical technique (acceptable for publication in a subsequent edition of this book) that will let honest players directly beat dealer-partner Neocheating, especially in high-stake casino poker, as described in Chapters 1, X, and Xl. Only with that answer will the Neocheater have no out — no long-range survival.

That information will complete this book and eventually seal the coffin on all cheaters. With that last loophole closed, anyone who reads this book can prevent any cheater or Neocheater from operating profitably.

Statistically, the alert player knowledgeable about Neocheating can actually increase his advantage in full games (7 or more players) in which unbeatable dealer-partner Neocheating is occurring. While he cannot beat the dealer-partner Neocheaters directly, by being aware of their all-knowing betting position, he can actually gain more money from the other players than he will lose to the dealer-partner Neocheaters. By assuming the dealer always knows everyone's hole cards (thus making his partner's move always correct), a knowledgeable player can use their moves to read more accurately the other players. For example, if he reads the Neocheater for the best hand or the greatest advantage but the Neocheater suddenly folds, his folding signals that another player has a well-hidden, even more powerful hand or advantage. Such information can eventually save the knowledgeable player considerable money, especially in the "big" pots, thereby increasing his overall profits.

Or, as another example, suppose the knowledgeable player is competing with the dealer-partner Neocheater for catching the best hand, but should fold if another player has already caught an even better hand. If the Neocheater bets, the knowledgeable player can read the other player as not having caught his hand. Then if the knowledgeable player catches his hand and the Neocheater folds, the odds favor the knowledgeable player holding the best hand. He can then bet more aggressively or call a bluff more confidently against opponents with better appearing hands.

In other words, the knowledgeable player, through his awareness of Neocheating, can capture some of the advantages created by dealer-partner Neocheaters. If the game has sufficient opponents to exploit such rubbed-off advantages, the knowledgeable player can gain enough advantages to actually increase his winnings because of the Neocheaters.

Still, he cannot directly beat the dealer-Neocheaters. And, in games with too few noncheating opponents, he cannot gain enough advantages over those opponents to offset his losses to the Neocheaters.

## Table 5
## NEOCHEATING BEYOND CARDS

| AREA OF ENDEAVOR | EXAMPLES OF MASTER NEOCHEATERS | NEOCHEATING CRITERIA | |
|---|---|---|---|
| | | EASY TO EXECUTE | UNASSAILABLE |
| Business | Prosperous but dishonest stock and real estate brokers. | Mislead customers or clients by taking advantage of superior authority. | Appear to work for customer's best interest. |
| Banking | International bankers who gain advantages and profits through governments. | Glean unearned money by manipulating government funds and favors. | Nothing is illegal about their manipulations. |
| Politics | Most elected heads of states | Live by machinations that never involve the effort of productive achievement. | Traditionally accepted as good or at least necessary. |
| Religion | Most religious leaders. | Need no genuine effort to extract a respectable living from producers. | As with politicians, traditionally accepted as good and needed. |

215

## Table 5
## NEOCHEATING BEYOND CARDS

| AREA OF ENDEAVOR | EXAMPLES OF MASTER NEOCHEATERS | NEOCHEATING CRITERIA | |
|---|---|---|---|
| | | EASY TO EXECUTE | UNASSAILABLE |
| Social | Dishonest Don Juans. | Manipulate partners through vulnerable emotions. | Others cannot prove bad intent. |
| Media | Many of the best-known TV commentators, journalists, editorial writers, performers, authors. | Foist inaccurate, dishonest, or out-of-context "facts" on trusting followers. | Others cannot prove immorality of author, actor, newscaster. |
| Education | Certain professors, teachers, nutritionists who build careers through ideas based on "big lies", empiricisms, myths, and mysticism | Exploit students and followers through power of teaching positions. | Others cannot prove career-enhancing or ego-boosting abuses of power and authority. |

216

**Table 5**
**NEOCHEATING BEYOND CARDS**

| AREA OF ENDEAVOR | EXAMPLES OF MASTER NEOCHEATERS | NEOCHEATING EASY TO EXECUTE | NEOCHEATING CRITERIA UNASSAILABLE |
|---|---|---|---|
| Science | Most so-called environmentalists, and all politically or socially oriented "scientists" who build careers by using facts out of context. | Gain prestige with comfortable income and security. | Appear to be acting in society's best interest when actually generating unearned prestige undermining productive achievement. |

217

Book 4
Neocheating: The Unbeatable Weapon